WEBSTER'S
BASIC DICTIONARY

Minerva Books, Ltd.
New York, NY

ISBN: 0-8056-5622-7

Printed in the United States of America

About This Dictionary

In order to make this dictionary a valuable "tool" for anyone concerned with the English language, the lexicographers who have compiled this book have tried to make it easy-to-use as well as contemporary. It would be of little use to you to have a dictionary that featured thousands of foreign, obscure, and antiquated terms. Thus, these words have been trimmed down to the basics — words that may still be in use after hundreds of years as well as those foreign words that you may encounter on a steady basis (**du jour**). In addition, we have included many of the more contemporary words that have come into use throughout the last several years, especially in the fields of science and computers. Words and terms such as **desktop publishing** and acronyms such as **ASCII** and **DOS** are important inclusions that assure the contemporary nature of this dictionary.

To use this dictionary, it is necessary for you to understand how it is organized. We've organized the words in paragraphs, featuring the root word in a larger, bold typeface. The words that are derived from this root word, or those that are related to it, are also in bold type. Thus, the word **execute** will include derivative words such as **execution**, **executioner**, and **executive**. If there are alternative spellings for the words, they are included. If there are unique plural forms of the word, these are included also.

In the next section is a list of abbreviations which appear throughout this dictionary. This includes the parts of speech, in order for you to recognize how the entry word is used. (Since this is not a grammar book, you will have to look elsewhere to determine what a *noun* is in contrast to a *verb transitive*.) You will find the word **lady** as a *noun* (*n.*) and the word **lag** as a *verb intransitive* (*v.i.*). However, the word **laggard** is a *noun* and an *adjective*, and the differing definitions are provided.

For many of the words where there may be a question of how to pronounce them, there are accent marks (ʹ) to show syllable emphasis as well as pronunciation guides. For example, look at the word **banquet**.

banq′uet (bang′-kwet) *n.* feast. *-v.i.* feast. - *v.t.* give a feast to
-**banq′ueter** *n.* [F., dim of *banc*, bench]

This is a complete entry. First you are provided with the root word;
banquet. In order for you to know that the accent is on the first syllable,
there is an accent mark (′). Following the root word is a pronunciation
guide in parentheses. The first syllable is pronounced like the word
bang; the second sounds like *kwet*. The parts of speech follow. This
word can be used in several ways: as a *noun*, *verb intransitive*, *verb
transitive*. The associated word is **banqueter**, which is a *noun* . Finally,
the derivation of the word is given, the diminutive (dim) of the French
word *banc*.

We do not provide the accent marks with words of one syllable, or
those with a silent *e* at the end of the word.

Most pronunciation guides are self-explanatory. For example, the
second syllable in the word **baroque** is pronounced as a *k*, and the
pronunciation guide provides the letter (-k-). As a guide for you, following are the common pronunciations that we use:

ch	chip	ng	ring
CH	chord	s	sweet
g	go	th	thin
hw	where	TH	this
j	juice, gene	y	yes
ng	French nasal sound	zh	measure

As you saw from the example above, the derivation or etymology
of the main word is provided at the end of most entries in square brackets.
Like the rest of this dictionary, we've tried to make it easy to use and in
most cases have given the primary origin for a word, usually the Latin
or Anglo-Saxon derivation. From time to time, where it would enhance
your understanding of the derivation of the word, a somewhat more
detailed explanation is provided.

Finally, when entries contain prefixes, we have offered only a
handful of the words that can be created by the use of the prefix. A prefix
such as **anti-** can be used to create hundreds of words. We have offered
only a few, but suggest that you see the words without the prefix.

Abbreviations Used In This Book

a.	adjective	*interj.*	interjection
abbrev.	abbreviation	*lang.*	language
adv.	adverb	*lit.*	literally
alg.	algebra	*maths.*	mathematics
arch.	archaic	*med.*	medicine
archit.	architecture	*mil.*	military
astron.	astronomy	*mod.*	modern
avoir.	avoirdupois	*mus.*	music
bot.	botany	*myth.*	mythology
cap.	capital	*n.*	noun
cp.	compare	*n. masc.*	noun masculine
char.	character	*naut.*	nautical
chem.	chemistry	*obj.*	objective
colloq.	colloquial	*obs.*	obsolete
comp.	comparative	*opp.*	opposite
compute.	computers	*orig.*	origin (-ally)
conj.	conjunction	*p.p.*	past participle
contr.	contraction	*p.t.*	past tense
const.	construction	*perh.*	perhaps
corrupt.	corruption, corrupted	*pert.*	pertaining to
dial.	dialect, dialectal	*philos.*	philosophy
dem. pron.	demonstrative pronoun	*phot.*	photography
dim.	diminutive	*phys.*	physics
e.g.	for instance	*pl.*	plural
elec.	electricity	*poet.*	poetry, poetical
esp.	especially	*polit.*	politics
euph.	euphemism	*poss.*	possessive
fem.	feminine	*pref.*	prefix
fig.	figuratively	*prep.*	preposition
fort.	fortification	*pres. p.*	present participle
fr.	from	*print.*	printing
gen.	generally	*prob.*	probably
geog.	geography	*pron.*	pronoun
geol.	geology	*pros.*	prosody
gram.	grammar	*prov.*	provincial
hist.	history	*psych.*	psychology
ident.	identical	*q.v.*	which see
i.e.	that is	*redupl.*	reduplication
imit.	imitation, imitative	*reflex.*	reflexive
impers.	impersonal	*rhet.*	rhetoric
infin.	infinitive	*rel. pron.*	relative pronoun
intens.	intensive	*sing.*	singular

sl.	slang		*v.*	verb
superl.	superlative		*var.*	variant, variation
surg.	surgery		*v. aux.*	auxiliary verb
trans.	transitive		*v.i.*	verb intransitive
trig.	trigonometry		*v.s.*	(*vide supra*) see above
ult.	ultimately		*v.t.*	verb transitive
usu.	usually		*zool.*	zoology

Word Derivations

AF.	Anglo-French		ME.	Middle English
Afr.	African		Med. L.	Medieval Latin
Am. Amer.	American		Mex.	Mexican
Arab.	Arabic		Mod. L.	Modern Latin
Aram.	Aramaic		Mongol.	Mongolian
Austr.	Australian		N.	North
Braz.	Brazilian		Norw.	Norwegian
Can. F.	Canadian French		O.	Old
Carib.	Caribbean		OE.	Old English
Celt.	Celtic		OF.	Old French
Chin.	Chinese		OHG.	Old High German
Dan.	Danish		ON.	Old Norse
Du.	Dutch		ONF.	Old North French
E.	English		Pers.	Persian
F.	French		Peruv.	Peruvian
Flem.	Flemish		Port.	Portuguese
G.	Greek		Rom.	Romany
Gael.	Gaelic		Russ.	Russian
Ger.	German		S.	South
Heb.	Hebrew		Sans.	Sanskrit
Hind.	Hindustani		Sc.	Scottish, Scots
Hung.	Hungarian		Scand.	Scandinavian
Ice.	Icelandic		Slav.	Slavonic
Ind.	Indian		Sp.	Spanish
Ir.	Irish		Sw.	Swedish
It.	Italian		Teut.	Teutonic
Jap.	Japanese		Tibet.	Tibetan
L.	Latin		Turk.	Turkish
LL.	Low or Late Latin		U.S.	United States
M.	Middle		VL.	Vulgar Latin
Malay	Malay		W.	Welsh, West

A

a, an *a.* one; any. [OE, an, one]

aard'vark *n.* S. African ant-bear. [Du. *aarde*, earth, *Larken*, pig]

A-bomb *n.* atomic bomb.

ab'aca *n.* Indian plantain, Manila hemp. [Malay]

ab'acus *n-* flat piece at the top of a column; frame with parallel wires on which slide beads for counting. [L. -G. *abax*, tablet, reckoning board]

abalo'ne (-one) *n.* shellfish yielding mother-of-pearl. [Sp. Amer.]

aban'don *v.t.* give up altogether.

aban'doned *pp.* and *a.* given up, *esp.* to evil. -aban'donment *n.* [F. *abandonner*]

abase' *v.t.* lower, humiliate. -abase'-ment *n.* [F. *abaiser*. See base]

abash' *v.t.* confuse, make ashamed. -abash'ment *n.* [F. *ébahir*, astound]

abate' *v.t.* lessen. *-v.i.* become less. abate'ment *n.* [F. *abatire*, beat off]

ab'bey *n.* monastery or nunnery under an abbot, abbess. [abbot] **abb'ot** *n.* head of a monastery. -abb'ess *fem.* -abb'acy *n.* office of abbot. [OE. *abbod*, fr. L. *abbas*, father]

abbreviate *v.t.* shorten or abridge. -abbrevia'tion *n.* [L. *abbreviate*]

ab'dicate *v.t.* give up formally. *-v.i.* give up power or office, *esp.* the throne. abdica'tion *n.* [L. *abdicate*]

abdo'men *n.* belly. -abdom'inal *a.* [L.]

abduct' *v.t.* carry off, kidnap. -abduction *n.* [L *abducere*, lead away]

aberration *n.* wandering, *esp.* mental disorder, 'wandering of wits.'—aberr'ant *a.* [L. *aberrare*, wander away]

abet' *v.t.* help in something bad. -abett'er, abett'or *n.* [OF. *abeter*, egg on]

abey'ance *n.* suspension from use or action. [OF. *abéance*, fr. *aboer*, gape at]

abhor' *v.t.* dislike very strongly; loathe, detest. -abhorr'ence *n.* -abhor'ent *a*, [L. *ab-horrere*, shrink from]

abide' *v. i.* stay, reside; await. *-v.t.* endure, put up with. [OE. *abidan*]

ab'igail *n.* lady's maid. [Biblical character]

abil'ity *n.* capacity, power, skill. [L. *habilis*, easy to hold]

a'ble *a.* capable, clever, having power or skill. -a'bly *adv.* [L. *habilis*, fit]

ablu'tion *n.* washing; ceremonial cleansing. [L. *abluere*, wash away]

ab'negate *v.t.* give up, renounce. abnega'tion *n.* [L. *abnegare*, deny]

abnorm'al *a.* irregular; not usual; not according to type; exceptional. [L. *ab*, from, *norma*, rule]

aboard' *adv.* on board, on a ship, train or plane. *-prep.* on board of. [board]

abode' *n.* home, dwelling. [abide]

abolish *v.t.* do away with. -aboli'tion *n.* -aboli'tionism *n.* -aboli'tionist *n.* one who wishes to do away with, *esp.* an evil, *e.g.* , slavery. [F. *abolir*]

aborigines (-ji-nez) *n. pl.* original in-

habitants of a country. -aborig'inal *a.* [L. *ab origine*, from the beginning]

abort' *v.t.* miscarry-abor'tion *n.* something misshapen or unnatural. abor'tive *a.* prematurely born; come to nothing. [L. *aboriri*, miscarry]

abound' *v.t.* be plentiful. [F. *abonder* L. *abundare*, overflow]

about' *adv.* on all sides; nearly; up and down; out, astir. *-prep.* round; near; dealing with. [OE. *onbutan*]

above' *adv.* in a higher place. *-prep.* on top of, higher; more than. [OE. *abufan*]

abridge' *v.t.* cut short, abbreviate. -abridg'ment *n.* [F. *abreger*]

abroad' *adv.* out of house or country; at large. [ME. *on brede*, on breadth]

ab'rogate *v.t.* cancel, put an end to. -abroga'tion *n.* [L. *abrogare*, call ofl]

abrupt' *a.* hasty; steep; sudden; blunt. -abrupt'ly *adv.* -abrupt'ness *n.* [L. *abrumpere*, break off]

ab'scess (-ses) *n.* collection of pus in the tissues. [L. *abscedere*, go away]

abscond' (-sk-) *v.i.* withdraw; decamp. [L. *abscondere*, hide away]

ab'sent *a.* away, not present. -(absent') *v.t.* keep away. -ab'sence *n.* -absentee' *n.* one away; one who habitually stays away. -absentee'ism *n.* practise of a landlord living away from his estate, or a man absenting himself from his work. ab'sently *adv.* -ab'sent-mind'ed *a.* inattentive, preoccupied. -ab'sent-mindedness *n.* [L. *absens*, away]

ab'sinthe (ab'sinth) *n.* wormwood; liqueur flavored with wormwood. [F.]

ab'solute *a.* not limited, unconditional; entire, pure (as absolute alcohol). ab'solutely *adv.* -ab'soluteness *n.* [L. *absolvere*, set free]

absolve' *v.t.* free from, pardon. -absolu'tion *n.* [L. *absolvere*, set free]

absorb' *v.t.* suck up, drink in; engage the whole attention of -absorb'ent *a.* and *n.* -absorp'tion *n.* -absorp'tive *a.* [L. *absorbers*, suck away]

abstain *v. i.* keep from, refrain, *esp.* from strong drink. [L. *abstenere*, hold from]

ab'stract *a.* separate; existing only in the mind, not concrete. *-n.* summary, abridgment. -abstract' *v. t.* draw from, remove. -abstract'ed *a.* absent-minded. -abstraction *n.* -abstract'ly *adv.* [L. *abstrahere*, draw away]

absurd' *a.* silly, contrary to reason. -absurd'ity *n.* -absurd'ly *adv.* [L. *absurdus*, fr. *surdus*, deaf]

abundance *n.* great plenty. -abun'dant *a.* plentiful. -abun'dantly *adv.* [F. *abondance*]

abuse' *v.t.* misuse; miscall, address in rude language. *n.* abu'sive *a.* -abu'sively *adv.* -abu'siveness *n.* (L. *ab*, away from, *uti*, use]

abut' *v. i.* end on, border on. -abut'ment *n.* support, *esp.* for the end of a bridge. [OF. *abouter*, join at the end]

abyss' *n.* very deep gulf or pit. -abys'mal (-z-) *a.* -abys'mally *adv.* -abyss'al *a.* [G. *abyssos*, bottomless]

acad'emy *n.* higher school; society to advance arts or sciences. **-academ′ic** *a.* of an academy; theoretical. **-academ′ically** *adv.* **-academi′cian** *n.* [G. *akademeia*, garden where Plato taught]

accel′erate (aks-) *v.t.* and *i,* increase speed. **-accelera′tion** *n.* **-accel′erative** *a.* **-accel′erator** *n.* mechanism to increase speed, *esp.* in an automobile. [L. *accelerate,* fr. *celer,* swift]

ac′cent (aks-) *n.* stress of the voice; mark to show such stress; manner of speech peculiar to a district or individual. **-(sent′)** *v.t.* **-accen′tual** *a.* **-accen′tuate** *v.t.* **-accentua′tion** *n.* [F., fr. L. accentual note or tone]

accept′ (aks-) *v.t.* take, receive; admit, believe; agree to [L. *acceptare,* take]

ac′cess (-ks-) *n.* admission; entrance; attack; liberty to approach; means of approach. **-accessibil′ity** *n.* **-access′ible** *a.* easy to approach. **-access′ibly** *adv.* [L. *accedere,* go near to]

accessary *n.* helper, *esp.* in a crime. [*access*]

accessory *a.* additional. **-***n.* added or nonessential item of dress or equipment; accomplice, aid in crime (*access*)

ac′cidence (-ks-) *n.* part of grammar dealing with changes in the form of words, *e.g.,* plurals. [for accidents]

ac′cident (-ks-) *n.* something happening by chance; mishap; quality not essential. **-acciden′tal** *a.* happening by chance. **-***n.* (*mus.*) sharp, flat or natural, not of the key. **-acciden′tally** *adv.* [F.]

acclaim′ *v.t.* applaud, receive with applause. **-acclama′tion** *n.* **-acclam′a-tory** *a.* [L. *acclamare,* shout to]

accolade′ *n.* part of the ceremony of conferring knighthood, a light stroke with a flat of the sword. [F.]

accomm′odate *v.t.* fit; harmonize; supply. **-accomm′odating** *a.* obliging. **accommoda′tion** *n.* lodgings; loan; adjustment or compromise; obligingness. [L. *accommodate,* fit]

accom′pany *v.t.* go with; join with. **accom′paniment** *n.* something which accompanies, *esp.* (*mus.*) the instrumental part which goes with, *e.g.,* a vocal solo. **-accom′panist** *n.* one who plays an accompaniment. [F. *accompagner*]

accom′plice *n.* companion in evil deeds. [Earlier *complice,* fr. L. *complex,* woven together]

accom′plish *v.t.* carry out; finish. **accom′plished** *a.* complete, perfect; socially talented. **-accom′plishment** *n.* completion; a personal ability, talent. [F. *accomplir*]

accord′ *v.t.* compose, settle. **-***v.i.* agree. **-***n.* agreement, harmony. **-accord′-ance** *n.* **-accord′ant** *a.* **-accord′ing** *adv.* [L. *ad,* to, *cor, cordis,* heart]

accord′ion *n.* wind instrument worked by a bellows in the hands, a concertina. [See **accord**]

account′ *v.t.* reckon, judge. **-***v.i.* give a reason; make a statement of money. **-***n.* statement of monies; report, description. **-ac-**

countabil′ity *n.* **-account′able** *a.* responsible. **-account′ant** *n.* professional reckoner, one skilled in accounts. [OF. *aconter,* reckon]

accountancy *n.* the office or work of an accountant. [OF. *acconter*-L. *ad,* to, *computare,* to reckon]

accumulate *v.t.* amass. **-***v.i.* grow into a mass, increase. **-accumula′tion** *v.* **-accu′mulator** *n.* electrical storage battery. [L. *cumulare,* heap up]

ac′curate *a.* exact, correct. **-ac′curacy** *n.* **-ac′curately** *adv.* **-ac′curateness** *n.* [L. *accurare,* give care to]

accurs′ed, accurst′ *a.* under a curse; hateful. [*a-, intens.* and cursed]

accuse′ *v.t.* charge with wrongdoing; blame. **-accusa′tion** *n.* **-accu′sative** *n.* Latin case of nouns indicating an object. **-accu′satory** *a.* **-accu′ser** *n.* [L. *accusare,* call to account]

accus′tom *v.t.* make used to, familiarize. **-accus′tomed** *a.* [OF. *acostumer*]

acer′bity *n.* sour, bitterness; severity of manner. [L. *acerbitas*]

ace′tic *a.* derived from or having the nature of vinegar. [L. *acetum,* vinegar]

acet′ylene *n.* gas made from calcium carbide and water, burning with a bright flame. [*acetic*]

ache (ak) *n.* continuous pain. **-***v.i.* be in pain. **-ach′ing** *a.* [OE. *acan*]

achieve′ *v.t.* finish, accomplish, perform successfully. **-achieve′ment** *n.* something accomplished; high exploit; coat of arms. [F. *achever*]

achromat′ic *a.* free from or not showing color, as of a lens. **-achro′matism** *n.* [G. *achrom, atos*]

ac′id *a.* sharp, sour. **-***n.* sour substance; (*chem.*) one of a class of compounds which combine with bases (alkalis, oxides, *etc.*) to form salts. **-acid′ify** *v.t.* **-acid′ity** *n.* [L. *acidus-acere,* be sour]

acknow′ledge (-nol′ -) *v.t.* admit, own, recognize. **-acknow′ledgment** *n.* [ME. *knowlechen,* perceive]

ac′me *n.* highest point. [G. *akme,* point]

ac′ne *n.* skin disease; pimple. [G. *akme,* point]

a′corn *n.* fruit of the oak. [OE. *æcern,* fruit of the open country]

acous′tic *a.* pertaining to hearing. **acous′tics** *n. pl.* science of sounds. **acoustic guitar** *n.* one not amplified by electronic means. [G. *akoustikos*]

acquaint′ *v.t.* make to know, inform. **-acquaint′ance** *n.* personal knowledge; person known. **-acquaint′anceship** *n.* [OF. *acointier*-L. *ad,* to, *cognitus,* known]

acquiesce′ *v.i.* agree in silence; consent. **-acquiescence** *n.* **-acquiescent** *a.* [L. *acquiescere,* rest]

acquire′ *v.t.* gain, get. **-acquire′ment** *n.* **-acquisi′tion** *n.* act of getting; thing gained. [L. *acquirere*]

acquit′ *v.t.* settle, discharge, as a debt; behave (oneself); declare innocent. **acquit′al** *n.* act of declaring innocent in a court. **-**

acquitt'ance *n.* discharge of a debt. [F. *acquitter*]

a'cre (*a'*-ker) *n.* measure of land, 4840 square yards. -pl. lands, estates. [OE. *wer*, field]

ac'rid *a.* bitter and hot to the taste; irritating. -acrid'ity *n.* -ac'ridness *n.* [irreg. formation fr. L. *acer*, sharp]

ac'rimony *n.* bitterness of feelings or language. -acrimo'nious *a.* sharp, biting, severe. [L. *acrimonia*]

ac'robat *n.* performer of skilled gymnastic feats. -acrobat'ic *a.* -acrobat'ics *n. pl.* his art- [G. *akrobatos*, tiptoe walking]

acrophobia *n.* fear of heights. [G. *akron*, point, *phobos*, fear]

across *adv.* and *prep.* crosswise; from side to side. [For on or in cross]

acros'tic *n.* poem in which the first or last letters of the lines, in order, spell a word or words. [G. *akros*, extreme, and *stichos*, row or verse]

act *n.* thing done, deed; process of doing; law or decree; section of a play. -v.t. perform, as in a play. -v.i. exert force; work, as a mechanism; behave. -ac'ting *n.* performance of a part; working. -ac'tion *n.* -activity; operation; gesture; battle; lawsuit. [F. *acte* fr. L. *agere*, do]

act'ual *adv.* real; existing in the present; not imaginary or bygone. -actual'ity *n.* ac'tually *adv.* [l. *actualis*]

ac'tuary *n.* registrar; one who makes calculations for insurance companies. -actua'rial *a.* [L. *actuarius*, recorder]

ac'umen *n.* sharpness of wit. [L.]

acute *a.* sharp; sensitive; keen, shrewd; critical. -acute'ly *adv.* -acute'ness *n.* [L. *acutus*, sharpened]

ad'age *n.* old saying, proverb. [F.]

ada'gio *a.* and *adv.* (*mus.*) slowly. -*n.* slow movement. [It. *ad agio*, at ease]

ad'amant *n.* very hard stone; diamond. -*a.* very hard, unbreakable; unyielding. -adamant'ine *a.* [G. *adamas*, invincible, not to be broken or tamed]

adapt' *v.t.* fit; modify; alter for a new use. [L. *adaptare*]

add *v.t.* and *i.* join; put something on; say further. -adden'dum (*pl.* -a) something to be added. -addi'tion *n.* -addi'tional *a.* [L. *addere*, put to]

ad'dict *n.* one given up to something, usually an evil, *e.g.*, drug-addict. **addict'ed** *a.* -addic'tion *n.* [L. *addictus;-addicere*, make over]

address' *v.t.* speak to; direct; dispatch; mark a destination, as on an envelope. -address (a speech; direction on a letter.-**addressee'** *n.* person to whom a letter *etc.* is directed. -address'es *n. pl.* courtship. [F. *adresser*, make straight]

ad'enoids *n. pl.* small growths at the back of the nasal passage. [G. *aden*, acorn]

adept' *a.* skilled. -(ad'-) *n.* expert; alchemist. [L. *adeptus*, having attained]

ad'equate *a.* sufficient, suitable; equal to. -ad'equacy *n.* -ad'equately *adv.* [L.

adæquatus, made equal to]

adhere' *v.i.* stick to; become or remain firm, in an opinion *etc.* -adhe'rent *n.* and a. -adhe'sion *n.* -adhe'sive *a.* [L. *adhærere*, stick]

ad'it *n.* horizontal entrance into a pit or mine. [L. *adire*, go in]

adja'cent *a.* lying close to; contiguous. -adja'cency *n.* [L. *adjacere*]

adjective *n.* word added to a noun to show quality or circumstance. -adjecti'val *a.* [L. *adjectivus*, added]

adjoin' *v.t.* and *i.* add; be next to. **adjoin'ing** *a.* [F. *adjoindre*]

adjourn' (a-jurn') *v.t.* and *i.* put off, postpone; end a meeting; move to another place. -adjourn'ment *n.* [F. *ajourner*, fr. OF. *journ*, day]

adjudicate *v.t.* and *i.* try, judge; sit in judgment. -adjudica'tion *n.* -adju'diator *n.* [L. *adjudicate*]

a'junct *a.* joined, added. -*n.* person or ing added. [L. *adjungere*, add to]

adjure' *v.t.* beg, entreat; charge on oath. -adjura'tion *n.* [L. *adjurare*, swear]

adjust' *v.t.* set right; make exact or suitable; arrange. -adjust'able *a.* -adjust'ment *n.* [F. *ajuster*, fr. *juste*, right]

ad'jutant *n.* military officer who assists the commanding officer of a unit. **ad'jutancy** *n.* [L. adjutare, help]

admin'ister *v.t.* manage; look after; dispense, as justice *etc.*; supply. **admin'istra'tion** *n.* -admin'istrative. *a.* -admin'istrator *n.* [L. *administrate*]

ad'miral *n.* naval officer of very high or great rank. -ad'miralty *n.* board which controls the British Navy; buildings of that board. [F. *amiral*, fr. Arab. *amir-al* (*bahr*), prince of the (sea)]

admire' *v.t.* look on with wonder and pleasure; respect highly; love or esteem. **admirable** *a.* -ad'mirably *adv.* admiration *n.* -admir'er *n.* -admir'ingly *adv.* [L. *admirari*, wonder at]

admit' *v.t.* let in; allow; accept as true; grant. -admissibil'ity *n.* -admiss'ible *a.* -admiss'ibly *adv.* -admis'sion *n.* -admitt'ance *n.* [L. *admittere*, send to]

admon'ish *v. t.* warn; reprove gently; advise. -admoni'tion *n.* -admon'itory *a.* [earlier *amonest*, OF. *amonester*, advise]

adoles'cent *a.* growing to manhood; not fully adult. -*n.* youth. -adoles'cence *n.* [L. *adolescere*, grow up]

adopt' *v.t.* take into relationship, *esp.* as one's child; take up, as a principle, resolution, idea. [L. *adoptare*, choose for oneself]

adore' *v.t.* and *i.* worship; love intensely. -ador'able *a.* -adora'tion *n.* -ador'er *n.* [L. *adorare*, worship, pray to]

adorn' *v.t.* beautify, embellish, deck. -adorn'ment *n.* [L. *adornare*]

adre'nal *a.* near the kidneys. **-adre'nal** glands, two small ductless glands over the kidneys. -adre'nalin *n.* secretion of these glands, taken from animals for use in medicine; powerful astringent drug. [L. *ad*, to, *renes*, kidneys]

adrift' *a.* and *adv.* floating free; loose; without aim or direction. [*on drift*]

adroit' *a.* skilful, expert, clever; dexterous. -**adroit'ly** *adv.* -**adroitness** *n.* [F. , orig. *àd droit*, rightly]

ad'ult *a.* -grown-up, mature. -*n.* grownup person. [L. *adolescere, adult-*, grow]

adul'terate *v.t.* corrupt; make impure by mixture. -**adul'terant** *a.* -**adultera'tion** *n.* -**adul'terator** *n.* [L. *adulterate*, corrupt]

advance' *v.t.* bring forward; promote; encourage; pay beforehand. -*v.i.* go forward; improve in rank or value. [F. *avancer*, put forward]

advantage *n.* gain; superiority. -*v.t.* benefit, promote. -**advanta'geous** *a.* -**advanta'geously** *adv.* [F. *avantage*]

ad'vent *n.* coming, arrival; the first or second coming of Christ; season of four weeks before Christmas. -**adven'tual** *a.* [L. *adventus–ad*, to, *venire*, come]

adven'ture *n.* remarkable happening; enterprise; risk; bold exploit; commercial speculation. -*v.t.* and *i.* risk; take a risk. -**adven'turer** *n. masc.* [F. *aventure*]

ad'verb *n.* word added to a verb, adjective or other adverb to modify the meaning. -**adverb'ial** *a.* [L. *adverbium*, fr. *ad*, to, *verbum*, word]

ad'verse *a.* opposed to; hostile; contrary to desire. -**ad'versary** *n.* enemy-**advers'ative** *a.* -**ad'versely** *adv.* -**advers'ity** *n.* distress, misfortune. [L. *advertere*, turn against]

advert' *v. i.* turn the mind or attention to; refer. -**advert'ence** *n.* -**advert'ency** *n.* -**advert'ent** *a.* -**advert'ently** *adv.* [L. *advertere*, turn to]

advertise *v.t.* and *i.* make known; give notice of, *esp.* in newspapers, bills *etc.* -**advert'isement** *n.* -**ad'vertiser** *n.* **ad'vertising** *n.* and *a.* [F. *avertir*, warn]

advice' *n.* opinion given; counsel; iformation, news (*esp.* in *pl.*). [F. *avis*]

advise *v.t.* and *i.* give an opinion to; recommend a line of conduct; inform. **advis'able** *a.* expedient. -**advised'** (-zd) *a.* considered, deliberate, as in well-advised. -**advi'sedly** *adv.* -**advi'ser**, advisor *n.* -**advi'sory** *a.* [F. *avis*]

ad'vocate *n.* defender; one who pleads the cause of another, *esp.* in a court of law. -*v.t.* uphold, recommend. **ad'vocacy** *n.* -**advoca'tion** *n.* [L. *advocatus*, called in]

ae'on *n.* age, or series of ages; period of time; eternity. [G. *aion*, age]

a'erate *v.t.* expose to, or mix with, air; charge with carbonic acid or other gas. -**a'erator** *n.* apparatus to do this. **aera'tion** *n.* [L. *aer*, air]

aer'ial *a.* belonging to the air; ethereal: -*n.* elevated wire to send out or receive radio signals. [L. *aer*, air]

a'erie, a'ery, ey'rie *n.* nest of a bird of prey, *esp.* an eagle. [F. *aire*]

aero- *prefix* having to do with air or aircraft. [L. *aer*, air] -**aerobat'ics** *n.* 'stunts' in aviation. -**a'erodrome** *n.* airfield. -**a'erogram** *n.* air

letter. **a'erolite** *n.* meteoric stone. -**a'eronaut** *n.* 'air-sailor', *esp.* one who flies in airships or balloons. -**aeronaut'ics** *n. pl.* science of air navigation.

aero'bia *n. pl.* bacteria that cannot live without air, [G. *aer*, air, *bios*, life]

aero'bics *n.* any system of sustained exercises designed to increase the amount of oxygen in the blood and strengthen the heart and lungs.

a'erosol *n.* suspension of fine solid or liquid particles in a gas; container for dispensing such.

aesthetic, esthetic *a.* relating to the principles of beauty and taste, and of art. -**aes'thete, es'thete** *a.* one who affects an extravagant love of art. **aesthetically, esthetically** *adv.* [G. *aisthesthai*, perceive]

afar' *adv.* from, at, or to a distance. [M. E. *on fer* and *offer*, becoming *a fer*]

af'fable *a.* easy to speak to, polite and friendly. -**af'fabil'ity** *n.* -**af'fably** *adv.* [F]

affair' *n.* business operation; any small matter; romantic attachment. -*pl.* matters in general; public business. [F. *affaire*, fr. *faire*, do]

affect' *v.t.* acton, influence; move the feelings of, make a show of, make pretense; assume. -**affecta'tion** *n.* show, pretense. -**affec'ted** *a.* making a pretense. **affec'tedly** *adv.* -**affec'ting** *a.* moving the feelings, pathetic. -**affec'tingly** *adv.* -**affec'tion** *n.* fondness, love. **affec'tionate** *a.* loving. -**affec'tionately** *adv.* [L. *affectare*, aim at, fr. *afficere*, apply oneself to]

affida'vit *n.* written statement on oath. [Late L. = he has sworn]

affiliate *v.t.* adopt; attach, as a society to a federation, *etc.*; attribute to, father on. -**affilia'tion** *n.* [L. *affiliate*]

affinity *n.* relationship; structural resemblance; attraction, *esp.* chemical attraction. -**affin'itive** *a.* [L. *affinitas*]

affirm' *v.t.* assert positively; maintain a statement. -*v.i.* make a solemn declaration, *esp.* without oath in a court of law. [L, *affirmare*, make firm]

affix' *v.t.* fasten to, attach. -**affix** *n.* addition, *esp.* to a word, as a suffix or prefix. [L. *affigere, affix-*, fix to]

afflict' *v.t.* give pain or grief, vex. -**afflic'tion** *n.* distress, that which afflicts. -**afflic'tive** *a.* [L. *affligere*]

af'fluent *a.* wealthy. -*n.* tributary stream. -**af'fluence** *n.* wealth, abundance. [L. *affluere*, flow towards]

afford' *v.t.* be able to buy, or. to sustain the expense of; produce, yield. [earlier *aforth*, OE. *geforthian*, fr. *forth*, forward]

affray' *n.* fight, brawl. [OF. verb *esfreier*, frighten. Verb in E. survives only in p. p. *afraid* = *affrayed*]

affront' *v.t.* insult openly; meet face to face. -*n.* insult; contemptuous treatment. [F. *affronter*, confront]

afire' *adv.* on fire; in an inflamed condition. [*fire*]

afresh' *adv.* again, anew. [*fresh*]

aft *adv.* towards or near the stern of a ship. [OE. *æftan*]

af'ter *adv.* behind; later. *-prep.* like or in imitation of-; behind; later than. *a.* behind; later; nearer to the stern of a ship. [OE. *æfter*, farther away]

af'ter- as prefix makes compounds, as after-birth *n.* membrane expelled after a birth. -af'terclap *n.* brief, dramatic recrudescence of an affair apparently closed. -aftercrop *n.* - afterdamp *n.* gas left after an explosion in a coalmine. -af'terglow *n.* light after sunset. -af'termath *n.* second mowing of grass; sequel, later or secondary results. af'ternoon *n.* -af'terthought *n.* af'terwards, af'terward *adv.* later. [OE. *Eeftanweard*]

again' *adv.* once more; back, in return; besides. [OE. *ongean*]

against' *prep.* opposite; in opposition to; in contact with; in exchange for. [*again*, with *gen. -es*, and *-t* added]

age *n.* length of time a person or thing has existed; period of time; period of history; maturity; a long time. *-v.t.* make old. *v. i.* grow old. *-a'ged a.* old. *-n. pl.* old people. -age'less *a.* -age'long *a.* [OF. *edage*, fr. L. *a!tas*, age]

agen'da *n.* things to be done; program of a business meeting. [L.]

a'gent *n.* person or thing producing an effect; cause; natural force; person authorised to carry on business or affairs for another. - a'gency *n.* instrumentality; business or place of business of an agent. [L. *agere*, do]

aggravate *v.t.* make worse; [colloq.] annoy. -ag'gravating *a.* -aggrava'tion *n.* [L. *aggravate*, make heavy]

aggregate *v.t.* gather into a mass. *-n.* sum total. -aggrega'tion *n.* -ag'gregative *a.* [L. *aggregate*, form into a rock]

aggres'sion *n.* unprovoked attack. aggress' *v.i.* -aggress'ive *a.* quarrelsome. - aggress'iveness *n.* -aggress'or *n.* [L. *aggredi, aggress-*, advance towards]

aghast' *a.* terrified; horror-stricken. [earlier *agast*, fr. OE. *æmstan*, terrify]

ag'ile (-j-) *a.* active, nimble. -ag'ilely *adv.* -agil'ity *n.* [F. , fr. L. *agere*, do]

ag'itate (-j-) *v.t.* keep in motion; disturb, excite; keep in discussion. -agita'tion *n.* - ag'itator *n.* [L. *agitare*]

agnos'tic *n.* one who holds that we know nothing of things outside the material world. -agnos'ticism *n.* [G. *a*, not, *gnostos*, knowing]

ago' *adv.* gone; since; past. [earlier *agone*, p. p. of OE. *agan*, pass]

ag'ony *n.* extreme suffering; violent struggle; death struggle. -ag'onize *v.i.* suffer great pain or sorrow. -ag'onizing *a.* [G. *agonia*, struggle for victory]

agorapho'bia *n.* morbid fear of crossing open spaces. [G. agora, market-place, phobos, fear]

agree' *v. i.* be of one mind; consent; harmonize; determine, settle; suit. agreeabil'ity *n.* -agree'able *a.* agreeableness *n.* - agree'ably *adv.* agree'ment *n.* [F. *agréer*, fr. L, *gratus*, pleasing]

ag'riculture *n.* art or practise of cultivating the ground. -agricult'ural *a.* agricult'uralist, agriculturist *n.* [L. *agricultural*, tillage of the field]

aground' *adv.* stranded. [on ground]

a'gue *n.* fever in periodic fits, with shivering; quaking. [F. *aigu*, sharp]

ahead' *adv.* in front of. [*a* and *head*]

ahoy' *int.* shout used at sea for hailing, calling attention. [ME. hoy]

aid *v.t.* help. *-n.* help, support; something helpful. [F. *aider* -L. *adjutare*]

AIDS *n.* acronym for acquired immune (or immuno-) deficiency syndrome.

ail *v.t.* trouble, afflict. *-v.i.* be ill. -ail'ing *a.* -ail'ment *n.* [OE. *eglan*]

ail'eron *n.* steadying flap on wing-tip of airplane. [F. -L. *ala*, wing]

aim *v.t.* and *i* . direct effort towards; try to; give direction to a weapon; strike or throw. *-n.* direction; endeavor; object, purpose. - aim'less *a.* without object. [OF. *esmer*, estimate]

air *n.* mixture of gases we breathe, the atmosphere; breeze; tune; manner; affected manner. *-pl.* affected manners. *v.t.* expose; dry or warm. [G. *aer*, fr. *aein*, blow]

air- used as a prefix makes compounds denoting things in, of, or having to do with the air, as air'balloon *n.* , including broadcasting by radiowaves, as air'time. -air' base *n.* -air brake *n.* air' chamber *n.* -air'-condition *v.t.* fit with system to keep the interior air atrequisite temperature *etc.* -aircraft *n.* -air'craft carrier *n.* -air'crew *n.* air'duct *n.* -air' force *n.* national organization dealing with military aircraft. -airgun *n.* gun discharged by force of compressed air. -air' hole *n.* -air' lane *n.* aircraft route. -air' lift *n.* organized air transport operation. -air'line *n.* organization dealing with transport by airplanes. -air'man *n.* -air'plane *n.* heavier-than-air flying machine -air'pocket *n.* part of the air where an airplane drops suddenly. -air'port *n.* station for passenger aircraft. air' power *n.* - air'tight *a.* not allowing the passage of air. -air'valve *n.* -air'way *n.* regular aircraft route. air'worthy *a.* fit for service in the air. airwor'thiness *n.*

aisle *n.* wing of a church, or lateral division of any part of a church; walk between seats in a church. [bad spelling of F. *aile*-fr. L. *ala*, wing]

ajar' *adv.* partly open. [ME. *on char*, on the turn]

alabaster *n.* kind of soft, white, semitransparent stone. [G. *alabastros*]

alack' *int.* cry of sorrow. -alack'-a-day *int.* [prob. change of *alas*, by association with lack, failure or shame]

alac'rity *n.* quickness, briskness. [L. *alacritas*]

alarm' *n.* notice of danger; sudden fright; call to arms. *-v.t.* warn of danger; frighten. -alarm'ing *a.* -alarm'ist *n.* one given to prophesying danger. -alarm-clock *n.* clock which rings a bell at a set hour to give warning of the time. [OF. *à l'arme*, fr. It. *all' arme*, to arms (cp. *alert*). With the *r* rolled it gives also *alarum.*

alas' *int.* cry of grief. [OF. *a las, ah*, weary]

al'bacore *n.* large kind of tunna fish. [Port.]

albatross *n.* large, long-winged seabird, remarkable for its flying powers. [fr. obs. *alcatras*, frigate-bird, influenced by L. *albus*, white]

albi'no *n.* person or animal with unusually white skin and hair and pink eyes, due to lack of pigment in the skin. **al'binism** *n.* [Sp. , fr. L. *albus*, white]

al'bum *n.* book of blank leaves, for collecting portraits, stamps, autographs *etc.* [L. *albus*, white]

albu'men *n.* constituent of animal and vegetable matter, found nearly pure in white of egg. **-albu'minoid** *a.* albuminous *a.* [L. , fr. *albus*, white]

al'chemy (-k-) *n.* earlier stage of chemistry, its main aims the turning of base metals into gold and the finding of an elixir of life. **al'chemist** *n.* [Arab. *alkimiya*, transmutation]

al'cohol *n.* liquid made in fermenting sugar *etc.* , and forming the intoxicating part of fermented drinks. **-alcohol'ic** *a.* **alcoholiza'tion** *n.* **-al'coholize** *v.t.* **al'coholism** *n.* a disease, alcohol poisoning. [Arab. *al koh'l*, fine powder used to darken the eyelids]

al'cove *n.* recess; arbor, bower. [Arab. *al qobbah*, the vault]

al'derman (awl'-) *n.* town councillor appointed for life or a long period and not elected like the ordinary councillors. [OE. *ealdormann*, elder, chief]

ale *n.* fermented malt beverage, beer. **ale'-house** *n.* [OE. *ealu*]

alert' *a.* watchful; brisk. -n. sudden attack or surprise; alarm signal. **alert'ness** *n.* [OF. *à l'érte*, It. *all'erta*, to the height (watchtower). cp. *alarm*]

al'gae *n. pl.* seaweed. **-al'gous** *a.* [L. *alga*]

al'gebra *n.* method of calculating, using letters to represent the numbers and signs to show relations between them, making a kind of abstract arithmetic. **-algebra'ic, algebra'ical** *a.* **-al'gebraist** *n.* [Arab. *al-jebr*, joining of broken parts]

al'gesia *n.* the capacity to feel pain. [G. *algesis*, sense of pain]

a'lias *adv.* otherwise. -n. assumed name. [L.]

al'ibi *n.* plea that a person charged with a crime was somewhere else when it was conunitted. [L. = other-where]

a'lien *a.* foreign; different in nature; adverse. -n. foreigner. **-alienabil'ity** *n.* **-a'lienable** *a.* capable of being transferred, as property not entailed. **a'lienate** *v.t.* transfer; estrange. **alienation** *n.* **-a'lienism** *n.* **-a'lienist** *n.* doctor who specializes in treatment of mental disease. [L. *alienus*, foreign]

align', **aline'** *v.t.* bring into line. **align'ment**, **aligne'ment** *n.* [F. *ligne*, line]

alike' *a.* like, similar. [ME. *yliche*]

al'iment *n.* food. **-v.t.** feed, support. **aliment'ary** *a.* **-alimenta'tion** *n.* [L. *alimentu-alere*, nourish]

al'imony *n.* income allowed to a man or woman legally separated from his or her spouse. [L. *alimonia*, maintenance]

al'kali *n.* substance which combines with acid and neutralizes it, forming a salt. Potash, soda *etc.* are alkalis. **-al'kaline** *a.* **-alkalin'ity** *n.* **-al'kalize** *v.t.* **-al'kaloid** *n.* [Arab. *al-qali*, burnt ashes of certain plants]

all (awl) *a.* the whole of, every one of. *adv.* wholly, entirely. -n. the whole, everything. [OE. *all, eall*]

allege' *v.t.* and *i.* plead, bring forward as an argument; assert. **-allega'tion** *n.* [L. *allegare*, quote]

alle'giance *n.* duty of a subject to his government or superior; loyalty. [*See* liege]

alleg'ro *adv.* (*mus.*) briskly. [It.]

alle'viate *v.t.* make light, ease, lessen. **allevia'tion** *n.* **-alle'viator** *n.* (Late L. *alleviate*, fr. *levis*, light]

allitera'tion *n.* beginning of two or more words in close succession with the same sound, as *e.g.* , Sing a song of Sixpence. **-allit'erate** *v.i.* **-allit'erative** *a.* [L. *ad*, to, and *littera*, letter]

al'locate *v.t.* place; assign as a share. **-allocation** *n.* apportionment [VL. *allocare*, fr. *locus* place]

allot' *v.t.* give out; distribute as shares. **allot'ment** *n.* **-allott'ee** *n.* [OF. *aloter. See* lot]

allow' *v.t.* acknowledge; permit; give, grant. **-allow'able** *a.* **-allow'ably** *adv.* **-allow'ance** *n.* [OF. *allouer*]

alloy' *v.t.* mix metals; debase. -n. mixture of two or more metals. **alloy'age** *n.* [F. *aloi*, fr. L. *alligare*, bind]

allude' *v. i.* mention lightly, make indirect reference to; refer to. **-allu'sion** *n.* **-allu'sive** *a.* **-allu'sively** *adv.* [L. *alludere, allus-*, play on]

allure' *v.t.* entice, win over; fascinate. **allure'ment** *n.* **-allu'ring** *a.* **-allu'r-ingly** *adv.* [*lure*]

allu'vial *a.* deposited by rivers. **-allu'vion** *n.* land formed by washed-up earth and sand. **-allu'vium** *n.* water-borne matter deposited on lower lands. [L. *alluvius*, washed against]

ally' *v.t.* join in relationship by treaty, marriage or friendship. **-allied'** *a.* **-al'ly** *n.* confederate; state or sovereign bound to another by treaty. **-pl.** **ai'lies.** [F. *allier*]

almond (am'-) *n.* kernel of the fruit of a tree related to the peach; the tree. [OF. *alamande*]

almost (awl'-) *adv.* nearly, all but. [OE. *eallmæst*]

alms (amz) *n.* gifts to the poor. **-alm'oner** *n.* distributor of alms. **-alm'onry** *n.* place of distribution of alms. [OE. *aelmesse*, fr. G. *eleemosyne*, pity; almoner through OF. *almosnier*]

aloe *n.* genus of plants of medicinal value, found chiefly in S. Africa. **-pl.** bitter drug made from the plants; American plant of the amaryllis family [G.]

aloft' *adv.* on high; overhead; (*naut.*) at the masthead. [ON, *a lopt*, in the air]

alone' *a.* single, solitary. *-adv.* separately. [all one]

aloof' *adv.* at a distance; apart; with reserve. **-aloof'ness** *n.* [fr. Du. *to loef*, to windward]

aloud' *adv.* with loud voice; audibly; not in a whisper. [*loud*]

al'phabet *n.* set of letters used in writing a language. -alphabet'ic, **alphabetical** *a.* in the order of the letters. **-alpha-bet'ically** *adv.* [G. *alpha beta*, A, B, the first two G. letters]

alread'y (awl-red'i) *adv.* before, previously. [*all ready*, prepared]

al'so (awl'-) *adv.* further, too; in addition; besides. [OE. *eallswa*]

al'tar (awl'-) *n.* raised place, stone, etc. on which sacrifice may be offered; in a Christian Church, table on which the priest consecrates the Eucharist. [L. *altare*]

al'ter (awl'-) *v.t.* change, make different. -*v.i.* become different. [F. *altirer*, fr. L. *alter*, other]

alterca'tion (awl-) *n.* dispute, wrangling. -**al'tercate** *v. i.* -**al'tercative** *a.* [L. *allercari*, disputer]

al'ternate *v.t.* cause to occur by turns. *v.i.* happen by turns-**alter'nate** *a.* one after the other, by turns. -**alter'nately** *adv.* [L. *alternate*, fr. *alter*, other]

al'ternator *n.* generator of alternating current. -**al'ternating current**, electric current which flows in alternate directions. [L. *alter*, other]

although' *conj.* notwithstanding that. [all though]

altim'eter *n.* instrument for measuring heights. [L. *altos*, high, and *meter*]

at'titude *n.* height. [L. *altitudo*]

al'to *n.* (*mus.*) male voice of highest pitch or female of the lowest; part written for it; contralto part. [It. , fr. L. *altus*, high]

altogeth'er (awl-) *adv.* entirely. [three words in OE. *See* **together**]

al'truism *n.* principle of living and acting for the good of others. **-altruist'ic** *a.* -**altruist'ically** *adv.* [F. *altruisme*]

alum'inum *n.* metal like silver, very light. [fr. *alum*]

alum'nus *n.* graduate or pupil of a school or college. -*pl.* alum'ni. [L. *alere*, nourish]

al'ways (awl'-) *adv.* at all times; for ever. -also **always** [*all* and *ways*]

amass' *v.t.* collect in quantity. -amass'able *a.* [F. *amasser*]

am'ateur (-ur) *n.* one who carries on an art, study, game *etc.* for the love of it, not for money. -*a.* imperfect, like the work of an amateur; not professional. -amateur'ish *a.* -amateur'ishly *adv.* am'ateurism *n.* [F. fr. L. *amator*, lover]

am'atory *a.* relating to love or lovers. [L. *amatorius-amare*, love]

amaze' *v.t.* surprise, greatly astound. -amazement *n.* -ama'zing *a.* -amazingly *adv.* [OE. *amasian*]

ambassador *n.* representative of the highest rank sent by one state to another. -ambassado'rial *a.* -ambass'adress *n. fem.* [F. *ambassadeur*]

am'bergris *n.* gray substance secreted by the spermaceti whale, and used in perfumery. [F. *ambre gris*, gray amber]

am'bient *a.* surrounding, encompassing. -

n. air, sky. [L. *ambi*, about, *iens, ient-*, going]

ambiguous *a.* of double meaning; doubtful. -ambigu'ity *n.* [L. , fr. *amb* and *agere*, lit. , drive both ways]

am'bit *n.* circuit; space around; sphere of action. [L. *ambitus*, going round]

ambi'tion *n.* desire of power, fame, honor; object of that desire. -ambi'tious *a.* -ambi'tiously *adv.* -ambi'tiousness *n.* [L. *ambitio*, going about for votes-*ambire*, go round]

ambivalence, ambiv'alency *n.* in one person, opposite emotional reactions to the same thing; -ambiv'alent *a.* [L. *ambi*, both, *valere*, be strong]

am'ble *v.i.* of a horse, move with both legs together one side, then the other; move at an easy pace. -*n.* this movement. am'bler *n.* [L. *ambulate*, walk]

ambulance *n.* special carriage for the sick or wounded; movable hospital. [F. earlier *hôpital ambulant*, fr. L. *ambulate*, walk]

am'bush *n.* a lying in wait. -*v.t.* waylay, attack from hiding. [OF. embusche, hiding in the woods]

ame'liorate *v.t.* and *i.* make better, improve. [L. *ad*, to, *melior*, better]

ame'nable *a.* easy to be led or controlled. -amenabil'ity, ame'nableness *n.* -ame'nably *adv.* [F. *amener*, lead]

amend' *v. i.* grow better. -*v.t.* make better, improve; alter in detail-amendment *n.* -amends' *n. pl. reparation*. [F. *amender* -L. *ex* and *mendum*, fault]

amen'ity *n.* pleasantness. -*pl.* pleasant ways, civilities. [F. *amenité*]

am'ethyst *n.* bluish-violet precious stone. [G. *amethystos*, a-, not, *methyein*, be drunken. The stone was supposed to be a charm against drunkenness]

a'miable *a.* friendly, kindly. -amiabil'ity *n.* -a'miableness *n.* -a'miably *adv.* [F. *aimable*, lovable, fr. L. *amare*, love]

am'icable *a.* friendly. -amicabil'ity *n.* -am'icably *adv.* [Late L. *amicabilis*]

amid', amidst' *prep.* in the middle of, among. [OE. *on middan*]

am'ity *n.* friendship. [F. *amitio*]

ammo'nia *n.* pungent alkaline gas. ammo'niac *a.* -ammo'niated *a.* -ammo'nium *n.* hypothetical base of ammonia. [fr. *sal ammoniac*, salt said to have been first obtained in a region named after the god (Jupiter) *Ammon*]

am'monite *n.* fossil spiral shell of extinct mollusk. [fr. horn of (Jupiter) *Ammon*]

ammuni'tion *n.* cartridges, powder *etc.* for firearms; formerly, all military stores [F. *l'ammunition*, for *in munition*. *See* **munition**]

amne'sia *n.* loss of memory. [G.]

am'nesty *n.* general pardon. [G. *amnesia*, oblivion]

amoeb'a *n.* simplest microscopic animal, a unit mass which constantly changes its shape. [G. *amoibe*, change]

among' (-mu-), **amongst'** *prep.* mixed with, or the number of [OE. *on gemang*, fr. *gemang*, crowd]

am'orous *a.* easily moved to love; in love.

-am'orously *adv.* -am'orousness *n.* [F. *amoreux*]

amorph'ous *a.* shapeless; uncrystallized. -amorph'ism *n.* [G. *amorphos*]

amort'ize *v.t.* reduce or pay a debt through a sinking fund; convey to a corporation. [L. *ad*, to, *mortem*, death]

amount' *v. i.* come to, be equal to. -*n.* sum total; result; quantity. [OF. *amonter*, mount up]

amour' *n.* love intrigue or illicit love affair. -amour' propre (-pr), self-esteem. [F., fr. L. *amor*, love]

am'père *n.* unit of current of electricity, the amount one volt can send through one ohm. [fr. *Ampère*, F. physicist]

am'persand *n.* character &. [and per se, '*land*' by itself]

amphib'ious *a.* living both on land and in water. -amphib'ian *n.* (G. *amphi*, on both sides, *bios*, life)

amphithe'ater *n.* building with tiers of seats round an arena. [G. *amphi*, both sides, *theatron*, theater]

am'ple *a.* big enough, full, spacious. -am'pleness *n.* -amplifica'tion *n.* amplica'tory *a.* -am'plifier *n.* thermionic valve to increase power level of electric currents; apparatus to augment the output of sound. -am'plify *v.t.* make bigger, louder *etc.* -am'plitude *n.* spaciousness. -am'ply *adv.* fully. [F.]

am'putate *v.t.* cut off (a limb *etc.*) amputation *n.* [L. amputate]

am'ulet *n.* something carried, worn, as a charm against evil *etc.* [F. *amulette*]

amuse' *v.t.* divert; occupy pleasantly; excite a sense of fun. -amu'sement *n.* amu'sing *a.* -amu'singly *adv.* [F. *amuser*, make to muse. See muse]

an. See *a.*

anacon'da *n.* large water-snake of S. America. [orig. uncertain]

anad'romous *a.* of fish, ascending rivers to spawn. (G. *ana*, up, *dromos*, run)

anaero'bia *n.* *pl.* bacteria able to live without air. anerob'ic *a.* [G. *a.* without, *aer*, air, *bios*, life]

an'agram *n.* word or sentence made by arranging in different order the letters of another word or sentence, *e.g.*, ant from tan. -anagrammat'ical, *a.* -anagramm'atist *n.* (G. *anagramma*)

analge'sic *n.* anodyne, pain-killer. analge'sia *n.* painlessness. [G. *an*, not, *algein*, feel pain]

anal'ogy *n.* agreement or likeness in certain respects; correspondence. analo'gical *a.* -analog'ically *adv.* anal'ogize *v.t.* -anal'ogist *n.* analogous *a.* having similarity or correspondence. -anal'ogously *adv.* (G. *analogia*]

anal'ysis *n.* separation or breaking up of anything into its elements or component parts. -*pl.* anal'yses -an'alyze *v.t.* an'alyst *n.* -analyt'ical *a.* analytically *adv.* [G., fr. *lyein*, loose]

an'archy *n.* lack of government in a state;

lawlessness; confusion. anarch'al *a.* -anarch'ically *adv.* an'archism *n.* system of certain revolutionaries, aiming at a society with no government, in which each man should be a law to himself. -an'arch, an'archist *n.* [G. *anarchia*]

anath'ema *n.* solemn curse; anything accursed. -anath'ematize *v.t.* [G. offering; later, something devoted to evil]

anat'omy *n.* dissection of a body; science of the structure of the body; detailed analysis or examination. [G. *ena*, up, *temnein*, cut]

an'cestor *n.* forefather. -anees'tral *a.* -an'cestry *n.* [L. *ante*, before, *cedere*, go]

anch'or (-k-) *n.* implement for chaining a ship to the bottom of the sea. -*v.t.* fasten by an anchor. -*v.i.* cast anchor. anch'orage *n.* suitable place for anchoring. [L. *ancoral*]

anchorite, anch'oret *n.* hermit; one who has retired from the world, *esp.* for religion. [F., fr. G. *anachoretes*]

an'cient *a.* old; belonging to a former age; time-worn. -*n.* old man; one who lived in an earlier age (*esp.* in *pl*) anciently *adv.* [F. *ancien*]

an'cilary *a.* subordinate; subservient. [L. *ancilla*, maidservant]

and *conj.* in addition, used to join words and sentences, to introduce a consequence *etc.* [OE. *and, end*]

an'ecdote *n.* very short story, dealing with a single incident. -anecdot'al *a.* [G. = *unpublished*]

anem'ia *n.* lack of blood. -anem'ic *a.* [G. *an-*, not, *hainia*, blood]

anemom'eter *n.* instrument to measure the strength of wind, a wind-gauge. anemomet'ric *a.* -anemom'etry *n.* [G. *anemos*, wind, and meter]

anem'one (-ni) *n.* wind-flower. -sea-anem'one *n.* plant-like marine animal. [G., fr. *anemos*, wind]

anent' *prep.* concerning. [OE. *on-efen*, on even with]

anesthet'ic *a.* causing insensibility. -*n.* drug that does this. -anesthe'sia *n.* state of insensibility. -anesthet'ically *adv.* anes'thetize *v. t.* -anes'thetist *n.* [G. *anaisthetos*, without feeling]

anew' *adv.* afresh. [earlier of new]

an'gel (anj-) *n.* divine messenger; ministering spirit; person with the qualities of such a spirit, as gentleness, purity *etc.* -angel'ic *a.* -angel'ically *adv.* [G. *angelos*, messenger]

ang'er *n.* wrath, strong emotion including a sense of injury and a desire to retaliate. -*v.t.* rouse this emotion in. -ang'rily *adv.* ang'ry *a.* [ON. *angr*]

angi'na *n.* severe inflammation of the throat; quinsy. -angi'na pec'toris, heart disease marked by spasms of severe pain. [L., fr. *anguere*, strangle]

ang'le *v.t.* fish. -*n.* book. ang'ler *n.* angling *n.* [OE. *angel*]

ang'le *n.* corner; meeting of two lines. ang'ular *a.* -angular'ity *n.* [F., fr. L. *angulus*, corner]

ang'uish (-ng-gw-) *n.* great pain, mental or

bodily. [L. *anguere*, strangle]

an'ile   *a.* old-womanish, senile. (L. *anus*, old woman]

an'iline   *n.* product of coal-tar which yields dyestuffs. [F. *anil*, fr. Arab, *al-nil*, the indigo. Aniline was first gotten from indigo]

an'imal   *n.* being having life, feeling, power of voluntary motion; beast. -*a.* of or belonging to animals; sensual. **an'imalism** *n.* -**an'imally** *adv.* [L. *animale*, having breath of life]

an'imate   *v.t.* to give life to; enliven; actuate. -**an'imated** *a.* -**anima'tion** *n.* [L. *animare*]

an'imism   *n.* primitive religion, the belief that natural effects are due to spirits, that inanimate things have spirits. -**an'imist** *n.* -**animist'ic** *a.* [L. *animus*, spirit]

animos'ity   *n.* hatred. enmity. -**an'imus** *n.* actuating spirit; enmity. [L. *animus*, spirit]

an'ise   *n.* plant with aromatic seeds used for flavoring. -**an'iseed** *n.* liqueur or preparation of the seeds. [F. *anis*]

an'kle   (ang-kl) *n.* joint between the foot and the leg. -**ank'let** *n.* ornament or ring for the ankle. [OE. *ancleow*]

ankylosaus   *n.* any plant-eating dinosaur of the Cretaceous period of the suborder *ankylosauria* which has short legs and armour of bony plates.

an'nals   *n. pl.* record of events set down year by year. -**an'nalist** *n.* [L. *annales (libri)*, year-(books)]

annat'to   *n.* bright orange dye used for cloth, foodstuffs *etc.* -also **anat'ta**. [native S. American word]

anneal   *v.t.* toughen metal or glass by heating and slow cooling. -**anneal'ing** *n.* [OE. *anælan*, set on fire, bake]

annex   *v.t.* add, attach; take possession of, *esp.* territory. -**annexa'tion** *n.* **an'nexe** *n.* something added; supplementary building. [F. *annexer*, fr. L. *nectere*, bind]

anni'hilate   (-ni'-hi-) *v.t.* reduce to nothing, destroy. -**annihila'tion** *n.* **anni'hilative** *a.* -**anni'hilator** *n.* [Late L. *annihilate*, fr. *nihil*, nothing]

anniver'sary   *a.* yearly. -*n.* day on which an event happened or is celebrated. [L. *annus*, year, *vertere*, turn]

an'notate   *v.t.* make notes upon. **annota'tion** *n.* -**an'notator** *n.* [earlier *annote*; F. *annoter*. *See* note]

announce   *v.t.* make known, proclaim. -**announce'ment** *n.* -**announ'cer** *n.* one who announces, *esp.* a broadcasting official who reads out the news and announces items in the program. [F. *annoncer*, fr. L. *nuntius*, messenger]

annoy   *v.t.* trouble, vex; tease. **annoy'ance** *n.* [OF. *enoier*, fr. L. *in odio*, in hatred]

ann'ual   *a.* yearly. -*n.* plant which lives only a year; book published every year. -**annualize** *v.t.* to calculate for a shorter period as though on the basis of a full year. -**ann'ually** *adv.* [Late L. *annualis*, fr. *annus*, year]

annu'ity   *n.* sum paid every year. **annu'itant** *n,* one who receives such a sum. [F. *annuité*-L. *annus*, year]

annul'   *v.t.* reduce to nothing, abolish.

annul'ment *n.* [L. *annulare*, reduce to naught, *nullum*]

an'nular   *a.* ring-shaped. -**an'nulated** *a.* formed in rings. -**annula'tion** *n.* **an'nulet** *n.* a small ring. [L. *annularis*, fr. *annulus*, ring]

an'ode   *n.* (*elec.*) positive pole, or point of entry of a current-opposite to **cathode**. [G. *anodos*, way up]

anoint   *v.t.* smear with oil or ointment; consecrate with oil. -**anoint'ment** *n.* **The Anoint'ed** *n.* the Messiah. [OF. *enoindre* -L. *ungere*]

anon'   *adv.* in a short time; by and by. [OE. *on an*, *in* one]

anon'ymous   *a.* nameless, *esp.* without an author's name. **anonym'ity** *n.* **anon'ymously** *adv.* [G. *anonymos*]

anorex'ia, anorex'y   *n.* loss of appetite. [G. *an*, not, *orexis*, longing]

anoth'er   (-u-) *pron.* one other, a different one. [for another]

anoxemia   *n.* deficiency or reduction of exygen in the blook: -**anoxaem'ic**, **anoxem'ic**. *adj.*

an'swer   *v.t.* reply to; pay, meet; satisfy; suit. -*v.i.* reply, prove suitable; *n.* reply; solution; acknowledgment. -**an'swerable** *a.* that can be answered; accountable. -**an'swerer** *n.* [OE. *andswarian*, swear back]

ant   *n.* small social insect, proverbial for industry, the emmet. -**ant'eater** *n.* S. American animal which feeds on ants by means of a long sticky tongue. -**ant'hill** *n.* mound raised by ants in building their home [OE. *aemette*]

ant, prefix for anti- before a vowel, as antacids **antal'akli**. *See* words in anti-. **antagonist** *n.* opponent. -**antag'onize** *v.t.* -**antag'onism** *n.* -**antagonis'tic** *a.* hostile. -**antagonis'tically** *adv.* [G. *agonizesthai*, contend]

antarctic   *a.* of the south polar regions. -*n.* these regions [G. *anti-* and *arctic*]

ante-   *prefix* before [L. *ante*] found in compound words, as antechamber *n.* room leading to a chief apartment. **antedate** *v.t.* date before the true time; assign to an earlier date; anticipate. **antemerid'ian** (*abbrev.* ᴀ ᴍ.) *a.* before noon; between midnight and noon etc.

antece'dent   *a.* going before. -*n.* (*gram.*) noun *etc.* to which a relative pronoun refers. -*n. pl.* one's past history, record. [L. *antecedere*, go before]

an'telope   *n.* deer-like ruminant animal, remarkable for grace and speed. [Late G. *antholops*]

antenn'a   *n.* (*pl.* **antenn'ae**) insect's feeler; (radio) elevated conducting wire, an aerial. [L. = *sail-yard*]

ante'rior   *a.* before; earlier; in front. [L. *compar.* fr. *ante*, before]

an'them   *n.* piece of Scripture set to music for singing in churches; piece of sacred music (originally sung in alternate parts by two choirs). [OE. *antefu*, fr. G. *anti-*, against, *phone*, sound]

an'ther   *n.* top of the pollen-bearing stamen in a flower. (G. *anthos*, flower]

anthol'ogy   *n.* collection of choice poems, literary extracts *etc.* -**anthol'ogist** *n.* maker of such. [G. *anthologia*, gathering of flowers]

an'thracite *n.* hard, carbonaceous coat burning almost without flame or smoke. [G. *anthrakites*, coal-like]

an'thrax *n.* infectious disease of sheep and cattle, which can be transmitted to man. [G. = *carbuncle*]

anthropog'eny *n.* study of man's origin. [G. *anthropos*, man, *genes*, birth]

anthropography *n.* the branch of anthropology that deals with the geographical distribution of humans by skin color, language, customs, *etc.* -anthropograph'ic. *a.*

an'thropoid *a.* like man (of certain apes). [G. *anthropos*, man]

anthropol'ogy *n.* scientific study of the human race. -anthropolog'ical *a.* anthropol'ogist *n.* [G. *anthropos, logos*, word]

anthropomorph'ism *n.* ascription of human form and qualities to the Deity. [G. *anthropos*, man, *morphe*, form]

anti- *prefix* against; ant- before a vowel. [G. *anti*] Makes compounds as antiair'craft *a.* -anticath'olic *a.* An'tichrist *n.* -anticli'max *n.* anticli'nal *a.* sloping in opposite directions. -anticy'clone *n* -anti'dumping *a.* pertaining to laws or practices that discourage importing of goods and selling below cost. -an'tidote *n.* counter-poison. -antinuclear *a.* opposed to nuclear weapons. -antisep'tic a. and *n.* antispasmod'ic a. and *n.* -antitoxéin *n.* an'titrade *n.* wind contrary to trade wind. *etc.* (see word without prefix]

an'tibody *n.* protective substance forming in the blood in response to the presence of toxins *etc.* [*body*]

an'tic a. odd, grotesque. -*n.* grotesque figure or movement, an odd trick. [It. *antico* -L. *antiquus*, ancient]

antici'pate *v.t.* be beforehand; take or consider before the due time; foresee; enjoy in advance; expect. -anticipa'tion *n.* -anti'cipative, anticipatory *a.* [L. *anticipare*, take beforehand]

an'timony *n.* brittle, bluish-white metal. [Med. L. *antimonia*]

antiox'idant *n.* substance that inhibits or slows oxidation and therefore checking the deterioration it causes to tissue. -antioxidant. *a.*

antip'athy *n.* dislike. -antipathetic *a.* [G. *antipatheia*, fr. *pathos*, feeling]

an'tiphon *n.* anthem *etc.*, in which alternate lines or verses are alternately sung by two choirs. [G. *anti*, in return, *phone*, voice]

antip'odes *n. pl.* region of the globe exactly opposite ours. -antip'odal *a.* [G. , fr. *pous*, *pod-*, foot. Originally the people on the other side of the world, whose feet are opposite ours]

antique' *a.* ancient; old-fashioned -*n.* relic of former times. -antiqua'rian, antiquary *n.* student or collector of old things. - an'tiquated *a.* out of date. anti'quity *n.* great age; former times. [F. , fr. L. *ante*, before]

antirrhi'num *n.* snapdragon, a flowering garden plant. [G. *anti*, against, *rhis, rhin-*, nose]

anti-Semitism *n.* hostility or prejudice against the Jews. -an'ti-Semi'tic *a.* an'ti-Sem'ite *n.* [*See* Semitic]

anitiso'cial *a.* acting against the common good, or the customs *etc.* of society. [social]

antith'esis *n.* contrast; opposite; opposition of ideas. -antithet'ical *a.* antithe'tically *adv.* [G. fr. tithenai, place]

antitox'in *n.* substance formed in the body to counteract a disease or poison; appropriate serum injected into the bloodstream for the prevention of certain diseases. [G. *anti-*, *loxicon*, poison]

ant'ler *n.* deer's horn; branch of that horn. -ant'lered *a.* [VL. *ante ocularis ramus* branch before the eye]

an'tonym *n.* word of which the meaning is the opposite of another. [G. *anti*, against, *and onyma*, name]

anxiolytic *n.* drug that relieves tension or anxiety; tranquilizer. - anxiolytic *a.*

anx'ious *a.* troubled, uneasy, *esp.* about something doubtful or in the future. -anxi'ety *n.* anxiously *adv.* [L. *anxius*, fr. *angere*, compress]

an'y *a.* and *pron.* one indefinitely; some. - an'ybody *n.* -an'yhow *adv.* an'ything *n.* - an'yway *adv.* -an'ywhere *adv.* [OE. *aenig*, fr. *an*, one]

aorta *n.* great artery which rises from the left ventricle of the heart and sends its branches all through the body. -aort'al *a.* [G. *aorte*, what is hung up]

apart' *adv.* separately; aside. [F. *à part*]

apart'heid (a-part-had) *n.* idea of segregation of races. [*Afrikaans*]

apart'ment *n.* room, or suite of rooms, in a house, *usu.* rented as a self-contained lodging. [F. *appartement*, orig. 'separation']

ap'athy *n.* want of feeling; indifference-apathet'ic *a.* -apathet'ically *adv.* [G. *apatheia*]

ape *n.* monkey; monkey with no tail; imitator. -*v.t.* imitate. -a'pish *a.* -a'pishly *adv.* [OE. *apa*]

apéritif' *n.* drink to whet the appetite. [F. -L. *aperire*, open]

ap'erture *n.* opening. [L. *aperture*]

a pex *n.* (*pl.* a'pexes, a'pices) top or peak of anything. [L. = *summit*]

apha'sia *n.* dumbness due to brain disease. [G. *a-*, not, *phasis*, speech]

aphorism *n.* maxim, pithy saying aph'orist *n.* -aphoris'tic *a.* [G. *aphorismos*, definition]

aphrodisiac *a.* exciting to sexual intercourse. -*n.* that which so excites. [G. *Aphrodite*, goddess of love]

a'piary *n.* place where bees are kept. - a'pian, apiar'ian *a.* -a'piarist *n.* bee-keeper. -a'piculture *n.* [L. *apiarium*, fr. *apis*, bee]

apiece' *adv.* for each. [orig. two words]

aplenty *a., adv.* abundant, enough; in supply.

aplomb' *n.* self-possession, coolness. [F. phrase *à plomb*, perpendicular, fr. *plomb*, lead, plummet]

apoc'rypha *n.* religious writing of doubtful

authenticity, or excluded from the Canon, *esp.* the fourteen books or parts of books known as the Apocrypha of the Old Testament, found in the Septuagint but not in the Hebrew Canon. **apoc'ryphal** *a.* [L. fr. G. *apokryphos*, hidden away]

ap'ogee *n.* point of the sun's or moon's orbit farthest from the earth; the highest point. [F. , fr. G. *apo*, off, *ge*, earth]

apolitical *a.* not concerned or interested in politics. **-apolitically** *adv.*

ap'ologue *n.* moral fable or parable; allegory. [G. *apologos*, fable]

apol'ogy *n.* something spoken in defense; acknowledgment of an offence and expression of regret; poor substitute (with for). - **apologet'ic** *a.* **-apologetically** *adv.* - **apologet'ics** *n.* branch of theology charged with the defence of Christianity. **-apol'ogize** *v.i.* **-apol'ogist** *n.* [G. *apologia*, speaking away]

ap'oplexy *n.* sudden stroke, causing loss of sensation and motion, usually through haemorrhage in the brain. **-apoplec'tic** *a.* [G. *apoplexia*, disablement]

apos'tasy *n.* abandonment of one's religious or other faith. **-apos'tate** *n.* [G. *apostates*, one who stands away]

apos'trophe (-e-fi) *n.* a turning away from the subject of a speech to address some person present or absent; mark (') showing the omission of a letter or letters in a word. - **apos'trophize** *v.t.* [G. , fr. *strephein*, turn]

apoth'ecary *n.* old name for one who prepares and sells drugs, druggist. [G. *apotheke*, storehouse]

appall' (-awl') *v.t.* dismay, terrify. **appall'ing** *a.* [OF. *apalir*, make pale]

appara'tus *n.* equipment, instruments, for performing any experiment or operation. [L. fr. *apparare*, make ready]

appa'rent *a.* seeming; obvious. **appa'rently** *adv.* [L. *apparere*, appear]

appari'tion (-i'-shun) *n.* appearance, *esp.* of a ghost or other remarkable thing. [L. *appar-ere*, appear]

appeal' *v. i.* call upon, make earnest request; refer to, have recourse to; refer to a higher court. *-n.* request, reference, supplication. - **appeal'able** *a.* **-appeal'-ing** *a.* **-appeal'ingly** *adv.* **-appell'ant** *n.* one who appeals to a higher court. **-appell'ate** *a.* [F. *appeler*]

appear' *v. i.* become visible; come before; see, be plain. **-appear'ance** *n.* (OF. *apareir* -L. *apparere*)

appease' *v.t.* pacify, quiet, allay. - **appease'able** *a.* **-appease'ment** *n.* policy of conciliation by concessions to avoid war *etc.* [OF. *a pais*, at peace]

appella'tion *n.* name. **-appell'ative** *n.* generic name. *-a.* [*See* appeal]

append' *v.t.* join on, add. **-appen'dage** *n.* **-appen'dix** (*pl.*) **appendices'** **-ixes** *n.* [L. *appendere*, hang on]

appendici'tis *n.* inflammation of the vermiform appendix, a prolongation of the intestine. [*append*]

ap'petite *n.* desire, inclination, *esp.* desire

for food. **-ap'petize** *v.t.* **-appeti'zer** *n.* - **appeti'zing** *a.* **-appeti'zingly** *adv.* [F. *apetit*, fr. L. *petere*, seek]

applaud' *v.t.* praise by handclapping; praise loudly. **-applaud'er** *n.* **applaud'ing** *a.* - **applaud'ingly** *adv.* **-applause'** *n.* [L. *ap-plaudere*, clap]

applied' *a.* used for a practical or utilitarian purpose, as applied art, sci'ence. [*apply*]

apply' *v.t.* lay or place on; administer; bring into operation; devote, employ. **appli'ance** *n.* **-applicabil'ity** *n.* applicable *a.* **-ap'plicably** *adv.* **-applicant** *n.* **-apptica'tion** *n.* [L. *ap-plicare*, bend to]

appoint' *v.t.* fix, settle; name to an office; equip. **-appoint'ment** *n.* *-n. pl.* equipment. (F. , fr. *a point*, fitly]

appor'tion *v.t.* divide out in shares. **appor'tionment** *n.* [*See* portion]

ap'posite *a.* suitable, apt. **-ap'positely** *adv.* **-ap'positeness** *n.* **-apposi'tion** *n.* proximity; placing of one word beside another in explanation. **-appos'itive** *a.* [L. *appositus*, put against]

appraise' *v.t.* set a price on, value. - **apprais'able** *a.* **-apprais'al** *n.* **appraise'ment** *n.* **-apprais'er** *n.* [F. *ap-procier*, fr. L. *pretium*, price]

appre'ciate (-shi-) *v.t.* estimate justly; be sensible of good qualities in the thing judged. *-v.i.* rise in price. **-appre'ciable** *a.* - **appre'ciably** *adv.* **-apprecia'tion** *n,* - **appre'ciative** *a.* **-appre'ciator** *n.* [Late L. *ap-pretiare*, fr. *pretium*, price]

apprehend' *v.t.* take hold of, seize by authority; recognize, understand; fear. - **apprehensibil'ity** *n.* **-apprehen'sible** *a.* - **apprehen'sion** *n.* **-apprehen'sive** *a.* - **apprehen'siveness** *n.* [L. apprehendere, take hold of]

apprise' *v.t.* inform; acquaint. [F. appris, p. p. of *apprendre*, learn, teach]

approach' *v. i.* draw near; come near in quality, condition *etc.* *-v.t.* come near to; *n.* a drawing near; means of reaching; approximation. **-approachabil'ity** *n.* approach'able *a.* [F. *approcher*, fr. L. *proprius*, nearer]

approba'tion *n.* sanction, approval. [L. *ap-probate*, test, try]

appro'priate *v.t.* take to oneself *-a.* suitable, fitting. [Late L. *appropriate*, fr. *proprius*, own]

approve' *v.t.* think well of, commend. - **approv'al** *n.* **-approv'er** *n.* **approv'ingly** *adv.* [F. *approuver*]

approx'imate *a.* nearly resembling; nearing correctness. *-v.t.* bring close. *v. i.* come near. **-approx'imately** *adv.* **-approxima'tion** *n.* **-approx'imative** *a.* [L. *proximus*, nearest]

a'près *prep.* after, following; used in hyphenated compounds. **aprè-ski** *adv.*, *a.* after skiing; pertaining to the time after akiing used for eating, drinking and socializing. - **après-ski** *n.* event that takes place after skiing.

ap'ricate *v.i.* sunbathe. **-aprica'tion.** [L. *apricari*, expose to sun]

a'pricot *n.* orange-colored fruit of the plum kind. *-a.* of the color of the fruit. [F. *abricot*, fr. Port. *albricoque*, which gave obs. *apricock*]

A'pril *n.* fourth month of the year. [L. *aprilis*]

a prio'ri *a.* of knowledge gained without actual experience; of reasoning from cause to effect. [L. *a*, from, *priori*, preceding]

a'pron (a'-) *n.* piece of cloth, leather etc. worn in front to protect the clothes, or as part of an official dress. [an *apron* was a *napron*, fr. F. *napperon*, fr. *nappe*, cloth. cp. *adder*]

apropos *adv.* to the purpose; appropriately; in reference (to). [F. *à propos*]

apse *n.* arched recess at the end of a church. -**ap'sidal** *a.* [earlier *apsis*, G. *felloe* of a wheel]

apt *a.* suitable; prompt, quick-witted, likely. -**apt'itude** *n.* -**apt'ly** *adv.* -**apt'ness** *n.* [L. *aptus*, fr. *apere*, fasten]

aquamarine *n.* precious stone, the beryl. -*a.* pale blue, sea-colored. [L. *aqua marina*, sea water]

aqua'rium *n.* (*pl.* **aqua'riums**, **aqua'ria**) tank or pond for keeping water animals or plants, usually in a natural setting. [L. *aqua*, water]

Aqua'rius *n.* the Water-bearer, 11th sign of the zodiac, which sun enters on 21st January. [constellation *Aquarius* -L. *aqua*, water]

aquat'ic *a.* living or growing in water, or having to do with water, -**aquat'ics** *n.* pl. water-sports. [L. *aqua*, water]

aq'ueduct *n.* artificial channel for water, *esp.* a bridge to carry water across a valley, a canal across an obstacle *etc.* [L. *aquae ductus*, water conduit]

a'queous *a.* watery. [L. *aqua*, water]

aq'uiline *a.* relating to an eagle; hooked like an eagle's beak. [L. *aquila*, eagle]

ar'able *a.* fit for plowing. [L. *arabilis*, fr. *arare*, plough]

arach'nida (-k-) *n.* class including spiders, scorpions, mites. -**arach'nid** *n.* one of these. [G. *arachns*, spider]

ar'biter *n.* (**ar'bitress** *fem.*) judge; umpire. -**arbit'rament** *n.* -**ar'bitrary** *a.* not bound by rules; despotic. -**arbitrarily** *adv.* -**ar'bitrate** *v. i.* act as arbiter, , decide a dispute. -**arbitra'tion** *n.* -**ar'bitrator** *n.* [L. = *judge*]

ar'bor *n.* garden seat enclosed by branches, plants; shaded walk. [earlier *erber*, fr. OF. *herbier*, herb-garden]

arbo'real, **arbo'reous** *a.* relating to trees. -**arbore'tum** *n.* place for cultivating specimens of trees. -**ar'bori-culture** *n.* forestry, cultivation of trees for timber *etc.* [L. *arbor*, tree]

arc *n.* part of a circle or other curve. [L. *arcus*, bow]

arc *n.* luminous electrical discharge between two terminals. -**arc'-lamp** *n.* **arc'-light** *n.* lamp that produces high-intensity light by the jumping of electric current in an arc between electrodes *usu.* made of carbon or metal. [L. *arcus*, bow]

arcade *n.* row of arches on pillars; covered walk or avenue. [F.]

arcane *a.* being understood only by those who have access to a special knowledge. [*See* **arcanum**]

arch *n.* curved structure in building, supporting itself over an open space by mutual pressure of the stones. -*v.t.* give, or make into, an arch. -**arched** *a.* **arch'way** *n.* [L. *arcus*, bow]

arch *a.* chief; roguish, sly. -**arch'ly** *adv.* -**arch'ness** *n.* -**arch**-*prefix* chief, *e.g.*, **archenemy** *n.* -**arch-her'etic** *n.* **arch-rogue'** *n.* [G. *archos*, chief. Meaning of 'roguish' arose from arch-rogue]

archaeol'ogy (-k-) *n.* study of ancient times from remains of art, implements *etc.* -**archaeolog'ical** *a.* -**archaeol'ogist** *n.* [G. *archaiologia*]

archaeop'teryx (-k-) *n.* oldest known fossil bird. [G. *archaios*, ancient, pteryx, wing]

archa'ic (-k-) *a.* old, primitive. -**archa'ically** *adv.* -**ar'chaism** *n.* obsolete word or phrase. [G. *archaios*, old]

archan'gel (-k-) *n.* angel of the highest order. [*angel*]

archbish'op *n.* chief bishop. **archbishopric** *n.* [*bishop*]

archduke' *n.* duke of specially high rank. -**archdu'cal** *a.* -**archduch'ess** *fem.* -**archduch'y** *n.* [*duke*]

arch'er *n.* one who shoots with a bow. **arch'ery** *n.* [L. *arcus*, bow]

arch'etype (-ki-) *n.* original pattern or model. -**arch'etypal** *a.* [G. *typos*, model]

Archimede'an *a.* pertaining to the Greek mathematician Archimedes

archipel'ago (-k-) *n.* sea full of small islands; group of islands. -*pl.* **archipel'agoes**. -**archipelag'ic** *a.* [G. *archi-*, chief, *pelagos*, sea. The Greek chief sea was the Aegean]

arch'itect (-k-) *n.* master-builder, one who designs buildings; any maker or contriver. -**architecton'ic** *a.* -**architec'tural** *a.* **archi'tecture** *n.* [G. *architekton*, chief builder]

ar'chitrave *n-* in architecture, lowest division of entablature resting immediately on top of column. [L. *trabs*, beam]

archives (-kivz) *n.* place where government records are kept. -*pl.* public records. -**arch'ival** *a.* -**arch'ivist** *n.* [G. *archeion*, public office]

arc'tic *a.* of northern polar regions; extremely cold. -*n.* region round the north pole. [G. *arktikos*, fr. *arktos*, bear, constellation of the Great Bear]

ar'dent *a.* fiery; passionate. -**ar'dency** *n.* -**ar'dor** *n.* [L. *ardere*, burn]

ard'uous *a.* laborious, hard to accomplish. -**ard'uously** *adv.* **arduousness** *n.* [L. *arduus*, steep]

a'rea *n.* open space; superficial contents of a figure: extent, scope. [L. open space]

are'na *n.* space in the middle of an amphitheater; place of public contest; place of action; battlefield. [L. = *sand*]

ar'gent *n.* silver. -*a.* silver, silvery white, *esp.* in heraldry. [L. *argentum*]

ar'gon *n.* inert gas forming part of the air. [G. *argos*, idle]

ar'gonaut *n.* sailor, *esp.* one who sailed in the Argo in search of the Golden Fleece; an octopod mollusk. [G. *Argo* and *nautes*, sailor]

ar'gosy n. richly-laden merchant ship. [earlier *ragusye*, ship of *Ragusa*]

ar'got n. slang; thieves' cant. [F.]

ar'gue v.i. prove; offer reasons; dispute. v.t. prove by reasoning; discuss- **ar'guable** a. - **ar'guer** n. -**ar'gument** n. **argumenta'tion** n. -**argumen'tative** a- [L- *arguere*, prove]

argus n. watchful person; guardian. [G. *myth*, giant with a hundred eyes which were transplanted to a peacock by Hera upon the giant's death.]

a'ria n. air or rhythmical song in a cantata, opera *etc*. [It.]

ar'id a. parched, dry; empty, uninteresting. -**arid'ity** n. [L. *aridus*]

aridisol n. soil low in organic matter but high in salt and magnesium, often found in deserts.

A'ries a. the Ram, 1st sign of the zodiac, which sun enters on *c*. 21st March [L.]

arise v.i. come up; spring up; ascend; rise up. [OE. *arisan*]

aristoc'racy n. government by the best in birth or fortune; nobility of a state; upper classes generally. -**ar'istocrat** n. **aristocrat'ic** a. -**aristocrat'ically** adv. [G. *aristos*, best, *kratos*, power]

arith'metic n. science of numbers; art of reckoning by figures. -**arithmet'ical** a. **arithmet'ically** adv. -**arithmeti'cian** n. [G. *arithmetike -arithmos*, number]

ark n. box, chest; Noah's vessel; place of refuge. [OE. *earc*, L. *arca*, coffer]

arm n. limb extending from shoulder to wrist; anything projecting from the main body, as a branch of the sea, the supporting rail of a chair *etc*. -v.t. give an arm to. -compounds as **arm'chair** n. **arm'ful** n. **arm'hole** n. -**arm'let** n. band worn on arm. -*etc*. [OE. *earm*]

arm n. weapon; branch of the army. -*pl*. weapons; war:the military profession. v.t. supply with weapons. -v.i.take up arms. -**arm'ament** n. -**armed** a. [L. *arma*, neut. P.]

arma'da (-a'-) n. fleet of armed ships. [Sp. p.p. of *armar*, arm]

armadill'o n. small American animal protected by bands of bony plates. [Sp. , dim. of *armado*, man in armor]

ar'mature n. apparatus for defense; piece of iron across the ends of a magnet; revolving part of a dynamo or motor. [F. . fr.L. *armatura*, armor]

arm'istice n. truce, suspension of fighting. [F. , fr. Mod. L. *armistitium*]

arm'or n. defensive covering or dress; plating of warships. -**arm'ored** a. protected by armour, as armored car, armored train. -**arm'orer** n. -**arm'ory** n. [L. *armare*, arm]

arm'y n. large body of men armed for warfare and under military command; host; great number. [F. *armée*, p. p. of *armer*, fr. L. *armare*, arm]

ar'nica n. kinds of plant including mountain tobacco, used as a remedy in apoplexy and (externally) for bruises. [Mod. L. , orig. unknown]

aro'ma n. sweet smell; peculiar charm. -**aromat'ic** a. -**aroma'therapy** n. the massaging of the skin with oils or creams containing fragrant plant extracts. [G. = *spice*]

around adv. on every side; in a circle. prep. on all sides of. [*round*]

arouse v.t. awaken. [*rouse*]

arpe'ggio (-j-) n. chord of which the notes are sounded in quick succession. [It. , fr. *ar- peggiare*, play the harp]

arraign (-an')v.t. accuse, indict, put on trial; call to account. -**arraign'er** n. **arraign'ment** n. [OF. *arainer*; Low L. *arrationare*, reason]

arrange v.t. set in order; settle, adjust; plan. -v.i. make agreement. -**arrange'ment** n. [F. *arranger*, fr. *rang*, rank]

ar'rant a. downright, notorious. -**ar'rantly** adv. [var. of *errant*, *q.v*. Errant (wandering), associated with thief, vagabond, *etc*. lost its meaning and came to be just an intensive epithet]

array v.t. set in order; dress; equip. adorn. -n. order, *esp*. military order; dress. [OF. *aréer*]

arrear n. state of being behind; anything unpaid or undone (usu. in *pl*.). [fr. adv. *arrear*, backward]

arrest v.t. stop; catch the attention; apprehend by legal authority. -n. seizure by warrant; making prisoner. -**arrest'ment** n. detention of a person arrested pending bail *etc*. [OF. *arester*]

arrive v.i. reach a destination; (with *at*) attain an object, achieve success. **arri'val** n. [F. *arriver*]

ar'rogate v.t. claim as one's own; claim proudly or unjustly. -**ar'rogance** n. aggressive conceit. -**ar'rogant** a. arrogantly adv. [L. *arrogare*, claim]

ar'row n. pointed weapon to be shot with a bow. -**ar'rowy** a. -**ar'row-head** n. metal part of an arrow. [OE. *arwe*]

ar'senal n. magazine of stores for warfare, guns, ammunition *etc*. [It. *arsenale*, fr. Arab. *al-sina'ah*, workshop]

ar'senic n. one of the chemical elements, a soft, gray metal; its oxide, a powerful poison. -**ar'senate** n. -**arsen'ical** a. -**arse'nious** a. [G. *arsenikon*]

ar'son n. crime of intentionally setting on fire houses, ships or other property. [OF. , fr. L. *ardere*, bum]

art n. skill; human skill as opposed to nature; skill applied to music, painting, poetry *etc*.; any one of the subjects of this skill; system of rules; profession or craft; contrivance, cunning, trick; -*pl*. certain branches of learning, languages, history *etc*. , as distinct from natural science. **art'ful** a. cunning, clever. -**art'fully**, -**artfulness** n. -**art'ist** n. one who practises a fine art, *esp*. painting; one who makes his craft a fine art. -**artis'tically** adv. -**art'istry** n. -**art'less** a. simple, unaffected. -**art'lessly** adv. -**art'lessness** n. [F. , fr. L. *ars*, fr. a root meaning 'fit together']

arterio'sclero'sis n. hardening of the arteries. [G. *arterial* artery, *skleros*, hard]

ar'tery n. tube carrying blood from the heart; any main channel of communications. -**arte'trial** a. [G. *arterial*]

arteriogram *n.* x-ray of an artery that has been injected with dye; **-arteriograph**.

arte'sian *a.* describes a well bored down until water is reached which rises by itself. [F. *artesien*, of Artois, where such a well was first bored]

arthri'tis *n.* inflammation of a joint, gout. **-arthrit'ic** *a.* [G. *arthron*, joint]

art'ichoke *n.* thistle-like, perennial, eatable plant. **jerusalem artichoke,** a different plant, a sunflower with tubers like the potato. [It. *articiocco*, of Arab. origin. Jerusalem here is corrupt. of It. *girasole*, sunflower]

art'icle *n.* clause, head, paragraph, section; literary composition in a journal *etc.*; rule or condition; commodity or object. *-v.t.* bind as an apprentice. [L. *artus*, joint]

artic'ulate *v.t.* joint; utter distinctly; form into words or syllables. *-v.i.* speak. *a.* jointed; (of speech) clear, distinct. **artic'ulately** *adv.* **-artic'ulateness** *n.* **articula'tion** *n.* [L. *articulate*, joint]

art'ifice *n.* contrivance, trick; cunning, skill. **-artif'icer** *n.* craftsman. [L. *artificiurn-ars*, art, *facere*, make]

artificial (-sh-) *a.* synthetic; made by art, not natural; affected; feigned. **-artificial'ity** *n.* **-artifi'cially** *adv.* **artificial silk',** *See* rayon. [*artifice*]

artill'ery *n.* cannon; troops who use them. [OF. *artillerie—artiller*, arm]

artisan' *n.* craftsman, mechanic. [F.]

as *adv.* conj. in that degree, so far, since, because, when, while, in like manner. [worn-down form of *also*]

asap, ASAP as soon as possible.

ascend' *v.i.* climb, mount up; rise; go back in time. *-v.t.* walk, climb, mount up. **-ascend'ancy** *n.* control, domination. **-ascend'ant** *a.* rising; above the horizon. *-n.* superiority. **-aseen'sion** *n.* **-ascent'** *n.* rise. [L. *ascendere*, climb up]

ascertain' *v.t.* and i. get to know, find out. **-ascertain'able** *a.* **-ascertain'ment** *n.* [earlier *acertaine*, OF. *acertener*]

ascet'ic *n.* strict permit; one who denies himself pleasures for the sake of conscience or religion. *-a.* rigidly abstinent, austere. **-ascet'ically** *adv.* **-asceticism** *n.* [G. *asketikos*]

ASCII computer code standardized to allow transmission of data between various hardware and software. [*American Standard Code for Information Interchange.*]

ascor'bic ac'id chemical substance identified with vitamin C. [G. *a-*, and *scorbutic*]

ascribe' *v.t.* attribute, assign. **ascribable** *a.* **-ascrip'tion** *n.* [L. *ad*, to, *scribere*, write]

asep'tic *a.* not liable to decay, or to blood-poisoning. **-asep'sis** *n.* [G. *a*, not, *septikos*, decaying]

ash *n.* familiar timber tree; its tough, white wood. **-ash'en** *a.* **-mount'ain ash,** rowan. [OE. *Tsc*]

ash *n.* dust or remains of any-thing burnt. *-pl.* dead body. **-ash'y, ash'en** *a.*, of ashes; pale. **-ash'-tray** *n.* tray for tobacco-ash. [OE. *æsc*]

ashamed' *a.* affected with shame. [*See* shame]

ashore' *adv.* on shore. [*a.* on, and *shore*]

aside' *adv.* to, or on, one side; privately; apart. *-n.* words spoken in an under-tone not to be heard by someone present. [on side]

as'inine *a.* of or like an ass; silly, stupid. **-asinin'ity** *n.* [L. *asinus*, ass]

ask *v. t.* request, require, question, invite. *-v.i.* make enquiry; make request. [OE. *ascian* or *acsian*]

askew' *a. adv.* aslant, awry. [*a.* and *skew*]

aslant' (-ant') *adv.* on the slant, obliquely. *-prep.* athwart, across. [on slant]

asleep' *a.* and *adv.* sleeping; at rest. [earlier on sleep]

asp *n.* small venomous snake, vipera aspis of S. Europe. [G. *aspis*]

aspar'agus *n.* plant cultivated for its young shoots, esteemed as a delicacy. [G. *asparagos*]

as'pect *n.* look, view, appearance. [L. *aspecere*, look at]

as'pen *n.* trembling poplar tree. *-a.* of or like aspen; tremulous, [*a.* which has replaced the *n.* asp, OE. *æsp*]

as'phalt, asphalttum *n.* black, hard, bituminous substance, a mineral pitch, used for paving *etc.* *-v.t.* pave with asphalt. **-asphal'tic** *a.* [G. *asphaltos*]

asphyx'ia *n.* suffocation. **-asphyx'iate** *v.t.* **-asphyx'iated** *a.* **-asphyxia'tion** *n.* [G. *asphygia*, pulse stoppage]

as'pic *n.* savory jelly containing game, fish, *etc.* [F. *= asp* (fr. its coldness)]

aspire' *v. i.* desire eagerly; aim at high things; tower up. [L. *aspirate*, breathe towards]

as'pirin *n.* drug used to relieve theumatic and neuralgic pains. [Trademark]

ass *n.* familiar quadruped of the horse family; stupid fellow. (OE. *assa*]

assail' *v.t.* attack, assault. **-assail'ant** *n.* [L. *ad salire*, jump at]

assas'sin *n.* one who kills by treacherous violence, usually for reward. **-assassinate** *v.t.* **-assassina'tion** *n.* [fr. Arab. *hashshashin*]

assault' *n.* sudden attack; attack of any kind. *-v.t.* make an attack on. [F. *assaut*, VL. *adsaltus.*]

assay' *v. i.* test the proportions of metals in an alloy or ore; test the fineness of a metal *etc.* *-n.* **-assay'er** *n.* **-assay'ing** *n.* [*See* essay, of which this is a variant]

assem'ble *v.t.* bring together, collect; put together, as machinery. *-v.i.* meet together. **-assem'blage** *n.* **-assem'bly** *n.* [F. *assembler-* Late L. *assimulare*, bring together]

assembler language *n.* computer coding system meant to resemble natural language, uses symbols and numerals as equivalents of machine language.

assent' *v. i.* concur, agree. *-n.* acquiescence, agreement. [F. *assentir*]

assert' *v.t.* declare strongly, insist upon. **-asser'tion** *n.* **-asser'tive** *a.* **-asser'tively** *adv.* [L. *asserere*, claim]

assess' *v.t.* fix the amount (of a tax or fine); tax or fine; fix the value, estimate, *esp.* for taxation. **-assess'able** *a.* **assess'ment** *n.* **-**

assess'or *n.* [fr. L. *assidere*, assess-, sit by as judge]

as'sets *n. pl.* property available to pay debts, *esp.* of an insolvent debtor. *-n. sing.* item of such property; thing of value. (F. *assez*, enough]

assid'uous *a.* persevering. -assidu'ity *n.* tireless application. -assid'uously *adv.* [fr. L. *assidere*, sit down to]

assign' (in') *v.t.* allot, apportion, fix; transfer; ascribe. -assign'able *a.* asignation *n.* appointment to meet, tryst. [L. *assignare*, allot by sign, *signum*]

assim'ilate *v.t.* make similar; convert into like substance; absorb into the system. - **assim'ilable** *a.* -assimila'tion *n.* policy of fully accepting people of all races and backgrounds into a culture. -assim'ilative *a.* [L. *assimilate*, make like, fr. *similis*, like]

assist' *v.t.* help, support. *-v.i.* be present. - assis'tance *n.* help, relief

assis'tant *n.* [L. *assistere*, stand by]

asso'ciate *v.t.* join with, unite. *-v.i.* combine, unite. *-n.* companion, partner, ally, friend. *-a.* joined, connected. -associa'tion *n.* - asso'ciative *a.* [L. *associare*, fr. *socius*, companion]

assort' *v.t.* classify, arrange. *-v.i.* match, agree with. -assort'ed *a.* varied assortment *n.* variety. [OF. *asorter*, see sort]

assume' *v.t.* take for granted; put on; claim, arrogate; pretend. *-v.i.* be arrogant. - assump'tion *n.* supposition; arrogance. - assump'tive *a.* [L. *assumere*, take to oneself]

assure' *v.t.* make safe; insure; tell positively; give confidence. -assu'rance *n.* assured' *a.* -assu'redly *adv.* [F. *assurer*, make sure, fr. L. *securus*]

as'ter *n.* perennial plant with late-blooming star-like flowers. (G. = *star*]

as'terisk *n.* star (*) used in printing. [G. *asterikos*, little star]

astern' *adv.* at the stern; behind; backwards. [See stern]

as'teroid *n.* small planet. [G. *aster*, star, *eidos*, form]

asth'ma (-sm-) *n.* chronic disease entailing difficulty in breathing, wheezing, tightness in the chest *etc.* asthmat'ic *a.* -asthmat'ically *adv.* [G.]

astigmatism *n.* defect of the eye in which the rays are not brought to a proper focus at one point. -astigmat'ic *a.* (G. *a-*, not, *stigma*, point]

astir' *adv.* on the move; out of bed; out of doors; in excitement. (on stir]

astonish, astound' *v.t.* amaze, surprise greatly. -aston'ishing *a.* astonishment *n.* [OF. *estoner*, VL. *extonere*, thunder-strike; ME, *astoun*, later *astound*; fr. p. p. *astoned* came a new verb *astony*, later *astonish*. See stun]

as'tral *a.* of the stars, starry; belonging to the spirit-world. [L. *astralis*]

astride' *adv.* with the legs apart; one leg on either side of [See stride]

astringent *a.* binding, contracting. *-n.* binding medicine. -astrin'gency *n.* [L. *astringere*, tighten]

astrocyte *n.* star-shaped cell found in the brain, spinal cord, and nervous tissue. - astrocytic *a.* -astrocytoma *n.*

astrolabe *n.* instrument formerly used to measure the altitude of the sun and stars. [G. *astron*, star, *lambanein*, take]

astrology *n.* science (formerly synonymous with astronomy) pert. to the influence of the stars on human and terrestrial affairs. - astrol'oger *n.* -astrolo'gical *a.* [G. *astrologia*, knowing of the stars (*aster*, star)]

astron'omy *n.* science or study of the heavenly bodies. -astron'omer *n.* -astronom'ical *a.* of astronomy; very great. [G. *astron*, star, *nomos*, law]

astrophysics *n.* study of the physical conditions of the heavenly bodies. [G. *astron*, star, and physics]

astute' *a.* crafty, cunning; shrewd, acute. - astute'ly *adv.* -astute'ness *n.* [L. *astutus*, fr. *astus*, crafty]

asy'lum *n.* refuge, sanctuary; home for the care of the unfortunate. *esp.* lunatics; formerly a refuge for criminals. [fr. G. *a-*, not, *syle*, right of seizure]

asymmet'rical *a.* lacking in symmetry or balance between parts, lop-sided. [G. *a-*, not, and *symmetry*]

at *prep.* near to, by, in; engaged on; in the direction of [OE. *æt*]

at'avism *n.* appearance of ancestral, not parental, characteristics in an animal or plant; reversion to an earlier type. atavis'tic *a.* [L. *atavus*, great-grandfather's - grandfather]

atax'ia, atax'y *n.* impaired co-ordination (through disease) of the muscles controlling voluntary movement. [G. *a-*, not, *taktos*, arrange]

at'elier *n.* studio, workshop. [F.]

a'theism *n.* disbelief in the existence of God. [fr. G. *a-*, not, *theos*, God]

athirst' *a.* thirsty. [See thirst]

ath'lete *n.* one trained to physical exercises, feats or contests of strength. athlet'ic *a.* - athlet'icism *n.* -athlet'ies *n. pl.* sports of running, wrestling *etc.* [G. *athletes*, fr. *athlos*, contest]

athwart' *adv.* across, *esp.* obliquely. *prep.* across. (See thwart]

Atlan'tic *n.* the ocean between Europe, Africa and the American Continent; belonging to Atlas (*myth*). [fr. Mount Atlas in N. W. Africa]

at'las *n.* book of maps. [G. *Atlas*, a Titan who bore the world on his shoulders and whose image appeared on the title-page of old map books]

ATM *n.* automatic or automated teller machine operated by customers with magnetized cards to make financial transactions.

atmosphere *n.* mass of gas surrounding a heavenly body, *esp.* the earth. atmospher'ic *a.* -atmospher'ically *adv.* -atmospher'ics *n.* pl. noises in wireless reception due to electrical disturbances from the atmosphere. [G. *atmos*, vapor, *sphaira*, sphere]

at'oll *n.* ring-shaped coral island enclosing a

lagoon. [Maldive word]

at'om n. smallest particle of matter which enters into chemical combination; any very small particle. -atom'ic a. at'om bomb', bomb in which the explosion is caused by atomic energy. atom'ic en'ergy, energy derived from a sustained neutron chain reaction resulting from nuclear fission of the atom. [G. atomos, fr. a-, not, temnein, cut]

atomi'zer n. device for ejecting liquids in a fine mist-like spray. [atom]

atone v. i. give satisfaction or make reparation. -atone'ment n. [orig. , to reconcile, fr. adv. phrase at one]

atrocious (-shus) a. extremely cruel or wicked. -atro'ciously adv. -atro'city n. (L. atrox, cruel, fr. ater, black]

at'rophy n. wasting away in a living body with lessening of size and strength, emaciation. -v.i. waste away, become useless. -at'rophied a. [G. a-, not, trephein, nourish]

at'ropine n. poisonous alkaloid obtained from deadly nightshade. [G. Atropos, the Fate who cuts the thread of life]

attach' v.t. fasten, seize, connect, join to. -v.i. adhere. -attach'ment n. [F. attacher, It. attaccare. See attack]

attach'é (a-tash'a) n. member of an ambassadorés staff. -attach'é-case n. small rectangular handbag for papers. [F. = attached]

attack' v.t. fall upon violently; assault, assail; affect (of a disease). -n. assault; seizure. [F. attaquer, It. attaccare, join; F. and E. sense is fr. attaccare battaglia, join battle]

attain' v.t. arrive at, reach, gain by effort. [F. atteindre]

attempt' v.t. try, endeavor, make an effort or attack on. -n. trial, effort. [L. attentare, try]

attend' v.t. wait upon, accompany; wait for; be present at. -v.i. give the mind (to). [fr. L. attendere, stretch towards]

attenuate v.t. make thin or slender; weaken, reduce. -v.i. become weak or slender. -atten'uated a. -attenua'tion n. [L. attenuate, make thin, tenuis]

attest' v.t. bear witness to, certify. attesta'tion n. [L. attestari, bear witness]

at'tic n. low story above the cornice of a building; room in the roof. -a. of Athens; elegant. [Attica, Athens]

attire' v.t. dress, array. -n. dress. [OF. atirer, put in order]

at'titude n. posture, position; behavior, relation of persons expressing thought, feeling etc. [L, aptitudo, fr. aptus, fit]

attorn'ey (-tur'-) n. one legally authorized to act for another; a qualified practicioner of law, lawyer. [OF. atorner -Low L. atornare, appoint]

attract' v.t. draw towards, literally or figuratively; entice; cause to approach; charm, fascinate, -attrac'tion n. attractive a. - attrac'tively adv. - attractiveness n. [L. attrahere]

attribute v.t. ascribe, assign, refer to. (at'tribute) n. quality, property or characteristic of anything. -attrib'utable a.

attribu'tion n. -attrib'utive a. [L. attribuere-tribuere, pay tribute

attune' v.t. put in tune, harmonize. [at and tune

ATV n. pl. ATVs all-terrain vehicle; a vehicle with special wheels or tires for traversing rough terrain.

aubergine' (ō-ber-zhen') n. egg-plant; its fruit. [F. , fr. auberge, peach]

aub'urn a. reddish-brown. [fr. L. auburnus, whitish (the old meaning was light yellow)]

auc'tion n. public sale in which the bidder offers increase of price over another, and what is sold goes to the highest bidder. -auctioneer' n. auc'tion-bridge' n. card game. [L. augere, increase]

audacious a. bold, daring; insolent. auda'city n. [L. audax–audere, dare]

aud'ible a. able to be heard. audibil'ity n. -aud'ibly adv. [L. audire, hear]

aud'ience n. act of hearing; judicial hearing; formal interview; assembly of hearers. [F. , fr. L. audire, hear]

audiocassette n. tape enclosed in a case, used to record and play back sound; a sound tape recording. audiotape.

aud'it n. formal examination of accounts; periodical settlement. -v.t. examine (accounts). -aud'itor n. [L. auditus audire, hear]

audition n. sense of hearing; hearing, esp. test hearing of a performer.

audito'rium n. place for hearing.

aud'itory a. [L. audire, hear]

au'ger n. carpenter's tool for boring holes. [an auger was ME. a nauger OE. nafugar. cp. adder]

augment v.t. and i. increase, enlarge. (aug'-) n. increase. -augmenta'tion n. augment'ative a. [L. augmentare, fr. augere, grow]

august' a. majestic, dignified. -Aug'ust n. eighth month of the year. -August'an of Augustus, the Roman Emperor; hence classic, distinguished, as applied to a period of literature. [L. augustus, venerable; Augustus Caesar, 31 B.C.-14 A.D.]

aunt (ant) n. father's or mother's sister; uncle's wife. [OF. ante, fr. L. amita, paternal aunt]

aur'a n. (occultism) subtle emanation surrounding a person or thing; distinctive air or character. [L. aura]

aur'al a. of the ear. -aur'ally adv. [L. auris, ear]

aur'ic a. pertaining to gold. [fr. L. aurum]

aur'icle n. outside ear. -pl. upper-cavities of the heart. —auric'ular a. of the ear; known by ear, told in the ear, esp. of confession. [L. auris, ear]

auro'ra n. lights in the atmosphere to be seen radiating from the regions of the poles. The northern is called auro'ra borea'lis, and the southern auro'ra austra'lis. [L. = dawn]

aus'pice n. omen drawn from the observation of birds (usu. in pl.). -pl. patronage, favor. -auspi'cious a. of good omen, favorable. -auspi'ciously adv. [L. auspicium, fr. avis, bird, specere, behold]

austere' *a.* harsh, strict, severe. **austere'ty** *adv.* -**auster'ity** *n.* [G, *austeros*, making the tongue rough]

aus'tral *a.* southern. [L. *austr-alis auster*, south wind]

authentic *a.* trustworthy, real, genuine, true. -**authen'tically** *adv.* -**authen'ticate** *v.t.* -**authentica'tion** *n.* -**authenti'city** *n.* [G. *authentikos*, first-hand, fr. *authentes*, one who does things for himself]

auth'or *n.* originator, constructor; writer of a book; an author's writings. **auth'oress** *n. fem.* -**auth'orship** *n.* [L. *auctor*, fr. *augere*, make grow]

author'ity *n.* legal power or right; delegated power; permission; book, person *etc.* settling a question, entitled to be believed; body or board in control, *esp.* in *pl.* -**authoriza'tion** *n.* -**auth'orize** *v.t.* **author'itative** *a.* -**author'itatively** *adv.* [L. *auctoritas*, fr. *auctor, v. s.*]

autobiog'raphy *n.* biography or life of a person written by himself- **autobiog'rapher** *n.* -**autobiograph'ical** *a.* **autobiograph'ically** *adv.* [fr. G. *autos*, self, *bios*, life, *graphein*, write]

aut'ocrat *n.* absolute ruler. -**autoc'-racy** *n.* -**autocrat'ic** *a.* -**autocrat'ically** *adv.* [G. *autos*, self, *kratos*, power]

auto'cross *n.* an automobile sport testing driving speed and skill.

aut'omation *n.* the automatic control of successive production processes by electronic apparatus. [G. *autos*, self]

automa'ton *n.* self-acting machine, *esp.* one simulating a human being; (*fig.*) human being who acts by routine, without intelligence. -**automat'ic** *a.* -**automat'-ically** *adv.* -**autom'atism** *n.* [G. *automatos*, self-moving]

automo'bile *n.* a mechanical road vehicle *usu.* with four wheels and for passenger transportation. -**automo'bilist** *n.* [G. *autos*, self, and mobile]

auton'omy *n.* self-government. -**autonomous** *a.* [G. *autonomia*, self-rule]

autophyte *n.* any plant that makes its own food by synthesizing inorganic matter. -**autophytic** *a.* **autophytically.** *adv.*

autop'sy *n.* personal inspection; postmortem examination. [G. *aulopsia*, seeing for oneself -*autos*, self, *opsis*, sight]

aut'umn (-um) *n.* third season of the year, season of harvest; fall. -**autum'nal** *a.* -**autum'nary** *adv.* [L. *autumnus*]

auxil'iary *a.* helping, subsidiary. -*n.* helper; something subsidiary, as troops; verb used to form tenses of other verbs. [L. *auxilium*, help]

avail' *v. i.* be of value, of use. -*v.t.* benefit, help. -*n.* benefit, as in *be of little avail, etc.* -**availabil'ity** *n.* -**avail'able** *a.* -**avail'** oneself of, make use of. [F. *valoir*, be worth]

av'alanche (-sh) *n.* mass of snow and ice sliding down a mountain. [F. earlier *lavanche*; Late L. *labina*, landslide, influenced by *avaler*, descend]

av'arice *n.* greediness of wealth.

avari'cious *a.* -**avari'ciously** *adv.* [F.]

avast' *int.* (*naut.*) enough! stop! [Du. *houd vast*, hold fast]

avenge' *v.t.* take vengeance on behalf of (a person) or on account of (a thing). **aven'ger** *n.* -**aven'ging** *a.* [OF. *avengier*, fr. L. *vindicate*. *See* vengeance]

av'enue *n.* approach; double row of trees, with or without a road; handsome street. [F., fr. *avenir*, come to]

aver' *v.t.* declare true; assert. **aver'ment** *n.* [F. *avérer*, fr. L. *verus*, true]

av'erage *n.* mean value or quantity of a number of values or quantities; (formerly meant charge over and above freight at sea; loss from damage *etc.*). -*a.* medium, ordinary. -*v.t.* fix or calculate a mean. *v.i.* exist in or form a mean. [orig. unknown]

avert' *v.t.* turn away, ward off. -**averse'** *a.* disinclined, unwilling. -**aver'seness** *n.* -**aver'sion** *n.* dislike. [L. *avertere*, turn from]

a'viary *n.* place for keeping birds. **a'viarist** *n.* [L. *aviarium*, fr. *avis*, bird]

avia'tion *n.* art of flying by mechanical means. -**a'viator** *n.* -**av'ion** *n.* French word for airplane. [F. , fr. L. *avis*, bird]

avoca'do *n.* pear-shaped edible fruit of a tropical American tree of the laurel family. [Sp.]

avoca'tion *n.* employment, business; (formerly, distraction from business, diversion). [L. *avocatio*, calling away]

avoid' *v.t.* keep clear of, escape; (*law*) annul, invalidate. -**avoid'able** *a.* **avoidance** *n.* [OF. *esvuider*, empty out]

avow' *v.t.* own, acknowledge. -**avow'able** *a.* -**avow'al** *n.* -**avowed'** *a.* **avow'edly** *adv.* [F. *avouen*-Low *uotare*, vow]

avuncular *a.* of, like, an uncle. [L. *avunculus*, uncle]

AWACS *n.* acronym for airborne warning and control system

await' *v.t.* wait or stay for; be in store for. [ONF. *awatier*. *See* wait]

awake', **awa'ken** *v.t.* rouse from sleep, stir. -*v.i.* cease from sleep; bestir oneself; become aware, not sleeping. **awakening** *n.* [OE. *awæcnan*]

award' *v.t.* adjudge. -*n.* judgment of an arbiter, final decision. [fr. OF. *eswarder*. *See* guard, ward]

aware' *a.* informed, conscious. **awareness** *n.* [OE. *sewer*]

awash' *adv.* level with the surface of water, washed over by waves. [*a*-and *wash*]

away' *adv.* absent, apart, at a distance. [OE. *onweg*, on the way]

awe *n.* dread mingled with reverence. *v.t.* fill with awe. -**aw'ful** *a.* inspiring awe; dreadful; very bad. -**aw'fully** *adv.* **awe'some** a. [ON. *agi*, fear]

awhile' *adv.* for a time. [*See* while]

awk'ward *a.* clumsy, ungainly; difficult to deal with; embarrassed. -**awk'wardly** *adv.* -**awk'wardness** *n.* [orig. *adv.* , with suffix *-ward* on *old awk*, backhanded]

awl *n.* pointed tool for boring small holes, *esp.* in leather. [OE. *æl*] awn'ing n. covering of canvas etc. to shelter from sun. [orig. unknown]

awry' adv. crookedly, perversely. a. crooked, distorted; wrong. [earlier onwry. See wry]

ax, axe n. tool with iron blade for hewing or chopping. [OE. æx]

axel n. jump performed in competitive figure skating in which a skater leaps from the outer front edge of one skate, does 1½ turns in the air, and lands on the outer back edge of the other skate.

ax'iom n. self-evident truth; received principle. -axiomat'ic a. [G. axioma, fr. axioein, take for granted]

ax'is n. straight line round which a body revolves; line or column about which parts are arranged; (politics) German-Italian (Nazi-Fascist) alliance in World War II. [L. = pivot]

ax'le, ax'le-tree n. rod on which a wheel turns. [ON. äxul-tre]

ayatollah n. one of a class of Iranian Shiite religious leaders. [Pers. and Arab., aya, sign, Allah, god]

aza'lea n. genus of shrubby plants allied to the rhododendron, with fine white, yellow or red flowers. [fr. G. azaleas, dry]

az'imuth n. arc between zenith and horizon; its angular distance from the meridian. [Arab. as-sumut, the way]

AZT n. azidothymidine, a drug used to treat the AIDS virus. [Trademark]

az'tec a. /n. (member) of ruling race (and language) in Mexico before Spanish Conquest. [Azteca, native name of tribe]

az'ure a. clear blue, sky-colored. -n. delicate blue; the sky. [orig. the lapis lazuli, fr. Arab. azward, Pers. lajward, Place in Turkestan, where it was procured]

B

bab'ble v.i. speak like a baby; talk idly. -v.t. utter idly. -n. chatter, idle talk. -bab'bler n. -bab'bling, bab'ble ment n. [imit. of infant speech]

ba'bel n. confusion of sounds; scene of confusion. [Tower of Babel (Gen. xi), understood as confusion, but prob. Assyr. bab-ilu, gate of the gods]

baboon' n. species of large monkey, with long face and dog-like tusks. [F. babouin]

ba'by n. infant child. -babe n. ba'byhood n. -ba'byish a. -ba'by boom' large increase in the birth-rate, esp. as occurred in the years following the end of World War II. -ba'by carr'iage light vehicle for transporting a baby. [earlier baban. imit. of baby speech]

baccalau'reate n. university degree of bachelor. -baccalau'rean a. [See bachelor]

bac'chanal (-ka-) n. worshipper of Bacchus; reveller. -bacchana'lian a. [L. bacchanalis-Bacchus, god of wine]

bach'elor n. unmarried man; one who takes his first degree at a university; young knight. -bach'elorhood n.— bach'elorship n. [Low. L. baccalarius, cowherd]

bacil'lus n. (pl. bacil'li) microbe, minute organism causing disease. -bacil'liform a. -bacill'ar, bacill'ary a. [Late L. , dim. of baculus, rod]

back n. hinder part.; situated behind. -v.t. support; make recede. -v.i. move away to the rear. -v. to the rear; to a former condition; in return. back'beat n. the second and fourth beats in music written in even time or, in more complex time signatures, the last beat of the bar. -back'er n. one who supports another, esp. in a contest. -back'fire v.i. ignite wrongly, as a gas-burner etc. -back-gam'mon n. board game played with pieces and dice. -back'-ground n. space at the back; space behind the chief figures of a picture etc. -back'-hand n. stroke with the hand turned backward; writing that slopes to the left. -back' talk n. insolent rejoinder. -back'-ward, back'wards adv. to the rear; to the past; from a better to a worse state. a. lagging behindhand. -back'wardness n. -back'water a to reverse propellers to stop a ship or make it go backwards. [OE. bæc]

ba'con n. cured pig's flesh. [OE.]

bacte'rium n. microbe, disease-germ - bact'ria pl. -bacte'rial a. -bacteri ol'ogist n. -bacteriol'ogy n. study of bacteria. [G. bakerion, little staff]

bad a. not good; evil, wicked; faulty. -bad'ly adv. -bad'ness n. [ME. badde]

badge n. mark or sign. (ME. bage]

badg'er n. burrowing night animal, about the size of a fox. -v.t. hunt eagerly, worry, as dogs a badger. [orig. uncertain]

badinage' (-azh') n. light playful talk, banter, chaff. [F.]

bad'minton n. game like lawn-tennis, but played with shuttlecocks. [Badminton, Duke of Beaufort's house]

baf'fle v.t. check, frustrate. [orig. uncertain]

bag n. sack, pouch; measure of quantity. -v.i. swell out. -v.t. put in a bag; kill, seize, as game etc. -bagg'y a. loosely bulging. [ON. baggi]

bagatelle' n. trifle; game played with nine balls and cue on a board. [F.]

bagg'age n. portable luggage of an army; any luggage; saucy or worthless woman. [F. bagage]

bag'pipe n. musical wind-instrument consisting of a leather wind-bag and pipes. -bag'piper n. [bag and pipe]

bail n. (law) security given for a person's reappearance in court; one giving such security. -v.t. release on security. [OF., fr. bailler, give]

bail n. pole separating horses in a stable. [OF., fr. L. baculum, stick]

bail v.t. empty out water from a boat. bail' out v.i. drop from an airplane by parachute. -bail'er n. [obs. bail, bucket]

bail'iff n. a minor officer in a court of law; sheriffs officer; land steward. bail'iwick n. jurisdiction of a bailiff. [OF. bailif]

bait n. food put on a hook to entice fish; any lure or enticement; refreshment on a journey. -v.t. set a lure; feed and water; annoy, persecute. -v.i. take refreshment on a journey. [ON. beita, cause to bite]

baize *n.* coarse woollen cloth. [earlier haves (*pl.*) fr. color *bay*]

bake *v.t.* cook or harden by dry heat, to cook in oven. *-v.i.* make bread; become scorched. -ba'ker *n.* -ba'kery. -ba'ker's doz'en, thirteen. [OE. *bacan*]

bal'ance *n.* pair of scales; equilibrium; surplus; sum due on an account; difference of two sums. *-v.t.* weigh; bring to equilibrium; adjust. *-v.i.* have equal weight; be in equilibrium. -bal'ance-sheet *n.* list of assets and liabilities. -bal'ance-wheel *n.* regulating wheel of a watch. [L. *bilanx- bis*, twice, and *lanx*, platter]

bal'cony *n.* platform projecting from the wall of a building; second gallery of a theater. -bal'conied *a.* [It. *balcone*]

bald (bawld) *a.* hairless (featherless *etc*); plain, meager. -bald'head *n.* -bald'ly *a.* -bald'ness *n.* [earlier *balled*, fr. Welsh *bal*, white on the brow]

bale *n.* bundle or package. *-v.t.* make into bundles. [OF. = ball]

bale *n.* evil, mischief, woe. -bale'ful *a.* bale'fully *adv.* -bale'fulness *n.* -bale'fire *n.* beacon, bonfire. [OE. *bealo*, woe]

balk (bawk) *n.* strip of land left unploughed; squared timber, beam; hindrance. *-v.t.* hinder. *-v.i.* swerve, pull up. [OE. *balca*, ridge]

ball (bawl) *n.* anything round; globe, sphere; bullet; game played with ball. [ON. *bollr*]

ball (bawl) *n.* assembly for dancing. -ball'room *n.* [F. *bal*]

ball'ad *n.* simple spirited narrative poem; simple song. [F. *ballade*, orig. a dancing-song]

ballade' *n.* form of poem. [F.]

ball'ast *n.* heavy material put in a ship to give steadiness by added weight. *-v.t.* load thus. [obs. *last*, burden]

balleri'na (-e'-) *n.* dancer, *esp.* premiere in a ballet, [It.]

ball'et (-ā-) *n.* theatrical dance. [F.]

ballis'tics *n.* science of projectiles. -ballis'tic *a.* [L. *ballista*, Roman military engine—G. *ballein*, throw]

balloon' *n.* early form of aircraft, raised by large gas-filled bag; inflated toy. *-v.i.* go up in a balloon; puff out. -balloon'ist *n.* [F. *ballon*]

ball'ot *n.* method of voting secretly by putting balls or tickets into a box. *-v.i.* vote by this method. -ball'ot-box *n.* [It. *ballotta*, dim. of *balla*, ball]

balm (bam) *n.* aromatic substance; healing or soothing ointment; anything soothing. -balm'iness *n.* -balm'y *a.* [L. *balsamum*. See balsam]

bal'sam (bawle-) *n.* resinous aromatic substance. -balsam'ic *a.* [L. *balsamum*]

bamboo' *n.* large Indian reed, with hard, hollow stem. [Malay orig.]

bamboo'zle *v.t.* confound or mystify, confuse, puzzle. [arbitrary formation]

ban *n.* denunciation, curse; proclamation. *-v.t.* curse, forbid; outlaw. -banns *n.* *pl.* proclamation of marriage. [OE. *bannan*, summon, later curse]

banal', ba'nal *a.* commonplace, trivial. -

banal'ity *n.* [F.]

bana'na (-an-) *n.* tall tropical or subtropical tree; its fruit. [Sp. or Port. fr. native Guinea name]

ban'co *interj.* call in gambling games such as chemin de fer and baccarat by a player or bystander who wishes to bet against the entire bank. [It. *banco*, bank]

band *n.* strip used to bind; bond. -ban'dage *n.* strip of cloth used by surgeons for binding. [*bind*]

band *n.* company, troop; company of musicians. *-v.t.* and *i.* join into a band. [F. *bande*]

bandann'a *n.* patterned, colored silk or cotton handkerchief [Hind. *bhandknu*, method of dyeing]

band'box *n.* light box for hats *etc.* [orig. a box for *bands*, collars]

ban'dit *n.* outlaw; robber. [It. *bandito*. See ban]

bane *n.* ruin, destruction; poison. -bane'ful *a.* -bane'fully *adv.* -bane'-fulness *n.* [OE. *bana*, murderer]

bang *n.* heavy blow; sudden loud noise, explosion. *-v.t.* beat, strike violently; slam; make a loud noise. [ON. *banga*, beat, of imit. orig.]

bang'le (-ngé-gl) *n.* ring worn on arm or leg [Hind. *bangri*]

ban'ish *v.t.* condemn to exile; drive away. -ban'ishment *n.* [F. *bannir*, proclaim outlaw. cp. *ban*]

ban'ister *n.* corrupt, of baluster (q.v.)

ban'jo *n.* musical instrument, having a body like a flat drum, a long neck and strings played with the fingers. [earlier *banjore*, corrupt. of old bandore; L. *pandura*]

bank *n.* mound or ridge of earth; margin of a river, lake *etc.*; rising ground in the sea. *-v.t.* and *i.* enclose with a ridge; pile up; of an airplane, tilt inwards in turning. [ME. *banker*]

bank *n.* establishment for keeping, lending, exchanging *etc.* money. *-v.t.* put in a bank. *-v.i.* keep or deal with a bank. -bank'er *n.* -bank'ing *n.* [fr. It. *banca*, orig. a money-changer's bench]

bank *n.* bench in a galley; row or rank. [OF. *banc*, bench]

bank'rupt *n.* one who fails in business, cannot pay his debts. *-a.* insolvent. -bank'ruptcy *n.* insolvency. [earlier *bankrout*, fr. It. *banca rotta*, broken bank]

bann'er *n.* flag bearing a device; a country's flag. [F. *bannière*]

banq'uet (bang'-kwet) *n.* feast. *-v.i.* feast. *-v.t.* give a feast to -banq'ueter *n.* [F., dim. of *banc*, bench]

ban'tam *n.* dwarf variety of domestic fowl; boxing weight. [place in Java]

ban'ter *v.t.* make fun of *-n.* raillery in fun. [orig. unknown]

bant'ing *n.* slimming dietary. [W. Banting, its inventor]

baptize' (-iz') *v.t.* immerse in or sprinkle with water ceremonially; christen. -bap'tism *n.* -baptis'mal (-iz') *a.* baptis'mally *adv.* -bap'tist *n.* believer in baptism by immersion only. [G. *baptizein*, immerse]

bar *n.* rod of any substance; bank of sand at the mouth of a river; rail in a law-court; body of lawyers; counter where drinks are served; shop where alcoholic drinks are served and consumed. -*v.t.* make fast; obstruct; hinder, shut out (in); except. *prep.* except. -**bar'code** *n.* a machine-readable arrangement of numbers and parallel lines of different widths printed on a package, which can be electronically scanned at a checkout to give the price of the goods and to activate computer stock-checking and reordering. [F. *barre*]

barb *n.* curved jag on the point of a spear, fish-hook *etc.* -*v.t.* furnish with such jags. [fr. L. *barba*, beard]

bar'barous *a.* savage, brutal, uncivilized. -**barba'rian** *n.* -**bar-** **bar'ic** *a.* -**bar'barism** *n.* -**barbar'ity** *n.* -**bar'barously** *adv.* [G. *barbaros*, foreign]

bar'bary ape *n.* magot; small, tailless ape of Gibraltar and Africa. [Barbary]

bar'ber *n.* one who shaves beards and cuts hair. [L. *barba*, beard]

bar'bital *n.* an addictive, hypnotic drug, veronal. -**barbitu'ric a'cid**, an acid derived from urea. -**barbitu'rate** *n.* salt or ester of barbituric acid; any of a variety of sedative or hypnotic drugs. [fr. *usnea barbata* (lichen) and *uric* acid]

bar'carolle *n.* boat-song, gondolier's song. [It. *barca*, boat]

bard *n.* poet, minstrel, *esp.* among the Celtic races. -**bard'ic** *a.* [Gael.]

bare *a.* uncovered; naked; poor, scanty. *v.t.* make bare. -**bare'ly** *adv.* -**bare'ness** *n.*, -**bare'back** *a.* and *adv.* without a saddle. -**bare'faced** *a.* impudent. -**bare'foot** *a.*

bar'gain (-gin) *n.* contract or agreement; favourable purchase -*v.i.* make a bargain; chaffer. [OF. *bargagne*]

barge *n.* flat-bottomed freight boat; state or pleasure boat. -**barge'man**, **bargee'** *n.* [fr. L. *barca*, bark, boat]

baritone *n.* voice between tenor and bass. *a.* having such a voice. [G. *barus*, heavy, *tonos*, tone]

ba'rium (bā-') *n.* metal element. -**bar'ic** *a.* [fr. G. *barus*, heavy]

bark *n.* rind of a tree. -*v.t.* strip the bark from; rub off (skin). [ON. *börkr*]

bark *v.i.* utter a sharp cry, *esp.* of a dog. -*n.* cry of a dog *etc.* [OE. *beorcan*]

bar'ley *n.* hardy grain used for food and for making malt liquors and spirits. [OE. *bærlic a.*]

barn *n.* building to store grain, hay *etc.* -**barn'door**, **barn'yard** *a.* rustic. [OE. *bern* for *bere-ærn*, barley-house]

bar'nacle *n.* shellfish which sticks to rocks and bottoms of ships. -**bar'nacle goose** *n.* species of wild goose. [fr. OF. *bernaque*]

barom'eter *n.* instrument to measure the weight or pressure of the atmosphere, indicate weather changes. -**bar'ograph** *n.* recording barometer. -**baromet'ric** *a.* [G. *baros*, weight]

bar'on *n.* title of nobility, in Britain a peer of the lowest rank. -**bar'oness** *fem.* -**bar'onage** *n.* -**baro'nial** *a.* **bar'ony** *n.* -**bar'on of beef'**, double sirloin. [F.]

bar'onet *n.* in Britain the lowest heredi tary title, inferior to baron but superior to knight. -**bar'onetage** *n.* -**bar'onetcy** *n.* [dim. of *baron*]

baroque' (-k) *a.* in art, extravagantly orna-mented; irregularly shaped. [F.]

barr'ack *n.* building for soldiers; huge bare building. [F. *baraque*, bul]

barracuda (-ōō-) *n.* voracious W. Indian fish. [orig. unknown]

barr'age (-azh) *n.* dam built across a river; curtain of shellfire (barrage balloons) to cover an attack *etc.* -**barr'age-balloon** *n.* [F.]

barr'el *n.* round wooden vessel, made of curved staves bound with hoops; quantity held by such vessel; anything long and hollow, as tube of a gun. -*v.t.* put in a barrel. -**barr'elled** *a.* [F. *baril*]

barr'en *a.* unfruitful, sterile; unprofitable. -**barr'enness** *n.* [OF. *brehaing*]

barr'icade *n.* improvised fortification against an enemy. -*v.t.* obstruct; fortify. [F., fr. *barrique*, cask]

barr'ier *n.* fence, obstruction; any obstacle. [F. *barrière*, fr. L. *barra*, bar]

barring *prep.* excepting.

barr'ister *n.* in Britain lawyer in the higher law courts. [fr. *bar* of the Inns of Court]

barr'ow *n.* small wheeled hand carriage. [OE. *bearwe*, bier]

bar'ter *v.i.* traffic by exchange of things. -*v.t.* give (one thing) in exchange for another. -*n.* traffic by exchange. [OF. *barater*, haggle]

base *n.* bottom, foundation; starting point; fixed point. -*v.t.* found, establish. -**bas'sic** *a.* -**base'less** *a.* -**base''ment** *n.* lowest story of a building; room or rooms in a building which are below ground level. [G. *basis*, step, pedes-tal]

base *a.* low, mean; despicable. -**base'ly** *adv.* -**base'ness** *n.* -**base'-born** *a.* **base-mind'ed** *a.* [VL. *bassus*, stumpy]

base'ball *n.* ball game played by two teams of nine players on an open field and in which the runner must complete a circuit of four bases to score; the ball used in this game. [fr. 'prisoners' base', where *base* is for *bars*]

bash *v.t.* smash in. [orig. unknown]

bash'ful *a.* shy, modest, wanting con-fidence. -**bash'fully** *adv.* -**bash'fulness** *n.* [*abash*]

ba'sic. *See* base.

BA'SIC *n.* a computer programming lan-guage that uses common English terms. [fr. *beginner's all-purpose symbolic instruction code*]

basil'ica *n.* large Roman hall with colon-nades and apse; church built in this style. [L. -G. *basilike*, king's house, palace]

ba'sin *n.* deep circular dish; a sink; dock; hollow holding water; land drained by a river. [F. *bassin*]

ba'sis *n.* foundation, groundwork. [G.]

bask (-a-) *v.i.* lie in warmth and sunshine. [ON. *bathask*, bathe]

bas'ket n. vessel made of interwoven twigs, rushes etc. [orig. doubtful]

Basque (bask) n. name of people of W. Pyrenees in Spain and France; their non-Aryan language. [F.]

bas-relief (ba-) n. sculpture in which the figures do not stand out much. [It. bassorilievo. See base and relief]

bass (bas) n. lowest part in music; man's lowest voice; one having such a voice. -a. low in the scale, deep. [It. basso, base]

bass (bas) n. sea-fish of the perch family. [OE. bærs]

bas'sinet n. baby-carriage or cradle. [orig. doubtful]

bassoon' n. wood-wind instrument. -bassoon'ist n. [F. basson. See bass]

baste v.t. beat with a stick. -ba'sting n. [Jocular use of v.i. baste, anoint]

baste v.t. drop melted fat over (roasting meat). [OF. basser, soak]

baste v.t. sew together loosely. [OF. bastir, build; OHG. bestan, sew]

bat n. heavy stick; flat club, esp. as used in baseball, cricket, etc. -v.i. use the bat in a game. -bat'ter n. -bat'ting n. [OE. batt, club]

bat n. mouse-like flying animal of nocturnal habits. [ME. bakke]

batch n. quantity of bread baked at one time; any quantity or number; set. [ME. bache, fr. bake]

bath (-a'-) n. water to plunge the body in; act of bathing; vessel for bathing. -v.t. wash. -bath'house n. -bath'room n. bath'tub n. [OE. bæth]

bathe (-aTH) v.t. and i. wash. -ba'ther n. -ba'thing n. [OE. bathian]

ba'thos n. ludicrous descent from the elevated to the mean in writing or speech. [G. = depth]

bat'on n. staff, esp. of a policeman, conductor or marshal. [F. bâton]

battalion (-yun) n. division of the army consisting of several companies and units of soldiers; troops in battle array. [F. bataillon. See battle]

bat'ten v.i. grow fat; live luxuriously. [Ice. batna, grow better]

bat'ter v.t. strike continuously. -n. ingredients beaten up with liquid into a paste. -bat'tering-ram n. former military engine for beating down walls etc. [F. battre, beat]

bat'tery n. number of cannon; place where they are mounted; unit of artillery, men horses and guns; (law) assault by beating; (electr.) set of voltaic cells in which electric current is stored. [F. batterie]

bat'tle n. fight between armies. -v.i. fight, struggle. [F. bataille]

bau'ble n. jester's stick; trifle, trinket. [OF. baubel, toy]

baux'ite n. aluminum-yielding clay. [F. les Beaux, near Arles]

bawd n. procurer, procuress; prostitute; keeper of brothel. -bawd'y a. lewd. -bawd'y-house n. brothel. [M. E. bawdstrot, pander]

bawl v.i. shout; speak noisily. -n. shout. [orig. uncertain]

bay a. reddish-brown. -n. horse of this colour. [fr. L. badius]

bay n. wide inlet of the sea. [Late L. baia]

bay n. space between two columns; recess. -bay'-window n. window in a recess. [F. baie, fr. bayer, gape]

bay n. laurel-tree. -pl. honorary crown of victory. [F. baie, berry]

bay n. bark; cry of hounds in pursuit. v.i. bark. v.t. bark at. [earlier abay, OF. abaier, bark]

bay'onet n. stabbing weapon fixed to a rifle. -v.t. stab with a bayonet. [F. baionette, perh. fr. Bayonne]

bazaar' (-zar') n. Eastern market; fancy fair; a sale for charity; a shop, usu. selling goods cheaply. [Pers. bazar, market]

bazoo'ka n. portable anti-tank gun. [orig. uncertain]

be v.i. live; exist; have a state or quality. [OE. beon, exist]

beach n. shore of the sea. -v.t. run on the shore. [orig. unknown]

beac'on n. signal-fire; sea-mark; radio transmitter to guide ships or aircraft; traffic lights. [OE. beacn]

bead n. little ball pierced for threading on a string; narrow molding; flange of tire. -bead'ed a. -bead'ing n. -bead'y a. [OE. gebed, prayer (beads of rosary)]

bea'gle n. small hound. [ME. begle]

beak n. bill of a bird; anything pointed or projecting. [F. bec]

beak'er n. large drinking-cup; glass vessel used by chemists. [ON. bikarr]

beam n. long squared piece of wood; ship's widest part; bar of a balance; shaft of light. -v.t. emit in rays. -v.i. shine. -a. (of radio transmission) in a controlled direction. -beam-ends n. pl. ship's side. [OE. = tree]

bean n. any of various kinds of leguminous plants and their seeds. [OE.]

bear (-a-) v.t. carry; support; endure; produce; press (upon). -born pp. brought into being. -borne pp. carried. [OE. beran]

bear n. heavy, partly-carnivorous quadruped; rough fellow; speculator for a fall in stocks. [OE. bera]

beard n. hair on the chin; similar growth in plants. -v.t. defy. [OE.]

beast n. animal; four-footed animal; brutal man; -beast'liness n. -beast'ly a. [OF. beste]

beat v.t. strike repeatedly; overcome. -v.i. throb; sail against the wind. -n. stroke; pulsation; regularly-trodden course. [OE. beatan]

beat'ify (be-at'-) v.t. make happy; pronounce in eternal happiness (the first step in canonisation). -beatif'ic a. -beatifica'tion n. -beat'itude n. [L. beatus, blessed, facere, make]

beaut'y n. loveliness, grace; beautiful person or thing. -beaut'eous a. -beautic'ian n. keeper of a beauty-parlor. [F. beauté]

beav'er n. amphibious rodent quadruped; its fur; hat made of the fur. [OE. beofor]

because' adv. and conj. by reason of; on account of. [earlier *by cause*]

beck *n.* sign, gesture; nod. [fr. obs. v. *beck*, *beckon*]

beck'on *v.i.* make a silent signal. -*v.t.* call by anod, or movement of the finger. [OE. *bicnan*, fr. *beacn*, sign, beacon]

become (-kum') *v.i.* come to be. -*v.t.* suit. -becom'ing *a.* suitable to; graceful. [OE. *be-cuman*, fr. *come*]

bed *n.* couch or place to sleep on; place in which anything rests, in architecture *etc.*; bottom of a river; layer, stratum; garden plot. -*v.t.* lay in a bed; plant. -bed'ding *n.* -bed'ridden *a.* -bed'rock *n.* -bed'room *n.* -bed'stead *n.* [OE. *bedd*]

bedev'il *v.t.* to torment greatly, to frustrate repeatedly. [*devil*]

bed'lam *a.* place of uproar; lunatic asylum. -bed'lamite *n.* [*Bethlehem* (Hospital of St. Mary of Bethlehem, London, converted into lunatic asylum)]

bee *n.* insect that makes honey; bee-like association of persons in some activity, as sewing-bee, spelling-bee. -bee'hive *n.* -bee'line *n.* shortest route. -bees'wax *n.* [OE. *beo*]

beech *n.* common tree with smooth silvery bark and small nuts. -beech'en *a.* -beech'mast *n.* beech nuts. [OE. *bece*]

beef *n.* flesh of an ox or cow. -beef'y *a.* fleshy, stolid. [F. *boeuf*, ox]

beer *n.* fermented alcoholic beverage made from malt and hops. [OE. *beor*]

beet *n.* plant with a carrot-shaped root, used as a vegetable (red variety) or to extract sugar (white variety). [OE. *bete*]

beet'le *n.* coleopterous insect. [OE. *bitela-bitan*, bite]

befit *v.t.* be suitable to. -befitt'ing *a.* -befitt'ingly *adv.* [*fit*]

before *prep.* in front of, in presence of, in preference to; earlier than. -*adv.* ahead; earlier; in front; in advance. -*conj.* sooner than. [OE. *beforan*]

befriend (-rend') *v.t.* help. [*friend*]

beg *v.t.* ask earnestly, beseech; take for granted, *esp.* in begging the question, taking for granted what ought to have been proved. -*v.i.* ask for or live on alms. -beg'gar *n.* -beg'garly *a.* -beg'gary *n.* [OF. *begard*, fr. Med. L. *begardus*, member of a certain mendicant order. The *v.* is fr. the *n.*]

beget *v.t.* produce, generate. -begett'er *n.* [OE. *begilan*, fr. *get*]

begin *v.i.* take rise; commence. -*v.t.* enter on, originate. -beginn'er *n.* beginn'ing *n.* [OE. *beginnan*]

begrudge *v.t.* grudge, envy anyone the possession of something; give unwillingly. [*grudge*]

beguile (-gil') *v.t.* cheat; wile away. -beguile'ment *n.* -begui'ler *n.* [*guile*]

behalf (-haf') *n.* favour, benefit (in phrases such as *on behalf of*). [fr. *by* (*the*) *half*; OE. *healf*, half side]

behave *v.i.* bear, carry, conduct (oneself). -beha'vior (-yer) *n.* conduct. -beha'viorism *n.* psychological approach based on the (ob-

jective) study of reaction to external stimulus. [*have*]

behead *v.t.* cut off the head. [*head*]

behind (-hi'-) *prep.* in the rear of. -*adv.* in the rear. -behind'hand *a.* in arrears, tardy. -*adv.* [OE. *behiadan*]

behold *v.t.* watch, see. -behold'en *a.* bound in gratitude. -behold'er *n.* onlooker. [OE. *behealdan*]

beige (-ezh) *n.* fabric of undyed wool; its color. *a.* [F.]

be'ing *n.* existence; creature. [*be*]

bela'bor *v.t.* beat soundly. [*labor*]

bela'ted *a.* tardy, late. [*late*]

belay *v.t.* (*naut.*) fasten a running rope by coiling it round a cleat. [*lay*]

belch *v.i.* void wind by the mouth. -*v.t.* eject violently; cast up. -*n.* emission of wind *etc.* [OE. *bealcian*]

bel'fry *n.* bell-tower. [OHG. *bergfrid*, guard-peace, watchtower]

belie *v.t.* falsify; counterfeit; speak falsely of [OE. *beleogan*, deceive]

believe *v.t.* regard as true; trust in. -*v.i.* have faith; suppose. -belief' *n.* believable *a* [ME. *beleven*]

belit'tle *v.t.* cause to appear small; make small. -belit'tlement *n.* [*little*]

bell *n.* hollow metal vessel to give a ringing sound when struck; anything shaped like a bell; sound of a bell. -bell'buoy *n.* [OE. *belle*]

bel'ladonna *n.* deadly nightshade; narcotic drug made from it. [It. *bella donna*, fair lady]

belle *n.* beautiful woman; fairest lady (*e.g.* at a ball). [F.]

bel'licose *a.* war-like. [L. *bellicosus*]

belli'gerent (-ij'-) *a.* waging war. -*n.* nation or person taking part in war. [L. *belligerare*, wage war (*bellum*)]

belf'jar *n.* bell-shaped glass jar used in laboratories.

bel'low *v.i.* roar like a bull; shout. -*n.* roar of a bull; any deep cry or shout. [OE. *bylgan*]

bel'lows *n.* instrument for making a blast of air (to blow up a fire *etc.*). [fr. OE. *bielg*, belly]

bel'ly *n.* part of the body which contains the bowels; stomach. -*v.t.* and *i.* swell out. [OE. *belg*]

belong *v.i.* be the property or attribute of, be connected with. [earlier *long*, as though 'go along with']

belov'ed (-luv'-) *a.* much loved. (fr. obs. v. *belove*]

below *adv.* beneath; unworthy of. -*prep.* lower than. [*by low*]

belt *n.* band; girdle. -*v.t.* furnish, surround, or mark, with a belt. [OE.]

bemoan *v.t.* lament, show grief by moaning. [*moan*]

bemuse *v.t.* stupefy, confuse; -bemused' *a.* [*muse*]

bench *n.* long seat; seat or body of judges *etc.* -*v.t.* place on a bench. [OE. *benc*]

bend *v.t.* curve or bow. -*v.i.* take a curved shape. -*n.* curve. [OE. *bendan*]

beneath *prep.* under, lower than. -*adv.* in a lower position. [OE. *beneothan*]

benedic'tion n. invocation of the divine blessing. [L. benedictio]

ben'efit n. advantage, favor, profit, good. -v.t. do good to. -v.i. receive good. -benefac'tion n. -benefac'tor n. benefactress fem. -ben'efice n. ecclesiastical living. -benef'icence n. -benef'icent a. -benefi'cently adv. benefi'cial a. -benefi'cially adv. -benefi'ciary n. [L. benefactum, well done]

benev'olent a. kindly, charitable. -benev'olence n. - benev'olently adv. [L. bene, well, volens, wishing]

benign' (-in) a. kindly, mild, gentle; favourable. [L. benignus]

bent n. kind of wiry grass. [OE. beonot- (in place-names)]

bent n. inclination, turn of mind. [bend]

ben'zene n. tarry liquid distilled from oil; by-product of coal-tar. -ben'zine n. distillate of petroleum. [earlier benjoin, fr. Arab. luban jawi, Java frankincense]

bequeath' (-th) v.t. leave by will. -bequest' n. act of bequeathing; legacy. [OE. becwethan-be- and cwethan, say]

bereave' v.t. rob of -bereave'ment n. [OE. bereafian, plunder]

beret' (be'-rā) n. woolen cap, orig. of the Basques. [F.]

berr'y n. small stoneless fruit. -berr'ied a. bearing berries. [OE. berie]

ber'serk a. frenzied with rage; filled with the fighting fury of a berserk. -n. Norse warrior. [Ice. berserkr]

berth n. shipés anchoring place; place to sleep in a ship; employment, situation. v.t. moor. [bear, in naut. sense of direction]

ber'yl n. greenish or bluish precious stone; aquamarine. -beryl'lium n. the white metal glucinium. [G. beryllos]

beseech' v.t. entreat, implore. [ME. sechen, seek]

beside' prep. by the side of, near; distinct from. -besides' adv. and prep. in addition, otherwise, over and above. [OE. bi sidan by the side]

beseige' v.t. invest, beset with armed forces; throng round [seige]

best a., adv. superlative of good or well. v.t. defeat. -best-man n. groomsman at a wedding. -best-sel'ler n. book with large sales. [OE. bet(e)st. See **better**]

bes'tial a. like a beast; rude; brutal. -bestial'ity n. [L. bestialis]

bestow' v.t. give; put away; accommodate. -bestow'al n. [stow]

bestride' v.t. sit or stand over with legs apart. [OE. bestridan, sit on a horse]

bet n. wager. -v.t. and i. wager. [prob. shortened fr. abet]

betimes' adv. early, in good time; seasonably. [earlier betime, by time]

betray' v.t. give up treacherously; be disloyal to; mislead; reveal, show signs of. -betray'al n. -betray'er n. [L. tradere, hand over]

betroth' (-oth') v.t. bind to marry, affiance. -betroth'al n. -betrothed' a.and n. [ME. bitreuthien]

bett'er a. and adv. comparative of good and well. -v.t. and i. improve. -bett'er oneself, improve one's (financial etc.) conditions. [OE. betera, compar. of a lost stem *bat-]

between', betwixt' prep. in the middle of two, of space, time etc.; in the middle or intermediate space. -adv. midway. [OE. betweonum, by twain, and OE. betweox, fr. twisc, twofold]

bev'el n. slant, diagonal surface; tool for setting off angles. -a. slanted. -v.t. cut away to a slope. [cp. F. biveau]

bev'erage n. liquor for drinking. [OF. bevrage, fr. beivre, L. bibere, drink]

bev'y n. flock of birds, esp. quails; company, esp. of ladies. [AF. bevee, further orig. unknown]

beware' v.i. be on one's guard. [ware]

bewil'der v.t. puzzle, lead astray. bewil'dering a. -bewil'deringly adv. -bewil'derment n. confusion of mind. [fr. obs. wildern, wilderness]

bewitch' v.t. affect by witchcraft; charm, fascinate. -bewitch'ing a. enchanting. -bewitch'ingly adv. [witch]

beyond' adv. farther away. -prep. on the farther side of; later than; surpassing, out of reach of. [OE. begeondan]

bez'el n. part of a setting which holds a precious stone. [OF. bisel]

bi'as n. slant; one-sided inclination; leaning, bent; swaying impulse. -v.t. influence. -bi'ased a. prejudiced. [F. biais]

bib n. cloth put under a child's chin. [ME. bibben, fr. L. bibere, drink]

Bi'ble n. Old and New Testaments, the sacred writings of the Christian Church. -bib'lical a. [G. biblia, books]

bibliog'raphy n. history and description of books. [G. biblion, book, graphein, write]

bi'centennial n. the day celebrating an event exactly 200 years previously. [fr. bi-, two, L. centenarius, century]

bi'ceps (-s-) n. two-headed muscle, esp. the muscle of the upper arm. [L. bis, twice, caput, head]

bick'er v.i. quarrel; quiver, flash. -bick'ering n. [orig. uncertain]

bi'cycle n. vehicle with two wheels, one in front of the other, propelled by pedals worked by the rider. -bi'cyclist n. [F. fr. bi-, two, and G. kyklos, wheel]

bid v.t. offer; command. -n. offer, esp. of a price at an auction sale. -bid'der n. -bid'ding n. [confusion of OE. beodan, offer, and biddan, request]

bide v.i. remain. -v.t. await. [OE. bidan, remain]

bienn'ial (bi-en'-) a. happening every two years; lasting two years. -n. plant which lives two years. -bienn'iatly adv. [L. biennium, two years]

bifo'cal (bi-fō'-) a. having two foci, esp. of spectacle lenses designed for near and distant vision. [bi-, two, and focal]

bifur'cate a. having two branches; forked.

-v.t. and i. -bifurca'tion n. [L. bifurcus, two-pronged]

big a. large, great; pregnant; haughty. -big'ness n. [orig. unknown]

big'amy n. crime of having two husbands or two wives at once. -big'amist n. [bi-, two, and G. gamos, marriage]

big'ot n. one blindly or obstinately devoted to a party or creed. -big'oted a. -big'otry n. narrow zeal. [F.]

bilat'eral (bi-) a. two-sided. [lateral]

bile n. fluid secreted by the liver; (fig.) anger, bitter temper. -bil'ious a. bil'iousness n. [L. bilis]

bilge n. bottom of a ship's hull; foulness collecting therein. -v.i. spring a leak. bilge'-water n. [form of bulge]

biling'ual (bi) a. having or written in two languages. -biling'ualism n. [fr. bi-, two, and L. lingua, tongue]

bill n. tool for pruning; halberd, an old weapon. [OE. bil, sword]

bill n. bird's beak. -v.i. join bills, as doves; caress. [OE. bile]

bill n. note of charges; banknote; draft of proposed law; advertisement; commercial document. -v.t. announce by advertisement. -bill'board n. a large surface designed to exhibit bills for advertising bill'fold n. a folding pouch designed to carry paper money and other small personal belongings. [Late L. billa, bulla, seal]

bill'iards (-ly-) n. game played on a table with balls and cues. (F. bille, ball, billard, cue]

bill'ion n. a thousand millions. [F.]

bill'ow n. great swelling wave. -v.i. rise in waves. [ON. bylga]

bimonth'ly (bi-) a. and adv. every two months; twice a month. [month]

bin n. receptacle for storing corn, wine etc., or for refuse. [OE. binn, manger]

bi'nary (bi'-) a. twofold. -n. double star, two stars revolving round the same center of gravity. [L. bini, two by two]

bind (-i-) v.t. tie fast; tie round, gird, tie together; unite; put (a book) into a cover. -bind'er n. -bind'ery n. [OE. bindan]

binge (-j-) n. (sl.) party or celebration, carouse, spree. [origin unknown]

binn'acle n. box in which a ship's compass is kept. [earlier bittacle, fr. L. habitaculum, little dwelling]

binoc'ular a. adapted to both eyes. -n. telescope made for two eyes (usu. in pl.). (L. bini, two together, oculus, eye]

bino'mial a. (alg.) quantity consisting of two terms, e.g., a+b [L. bi-, twice, and nomen, a name, a term]

bi'o- prefix meaning life. [G. bios] forms compounds as biochemistry n. chemistry of living things. -biodynam'ics n.

biodegrad'able a. capable of decomposition by natural means. [L. gradus, degree]

biog'raphy n. story of a person's life. biog'rapher n. -biograph'ical a. biograph'ically adv. (G. graphein, write]

biol'ogy n. science of life. -biolog'ical a. -

biolog'ically adv. -biol'ogist n. [G. logos, discourse]

bion'ics n. study of relation of biological and electronic processes -bion'ica. having physical functions augmented by electronic equipment. [fr. G. bios, life, and electronic]

bio'rhythm n. a cyclically recurring pattern of physiological states in an organism or organ, believed by some to affect physical and mental states and behavior. -bio'rhythmic adv. [G. rhythmos, rhythm]

bipart'ite a. composed of two parts or parties. [part]

bi'ped (bi'-) n. two-footed animal. [L. bipes-bi-, two, pes, foot]

bi'plane (bi-') n. airplane with two planes in each wing. [bi-, two, and plane]

birch n. tree with smooth white bark; rod for punishment, made of birch twigs. -v.t. flog. [OE. birce]

bird n. feathered animal. [OE. bridd]

birth n. bearing or being born of, offspring; parentage. [ON. byrth]

bis'cuit (-kit) n. a soft bread in small cakes; pottery clay that has been fired once prior to glazing. -a. pale brown. [F., fr. L. bis coctus, twice baked]

bisect' (bi-) v.t. cut in equal halves. bisect'or n. [L. bi-, two, secare, cut]

bish'op n. clergyman in charge of a diocese; spiritual overseer. -bish'opric n. [G. episkopos, overseer]

bi'son (bi'-) n. large wild ox, buffalo. [L.]

bit n. fragment, piece, bite; in computing, smallest unit of information. [OE. bita]

bit n. biting part of a tool; mouthpiece of a horse's bridle. -v.t. put the bit in. [OE. bite, bite]

bitch n. female dog. [OE. bicce]

bite v.t. cut into with the teeth; cut into generally; corrode. -n. act of biting; wound made by biting; mouthful. -bi'ter n. -bi'ting a. mordant, sarcastic. [OE. bitan]

bitt'er a. harsh-tasting; sharp, painful; stinging. -bitt'erly adv. -bitt'erness n. -bitt'ers n. pl. bitter medicines or essences. [OE. biter]

bit'umen n. any of various flammable mineral substances, e.g., petroleum, asphalt etc. -bitu'minous a. [L.]

bi'valve (bi-') a. having a double shell. n. mollusk with such a shell. [L. bi-, two, valva, valve]

biv'ouac (-ōō-ak) n. temporary resting place of troops, without tents. -v.i. pass the night in the open. [F.]

bizarre' a. quaint, fantastic. [F.]

black a. without light; dark; of the darkest color. -n. darkest color; black paint or fabric; a person of a black-skinned race. -black'en v.t. and i. -black'-mar'ket n. illicit dealings in rationed (smuggled etc.) goods; scene of such transaction. -black'out n: temporary loss of memory or consciousness; obscuring or extinguishing of lights to make dark. -v.t. and i. -black'shirt n. fascist. -black widow n. venomous spider. [OE. blæc]

black'mail n. money extorted by threats. -v.t. extort thus. [mail]

black'smith *n.* smith who works in iron, black metal. (*black* and *smith*)

bladd'er *n.* membraneous bag to contain liquid, *esp.* as part of the body; inflated bag. [OE. *blæddre*]

blade *n.* leaf; leaf-like part of anything; edge of a tool; sword; dashing fellow; flat of an oar. [OE. *blæd*, blade (of oar)]

blame *v.t.* find fault with; censure. *-n.* censure, culpability. [F. *blâmer* - G. *blasphemein*, speak ill of]

blanch *v.t./i.* whiten, drain color from. [F. *blanc*, white]

bland *a.* smooth in manner. **-bland'ish** *v.t.* **-bland'ishment** *n.* [L. *blandus*]

blank *a.* without marks or writing; empty; vacant, confused; (of verse) without rhyme. *-n.* empty space; lottery ticket not drawing a prize; void. *-v.* in sport, to prevent another team from scoring any points. **-blank'ly** *adv.* [F. *blanc*, white]

blank'et *n.* woollen bed-covering. *-v.t.* cover with a blanket; cover. [F. *blanc*]

blare *v.i.* roar; trumpet. *-n.* trumpet sound; roar. [*imit.*]

bla'sé (bla'zā) *a.* bored; satiated with pleasure. [F.]

blaspheme' *v.i.* talk profanely. *-v.t.* speak irreverently of. [G. *blasphemein*]

blast (-ast) *n.* current of air; gust of wind; explosion. *-v.t.* blow up; blight, ruin. [OE. *blæst*, strong gust]

blaze *n.* bright flame of fire; brightness; outburst; white mark on animal's face. *v.i.* burn fiercely, brightly; burn with passion etc. [OE. *blæse*, torch]

blaze *v.t.* proclaim, publish (as with trumpet). [ON. *blasa*, blow]

bla'zer *n.* light flannel sports jacket, often colored. [*blaze*]

bleach *v.t.* whiten. *-v.i.* become white. [OE. *blæcan*, fr. *blæc*, pale]

bleak *a.* cold and cheerless; exposed; originally pale. [ON. *bleikr*]

bleat *v.i.* cry, as a sheep. *-n.* sheep's cry. [OE. *blætan*]

bleed *v.i.* lose blood. *-v.t.* draw blood from; extort money from. [OE. *bledan*]

blem'ish *v.t.* mar, spoil. *-n.* disfigurement, stain, defect. [F. *blêmir*, stain]

blend *v.t.* mix. *-n.* mixture. **-blend'er** *n.* a machine for cutting food up finely, or reducing it to a liquid pulp. [ON. *blanda*, mix]

bless *v.t.* consecrate; give thanks to; invoke happiness on; make happy. **bless'edness** *n.* **-bless'ing** *n.* [OE. *bletsian*, consecrate (with blood)]

blight (blit) *n.* mildew; plant disease; baneful influence. *-v.t.* affect with blight; spoil. [orig. uncertain]

blimp *n.* small non-rigid type of airship; old fogey. [Colonel *Blimp* of David Low's cartoons]

blind (-i-) *a.* lacking sight; heedless, random; dim; closed at one end; concealed, as *blind corner. -v.t.* deprive of sight. *-n.* something cutting off light; screen for a window; pretext.

-blinders *n. n. pl.* leather covers to prevent a horse from seeing in any direction but straight forward. [OE.]

blindside *v.t.* to attach or hit someone from an angle whereby they do not detect of anticipate the attack; take by surprise; to attach someone's weak spot.

blink *v.i.* look with half-closed eyes; wink; shine unsteadily. *-v.t.* shut the eyes to, shirk. *-n.* gleam; glimpse; glance. **-blink'ers** *n.pl.* blinders [OE. *blencan*, deceive]

bliss *n.* perfect happiness. **-bliss'ful** *a.* **-bliss'fully** *adv.* **-bliss'fuliness** *n.* [OE. *bliths*, fr. *blithe*]

blis'ter *n.* bubble on the skin; plaster to produce one. *-v.t.* raise a blister. [OF. *blestre*]

blitz *n.* sudden fierce onslaught, *esp.* from the air. [Ger. = lightning]

blitz'krieg (-kreg) *n.* lightning attack; raids by heavy bombers. [Ger. *blitz*, lightning, *krieg*, war]

blizz'ard *n.* blinding storm of wind and snow. [orig. uncertain]

bloat'ed *a.* swollen. [fr. ON. *blautr*, soft]

blob *n.* spot, globule. [imit. a bubble]

bloc *n.* combination, *e.g.* , of nations, for a common aim. [F.]

block *n.* solid piece of wood, a stump; any compact mass; obstacle; stoppage; pulley with frame; group of houses; stupid person. *-v.t.* obstruct, stop up; shape on a block; sketch. **-blockade** *n.* shutting of a place by siege. *-v.t.* close by siege. **-block'head** *n.* unintelligent person [F. *bloc*]

blond, **blonde** *a.* light golden-brown; fair. *-n.* one who is fair. [F. *blond*]

blood *n.* (blud) red fluid in the veins of men and animals; race, kindred; good parentage; temperament; passion. *-v.t.* draw blood from; harden to blood-shed. **-blood'ily** *adv.* **-blood'less** *a.* **-blood'y** *a.* **-blood-bank** *n.* classified store of human blood preserved in dried or plasma form for use in transfusion. **-blood count** *n.* amount of red and white corpuscles in given quantity of blood. **-blood-transfusion** *n.* transference of blood of one person to another of same blood group. **-blood'vessel** *n.* [OE. *blod*]

bloom *n.* flower of a plant; blossoming; prime, perfection; glow; powdery deposit on fruit. *-v.i.* be in flower; flourish. **-bloom'ing** *a.* [ON. *blom*]

bloss'om *n.* flower; flower-bud. *-v.i.* flower. [OE. *blostm*]

blot *n.* spot, stain; blemish; disgrace. *-v.i.* spot, stain; obliterate; dry with blotting paper. [orig. uncertain]

blotch *n.* dark spot on the skin. *-v.t.* make spotted. **-blotch'y** *a.* [OF. *bloche*]

blot'ter *n.* a book in which records are held temporarily before being entered into a permanent register. [orig. uncertain]

blouse (-ow-) *n.* light, loose upper garment; woman's loose bodice. **-blousson** *n.* very loose-fitting blouse gathered at the waist by elastic. [F.]

blow *v.i.* make a current of air; pant; sound a blast. *-v.t.* drive air upon or into; drive by current of air; sound; spout (of whales); boast; fan, -n. blast. [OE. *blawan*]

blow v.i. blossom. [OE. *blowan*]

blow n. stroke or knock; sudden calamity, [orig. uncertain]

blubb'er n. fat of whales; weeping. -v.i. weep [imit. formation, with first meaning of bubble]

blue a. of the color of the sky or shades of that color; livid; (sl.) depressed. -n. the color; paint, clothing etc. of that color. -v.t. make blue; dip in blue liquid. -blu'ish a. -blue baby n. baby suffering from congenital cyanosis. -blue-pen'cil v.t. correct or edit. -blue'-print n. copy of a drawing made by the action of light on sensitised paper, in which the lines are white on a blue ground; proposal for action. -blue rib'bon a. of high and respected quality. [F. *bleu*]

bluff a. steep; abrupt; rough and hearty blunt frank. -n. cliff, high steep bank. [obs. Du. *blaf*]

bluff v.t. deceive by pretence of strength. [cp. Du. *verbluffen*]

blun'der v.i. flounder; make a stupid mistake. -n. gross mistake. [ME. *blondren*, confuse]

blunt a. having dull edge or point; abrupt of speech. -v.t. dull -blunt'ly adv. -blunt'ness n. [orig. unknown]

blur n. spot, stain. -v.t. stain; obscure, dim. [orig. unknown]

blurb n. publisher's recommendation on book-jacket. [coined in U.S.A. by Gelett Burgess]

blurt v.t. utter suddenly or unadvisedly. [imit.]

blush v.i. become red in the face; be ashamed. -n. red glow on the face; flush of color. [OE. *blyscan*, shine]

blus'ter v.i. of wind, blow boisterously; swagger; bully. -n. blast. [orig. uncertain]

bo'a n. genus of snakes which kill by crushing; long coil of fur or feathers worn round the neck by ladies. [L.]

boar n. male of the swine. [OE. *bar*]

board n. broad, flat piece of wood; table, meals; authorized body of men; thick stiff paper. -pl. theater, stage. -v.t. cover with planks; supply food daily; enter a ship; attack -v.i. take daily meals. -board'ing-school n. -on board', in or into a ship. [OE. *bord*, plank, table, side of ship]

boast n. brag, vaunt. -v.i. brag. -v.t. brag of, have to show. [AF. *bost*, clamor]

boat n. small open vessel; ship generally. -v.i. sail about in a boat. boat'er n. flat straw hat. -boat'hook n. -boat'house n. - boat'ing n. [OE. *bat*]

bob n. pendant; slight blow; knot of hair, ribbon etc.; weight of a plumb-line etc. v.i. move up and down. -v.t. move jerkily; cut (women's hair) short. -bobbed a. [orig. uncertain]

bobb'in n. small round stick on which thread is wound. [F. *bobine*]

bobb'y sock n. (sl.) ankle-sock. bobbysox'er n. girl in her teens. [orig. uncertain]

bobeche n. cup, ring, or disk with a center hold placed on a candle below the wick to catch the drippings. [F.]

bob'sled, bob'sleigh n. sledge made of two smaller ones tied together; racing sled. [sleigh]

bode v.t. portend, prophesy. -bode'ful a. ominous. [OE. *bodian*, announce]

bod'ice (-is) n. upper part of a woman's dress. [for (pair of) bodies, i.e., stays]

bod'kin n. small dagger; tool for piercing holes; large blunt needle. [ME. *boidekin*]

bod'y n. whole frame of a man or animal; main part of such frame; main part of anything; substance; mass; person; number of persons united or organized; matter, opposed to spirit. -v.t. give form to. -bod'iless a. -bod'ily a. and adv. - bod'yguard n. [OE. *bodig*]

bog n. wet, soft ground. -v.t. entangle in such ground. -bogg'y a. [Ir. Gael. *bogach*, fr. *bog*, soft]

bo'gey n. in golf, score of one over par at a hole. [Colonel *Bogey*, imaginary player]

bogg'le (-gl) v.i. stop at, hesitate; make difficulties; bungle, fumble. -bogg'ler n. [orig. to start with fright, as though at a ghost. See bogle]

bo'gus a. sham. [orig. unknown]

Bohe'mian n. Czech; unconventional person, esp. if artist, actor or the like; [F. *bohemien*, gypsy]

boil n. inflamed swelling. [OE. *byl*]

boil v.i. bubble up from the action of heat; be agitated, seethe; be cooked by boiling. -v.t. cause to bubble up; cook by boiling. -boil'er n. vessel for heating water or generating steam. -boil'ingpoint n. [F. *bouillir*]

bois'terous a. wild, noisy; turbulent. - bois'terously adv. -bois'terousness n. [ME. *boistous*]

bold a. daring, fearless; presumptuous; well-marked, prominent. -bold'ly adv. - bold'ness n. [OE. *bald*]

boll n. seed-vessel or pod. -boll'-wee'vil n. insect pest ravaging American cotton crops. [OE. *bolla*]

bol'ster n. long pillow; pad, support. v.t. support, uphold. [OE.]

bolt (bō-) n. bar or pin; arrow; rush, running away; discharge of lightning. -v.t. fasten with a bolt; swallow hastily. -v.i. rush away; break from control. -bolt'-hole n. underground refuge, hide-out. [OE. = heavy arrow]

bomb (bom) n. explosive projectile usually dropped from aircraft; grenade. v.t. attack with bombs. -bombard' v.t. shell. -bombard'ment n. - bomb'er n. bomb-dropping airman, airplane. [L. *bombus*, a humming]

bom'bast n. inflated language. -bombas'tic a. (OF. *bombace*, cotton-wool]

bo'nafi'de a. true, genuinely, sincerely. - bona fides n. good faith, sincerity. [L. = good faith]

bonan'za n. rich vein of gold; lucky strike. [Sp. = fair weather]

bond n. that which binds; link, union; written promise to pay money or carry out a contract. -v.t. bind; store goods until duty is paid on them. [band]

bone *n.* hard substance forming the skeleton of animals; piece of this. *-v.t.* take out bone. **-bone'less** *a.* **-bone'meal** *n.* **-bo'ny** *a.* [OE. *ban*]

bon'fire *n.* open-air fire to express joy, burn rubbish *etc.* [for *bone-fire*]

bonn'et *n.* hat or cap, *usu.* worn by a woman. [F., for *chapeau de bonnet*, perh. some unknown material]

bo'nus *n.* extra payment. [L. *bonum*, something good]

boo'gie-woo'gie *n.* jazz piano-playing with variations on simple melody and persistent bass rhythm. [imit.]

book *n.* collection of sheets of paper bound together; literary work; main division of a work. *-v.t.* enter in a book. **-book'ish** *a.* **-book'let** *n.* **-book'binder** *n.* **-book'binding** *n.* **-book'case** *n.* and other compounds. [OE. *boc*, beech, *boc stæf*, beech-staff, letter]

boom *n.* long spar; barrier. [Du.]

boom *v.i.* hum; roar. *-n.* hum or roar. [ME. *bommen*]

boom *n.* sudden commercial activity; prosperity. *-v.i.* become active, prosperous. *-v.t.* push into prominence. [orig. uncertain]

boom'erang *n.* Australian hardwood missile, designed to return to the thrower. [native]

boon *n.* favour; thing asked for. [ON. *bon*, petition]

boor *n.* rustic; rude fellow. **--boor'ish** *a.* [Du. *boer*, peasant]

boost *v.t.* help forward; push, advertise forcefully. *-n.* help forward; advertisement. [orig. unknown]

boot *n.* covering for the foot and lower leg. [F. *botte*]

boot *n.* profit, use. **-boot'less** *a.* **-to boot'**, in addition. [OE. *bot*]

booth *n.* hut or stall. [ON. *buth*]

boot'legger *n.* smuggler, *esp.* an illicit importer of alcoholic liquor **-boot'leg** *v.t.* and *i.* smuggle. [fr. smuggling of bottles of liquor in the *leg* of a long *boot*]

boot'y *n.* plunder, spoil. [F. *butin*]

bor'der *n.* margin; frontier; limit, boundary; flowered edge adjoining a walk, lawn *etc.* *-v.t.* put on a margin, edging; adjoin. *-v.i.* resemble. *-v.i.* resemble (with on); be adjacent (with upon). **-bor'derer** *n.* [F. *bordure*, edge]

bore *v.t.* pierce, making a hole; weary. *-n.* hole; size or cavity of a gun; wearisome person. **-bore'dom** *n.* **-bo'rer** *n.* [OE. *borian*, pierce]

bore *n.* tidal wave in a river. [orig. uncertain]

born, borne. *See* bear.

bo'ron *n.* non-metallic element found in borax *etc.* [*borax*]

bor'ough (bur'-e) *n.* town with a corporation. [OE. *burg*, *burh*, fort]

bor'row *v.t.* and *i.* obtain on loan or trust; adopt from abroad. **-bor'rower** *n.* [OE. *borgian*, fr. *borg*, pledge]

bor'zoi *n.* Russian wolf-hound. [Russ.]

bo'som *n.* human breast; dress covering it; seat of the passions and feelings; expanse. [OE. *bosm*]

boss *n.* knob or stud. *-v.t.* ornament with bosses. [F. *bosse*, hump]

boss *n.* employer; person in charge. [Du. *baas*]

bossa nova *n.* Brazilian dance music blending elements of jazz and samba.

bot'any *n.* science of plants. **-botan'ic, botanical** *a.* **-bot'anize** *v.i* **-bot'anist** *n.* [G. *botane*, plant]

botch *v.t.* patch or put together clumsily; bungle. *-n.* clumsy patch; bungled piece of work. **-botch'er** *n.* [ME. *bocchen*, patch]

both *a.* the two. *-adv.* and *conj.* as well; for the one part. [ME. *bathe*]

both'er (-TH-) *v.t.* pester, perplex. *-v.i.* fuss, be troublesome. *-n.* trouble, fuss. [orig. unknown]

bot'tle *n.* vessel for holding liquids; contents of such vessel. *-v.t.* put in a bottle. [F. *bouteille*]

bot'tle *n.* truss of hay. [OF. *botel*]

bot'tleneck *n.* narrow retarding passage; hold-up in traffic or in production of a manufactured good for lack of essential component *etc.* [*bottle-neck*]

bott'om *n.* lowest part; bed of a sea, river *etc.* sitting part of the human body; ship; staying power, stamina. *-v.t.* put a bottom to; base. [OE. *botm*]

bot'ulism *n.* form of food poisoning. [L. *botulus*, sausage]

bou'doir *n.* lady's private room. [F. *bouder*, pout, sulk]

bough (bow) *n.* branch of a tree. [OE. *bog*, arm, shoulder]

boul'der *n.* large stone rounded by action of water. [ME. *bulderston*]

boul'evard *n.* broad tree-lined promenade. [F. = rampart. *See* bulwark]

bounce *v.i.* bound, like a ball; throw oneself about; boast, exaggerate. *-n.* leap, spring, rebound; boast. [ME. *bunsen*, thump]

bound *n.* limit, boundary. *-v.t.* limit. close in. **-bound'ary** *n.* **- bound'ed** *a.* **-bound'less** *a.* [AF. *bounde*]

bound *v.i.* spring, leap. *-n.* spring or leap. **-bound'er** *n.* boisterous, vulgar fellow. [F. *bondir*]

boun'ty *n.* liberality; gift; premium. [F. *bonté-* L. *bonitatem-bonus*, good]

bouquet' *n.* bunch of flowers; perfume of wine. [F.]

bourgeois' (-jois') *n.* former name for 9-point printing type. [F.]

bourn *n.* small stream; in Scots, burn. [*burn*]

bout *n.* turn, round; attempt; contest. [earlier *bought*, bend. *See* bight]

bo'vine *a.* of the ox; oxlike, dull, stolid. [L. *bovinus*]

bow (bō) *n.* bend, bent line; rainbow; weapon for shooting arrows; looped knot of ribbon *etc.*; instrument for playing violin. **-bow'man** *n.* archer. [OE. *bogs*]

bow (bow) *v.i.* bend the body in respect, assent *etc.*; submit. *-v.t.* bend downwards; cause to stoop; crush. *-n.* inclination in respect. [OE. *bugan*]

bow (bow) *n.* fore end of a ship; stem. [LG.

bug, shoulder]

bow'el (-ow'-) n. intestines. -pl. entrails; interior; seat of emotions; pity, feeling. [OF. bouel]

bowl (-ō-) n. round vessel, a deep basin; drinking-cup; hollow part of anything. [OE. bolle]

bowl (-ō-) n. wooden ball. -v.t. and i. roll or throw a ball in various ways. [F. boule]

bow'sprit (bow'-) n. spar projecting from the bow of a ship. [Du. boegspriet]

box n. tree yielding hard smooth wood; its wood; case, generally with a lid; contents of such case; small house or lodge; driver's seat; compartment. -v.t. put in a box; confine. [OE., fr. L.]

box n. blow. -v.t. cuff. -v.i. fight with the fists, esp. with gloves on. -box'er n. one who so fights; a breed of dog. [orig. uncertain]

boy n. male child; lad; young man; native servant. [ME. boi]

boy'cott v.t. refuse to deal with. -n. concerted refusal to deal with. [fr. treatment of Capt. Boycott by the Irish Land League in 1880]

brace n. clasp, clamp; pair, couple; strut, support; carpenter's tool for turning boring instruments. -pl. suspenders. -v.t. stretch, strain, string up, support, make firm. [OF. brasse, pl. two arms]

brace'let n. wrist-ornament. [F.]

brack'et n. support for a shelf -pl. in printing, the marks [] used to enclose words. -v.t. enclose in brackets; couple, connect; (artillery) range by dropping shells nearer and farther than a mark. [earlier bragget, fr. F. brogue]

brackish a. saltish. [fr. Du. brak]

brad n. small nail. -brad'awl n. tool to pierce holes. [ON. broddr, spike]

brag v.i. boast, bluster. -n. boastful language. -braggado'cio (-shyō) n. -bragg'art n. [OF. braguer]

braid v.t. plait; trim with braid. -n. plaited cord; woven band; plait of hair. [OE. bregdan]

braille (brāl) n. system of printing for the blind; letters used, consisting of raised dots. [Louis Braille, inventor]

brain n. nervous matter in the skull; intellect. -v.t. dash out the brain. -brain'less a. -brain'y a. [OE. brægen]

braise v.t. stew in covered pan, originally between layers of hot charcoal. [F.]

brake n. fern; place overgrown with ferns; thicket. [orig. uncertain]

brake n. instrument for retarding the motion of a wheel; wagonette. -v.t. apply a brake to. -brake'van n. [OF. brac-L. brachium, arm]

bram'ble n. prickly shrub, the blackberry. -bram'bly a. [OE. bræmbel]

bran n. sifted husks of corn. [F.]

branch (-a-) n. limb of a tree; anything like a limb; subdivision, section; subordinate department of a business. -v.i. bear branches; divide into branches; diverge. -branch'y a. [F. branche]

brand n. burning piece of wood; mark made by a hot iron; trade-mark; sword; class of goods; mark of infamy. -v.t. burn with an iron; mark. [OE.]

bran'dish v.t. flourish. [F. brandir, flourish a brand, sword]

bran'dy n. spirit distilled from wine. (Du. brandewijn, burnt wine]

brash n. rash, eruption; belching of acid water from stomach; hedge-clippings; rock, ice fragmental. loud, arrogant, ambitious; brittle. [F. brèche]

brass n. alloy of copper and zinc; brass memorial tablet in a church; (sl.) money; impudence. -brass'y a. [OE. bræs]

brassière n. (abbrev. bra) woman's undergarment supporting the breasts. [F.]

brat n. contemptuous name for a child. (orig. uncertain)

brava'do (-va'-) n. boastful display of boldness; swagger. [Sp. bravado]

brave a. bold, courageous; splendid; finely dressed. -n. Indian warrior. -v.t. defy, meet boldly. -brave'ly adv. -bra'very n. [F.]

bra'vo int. well done! [It.]

brawl v.i. quarrel noisily; flow noisily. n. noisy quarrel. -brawl'er n. [F. brailler, be noisy]

brawn n. muscle; thick flesh; strength; preparation of chopped meat. -brawn'y a. [OF. braon, fleshy part]

bra'zen a. (made) of brass; forward. -v.t. (with "out") face accusation etc. with impudence. [brass]

bra'zier n. pan for burning charcoal. [F. brasier, fr. braise, hot coals]

breach n. break, opening; breaking of rule, duty, law, promise; quarrel. -v.t. make a gap in. [F. breche]

bread (-ed) n. food made of flour or meal baked; food; livelihood. [OE.]

breadth (-edth) n. extent across, width; largeness of view, mind. [OE. brad]

break (brāk) v.t. part by force; shatter, crush, bruise, burst, destroy, frustrate; make bankrupt; discard; loosen, dissolve; tell with care. -v.i. become broken, shattered; divided; open, appear; crack, give way; part, fall out. -n. fracture; gap, opening; dawn; separation, interruption. -break'age n. -break'down n. break-even point n. point at which profit and loss are equal; point when the return equals the investment. [OE. brecan]

bream n. small freshwater fish. [F. brème]

breast (-est) n. human chest; woman's mammary gland; affection; any protuberance. -v.t. face, oppose; mount. -breast'plate n. [OE. breost]

breath (-eth) n. air taken into and put out from the lungs; life; power of breathing; very slight breeze. -breathe (-ēTH) v.i. inhale and exhale air from the lungs; live; pause, rest. -v.t. inhale and exhale; utter softly; exercise. -brea'ther (-TH-) n. -brea'thing (-TH-) n. breath'less a. [OE. bræth, exhalation]

breech n. lower part of the body behind; hinder part of anything, esp. of a gun. -v.t. put into breeches. -breech'es n. pl. britches. -breech-load'er n. [OE. brec]

breed v.t. generate, bring forth; give rise to; rear. -v.i. be produced, -be with young. -n. offspring produced; race, kind. -breed'er n.

-**breed'ing** n. [OE. *bredan*, keep warm, cherish]

breeze n. gentle wind; wind; rumor; quarrel; something easily achieved. -breez'ily adv. -**breez'y** a. windy; bright, lively. [F. *brise*]

breth'ren n. pl. brothers. [*brother*]

brev'ity n. shortness. [L. *brevis*, short]

brew (-ōō-) v.t. prepare a beverage by fermentation, as beer from malt *etc.*, or by infusion, as tea *etc.*; plot, contrive. -v.i. be in preparation. [OE. *breowan*]

bri'ar n. See **brier**.

bri'ar a. only in briar pipe, one made of a heather root. [F. *bruyère*, heather]

bribe n. gift to corrupt; allurement. -v.t. influence by a bribe; win over; pervert. -bri'ber n. -bri'bery n. [F. = fragment, broken meats]

brick n. oblong mass of hardened clay; any oblong block. -v.t. lay or pave with bricks. [F. *brique*]

bri'dal n. wedding. -a. belonging to a wedding. [OE. *brydealu*, bride-ale, feast]

bride n. woman about to be, or just, married. -bride'groom n, man about to be, or just, married. -brides'maid n. bride's attendant. [OE. *bryd*]

bridge n. structure for crossing a river *etc.*; raised narrow platform on a ship; upper part of the nose; part of a violin supporting the strings. -v.t. make a bridge over. [OE. *brycg*]

bridge n. card game. [Russ. *biritch*]

bri'dle n. headgear of horse-harness; curb or restraint. -v.t. put a bridle on; restrain -v.i. throw up the head. -bri'dle-path n. [OE. *bridel*]

brief a. short; concise. -n. summary of a case for the use of counsel; papal letter. -n. pl. underpants. [F. *bref*]

bri'er, bri'ar a. prickly shrub, *esp.* the wild rose. [earlier *brere*, OE. *brær*]

brig n. two-masted, square-rigged ship. [shortened fr. *brigatine*]

brigade' n. sub-division of an army, under a general; organized band. -v.t. join units into a brigade. -brigadier-gen'-eral n. [F.]

brig'and n. robber. [F.]

bright (brit) a. shining, full of light; lively; cheerful; clever; illustrious. -bright'en v.t. and i. -bright'ly adv. -bright'ness n. [OE. *beorht*]

brill n. white-spotted flat-fish like turbot. [orig. unknown]

brill'iant (-lya-) a. and n. shining; sparkling; splendid. -brill'iance, brilliancy n. -brill'iantly adv. [F. *brillant*]

brim n. margin or edge, *esp.* of a river, cup, hat. [ME. *brymme*]

brim'stone n. sulfur. [ME. *bernston*, *brinston*, burnt stone]

brine n. salt water; pickle. -bri'ny a. salt. -n. (*sl.*) the sea. [OE. *bryne*]

bring v.t. fetch; carry with one; cause to come. [OE. *bringan*]

brink n. edge of a steep place; utmost edge of anything. [ME. *brenk*]

brisk a. active, lively, sharp. -v.t. enliven. -v.i. cheer up -brisk'ly adv. -brisk'ness n. [W.

brysg]

bris'ket n. breast of an animal (as a joint). [F. *brechet*]

bris'ling n. Norwegian sprat. [Norw.]

bris'tle (-is'l) n. short, stiff hair. -v.i. stand erect -v.t. erect like bristles. -bris'tliness n. -bris'tly a. [ME. *brustel*]

brit'ches n. pl. short trousers *usu.* for men, gathered and fastened at the knee. [OE. *brec*]

Brit'ish a. of pert. to Britain -Brit'on n. native of Britain [OE. *Brit*, Briton]

brit'tle a. easily broken, fragile. -britt'leness n. [OE. *breotan*, break]

broach n. boring tool; split. -v.t. pierce (a cask); open, begin. [F. *broche*, spit]

broad (-awd) a. wide, ample, open; outspoken; coarse; general; tolerant; of pronunciation, dialectal. -broad'en v.t. and i. -broad'ly adv. -broad'cast a. scattered freely. -v.t. scatter, as seed; send out radio messages, music *etc.* for general reception. -broad'cloth n. -broad'gauge n. and a. -broad'-mind'ed a. tolerant, not narrow in ideas. [Sp. *brocado*]

broc'coli n. hardy kind of cauliflower. [It. = sprouts]

brochure' (-shōōr) n. pamphlet. [F., fr. *brocher*, stitch]

brogue (-ōg) n. dialectal pronunciation, *esp.* the Irish pronunciation of English. [orig. uncertain]

broil n. noisy quarrel, tumult; confusion. [F. *brouiller*, mix up]

broil v.t. cook over hot coals or direct heat; grill. -v.i. be heated. -broiler n. apparatus for cooking under direct heat. [F. *brôler*, burn]

bro'ker n. one employed to buy and sell for others; dealer; one who values goods distrained for rent. - bro'kerage n. payment to a broker. [OF. *brocheor*]

bro'mide n. photograph printed on paper treated with silver bromide; sedative drug; user of clichés. [G. *brōmos*, stink]

bro'mine n. gaseous element allied to chlorine. -bro'mate n. -bro'mic a. [G. *brōmos*, stink]

bron'chi (-ng'-ki) n. pl. branches of the windpipe. -bron'chial a. -bronchi'tis n. [G. *bronchos*, windpipe]

brontosaur'us n. extinct giant lizard. [G. *bronte*, thunder, *sauros*, lizard]

bronze n. alloy of copper and tin. -a. the appearance of bronze to. -bronzed a. coated with, or colored bronze; sunburnt. [F.]

brood (-ōō-) n. family of young, *esp.* of birds; tribe, race. -v.t. sit, as a hen on eggs; meditate, think anxiously about. -brood'y a. -brood'ing a. [OE. *brod*]

brook (-ōō-) n. small stream. -brook'let n. [OE. *broe*]

brook (-ōō-) v.t. put up with, endure. [OE. *brucan*, use]

broom (-ōō-) n. yellow-flowered shrub; brush for sweeping (orig. of twigs), -broom'stick n. [OE. *brom*]

broth n. decoction of meat, usually with vegetables. [OE.]

broth'el n. house of prostitutes. [ME. = vile

person, fr. OE. *breothan*, go to ruin. Sense is by confusion of *brothel-house* with *bordel*, F. *bordel*, little house]

broth'er (-uTH'-) *n.* son of the same parents; anyone closely united with another. -**broth'erhood** *n,* relationship; fraternity, company. -broth'erliness *n.* - broth'erly *a.* -broth'er-in-law *n.* brother of a husband or wife; husband of a sister. [OE. *brothor*]

brow *n.* ridge over the eyes; forehead; edge of a hill. -brow'beat *v.t.* bully. [OE. *bru*, eyelid, eyebrow]

brown *a.* of a dark color inclining to red or yellow. -*n.* the color. -*v.t.* or *i.* make or become brown. [OE. *brun*]

brown'ie *n.* household spirit or goblin in Scots folklore; member of a junior formation of the girl scouts; a chocolate cookie. [*brown*]

browse *v.i.* feed on shoots and leaves; study desultoriy, as books. [fr. obs. *n. browse*, young shoots]

bruise (-ōōz) *v.t.* injure by a blow or pounding; oppress. -*n.* contusion; discolored lump raised on the body by a blow. -bruis'er *n.* boxer, prizefighter. [OF. *bruiser*]

brunch *n.* combination of breakfast and lunch. [*breakfast, lunch*]

brunette' *n.* woman with dark hair or of dark complexion, [F.]

brunt *n.* shock of an attack; chief stress of anything. [orig. a blow; orig. uncertain]

brush *n.* small shrubs; thicket; backwoods. [F. *brousse*, faggots]

brush *n.* utensil for sweeping; tool of hair used by painters; bushy tail; skirmish, fight; bundle of wires, or anything like a broom. -*v.t.* remove dust, clean with a brush; touch lightly. -*v.i.* move lightly. [F. *brousse*, faggots]

brusque (-sk) *a.* rough in manner. [F.]

brute (-ōō-) *n.* one of the lower animals; man like such animal. -*a.* animal; sensual; stupid. -bru'tal *a.* -bru'talize *v.t.* -brutal'ity *n.* - bru'tally *adv.* -bru'tish *a.* [L. *brutus*, dull, stupid]

bubb'le *n.* hollow globe of liquid, blown out with air; anything empty; swindle. -*a.* deceptive; transient. -*v.i.* form bubbles, rise in bubbles. -bubb'ly *a.* [earlier *burble*, of imit. orig.]

buck *n.* male deer, or other male animal; dandy. -*v.t.* of a horse, attempt to throw a rider by jumping upwards; to oppose in a direct manner. -buckjumper *n.* -buck'shot *n.* large shot. -buck'skin *n.* [OE. *buce*]

buck'et *n.* vessel, usually round with an arched handle, for water *etc.* -buck'etful *n. [OE. buc,* pitcher]

buck'le *n.* metal instrument with rim and tongue, for fastening straps, bands *etc.* -*v.t.* fasten with a buckle. -*v.i.* warp, bend. [F. *boucle*, boss of shield]

bud *n.* first shoot of a plant, leaf *etc.;* unopened flower. -*v.i.* begin to grow -*v.t.* graft. [ME. *bodde*]

budge *v.i.* move, stir. [F. *bouger*]

budg'et *n.* bag and its contents; annual financial statement; collection of things. -*v.t.* prepare a financial statement. [OF. *bougette*, wallet]

buff *n.* leather made from buffalo or ox hide; its light yellowish color; bare skin. [*buffalo*]

buff'alo *n.* any of several species of large oxen. [Port. *bufalo* - G. *bous*, bull]

buff'er *n.* contrivance to lessen the shock of concussion. [fr. obs. v. *buff*, imit. of muffled blow]

buff'et *n.* blow, slap; misfortune. -*v.t.* strike with the fist; contend against. -buff'eting *n.* [OF.]

buff'et *n.* sideboard; refreshment bar. [F.]

buffoon' *n.* clown; fool. -buffoon'ery *n.* [F. *bouffon*]

bug *n.* small blood-sucking insect; any insect. [OE. *budda*, beetle]

bu'gle *n.* hunting-horn; instrument like a trumpet. -bu'gler *n.* (for *bugle-horn* fr. L. *buculus,* fr. *bos*, ox]

bu'gle *n.* glass bead, usually black. [*bugle* ox, fr. its horny appearance]

build (bild) *v.t.* erect, as a house, bridge *etc.;* form, construct. -*v.i.* depend (on). -*n.* make, form. - build'er *n.* -build'ing *n.* [OE. *byldan*]

bulb *n.* rounded stem or shoot of the onion and other plants; anything resembling this, as electric light bulb. -*v.i.* form, bulbs. -bulb'ous *a.* [L. *bulbus*, onion]

bulge *n.* swelling, protuberance. -*v.i.* swell out [L. *bulge*, knapsack]

bulk *n.* size, volume; greater part; cargo. -*v.i.* be of weight or importance. -bulk'iness *n.* -bulk'y *a.* large; unwieldy. [ON. *bulki*, heap, cargo]

bulk'head *n.* partition in the interior of a ship. [fr. ON. *balkr*, beam]

bull (-ōō-) *n.* male of cattle; male of various other animals; speculator for a rise in stocks. -bull'ock *n.* castrated bull -bull's-eye *n.* boss in glass; lantern; middle part of a target. [ME. *bole*]

bull (-ōō-) *n.* Papal edict, bearing Pope's seal. [L. *bulla*, seal]

bull'dog *n.* powerfully-built dog of great courage and tenacity. *a.* brave, tenacious. [*bull* and *dog*]

bull'dozer *n.* powerful machine for leveling ground. [orig. uncertain]

bull'et (-ōō-) *n.* metal ball discharged from a rifle, pistol *etc.* [F. *boulet*, cannonball]

bull'etin (-ōō-) *n.* official report; brief official statement reporting on an event; news report. [F. fr. L. *bulla*, seal]

bull'ion *n.* uncoined gold or silver, in mass. [F. *bouillon*, boiling]

bull'y *n.* rough, overbearing fellow. -*v.t.* intimidate, overawe; ill-treat. [orig. uncertain]

bul'wark (-ōō-) *n.* raised side of a ship; breakwater; rampart; any defense or means of security. -*v.t.* protect. [orig. *rampart*, fr. *bole*, tree, and work]

bum *n.* buttocks; one who has no fixed occupation and who sponges off others [*bump*]

bum'ble-bee *n.* large bee, the humblebee. [imit.]

bump *n.* heavy blow, dull in sound; swelling caused by a blow; protuberance. -*v.t.* strike against. -bump'er *n.* full glass. *a.* full, abundant. [imit.]

bumper stick'er *n.* paper advertisement, slog, or saying with sticky backing for placement on bumper of a vehicle.

bump'kin *n.* rustic. [orig. uncertain]

bun *n.* small sweet cake; round mass of hair. [ME. *bunne*, small loaf]

bunch *n.* number of things tied or growing together; cluster; tuft, knot. *-v.t.* put together in a bunch. *-v.i.* draw together into a cluster. *-bunch'y* *a.* [orig. uncertain]

bun'dle *n.* package; number of things tied together. *-v.t.* tie in a bundle; send (off) without ceremony. *-v.i.* pack and go (with off *etc.*) [*bind*]

bung'alow (bung'ga-lō) one storied house. [Hind. *bangla*, or Bengal]

bung'le (bung'gl) *v.t.* do badly for lack of skill, manage awkwardly. *-v.i.* act clumsily, awkwardly. *-n.* blunder, muddle. [orig. uncertain]

bun'ion *n.* inflamed swelling on the foot. [perh. It. *bugnone*, swelling]

bunk *n.* box or recess for sleeping in. *esp.* in a ship's cabin [Du. *bank*, bench]

bunk'er *n.* receptacle for coal, *esp.* in a ship; sandy hollow on a golf-course. [perh. ON. *bunke*, ship's hold]

bun'ny *n.* pet name for rabbit. [*bun*]

bunt *n.* disease of wheat; the fungus. [orig. unknown]

bunt'ing *n.* bird allied to the lark. [ME. *bountyng*]

bunt'ing *n.* worsted material for flags; flags *etc.* made from it. [orig. uncertain]

buoy (boi) *n.* floating mark anchored in the sea; something to keep a person afloat. *-v.t.* mark with a buoy; keep from sinking; support. *-buoy'ancy* *n.* *-buoy'ant* *a.* [L. *boia*, chain (by which the buoy was secured)]

bur, burr *n.* prickly head of a plant; rough ridge or edge; accent associated with trilled gutteral *r-* sound, *esp.* of north of England and Scotland. [ME. *borre*]

burd'en, burth'en (-TH-) *n.* load; weight; cargo; anything difficult to bear. *-v.t.* load, encumber. *-burden'some* *a.* [OE. *byrthen*]

burd'en *n.* chorus of a song; chief theme. [F. *bourdon*, humming tone]

bu'reau *n.* writing-desk; office, *esp.* for public business. [F. = *office*, earlier *desk*, and earlier still its cloth covering; OF. *burel*, a coarse cloth]

bureauc'racy (-ok'-) *n.* government by officials; body of officials. *-bu'reaucrat* *n.* *-bureaucrat'ic* *a.* [*bureau* and G. *kratein*, govern]

burette' *n.* graduated glass tube for measuring liquids; cruet bottle. [F.]

bur'geon (-jen) *n./v.i.* sprout, bud. [F. *bourgeon*]

bur'glar *n.* one who breaks into a house by night with intent to steal. [prob. fr. OE. *burg*, dwelling]

bur'gundy *n.* red wine of Burgundy.

burlesque' (-esk') *n.* travesty, grotesque imitation, mockery. *-v.t.* caricature. *-a.* mocking,

derisively imitative. [It. *burlesco*, fr. *burla*, jest]

bur'ly *a.* sturdy, stout. *-bur'liness* *n.* [ME. *borlich*, massive]

burn *n.* small stream. [OE. *burne*]

burn *v.t.* destroy or injure by fire. *-v.i.* be on fire, literally or figuratively; shine; be consumed by fire. *-n.* injury or mark caused by fire. *-burn'er* *n.* *-burn'ing* *a.* [OE. *burnan*]

burn'ish *v.t.* make bright by rubbing, polish. *-n.* lustre, polish. *-burn'isher* *n.* [F. *brunir*, make bright]

burr'ow (-ō) *n.* hole of a rabbit *etc.* *-v.t.* make holes in the ground, as a rabbit; bore; conceal oneself. (var. of borough; OE. *beorgan*, protect]

burs'ar *n.* treasurer, *esp.* of a college; one who holds a bursary or scholarship. *-burs'ary* *n.* [Med. L. *bursarius*, purse bearer. *See* purse]

burst *v.i.* fly asunder; break into pieces; break open violently; break suddenly into some expression of feeling. *-v.t.* shatter; break violently. *-n.* a bursting explosion; outbreak; spurt; (*sl.*) drunken spree. [OE. *berstan*]

bur'y (ber'-i) *v.t.* put underground; put in a grave. *-bur'ial* *n.* [OE. *brygan*]

bus *n. See* omnibus.

bus'by *n.* fur hat worn by hussars. [orig. uncertain]

bush (-ŏŏ-) *n.* shrub; woodland, thicket; backwoods, interior of S. Africa and Australia. *-bush'y* *a.* *-bush'man* *n.* member of nomadic S. African tribe; Australian bushdweller. *-bush-whacker* *n.* one who ranges in bush; guerilla fighter; lout. [ME. *bush, busk*]

bush'el *n.* dry measure of eight gallons. [OF. *boissel*, dim. of *boiste*, box]

bust *n.* sculpture representing the head and shoulders of the human body; upper part of the body. [F. *buste*]

bus'tle (-sl) *v.i.* be noisily busy; be active. *-n.* fuss, stir. *-bus'tier* *n.* [obs. *buskle*, make hurried preparations]

bus'y (biz'-i) *a.* actively employed; diligent; meddling; occupied. *-v.t.* occupy. *-bus'ily* *adv.* *-bus'iness* (biz'-nis) *n.* affairs, work, occupation. *-bus'ybody* *n.* meddler. *-bus'yness* *n.* [OE. *bysig*]

but *prep.* and *conj.* without; except; only; yet; still; besides. [OE. *butan, beutan*, outside]

butch'er (-ŏŏ-) *n.* one who kills animals for food, or sells meat; bloody or savage man. *-v.t.* slaughter, murder. [F. *boucher* fr. *bouc*, goat]

but'ler *n.* servant in charge of the wine cellar; chief servant [OF. *bouteillier*, bottler]

butt *n.* target; object of ridicule. [F. *but*, end, aim]

butt *n.* thick end of anything; stump. [orig. uncertain]

butt *v.t.* and *i.* strike with the head; push. *-n.* blow with the head, as of a sheep. *-butt'er* *n.* [F. *bouter*, thrust]

butt'er *n.* oily substance produced from cream by churning. *-v.t.* spread with butter; flatter grossly. *-butt'ery* *a.* *-butt'ercup* *n.* meadow plant with golden-yellow flowers.

-butt'erfly n. -butter'milk n. -butt'erscotch n. sweetmeat. [OE. *butere*, fr. L. *buty-rum*]

butt'ock n. rump, protruding hinder part (*usu.* in *pl.*). [prob. dim of *butt*, thick end]

butt'on n. knob or stud, *esp.* for fastening dress; badge; bud. -v.t. fasten with buttons. [F. *bouton*, bud]

butt'ress n. structure to support a wall; prop. -v.t. support. [OF. *bouterez*, supports, fr. *bouter*, thrust]

bux'om a. full of health, gay, lively. [orig. 'obedient,' fr. OE. *bugan*, bow]

buy (bi) v.t. get by payment; obtain in exchange for something; bribe. -buy'er n. [OE. *bycgan*]

buzz v.i. make a humming sound. -n. humming; sound of bees. -buzz'er n. signalling device. [imit.]

buzz word n. word or phrase that was part of a special vocabulary or jargon that comes into vogue in a community or culture.

buzz'ard n. bird of prey of the falcon family; any of the large birds of prey. [OE. *busard*]

by *prep.* near; beside; with, through. *adv.* near, close; out of the way; beyond. -by'-and-by, soon. -by'gone a. past. -by'-pass n. road to divert traffic from busy main road. -by'-product n. -by'-way n. [OE. *bi*]

bye n. side issue; passing through to the next round in a tournament without playing a match. [*by*]

by'law, bye'law n. local law made by a subordinate authority. [ME. *bilaw*, fr. *bi*, borough]

byte n. in computing, sequence of bits processed as a single unit of information. [perh. *bite*]

C

cab n. carriage for public transport; taxicab; covered part of a vehicle or machine (*esp.* a locomotive, truck or tractor) which accommodates the driver. -cab'man, cab'by n. [F. *cabriolet*, light carriage]

cabal' n. secret plot; small body of people engaged in one. -v.i. plot, intrigue. [Heb. *quab-balah*, tradition, mystical interpretation]

cab'aret n. small tavern; restaurant entertainment. [F.]

cab'bage n. green vegetable with large round head. [fr. L. *caput*, head]

cab'in n. hut, small room, *esp.* in a ship. -v.t. shut up, confine. **cab'in-boy** n. [F. *cabane*, hut]

cabinet n. case of drawers for things of value; private room; committee of politicians governing a country. -cab'inet maker n. maker of cabinets, furniture. [dim. of *cabin*]

ca'ble n. strong rope; submarine telegraph line; message sent by such line. -v.t and i. telegraph by cable. -cablegram n. [Late L. *capulum*, halter]

caboose' n. ship's galley; guardés van in freight train. [early Du. *cabuse*]

caca'o n. earlier and correct form of cocoa; tropical tree with seeds from which chocolate and cocoa are made. [Mex. *cacanatt*, cacao tree]

cache (-ash) n. hidden store; secret hiding-place. [F. *cacher*, hide]

cack'le v.i. make a chattering noise, as a hen. -n. cackling noise; empty chatter. -cack'ler n. [imit.]

cacophony n. disagreeable sound, discord of sounds. -cacoph'onous a. [G. *kakophonia*, ill sound]

cac'tus n. prickly desert plant. [L.]

cad n. vulgar fellow; no gentleman [*cadet*]

CAD n. (*compute.*) use of computers to prepare and test mechanical designs and engineering and architectural drawings. [computer *assisted design*]

cadav'erous a. corpse-like; sickly-looking. [fr. L. *cadaver*, dead body]

cadd'ie n. golfers attendant. [fr. *cadet*]

ca'dence n. fall or modulation of voice, music or verses. [F., L. *cadere*, fall]

cadet' n. younger son or brother; student in a naval or military college. [F.]

ca'dre (ka-der) n. nucleus, framework, *esp.* the permanent skeleton of a regiment; cell of a revolutionary political party; indoctrinated member of that cell or similar organization. [F.]

caesarean, cesarean n. (birth) delivery by incision. [confusion of L. *caedre, caes-*, cut, with *Caesar*]

caesu'ra n. natural pause in a line of verse. [L. *cædere, cæs-*, cut off]

caf'e' n. coffee-house; restaurant serving drinks and light meals. [F. *coffee*]

cafeteria n. restaurant where patrons serve themselves from a counter. [Amer. Sp.]

caffeine n. alkaloid in tea and coffee. [F. *cafeine*]

cage n. place of confinement; box with bars, *esp.* for keeping animals or birds. -v.t. put in a cage, confine. -cage'bird n. [F., fr. L. *caves*, hollow]

cajole' v.t. cheat by flattery. -cajole'ment n. -cajo'ler n. -cajo'lery n. [F. *cajoler*]

cake n. piece of dough baked; fancy bread; flattened hard mass. -v.t. and i. make into a cake. -cake'-walk n. orig. dance performed by black Americans competing for cake. [ON. *kaka*]

cal'amine n. a zinc ore. [Low L. *calamine*]

calamity n. great misfortune; distress, disaster. -calam'itous a. [L. *calamitas*]

calcareous a. like or containing lime. [L. *calx*, lime]

cal'cine v.t. reduce to lime; burn to ashes. -v.i. burn to ashes. [L. *caix*, lime]

cal'cium n. metal derived from lime compounds. -cal'cic a. [L. *calx*, lime]

calculate' v.t. reckon, compute. -v.i. make reckonings. -cal'culable a. -calculating a. - calculaétion n. -calculator n. a person who calculates; a machine which carries out calculations. -cal'culus n. stone in the body; method of mathematical calculation. [L. *calculus*, pebble]

cal'dron, caul'dron n. large kettle or boiler. [fr. L. *calidus*, hot]

cal'endar n. table of months and days; list of

documents, register. [L. *calendae*, first days of months]

calf (kaf) *n*. young of the cow, also of various other animals; leather made of calfs skin. **-calves** (kavz) *pl*. **-calve** *v. i*. give birth to a calf. [OE. *cealf*]

calf (kaf) *n*. fleshy hinder part of the leg below the knee. [ON. *kalfi*]

caliber *n*. size of the bore of a gun; capacity; character. [F.]

cal'ico *n*. cotton cloth. [*Calicut*, India]

calipers, callipers *n*. instrument for measuring diameters. [same as *calibre*]

call (kawl) *v.t.* announce; name; summon. *-v.i.* shout; pay a short visit. *-n*. shout; animal's cry; visit; invitation. **-call'er** *n*. visitor. **-call'ing** *n*. vocation, occupation. [ON. *kalla*, cry loudly]

calligraphy *n*. handwriting; penmanship. [G. *kallos*, beauty, graphein, write]

callisthen'ics *n. pl*. exercises to promote strength and grace. [G.*kallos*, beauty, *sthenos*, strength]

call'ous *a*. hardened, unfeeling. **-callos'ity** *n*. hard lump on the skin. **-call'ously** *adv*. **-call'ousness** *n*. [L. *callosus*, thick-skinned]

call'ow *a*. unfledged; raw, inexperienced [OE. *calu*, bald]

calm (kam) *n*. stillness, want of wind. *-a*. still, quiet. *-v.t.* and *i*. become, make, still or quiet. **-calm'ly** *adv*. **-calm'ness** *n*. [F. *calme*]

cal'orie, cal'ory *n*. unit of heat; unit expressing the heat or energy potential of food when digested. **-calorific** *a*. heatmaking. **-calorim'eter** *n*. heat-meas uring instrument. [fr. L. *color*, heat]

cal'umny *n*. slander. [L. *calumnia*]

ca'lyx *n*. covering of a bud. [G. *kalyx*]

cam *n*. device to change a rotary motion to a reciprocating one. [*comb*]

CAM *n*. (*compute*) application of computers to certain manufacturing tasks. [computer aided *m*anufacturing]

cam'ber *n*. slight convexity on surface, *esp*. of road. *-v.i.* to arch slightly. [L. *camerare*, vault]

cam'bric (ka'-) *n*. fine white linen. [fr. *Cambrai*, in France]

cam'el *n*. animal of Asia and Africa, with a hump (or two humps) on its back, used as a beast of burden. [G. *kamelos*]

camell'ia *n*. Eastern evergreen shrub with beautiful rose or white flowers. [G. J. *Kamel*, Jesuit and botanist]

cam'eo *n*. stone of two layers cut in ornamental relief. [It. *cammeo*]

cam'era *n*. apparatus used to make photographs; judge's private room. **-cam'era-man** *n*. photographer attached to newspaper or film company. **-cam'era obscu'ra** *n*. darkened room in which rotating apparatus reflects pictures of surrounding country on screen. [L. *chamber*]

cam'isole *n*. under-bodice. [F.]

cam'omile *n*. aromatic creeping plant used in medicine. [G. *chamaimelon*, earth appie]

camouflage (-azh) *n*. disguise; means of deceiving enemy observation. *-v.t.* disguise. [F.]

camp *n*. tents of an army; military quarters; travellers' resting-place. *-v.i.* form or lodge in a camp. **-camp'er** *n*. **-camp'ing** *n*. [L.*campus*, field]

campaign' *n*. time in which an army keeps the field; series of operations. *-v.i.* serve in a war. **-campaigner** *n*. [L. *campania*, open country]

campani'le *n*. bell-tower. [It.]

cam'phor *n*. solid essential oil with aromatic taste and smell. **-cam'phor- ated** *a*. [Malay. *kapur*, chalk]

camp'us *n*. college grounds. [L. = field]

can *v.i.* be able; having the power; be allowed. [pres. of OE. *cunnan*, know]

can *n*. vessel, usually of metal, for holding liquids. *-v.t.* put, or preserve, in a can **-cannery** *n*. factory where foods are canned. [OE. *canne*]

canal' *n*. artificial watercourse, duct in the body. **-canaliza'tion** *n*. **-can'alize** *v.t.* cut canal through; convert into canal; direct (thoughts *etc*.) into particular channel. [L. *canalis*, water-pipe]

canard' *n*. lying rumour; false report. [F.]

cana'ry *n*. yellow singing-bird; light wine. [*Canary* Islands]

can'cel *v.t.* cross out; annul, abolish, suppress. **-cancella'tion**, cancelation *n*. [L. *cancellare*, mark lattice-wise]

Can'cer *n*. malignant growth or tumor; the Crab, 4th sign of the zodiac, which sun enters about midsummer. [L. = crab]

candela'brum (-a-) *n*. branched ornamental candlestick. *-pl*. candelabra. [L.]

can'did *a*. frank, open, impartial. **-can'didly** *adv*. **-can'didness** *n*. **-can'dor** *n*. [L.*candidus*, white]

candidate *n*. one who seeks an office, appointment, privilege *etc*. [L. *candidatus*, one wearing a white toga]

can'dle *n*. stick of wax with a wick; light. **-can'dlestick** *n*. **-can'dlepower** *n*. unit, standard for measuring light. [L. *candela*]

can'dor. See candid.

can'dy *n*. (sweetmeat of) crystallized sugar. *-v.t.* preserve with sugar. *-v.i.* become encrusted with sugar. **-can'died** *a*. [fr. *silgar*-candy, F. *sucre candi*, fr. Arab. *qand*, sugar]

cane *n*. stem of a small palm or large grass; walking-stick. *-v.i.* beat with a cane. [G. *kanna*, reed]

ca'nine *a*. like or pertaining to the dog. [L. *canes*, dog]

canister *n*. box or case, usually of tin. [L. *canistrum*, bread-basket]

cank'er *n*. eating sore; anything that eats away, destroys, corrupts. *-v.t.* infect, corrupt. *-v.i.* become cankered. **-cank'er-worm** *n*. [L. *cancer*, crab]

cannibal *n*. one who eats human flesh. *-a*. **-cann'ibalism** *n*. [Sp. *canibal*, for *Caribal*, Carib]

cann'on *n*. ancient (unrifled) piece of ordnance; modem weapon used in aircraft. [F. *canon*, fr. L. *canna*, reed, tube]

cann'y *a*. shrewd; cautious; crafty. **-cann'ily**

adv. -**cann'iness** *n.* [*See* **can**]

canoe' *n.* boat made of a hollow trunk or of bark or skins; light boat.**canoe'ist** *n.* [orig. *canoa*, Sp. fr. Haiti]

can'on *n.* law, rule, *esp.* of the church; standard; body of books accepted as genuine; list of saints. [G. *kanon*, rule]

can'on *n.* church dignitary, member of a cathedral chapter. -**canon'ical** *a.* [L. *canonicus*, regular priest]

can'opy *n.* covering over a throne, bed *etc.* -*v.t.* cover with a canopy. [G. *konopeion*, couch with mosquito curtains, fr. *konops*, gnat]

cant *n.* hypocritical speech; whining; language of a sect; technical jargon, slang, *esp.* of thieves. -*v.i.* use such language. [ONF. = singing]

cant *n.* inclination from the level. -*v.t.* and *i.* tilt. [Med. L. *cantus*, edge, corner]

cantaloupe (-loop) *n.* variety of melon. [*Canwupo*, town in Italy]

cantankerous *a.* cross-grained, ill-natured. [ME. *contak*, strife]

canteen' *n.* small tin vessel; shop or refectory in a camp, barracks or factory; case of cutlery *etc.* [F. *cantine*]

can'ter *n.* easy galloping pace. -*v.i.* move at this pace. -*v.i.* make to canter. [short for *Canterbury* pace, pilgrim's pace on the Old Kent Road]

can'ticle *n.* hymn. [L. *canere*, sing]

cantilever *n.* large bracket supporting balcony *ete.* -**can'tilever bridge**', bridge built on cantilever principle. [Sp. *can*, support; F. *lever*, raise]

can'to *n.* division of a poem. [It.]

can'vas *n.* coarse cloth of hemp, used for sails, painting on, *etc.*; sails of a ship; picture. [F. *canevas*, fr. L. *cannabis*, hemp]

canvass *v.t.* sift, discuss, examine; solicit votes, contributions *etc.* -*n.* solicitation. -**can'vasser** *n.* [*canvas*]

can'yon *n.* deep gorge, ravine. [Sp. *cañon*]

cap *n.* covering for the head; lid, top or other covering. -*v.t.* put a cap on; confer a degree upon; outdo; raise the cap in respect. [OE. *ceppe*, hood]

ca'pable *a.* able, gifted; having the capacity, power. -**capabil'ity** *n.* [F.]

capa'city (-as'-) *n.* power of holding or grasping; room; volume; character; ability, power of mind. -**capa'cious** *a.* roomy. [F. *capacité*- L. *capere*, hold]

cape *n.* covering for the shoulders. [F.]

cape *n.* point of land running into the sea. [F. *cap*, fr. L. *caput*, head]

ca'per *n.* pickled flower-bud of a shrub growing in Sicily. [L. *capperis*]

ca'per *v.i.* skip or dance. -*n.* frolic; freak. [It.*capriola*; L. *caper*, goat]

capillary *a.* hair-like. -*n.* tube with very small bore, *esp.* a small vein. [L. *capillaris*, fr. *capillus*, hair]

cap'ital *n.* headpiece of a column; chief town; large-sized letter; money, stock, funds. *a.* affecting life; serious; chief, leading; excellent. [L. *capitalis*, fr. *caput*, head]

capitation *n.* census; poll-tax. [L. *caput*, head]

Cap'itol *n.* temple of Jupiter in Rome; house of Congress or state legislature in U.S. [L. *Capitolium*]

capitulate *v.i.* surrender on terms. -**capitula'tion** *n.* [Med. L. *capitulate*, draw terms under 'heads'; fr. *caput*, head]

ca'pon *n.* castrated cock. -**ca'ponize** *v.t.* [G. *kapon*]

caprice' *n.* whim, freak. -**capricious** *a.* **capri'ciousness** *n.* [F.]

Capricorn *n.* the Goat, 10th sign of zodiac, which sun enters in midwinter. [L. *caper*, goat, *cornu*, horn]

capsize' *v.t.* upset.-*v.i.* be upset over turned. [orig. uncertain]

cap'stan *n.* machine turned by spokes, or power, to wind a cable, *esp.* to hoist an anchor on board ship. [fr. L. *capistrare*, fasten with a rope]

cap'sule *n.* seed vessel of a plant; gelatin case for a dose of medicine. [L. *capsula* dim. of *capsa*, case]

cap'tain *n.* leader, chief; commander of a vessel, company of soldiers. [F. capitaine. [fr. L. *caput*, head]

cap'tion *n.* title, of an article, picture *etc.* [orig. a law term meaning arrest. [fr. L. *capere*, take]

cap'tive *n.* one taken prisoner, kept in bondage.; taken, imprisoned. -**captivate** *v.t.* fascinate. -**cap'tivating** *a.* -**capti'vity** *n.* [L. *captivus*]

cap'ture *n.* seizure, taking. -*v.t.* seize, catch, make prisoner. -**cap'tor** *n.* [L. *captura*, fr. *capere*, take]

car *n.* wheeled vehicle, railroad or tramway carriage; automobile. [L. *carrus*]

carafe *n.* water jug, decanter. [Ital. *caraffa*, flagon]

car'amel *n.* dark substance obtained from sugar on heating; sweet-meat. [L. *cunna mellis*, (mel) honey]

car'apace *n.* upper shell of tortoise *etc.* [F. -Sp. *carapacho*]

car'at *n.* small weight used for gold, diamonds *etc.*; proportional measure of twenty-fourths used to state the fineness of gold. [G. *keration*, carob fruit, small weight]

car'avan *n.* company of merchants *etc.* traveling together, *esp.* in the East; covered van or house on wheels, trailer. [Pers. *karwan*, company of merchants or ships; *sarai*, mansion, inn]

car'away *n.* plant with aromatic seeds; the seeds. [Sp. *carvi*, for G. *karon*]

car'bide *n.* compound of carbon with an element, *esp.* calcium carbide. [*See* **carbon**]

car'bine, car'abine *n.* short rifle. [F. *carabine*]

carbolic a'cid *n.* acid made from coal-tar and used as a disinfectant.[fr. carbon, by analogy with alcholic **car'bon** *n.* non-metallic element, substance of pure charcoal, found in all organic matter. -**car'bonate** *n.* -**carbon'ic** *a.* -**car'bon copy** *n.* written duplicate made

by interleaving sheets of carbon paper. -
car'bon diox'ide, gas exhaled from the lungs.
-car'bon monoxide odorless poisonous gas
from car exhausts *etc.* -carbon'ic acid *n.*
carbon dioxide, compound formed by combination of carbon dioxide and water. [L.
carbo]
car'buretor *n.* apparatus for mixing oil
vapor and air in an engine. [*carbon*]
car'cass, car'case *n.* dead body of an
animal; orig. skeleton. [F. *carcasses*]
carcinoma *n.* cancerous growth. -
carcino'sis *n.* spread of cancer in body. [G.
karkinōma, crab]
card *n.* pasteboard; small piece of pasteboard
with a figure for playing games, or with a name
and address *etc.*; dial of a compass. -
card'board *n.* pasteboard. [G. *charles,* leaf
of papyrus]
card *n.* instrument for combing wool *etc.* -*v.t.*
comb (wool). [L. *carduus,* thistle]
car'diac *a.* pert. to heart; heart stimulant or
cordial. -car'diograph *n.* instrument recording heart movements-car'diogram *n.* graph
of these. -car'dioid *a.* heart-shaped. -car'dio-
pulmonary *a.* relating to, or affecting, the
heart and lungs. [G. *kardia,* heart]
car'digan *n.* knitted woollen jacket,
waistcoat.[7th Earl of *Cardigan*]
car'dinal *a.* chief, principal. -*n.* prince of the
R.C. Church; member of the pope's council.
-car'dinalate *n.* -cardinal numbers, the
simple numbers 1, 2, 3 *etc.* -cardinal points,
North, South, East and West. [G. *cardinals,*
essential, fr. *cardo,* hinge]
care *n.* anxiety; pains, heed; charge, over-
sight.-*v.i.* be anxious; be disposed (to); have
regard or liking (for). -care'free *a.* -care'ful
a. -care'fully *adv.* -care'fulness *n.* -care'less
a. -care'lessness *n.* -care'taker *n.* [OE. *caru,*
n., cearian v., sorrow]
careen' *v.t.* lay a ship over on her side for
cleaning or repair. -*v.i.* heel over. [L. *carina,*
keel]
career' *n.* course through life; course of action, height of activity; course, running.-*v.i.*
run or move at full speed. [F. *carriare,*
racecourse]
caress' *v.t.* fondle, embrace, treat with affection. -*n.* act or expression of affection. [L.
carus, dear]
car'et *n.* mark inserted to show where something has been omitted. [L. *caret,* there is
wanting]
car'go *n.* ship's load. [Sp. *cargar,* load]
caricature *n.* likeness exaggerated or distorted to appear ridiculous. -*v.t.* portray in this
way. [It. *caricatura,* lit. an overloading]
ca'ries *n.* tooth or bone decay. [L.]
carill'on *n.* peal of bells; tune played on
them. [F.]
car'mine *n.* warm crimson color. -*a.* [L. *car-
minus,* fr. Arab. *qarmazi,* crimson]
carn'age *n.* slaughter. [L. *caro,* flesh]
car'nal *a.* fleshly, sensual; worldly. [L. *car-
nalis,* of the flesh]
carnation *n.* flesh color; cultivated flower,
double-flowering variety of the clove pink.

[fr. L. *caro,* flesh]
car'nival *n.* revel; season of revelry before
Lent. [F. *carnaval*]
carnivorous *a.* flesh-eating. carn'i- vore *n.*
-*pl.* carnivore. [L. *carnivorus*]
car'ol *n.* song of joy or praise. -*v.i.* and t. sing
or warble. -car'olhng *n.* [OF. *carole*]
carouse' *n.* drinking-bout.-*v.i.* hold a drinking bout.-carous'al *n.* -carous'er *n.* [fr. phrase
drink carouse, Ger. *gar aus,* quite out]
carouser. See carrousel.
carp *n.* freshwater fish. [P. *carpe*]
carp *v.i.* catch at small faults or errors; cavil.
[ON. *karpa,* chatter, influenced by L. *carpere,*
pluck]
carpenter *n.* worker in timber, as in building,
etc. car'pentry n. [L. *carpentari, carpentum,*
chariot]
car'pet *n.* cloth floor-covering. -*v.t.* cover a
floor. -car'pet-bag *n.* carpetbagger *n.* political adventurer. car'pet-sweep-er *n.* [Med. L.
carpita, patchwork]
carriage *n.* act or cost of carrying; vehicle;
bearing, conduct.-carr'iage- horse *n.* [ONF.
cariage, fr. *carier,* carry]
carr'ion *n.* rotting dead flesh. *a.* [ONF.
caroigne]
carr'ot *n.* plant with a reddish, eatable root.-
carr'oty *a.* red. [G. *karoton*]
carrousel, carouser *n.* merry-go round; circular belt on which items are placed for collection or distribution, as luggage at an airport
etc. [F.]
carr'y *v.t.* convey, transport; capture; effect;
behave. -*v.i.* reach, of a projectile, sound. -*n.*
range. -carr'ier *n.* one who, that which, carries goods; kind of pigeon; (*colloq.*) aircraft
carrier; person who transmits disease to
others, though himself immune. [ONF.
carier, fr. *car,* vehicle]
cart *n.* two-wheeled vehicle without springs.
-*v.t.* convey in such vehicle; carry. -cart'age
n. -cart'er *n.* -cart'-wright *n.* [ON. *kartr*]
cartilage *n.* firm elastic tissue in the body of
vertebrates; gristle. cartila'ginous (-aj-) *a.* [L.
cartilage]
cartography *n.* map or chartmaking.
carto'grapher *n.* [L. *charta,* map; G.
graphein, describe]
car'ton *n.* pasteboard container. [F.]
cartoon' *n.* design for a painting; satirical
illustration in a journal, *esp.* relating to current
events. cartoon'ist *n.* [F. *carton*]
cartridge *n.* case containing the charge for a
gun. [F. *cartouche,* fr. It.*cartoccio,* roll of
paper, fr. *carta,* card]
carve *v.t.* cut; hew, sculpture, engrave; cut up
(meat). -carv'er *n.* car'very *n.* an eating establishment at which customers pay a set price
and may then have unrestricted helpings of
food from a variety of meats, salads, and other
vegetables. -carv'ing *n.* [OE. *coerfan,* cut]
cascade' *n.* waterfall; anything resembling
this. -*v.i.* fall in cascades. [F.]
case *n.* instance; state of affairs; condition;
lawsuit; grounds for a suit. [orig. 'what
befalls'; F. *cas,* fr. L. *cadere,* fall]
case *n.* box, sheath, covering; any receptacle;

box and its contents. -v.t. put in a case -
case′harden v.t. a process to harden steel by
combining it with carbon. -**case′**-hardening
n. [ONF. casse, fr. L. capere, hold]
case′ment n. window frame; window opening on hinges. [for encaseraent, OF.
enchâssement. See sash]
cash n. money, coin. -v.t. turn into or exchange
for money. -**cashier′** n. -**cash′book** n. -
cash′less adv. functioning, operated, or performed without using coins or banknotes for
money transactions but instead using credit
cards or electronic transfer of funds. -**cash′**
register n. recording till. [orig. 'moneybox';
It.cassa, fr. L. capere, hold]
cashew′ n. S. American tree with kidney-
shaped nuts. [Braz. acajoba]
cashier′ v.t. discharge, dismiss in disgrace.
[L. cassare, make void]
cash′mere n. shawl; soft fabric of goat's hair.
[Kashmir]
casi′no n. building with gaming tables, public
dance-halls etc. [It.]
cask n. barrel. [Sp. casco, pot, helmet]
cask′et n. small case or box for jewels etc.;
coffin, usu. of ornate kind. [F. cassette, small
case]
casserole n. fireproof dish for cooking and
serving meat etc. [F.]
cassette′ n. plastic container for film, magnetic tape etc. [OF. casse, case]
cass′ock n. long, black tunic worn by clergymen. **cass′ocked** a. [F. cassaque]
cast (-a-) v.t. throw or fling; shed; throw
down; allot, as parts in a play; found, as metal.
-v.i. cast about, look around. -n. throw; thing
thrown; distance thrown; squint; mold; manner, quality, tinge, color, degree; set of actors.
[ON. kasta]
caste n. section of society in India; social rank.
[Port. caste, race]
castigate v.t. chastise; punish or rebuke
severely. -**castiga′tion** n. -**cas′tigator** n. [L.
castigate]
cas′tle (kas′l) n. fortress; country mansion.
[L. castellum]
cas′trate v.t. remove the testicles, deprive of
the power of generation. -**castra′tion** n. [L.
castrate]
cas′ual (-zh-) a. accidental; unforeseen; occasional; unmethodical. -**cas′ually** adv. -
cas′ualty n. accident; loss in war. [L. casualis,
fr. cadere, fall]
cat n. tame or wild animal of the genus Felis;
spiteful woman; piece of wood tapered at both
ends; nine-lashed whip. -**catt′y** a. -**cat′-fish**
n. fish with features like cat. -**cat′gut** n. cord
made of intestines of animals. [ONF. -Late L.
cattus]
cat′aclism n. upheaval. [G. kataklysrnos]
cat′acomb n. underground gallery for burial.
[Late L. Catacumbas]
catalepsy n. state of trance; disease causing
it. -**catalep′tic** a. [G. kata, down, lepsomai, I
seize]
catalogue, cat′alog (-og) n. descriptive list. -
v.t. make a list of; enter in a catalogue. [G.
katalogos, fr. legein, choose]

catal′ysis n. chemical change effected by
catalyst. -**cat′alyst** n. substance producing
chemical change in another sub stance
without itself changing. [G. kata, down, luein,
loose]
cat′apult n. small forked stick with an elastic
sling used by boys for throwing stones;
formerly an engine of war for hurling arrows,
stones etc. [fr. G. katapeltes, fr. pallein, throw]
cat′aract n. waterfall; defect in an eye, causing blindness. [G. katarhaktes]
catastrophe n. climax of a tragedy; great
disaster. [G. katastrophe]
catch v.t. take hold of, seize; understand. -v.i.
be contagious; get entangled. -n. seizure; anything that holds, stops etc.; that which is
caught; form of musical composition; advantage taken or to be gained; hidden difficulty or drawback. -**catchword** n. cue; popular
phrase. [ONF. cachier]
catechize (-k-) v.t. instruct by question and
answer; question. -**catechet′ic** a. -
catechet′ics n. -**cat′echism** n. -**catechist** n.
-**catechu′men** n. one under instruction in
Christianity. [G. katechizein]
category n. class or order; division. -
categorical a. positive; what may be affirmed
of a class. -**categor′ically** adv. -**cat′egorize**
v.t. [G. kategoria, assertion]
ca′ter v.i. provide food, entertainment etc. -
ca′terer n. -**ca′tering** n. [ME. acatour, buyer,
fr. OF. achater, buy]
caterpillar n. hairy grub of a moth or butterfly. -**cat′erpillar-wheel** n. endless band instead of a wheel for vehicles crossing rough
ground. [OF. chatepelose, hairy cat]
cathedral n. principal church of a diocese.
-a. pertaining to a cathedral. [orig. a. in
cathedral church, fr. G. kathedra, seat (i.e., of
the bishop)]
cath′ode n. negative pole in electricity. [G.
kata, down, hodos, way]
cath′olic a. universal; including the whole
body of Christians; relating to the Roman
Catholic Church. -n. adherent of the R.C.
Church. [G. katholikos, universal]
cat′sup n. sauce of tomatoes, mushrooms etc.
[Malay kechap]
catt′le n. beasts of pasture, esp. oxen, cows.
-sometimes horses, sheep. [L. capitale, stock,
fr. caput, head]
cau′cus n. private political meeting or group.
[perh. fr. Algonquin cawcawaasough, coun-
sellor]
caul n. membrane covering head of some in-
fants at birth; openwork head covering. [OF.
cale, small cap]
cauldrons See caldron.
cauliflower (kol′-) n. cabbage with an
eatable white flower-head. [L. caulis, cabbage, and flower]
caulk, calk (kawk) v.t. press oakum into the
seams of a ship, to make it watertight. [Late
L. calicare, stop up with lime, calx]
cause (-z) n. that which produces an effect;
reason; origin; motive, purpose; lawsuit; party
principle. -v.i. bring about, make to exist.-
caus′al a. -**causa′tion** n. -**cause′less** a. [L.

causa]

caust'ic *a*. burning; bitter, severe. -*n*. corrosive substance. -**caus'tically** *adv*. [G. *kaustikos*]

cauterize *v.t*. burn with a caustic or hot iron. -**cauteriza'tion** *n*. [G. *kauterion*, hot iron]

ca'ution *n*. heedfulness, care; warning. -*v.t*. warn. -**cau'tionary** *a*. -**cau'tioner** *n*. - **cau'tious** *a*. -**cau'tiously** *adv*. -**cau'tiousness** *n*. [L. *cautio*, fr. *cavere*, beware]

cavalcade' *n*. column or procession of persons on horseback; procession of vehicles. -**cavalier'** *n*. horseman; courtly gentleman; adherent of the King in the English Civil War. -*a*. careless disdainful. -**cavalier'ly** *adv*. - **cav'alry** *n*. mounted troops. [F., fr. L. *caballus*, horse]

cave *n*. hollow place in the earth; den. - **cav'ern** *n*. deep cave. -**cav'ernous** *a*. - **cav'ernously** *adv*. -**cav'ity** *n*. hollow opening. (L. *cavus*, hollow]

cave in, fall in; collapse; submit. [fr. earlier E. dialect *calve in*]

cav'eat (kaévi-at) *n*. a notice or warning, esp. a notice to suspend proceedings in a court of law. [L.]

caviar' *n*. salted sturgeon roe; (*fig*.) some thing too fine for the vulgar taste. [Turk. *khavyar*]

cayenne', cayenne'-pep'per *n*. very pungent red pepper. [Braz.]

cay'man *n*. kind of alligator. [Sp. Port.(orig. perh. Carib) *caiman*]

cease *v.i*. stop, give over. -*v.t*. discontinue. - **cease'less** *a*. -**cease'lessly** *adv*. [F. *cesser*-L. *cessare*, give over]

ce'dar *n*. large spreading evergreen tree; its wood. [fr. G. *kedros*]

cede *v.t*. yield, give up, *esp*. of territory. [L. *cedere*, yield]

cei'ling *n*. inner roof, *usu*. plastered; upper limit. -**ceil** *v.t*. [F. *ceil*, heaven, fr. L. *call*, canopy]

celebrate *v.t*. make famous; mark by ceremony (event of festival); perform with due rites. -**cel'ebrant** *n*. -**cel'ebrated** *a*. famous. -**celebra'tion** *n*. -**celeb'rity** *n*. fame; famous person. [L. *celebrate*]

cel'ery *n*. vegetable with long white eatable stalks. [F. *cgleri*]

celestial *a*. heavenly, divine. [L. *cœlestis*, fr. *cxlum*, heaven]

celibacy *n*. single life, unmarried state. - **cel'ibate** *a*. [L. *cœlebs*, unmarried]

cell *n*. small room; small cavity; unit-mass of living matter. -**cell'ular** *a*. -**cell'ude** *n*. [L. *cella*]

cell'ar *n*. underground room for storage. [L. *cellarium*, set of cells]

cell'o (ch-) *n*. for violoncello (*q.v.*). cellophane *n*. transparent material chiefly used for wrapping. [Trademark]

celluloid *n*. synthetic substance made from cellulose; substitute for bone, ivory, *etc*. [Trademark] [L. *cella*]

cellulose *n*. cell membrane of plants and wood; group of carbohydrates. *a*. containing cells. [L. *cella*]

cement' *n*. mortar; anything used for sticking together. -*v.t*. unite with cement; unite firmly. [F. *ciment*]

cem'etery *n*. burying-ground. [fr. G. *koimeterion*, sleeping-place]

cen'sor *n*. supervisor of morals; one who examines plays, books, news *etc*. before publication. -**censo'rial** *a*. -**censo'rious** *a*. fault-finding. censo'riously *adv*. -**censo'riosness** *n*. -**cen'sorship** *n*. [L. = judge of morals]

cen'sure *n*. blame; reproof. -*v.t*. blame, reprove. cen'surable *a*. -**cen'surably** *adv*. [L. *censure*, judgment]

cen'sus *n*. official counting of the inhabitants of a country; any official counting. [L.]

cent *n*. hundred; hundredth part of a dollar. per cent', in, to, by each hundred. [L. *centum*]

centennial *n*. hundred years; celebration of a hundredth anniversary. -*a*. pertaining to a hundred. -**centena'rian** *n*. one a hundred years old. *a*. lasting a, or happening every, hundred years. -**cente'nary** *n*. centennial. (L. *centenarius*]

cen'ter *n*. mid-point of anything; pivot, axis; point to which, or from which, things move or are drawn. -**cen'tral** *a*. [L. *centrum*]

centigrade *a*. having a hundred degrees. [L. *centum*, hundred, *gradus*, degree]

centigram *n*. one hundredth part of gram. [L. *centum*, hundred]

centimeter *n*. one hundredth part of meter. [L. *centum*, hundred]

centipede *n*. small segmented animal with many legs. [L. *centipeda-centum*, hundred, *pes, ped-*, foot]

centurion *n*. commander of a hundred men. [L. *centurio*]

cen'tury *n*. hundred years; unit of one hundred. [L. *centenarius*]

ceram'ics *n.pl*. potter's art. -**ceram'ic** *a*. [G. *keramos*, potter's earth]

ce'real *a*. pertaining to corn. -*n*. grain used as food (*usu. pl*.). [L. *cerealis*, fr. *Ceres*, goddess of agriculture]

cer'ebral *a*. pertaining to the brain. - cerebra'tion *n*. brain action. cer'ebro-spi'nal *a*. [fr. L. *cerebrum*, brain]

cer'emony *n*. sacred rite; formal observance; usage of courtesy; formality. [L. *cœrimonia*]

cer'tain *a*. sure, settled, fixed, inevitable; some, one; of moderate (quantity, degree *etc*.). cer'tainly *adv*. cer'tainty *n*. -cer'titude *n*. [F., fr. L. *cerius*]

cer'tify *v.t*. make known as certain; declare formally. -**certifica'tion** *n*. -**certif'icate** *n*. written declaration. -*v.t*. give a written declaration. -cer'tifier *n*. [L. *cerius*, sure, *facere*, make]

cesa'rian. See caesarian.

cesium, caesium *n*. a silver-white alkaline metal. [L. *caesius*, bluish-gray]

cessation *n*. a ceasing or stopping. [L. *cessatio*. See cease]

cess'pool *n*. pit in which filthy water collects, a receptacle for sewage. [orig. uncertain]

chafe *v.t*. make hot by rubbing; fret or wear

by rubbing; irritate. -cha′fing-dish n. - cha′fing-gear n. [F. chauffer]

chaff (-af) n. husks of corn; worthless matter; banter, making fun. [OE. ceaf]

chag′rin (sh-) n. vexation, disappointment.- v.t. vex. [F, = sad]

chain n. series of links or rings each passing through the next; fetter; anything that binds; connected series of things or events; surveyor′s measure, -v.t. fasten with a chain; confine. makes compound nouns as -chain- arm′or, chain-mail, chain-shot, chain′stitch etc. [F. chatne, fr. L. catena]

chair n. movable seat; seat of authority; professor′s seat, or his office; iron support for a rail on a railway. -v.t. carry in triumph. - chair′nian n. one who presides. chair′manship n. [F. chaire, fr. G. kathedra]

chal′et n. Swiss Alpine wooden hut; wooden villa. [F.]

chalice n. cup, esp. Communion Cup. - chal′iced a. cup-shaped. [L. colix, cup]

chalk (chawk) n. white substance, carbonate of lime. -v.t. rub or mark with chalk. -v.i. mark with chalk; keep a reckoning. chalk′iness n. -chalk′y a. [OE. cealc, L. calx, lime]

challenge v.t. call to fight; call to account; dispute; claim; object to. -chall′engeable a. chall′enger n. [L. calumnia, false accusation]

cha′mber n. room; room for an assembly; assembly or body of men; compartment; cavity. -cha′mberlain n. officer appointed by a king etc. for domestic and ceremonial duties. -cha′mber-maid n. servant with care of bedrooms. -cha′mber-pot, cha′mber n. vessel for urine. [F. chambre, fr. L. camera, vault]

chameleon (ka-) n. small lizard famous for its power of changing color. [G. chamaileon, dwarf lion]

cham′ois n. goat-like mountain animal; soft leather. [F.]

champagne′ (sham-pan) n. sparkling white wine of Champagne, France. cham′pion n. one who fights for another; one who defends a cause; in sport etc., one who excels all others; hero. -v.t. fight for, maintain. -cham′pionship n. [F., fr. Late. L. campio, fighter in the arena]

chance (-a-) n. that which happens; fortune; risk; opportunity; possibility; probability.-v.t. risk. -v.i. happen- a. casual, unexpected. [F, fr. OF. cheoir, fall; orig. ′fall′ of dice]

chan′cery n. office of a chancellor; court of equity. [orig, a court presided over by the Lord Chancellor, a chancellery]

change v.t. alter or make different; put for another; exchange, interchange.-v.i. alter; put on different clothes. -n. alteration, variation; variety; conversion of money; small money; balance received on payment. -change′ling n. child substituted for another by the fairies. [F. changer]

chann′el n. bed of a stream; deeper part of a strait, bay, harbor; groove; means of passing or conveying.-v.t. groove, furrow. [L. canalis]

chant v.t. and i. sing. -n. song; church melody. -chant′er n. -chant′ry n. -endowment or chapel for singing masses. -chant′y (sh-) n. sailor′s song. [F. chanter, fr. L. cantare, sing]

Chan′ukah. See Han′ukkah.

cha′os (ka) n. disorder, confusion; state of the universe before the Creation. [G.]

chap v.t. crack; strike. -v.i. fissure. -n. crack in the skin. -chapped a. [related to chip, chop]

chap n. fellow. [for chapman, pedlar]

chap′el n. subordinate place of worship, as one attached to a garrison, house, prison etc., and not a cathedral or parish church; division of a church with its own altar. [orig. sanctuary where was deposited the cappella, or sacred cloak, of St.Martin]

chap′eron (sh-) n. one who attends a young unmarried lady in public as a protector. -v.t. [F. = hood]

chap′lain n. clergyman attached to a chapel, regiment, ship of war, institution etc. - chap′laincy n. [F. chapelain. See chapel]

chap′ter n. division of a book; section, heading; assembly of the clergy of a cathedral etc. organized branch of a society, fraternity. [L. capitulum, dim. of caput, head; the church chapter was a meeting at which a chapter was read]

char v.t. scorch, burn, reduce to charcoal. [fr. charcoal]

char, chore n. odd job. -pl. household tasks. -v.i. -char′woman n. domestic cleaner, scrub-woman. [OE. cierran, turn]

character (ka-) n. letter, sign, or any distinctive mark; essential feature; nature; total of qualities making up an individuality; moral qualities; reputation of possessing them; statement of the qualities of a person who has been in one′s service; person noted for eccentricity; personality in a play or novel. - characteriza′tion n. characterize v.t. characteristic a. characteris′tically adv. char′acterless a. [G. character, tool for stamping]

charade′ (shar-ad) n. riddle, often acted, on the syllables of a word. [F.]

char′coal n. black residue of wood, bones etc. by smothered burning; charred wood. char′coal-burner n. [orig. uncertain]

charge v.t. fill; load; lay a task on, enjoin, command; deliver an injunction; bring an accusation against; ask as a price; fill with electricity. -v.i. make an onset.-n. that which is laid on; cost; price; load for a gun etc.; command, exhortation; accusation; accumulation of electricity. -pl. expenses. - charge′able a. char′ger n. officer′s horse. [F. charger, Low L. carricare, load]

char′iot n. two-wheeled war vehicle drawn by horses; state carriage. -charioteer′ n. [F., fr. char, car]

charity n. love, kindness; disposition to think kindly of others; practical kindliness, alms-giving. char′itable a. -charitably adv. [F. charitg, fr. L. caritas-carus, dear]

charlatan (sh-) n. quack. -charl′atanry n. [It. ciarlatano, prattler]

Charleston n. orig. a black American dance, adaptation of this as ballroom dance. [Charleston, S. Carolina]

charm n. magic spell; thing worn to avert evil; anything that fascinates; attractiveness.

chart 39 **chill**

-v.t. bewitch; delight, attract.-charmed a. -
charm′er n. -**charm′ing** a. -**charm′ingly**
adv. [F. charme, fr. L. carmen, song, incanta-
tion]
chart n. map of the sea; diagram or tabulated
statement. -**chart′-house** n. (Nautical). [L.
charta, paper]
chart′er n. writing in evidence of a grant of
privileges etc.; patent. -v.t. establish by
charter; let or hire. [L. chartula, dim. of charta, paper]
chase v.t hunt, pursue; drive from, into etc.
-n. pursuit, hunting; thing hunted; hunting-
ground. [F. chasser]
chase v.t decorate with engraving. -**cha′ser**
n. **cha′sing** n. [for enchase, F. enchâsser,
enshrine]
chasm (kazm) n. deep cleft; abyss. [G. chas-
ma]
chassis n. framework, wheels and machinery
of a motor-car; underframe of an airplane. [F.]
chaste a. pure; modest; virtuous; (art) in
good taste. -**chaste′ly** adv. -**chas′tity** n. [L.
castus, pure]
cha′sten (-an-) v.t free from faults by punishment; restrain, moderate. -**chastened** a.
[chaste]
chastise′ v.t inflict punishment on; reduce to
order. **chas′tisement** n. [chaste]
chat v.t talk idly or familiarly. -n. familiar talk;
idle talk; genus of small birds, as stonechat,
whinchat etc. -**chatt′ily** adv. **chatt′y** a. [chat-
ter]
chatt′el n. any movable property (usu. in pl.).
[fr. Late L. capitale, goods, property. See cat-
tle]
chatt′er v.i. talk idly or rapidly; rattle the
teeth. -n. idle talk. -**chatt′erbox** n. -**chatt′erer**
n. -**chatt′ering** n. [imit.]
chauffeur′ n. professional automobile
driver. [F. = stoker]
chauvinism n. noisy patriotism; smug sense
of superiority; jingoism. [Chauvin, French
soldier]
cheap a. low in price; inexpensive; easily obtained; of little value or estimation. [OE. ceap,
a bargain]
cheat v.t. deprive of by deceit, defraud; impose upon. -v.i. practise deceit.-n. fraud. [for
escheat, confiscate]
check v.t. stop; restrain; hinder; repress; control; examine. -n. threatening the king at chess;
repulse; stoppage; restraint; token, ticket;
order for money; bill; a mark (√) indicating
approval of the affirmative. -**checkered** a.
marked in squares; uneven, varied. -
check′ers pl. (dial) boardgame using the
same board as for chess. -**cheek′mate** n. in
chess, the final winning move; any overthrow,
defeat.-v.t. make the movement ending the
game; defeat. [F. échec, fr Pers. shah, king
(in danger); checkmate fr. F. échec et mat, fr.
shah mat, the king is dead]
Ched′dar n. kind of cheese. [first made at
Cheddar, Somerset]
cheek n. side of the face below the eye; impudence. -v.t. address impudently. -**cheek′ily**
adv. -**cheek′y** a. [OE. ceace, cheek, jaw]

cheer n. mood; mirth, joy; food; shout of approval. -v.t. comfort; gladden; encourage, esp.
by shouts. -v.i. shout applause. [F. (bonne)
chère-Low L. cara, face]
cheese n. curd of milk coagulated, separated
from the whey and pressed. [OE. ciese, fr. L.
caseus]
chee′tah n. Indian leopard. [Hind. chita]
chef (sl.) n. head cook. [F. chef de cuisine]
chemistry (k-) n. science which treats of the
properties of substances and their combinations and reactions. -**chem′ical** a. -
chem′ically adv. -**chem′ist** n. [See alchemy]
chenille′ n. velvety cord used in embroidery
etc. [F. = caterpillar]
cher′ish v.t. treat with affection; protect; encourage. [F. chérir]
cher′ry n. small red stone-fruit; the tree. -a.
ruddy. [fr. G. kerasion]
cher′ub n. winged child, angel. -**cherubim**,
cher′ubs pl. -**cheru′bic** a. [Heb. krub, pl.
krubim]
chess n. game of skill played by two persons
with 32 'pieces' on a board of 64 squares.
-**chess′board** n. -**chess′men** n.pl. the pieces
used in chess. [F. of echec. See **check**]
chest n. box; coffer; upper part of the trunk
of the body. [OE. cist, fr. L. cista]
chest′nut (-an-) n. large reddish-brown nut
growing in a prickly husk; tree earing it; (sl.)
hoary joke. -a. reddishbrown. [for chesteine-
nut, fr. OF. chastaigne, G. kastanea]
chev′ron (sh-) n. V-shaped band of braid
used as a badge in the armed forces. [F.]
chew v.t. grind with the teeth. -**chew′ing-**
gum n. [OE. ceowan]
chic n. style, elegance. -a. [F.]
chicane′, **chicanery** a. quibbling trick, artifice. -**chicane′**-v.i. quibble, use tricks. [F.]
Chican′o n. an American citizen of Mexican
descent. [fr. Sp. Mejicano]
chick n. short for chicken; young of birds,
esp. of the domestic fowl. -**chick′enheart′ed**
a. -**chick′en-pox** n. mild contagious fever.
[OE. cicen]
chic′ory n. salad plant of which the root is
ground and mixed with coffee. [fr. G. kichora,
endive]
chide v.t. scold, reprove. [OE. cidan]
chief n. head or principal person. -a. principal, foremost, leading. -**chiefly** adv. [F. chef,
fr. L. caput, head]
chieftain n. leader or chief of a clan or tribe.
[OF. chevetain, another form of capitaine,
captain]
chiff′on (sh-) n. gauzy material. -**chiffonier′**
n. ornamental cupboard. fF.]
chi′gnon n. back-hair twisted into roll or bun.
[F.]
child (-i-) n. infant; boy or girl; son or
daughter. **child′ren** n.pl. **child′bed** n. state of
a woman giving birth to a child. -**child′birth**
n. -**child′hood** n. -**child′ish** a. -**child′ishly**
adv. -**child′less** a. -**child′like** a. [OE. cild]
chil′i, **chil′e**, **chilli** n. hot pepper, fruit of the
capsicum. [Mex. fr. Nanuali, chilli]
chill n. coldness; cold with shivering; any-

thing that damps, discourages. [OE. *ciele*, cold]

chime *n*. sound of bells in harmony; set of bells. -*v.i.* ring harmoniously; agree. *v.i.* strike (bells). -chime in', come into a conversation with agreement. [L. *cymbalum*, cymbal]

chim'ney *n*. passage for smoke. -chim'ney-sweep *n*. [L. *caminus*, furnace]

chimpanzee' *n*. African anthropoid ape, [native]

chin *n*. part of the face below the mouth. [OE. *cin*]

chi'na *n*. fine earthenware. [fr. *China*]

chink *n*. cleft, crack. [OE. *cinu*]

chink *n*. sound of pieces of metal knocking together. -*v.i.* make this sound. -*v.t.* cause to do so. [*imit.*]

chintz *n*. cotton cloth printed in colors. [*pl.* of Hind. *chint*, spotted cotton]

chip *v.t.* chop or cut into small pieces; break little pieces from; shape by cutting off pieces. -*v.i.* break off. -*n*. small piece broken off, thin fried slices of potato; counter used as a token in gambling and games; tiny wafer of silicon forming an integrated circuit in a computer. [related to *chop*]

chipmunk *n*. small squirrel of n. Amer. [Indian name *achitamon*]

chiropractic *n*. and *a*. treatment of diseases by manipulating joints, *esp.* of the spine. -chiroprac'tor *n*. [G. *cheir*, hand, *praktikos*, concerned with action]

chis'el (-zl) *n*. cutting tool, usually a bar of steel with an edge across the main axis. -*v.t.* cut or carve with a chisel. [ONF, fr. L. *cmdere*, cut]

chit *n*. note; order, pass. [Hind. *chitthi*]

chiv'alry (sh-) *n*. bravery and courtesy; feudal system of knighthood. -chivalrous *a*. -chiv'alrously *adv*. [F. *chevaterie*, fr. *cheval*, L. *caballus*, horse]

chlo'rine *n*. yellowish-green gas with a suffocating action on the lungs. chlo'rate *n*. -chlo'ride *n*. -chlo'rinate *v.t.* [G. *chlaros*, yellowish-green]

chloroform (kl-) *n*. liquid used as an anaesthetic. -*v.t.* put to sleep with this drug. [fr. *chlor*ine and *form*ic acid]

chlorophyll (kl-) *n*. coloring matter of plants. [G. *chloros*, green, *phyllon* leaf]

chock *n*. block, wedge. [ONF. *choque*]

chocolate *n*. paste of cacao-tree seeds; sweetmeat or drink made from it. -*a*. dark brown. [Mex. *chocolatl*]

choice *n*. act or power of choosing; alternative; something chosen. -*a*. select, fine, worthy of being chosen. -choice'ly *adv*. [F. *choisir*, choose]

choir (kwir) *n*. band of singers, *esp.* in a church; part of a church set aside for them. [F. *chœur*-L. *chorus*]

choke *v.t.* throttle; stop up; smother, stifle; obstruct.-*v.i.* suffer choking. -*n*. act or noise of choking; device to regulate flow of gas *etc*. -choked *a*. -choke'-bore *n*. gun narrowed towards the muzzle, to concentrate the shot.-choke'-damp *n*. carbonic gas in coal-mines. [OE. *aceocian*]

chol'er (k-) *n*. bile; anger. -chol'eric *a*. [G. *cholera*, biliousness, fr. *chole*, bile]

chol'era (k-) *n*. deadly disease marked by vomiting and purging. [See *choler*]

choose *v.t.* take one thing rather than another; select.-*v.i.* will, think fit.choos'er *n*. [OE. *ceosan*]

chop *v.t.* cut with a blow; cut in pieces. *n*. hewing blow; slice of meat containing a rib. [ME., related to *chap* and *chip*]

chop *v.t.* exchange, bandy, *e.g.* chop logic, chop and change. [OE. *ceapian*, barter]

chop, chap *n*. jaw (*usu*. in *pl*.). -chop'-fallen *a*. dejected. [*orig*. uncertain]

chord (k-) *n*. string of a musical instrument; straight line joining the ends of an arc. [G. *chorde*, intestine]

chord (k-) *n*. harmonious simultaneous union of musical notes. [*accord*]

choreography *n*. art, notation of (ballet-) dancing; arrangement of ballets. [G. *choros*, dance]

chort'le *v.i.* chuckle; laugh in triumph. [coined by Lewis *Carroll*]

chor'us *n*. band of singers; combination of voices singing together; refrain. -*v.t.* sing or say together. [L., fr. G. *choros*, band of singers]

chrism *n*. holy oil; unction; confirmation. chrismal *a*. -*n*. pyx; christening veil. [G. *chrisma*]

Christian (kris'tyan) *n*. follower of Christ. -*a*. following Christ; relating to Christ or his religion. -chris'ten (krisén) *v.t.* baptize, give a name to. chris'tendom (-an-) *n*. all Christian countries. -chris'tianize *v.t* -Christian'ity *n*. religion of Christ. -Chris'mas *n*. festival of the birth of Christ. -Chris'tian name, name given at christening, individual name. -Chris'tian Sci'ence, religious system founded by Mary Baker Eddy, in America. [G. *christós*, anointed]

chromatic (k-) *a*. relating to color; (*mus*.) of a scale proceeding by semi-tones. [G.*chrome*, color]

chrome (k-) *n*. chromium or compound of it; chrome-yellow. chro'mium *n*. metallic element. [L. *chrome*, color]

chromosome *n*. microscopic body found in cell during division. [G. *chrome*, color]

chron'ic (k-) *a*. lasting a long time. -chron'icle *n*. record of events in order of time. -*v.t.* record. -chron'icler *n*. -chronological *a*. -chronolo'gically *adv*. chronol'ogist *n*. -chronol'ogy *n*. -chronom'eter *n*. instrument for measuring time exactly. -chronomet'rical *a*. -chronom'etry *n*. [G. *chronos*, time]

chrysalis *n*. resting state of an insect between grub and fly; case from which it emerges. [G. *chrysallis*, fr. *chrysos*, gold (fr. the gold-colored sheath of butterflies)]

chrysanthemum *n*. autumn-blooming plant with large handsome flowers. [G. *chrysos*, gold, *anthemon*, flower]

chuck *v.t.* tap, as under the chin; throw. -*n*. tap; throw. [F. *choquer*, shock]

chuck'le *v.i.* laugh in a quiet manner -*n*. such laugh. [*imit*.]

chunk *n.* lump; thick piece. [*See* chock]

church *n.* building for Christian worship; whole body of Christians; clergy; body or md of Christians. *-v.t.* give thanks on behalf of (a woman) after childbirth *etc.* [OE. *eirice*, fr. G. *kyriakon*, of the Lord]

churn *n.* vessel for making butter. *-v.t.* shake up (a liquid). [OE. *cyrin*]

chute *n.* waterfall; channel for logs, rubbish *etc.* [F. = fall]

chut'ney *n.* condiment of fruits, spices *etc.* [Hind. *chatni*]

cica'da *n.* chirping insect. [L. = *cricket*]

cicatrix, **cic'atrice** *n.* scar of a wound. [L.]

ci'der *n.* drink made from apples. [F. *cidre*-G. *sikera*, strong drink]

cigar' *n.* roll of tobacco-leaves for smoking. **cigarette'**, **cigaret'** *n.* finely cut tobacco rolled in paper for smoking. [Sp. *cigarro*; F. *cigarette*]

cinch *n.* saddle girth; (*sl.*) firm grip; walkover; certainty. [Sp. *cincha*]

cin'der *n.* piece of glowing coal; partly burnt coal. [OE. *sinder*, slag]

cin'ema *n.* motion pictures; building where these are shown. [for *cinematograph*]

cinemat'ograph *n.* apparatus for throwing moving pictures on a screen by means of light. [G. *kiaema*, motion]

cinnamon *n.* spicy bark of a tree in Ceylon; the tree. *-a.* of a light brown color. [Heb. *qinnamon*]

ci'pher, **cy'pher** *n.* arithmetical symbol 0; figure; person of no importance; monogram; secret writing. *-v.i.* work at arithmetic. [Arab. *sifr*, empty]

cir'cle (ser-kl) *n.* perfectly round figure; ring; company of persons gathered round another, or round an object of interest; seance; class or division of society. *-v.t.* surround. *-v.i.* move round. **-cir'cular** *a.* round; moving round. *-n.* letter sent to several (a circle of) persons. **circ'ulate** *v.i.* move round; pass from place to place; come to readers. *-v.t.* send round. **circula'tion** *n.* [L. *circulus*, dim. of *circus*, ring]

cir'cuit (-kit) *n.* a moving round; area; round of visitation, *esp.* of judges; district; path of an electric current. **-circu'itous** *a.* **-circu'itously** *adv.* [L. *circuitus*, a going round]

circumcise *v.t.* cut off the foreskin of - **circumcis'ion** *n.* [L. *circumcidere*, cut round]

circumference *n.* boundary line, *esp.* of a circle. [L. *circumferential* periphery]

circumflex *n.* accent (^) on a vowel or syllable *-a.* bending or winding round. [L. *flectere*, *flexum*, to bend]

circumlocution *n.* roundabout speech. [L. *circumlocution* a talking round]

circumnav'igate *v.t.* sail round. [*See* navigate]

circumscribe' *v.t.* confine, bound, limit, hamper. [L. *circumscribere*, write (draw lines) round]

circumspect *a.* watchful, prudent. [L. *circumspicere*, look around]

circumstance *n.* detail; event, matter of fact. *-pl.* state of affairs; condition in life; surroundings or things accompanying a certain action. **-circumstan'tial** *a.* depending on details; particular as to details; indirect. [L. *eir-cumstare*, stand round]

circumvent *v.t.* outwit. [L. *circumvenire*, come round]

cir'cus *n.* circular building for public shows; entertainment of horse-riding, clowning *etc.*; group of houses built in a circle. [L.]

cirr'us *n.* high fleecy cloud. [L. = curl]

cit'adel *n.* fortress in or near a city [fr. It. *citadella*, dim. of *city*, city]

cite *v.t.* summon; quote; bring forward as proof **-cita'tion** *n.* [L. *ciiare*, call]

cit'izen *n.* inhabitant of a city; townsman; member of a state. **-citizenship** *n.* [fr. OF. *citeain*]

cit'ron *n.* fruit like a lemon; the tree. **-citrus** *a.* **-cit'rica.** of the acid of the lemon and citron. [F., fr. L. *citrus*, citrontree]

cit'y *n.* large town; (properly) town made city by charter. [F. *cite*, fr. L. *civitas*, fr. *civis*, citizen]

civ'ic *a.* pertaining to a city or citizen. **-civics** *n.* science of municipal and national life of service. [L. *civicus*, citizen]

civ'il *a.* relating to citizens or the state; refined, polite, not barbarous; not military; (*law*) not criminal. **-civil'ian** *n.* nonmilitary person. **-civiliza'tion** *n.* **civ'ilize** *v.t.* refine, bring out barbarism. **-civ'ilized** *a.* **-civil'ity** *n.* politeness. **-civ'illy** *adv.* [L. *civilis*]

claim *v.t.* call for; demand as a right. *-n.* demand for a thing supposed due; right; thing claimed. **-claim'ant** *n.* **-clam'ant** *a.* demanding attention. [L. *clamare*, shout]

clairvoy'ancy *n.* second sight, supersensory vision. **-clairvoy'ant** *n.* and *a.* [F. *clair*, clear, *voir*, see]

clam *n.* bivalve shellfish. [OE. = fetter]

clamm'y *a.* moist and sticky. **-clamm'iness** *n.* [earlier *claymy*]

clam'or *n.* loud shouting; outcry, noise. *v.i.* shout; call noisily (for). **-clam'orous** *a.* **clam'orously** *adv.* [L. *clamor*. *See* claim]

clamp *n.* tool for holding or pressing. *v.t.* fasten with clamps. [Du. *clamp*]

clan *n.* tribe or collection of families under a chief, and of supposed common ancestry; sect, group. [Gael. *clann*]

clandestine *a.* secret; sly. **-clandestinely** *adv.* [L. *clandestinus*]

clang *n.* loud ringing sound. *-v.i.* make such sound. *-v.t.* strike together with a clang. **clang'or** *n.* [L. *clangere*; imit. orig.]

clank *n.* short sound as of pieces of metal struck together. *-v.t.* and *i.* cause, or move with, such a sound. [imit.]

clap *n.* hard, explosive sound; slap. *-v.i.* strike with this noise; strike the open hands together; applaud. *-v.t.* strike together; pat; applaud; thrust suddenly, impose abruptly. [imit.]

clar'et *n.* red Bordeaux wine. [OF. (*vin*) claret, clear (wine)]

clar'ify *v.t.* make clear; purify **-clarification** *n.* [L. *clarificare*] clar'ity n. clearness. [L. claritas]

clash n. loud noise, as of weapons striking together; conflict, collision. -v.i. make a clash; come into conflict.-v.t. strike together to make a clash. [imit.]

clasp n. hook or other means of fastening; embrace; military decoration. -v.t. fasten; embrace, grasp. -clasp-knife n. [orig. uncertain]

class n. rank of society; division of pupils; division by merit; qualify; any division, order, kind, sort.-v.t. assign to the proper division. -classifica'tion n. -class'ify v.t. arrange methodically in classes. [L. classes, division of the Roman people]

class'ic, classical a. of the first rank of Greek and Roman authors; of the highest rank generally, but esp. of literature; resembling in style the Greek writers; refined, chaste; famous. -class'ically adv. -class'icism n. -class'icist n. (See class)

clause (-z) n. part of a sentence; article; n a formal document. [F., fr. L. clausa]

claustrophobia n. morbid fear of enclosed spaces. [L. clausus-claudere, shut; G. phobos, fear]

clavichord (-k-) n. obsolete musical instrument like a spinet. [Mod. L. clavichordium, key string]

clav'icle n. collar-bone. -clavic'ular a. [L. clavicula, dim. of clavis, key]

claw n. hooked nail of a bird or beast; foot of an animal with hooked nails; anything like a claw. -v.t. tear with claws; grip. [OE. clawu]

clay n. stiff viscous earth; earth generally; human body. clay'ey a. [OE. clæg]

clean a. free from dirt, stain or any defilement; pure; guiltless; trim, shapely. adv. so as to leave no dirt; entirely. -v.t. free from dirt.-clean'er n. -clean'liness (klen-) n. -clean'ly (klen'-) a. -clean'ly adv. cleanness n. -cleanse (klenz) v.t. [OE. claene]

clear a. free from cloud; pure, undimmed, bright; free from obstruction or difficulty; plain, distinct; without defect or drawback; transparent.-ado. wholly, quite. v.t. make clear; acquit; pass over or through; make as profit; free from cloud; obstruction, difficulty; free by payment of dues. -v.i. become clear, bright, free, transparent. -clearinghouse n. place where cheques are exchanged. -clear'ing-station n. place from which wounded are removed; place where items are kept prior to being removed. clear-sight'ed a. [F. clair, fr. L. clarus]

cleat n. wedge; (naut.) block to which ropes are made fast; porcelain insulation. [See clod, clot]

cleek n. large hook used in fishing; golf club with iron head. [ME. = clutch]

clef n. mark to show the pitch in music. [F., fr. L. clavis, key]

cleft n. opening made by cleaving; crack, fissure. [cleave]

clench v.t. make fast; set firmly together; grasp; drive home. [OE. -clencan, in beciencan, make to cling]

clere'story n. upper part of a church with a row of windows. [clear ('lighted') storey]

clergy n. appointed m; nisters of the Christian church. -cler'gyman n. [L. clericus. See clerk]

cler'ic n. belonging to the clergyman. clergyman. -cler'ical a. [See clerk]

clerk (-ark) n. clergyman or priest; one who leads the responses in church; an officer in charge of records, correspon dence etc. of a department or corporation; subordinate in an office; salesperson. [L. clericus, fr. G. kleros, heritage]

clev'er a. able, skillful, adroit.clev'erly adv. -clev'erness n. [orig. uncertain]

cli'ché n. stereotyped hackneyed phrase. [F., fr. clicher, click, sound made in stereotyping]

click n. short, sharp sound, as of a latch in the door. -v.i. [imit.]

cli'ent n. customer, one who employs a professional man. -clientele' n. body of clients. [L. cliens]

cliff n. steep rock face. [OE. clif]

climate n. the average weather conditions of a region. [G. klinw, klimatos, slope]

cli'max n. highest point, culmination; arrangement of language to rise in dignity and force; point of greatest excitement, tension, in a play, story etc. [G. klimax, ladder]

climb (klim) v.t and i. mount by clutching, grasping, pulling; creep up, mount, ascend. climb'er n. -climb'ing n. [OE. climban]

clinch v. clench (q.v.).

cling v.i. stick fast, be attached; remain by. [OE. clingan]

clinic n. relating to practical instruction in medicine in hospitals. -n. place or meeting for medical examination or teaching (also clinique'). -clin'ical a. clin'ically adv. [G. kline, bed]

clink n. sharp metallic sound. -v.t. and i. make or cause to make such sound. [imit.]

clink'er n. hard slag. [Du. blinker]

clip v.t. grip, clutch, hug. -n. device for gripping. [OE. clyppan]

clip v.t. cut with scissors or shears; cut short.- n. the wool shorn at a place or in a season. -clip'ping n. something clipped off, esp. article cut out of a publication. clipp'er n. [ON. kappa]

clipp'er n. fast sailing-ship formerly employed to carry tea, wool etc.; fast transworld airplane. [clip, shear]

clique (ik) n. small exclusive set; faction, gang. [F.]

cloak n. loose outer garment; disguise, pretext.-v.t. cover with a cloak; disguise, conceal. [earlier cloke, fr. Late L. clocca, bell (shape of garment)]

clock n. instrument for measuring time; ornament on the side of a stocking. [orig. 'bell;' fr. Late. L. clocca]

clod n. lump of earth; blockhead. [clot]

clog n. obstruction, impediment, woodensoled shoe; v.t. gather in a mass and cause stoppage; choke up. -clog'-dance n. [orig. unknown]

clois'ter n. covered arcade; convent-v.t. confine in a cloister, or within walls. [L- *claudere*, *claus*-, close]

close (-a) *a.* shut up; confined; secret; unventilated, stifling; reticent; niggardly; compact; crowded; strict, searching. *adv.* nearly, tightly. -*n.* shut-in place; precinct of a cathedral. - **close'ly** *adv.* -**close'ness** *n.* -**close'-up** *n.* photograph or film sequence taken at short range. [L. *claudere*, close]

close (-z) *v.t.* shut; stop up; finish. -*v.i.* come together, grapple. -*n.* end. [L. *claudere*]

clos'et (-z-) *n.* small private room; a cabinet, recess or cupboard for storage of e. g. household utensils or clothes. -*v.t.* shut up in a closet; conceal. [OF. dim. of *clas*, fr. L. *claudere*]

clot *n.* mass or lump. -*v.t.* form into lumps. [OE. *clod*-, in compounds]

cloth (-th) *n.* woven fabric. clothes (-TH-) *n. pl.* dress; bed-coverings. -clothe *v.t.* put clothes on. clo'thier *n.* clo'thing *n.* [OE. *clath*]

cloud *n.* vapor floating in the air; state of gloom; great number or mass. -*v.t.* overshadow, dim, darken. -*v. i.* become cloudy. -**cloud'less** *a.* -**cloud'y** *a.* [OE. *clud*, mass]

clout *n.* piece of cloth; blow, cuff. -*v.t.* patch. [OE. *clut*]

clove *n.* dried flower-bud of an Eastern tree, used as a spice. -**clove'-pink** *n.* clove-scented pink. [L. *clavus*, nail]

clo'ven *a.* split. -**clo'ven hoof**, divided hoof of cattle *etc.*; (*fig.*) sign of the devil's agency. [*cleave*]

clo'ver *n.* low-growing forage plant, trefoil. [OE. *clafre*]

clown *n.* rustic; jester. **clown'ish** *a.* [perh. fr. Du. *kloen*, clew, hoyden]

cloy *v.t.* weary by sweetness, sameness *etc.* [earlier *accloy*, fr. F. *enclouer, prick*, spike with a nail]

club *n.* thick stick; bat; one of the suits at cards; association for a common object.-*v.t.* strike with a club; put together. -*v.i.* join for a common object. [ON. *klubba*]

cluck *n.* noise of a hen. -*v.i.* make that noise. [OE. *cloccian*]

clue *n.* ball of thread; thread used as a guidance, trail; indication, *esp.* of the solution of a mystery. [OE. *cliwen*, ball of thread]

clump *n.* cluster of trees or plants; compact mass; lump; thick additional sole. -*v.i.* walk heavily. [Du. *klomp*]

clum'sy (-z-) *a.* awkward, unwieldy, badly made or arranged. -**clum'sily** *adv.* -**clum'siness** *n.* [earlier *clumsed*, ME. *clumsen*, benumb]

clus'ter *n.* group, bunch. -*v.t.* and *i.* gather, grow in a cluster. [OE. *clyster*]

clutch *v.t.* grasp eagerly, snatch. -*v.i.* make a snatch at.-*n.* grasp, tight grip; device for connecting and disconnecting parts of machinery, *e.g.* a motor engine. [OE. *clyccan*]

clutch *n.* brood of chickens; 'setting' of eggs for hatching. [fr. obs. v. *clerk*, ON. *klekja*, hatch]

clutt'er *n.* litter, confusion. -*v.t.* and *i.* [*clot*]

coach *n.* large four-wheeled carriage; passenger car on a railroad; a class of travel in air transportation which is lower than first class; tutor; trainer in rowing *etc.* -*v.i.* ride in a coach. -*v.t.* tutor; train. -**coach'man** *n.* [F. *coche*]

coagulate *v.t.* and *i.* curdle, form into a mass. **coag'ulant** *n.* -**coag'ulated** *a.* -**coagula'tion** *n.* [L. *coagulate*]

coal *n.* glowing ember; mineral consisting of carbonized vegetable matter, used as fuel. -*v.t.* supply with coal. -*v.i.* take in coal. [OE. *col*]

coalesce' (-es-) *v.i.* unite. -**coales'cence** *n.* **coali'tion** *n.* alliance, *esp.* of parties. [L. *coalescere*, grow together]

coarse *a.* rough, harsh; unrefined; indecent; gross. [ME. *cars*, fr. AF. *cros*, F. *gros*]

coast *n.* sea-shore. -*v.i.* and t. sail by the coast. -**coast'er** *n.* [L. *costa*, rib]

coat *n.* outer garment; animal's fur or feathers; covering; layer. -*v.t.* clothe, cover with a layer. -**coat-of-arms** *n.* heraldic bearings. [OF. *cote* fr. L. L. *cotta*]

coax *v.t.* wheedle, cajole, persuade [earlier *cokes, cox*]

co'balt *n.* a metal; blue pigment made from it.(Ger. *kobalt*, fr. *kobold*, demon]

cob'ble *v.t.* patch roughly, as shoes. -**cobb'ler** *n.* [orig. uncertain]

COB'OL *n.* computer programming language for general commercial use. [fr. common business oriented language]

co'bra *n.* poisonous hooded snake. [Port., fr. L. *colubra*, snake]

cob'web *n.* spider's web. [ME. *coppeweb*, fr. *coppe*, spider]

C'oca-Co'la *n.* carbonated soft drink. [Trademark]

cocaine' *n.* alkaloid drug used as an anaesthetic. [*coca*, American shrub]

cock *n.* male bird; tap for liquids; hammer of a gun; its position drawn back; upward turn. -*v.t.* set or turn assertively; draw back (gun hammer). [OE. *cocc*]

cockatoo' *n.* crested parrot. [Malay *kakatua*; imit. of cry]

coc'kle *n.* kind of shellfish. [F. *coquille*]

cock'ney *n.* native Londoner; his dialect. [ME. *cokenay*, townsman]

cock'pit *n.* the place where game-cocks fought; the pilot's space in an airplane. [*cock* and *pit*]

cockroach *n.* a black or brown beetle known particularly for its habit of infesting houses and associated with insanitary conditions. [Sp. *cucaracha*]

co'co *n.* tropical palm. -**co'conut** *n.* very large hard nut from the coco palm. [Sp. = ugly-face, bogey (fr. marks at end of the shell)]

co'coa *n.* powder made from the seed of the cacao, a tropical tree; drink made from the powder, [corrupt.of *cacao*. fr. Mex. *cacauatl*]

cocoon' *n.* sheath of an insect in the chrysalis stage. [F. *cocon*, L. *concha*, shell]

cod *n.* large sea fish. [orig. uncertain]

co'da *n.* passage completing and rounding off a musical composition. [L. *canda*, tail]

cod'dle *v.t.* nurse excessively, take too great care of. [orig. uncertain]

code *n.* collection of laws; system of signals.

-codifica'tion n. -co'dify v.t [F. fr. L. cortex, set of tablets; book]

cod'icil n. addition to a will. [L. codicillus, dim. of codex. See code]

coefficient n. joint agent or factor. [fr. L. coefficere. See effect]

coerce' v.t. force. -coer'cion n. coer'cive a. [L. coercere, fr. arcere, restrain]

coeta'neous a. contemporary, of same age. [L. aetas, age]

co-exist' v.i. exist together. -coexistence n. -coexist'ent a. [See exist]

coff'ee n. seeds of a shrub originally from Arab; drink made from these seeds. [Turk, qahveh, Arab. qahweh, wine]

coff'in n. box for a dead body. -v.t. put into a coffin. [L. cophinus, G. kophinos, basket]

cog n. one of a series of teeth on a wheel. [ME. cogge]

co'gent a. forcible, convincing. -co'gency n. -co'gently adv. [L. cogere, constrain-co, together, agere, drive]

cog'itate v.i. think, reflect.-v.t. plan. -cogita'tion n. [L. cogitare]

cogn'ac n. fine French brandy. [made in Cognac, Charente]

cogni'tion n. perception; act of knowing. [L. cognoscere, cognit-, know]

cognizance n. knowledge, awareness, observation. [L. cognoscere, know]

cohab'it v.i. live together as husband and wife. [L. co and habitare, dwell]

co'hort n. troop; tenth of a legion. [L. cohors, company of soldiers]

coif n. close-fitting cap or hood. [F. coiffecap]

coiffure' n. style of hairdressing. -coiffeur n. hairdresser. -coiffeuse' fem. [F.]

coil v.t. lay in rings; twist into a winding shape. -v.i. twist; take up a winding shape. -n. series of rings. [OF. coiner, collect]

coin n. piece of money; money. -v.t. make into money, stamp; invent.-coin'age n. [L. cuneus, wedge (a stamping die being like a wedge)]

coincide' v.i. happen together; agree exactly. -coin'cidence n. coincident; coincidental a. [Med. coincidere, fall together. See incident]

coi'tion n. sexual intercourse. [L. coitio]

coke n. popular name for the beverage Coca-Cola.

coke n. residue left from the distillation of coal. [orig. uncertain]

col'ander n. sieve. [L. colare, strain]

cold a. lacking heat; indifferent, apathetic; dispiriting. -n. lack of heat; common ailment marked by nasal catarrh etc. -cold'ly adv. -cold'ness n. -cold feet, (sl.) fear, timidity. -cold stor'age n. storing perishable goods at artificially reduced temperatures. cold war, diplomatic, economic but non-military hostility. [OE. ceald]

coleop'tera n. pl. order of winged insects, the beetles. [G. koleos, sheath, pteron, wing]

col'ic n. severe intestinal pain. [fr. G. kolon, lower intestine]

collaborate v.i. work with another, esp. in literature. -collabora'tion n. -collaborator n. one who works thus; native who collaborates with the enemy in an occupied country. [L. collaborare, fr. laborare, work]

collapse' v.i. fall together, give way; lose strength, fail. -n. act of collapsing. collaps'ible a. [L. labi, laps-, slip]

coll'ar n. band worn round the neck. v.t. seize, capture. [L. collum, neck]

collate' v.t. compare carefully; appoint to a benefice. -colla'tion n. bringing together for comparison; light repast. [L. collatus, fr. conferre, bring together]

collateral a. accompanying; subordinate; of the same stock but a different line. -n. kinsman. [L. latus, side]

colleague n. associate, companion in an office, employment. [L. college]

collect' v.t. gather, bring together. -v.i. come together. -collec'ted a. gathered; calm. [L. colligere, collect-, gather together]

coll'een n. girl. [Ir. cailin]

coll'ege n. society of scholars; place of higher education; association. -colle'gian n. -colle'giate a. [L. collegium, fr. legere, gather]

collide' v.i. strike or dash together; come into conflict. -colli'sion n. [L. collidere, fr. laedere, hurt]

coll'ie n. Scottish sheep-dog. [orig. uncertain]

coll'oid n. gummy substance. colloidal a. gummy. [G. kolla, glue, eidos, form]

coll'oquy n. conversation. -collo'quial a. conversational, informal. -collo'quialism n. [L. colloqui, converse]

collu'sion n. arrangement, action in secret with another. -collu'sive a. [L. colludere, collus-, play together]

co'lon n. mark (:) indicating a division of a sentence. [G. kolon, limb, part of a sentence]

co'lon n. lower intestine. [See colic]

colonel (kur'-nel) n. commander of a regiment; rank between lieutenant colonel and brigadier general. [It. colonello, column (i.e., 'support' of regiment)]

colonnade' n. row of columns. [F.]

col'ony n. body of people who settle in a new country; country so settled. [L. colonia, fr. colere, till]

col'ophon n. publisher's imprint or device. [G. kolophen, summit, finishing touch]

coluss'us n. huge statue; very big man. -coloss'al a. huge. [L.]

col'or (kule-er) n. hue, tint; complexion; paint or anything giving color; race, when associated with skin-color. -pl. flags. -v.t. stain, dye, paint, give color to; disguise; misrepresent.-v.i. become colored; blush. -col'orblind'ness n. the inability to distinguish between certain colors. -col'ored a. having color; of a race other than white; black. -col'orful a. of bright colors; exaggerated. -col'oring n. act of applying color; natural color. [L. color]

colt n. young of the horse. -colts'foot n. yellow-flowered plant formerly used in medicine, [OE.]

col'umbine a. of, like, a dove. -n. flowering plant with petals resembling doves. [L. columba, dove]

col'umn (-um) *n.* long vertical cylinder, pillar; division of a page; body of troops; anything like these. **-colum'nar** *a.* **-col'umnist** (-um-ist) *n.* writer of a periodical column. [L. *columna*-G. *kolone*, hill]

co'ma *n.* stupor, unnatural sleep. **-co'matose** *a.* [G. *koma*]

comb *n.* toothed instrument for arranging hair, or ornamenting it; cock's crest; mass of honey-cells. *-v.t.* apply a comb to. [OE. *comb*, Ice. *kambri*]

com'bat *v.i.* fight.*-n.* a fight. **com'batant** *n.* **-com'bative** *a.* [F.]

combine' *v.t.* and *i.* join together; ally. **-com'bine** *n.* group of companies or political associates. **-combina'tion** *n.* [Late L. *combinare*, put two-and-two (*bini*) together]

combus'tion *n.* burning. [Late L. *combustion* fr. *comburere*, burn]

come (kum) *v.i.* approach, arrive, move towards; reach; happen (to); originate (from); get to be, become; turn out to be. [OE. *cuman*]

com'edy *n.* drama dealing with the lighter side of life, ending happily, or treating its subject humorously; play of this kind. **-come'dian** *n.* player in comedy. [I. *comoedia*]

come'ly (kum'-) *a.* fair, pretty; seemly. **come'liness** *n.* [OE. *cymlic*]

com'et *n.* heavenly body like a star or planet w i th a tail of light. **com'etary** *a.* [G. *kome*, head of hair]

com'fort (kum'-) *v.t.* console, cheer, gladde *-n.* consolation; well-being, ease; means of consolation or ease. **-com'fortable** *a.* **-com'fortably** *adv.* **com'forter** *n.* one who comforts; baby's 'dummy'. [Late L. *confortare*, strengthen]

com'ic *a.* relating to comedy; funny, laughable. **-com'ical**. **-com'ically** *adv.* [G. *komikos*]

comm'a *n.* mark (,) separating short parts of a sentence. [G. *komma*, piece cut off, short clause]

command' *v.t.* order; rule; compel; have in one's power; overlook; dominate. *-v.i.* exercise rule. *-n.* order, rule; power of controlling, ruling, dominating; overlooking; post of one commanding; his district. **commandant'** *n.* **-commandeer'** *v.t.* seize for military service. **-command'er** *n.* **-command'ment** *n.* [L. *mandare*, enjoin]

command'o *n.* military body detailed for special or dangerous service; member of this body. [Port.]

commem'orate *v.t.* celebrate, keep in memory by ceremony. **-commemora'tion** *n.* **-commem'orative** *a.* [L. *commemorate. See* memory]

commence' *v.t.* and *i.* begin. **-commence'ment** *n.* the act of commencing; ceremony at which degrees or diplomas are conferred. [F. *commencer*-L. *com* and *initiare*, begin]

commend' *v.t.* praise; commit, entrust. **-commendable** *a.* praiseworthy. [L. *commendare*]

commens'urate *a.* in proportion, adequate; equal in size or length of time. [L. *mensurare*, measure]

comm'ent *n.* note, collection of notes; remark; criticism. *-v.i.* make remarks, notes, criticisms. **-comm'entator** *n.* [L. *commentari*]

comm'entary *n.* series of comments; book of notes or comments on another book. **-runn'ing commentary**, comments on a game *etc.* as it proceeds. [*comment*]

comm'erce *n.* buying and selling; dealings, intercourse. **-commer'cial** *a.* **-commercialize** *n.* [L. commercium, fr. *merx*, merchandise]

commis'erate (-z-) *v.t.* pity, condole with. **commisera'tion** *n.* [L. *commiserari*, bewail with]

commis'sion *n.* doing, committing; something entrusted to be done; payment by a percentage for doing something; delegate -d authority; body entrusted with some special duty. *-v.t.* give an order for; authorize, give power to. **-commis'sioner** *n.* [L. *commission* fr. *committere*, entrust]

commit' *v.t.* entrust, give in charge; perpetrate, be guilty of, compromise, entangle. **-committee'** *n.* person to whom something is committed. **-commit'ment** *n.* **-committ'al** *n.* [L. *committere*, entrust]

committ'ee *n.* body appointed or elected for some special business, usually from some large body. [orig. one person entrusted with a duty *etc.* [fr. L. *committere*, entrust]

commode' *n.* chest of drawers; stool containing a chamber-pot. [L. *commodus*, fit]

commo'dious *a.* roomy, convenient. **commo'diously** *adv.* [L. *commodus*, fit]

commodity *n.* article of trade, anything meeting a need. [L. *commodus, fit*]

comm'odore *n.* naval officer ranking between captain and rear-admiral; senior captain in shipping line; president of a yacht club. [orig. uncertain]

comm'on *a.* shared by or belonging to all, or several; public, general; ordinary, usual, frequent; inferior, vulgar. *-n.* land belonging to a community, unenclosed land not belonging to a private owner. *pl.* ordinary people; the lower house of the British Parliament; rations, food provided daily. **-comm'onality** *n.* general body of the people. **-comm'oner** *n.* **-comm'only** *adv.* **comm'onplace** *a.* ordinary, trivial. *-n.* **-comm'onwealth** *n.* state. [L. *communis*]

commo'tion *n.* stir, disturbance, tumult. [L. *movere, mot-*, move]

commune' *v.i.* have intimate intercourse. **commu'nicable** *a.* **-commu'nicant** *n.* one who receives Communion. **-commu'nicate** *v.t.* impart, give a share. *v.i.* give or exchange information; receive Communion. **communica'tion** *n.* act of giving, *esp.* information; information, letter, message. **commu'nion** *n.* fellowship; body with a common faith; sharing. **-Commu'nion** *n.* participation in the sacrament of the Lord's Supper; that sacrament, Eucharist. [L. *communes*, common]

comm'unism. See community.

commu'nity *n.* state; body of people with

something in common, *e.g.*, district of residence, religion; joint ownership. - **comm'une** *n.* small administrative district; organization where property and responsibilities are shared in common. -**commu'nal** *a.* common, shared by a number. **comm'unism** *n.* doctrine that all goods, means of production *etc.* should be the property of the community. [L. *communes*, common]

commute' *v.t.* exchange; change (a punishment *etc.*) into something less; change (a duty *etc.*) for a money payment; (*elec.*) reverse current. commuta'tion *n.* [L. *mutare*, change]

com'pact *n.* agreement, covenant. [L. *compacisci*, agree together]

compact' *a.* neatly arranged or packed; solid, concentrated; terse. com'pact *n.* pocket-sized vanity case. -**compact disk** digital disk on which music, video, or computer data is encoded and read by a laser device. -compact'ly *adv.* -compact'ness *n.* [L. *compingere, compact-*, join together]

compan'ion *n.* mate, follow, comrade, associate. compan'ionable *a.* . compan'ionship *n.* [L. *companio*, messmate, fr. *panes*, bread]

compan'ion *n.* raised cover over a staircase from the deck to the cabin of a ship; deck skylight. [Du. *kampanje*]

com'pany *n.* assembly; society; association of people for trade *etc.*; ship's crew; part of a battalion. [*companion*]

compare' *v.t.* notice or point out the likenesses and differences of anything; liken or contrast; make the comparative and superlative of an adjective or adverb. - *v.i.* be like; compete with. -**com'parable** *a.* -compar'ative *a.* that may be compared; not absolute; relative, partial. -compar'atively *adv.* -compar'ison *n.* [L. *comparare*]

compartment *n.* division or part divided off, a section; division of a railway car *etc* . [L. *com* and *partiri*, share, fr. *pars*, share]

com'pass (kum'-) *n.* instrument for showing the north; instrument for describing circles (usu. in *pl.*); circumference, measurement round; space, area, scope, reach. -*v.t.* contrive; surround; attain. [VL. *compassare*, go round, fr. *passus*, step]

compassion (-shun) *n.* pity, sympathy. compassionate *a.* -compas'sionately *adv.* [L. *com*, with, *pati, pass-*, suffer]

compatible *a.* consistent, agreeing with. -compatibil'ity *n.* compat'ibly *adv.* [Med. L. *compatibilis*, sharing in suffering, fr. *pati*, suffer]

compel' *v.t.* force, oblige, bring about by force. -compul'sion *n.* compul'sory *a.* [L. *compellere*, drive together]

compendium *n.* abridgment or summary; epitome. [L. = what is weighed together]

com'pensate *v.t.* make up for; counterbalance. -compensa'tion *n.* [L. *compensate*, weigh together]

compete' *v.i.* strive, vie (with). - competi'tion *n.* -compet'itive *a.* compet'itor *n.* [L. *competere*, seek in common]

competent *a.* able, skillful; properly qualified; proper, due, legitimate, suitable, sufficient.-com'petence, com'petency *n.* - com'petently *adv.* [L. *compelere*, be convenient]

compile' *v.t.* make up (*e.g.*, a book) from various sources or materials; put together. - compila'tion *n.* -compi'ler *n.* [L. *compilare*, plunder]

compiler *n.* (*compute.*) computer program that translates a program written in high-level language into machine languge that the compute can execute.

complacent *a.* self-satisfied. - com'plaisance *n.* obligingness, willingness to please. com'plaisant *a.* [L. *complacere*, please greatly]

complain' *v.i.* grumble; bring a charge, make known a grievance; (with of) make known that one is suffering from. -complain'ant *n.* -complaint' *n.* statement of a wrong, a grievance; an illness. [L. *plangere*, beat the breast]

complete *a.* full, finished, ended, perfect.-*v.t.* finish; make whole, full, perfect. -complement *n.* something completing a whole; full allowance, equipment, *etc.* - complement'ary *a.* -complete'ly *adv.* - complete'ness *n.* -comple'tion *n.* [L. *cornplere*, complete, fill up]

com'plex *a.* intricate, compound, involved-*n.* psychological abnormality, obsession. - complex'ity *n.* [L. *complectere*, plait together]

complexion (-ek'-shun) *n.* look, color, *esp.* of the skin. [F., fr. L. *complexio*]

complicate *v.t.* make intricate, involved, difficult. -complica'tion *n.* [L. *eomplicare*, fold together]

complicity *n.* partnership in wrongdoing. [*See* accomplice]

compliment *n.* remark neatly expressing praise. -*pl.* expression of courtesy, formal greetings. -*v.t.* praise, congratulate. - complement'ary *a* . [Sp. *cumplimiento*, a 'fulfilling' of an act of courtesy; same word as *complement*]

comply' *v.i.* consent, yield, do as asked. - compli'ance *n.* compli'ant *a.* [It.*complire*, fr. Sp. *cumplir*, satisfy requirements, fr. L. *complere*, fill up]

component *n.* part, elemental. composing, making up. [L. *componere*, put together]

comport' *v.t.* conduct or carry (oneself). - *v.i.* agree, accord (with). [L. *portare*, carry]

compose' *v.t.* make up; write, invent; arrange, put in order; settle, adjust; calm. -composed' *a.* calm. compo'ser *n.* author of a musical work. -com'posite *a.* compound, not simple. -compo'sure *n.* calmness. [F. *composer*]

compound' *v.t.* mix, make up, put together; compromise, make a settlement of debt by partial payment; condone. -*v.i.* come to an arrangement, make terms. -com'pound *a.* not simple; composite, mixed. -*n.* mixture, joining; substance, word *etc.* made up of parts. [L. *componere*, put together]

comprehend' *v.t.* understand, take in; include, comprise. [L. *comprehendere*, grasp]

compress *v.t.* squeeze together; make smaller in size, bulk. -**com'press** *n.* pad of wet lint *etc.* applied to a wound, inflamed part *etc.* **compress'ible** *a.* **compres'sion** *n.* [L. *premere, press-*, press]

comprise *v.t.* include, contain. [F. *compris, pp.* of *comprendre*, comprehend]

compromise *n.* meeting halfway, coming to terms by giving up part of a claim. -*v.t.* expose to risk or suspicion. *v.i.* come to terms. [L. *compromittere*, put before an arbiter]

compulsion. *See* compel.

compute' *v.t.* reckon, estimate. - **computa'tion** *n.* -**comput'er** *n.* a machine, *usu.* electronic, capable of carrying out calculations and other complex functions at high speeds. -**comput'erize** *v.t.* equip with, perform by a computer. [L. *computare*]

com'rade *n.* mate, companion, friend. - **com'radeship** *n.* [Sp. *camorada*, roomful, later room-mate; fr. L. *camera*, room]

con *v.t.* direct the steering of a ship. -**conn'ing-tower** *n.* [earlier cond, condy, fr. F. *conduire*, guide]

con *v.t.* trick, swindle. -*n.* [fr. *confidence* trick]

concatenation *n.* series of links; chain (of events *etc.*). -**concat'enate** *v.t.* [L. *con*, together, *catena*, chain]

con'cave *a.* hollow, rounded inwards. - **concav'ity** *a.* [L. *cavus*, hollow]

conceal' *v.t.* hide, keep secret. concealment *n.* [L. *celare*, hide]

concede *v.t.* admit, grant; yield. - **conces'sion** *n.* -**concess'ive** *a.* [L. *cedere, cess-*, give away]

conceit' *n.* vanity, overweening opinion of oneself; far-fetched comparison. -**conceit'ed** *a.* conceive **conceive'** *v.t.* become pregnant with; take into the mind, think of, imagine; understand. -**conceiv'able** *a.* -**conceiv'ably** *adv.* [F. *concevoir*, fr. L. *concipere*]

concentrate *v.t.* reduce to small space; increase in strength; gather to one point. - *v.i.* come together; devote all attention. - **concentra'tion** *n.* -**concentra'tion camp**, camp for political prisoners *etc.* [L. *concentrum*]

concentric *a.* having a common center. [L. *cum* and *centrum*, center]

con'cept *n.* idea, abstract notion. - **concep'tual** *a.* -**concep'tion** *n.* conceiving, idea [L. *concipere*, conceive]

concern' *v.t.* to relate or belong to; to interest, affect, trouble, involve. -*n.* affair, importance, business, establishment. **concern'ing** *prep.* respecting. [L. *cernere*, have regard to]

concert' *v.t.* arrange, plan together. -**con'cert** *n.* musical entertainment; harmony, agreement. **concert'ed** *a.* mutually arranged. **concer'to** (cher-) *n.* musical composition for solo instrument and orchestra. **concerti'na** *n.* musical instrument with bellows and keys. [F. *concerted*]

concierge' (kong-si-erzh) *n.* French doorkeeper, porter, caretaker. [F.]

conciliate *v.t.* pacify, gain friendship. [L.

conciliate, bring together in council]

concise' *a.* brief, in few words. -**concise'ly** *adv.* -**concise'ness** *n.* concision (-sizhn) *n.* [L. *concisus*, fr. *cwdere*, cut]

conclude *v.t.* end, finish; settle; *v.i.* come to an end; infer, deduce; decide. **conclu'sion** (-oo'shn) *n.* -**conclu'sive** *a.* decisive, convincing. -**conclu'sively** *adv.* [L. *concludere*]

concoct *v.t.* make a mixture, prepare with various ingredients; make up; devise, as a plan. -**concoc'tion** *n.* [L. *concoquere*, boil together]

conc'ord *n.* agreement. -**concord'ance** *n.* agreement; an index to the words of a book. **concord'ant** *a.* [L. *Concordia*]

concourse *n.* crowd; a flocking together. [L. *concurrere*, concur, run together]

con'crete *a.* solid; consisting of matter, facts, practice, *etc.*; not abstract. -*n.* mixture of sand, cement, *etc.*, used in building -**concrete'ly** *adv.* [L. *concrescere, concretum*, grow together]

concubine *n.* woman living with a man as his wife, but not married to him. **concu'binage** *n.* [fr. L. *con*, together, and *cubare*, lie]

concur' *v.i.* agree, express agreement; happen together. -**concur'rence** *n.* concur'rently *adv.* [L. *concurrere*, run together]

concussion (-shn) *n.* violent shock; injury by blow, fall, *etc.* [L. *concussion*, shaking together]

condemn' *v.t.* blame; find guilty; doom; find unfit for use. **condem'natory** *a.* **condemna'tion** *n.* [L. *condemnare*]

condense' *v.t.* concentrate, make more solid; turn from gas into liquid; compress. - *v.i.* turn from gas to liquid. **condensa'tion** *n.* **conden'ser** *n.* (*elec.*) apparatus for storing electrical energy for reducing vapors to liquid form; lens, mirror for focusing light. [L. *condensare*]

condescend' *v.i.* stoop, deign; be gracious; patronize. condescen'sion *n.* [Late L. *condescendere*, come down]

condiment *n.* relish, seasoning. [L. *condimentum condire*, pickle]

condition *n.* thing on which a statement or happening or existing depends; stipulation; state of circumstances of anything. -*v.t.* be essential to the happening or existence of; stipulate; make fit (for). -**condi'tioned reflex** *n.* response automatically produced by stimulus repeatedly applied. [L. *condicio*, discussion]

condole' *v.i.* grieve with, offer sympathy. condo'lence *n.* [L. *condolere*, suffer with]

condominium *n.* joint rule; an apartment in a house consisting of individually owned apartments; an apartment in such a house. *abbrev.* con'do. [L]

condone' *v.t.* overlook, forgive, treat as not existing. [L. *condonare*, remit]

con'dor *n.* S. Ameriran vulture. [Sp., fr. Peruvian *cuntur*]

conduct *v.t.* lead, direct, manage. -**con'duct** *n.* behavior; management. -**conduc'tor** *n.* **conduc'tion** *n.* conduc'tive *a.* -**conductiv'ity**

n. power to conduct heat, electricity. [L. *conducere*]

con'duit (-dit) *n.* channel or pipe for water. [F., fr. L. *conducere*, lead]

cone *n.* solid figure with a circular base and tapering to a point; any object in this shape; fruit of the pine, fir, *etc.* -**con'ic**, **con'ical** *a.* **co'nifer** *n.* tree bearing cones. coniféerous *a.* [G. *konos*, peak]

confection *n.* prepared delicacy, sweetmeat; made-up millinery, *etc.* -**confectioner** *n.* dealer in cake, pastry, sweets, *etc.* -**confec'tionery** *n.* [L. *conficere*, make up]

confederate *a.* united in a league-*n.* ally; accomplice. -*v.t.* and *i.* unite. [L. *confœderatus*, fr. *fœdus, fœderis*, treaty, league]

confer' *v.t.* grant, give. - *v.i.* talk with, take advice. -**confer'ment** *n.* -**con'ference** *n.* [L. *conferre*, bring together]

confess' *v.t.* admit, own, acknowledge, declare; (of a priest) to hear the sins of. *v.i.* acknowledge; declare one's sins orally to a priest. -**confes'sor** *n.* priest who hears confessions; person who keeps his faith under persecution, but without martyrdom; one who confesses. [L. *confiteri, confessus*, acknowledge]

confetti *n.* small shaped pieces of colored paper for throwing at carnivals and weddings [It.]

confide' *v.i.* trust (in). *v.t.* entrust. -**confidant'** *n.* one entrusted with smrets. -**con'fidence** *n.* trust; boldness, assurance; intimacy. **con'fident** *a.* -**con'fidently** *adv.* [L. *fidere*, trust]

configuration *n.* shape, aspect; outline. [L. *figurare*, fashion]

confine' *v.t.* shut up, imprison; keep within bounds; keep in house, bed. -**con'fines** *n.pl.* boundaries. -**confine'ment** *n.* restraint, imprisonment; child bed. [L. *confinis*, bordering]

confirm' *v.t.* make strong, settle; make valid, ratify; make sure, verify; administer confirmation to. -**confirma'tion** *n.* making strong, valid, certain, *etc.*; rite administered by a bishop to confirm baptized persons in the vows made for them at baptism. [L. *confirmare*]

confiscate *v.t.* seize by authority. -**confisca'tion** *n.* confiscatory *a.* [L. *confiscare*, seize for the treasury, *liscus.* cp. *fiscal*]

conflagration *n.* great fire. [L. *confl agration*, burn up]

con'flict *n.* struggle, trial of strength; variance. -**conflict'** *v.t.* be at odds with, inconsistent with; clash. [L. *conflictusfligere*, strike]

conform' *v.t.* and *i.* comply, adapt to rule, pattern, custom, *etc.* [L. *conformare*, give same shape]

confound' *v.t.* baffle, bring to confusion, defeat; mix up. [F. *confondre*-L. *confundere, confusum*, pour together]

confront' (-unt) *v.t.* face; bring face to face with. -**confronta'tion** *n.* [F. *confronter*, fr. front, brow]

Confu'cian *a.* of, or pertaining to, the Chinese philosopher Confucius (d. 478 B.C.)

confuse' *v.t.* disorder, mix mentally. -**confu'sion** *n.* [*See* confound]

congeal' *v.t.* and *i.* solidify by freezing or otherwise. -**congela'tion** *n.* [L. *congelare*, freeze together]

congenial *a.* suitable, to one's liking; of kindred disposition. -**conge'nially** *adv.* -**congenial'ity** *n.* [Mod. L. *congenialis*, suiting one's genius]

congenital (-je-) *a.* born with one, dating from birth. [L. *congenitus*]

congestion *n.* abnormal accumulation of blood, population, *etc.*; over-crowding. -**conges'ted** *a.* [L. *congestio*]

conglomerate *a.* gathered into a ball. -*v.t.* and *i.* -*n.* rock of rounded pebbles cemented together-puddingstone. **conglomera'tion** *n.* confused mass. [L. *conglomerate*]

congratulate *v.t.* felicitate, offer expression of pleasure at another's good fortune, success, *etc.* -**congratula'tion** *n.* congratulatory *a.* [L. *congratulari*]

congregate (-ng-g-) *v.i.* flock together; assemble. -**congrega'tion** *n.* assembly, *esp.* for religious worship. [L. *grex, gregis*, herd]

cong'ress (-ng-g-) *n.* meeting; a formal assembly for discussion; a legislative body. **congres'sional** *a.* [L. *congredi*, congresses, go together]

congruent (-ng-groo-) *a.* fitting together; suitable, accordant. -**cong'ruence** *n.* **cong'ruous** *a.* -**congru'ity** *n.* [L. *congruere*, rush together]

conjecture *n.* guess. -*v.t.* and *i.* guess. -**conjec'tural** *a.* [L. *conjecture*, fr. *conjicere*, conjecture, throw together]

con'jugal *a.* of marriage; between married persons. -**conjugal'ity** *n.* [L. *conjunx*, spouse, *lit.* joined together]

conjugate *v.t.* inflect a verb in its various forms (past, present, *etc.*). -**conjuga'tion** *n.* [L. *conjugate*]

conjunction *n.* part of speech joining words, phrases, *etc.*; union; simultaneous happening. -**conjunc'ture** *n.* combination of circumstances, decisive point. [L. *conjungere*, join together]

conjure' *v.t.* implore solemnly. -**con'jure** (kunjer) *v.t.* and *i.* produce magic effects by secret natural means; invoke devils. [L. *conjurare*, swear together]

connote *a.* innate, congenital. -**conna'tion** *n.* **connat'ural** *a.* of the same nature. [L. *nasci, natus*, be born]

connect' *v.t.* and *i.* join together, unite; associate -**connec'tion, connex'ion** *n.* -**connect'ive** *a.* [L. *nectere*, bind]

connoisseur (kon-e-ser) *n.* critical expert in matters of taste. [OF. *conoisseur*, fr. L. *cognoscere*, know]

connote *v.t.* imply, mean in addition to the chief meaning. **connota'tion** *n.* [Med. L. *connotare*]

connubial *a.* connected with marriage. [L. *conubium*, marriage]

con'quer (-ker) *v.t.* win by war; overcome, defeat. -*v.i.* be victorious. -**conqueror** (-ke) *n.*

-con'quest n. [L. quæxrere, seek]

con'science (-shens) n. mental sense of right and wrong. conscien'tious a. [L. conscienlia, knowledge within oneself]

con'scious (-shus) a. aware, awake to one's surroundings and identity, in one's senses. -con'sciously adv. con'sciousness n. [L. conscius, aware]

con'script n. one compulsorily enlisted for military service. -conscrip'tion n. [L. conscribere, write together, enroll]

con'secrate v.t. make sacred. -consecration n. [L. consecrate]

consec'utive a. orderly; in unbroken succession; expressing consequence. -consec'utively adv. [L. consequi, con and sequi, secutus, follow]

consen'sus n. agreement (of opinion etc.); general trend. [consent]

consent' v.i. agree to, comply. -n. agreement, acquiescence. [L. consentire, feel together]

con'sequence n. result, effect, what follows on a cause. con'sequent a. -consequen'tial a. self-important. con'sequently adv. [L. consequential fr. consequi, follow]

conserve' v.t. keep from change or decay. conser'vancy n. board controlling a river or port, its fisheries etc. -conserva'tion n. -conser'vative a. and n. -conser'vatory n. greenhouse. [L. conser-vare, protect]

consid'er v.t. think over; examine; make allowance for; esteem; be of opinion that. -considera'tion n. -consid'erable a. important; somewhat large. consid'erably adv. -consid'erate a. thoughtful for others; careful. consid'erately adv. [L. considerate]

consign' v.t. commit or hand over to; entrust to a carrier. -consign'er n. consignee' n. consign'ment n. [L. corwignare, fr. signum, sign]

consist' v.i. be composed of-, agree with, be compatible. consist'ent a. agreeing (with); constant. [L. consistere, stand firm]

console' v.t. comfort in distress. [L. consolari, comfort]

consolidate v.t. make firm; combine into a connected whole. -consolida'tion n. [L. consolidate, fr. solidus, solid]

consonant n. sound making a syllable only with a vowel, a non-vowel. -a. agreeing with, in accord. -con'sonance n. [L. consonare, sound with]

con'sort n. ship sailing with another; husband or wife, esp. of a queen or king. -consort' v.i. associate, keep company with. [L. consors, fr. sors, fate]

consortium (-shi-) n. society; fellowship; international banking combine. [L. = partnership]

conspic'uous a. striking to the eye, very noticeable; eminent. -conspic'uously adv. [L. conspicere, see clearly]

conspire' v.i. combine for an evil purpose, plot. conspir'ator n. -conspir'acy n. -conspirator'ial a. [L. conspirare, lit. breathe together]

con'stable n. officer of the peace; governor of a royal fortress; British policeman. [Late

L. comes stabuli, count of the stable, marshal]

con'stant a. fixed, unchanging; steadfast; always duly happening or continuing. -con'stantly adv. con'stancy n. [L. constare, stand together]

constella'tion n. group of stars. [L. constellation, cluster of stars. -stellar, star]

consterna'tion n. terrifying sense of disaster; dismay. [L. cowternatio]

constipa'tion n. difficulty in emptying the bowels. con'stipate v.t. affect with this disorder. [L. constipare, press together]

constitute v.t. set up, establish, make into, found, give form to. -constitu'tion n. make, composition; basic physical condition; disposition; body of principles on which a state is governed. -constitu'tional a. relating to a constitution; in harinony with a political constitution. -n. walk taken for health. -constituency n. a body of people entitled to elect a representative in government; the geographical location of this body. [L. constituere, place together]

constrain' v.t. force, compel; urge. -constraint' n. compulsion; restraint; embarrassment. [L. constringere, tighten]

constric'tion n. compression, squeezing together. [L. constriction pressing together]

construct' v.t. to make, build, form, put together. -construc'tion n. -construc'tive a. -construc'tively adv. [L. con struere, constructum, pile together, build]

construe' v.t. interpret, analyze, grammatically; translate. [L. construere, pile together]

con'sul n. state agent residing in a foreign town; in ancient Rome, one of the chief magistrates. [L]

consult' v.t. and i. seek counsel, advice or information (from). -consul'tant n. one who consults or advises; specialist (in medicine etc.). consulta'tion n. [L. consultare]

consume' v.t. make away with; use up; eat or drink up; destroy. -consump'tion n. using up; destruction; wasting of the body by tuberculosis. -consump'tive a. [L. consumers, use up]

con'summate v.t. complete, finish. -consumm'ate a. of the greatest perfection or completeness. [L. summus, highest]

con'tact n. touching; being in touch; person contacted. -v.t. get into touch with. conta'gion (-jn) a. passing on of disease by touch, contact; physical or moral pestilence. -conta'gious a. [L. tangere, touch]

contain' v.t. hold; have room for; include; restrain (oneself). contain'er n. [L. tenere, hold]

contam'inate v.t. stain, sully, infect. -contaminant n. substance or thing that infects, pollutes, or corrupts. [L. contamen, contagion]

con'template v.t. gaze upon; meditate on; intend, purpose. [L. conlemplari; orig. of augurs viewing a templum in the sky. cp. templo]

contem'porary a. existing at, or lasting, the same time; of the same age. -n. one existing at the same time. -contempora'neous a. -

contempora'neously adv. [L. tempus, tempor, time]

contend' v.i. strive, fight, dispute. con ten'tion n. -conten'tious a. -conten'tiously adv. [L. tendere, stretch]

content' a. satisfied. -v.t. satisfy. -n. satisfaction. -con'tent n. holding capacity; pl. that contained. -content'ment n. [L. continere, contain]

contest' v.t. dispute, debate, fight for. - con'test n. debate; conflict, strife; competition. -contes'tant n. -contes'table a. [L. contestari, call to witness]

con'text n. what comes before and after a passage, words, esp. as fixing meaning. [L. contexere, weave together]

contiguous a. touching; adjoining; neighboring. -contigu'ity n. [L. contiguus, fr. contingere, touch]

continent a. self-restraining; sexually chaste. -con'tinence n. [L. continere, hold together]

continent n. large continuous mass of land, a main division of the earth. -The Con'tinent, European mainland. continen'tal a. [L. continere, hold together]

contingent (-j-) a. uncertain; depending for occurrence (on); accidental. -n. quota of troops supplied by an ally, an organization, etc. -contin'gency n. [L. contingere, relate to]

contin'ue v.t. and i. go on, carry on, last, remain, keep in existence, prolong, resume. -contin'ual a. -contin'ually adv. continuance n. -continua'tion n. -contin'uity n. contin'uous a. -contin'uously adv. [L. continuare]

contort' v.t. twist out of normal shape; writhe. contor'tion n. [L. contorquere, contortum, twist together]

con'tour (-oor) n. outline of shape of anything, esp. mountains, coast, etc. -contour (line) n. line on a map showing uniform elevation. [F., fr. contourner, follow the outline]

contraception n. birth-control; prevention of conception, usu. by artificial means. - contracep'tive a. and n. [L. contra and conception]

con'tract n. bargain, agreement; formal writing recording an agreement; agreement enforceable by law. -contract' v.i. enter into an agreement; become smaller. -v.t. agree upon; incur, become involved in; make smaller; shorten. [L. contrahere, draw together]

contradict' v.t. deny; be at variance with. -contradic'tory a. -contradic'tion n. [L. contradicere, speak against]

contradistinction n. difference marked by contrasting opposite qualities. [L. contra, opposite, and distinction]

contralto n. voice, or part, next above alto; singer of that voice. [It.]

contraption n. (sl.) contrivance; odd device or appliance. [orig. uncertain]

con'trary a. opposed; opposite, other. n. something the exact opposite of another. adv. in opposition. -con'trarily adv. -contrari'ety n. -con'trariwise adv. [L. contraries]

contrast' (-a-) v.t. bring out differences; set in opposition for comparison. -v.i. show great difference. -con'trast n. striking difference; something showing a marked difference; placing, comparison, to bring out differences. [Late L. contrastare, stand against]

contribute v.t. give or pay to a common fund; help to a common result. -v.i. give or pay or help in a common fund or effort. - contribu'tion n. -contrib'utor n. contrib'utory a. contrib'utive a. [L. contribuere. See tribute]

con'trite a. sorrowing for wrong-doing. - contri'tion n. -con'tritely adv. [L. conterere, contrit-, bruise]

contrive' v.t. devise, invent, design; succeed in bringing about. -contri'ver n. - contri'vance n. [F. controuver]

control' v.t. command, dominate, regulate; direct, check, test. -n. domination; restraint; direction; check; (spiritualism) medium's spirit-guide. -pl. controlling levers etc. of car, plane; -control'lable a. -controlled substance n. drug whose possession and use is restricted by law. [OF. contre-rolle, duplicate register]

controversy n. dispute, debate, esp. a dispute in the press and of some duration. [L. controversus, turned against]

contuse' v.t. bruise. -contu'sion n. [L. tundere, tusum, beat, bruise]

conundrum n. riddle, esp. one with a punning answer. [orig. uncertain]

convalescent a. recovering from illness. -n. person recovering from sickness. convales'cence n. [L. convalescere, grow strong]

convection n. (elec.) transmission of heat through liquid or gases. -convective a. [L. convectio-vehere, carry]

convene' v.t. call together. - v.i. assemble. - conven'er n. one who calls a meeting; chairman of a committee. [L. convenire, come together]

convenient a. handy; favorable to needs, comfort; well-adapted to one's purpose. - conve'niently adv. -conve'nience n. [L. convenire, come together]

con'vent n. community of monks or nuns; their building. -conven'tual a. [convene]

convention n. a calling together; assembly; treaty, agreement; rule or practice based on agreement; accepted usage, esp. one grown quite formal; deadening. -conven'tional a. -conven'tionally adv. -conventionality n. [convene]

converge' v.i. approach, tend to meet. - conver'gent a. conver'gence n. (Late L. convergere, incline together]

converse' v.i. talk (with). -con'verse n. talk. -con'versant a. familiar with, versed in. [L. conversari, dwell with]

con'verse a. opposite, turned round. n. opposite, statement with the terms of another interchanged or turned round. [L. conversus, turned about]

convert' v.t. apply to another purpose; change, transform; cause to adopt a religion, an opinion. **-con'vert** *n*. converted person. **-convert'ible** *a*. being capable of transformation. *-n*. automobile with a collapsible roof. [L. *converters*, turn about]

con'vex *a*. curved outwards, like any part of the surface of an egg; opposite of concave. **-convex'ity** *n*. [L. *conuexus*]

convey' *v.t.* carry, transport; impart, communicate; make over, transfer. **-convey'ance** *n*. carriage, vehicle; (law) transfer of property. **-convey'ancer** *n*. one skilled in the legal forms of transferring property. **-convey'ancing** *n*. [OF. *conveier*, fr. L. *via*, way; orig. *escorl*]

convict' *v.t.* prove or declare guilty. **-con'vict** *n*. criminal undergoing penal servitude. **convic'tion** *n*. a convicting, verdict of guilty; a being convinced, firm belief, state of being sure. **-convince'** *v.t.* bring to a belief, satisfy by evidence or argument. [L. *convincere*, fr. *vincere*, vanquish]

convoy *v.t.* escort for protection, as ships, war supplies, *etc*. **-con'voy** *n*. party (of ships, troops, *etc*.) conveying or convoyed. [same as *convey*]

convulse *v.t.* shake violently; affect with violent involuntary contractions of the muscles. **-convul'sive** *a*. **-convul'sively** *adv*. **-convul'sion** *n*. [L. *convel- lere*, fr. *vellere*, *vulsum*, pluck]

cook *n*. one who prepares food for the table. **-** *v.i.* act as cook; undergo cooking. **-** *v.t.* prepare (food) for the table, *esp*. by heat; (*sl.*) falsify accounts, *etc*., **cookbook** book of cooking recipes. [OE *coc*, fr. L. *coquus*]

cook'ie, cooky *n*. plain bun; one of many kinds of sweet, flat baked cakes, *usu*. hard or semi-hard. [*cook*]

cool *a*. moderately cold; unexcited, calm; lacking friendliness or interest. *-v.t.* and *i*. make or become cool. *-n*. cool time, place, *etc*. [OE. *col*]

coop *n*. cage or pen for fowls. *-v.t.* shut up in a coop; confine. **-coop'er** *n*. one who makes casks. **coop'erage** *n*. [L. *cupa*, vat, cask]

cooperate *v.i.* work together. **-co'operation** *n*. working together; production or distribution by cooperators who share the profits. **-co'operative** *a*. **-co'operator** *n*. [fr. L. *co-*, together, and *opus*, work]

coordinate *a*. equal in degree, status, *etc*. *-v.t.* place in the same rank; bring into order as parts of a whole. *-n*. coordinate thing; any set of numbers defining the location of a point. **-co'ordination** *n*. [L. *ordo, ordin-*, order]

cop *n*. conical ball of thread or spindle. [OE. *cop, copp*]

cope *v.i.* contend, deal with. [perh. fr. F. *coupler*, grapple]

co'pious *a*. plentiful, full, abundant; copiously *adv*. **co'piousness** *n*. [L. *copia*, plenty]

copp'er *n*. reddish malleable ductile metal; bronze money, bronze coin; large vessel for boiling clothes. *-v.t.* cover with copper. **-copp'ersmith** *n*. one who works in copper. [L. *Cyprium aes*, bronze from Cyprus, G. *Kypros*]

copperhead *n*. venomous snake of *n*.

America. [*See* copper]

cop'ula *n*. word acting as a connecting link in a sentence; connection. **-cop'ulate** *v.i.* unite sexually. **-copula'tion** *n*. **-cop'ulative** *a*. [L. *copula bond*, couple, fr. *co-*, together, *apere*, fit]

cop'y *n*. imitation; single specimen of a book; piece of writing for a learner to imitate; matter for printing. *-v.t.* make a copy of, imitate. **-cop'yright** *n*. legal exclusive right to print and publish a book, article, work of art, *etc*. *-a*. protected by copyright *v.t.* protect by copyright. **-cop'yist** *n*. [L. *copia*, abundance]

coquette' *n*. woman who plays with men's affections. **-coquett'ish** *a*. **-coquet'** *v.i.* co'quetry *n*. [F.]

cor'al *n*. hard substance made by sea polyps and forming pink or red or white growths, islands, reefs; ornament or toy of coral. **-cor'alline** *a*. [L. *corallum*]

cord *n*. thin rope or thick string; rib on cloth, ribbed fabric; electrical wire with protective coating; measure of cut wood, usually 128 cub. ft. *-v.t.* fasten or bind with cord. **-cord'age** *n*. **cord'uroy** *n*. ribbed cotton stuff. *-a*. **-cord'uroy road'**, swamp road of transverse logs. [G. *chortle*, gut; *corduroy* is of unknown origin]

cordial *a*. hearty, sincere, warm. *-n*. stimulating medicine or drink cordially. [L. *car, cordis*, heart]

cord'ite *n*. cord-like smokeless explosive. [fr. *cord*]

cord'on *n*. a chain of troops or police; ornamental cord; fruit-tree grown as a single stem. [F. dim of *corde*, cord]

cord'uroy. See **cord**.

core *n*. horny seed-case of apple and other fruits; central or innermost part of anything. [perh. fr. L. *car*, heart]

co-respondent *n*. person proceeded against together with the respondent in a divorce suit. [*respondent*]

Corin'thian (-th-) *a*. of Corinth; of the Corinthian order of architecture, ornate Greek. *-n*. native of Corinth; man of fashion. [*Corinth*]

cork *n*. bark of cork-oak; piece of it, *esp*. a round piece used as a stopper. *-v.t.* stop up with a cork; stop up generally. **cork'y** *a*. light, buoyant. **-cork'screw** *n*. tool for pulling out corks. [Sp. *alcorque*, cork-shoe, slipper; of Arab. orig.]

corn *n*. grain, fruit or cereals; a grain; maize. *-v.t.* preserve (meat) with salt. **-corn'ball** *n*. person given to mawkish or unsophisticated behavioral. another word for corny. **corn'crake** *n*. bird, the landrail. **-corn'flower** *n*. blue flower growing in cornfields. **-corn row** *n*. hairstyle of narrow braids plaited in rows close to the scalp. **-corn'starch** *n*. maize flour. [OE. *corn*]

corn *n*. horny growth on foot or toe. [OF., fr. L. *cornu*, horn]

corn'ea *n*. horny membrane covering the front of the eye. [for L. *cornea tela*, horny web]

corne'lian *n*. precious stone, a reddish chalcedony. [L. *cornu*, horn]

corn'er *n.* part of a room where two sides meet; remote or humble place; point where two walls, streets, *etc.* meet; angle, projection; buying up of the whole existing stock of a commodity. -*v.t.* drive into a position of difficulty, or one leaving no escape; establish a monopoly- [L. *cornu*, horn]

corn'et *n.* trumpet with valves; formerly lowest-grade cavalry officer, sublieutenant. [L. *cornu*, horn]

corn'ice *n.* projecting source near the top of a wall; ornamental molding at junction of wall and ceiling. [F. *corniche*]

cornuco'pia *n.* symbol of plenty, a goat's horn overflowing with fruit and flowers. [L. *cornu copice*, horn of plenty]

coroll'a *n.* flower's inner envelope of petals. [L. dim. of *corona*, crown]

cor'ollary *n.* proposition that follows without proof from another proved; natural consequence. [L. *corolla*, a garland]

coro'na *n.* crown, top; top part of a cornice; sun's luminous envelope; moon's halo during a solar eclipse. -**cor'onary** *a.* of a crown; of the crown of the head; as a circle; relating to the arteries which supply blood to the heart. [L. *corona*, crown]

coronation *n.* ceremony of crowning a sovereign. [OF. *coroner*, crown]

cor'oner *n.* officer who holds inquests on bodies of persons supposed killed by violence, accident, *etc.* -**cor'onership** *n.* [A.F. *corouner*, fr. *coroune*, crown]

corp'oral *n.* non-commissioned officer below a sergeant. [OF. *corporal*, fr. L. *corpus*, body]

corp'oral *a.* of the body; material, as opposed to spiritual. -**corporal'ity** *n.* [L. *corporalis*, fr. *corpus*, body]

corporation *n.* body of persons legally authorised to act as an individual; authorities of a town or city; (*colloq.*) rotundity of figure. -**cor'porate** *a.* [fr. L. *corporate*, to embody]

corps *n.* military force, body of troops. [F. = body; L. *corpus*]

corpse *n.* dead body of human being. [L. *corpus*]

corp'ulent *a.* bulky of body, fat. -**cor'pulence** *n.* [L. *corpulentus*, fr. *corpus*]

corpuscle (-usl) *n.* minute organism or particle, *esp.* the red and white corpuscles of the blood. [L. *corpusculum*, dim. of *corpus*, body]

corral' *n.* enclosure for cattle. -*v.t.* enclose in a corral. [Sp., fr. *correr* - L. *currere*, run. *See* kraal]

correct' *v.t.* set right; rebuke, punish; counteract; neutralize. -*a.* right, exact, accurate, in accordance with facts or a standard. [L. *corrigere*, *correct*-, fr. *regere*, rule]

corr'elate *v.t.* bring into mutual relation. -*n.* either of two things or words necessarily implying the other. -**correlation** *n.* [*relate*]

corr'espond' *v.i.* exchange letters; answer or agree with in some respect. -**correspond'ence** *n.* **correspon'dent** *n.* [*respond*]

corr'idor *n.* a passage in a building,

railyway-train, *etc.* [It. *corridore*, fr. *correre*, L. *currere*, run]

corr'igible *a.* able to be corrected. [L. *corrigere*, correct]

corrob'orate *v.t.* confirm, support (a statement, *etc.*). -**corrobora'tion** *n.* -**corrob'orative** *a.* [L. *corroborate*, strengthen]

corrode' *v.t.* eat away, eat into the surface of (by chemical action, disease, *etc.*). -**corro'sive** *a.* -**corro'sion** *n.* [L. *rodere*, *ros*, gnaw]

corr'ugated *a.* wrinkled, bent into ridges. -**corruga'tion** *n.* [L. *corrugatus*, fr. *ruga*, wrinkle]

corrupt' *v.t.* make rotten; pervert, make evil; bribe. - *v.i.* rot. *a.* tainted with vice or sin; influenced by bribery; spoilt by mistakes, altered for the worse (of words, literary passages, etc.) [L. *corrumpere*, *corrupt*-, lit. break up]

cor'sage *n.* bodice of a woman's dress; flowers *etc.* to wear on it. [OF.]

cors'et *n.* stiffened inner bodice; stays. [F., dim of OF. *cars*, body]

cortège' (-ezh') *n.* funeral procession. [F.]

cortisone *n.* synthetic hormone, used *esp.* in treatment of rheumatoid arthritis. [fr. L. *cortex*, covering (of the kidneys)]

corundum *n.* aluminous minerals of great weight and hardness. [Tamil *kurundum*]

corvette' *n.* small naval escort ship. [F.]

cosine *abbrev.* **cos** (kos) *n.* (*trigonometry*) in a right-angled triangle, the cosine of an acute angle is the ratio of its adjacent side to the hypotenuse. [*co-* for complement, and L. *sinus*, a bay]

cosmetic *n.* a preparation to beautify the skin. [G. *kosmos*, order, adornment]

cos'mic (kos'-) *a.* relating to the universe; of the vastness of the universe. -**cos'mic rays**, shortest known electromagnetic waves. -**cosmol'ogy** *n.* the science or the study of the universe. -**cosmolog'ical** *a.* -**cosmol'ogist** *n.* -**cosmog'raphy** *n.* description or mapping of the universe. -**cosmog'rapher** *n.* -**cosmograph'ic** *a.* -**cosmopol'itan** *a.* relating to all parts of the world -**cos'mos** *n.* universe; ordered system, as opposed to chaos. [G. *kosmos*, order (the name given by Pythagoras to the universe)]

cost *v.t.* entail the payment, or loss, or sacrifice of; have as price. -*n.* price; expenditure of time, labor, *etc.* -*pl.* expenses of a lawsuit. -**cost'ing** *n.* system of calculating cost of production. -**cost'ly** *a.* of great price or value; involving much expenditure, loss, *etc.* -**cost'liness** *n.* [L. *constare*, fr. *stare*, stand]

cos'tal *a.* of, pert. to -ribs. -**cos'tate** *a.* ribbed. [L. *costa*, rib]

cos'tume *n.* style of dress; outer clothes; set of outer clothes for a woman; theatrical clothes. -**costu'mier** *n.* [It. *costume*, custom, fashion]

cot *n.* swinging bed an board ship; light or folding bed. [Hind. *khat*]

cote *n.* shelter for animals. [OE. *cot*]

co'terie *n.* literary or social *etc.* circle or clique. [F.]

cott'age *n.* small house. **-cott'ager** *n.* [AF. *cotage*, fr. OE. *cot*]

cott'on *n.* plant; the white downy fibrous covering of its seeds; thread, cloth made of this fibre. **-cott'on-wool** *n.* wadding of raw cotton. [Arab, *qutn*]

cott'on *v.i.* take (to); agree (with). [orig. unknown]

couch *v.t.* put into (words); lower (a lance) for action; cause to lie down. **-v.i.** lie down, crouch. **-n.** piece of furniture for reclining on by day, sofa; bed, or what serves for one. [F. *coucher*, OF. *colchier*, fr. L. *collocare*, place together]

cou'gar *n.* large cat-like American beast of prey; puma. [native name]

cough (kof) *v.i.* expel air from the lungs with sudden effort and noise, often to remove an obstruction. **-n.** act of coughing; ailment or affection of coughing. [imit.origin]

coulomb' (-om) *n.* unit of measurement of electric current.[C.A. de *Coulomb*]

council *n.* any deliberative or administrative body; one of its meetings. **-coun'cilor, coun'cillor** *n.* [L. *concilium*, assembly]

coun'sel *n.* deliberation or debate; advice; intentions; barrister or barristers. **- v.t.** advise, recommend. **-coun'selor, counsellor** *n.* [L. *consilium*, plan]

count *v.t.* reckon, calculate, number; include; consider to be. **- v.i.** be reckoned in; depend or rely (on); be of importance. *n.* reckoning; item in a list of charges or indictment; act of counting. **-count'less** *a.* **-count'ing-house** *n.* room or building or actions. [L. *computare*, reckon]

count *n.* European nobleman of rank corresponding to British earl. **-count'ess** *n. fem.* wife or widow of a count or earl. [L. *comes, commit-*, a companion]

countenance *n.* face; its expressions support, patronage. **-v.t.** give support, approval. [L. *continentia*, demeanor]

count'er *n.* table of a bank, shop, *etc.*, on which money is paid, *etc.*; disk or other object used for counting, *esp.* in card games; token. [F. *comptoir*, fr. L. *computare*, count]

count'er *n.* curved part of the stern of a ship. [orig. uncertain]

count'er *adv.* in the opposite direction; contrary. **- v.t.** oppose, contradict. **-counter culture** *n.* alternative lifestyle that opposes tradition and social norms. [*See* counter- *prefix*]

count'er *n.* fencing, *etc.*, parry. **- v.t.** and *i.* parry. [for *counter-parry*]

counter- *prefix* used to make compounds with meaning of reversed, opposite, rival, retaliatory. [L. *contra*, against]. **-counteract'** *v.t.* neutralize or hinder. **-counterac'tion** *n.* **-count'er-attack** *v.t.* and *i.* and *n.* attack after an enemy's advance. **-count'er-attraction** *n.* **-counterbal'ance** *n.* weight balancing or neutralizing another. **-count'er-blast** *n.* energetic declaration in answer- **-count'er-claim** *n.* (*esp. in law*) claim to off-set an opponent's **-count'er-clock'wise** *adv.* and *a.* **-count'er-irr'itant** *n.* **-irritant** applied to the skin to relieve internal co gestion *etc.* **-count'er-**march *v.i.* **-count'ermine** *v.i.* **-count'erplot** *n.* **-count'erpoise** *n.* weight *etc.* which balances another, equilibrium. **- v.t. -count'er-reforma'tion** *n.* **-count'errevolution** *n.* **-count'er-terr'orism** *n. etc.* etc. **counterfeit** (-fet) *a.* sham, forged false. **-n.** imitation, forgery. **-v.t.** imitate with intent to deceive; forge. **-counterfeiter** *n.* [F. *fait*, made]

countermand' *v.t.* cancel (an order); revoke. [L. *mandare*, order]

counterpart *n.* something so like another as to be mistaken for it; something complementary or correlative of another. [*counter* and *part*]

counterpoint *n.* melody added as accompaniment to another; art of so adding melodies. **-contrapun'tal** *a.* [It.*contrappunto*, accompaniment 'pricked against' notes of melody. *See* puncture]

countersign (-sin) *n.* signal or password used in answer to another. **- v.t.** sign a document already signed by another; ratify. [*sign*]

count'ess. *See* count.

coun'try *n.* region, district; territory of a nation, land of birth, residence, *etc.*; rural districts as opposed to town; nation. **country music** *n.* popular folk music of S.W and S.E. U.S. *usu.* accompanied by guitar, banjo, and other stringed instruments; cowboy music (also, **country and western music**). **-coun'tryside** *n.* any rural district or its inhabitants. **-coun'trified** *a.* rural in manner or appearance. [F. *controe*, Late L. *contrata*, (land) spread before one, *contra*]

coun'ty *n.* division of a country or state. [F. *comté*, fr. *comte*, count]

coup *n.* successful stroke. [F.]

coup'le *n.* two, a pair; leash for two hounds. **-v.t.** tie (hounds) together; connect, fasten together; associate, connect in the mind. **-v.i.** join, associate. **-coup'ler** *n.* **-coup'ling** *n.* coup'let *n.* pair of lines of verse, *esp.* rhyming and of equal length. [F., fr. L. *copula*, bond]

cou'pon *n.* detachable ticket entitling the holder to something, *eg.* periodical payment of interest, entrance to a competition, share of rationed goods, *etc.* [F., fr. *couper*, cut]

cou'rage (ku'-) *n.* bravery, boldness. **coura'geous** *a.* **-coura'geously** *adv.* [F., fr. L. *cor*, heart]

cou'rier (koo'-) *n.* express messenger; attendant on travelers. [F.*courrier*, fr. L. *currere*, run]

course *n.* movement or run in space or time; direction of movement; successive development, sequence; line of conduct or action; series of lectures, exercises, *etc.*; any of the successive parts of a dinner. **- v.t.** hunt. *v.i.* run swiftly, gallop about **-cours'er** *n.* swift horse. [F. *cours*, fr. L. *currere*, run]

court *n.* space enclosed by buildings, yard; number of houses enclosing a yard opening on to a street; section of a museum, *etc.*; area marked offer enclosed for playing various games; retinue and establishment of a sovereign; assembly held by a sovereign; body with judicial powers, place where they sit, one of their sittings; attention, homage,

flattery. - *v.t.* seek; woo, try to win or attract.
cour'teous *a.* polite. **-cour'teously** *adv.* -
cour'tesy *n.* **-cour'tier** *n.* one who frequents
a royal court. **-court'ly** *a.* ceremoniously
polite; characteristic of a court. **-court'liness**
n. **-court-mar'tial** *n.* court of naval or military
officers for trying naval or military offenses.
-court'ship *n.* wooing. **-court'yard** *n.* space
enclosed by buildings. **-courtesan'** (kor ti-
zan) *n.* prostitute, *esp.* highly-placed or
refined. [L. *cohors, cohort-*; cognate with *hortus*, garden]
cous'in (kuz'-) *n.* sons or daughter of an uncle
or aunt; person related to another by descent
from one ancestor through two of his or her
children. [Med. L. *cosinus*]
cove *n.* small inlet of coast, sheltered small
bay. [OE. *cofa*, recess]
cov'en (kuv'-) *n.* muster of witches. [*convention*]
cov'enant (ku-) *n.* contract, mutual agreement; compact. - *v.t.* agree to by a covenant.-
v.i. enter into a covenant. [L. *convenire*, come
together]
cov'er (ku-) *v.t.* be over the whole top of,
enclose; include; shield; protect; screen;
counterbalance. **-n.** lid, wrapper, envelope,
binding, screen, anything which covers. -
cov'ert *a.* secret, veiled. **-n.** thicket, place shel-
tering game. **-cov'ertly** *adv.* [F. *coucrir*, L.
cooperire]
cov'et (ku-) *v.t.* long to possess, *esp.* what
belongs to another. **-co'vetous** *a.* -
co'vetousness *n.* [L. *cupiditare*, desire]
cov'ey (ku-) *n.* brood of partridges or quail,
esp. flying together. [F. *couvée*, fr. *couver*,
brood. -L. *cubare*]
cow *n.* female ox; female of elephant, whale,
etc. **-cow'bane** *n.* water hemlock. **-cow'boy**
n. cattleman on a ranch. **-cow'-catcher** *n.*
fender on locomotive for clearing line. [OE.
cu]
cow *v.t.* frighten into submission, overawe.
[ON. *kuga*, oppress]
cow'ard *n.* one given to fear, fainthearted.
-cow'ardly *a.* **-cow'ardice** *n.* [F. *couard*, fr.
L. *cauda*, tail]
cow'er *v.i.* crouch, shrinking, in fear or cold.
[cp, Ger. *kauern*]
cowl *n.* monk's hooded cloak; its hood;
hooded top for chimney; (engine) bonnet. [L.
cucullus, hood of a cloak]
cox'swain (kok'sn), cox *n.* steerer of a boat,
esp. one in permanent charge of a boat. **-cox**
v.t. and *i.* act as coxswain. [earlier *cock-swain*]
coy *a.* shy; slow to respond, *esp.* to lovemaking. **-coy'ly** *adv.* **-coy'ness** *n.* [F. *coi*, fr. L.
quietus]
coyo'te *n.* N. American prairiewolf. [Mex.
coyote]
co'zy *a.* warm, comfortable, sheltered. -
co'zily *adv.* [origin uncertain]
CPU *n.* (*compute.*) portion of the computer
that performs calculations and controls its
primary functions. [central *processing unit*]
crab *n.* edible crustacean with ten legs, of
which the front pair are armed with strong
pincers, noted for sidelong and backward

walk. - *v.i.* (of aircraft) fly sideways. -
crabb'ed *a.* perverse; badtempered, irritable;
of writing, hard to read. [OE. *crabba*; the *a.*
fr. the crooked walk of the creature]
crabapple *n.* wild apple of sour taste. [perh.
fr. Gael, *craobh*]
crack *v.t.* break, split partially; break with
sharp noise; cause to make a sharp noise, as
of whip, rifle, *etc.* - *v.i.* make a sharp noise;
split; of the voice, lose clearness when changing from -boy's to man's. *n.* sharp explosive
noise; split, fissure; flaw. -(*sl.*) sharp witty
retort, wisecrack. -*a.* special, smart, of great
reputation for skill or fashion. **-crack'er** *n.*
explosive firework; a thin dry cake. [OE.
cracian; of imit.orig.]
cra'dle *n.* infant's bed on rockers; *fig.* earliest
resting-place or home; supporting
framework. - *v.t.* lay in, or hold as in, a cradle;
cherish in early stages. [OE. *cradol*]
craft *n.* skill, cunning; manual art; skilled
trade; members of a trade. **-crafts'man** *n.* -
crafts'manship *n.* **-craf'ty** *a.* cunning. -
craf'tily *adv.* [OE. *cræft*]
craft *n.* vessel of any kind for carriage by
water or air; ship; ships collectively. [fr. small
craft for vessels of small craft, power]
crag *n.* steep rugged rock. **-cragg'y** *a.* -
crags'man *n.* rock-climber. [*Celt.*]
cram *v.t.* fill quite full; stuff, force; pack tightly; feed to excess; prepare quickly for examination. **-n.** close-packed state; rapid
preparation for examination; information so
got; (*sl.*) lie. [OE. *crammian*, fr. *crimman*,
insert]
cramp' *n.* painful muscular contraction;
clamp for holding masonry, timber, *etc.*,
together. - *v.t.* hem in, keep within too narrow
limits. [OF. *crampe*]
cranberry *n.* red berry of a dwarf shrub.
[Ger. *kranbeere*, crane berry]
crane *n.* large wading bird with long legs,
neck and bill; machine for moving heavy
weights. **-v.i.** stretch the neck for better seeing.
[OE. *cran*]
cra'nium *n.* skull **-cra'nial** *a.* [Low L. G.
kranion, skull]
crank *n.* arm at right angles to an axis, for
turning a main shaft, changing reciprocal into
rotary motion, *etc.*; fanciful turn of speech;
fad; faddist. - *v.t.* and *i.* turn, wind. **-crank'y**
a. shaky; crotchety. [OE. *crane*]
crann'y *n.* small opening, chink. **-crann'ied**
a. [F. *cran*, notch]
crap(s) *n.* gambling game played with 2 dice.
[orig. unknown]
crape *n.* gauzy wrinkled fabric, usually of
black silk for mourning. [F. *crépe*, fr. L. *crispa*,
curly]
crash *n.* violent fall or impact with loud noise;
burst of mixed loud sound, *e.g.* of thunder,
breaking crockery; sudden collapse or
downfall. **-v.i.** make a crash: fall, come with,
strike with, a crash; collapse; of an airplane,
come to earth by, or with, an accident. [imit.
origin]
crash *n.* coarse linen for towels. [Russ.
krashenina, colored linen]

crass a. grossly stupid; gross. [L. *crassus*, thick, fat]

crate n. open-work case of wooden bars or wicker. [Du. *krat*, basket]

cra'ter n. mouth of a volcano; bow-shaped cavity, esp. one made by the explosion of a large shell, a mine, etc. [G. *krater*, mixingbowl]

cravat n. neckcloth; necktie; ascot. [F. *cravate*, Croatian (scarf); fr. the scarf worn by *Croats* in Thirty Years' War]

crave v.t. and i. have a very strong desire for, long for; ask. -**cra'ving** n. [OE. *crafi, an*, demand as a right]

cra'ven a. cowardly, abject. -n. coward. [OF. *craventer*, overthrow]

craw'fish, cray'fish n. crustacean like a small lobster. [corrupt. of ME. *crevesse*, F. *crevisse*]

crawl v.i. move along the ground on the belly or on the hands and knees; move very slowly; move stealthily or abjectly; swim with the crawl-stroke. -n. crawling motion; very slow walk; racing stroke at swimming. -**crawl'er** n. [ON. *krafla*, claw]

cray'on n. stick or pencil of colored chalk; picture made with crayons. [F.*crayon*, pencil, fr. *craie*, chalk]

cra'zy a. rickety, falling to pieces; full of cracks; insane, extremely foolish; madly eager (for). -**craze** v.t. make crazy. -n. general or individual mania. [F. *craser*, break]

cream n. oily part of milk; best part of anything. - v.i. form cream. -v.t. take cream from; take the best part from. -**cream'y** a. - **cream'ery** n. butter and cheese factory; shop for milk and cream. [L.*chrisma*, fr. G. *chrism*, anoint]

crease n. line made by folding; wrinkle- v.t. and i. make, develop, creases. [L.*crista*, ridge]

create v.t. bring into being; give rise to; make. -**crea'tion** n. -**creative** a. -**crea'tor** n. -**crea'ture** n. anything created; living being; dependent, tool. [L. *create*]

crèche (kresh, krash) n. public nursery for babies and young children. [F.]

cre'dence n. belief, credit; side-table for the elements of the Eucharist before consecration. -**creden'tials**n.pl.letters of introduction, esp.those given to an ambassador. [L.*credere*, believe]

cred'it n. belief, trust; good name; influence or honor or power based on the trust of others; trust in another's ability to pay; allowing customers to take goods for later payment; money at one's disposal in a bank, etc.; side of a book on which such sums are entered, - v.t. believe; put on the credit side of an account; attribute, believe that a person has. -**cred'ible** a. worthy of belief. -**cred'ibly** adv. -**credibil'ity** n. - **cred'itable** a. bringing honor. -**cred'itably** adv. -**cred'itor** n. one to whom a debt is due. -**credit'worthy** a. (of an individual or business enterprise) adjudged as meriting credit on the basis of such factors as earning power previous record of debt repayment, etc. - **cred'ulous**a. too ready to believe. -**credu'lity** n. [L. *credere*, believe]

creed n. a system of religious belief; summary of Christian doctrine; system of beliefs, opinions, principles, etc. [L. *credo*, I believe]

creek n. narrow inlet on the sea-coast. [ON. *kriki*, bend, nook]

creel n. basket, esp. angler's fishhawker's basket.[origin uncertain. cp. OF.*creil*, hurdle; *crates*, wickerwork]

creep v.i. make way along the ground, as a snake; move with stealthy, slow movements; go about abjectly; of skin or flesh, to feel a shrinking, shivering sensation, due to fear or repugnance. **creep'er** n. creeping or climbing plant. -**creep'y** a. uncanny, unpleasant; causing the flesh to creep. [OE. *creopan*]

cremation n. burning as a means of disposing of corpses; this process. -**cremate** v.t. -**crem'atory, cremator'ium** n. place for cremation. [L. *cremare*, burn]

crerno'na n. superior type of violin. [*Cremona*, Italy]

Cre'ole n. native of the West Indies or Sp. America descended from European ancestors; a person descended from French or Spanish ancestors settled in the U.S. Gulf states; languages associated with these cultures. [F. *croole*]

crèpe n. fabric with a crimped surface; a light, thin pancake. **crèp'erie** n. eating establishment that specializes in making pancakes; pancake house. [*See* crepe]

crescendo (-sh-) a., adv. and n. increase of loudness. [L. *crescere*, grow]

cres'cent n. moon as seen on the first or last quarter; any figure of this shape; row of houses on a curve. -a. growing, increasing. [L. *crescere*, grow]

crest n. comb or tuft on an animal's head; plume or top of a helmet; top of mountain, ridge, wave, etc.; badge above the shield of a coat of arms, also used separately on seals, plate, etc. - v.i. crown. -v.t. reach the top of. -**crest'fallen** a. cast down by defeat or failure. [L. *crest*]

cretaceous (-shus) a. chalky; (geol.) of the upper Mesozoic rocks. [L. *creta*, chalk]

cret'in n. deformed idiot. -**cret'inism** n. -**cret'inous** a. [Swiss *crestin*, Christ ian]

crev'ice (-is) n. cleft, fissure. -**crevasse'** n. deep open chasm in a glacier. [F. *crevasse*]

crew n. ship's or boat's company, excluding passengers; gang or set. **fearlier crue**, accrue, reinforcement. [fr. L. *crescere*, grow]

crew'el n. woolen embroidery yarn. [orig. uncertain]

crew neck n. rounded, close-fitting neckline on a sweater, shirt, or other top.

crib n. barred rack for fodder; child's bed usu. with high or with barred sides; cards thrown out at cribbage; a plagiarism; a translation. -v.t. confine in small space; copy unfairly. -**cribb'age**n. card game. [OE. *cribb*, ox-stall]

crick n. spasm or cramp, esp. in the neck. [orig. uncertain]

crick'et n. chirping insect. [F. *criquet*, fr. *cri-quer*,creak, crackle]

crick'et n. open-air game played with bats, ball, and wickets. -**crick'eter** n. -**crick'et-**

match n. [orig. uncertain]

crime n. violation of the law (usually of a serious offense): wicked or forbidden act; (military) offence against regulations. -v.t. charge (in army) with an offence against the regulations. -crim′inal a. and n. -crim′inally adv. -criminal′ity n. -criminol′ogy n. study of crime and criminals. [L. crimen]

crimp v.t. pinch with tiny parallel pleats. [Du. krimpen]

crim′son (-z-) a. of rich deep red. -n. the color. -v.t. and i. turn crimson. [O. Sp. cremesin, fr. Arab. qirmiz, kermes, cochineal insect]

cringe v.i. shrink, cower; behave obsequiously. [ME. crengen, succumb]

crin′kle v.t. wrinkle, make a series of bends, windings or twists in a line or surface. -v.i. wrinkle. -n. wrinkle, winding. -crin′kly a. [OE. crincan]

crinoline (-len) n. hooped petticoat. [orig. a stiff fabric of thread and horsehair. [F., fr. crin, horsehair, and lin, flax]

cripp′le n. one not having a normal use of the limbs, a disabled or deformed person. -v.t. maim or disable; diminish the resources of. [OE. crypel]

cri′sis n. turning point or decisive moment, esp. in illness; time of acute danger or suspense. [G. krisis, decision]

crisp a. brittle, but of firm consistence; brisk, decided; clear-cut; crackling; of hair, curly. [L. crispus, curled]

criterion (kri-) n. -(crite′ria pl). standard of judgment; standard; rule. [G.]

crit′ic n. one who passes judgment; writer expert in judging works of literature, art, etc. -crit′ical a. skilled in, or given to, judging; fault-finding; of great importance, decisive. -crit′icism n. -crit′ically adv. -crit′icize v.t. -critique′ n. critical essay, carefully written criticism. [G. kritikos, krinein, judge]

croak v.t. utter a deep hoarse cry, as a raven, frog; talk dismally. -n. such cry. -croak′er n. [imit. origin]

cro′chet (-she) n. kind of knitting done with a hooked needle. -v.t. and i. do such work. [F. dim. of croc, hook]

crock n. earthenware jar or pot; broken piece of earthenware; old broken-down horse. -(sl.) broken-down or unfit person. -crock′ery n. earthenware. [OE. crocc, pot]

croc′odile (krok′-) n. large amphibious reptile. -croc′odile-tears, hypocritical pretense of grief, the crocodile being fabled to shed tears while devouring human victims. [G. krokodeilos, lizard]

cro′cus n. small bulbous plant with yellow, white or purple flowers. [G. krokos]

Croe′sus n. very wealthy man. [Crœsus, king of Lydia]

croft n. small farm; small-holding, esp. in Scotland. -crof′ter n. [OE.]

crone n. withered old woman. [perh. fr. Ir. crion, withered]

cro′ny n. intimate friend [earlier chrony, contemporary. [G. chronos, time]

crook n. hooked staff, any hook, bend, sharp turn; (sl.) cheat; criminal. -v.t. bend into a hook or curve. -crook′ed a. bent, twisted; deformed; dishonest. [ON. krokr]

croon v.t. sing in an undertone; hum. -croo′ner n. entertainer who croons sentimental songs. [cp. Du. kreunen, groan]

crop n. year's produce of cultivation of any plant or plants, in a farm, field, country, etc.; harvest, lit. or lig.; pouch in a birds′ gullet; stock of a whip; hunting whip; cutting of the hair short, closely-cut head of hair. -v.t. and i. poll or clip; bite or eat down; raise produce or occupy land with it. [OE. cropp, head of herb, ear of corn, etc.]

cro′quet n. lawn game played with balls, mallets and hoops. [Breton dial. croquet, ident. with crochet (q.v.)]

croquette′ n. meat or fish ball, cake; rissole. [F.]

cross n. stake with a transverse bar, used for crucifixion. -the Cross, that on which Christ suffered; model or picture of this; symbol of the Christian faith; affliction; intermixture of breeds, hybrid. -v.t. place so as to intersect; make the sign of the cross on or over; pass across, over; meet and pass; mark with lines across, thwart, oppose; modify breed of animals or plants by intermixture. - v.i. intersect, pass over. -a. transverse; intersecting; contrary; adverse; out of temper. -cross′bow n. bow fixed across a wooden shoulder-stock. -cross′coun′try a. across fields or land. cross′eyed a. squinting. -cross-exam′ine v.t. examine a witness already examined by the other side. -cross′-word puzzle n. puzzle built up of intersecting words, of which some letters are common to two or more words, the words being indicated by clues. [L. crux]

crotch′et n. musical note, fad. -crotch′ety a. bad-tempered. [F. crochet, little hook]

crouch v.i. bend low for hiding, or to spring, or servilely. [orig. uncertain]

croup n. throat disease of children. [Sc. orig. a verb, croak]

croup n. hindquarters of a horse. [F. croupe]

croupier n. raker-in of the money on a gaming-table; vice-chairman of a dinner. [F. orig. one who rode on the croupe, behind another]

crow n. large black carrion-eating bird. [OE. crawe, imit. of cry]

crow, crow′bar n. iron bar, usually beaked at one end, for levering. [OF. cros, pl. of croc, crook]

crow (-ō) v.i. utter the cock's cry; utter joyful sounds; exult. -n. cry of the cock. [OE. crawan]

crowd v.i. flock together. -v.t. cram, force, thrust, pack; fill with people. -crowd out, exclude by excess already in. -n. throng, large number, mass. [OE. criudan, press, push]

crown n. monarch's headdress; wreath for the head; royal power; formerly, British coin of five shillings; various foreign coins; top of the head; summit or topmost part; completion or perfection of anything. -crown′-jew′els, jewels of regalia. - v.t. put a crown on. [L. corona]

CRT *n.* (*compute.*) output device the converts electric signals into visual form by beans of a controlled electron beam; computer screen. [cathode ray *tube*]

cru'cial *a.* decisive, critical. [fr. L. *crux*, cross, in the sense of fingerpost at cross-roads, decision-point]

cru'cify *v.t.* put to death on a cross. -**crucifix'ion** *n.* **cru'cifix** *n.* image of Christ on the cross. [L. *cruci figere* (*p.p. fixus*) fix on a cross]

crude *a.* in the natural or raw state; rough, unfinished, rude. -**crude'ly** *adv.* -**cru'dity** *n.* [L. *crudus*, raw]

cru'el *a.* delight in or callous to others' pain; merciless. -**cru'elty** *n.* -**cruelly** *adv.* [F. *cruel*, L. *crudetis*]

cru'et *n.* small stoppered bottle for vinegar, oil, *etc.*; stand holding such bottles, mustard-pots, *etc.* [OF. *cruie*, pot, F. *cruche*, jar]

cruise (-ooz) *v.i.* sail about without precise destination. -*n.* cruising voyage. -**cruise control** *n.* device that maintains the speed of a vehicle at a setting chosen by the driver. -**cruis'er** *n.* warship of less displacement and greater speed than a battleship. [Du. *kruisen*, fr. *kruis*, cross]

crumb *n.* small particle, fragment; soft part of bread. -*v.t.* reduce to, or cover with crumbs. -**crum'ble** *v.t.* and *i.* break into small fragments; decay. [OE. *cruma*]

crum'pet *n.* flat soft batter-cake, eaten with much butter. [fr. obs. *crump*, curl up]

crum'ple *v.t.* and *i.* make or become crushed, wrinkled, creased. **crum'pled** *a.* crushed, creased; bent, curled. [fr. obs. *crump*, curl up]

crunch *n.* sound made by chewing crisp food, treading on gravel, hard snow, *etc.* -*v.t.* and *i.* chew, tread, *etc.* with this sound. [earlier *craunch*, perhaps imit.]

crusad'e *n.* medieval Christian war to recover the Holy Land; campaign against evil. -*v.i.* engage in a crusade. -**crusa'der** *n.* [F. *croisade*, and Sp. *cruzada*, marked with a cross]

crush *v.t.* compress so as to break, bruise, crumple; break to small pieces; defeat utterly, overthrown. act of crushing; crowded mass of persons, *etc.* [OF. *cruissir*]

crust *n.* hard outer part of bread; similar hard outer casing on anything. - *v.t.* and *i.* cover with or form a crust. -**crust'y** *a.* having or like a crust, short-tempered. -**crust'ily** *adv.* [L. *crusta*, rind]

crustacean (-shn) *n.* hard-shelled animal, *e.g.* crab, lobster shrimp. -**crusta'ceous** (-shus) *a.* [L. *crusta*, rind]

crutch *n.* staff with a cross-piece to go under the armpit for the use of cripples; forked support. [OE. *crycc*]

crux (kruks) *n.* the most important point; (*fig.*) a cause of extreme difficulty or perplexity. [L. *crux, crucis*, a cross]

cry *v.i.* utter a call; shout; weep, wail. -*v.t.* utter loudly, proclaim. -*n.* loud utterance; scream, wail, shout; the characteristic call of an animal; watch-word; fit of weeping. [F. *crier*]

cryonics *n.* preservation of a dead body by deep-freezing.

crypt *n.* vault, *esp.* under a church. -**cryp'tic** *a.* secret, mysterious. -**cryp'togram** *n.* piece of cipher-writing. [G. *krypte*, vault; *cryptein*, hide]

crys'tal *n.* clear transparent mineral; very clear glass; cut-glass vessels; form assumed by many substances with a defi nite internal structure and external shape of symmetrically arranged plane surfaces. -**crys'tal-set**, wireless set in which a small crystal rectifies current. -**crystalline** *a.* -**crys'tal** *v.t.* and form into crystals; become definite. [G. *krystallos*, clear ice]

cte'noid *a.* comb-shaped, as the fins of some fishes. [G. *kteis, ktenos*, comb, *eidos*, form]

cub *n.* young of the fox and other animals; junior Boy Scout. -*v.t.* and *i.* bring forth (cubs). [perh. fr. Ir. *cuib*, whelp]

cube (kfi-) *n.* regular solid figure contained by six equal squares; cube multiplying a number by itself twice. -*v.t.* multiply thus. -**cu'bic** *a.* three-dimensional; of the third power. -**cu'bical** *a.* cube-shaped. -**cu'bism** *n.* style of art in which objects are presented to give the appearance of an assemblage of geometrical shapes. -**cu'bist** *n.* (G. *kybos*, a die]

cu'bicle *n.* small separate sleeping compartment in a dormitory. [L. *cubare*, lie]

cu'bit *n.* an old measure of length, about 18 inches. [L. *cubitus*, forearm, from elbow to finger-tips]

cuck'old *n.* husband of unfaithful wife. [OF. *eucu*, cuckoo)

cu'ckoo *n.* migratory bird named from its call. -**cuck'oo-clock**, clock chiming hours with cuckoo-call. [imit. orig.]

cu'cumber *n.* creeping plant with long fleshy green fruit, usually eaten as salad; the fruit. [L. *eucumis*]

cud *n.* food which a ruminant (*e.g.* cow) brings back into its mouth to chew. [OE. *cudu*]

cud'dle *v.t.* hug. -*v.i.* lie close and snug, nestle. [orig. uncertain]

cue *n.* pigtail; long tapering stick used by a billiard player. -**cue'ist** *n.* [F. *queue*, tail]

cue *n.* last words of an actor's speech as signal to another to act or speak; hint or example for action. [earlier 'q.,' for L. *quando*, when (to come in)]

cuff *n.* ending of a sleeve; wristband. [ME. *cuffe*]

cuff *v.t.* strike with the hand. -*n.* blow with the hand. [F. *coiffer*]

cuisine' *n.* cookery; kitchen department. [F.]

cul-de-sac *n.* street closed at one end; blind alley. [F.]

culinary *a.* of, or for, cooking. [L. *culinarius*, fr. *culina*, kitchen]

cull *v.t.* gather, select. [L. *colligere*, collect]

culminate *v.i.* reach the highest point; come to a climax. -**culmina'tion** *n.* [L. *culmen*, summit]

culpable *a.* blameworthy. -**culpabil' ity** *n.* -**cul'pably** *adv.* [L. *culpa*, fault]

cul'prit *n.* offender, one guilty of an offense; (*law*) prisoner about to be tried. [fr. OF. *cul. prest*, contr. of *culpable prest*, ready (to be

cult

58

curve

proved) guilty]

cult *n.* system of religious worship; pursuit of, or devotion to, some object. [L. *cultus*, fr. *colere*, cultivate]

cultivate *v.t.* raise (*crops*) on land; develop, improve, refine; devote attention to, practice, frequent. [L. *cultura*]

culture *n.* cultivation; state of manners, taste, and intellectual development at a time or place. **cul'tured pearl**, artificially grown real pearl. **-cul'tured** *a.* refined, showing culture. **-cul'tural** *a.* [Late L. *cultivate*, fr. *colere*, till]

culvert *n.* tunneled drain for the passage of water, under a road, *etc.* [orig. unknown]

cum'in *n.* eastern plant with seeds like caraway. [Heb. *kammon*]

cummerbund *n.* broad sash worn round waist. [Pers. *kamarband*, loin-band]

cumulative (-iv) *a.* representing the sum of items added by degrees; of shares, entitled to arrears of interest before other shares receive current interest. [L. *cumulus*, heap]

cu'mulus *n.* cloud shaped in rounded white masses. **-cu'muli** *pl.* [L. *cumulus*, heap]

cunn'ing *n.* skill, dexterity; selfish cleverness; skill in deceit or evasion; *-a.* having such qualities, crafty, sly. **-cunn'ingly** *adv.* [OE. *cunnan*, know]

cup *n.* small drinking vessel of china or earthenware with a handle at one side; any small drinking vessel; contents of a cup; various cup-shaped formations; cavities, sockets, *etc.* **-cup'board** *n.* closed cabinet, recess, or case with shelves, *esp.* one for crockery or provisions. [OE. *cuppe*; a cupboard was originally a table or sideboard]

Cu'pid *n.* Roman god of love. [L.]

cupidity *n.* greed of gain. [L. *cupere*, desire]

cu'pola *n.* dome; armored gunturret. [It. fr. L. *cupa*, cask]

cura're, cura'ri *n.* arrow poison of S. American Indians. **-cura'rine** *n.* poisonous alkaloid of curare. [*native*]

cur'ate *n.* clergyman who is a parish priest's appointed assistant. **-cur'acy** *n.* fone with a cure of souls. [fr. L. *cura*, care]

curator *n.* person in charge of something, *esp.* a museum, library, *etc.* **-cura'torship** *n.* [L. fr. *curare*, care]

curb *n.* chain or strap passing under a horse's lower jaw and giving powerful control with reins; any check or means of restraint; stone edging to a footpath or sidewalk. *-v.t.* apply a curb to (a horse); restrain. **-curb'stone** *n.* [F. *courber*, fr. L. *curvare*, bend]

curd *n.* coagulated milk. **-curd'le** *v.t.* and *i.* turn into curd, coagulate; of blood, to shrink with horror, *etc.* **-curd'y** *a.* (ME. *crudde*, prob. fr. OE. *crudan*, press]

cure *v.t.* heal, restore to health; remedy; preserve (fish, skins, *etc.*). *-n.* remedy; course of medical treatment; successful treatment, restoration to health. cure of souls, care of a parish or congregation. [L. *curate*, fr. *cura*, care]

cur'few *n.* ringing of a bell at a fixed evening hour, orig. as a signal to put out fires, now, under martial law, to mark the time for everyone to be indoors. [F. *couvrefew*, cover fire]

cu'rious *a.* eager to know, inquisitive; prying; puzzling, strange, odd; minutely accurate. **cu'riously** *adv.* **-curios'ity** *n.* eagerness to know; inquisitiveness; strange or rare thing. **-cu'rio** *n.* curiosity of the kind sought for collections. [L. *curiosus*, inquisitive caring for, fr. *cura*, care]

cu'rium *n.* radioactive inert gaseous element. [Marie and Pierre *Curie*]

curl *v.t.* bend into spiral or curved shape. *-v.i.* take spiral or curved shape or path. *-n.* spiral lock of hair; spiral or curved state or form or motion. **-cur'ly** *a.* **-curl'ing** *n.* game like bowls played with large rounded stones on ice. [ME. *crul*, curly]

curmudgeon (-jn) *n.* miser or churlish fellow. [orig. unknown]

curr'ant *n.* dried fruit of a Levantine grape; fruit of various plants allied to the gooseberry; plants. [orig. F. *raisins de Coraunte*, Corinth]

curr'ent *a.* in circulation or general use; going on, not yet superseded; fluent, running. *-n.* body of water or air in motion; flow of a river, *etc.*; tendency, drift, transmission of electricity through a conductor. **-curr'ently** *adv.* **-curr'ency** *n.* time during which anything is current; money in use; state of being in use. [L. *currere*, run]

curriculum *n.* (**curricula** *pl.*) course of study at school, college *etc.* [L., fr. *currere*, run]

curr'y *v.t.* rub down (a horse) with a comb; dress (leather); **-curry favor**, originally to *curry 'favel'*, 'the fawn-colored horse', a type of hypocrisy in an old allegory, hence to try to win favor unworthily, to ingratiate oneself. **-curr'ier** *n.* leather dresser. [OF. *correer*, prepare, fr. root of *ready*; for *favel*. See *fallow*]

curr'y *n.* preparation of a mixture of spices; dish flavored with it. *-v.t.* prepare a dish with curry. [Tamil *kari*, relish]

curse *n.* utterance intended to send a person or thing to destruction or punishment; expletive in the form of a curse; affliction, bane, scourge. *- v.t.* and *i.* utter a curse, swear at, afflict [OE. *curs*]

curs'ive *a.* written in running script. *-* curs'ory *a.* rapid, hasty, without attention to details. **-curs'orily** *adv.* [L. *cursivus*, fr. *currere*, run]

cursor *n.* (*compute.*) flashing pointer on CRT that can be moved by keys or mouse.

curt *a.* short, brief, rudely brief. **curt'ness** *n.* **-curt'ly** *adv.* [L. *curtus*, short]

curtail *v.t.* cut short, diminish. *-* curtail'ment *n.* [L. *curtus*, short]

cur'tain (-tin) *n.* cloth hung as a screen; screen separating audience and stage in a theater; end to an act or scene. *-v.t.* provide or cover with a curtain. **-curt'ain-fire** *n.* barrage. **-curt'ain raiser** *n.* short play coming before the main one. [Late L. *cortina*]

curt'sy *n.* woman's bow or respectful gesture made by bending the knees and lowering the body. [var. of *courtesy*]

curve *n.* line of which no part is straight, bent

line. -*v.t.* bend into a curve. -*v.i.* have or assume a curved form or direction. -**cury'ature** *n.* a bending; a bent shape. -**curvet'** *n.* horse's trained movement like a short leap over nothing. -*v.i.* to make this movement; frisk. -**curvilin'ear** *a.* of bent lines. [L, *curvus*, bent, *curvare*, bend]

cu'shion (koo'shn) *n.* bag filled with soft stuffing or air, to support or ease the body; pad, elastic lining of the sides of a billiard table. -*v.t.* provide or protect with a cushion. [F. *coussin*]

cusp *n.* point; horn of the moon; crown of a tooth; the meeting-point of two intersecting curves; the point of change; small architectural ornament. [L. *cuspis*, point]

cus'pidor *n.* spittoon. [*Port.*]

cuss *v.t.* and *i.* (*sl.*) curse, swear. -**cuss'ed** *a.* -**cuss'edness** *n.* contrariness. [*curse*]

cuss *n.* (*sl.*) fellow; creature. [*customer*]

cus'tard *n.* preparation of eggs and milk, flavored and cooked. [ME. *cruslade*, pie with a crust]

cus'tody *n.* safe-keeping, guardianship, imprisonment. -**custo'dian** *n.* keeper, caretaker, curator. [L. *custodial* fr. *custos*, keeper]

cus'tom *n.* fashion, usage, habit; busi ness patronage; *pl.* duties levied on imports. -**cus'tomary** *a.* -**cus'tomarily** *adv.* -**cus'tomer** *n.* one who enters a shop to buy, *esp.* one who deals regularly with it. -**cus'tomize** *v.t.* to build or alter to particular specifications. [OF. *coustume*, fr. L. *consuetudo*]

cut *v.t.* sever or penetrate or wound or divide or separate with pressure of an edge or edged instrument; pare or detach or trim or shape by cutting; divide; intersect; reduce, abridge; ignore (a person); strike (with a whip, *etc.*) -*n.* act of cutting; stroke, blow (of knife, whip, *etc.*); fashion, shape; incision; engraving; piece cut off, division. -**cutting edge** *n.* lead or forefront of a field; state-of-the-art. [orig. uncertain]

cutaneous *a.* of the skin. -**cu'ticle** *n.* outer skin. [L. *cutis*, skin]

cute *a.* (*sl.*) shrewd; cunning; engaging, attractive. [*acute*]

cut'las, cut'lass *n.* sailor's short, broad sword. [OF. *coutelas*, fr. *coutel*, knife]

cut'ler *n.* one who makes, repairs or deals in knives and cutting implements. -**cut'lery** *n.* knives, scissors. [OF. *coutelier*, fr. *coutel*, knife]

cut'let *n.* small piece of meat broiled or fried. [F. *cotelette*, double dim. of *cote*, rib, L. *costa*]

cyan'ogen *n.* poisonous gas, compound of carbon and nitrogen. -**cy'anide** *n.* compound of cyanogen. -**cyano'sis** *n.* blue jaundice. [G. *kyanos*, dark blue]

cy'cle (si'-) *n.* recurrent series or period; rotation of events; complete series or period; development following a course of stages; series of poems, etc.; bicycle. -*v.i.* move in cycles; use a bicycle. -**cy'clic, cy'clical** *a.* -**cy'clist** *n.* bicycle-rider. **cyclom'eter** *n.* instrument for measuring circles or recording distance travelled by a wheel, *esp.* of a bicycle.

[G. *kyklos*, circle]

cy'clone *n.* a system of winds moving round a center of low pressure; a circular storm. -**cyclon'ic** *a.* [G. *kyklos*, circle]

cy'clops *n.* mythical race of one-eyed giants. -**cyclope'an** *a.* gigantic. [G.]

cyg'net (sig'-) *n.* young swan. [dim. of F. *cygn*, swan]

cyl'inder (sil'-) *n.* roller-shaped solid or hollow body, of uniform diameter; piston chamber of an engine. -**cylin'drical** *a.* [G. *kylindein*, roll]

cym'bal (sim'-) *n.* one of a pair of cymbals. -*pl.* musical instrument consisting of two round brass plates struck together to produce a ringing or clashing sound. [G. *kymbalon*]

cyn'ic (sin'-) *n.* one of a sect of Greek philosophers affecting contempt of luxury and bluntness of speech; cynical person. -**cyn'ical** *a.* skeptical of or sneering at goodness; given to showing up human weakness, seeing the more unworthy motive in others; shameless in showing or admitting motives more commonly concealed. -**cyn'icism** *n.* [G. *kynikos*, doglike]

cy'press *n.* coniferous tree with very dark foliage; its wood; its foliage as a symbol of mourning. [L. *cupressus*]

cyst (si-) *n.* bladder or sac containing morbid matter. [G. *kystis*, bladder]

cytochemistry *n.* study of the chemical composition of cells.

Czar, Tzar, Tsar (zar) *n.* emperor or king *esp.* of Russia 1547-1917, or of Bulgaria in the Middle Ages and after 1908. -**Czari'na, Czarit'sa, Tsari'na, Tzarit'sa** *n. fem.*, the wife of a Russian Czar. [L. *Cæsar*]

Czech' (check) *n.* member, language of western branch of Slavs. [*Polish*]

D

dab *v.t.* strike feebly; apply with momentary pressure, *esp.* anything wet and soft. -*n.* slight blow or tap; smear; small flat roundish mass; small flat fish. [orig. uncertain]

dab'ble *v.i* splash about; be a desultory student or amateur (in). -**dab'bler** *n.* [obs. Du. *dabbelen*]

dace *n.* freshwater fish. [ME. *darce*]

dachshund *n.* short-legged long-bodied dog. [Ger. = badgerhound]

dac'tyl *n.* (*pros.*) foot of three syllables, long-short-short. [L. *dactylus*, finger]

dad, daddy *n.* child's name for father. **daddy-long-legs** *n.* insect or spider with long, ungainly legs, *esp.* the crane-fly or harvestman. [child's speech]

da'do *n.* lower part of a room wall when lined or painted separately. [It.]

daff'odil *n.* a yellow narcissus. [for earlier *affodil*, F. *aspodéle*]

daft *a.* foolish, crazy; fey; feeble-minded. [OE. *gedoefte*, meek, gentle]

dagg'er *n.* short, edged, stabbing weapon. [Med. L. *daggarius*]

dahl'ia (dal'-) *n.* garden plant with large, handsome flowers. [Dahl, Sw. botanist]

dail'y *a.* done, occurring, published, *etc.*, every day. -*adv.* every day, constantly. *n.* daily newspaper. [*day*]

dain'ty *n.* choice morsel, delicacy. -*a.* choice, delicate; pretty and neat; hard to please, fastidious. [OF. *deintie*, fr. L. *dignitas*, worthiness]

dair'y (daré-) *n.* place for dealing with milk and its products. [ME. *dey*, a woman, servant]

da'is (da-is) *n.* low platform, usually at one end of a hall. [F. fr. L. *discus*, table]

dais'y (-z-) *n.* small wild flower with yellow center and white petals. [OE. *dæges eage*, day's eye]

dais'ywheel *n.* a component of a computer printer in the shape of a wheel with many spokes that prints characters using a disk with characters around the circumference as the print element. [*daisy* and *wheel*]

Dalai' Lam'a head of Buddhist priesthood of Tibet. [Mongol. *datai*, ocean, *lama*, highpriest]

dale *n.* valley. [OE. *dxl*]

dall'y *v.i.* spend time in idleness or amusement or love-making; loiter. -**dall'iance** *n.* [OF. *dallier*, chaft]

dam *n.* mother, usually of animals. [var. of *dame*]

dam *n.* barrier to hold back a flow of waters. -*v.t.* supply, or hold with a dam. [Du.]

dam'age *n.* injury, harm -*pl.* sum claimed or adjudged in compensation for harm or injury. -*v.t.* do harm to, injure. [L. *damnum*, hurt, loss]

dam'ask *n.* figured woven material of silk or linen, *esp.* white table linen with design shown up by the light; color of the damask-rose, a velvety red. *a.* made of damask; colored like damask-rose. -*v.t.* weave with figured designs. [*Damascus*]

dame *n.* noble lady. [F., fr. L. *domina, fem.* of *dominus*, lord]

damn (-in) *v.t.* condemn to hell; be the ruin of, give a hostile reception to. -*v.i.* curse. -*interj.* expression of annoyance, impatience, *etc.* **dam'nable** *a.* deserving damnation, hateful, annoying. -**damna'tion**, *n.* -**dam'natory** *a.* [L. *damnare*, condemn to a penalty]

damp *a.* moist; slightly moist. -*n.* diffused moisture; in coal-mines, a dangerous gas. -*v.t.* make damp; deaden, discourage. -**damp'er** *n.* anything that discourages or depresses; silencing-pad in a piano; plate in a flue to control draught. [Du. *damp*, steam]

dam'sel (-z-) *n.* girl. [Fr. *demoiselle*, dim. of *dame*]

dance (-a-) *v.i.* move with rhythmic steps, leaps, gestures, *etc.*, usually to music; be in lively movement, bob up and down. *v.t.* perform (a dance); cause to dance. *n.* rhythmical movement; arrangement of such movements; tune for them; dancing party. -**dan'cer** *n.* [F. *danser*]

dandeîion *n.* yellow-flowered wild plant. [F. *dent de lion*, lion's tooth, from the edge of the leaf]

dand'ruff *n.* dead skin in small scales among the hair. [ON, *hrufa*, scab]

dan'dy *n.* a man who pays undue attention to dress; fashion; fop. [orig. uncertain]

dan'ger (dan'-j-) *n.* liability or exposure to injury or harm; risk, peril; originally meaning, subjection. -**dan'gerous** *a.* -**dan'gerously** *adv,* [F. fr. L. *dominium*, rule]

dan'gle (dang'gl) *v.t.* and *i.* hang loosely and swaying. [related to ding]

dank *a.* oozy, unwholesomely damp. [orig. uncertain]

dapp'er *a.* neat and precise, *esp.* in dress. [Du. *dapper*, brave, sprightly]

dapp'le *v.t.* and *i.* mark with rounded spots. -**dap'ple-gray'** *a.* gray marked with darker spots. [v. fr. *dapple-grey* for apple -grey]

dare *v.t.* venture, have the courage (to); defy. **dar'ing** *a.* bold. -*n.* adventurous courage. **dare'devil** *a.* reckless. -*n.* reckless person. [OE. *dearr*]

dark *a.* having little or no light; gloomy; deep in tint; dim, secret, mysterious, unenlightened; wicked. -*n.* absence of light or color or knowledge. [OE. *deorc*]

darling *n.* one much loved or very lovable. -*v.* beloved or prized. [OE. *deorling*, dim. of *dear*]

darn *v.t.* mend by filling (hole, *etc.*) with interwoven yarn. -*n.* place so mended. -**darn'ing** *n.* [orig. uncertain]

dart *n.* light javelin or other pointed missile; darting motion. -*pl.* indoor game, throwing darts at target. -*v.t.* cast, throw rapidly (a dart, glance, *etc.*). -*v.i.* go rapidly or abruptly, like a missile. [F. *dard*]

Darwin'ian *a.* of, pert. to Darwin and his theory of evolution. [Charles Darwin]

dash *v.t.* smash, throw, thrust, send with violence; cast down; tinge, flavor. -*v.i.* move or go with great speed or violence. *n.* rush, onset; vigor; smartness; small quantity, tinge; stroke (-) between words. -**dash'ing** *a.* spirited, showy. [prob. imit. orig.]

data *See* **datum.**

date *n.* stone-fruit of a date palm. IG. *daktylos*, finger]

date *n.* statement on a document of its time, or time and place of writing, time of an occurrence; period of a work of art, *etc.*; season, time; appointment. -*v.t.* mark with a date; refer to a date; court. -*v.i.* exist (from); betray time or period of origin. [L. *data.* given]

da'tum *n.*, **da'ta** *pl.* thing given, known, or assumed as the basis for a reckoning, reasoning, *etc.* -*n. pl.* collection of information, statistics *etc.* on a given subject. -**da'ta base** *n.* a systematized collection of data that can be accessed immediately and manipulated by a data-processing system for a specific purpose. **da'ta pro'cessing** *n.* the process of converting information into a form that can be machine-read so that it can be stored, used and updated by a computer. [L.]

daub *v.t.* coat, plaster, paint roughly. *n.* smear; rough picture. [F. *dauber*, fr. L. *dealbare*, plaster, fr. *albus*, white]

daught'er (dawt'-) *n.* female child, female descendant. -**daught'er-in-law** *n.* wife of a son. -**daught'erly** *a.* [OE. *dohtor*]

daunt *v.t.* frighten, *esp.* into giving up a purpose. -daunt'less *a.* not to be daunted. [F. *dompter,* L. *domitare,* tame]

dawn *v.i.* begin to grow light; to appear, begin. -*n.* first light, daybreak, first gleam or beginning of anything. -dawn'ing *n.* [earliest is *dawning,* fr. ON. *daga,* become day]

day *n.* time during which the sun is above the horizon; period of 24 hours; point or unit of time; daylight; time, period. -daily *a., adv.* and *n.* (see also under daily). -day'-dream, *n.* reverie. day'light *n.* natural light, dawn; (*fig.*) publicity, enlightenment. -day'light-sa'ving *n.* system of regulating the clock to maximize the daylight hours. [OE. *dæg*]

daze *v.t.* stupefy, stun, bewilder. -*n.* stupefied or bewildered state. [ON. *dasa*]

daz'zle *v.t.* blind or confuse or overpower with brightness, light, brilliant display or prospects. -*n.* brightness that dazzles the vision. [*daze*]

DBMS *n.* (*compute.*) computer programs that contruct, maintain, manipulate, and provide access to a database [*database management system*]

deac'on *n.* one in the lowest degree of holy orders; official of a free church. [G. *diakonos,* servant]

dead (ded) *a.* no longer alive; benumbed; obsolete; extinguished; lacking luster or movement or vigor; sure, complete. -*n.* dead person or persons (gen. in *pl.*, the dead). -dead'beat *a.* exhausted -*n.* one who consistently fails to pay debts; loafer. -dead'en *v.t.* -dead'-end *n.* blind alley; cul-de sac. -dead'heat *n.* race in which competitors finish exactly even. -dead'ly *a.* fatal; death-like. -dead of night, time of greatest sillness and darkness. -dead'reck'oning *n.* reckoning of ship's position by log and compass alone. [OE.]

deaf (def) *a.* wholly or partly without hearing; unwilling to hear. deaf'ness *n.* -deaf'en *v.t.* [OE.]

deal *v.t.* to distribute, give out. -*v.i.* to do business (with, in), deal with, handle, act in regard to. -*n.* a share; distribution; quantity. -deal'er *n.* one who deals; a trader. [OE. *n. dæl*]

dean *n.* head of a cathedral chapter; university or college official. dean'ery *n.* dean's house or appointment. [OF. *deien,* fr. L. *decanus;* orig. chief of ten monks]

dear *a.* beloved; costly, expensive. -*n.* beloved one. *adv.* at a high price. -dear'ly *adv.* -dear'ness *n.* -dearth (derth) *n.* scarcity. [OE. *deore*]

death (deth) *n.* dying; end of life; end, extinction; annihilation; personified power that annihilates, kills. -death'less a. immortal or destined to be immortal. -death'ly *a.* and *adv.* like death. -death'mask, plaster-cast of face after death. -death'-rate, annual proportion of deaths to population. -death'-trap, unsafe place, vessel, mine *etc.* -death-warrant, execution order. death'watch *n.* ticking beetle. [OE.]

debacle' (di-bakl') *n.* utter collapse, rout, disaster. [F.]

debate' *v.t.* discuss, dispute about. -u. *i.* engage in discussion; consider; reason out (with oneself). -*n.* discussion, controversy. deba'table *a.* -deba'ter *n.* [F. *débattre*]

debauch' (-tsh) *v.t.* lead away from virtue; spoil, vitiate; seduce. -*n.* bout of sensual indulgence. debauchee' (-osh-) *n.* -debauch'ery *n.* [F. *dobaucher*]

debenture *n.* bond of a company or corporation. [L. debere, owe]

debility *n.* feebleness, *esp.* of health. -debil'itate *v.t.* [L. *debilitas,* weakness]

deb'it *n.* entry in an account of a sum owed; side of the book in which such sums are entered. -*v.t.* charge, enter as due. [L. *debere,* owe]

debonair' *a.* genial, pleasant. [F. *débon naire.* orig. (of hawks) well-bred]

deb'ris *n.* fragments, rubbish. [F. *débris,* fr. *briser,* break]

debt (det) *n.* what is owed; state of owing. -debt'or *n.* [L. *debere,* owe]

debug *v.t.* (*compute.*) detect, trace, and eliminate mistakes in computer software.

debut' *n.* first appearance in public. de'butant *n.* (-ante fem.). [F.]

dec'ade *n.* period often years; set often. [G. *dekas,* group of ten]

dec'adent (or de-ca'-) *a.* declining, failing away. -dec'adence (or de-ca') *n.* [F. *decadent*]

dec'agon *n.* figure of ten angles. -decag'onal *a.* -dec'agram *n.* ten grams. -decahedron *n.* solid of ten faces. -decahe'dral *a.* -dec'aliter *n.* ten liters. -dec'alogue *n.* the ten commandments. dec'ameter *n.* ten meters. [G. *deka,* ten]

decant' *v.t.* pour off (liquid, wine, etc,) to leave sediment behind. -decant'er *n.* stoppered bottle for wine or spirits. [L. *canthus,* lip of jug]

decapitate *v.t.* behead. -decapita'tion *n.* [L. *caput,* head]

decay' *v.t.* and *i.* rot, decompose; fall off, decline. -*n.* rotting; a falling away, break up. [OF. *decair,* fr. *de* and L. *cadere,* fall]

decease' *n.* death. -*v.i.* die. -deceased' *a.* dead. -n, person lately dead. [L. *decessus,* departure]

deceive' *v.t.* mislead, persuade of what is false. [F. décevoir]

decel'erate *v.t.* and *i.* retard the speed of; slow down. [L. *de,* away from, *celer,* speed]

Decem'ber *n.* twelfth month. [L. *decem* (formerly) = tenth month]

de'cent *a.* seemly, not immodest; respectable; passable. -de'cency *n.* -de'cently *adv.* [L. *decere,* be fitting]

decentralize *v.t.* transfer (government functions *etc.*) from main center to local centers. [L. *de,* away from, and center]

deception *n.* deceiving; being deceived; trick. -decep'tive *a.* misleading, apt to mislead. [F. *deception*]

decibel *n.* 1/10th of bel; approx. smallest change in sound detectable by human ear. [*bel*]

decide' *v.t.* settle, determine, bring to resolution; give judgment. -*v.i.* determine, resolve. -deci'ded *a.* settled; resolute. -deci'dedly *adv.* certainly, undoubtedly. decis'ion (-zhn) *n.* [L.

decidere]

decid'uous *a.* of leaves, horns, *etc.*, falling periodically; of trees, losing leaves annually. [L. *decidere*, fall down]

dec'imal (des-)*a.* relating to tenths; proceeding by tens. *-n.* decimal fraction. **-dec'imal system**, system of weights and measures in which the value of each denomination is ten times the one below it. [L. *decem*, ten]

dec'imate *v.t.* kill a tenth or large proportion of. **-decima'tion** *n.* [L. *decem*, ten]

deci'pher *v.t.* turn from cipher into ordinary writing; make out the meaning of deci'pherable *a.* [*cipher*]

deck *n.* platform covering the whole or part of a ship's hull; pack of cards. *-v.t.* array, decorate. **deck'-chair** *n.* light folding chair of wood and canvas. [Du. *dek*, roof, covering]

declaim' *v.i.* and *t.* speak in oratorical style. **-declama'tion** *n.* **declam'atory** *a.* [L. *declamare*, cry out]

declare' (-at') *v.t.* announce formally; state emphatically; show; name (as liable to customs duty). *-v.i.* take sides (for). [L. *declarare*, make clear]

decline' *v.i.* slope or bend or sink downward; decay; refuse; make the case endings of nouns. *-n.* gradual decay, loss of vigor; wasting disease. **-declen'sion** *n.* a falling off, a declining; group of nouns. declinable *a.* **-declina'tion** *n.* downward slope or angle. [L. *declinare*, bend away]

decode' *v.t.* decipher a code message. [L. *de*, from, and *code*]

decompose' (de-, -oz) *v.t.* separate into elements, *-v.i.* rot. [*compose*]

décor' *n.* scenery on stage. [F.]

dec'orate *v.t.* beautify by additions; invest (with an order, medal, *etc.*). **-decora'tion** *n.* **-dec'orative** *a.* **-dec'orator** *n. esp.* a tradesman who paints and papers houses, [L. *decorare*, make fitting]

decor'um *n.* seemly behavior, usage required by decency or good manners. **-deco'rous** *a.* **-deco'rously** *adv.* [L.]

decoy' *n.* bird or person trained or used to entrap others; bait, enticement. [first in *decay-duck; coy* fr. Du. *kooi*, cage]

decrease' *v.t.* and *i.* diminish, make or grow less. **-de'crease** *n.* a lessening. [L. *decrescere-de*, from, *crescere*, grow]

decree' *n.* authoritative order; edict. *v.t.* order with authority, [L. *decretum*]

decrepit *a.* old and feeble. **-decrepitude** *n.* [L. *decrepitus*, fr. *crepare* creak]

decriminalize *v.t.* to remove the legal penalties from (some previously illegal act or practice); make no longer illegal. **-decriminali'zation** *n.* [*crime*]

decry' *v.t.* cry down, disparage. [*cry*]

dedicate *v.t.* devote to God's service; set aside entirely for some purpose; inscribe or address (a book, *etc.*) [L. *dedicare*]

deduce' *v.t.* draw as a conclusion from facts. **-deduct'** *v.t.* take away, subtract. **-deduction** *n.* deducting; amount subtracted; deducing; conclusion deduced; inference from general to particular. [L. *deducere*, lead down]

deed *n.* act; action or fact; legal document. [OE. *deed*]

deem *v.t.* judge, consider, hold to be true. [OE. *deman*]

deep *a.* extending far down or in or back; at or of a given depth; far down or back; profound; heartfelt; of color, dark and rich; of sound, low and full. *-n.* deep place. *-adv.* far down, *etc.* **-deep'en** *v.t.* **-deep'ly** *adv.* [OE. *deop*]

deer *n.* family of ruminant animals with deciduous horns in the male. **-deerhound** *n.* large rough-coated greyhound. [OE. *deor*, wild animal]

deface' *v.t.* mar the appearance of; blot out. **-deface'ment** *n.* [*face*]

defame' *v.t.* speak ill of, dishonor by slander or rumor. **-defama'tion** *n.* defam'atory *a.* [L. *diffamare*]

default' *n.* failure to act or appear or pay. **-in default of**, in the absence of *v.t.* and *i.* fail to pay. **-default'er** *n. esp.* a soldier punished for failure to comply with regulations. [*fault*]

defeat' *n.* overthrow; lost battle or encounter; frustration. *-v.t.* overcome. [F. *dofait*, undone]

def'ecate *v.t.* clear of impurities. **defecation** *n.* [L. *defcecare*]

defect' *n.* lack, falling short, blemish, failing. **-defec'tion** *n.* abandonment of a leader or cause. defect'ive *a.* incomplete, faulty. *-n.* one mentally or physically lacking. [L. *deficere*, undo]

defend *v.t.* protect, guard, uphold. **-defense'** *n.* **-defend'er** *n.* **-defens'ive** *a.* serving for defense. *-n.* position or attitude of defense. [L. *defenders*, ward off]

defer' *v.t.* put off. *-v.i.* procrastinate. **defer'ment** *n.* [L. *differre*, set aside]

defer' *v.i.* submit in opinion or judgment (to another). **-def'erence** *n.* respect for another inclining one to accept his views, etc. [L. *deferrer*, submit]

defi'cient (-ish'nt) *a.* wanting or falling short in something. **-def'icit** *n.* amount by which a sum of money is too small. [L. *deficere*, fail]

de'file *n.* narrow pass; march in file. *-v.i.* march in file. [F. *deliler*, march past]

defile' *v.t.* make dirty, pollute. defilement *n.* [OE. *fylan*, foul]

define' *v.t.* mark out, show clearly the form; lay down clearly, fix the bounds or limits of, state contents or meaning of defi'nable *a.* **-defini'tion** *n.* def'inite (-it) *a.* exact, precise, defined. def'initely *adv.* **-defin'itive** *a.* conclusive, to be looked on as final. **-defin'itively** *adv.* [F. *dgfinir*]

deflate' *v.t.* release air from (something inflated); remove excess of paper money in circulation. **-defla'tion** *n.* **-defla'tor** *n.* [coinage fr. *inflate*]

deflect' *v.i.* and *i.* make to turn, or turn, from a straight course. **-deflec'tion** *n.* [L. *deflectere*, bend aside]

deform' *v.t.* spoil the shape of, make ugly. **-deform'ity** *n.* **-deforma'tion** *n.* [L. *deformis*, ill-formed, ugly]

defraud' *v.t.* cheat. [*fraud*]

defray' *v.t.* provide the money for (expenses,

etc.). [F. *defrayer*]

deft *a.* skillful, neat-handed. **-deft'ly** *adv.* **-deft'ness** *n.* [OE. *gedxfte*, gentler]

defunct *a.* dead. [L. *defungi*, accomplish, *oneś* duty, finish]

defy *v.t.* set at naught; challenge to do, *esp.* something beyond expected power; offer insuperable difficulties. **defi'ance** *n.* **-defi'ant** *a.* **-defi'antly** *adv.* [F. *défier* -Low L. *dffidare*, renounce faith]

degenerate *v.i.* fall away from the qualities proper to race or kind. *a.* fallen away in quality. **-n.** [L. *degenerate*]

degrade *v.t.* reduce to a lower rank; dishonor; debase. **degrada'tion** *n.* **-degra'ded** *a.* [L. *gradus*, degree, step]

degree' *n.* step or stage in a process or scale or series; relative rank, order, condition, manner, way; university rank; unit of measurement of angles or temperature; form in the comparison of *a.* and *adv.* [F. *degré*, fr. L. *de* and *gradus*, step]

dehydrate *v.t.* deprive of water; dry by chemical means, as certain food-stuffs. [L. *de*, not, G. *hvdor*, water]

de'ify *v.t.* make a god of, treat as a god. **-deifica'tion** *n.* [fr. L. *deus*, god, and *facere*, make]

deign *v.i.* condescend, think fit. [F. *daigner*, fr. L. *dignari*, think fit]

deindustrializa'tion *n.* the decline in importance of manufacturing industry in the economy of a nation or area. **-deindustrialize** *v.* [*industry*]

de'ism *n.* belief in a god but not in revelation. **-de'ist** *n.* **-deis'tic** *a.* [L. *deus*, god]

de'ity *n.* divine status or attributes, a god; the Supreme Being. [L. *deus*, god]

deject' *v.t.* dispirit, cast down. **-deject'ed** *a.* **-dejec'tion** *n.* [L. *dejicere*]

delay' *v.t.* postpone, hold back. *-v.i.* be tardy, linger. **-n.** act of delaying; fact of being delayed. [F. *délai*]

delectable *a.* delightful. [L. *delectabilis*]

del'egate *v.t.* send as deputy; commit (authority, business, *etc.*) to a deputy. [L. *delegate*]

delete' *v.t.* strike out. **-dele'tion** *n.* **-delen'da** *n. pl.* things to be deleted. [L. *delere, deletunt*, destroy]

deleterious *a.* harmful. [G. *deleterios*]

deliberate *v.t.* and *i.* consider, debate. *a.* done on purpose; well-considered; without haste, slow. **delib'erately** *adv.* **-deliberation** *n.* **-delib'erative** *a.* [L. *deliberate*, weigh]

delicate *a.* dainty; tender; fastidious; exquisite; deft; ticklish; sensitive-, modest. **-del'icately** *adv.* **-del'icacy** *n.* [L. *delicatus*, fr. *lacere*, entice]

delicatessen *n.* food that is sold ready-prepared, such as cooked meats, salads, *etc.*; the store where such food is sold. **-del'i** *abbrev.* [Ger.]

delicious (-ish'us)*a.* very delightful or pleasing. **-deli'ciously** *adv.* **-deli'ciousness** *n.* [L. *delicix*, delight]

delight' (-lit')*v.t.* please highlv. *-v.i.* take great pleasure (in). **-n.** great pleasure. **-delight'ful**

a. [L. *delectare*]

delineate *v.t.* portray by drawing or description. **-delin'eator** *n.* **-delinea'tion** *n.* [L. *delineate*, fr. *linea*, line]

delinquent *n.* offender. **-delin'quency** *n.* [L. *delinquere*, fr. *linquere*, leave]

delirium *n.* disorder of the mind; raving, as in fever. **-delir'ious** *a.* **-delir'iously** *adv.* with wild excitement. [L.]

deliv'er *v.t.* set free; hand over; launch, send in, deal; give forth; disburden, as a woman at childbirth. **-deliv'ery** *n.* **-deliv'erance** *n.* [fr. L. *liberare*, set free]

dell *n.* wooded hollow. [OE.]

del'ta *n.* tract of alluvial land at the mouth of a river. [fr. its usual shape, the Greek fourth letter, *delta*, Δ]

delude' (-a-) *v.t.* deceive. **-delu'sion** *n.* false belief; hallucination. **-delu'sive** *a.* [L. *deludere*, play false]

del'uge *n.* flood, great flow, rush, downpour. *-v.t.* flood. [F. *deluge*]

delve *v.t.* and *i.* dig. [OE. *delfan*]

demagogue (-og) *n.* mob leader or agitator. [G. *dernagogos*, fr. *demos*, people, and *agogos*, leader]

demand' (-a-) *v.t.* ask as by right, ask as giving an order; call for as due or right or necessary-*n.* urgent request, claim, requirement; call for (a commodity). [L. *dem, andare*, entrust]

demarcation *n.* boundary line, its marking out. [Sp. *dernarcacin*]

demean' (-men') *v.t.* conduct oneself, behave, show specified bearing. **-demean'or** (-er) *n.* conduct, bearing. [F. *dérnener*, conduct]

demean' *v.t.* lower, degrade (oneself). [mean, in sense of low, base]

dement'ed *a.* mad; beside oneself [L. *dementare*, send out of one's mind]

demerit *n.* bad point; undesirable quality. [L. *demeritum*, desert]

demise' (-z) *n.* death; conveyance by will or lease; transfer of sovereignty on death or abdication. *-v.t.* convey to another. [F. *ettre*, put off]

demo'bilize *v.t.* disband (troops). **-demobiliza'tion** *n.* [*mobilise*]

democ'racy *n.* government by the people; state so governed. **-dem'ocrat** *n.* advocate of democracy. **democrat'ic** *a.* **-democrat'ically** *adv.* **-democ'ratize** *v.t.* **-democratiza'tion** *n.* [G. *demokratia, demos*, the people, *Kratein*, rule]

demog'raphy *n.* study of human population with emphasis on statistical analysis. [G. *demos*, people, *graphein*, draw]

demolish *v.t.* knock to pieces, destroy, overthrow. **demoli'tion** *n.* [L. *demoliri*, fr. *moles*, mass, building]

de'mon *n.* devil, evil spirit; person of prenatural cruelty or evil character or energy. **-demo'niac** *n.* one possessed by a demon. **-demoni'acal** *a.* **-demon'ica** *a.* of the nature of a devil, or of genius. [G. *daimon*]

dem'onstrate *v.t.* show by reasoning, prove; describe or explain by specimens or experiment. -v.i. make exhibition of political sympathy; make a show of armed force. -**demon'strative** a. conclusive; needing outward expression, unreserved; pointing out. [L. demonstrate]

demor'alize v.t. deprave morally; deprive of courage and discipline, morale. [F. démoratiser]

demote' v.t. reduce in rank; grade downwards. -**demo'tion** n. [motion]

demur' (-mer) v.i. raise objections, make difficulties. -n. hesitation, pause. [AF. demurer, stay]

demure' a. reserved, quiet, staid; affecting to be grave or decorous. -**demure'ly** adv. [AF. demurer, stay]

den n. cave or hole of a wild beast; lurking place; small room. [OE. denn]

dena'ture v.t. deprive of essential qualities. -**dena'tured al'cohol**, spirit made undrinkable. [nature]

deni'al. See deny.

denigrate v.t. blacken, defame. -**denigra'tion** n. [L. nigrare, blacken]

denizen n. inhabitant. [AF. deinz, fr. L. de intus, from within]

denominate v.t. give a name to -**denomina'tion** n. name, esp. one applicable to each individual of a class; distinctively named church or sect. -**denom'inator** n. number written below the line in a fraction, the divisor. [L. denominate]

denote' v.t. stand for, be the name of-, mark, indicate, show. -**denota'tion** n. [L. denotare]

denouement n. unravelling of a dramatic plot; final solution of a mystery. [F.]

denounce' v.t. speak violently against; accuse; give notice to withdraw from (a treaty, etc.). [F. dononcer]

dense a. thick, compact; stupid. -**dense'ly** adv. -**dens'ity** n. [L. densus]

dent n. hollow or mark left by a blow or pressure. -v.t. make a dent in. [dint]

dent'al a. of or relating to teeth or dentistry; pronounced by applying the tongue to the teeth. —**dent'ate** a. toothed. -**dent'istry** n. art of a dentist. -**denti'tion** n. teething; arrangement of teeth. -**dent'ure** n. set of teeth, esp. artificial. [L. dens, tooth]

denude' v.t. strip, make bare. -**denuda'tion** n. esp. removal of forest or surface soil by natural agency; erosion. [L. denudare]

deny' v.t. declare untrue or non-existent; contradict, reject; disown; refuse to give; refuse. **deni'al** n. **deni'able** a. [F.denier; L.denegare]

deodorize v.t. rid of smell. -**deodoriza'tion** n. -**deo'dorizer** n. [odour]

depart' v.i. go away; start; die; diverge, stray from. **depart'ure** n. [F. dopartir]

department n. division, branch province. -**department'al** a. -**department'- ally** adv. [depart]

depend' v.i. rely entirely; live (on); be contingent, await settlement or decision (on); hand down. -**depend'able** a. reliable. -**depend'ant** n. one for whose maintenance another is responsible. [L. dependere, hang from]

depict' v.t. give a picture of. -**depic'tion** [L. depingere, depict]

depil'atory a. removing hair. -n. substance that does this. -**depila'tion** n. [L. depilare, fr. pilus, hair]

deplete' v.t. empty, exhaust, or nearly. -**deple'tion** n. [L. deplere, deplete]

deplore' v.t. lament, regret. -**deplor'able** a. -**deplor'ably** adv. [L. deplorare]

deploy' v.i. of troops, ships, etc., to spread out from column into line. -**deploy'ment** n. [F. déployer]

depo'larize v.t. deprive of polarity. [polarize]

depo'nent n. one who makes a statement on oath, a deposition. [L. deponere, put down]

depop'ulate v.t. deprive of, reduce, population. -**depopula'tion** n. [populate]

deport' v.t. remove into exile; transport. -**deporta'tion** n. [F. deporter]

depose' v.t. remove from office, esp. of a sovereign. -v.i. make a statement on oath, give evidence. -**deposi'tion** n. [F. doposer, set down]

depos'it (-z-) v.t. set down; give into safe keeping, esp. in a bank; pledge for the carrying out of a contract. -n. act of depositing; thing deposited; pledge; sediment. -**depositor** n. [L. depositum, laid down]

dep'ot n. railroad or bus station; storage place for supplies, esp. military. [F. dépôt]

deprave' v.t. make bad, corrupt, pervert. -**deprav'ity** n. wickedness. [L. pravus, crooked, wrong]

dep'recate v.t. express disapproval of, advise against. -**dep'recatory** a. [L. deprecari, pray against]

depre'ciate (-shi-) v.t. lower the price or value or purchasing power of; belittle. v.i. fall in value. [L. depretiare]

depress' v.t. lower, in level or activity; affect with low spirits. -**depres'sion** (-shn) n. depressing; hollow; center of low barometric pressure; low spirits; low state of trade. -**depress'ible** a. [L. deprimere, depress-, press down]

deprive' v.t. strip, dispossess (of). -**depriva'tion** n. [L. privare, deprive]

depth n. deepness; degree of deepness; deep place, abyss; profundity; intensity. [deep]

depute' v.t. commit to (a substitute); point as substitute. -**dep'uty** n. substitute, delegate. [L. deputare, choose - lit. cut off]

derail' v.t. make (a train) leave the ails. -**derail'ment** n. [rail]

derange' v.t. throw into confusion or isorder; disturb; disorder the mind at; -**deranged'** a. disordered; out of one's mind, insane. -**derangement** n. [F. ranger]

derby n. a man's hat with dome-shaped crown and narrow brim; horse-race, usu. restricted to three-year-olds; race or competition in any sport, usu. with specific qualifications. [Earl of Derby]

der'elict a. abandoned, forsaken, esp. of ship. -n. thing forsaken, esp. a ship; son who has become unable to look after himself usu. as a result of alcoholism. -**derelic'tion** n.

neglect (of duty). [L. *derelictus*, forsaken]

deride´ *v.t.* laugh to scorn. -deris´ion, derisive *a.* -deris´ory *a.* futile. [L. *ridere*, laugh at]

derive´ *v.t.* get from; deduce; show the gin of-. -*v.i.* issue (from), be descended from). -deriva´tion *n.* -deriv´ative *a.* traceable back to something else. -*n.* thing or word derived from another. [L. *care*, lead water]

dermatol´ogy *n.* (*phys.*) science of the kin. -dermati´tus *n.* inflammation of the skin. [G. *derma*, skin]

derr´ick *n.* hoisting-machine. [*Derrick*, hangman at Tyburn, London, c. 1600]

derr´inger (-j-) *n.* small pistol. [Henry *Derringer*, gunsmith]

descend´ *v.i.* come or go down; slope down; swoop on or attack; stoop, condescend; spring from (ancestor, *etc.*); pass to an heir, be transmitted-*v.t.* go or come down. -descend´ant *n.* one descended from another. -descent´ *n.* [L. *descendere*, climb down]

describe´ *v.t.* give a detailed account of-, trace out (a geometrical figure, *etc.*); pass along (a course, *etc.*). -descrip´tive *a.* - descrip´tion *n.* detailed account; marking out; kind, sort, species. [L. *describere*, write down]

desecrate *v.t.* violate the sanctity of, profane; convert to evil uses. -desecra´tion *n.* - des´ecrator *n.* [opposite of *consecrate*]

desert´ (-z-) *n.* (*usu. pl.*) conduct or qualities deserving reward or punishment; what is due as reward or punishment; merit, virtue. [OF.]

desert´ (-z-) *v.t.* abandon, leave. -*v.i.* run away from service, *esp.* of soldiers and sailors. - deser´tion *n.* -desert´er *n.* [L. *deserere*, abandon]

des´ert (-z-) *n.* uninhabited and barren region. -a. barren, uninhabited, desolate. [L. *deserere, desert-*, abandon]

deserve´ (-z-) *v.t.* show oneself worthy of, have by conduct a claim to. -*v.i.* be worthy (of reward, *etc.*). -deserv´edly *adv.* -deserv´ing *a.* meritorious. [L. *deservire*, serve well]

desiccate *v.t.* to dry up. **desicca´tion** *n.* [L. *desiccate*, fr. *siccus*, dry]

design´ (-zin) *v.t.* plan out; purpose; set apart for a purpose; make working drawings for; sketch. -*n.* project, purpose, mental plan; outline, sketch, working plan; art of making decorative patterns, *etc.* -des´ignate (dez´-ig-) *v.t.* name, pick out, appoint to office. -*a.* appointed but not yet installed in office. - designa´tion *n.* name. [L. *designare*, mark out]

desire´ (-z-) *v.t.* wish for, long for; ask for, entreat. -*n.* longing; expressed wish; wish or felt lack; request; thing wished or requested. [F. *dosirer*, fr. L. *desider-are*, long for]

desist´ *v.i.* cease, give over. [L. *desistere*, stand back]

desk *n.* sloped board on which a writer rests his paper, a reader his book; table or other piece of furniture designed for the use of a writer or reader. [It. *desco* - L. *discus*, disk, table]

desktop publishing *n.* (*compute.*) use of computers in the preparation of typeset-quality publications, *e.g.* newsletters, reports, books, magazines, etc.

des´olate *n.* solitary; neglected, barren, ruinous; dreary, dismal, forlorn. -*v.t.* depopulate, lay waste; overwhelm with grief. desola´tion *n.* [L. *desolare*, leave alone, fr. *solus*, alone]

despair *v.i.* lose all hope. -*n.* loss of all hope; something causing this. despairing *a.* [L. *desperare*, give up hope]

despatch´. *See* dispatch.

desperate *a.* leaving no room for hope; hopelessly bad or difficult or dangerous; reckless from despair. -despera´tion *n.* - des´perately *adv.* -despera´do *n.* one ready for any lawless deed. [*despair*]

despise´ (-z) *v.t.* look down on. -des´picable *a.* base, contemptible, vile. -des´picably *adv.* -despite *n.* scorn; ill-will, malice, spite. -prep. in spite of. -despite´ful *a.* -despite´fully *adv.* [L. *despicere*, look down]

despond´ *v.i.* lose heart or hope. - despond´ent *a.* -despond´ency *n.* - despond´ently *adv.* [L. *despondere* (*animum*) give up (heart)]

des´pot *n.* tyrant, oppressor. [G. *despotes*]

dessert´ (-z-) *n.* fruit, *etc.*, served after dinner. [F., fr. *desseruir*, clear away]

destabilize *v.t.* to undermine or subvert (a government, economy, *etc.*) so as to cause unrest or collapse. -de´stabilization *n.* (L. *stabilis*, stable]

des´tine (-tin) *v.t.* predetermine, ordain or fix in advance; set apart, devote. -des´tiny *n.* power which foreordains; course of events or person's fate, *etc.*, regarded as fixed by this power. -destina´tion *n.* place to which a person or thing is bound; intended end of a journey. [L. *destinare*, make fast.]

des´titute *a.* in absolute want, in great need of food, clothing, *etc.* destitu´tion *n.* [L. *destitutus*, abandoned]

destroy´ *v.t.* make away with, put an end to, reduce to nothingness or uselessness. [L. *destruere*, 'unbuild']

des´ultory *a.* off and on, flitting from one thing to another, unmethodical. [L. *desultor*, circus rider, *lit.* leaper down]

detach´ (-tsh) *v.t.* unfasten, disconnect, separate. -detached´ *a.* standing apart, isolated. [F. *détacher* - See attach]

de´tail *n.* item or particular; treatment of anything item by item; small or unimportant part; party or man told off for a duty in the army *etc.* detail *v.t.* relate with full particulars; appoint for a duty. [F. *detail*]

detain´ *v.t.* keep under restraint; keep from going; keep waiting. -deten´tion *n.* [L. *detinere*, hold back]

detect´ *v.t.* find out or discover the existence or presence or nature or identity of. -detect´or *n.* device for detecting electrical waves. - detec´tion *n.* -detect´ive *a.* employed in or apt for detection. -*n.* policeman or other person employed in detecting criminals. [L. *detegere*, detect, uncover]

détente´ (da-tongt´) *n.* slackening of tension

in international crises. [F.]

deter' v.t. make to abstain (from); discourage, frighten. **-deterr'ent** a. [L. deterrere, frighten off]

detergent a. cleansing. -n. cleansing substance (for wounds, etc.); chemical substance which, added to water, removes dirt from fabrics etc. [L. detergere, wipe off]

dete'riorate v.i. and t. become or make worse. **-deteriora'tion** n. [L. deteriorate, make worse]

deter'mine v.t. make up one's mind, decide; fix as known; bring to decision; be the deciding factor in; law, end. -v.i. come to an end; come to a decision. **-deter'mined** a. resolute. **-deter'minism** n. theory that human ction is settled by forces independent of e will. [L. determinate]

detest' v.t. hate, loathe. [L. testari, execrate]

det'onate v.i. and t. explode with a loud report; set off an explosive. **-detona'tion** n. **-detonator** n. esp. a detonating apparatus as the fuse of a bomb, etc. [L. tonare, thunder down]

de'tour n. course which leaves the main route to rejoin it later. [F. detour, a turning aside]

detract' v.t. and i. takeaway (apart) from; belittle. [L. detrahere, detract-, draw away]

det'riment n. harm done, loss, damage. [L. detrimentum]

detri'tus n. gravel, debris, from wearing exposed surfaces. [L.]

deuce n. two at dice, cards, etc.; score of all at tennis. [F. deux, two]

deval'ue, devaluate v.t. reduce in value, esp. currency. **-devalua'tion** n. [value]

dev'astate v.t. lay waste. **-devasta'tion** n. [devastaire]

devel'op v.t. bring to maturity; bring, bring out; evolve. -v.i. grow to a maturer state. **-devel'oper** n. esp. photographic chemical; muscle exerciser. **-devel'opment** n. [F. dovelopper]

de'viate v.i. leave the way, turn aside, diverge. **-devia'tion** n. **-de'viator** n. [L. viare]

device n. contrivance, invention; fancy; scheme, plot; heraldic or semblematic or design. [F. devis]

dev'il n. personified spirit of evil; superhuman evil being, vice; fierceness in fighting; person of great wickedness, cruelty, etc.; one who devils for a lawyer or author; dish or devilled food. -v.t. **-dev'il's ad'vocate** n. one appointed to state the disqualifications of a person whom it is proposed to make a saint. [G. diabolos, slanderer]

de'vious a. roundabout; twisting; erring. (L. devius, out of the way)

devise' (-z-) v.t. plan, frame, contrive; plot; leave by will. [F. deviser, fr. L. dividire, divide]

devi'talize v.t. deprive of vitality, vigor. [vital]

devoid' a. empty of, lacking, free from. [obs. v. devoid, empty out; cp. avoid]

devote' v.t. set apart, give up exclusively (to a person, purpose, etc.). **devotee'** n. one devoted, worshipper. **-devo'ted** a. esp. very loyal or loving. [L. deuovere, devot-, vow]

devour' v.t. eat up, consume, destroy. **-devour'er** n. [L. devorare, swallow]

devout' a. earnestly religious; reverent. **-devout'ly** adv. [F. dóvot]

dew n. moisture from the air deposited as small drops on cool surfaces between nightfall and morning; any beaded moisture. -v.t. wet with, or as with, dew. [OE. deaw]

dexterity n. manual skill, neatness, adroitness. **dex'terous** a. neat-handed, skillful. [L. dexter, on the right hand]

dex'trose n. grape-sugar also made from starch; glucose. [L. dexter]

diabetes n. disease relating to an excess of sugar in the blood caused by the failure of the pancreas to produce insulin; urinary disease. **diabe'tic** a. [G. diabaiein, pass through]

diabol'ic, diabolical a. devilish. [See devil]

di'adem n. crown. [G. diadema, fillet]

diagnosis n. art or act of deciding from symptoms the nature of a disease; guess at the cause of anything. [G.]

diag'onal a. from corner to corner; oblique. -n. line from corner to corner. **-diag'onally** adv. [G. diagonios]

di'agram n. drawing, figure in lines, to illustrate something being expounded, as in a geometrical figure, weatherchart, etc. [G. diagramma]

di'al n. plate marked with graduations on a circle or arc on which something may be recorded (e.g., time on a sundial, dial of a clock, etc.); (sl.) face. -v.t. indicate on a dial; select a number on a telephone. [L. dies, day]

di'alect n. characteristic speech of a district; a local variety of a language. **-dialect'al** a. [G. dialektos, speech]

dialect'ic(s) n. art of arguing. **-dialect'ic** a. **-dialect'ically** adv. **-dialecti'cian** n. [G. dialektikos]

di'alogue, dialog n. conversation between two or more; literary work representing this; the conversational part of a novel, play, movie, etc. [G. dialogos, conversation]

dial'ysis n. (dial'yses pl.) (chem.) separation of substances by filtration. [G.]

diamanté n. fabric covered with sparkling particles; imitation diamond jewelry. [F. diamant, diamond]

diam'eter n. straight line passing from side to side of a figure or body through its centre; thickness; unit of magnifying power. **-diamet'rical** a. exact opposite. **-diamet'rically** adv. [G. diametros, measuring through]

di'amond n. very hard and brilliant precious stone; lozenge-shaped figure; card of the suit marked by (red) lozenges or diamonds. [F. diamant]

di'aper n. fabric with a small woven pattern; pattern of that kind; towel, etc., of the fabric; a baby's garment, made of cloth or another absorbent material, fitting between its legs and around its waist. **-di'apered** a. [OF. diaspre]

diaph'anous a. transparent; showing through (a mist, etc.) [G. diaphanes]

di'aphragm (-am) *n.* partition dividing the two cavities of the body, midriff, plate or disk wholly or partly closing an opening. [G. *diaphragma*]

diarrhoe'a *n.* excessive looseness of the bowels. [G. *diarrhoia*]

di'ary *n.* daily record of events or thoughts; book for such record. **di'arist** *n.* [L. *diarium*, daily allowance]

dias'pora *n.* dispersion of Jews from Palestine after Babylonian captivity; Jewish communities that arose after this; dispersion, as of people orig. of one nation. [G. *diaspeirein*, scatter]

di'astase *n.* organic ferment turning starch into sugar. [G. *diastases*, division]

dias'tole *n.* heart's dilating movement, opp. of systole, the contracting movement. [G.]

di'athermy *n.* curative treatment by heating parts of body by electric currents. [G. *dia*, through, *therme*, heat]

diaton'ic *a.* (*mus.*) of the natural major or minor scale. [G. *diatonikos*]

diatribe *n.* bitter speech of criticism, invective. [G. = a wearing away (of time)]

dice. *See* die.

dichotomy *n.* division into two. -**dichot'omize,** *v.t.* and *i.* -**dichot'omous** *a.* [G. *dicha*, in two, *temnein*, cut]

dicotyledon *n.* plant with two seed leaves or cotyledon. **dicotyle'donous** *a.* [G. *di-*, twice, *coty*, led on]

dictate' *v.t.* and *i.* say or read for exact reproduction by another on paper; prescribe, lay down. -**dic'tate** *n.* bidding. -**dicta'tion** *n.* **dicta'tor** *n.* one with absolute authority, supreme ruler. [L. *dictare*, say often]

dic'tion *n.* choice and use of words. -**dic'tum** *n.* (dic'ta) *a.* pronouncement, saying. [L. *dictio*, a speaking]

dictionary *n.* book setting forth, usually in alphabetical order, the words of a language with meanings, derivations, foreign equivalents, *etc.*; book of reference with items in alphabetical order. [Med. L. *dictionarium*, collection of sayings]

didac'tic *a.* instructive; meant, or meaning, to teach. -**didac'ticism** *n.* [G. *dieaktikos*]

die (di) *n.* cease to live; come to an end. **die'hard** *n.* one who resists (reform, *etc.*) to the end. [ON. *deyja*]

die (di) *n.* cube with sides marked one to six for games of chance; small cube of bread, *etc.*; (*pl.* dice); stamp for embossing, *etc.* (*pl.* dies). -**dice** *v.i.* to gamble with dice. -**di'cer** *n.* [F. *de*]

dies'el engine (dee-sl) *n.* oil-fuelled internal combustion engine. [R. *Diesel*]

di'et *n.* kind of food lived on; regulated course of feeding, restricted choice of foods; food. -*v.i.* follow a prescribed diet. -**di'etary** *n.* allowance or character of food, *esp.* in an institution, *etc.* -*a.* relating to diet. -**dietet'ic** *a.* -*n. pl.* science of diet. [G. *diaita*, system of life]

di'et *n.* parliamentary assembly in certain European countries. [Med. L. diets]

diff'er *v.i.* be unlike; disagree. -**diff'erence** *n.* unlikeness; degree or point of unlikeness; disagreement; remainder left after subtraction. **different** *a.* unlike. -**diff'erently** *adv.* -**differen'tial** *a.* varying with circumstances. **differential gear** *n.* mechanism in an automobile which allows the back wheels to revolve at different speeds when rounding a corner. **differen'tially** *adv.* -**differen'tiate** *v.t.* make different; develop into unlikeness. -*v.i.* discriminate. **differentia'tion** *n.* [L. *differre*, carry apart]

difficulty *n.* hardness to be done or understood; hindrance, obstacle; an obscurity; embarrassment. **difficult** *a.* not easy, hard, obscure; captious, hard to please. [L. *difficultas*]

diff'ident *a.* timid, shy. -**diff'idently** *adv.* -**diff'idence** *n.* [L. *diffidere*, distrust]

diffract' *v.t.* break up, as ray of light. [L. *diffringere*, *diffract*, break asunder]

diffuse' (-z) *v.t.* spread abroad. -*a.* (-s) loose, verbose. [L. *diffundere*, *diffus-*, pour apart]

dig *v.i.* work with a spade. -*v.t.* turn up with a spade; hollow out, make a hole in; get by digging; thrust into; delve. -**digg'er** *n.* one who digs; gold-miner; Australian. [OF. *diguer*]

digest' *v.t.* prepare (*food*) in the stomach, *etc.*, for assimilation; bring into handy form by sorting, tabulating, summarizing; reflect on; absorb; endure. -*v.i.* of food, to undergo digestion. **di'gest** *n.* methodical summary, *esp.* of laws. [L. *digerere*, *digest-*]

dig'it (-j-) *n.* any of the numbers 0 to 9; finger or toe. **dig'ital** *a.* using digits, *esp.* in a display. -**dig'ital recording** *n.* a sound recording process that converts audio signals into a series of pulses that correspond to the voltage level, which then can be stored on tape or on any other memory system. -**digita'lis** *n.* drug made from foxglove. [L. *digitus*, finger]

dig'nity *n.* worthiness, excellence, claim to respect; honorable office or title; stateliness, gravity. -**dig'nify** *v.t.* give dignity to. -**dig'nified** *a.* stately, majestic. -**dig'nitary** *n.* holder of high office. [L. *dignitas -dignus*, worthy]

digress' *v.t.* go aside from the main course, *esp.* deviate from the subject. [L. *digredi*, digress-step aside]

dike, dyke *n.* ditch; low wall; embankment. -*v.t.* wall or ditch. [OE. *dic*]

dilapidated *a.* ruinous, falling into decay. -**dilapida'tion** *n.* [L. *dilapidarei*, scatter stones apart]

dilate' (di-) *v.t.* widen, expand. -*v.i.* expand; talk or write at large (on). -**dilatation,** **dila'tion** *n.* [L. *dilatare*]

dilatory *a.* delaying, slow. [Late L. *dilatorious*, putting off (time)]

dilem'ma *n.* position in fact or argument offering choice only between two or more unwelcome courses. [G.]

dilettante (-ti) *n.* person with taste and knowledge of the fine arts as a pastime; amateur, dabbler. -*a.* amateur, desultory. [It. *dilettare*, delight]

dil'igent *a.* unremitting in effort, industrious. **dil'igence** *n.* industry; French stage-coach.

[L. *diligere*, delight in]

dill *n*. medicinal herb. [OE. *dile*]

dilute' *a*. reduce (a liquid) in strength by adding water or other matter. *-a*. weakened thus. **-dilu'tion** *n*. [L. *diluere, dilut-*, wash away]

dim *a*. indistinct, faint, not bright. *-v.t.* and *i*. make or grow dim. **-dim'ly** *adv*. **- dim'ness** *n*. [OE. *dimm*, dark]

dime *n*. U.S. 10 cent piece. [F. *disme*]

dimen'sion *n*. measurement, size. - **dimen'sional** *a*. [L. *dimensio*]

dimin'ish *v.t.* and *i*. lessen. **diminution** *n*. **dimin'utive** *a*. very small. *-n*. derivative word implying smallness. [L. *diminuere*, make less]

dim'ple *n*. small hollow in the surface of the skin, *esp*. of the cheek; any small hollow. *-v.t.* and *i*. mark with or break into dimples. [orig. uncertain]

din *n*. continuous roar of confused noises. *-v.t.* repeat to weariness, ram (opinion, *etc*.) into. [OE, *dyne*]

dine *v.i.* take dinner. *-v.t.* give dinner to. - **di'ning-room** *n*. room used for meals. **-di'ner** *n*. one who dines; railroad restaurant-car; inexpensive restaurant. [F. *diner*]

ding *v.t./i.* ring, resound, beat, knock; (Scot.) defeat; surpass. [ME. *dingen*]

dinghy (ding'gi) *n*. small boat; ship's tender. [Hind. *dingi*]

din'gy (-j-) *a*. dirty-looking, dull. **-din'giness** *n*. [orig. uncertain]

dinn'er *n*. chief meal of the day. [F. *diner*]

di'nosaur *n*. extinct giant reptile. [G. *deinos*, terrible, *sauros*, lizard]

di'ocese *n*. district or jurisdiction of a bishop. **dioc'esan** *a*. *-n*. bishop, or clergyman, or the people of a diocese. [F. *diocese*]

diox'ide *n*. oxide with two parts of oxygen to one of a metal. [*oxide*]

dip *v.t.* put partly or for a moment into a liquid; immerse, involve; lower and raise again; take up in a ladle, bucket, *etc*. *-v.i.* plunge partially or temporarily; go down, sink; slope downwards. *-n*. act of dipping; downward slope; hollow. **-dipp'er** *n*. [OE. *dyppan*]

diphtheria *n*. infectious disease of the throat with membranous growth. **diphtherit'ic** *a*. [G. *diphthera*, skin]

diphthong *n*. union of two vowel sounds in a single compound sound. [G. *diphthongos*, having two sounds]

diplo'ma *n*. document vouching for a person's title to some degree, honor, *etc*., - **diplo'macy** *n*. management of international relations; skill in negotiation; tactful or adroit dealing. **dip'lomat** *n*. one engaged in official diplomacy. [G. *folded paper*]

dire *a*, dread, terrible. [L. *dirus*]

direct' *v.t.* put in the straight way; address (a letter, *etc*.); aim, point, turn; control, manage, order. *-a*. straight; going straight to the point; lineal; immediate; frank, straightforward. - **direc'tion** *n*. a directing; body of directors; address, instruction; aim, course of movement. **-direct'or** *n*. one who directs; member of a board managing a company. **-direct'ory** *n*. book of names and addresses, streets, *etc*.

[L. *dirigere, direct-*, make straight]

dirge *n*. song of mourning. [L. *dirige*, in antiphon in Office for the Dead; *Dirige, Domine . . . viam meam*, Direct, O Lord. . . my way]

dirk *n*. short dagger orig. carried by Scottish clansmen. [orig. uncertain]

dirt'y *a*. unclean; soiled; mean. **-dirt** *n*. filth; mud, earth. **dirt'far'mer** *n*. farmer who farms his own land, usu. without the help of hired hands. **-dirt'ily** *adv*. **dirt'iness** *n*. [ON. *drit*, excrement]

dis- *prefix*, indicates negation, opposition, deprivation; in many verbs, it indicates the undoing of the action of the simple verb, *eg*. **-disembark'**, come out from what one embarked in; many verbs, nouns and adjectives in *dis*- mean the exact opposite of the simple word, *e.g.* **-disarrange'**, disorders **-dislov'al**; some verbs in *dis* - mean to deprive of the thing indicated by the simple word, *eg*. **-disembowel**. All such words are omitted, and the meaning should be sought under the simple word to which *dis*- is prefixed. [L.]

disa'ble *v.t.* incapacitate; disqualify; cripple. **disabil'ity** *n*. [*able*]

disaffected *a*. ill-disposed, inclined to sedition, disaffec'tion *n*. [*affect*]

disallow' *v.t.* reject the validity of (evidence *etc*.). [*allow*]

disappoint' *v.t.* fail to fulfill (hope) **-disappointment** *n*. [*appoint*]

disarm' *v.t.* li. take away weapons; reduce armaments; conciliate. **-disarm'ament** *n*. [*arm*]

disarray' *v.t.* throw into disorder; derange. *-n*. undress. [*array*]

disas'ter (-a-) *n*. calamity, a sudden or great misfortune. **-disas'trous** *a*. [orig. evil star. L. *astrum*]

disavow' *v.t.* disown; disclaim. **-disavowal** *n*. [OF. *desavouer*]

disband' *v.t.* and *i*. disperse. [*band*]

disburse' *v.t.* pay out money. **-disbursement** *n*. [F. *bourse*, purse]

disc *See* disk.

discard' *v.t.* and *i*. reject, or play as worthless (a card); give up; cast off. [OF. *descarter*, scatter]

discern' *v.t.* make out; distinguish. - **discern'ment** *n*. insight. **-discern'ible** *a*. [L. *discernere*, separate, sift]

discharge' *v.t.* unload; fire off; release; dismiss; let go, pay; emit. *-n*. a discharging; a being discharged; matter emitted; document certifying release, payment, *etc*. [OF. *descharger*, unload]

disci'ple *n*. follower, one who takes another as teacher and model. **-discipleship** *n*. - **dis'cipline** (-in) *n*. training that produces orderliness, obedience, self-control; result of such training in order, conduct, *etc*.; system of rules; maintenance of subordination in an army, school, *etc*. **-u-t**. train; chastise. **disciplin'arian** *n*. **-dis'ciplinary** *a*. [L. *discipulus*, pupil]

disclose' *v.t.* reveal, bring to light. - **disclo'sure** *n*. [*close*]

discon'solate *a*. unhappy, downcast; unconsoled. [console]

dis'cord n. absence of concord; difference, dissension; disagreement of sounds. [L. discordia]

discount' v.t. give present value of (a bill of exchange, etc.); detract from; allow for exaggeration in. -dis'count n. deduction made on discounting a bill, receiving payment for an account, etc. [OF. desconter, count off]

discourage (-kur-)v.t.reduce the confidence of; deter from; show disapproval of. -discour'agement n. [courage]

discourse n. speech, treatise, sermon; conversation. -discourse' v.i. speak, converse. -v.t. utter. [L. discursus, running to and fro]

discov'er (-kuv-) v.t. find out, light upon; make known. -discov'ery n. -discov'erer n. -discov'erable a. [cover]

discredit v.t. refuse to believe; disgrace, damage reputation. -n. -discreditable a. shameful; disgraceful. [credit]

discreet' a. prudent, knowing when to be silent. -discreet'ly adv. -discre'tion (-eshén) n. [discrete]

discrete' a. separate; disjoined. -discreteness n. -discret'ive a. [L. discretus, separated]

discrim'inate v.t. and i. detect or draw distinctions distinguish from or between. -discrimina'tion n. [L. discriminare, divide, discern]

disc'us n. a disk which is thrown to perform a track-and-field sport of that name. [G. diskos]

discuss' v.t. exchange opinions on; debate; consume (food or drink). -discus'sion n. [L. discutere, discuss-, agitate]

disdain' n. scorn, contempt. -v.t. scorn. [OF. desdain; cp. deign]

disease' n. illness; disorder of health. [OF. desaise, discomfort]

disembody v.t. remove from body, esp. of spirits; disband. -disembod'ied a. [embody]

disfig'ure (-get) v.t. mar the appearance of, deface. -disfig'urement n. -dis-figuration n. [figure]

disgrace' n. ignominy; cause of shame; loss of favor-v.t. bring shame or discredit upon. -disgrace'ful a. -disgrace'fully adv. [grace]

disgruntled a. dissatisfied; ill-humored. disgrun'tle v.t. [grunt]

disguise' (-giz) v.t. change the appear ance of, make unrecognizable; conceal, cloak; misrepresent. -n. false appearance; dress or device to conceal identity. [OF. desguiser, change costume]

disgust' n. violent distaste, loathing. v.t. affect with loathing. [OF. desgoust, now dogo (it, distaste)]

dish n. shallow vessel for food; portion or variety of food; contents of a dish. -v.t. put in a dish; serve up. [OE. disc, platter]

disheveled a. with disordered hair; ruffled, untidy, disorderly. [OF. deschevele, fr. chevel, hair]

dishonor n. disgrace; loss of honor -v.t. disgrace; to insult; refuse payment on. [honor]

disillusion n. freeing from illusion. v.t. undeceive. illusion -disinfect' v.t. free from in-

fection or germs; purify. -disinfect'ant a. 1n. germdestroying (agent). [infect]

disintegrate v.t. break up, crumble, fall to pieces. -disintegra'tion n. [integrate]

disinterested a. unbiased, impartial. [interest]

disk, disc n. thin circular plate; anything disk-like. -disk jock'ey n. (sl.) announcer on a radio program who introduces and plays recorded music. -disk drive n. in computer technology the unit that controls the mechanism for handling a diskette. -disk'ette n. floppy disk, used for storing information on a computer. [G. diskos, a round plate]

dislodge v.t. eject from a position, lodg ment. [lodge]

dis'mal (-z-) a. depressing, or depressed; cheerless, dreary. -dis'mally adv. [ME. in the dismal, L. dies mali, evil days]

dismantle v.t. deprive of defenses, furniture, etc.; remove equipment. [OF. desmanteier, strip]

dismay' v.t. dishearten, daunt. -n. consternation, horrified amazement. [OF. desmayer, deprive of power]

dismember v.t. tear or cut limb from limb; divide, partition. -dismem'berment n. [member]

dismiss' v.t. send away, disperse, disband; put away from employment, or from the mind. -dismiss'al n. [L. mittere, miss-, send]

disparage v.t. speak slightingly of; bring into disrepute. -dispar'agement n. [OF. desparagier, orig. marry unequally]

disparate a. essentially different, not related. -dispar'ity n. inequality. [parity]

dispassionate a. cool; unbiased. [passion]

dispatch, despatch' v.t. send off, send to a destination or on an errand; kill; eat up; finish off, get done with speed. -n. a sending off-, efficient speed; an official written message. -pl. state papers. [Sp. despachar, expedite]

dispel' v.t. clear away; banish. [L. dispellere, drive apart]

dispense' v.t. deal out; make up (a medicine), relax, not insist on; do without; administer. -v.i. make up medicines. -dispens'er n. -dispens'ary n. place where medicine is made up. -dispensation n. license or exemption; provision of nature or providence; act of dispensing. -dispens'able a. [L. dispensare, distribute by weight]

disperse' v.t. scatter. -dispersed' a. scattered; placed here and there. -disper'sion n. [F. disperser]

display' v.t. spread out for show; show, expose to view. -n. a displaying; show, exhibition; show, ostentation. [OF. despleier, L. displicare, unfold]

dispose' (-z) v.t. arrange; make inclined (to). -v.i. ordain, appoint. -dispose of, sell, get rid of; have authority over. -dispo'sal n. -disposi'tion n. arrangement; plan; inclination; east of mind or temper. [F. disposer]

dispute' v.i. debate, discuss. -v.t. call in question; debate, argue; oppose, contest; try to debar from. dis'putable a. -dis'putant n. -disputa'tion n. -disput-a'tious a. [L. dis-

putare, discuss]

disrupt' *v.t.* shatter, break in pieces, split. -**disrup'tion** *n.* -**disrup'tive** *a.* [L.*disrumpere*, disrupt-, break asunder]

dissect' *v.t.* cut up (a body, organism) for detailed examination; examine or criticize in detail. -**dissec'tion** *n.* -**dissec'tor** *n.* [L. *dissecare*, cut up]

disseminate *v.t.* spread abroad. -**dissemina'tion** *n.* -**dissem'inator** *n.* [L. *disseminate*, scatter seed]

dissent' *v.i.* differ in opinion; express such difference; disagree with the doctrine, *etc.*, of an established church. *n.* such disagreement. -**dissent'er** *n.* -**dissentient** *a.* and *n.* -dissen'sion n. [L. *dissentire*, differ in feeling]

dissertation *n.* formal discourse; treatise. [L. *dissertation*]

dissipate *v.t.* scatter, clear away; waste, squander. -*v.i.* disappear, clear away. -**diss'ipated** *a.* corrupted, dissolute. [L. *dissipate*, scatter]

dissociate *v.t.* separate, sever. dissociation *n.* [L. *socius*, companion]

dissolve' *v.t.* absorb or melt in a fluid; break up, put an end to, annul. -*v.i.* melt in a fluid; disappear, vanish; break up, scatter. -**dissol'uble** *a.* -**dissolu'tion** *n.* [L. *dissolvers*, loosen]

dissonant *a.* jarring, discordant in sound. -**diss'onance** *n.* [L. *dissonare*, sound diversely]

dissuade' (-sw-) *v.t.* advise to refrain, persuade not to. -**dissua'sion** *n.* -**dissua'sive** *a.* [L, *dissuadere-suadere*, advise]

dis'tance *n.* amount of space between two things; remoteness; excessive dignity. -*v.t.* leave behind, *esp.* in a race. -**dis'tant** *a.* -**dis'tantly** *adv.* [L. *distans, distantis*, fr. *distare*, stand apart]

distaste' *n.* dislike, aversion; disgust. -**distaste'ful** *a.* offensive to one's taste; unpleasant. [*taste*]

distemper *n.* disordered state of mind or body; disease of dogs. [L. *temperate*, mix, temper]

distend' *v.t.* and *i.* swell out by pressure from within. [L. *tendere*, stretch]

distill' *v.i.* pass over or condense from a still; trickle down. -*v.t.* obtain (a substance or part of it) in a purified state by evaporating and then condensing it.-**distill'ery** *n.* place where these are distilled. [L. *distillate*, trickle down]

distinct' *a.* clear, easily seen, sharp of outline; definite; separate, different. -**distinct'ly** *adv.* -**distinct'ness** *n.* distinction *n.* point of difference; act of distinguishing; eminence, high honor, high quality. -**distinct'ive** *a.* characteristic. -**disting'uish** *v.t.* class; make a difference in; recognize, make out; honor; make prominent or honored (*usu. refl.*). -*v. i.* draw a distinction, grasp a difference. -**disting'uishable** *a.* [L.*distinguere,-distinct-*, prick off]

distort' *v.t.* put out of shape; misrepresent, garble. -**distor'tion** *n.* [L. *distorquere, distort-*, twist apart]

distract' *v.t.* turn aside, divert; bewilder, drive mad. **distrac'tion** *n.* [L. *distrahere, distract-*, pull apart]

distraught' (-awt) *a.* bewildered, crazy. [fr. F. *distrait*, absentminded]

distress' *n.* severe trouble, mental pain; pressure of hunger or fatigue or want; (*law*) -distraint. -*v.t.* afflict, give mental pain to. -**distress'ful** *a.* [OF. *destresse*, fr. L. *distringere*, pull asunder]

distribute *v.t.* deal out; spread, dispose at intervals; classify. -**distrib'utive** *a.* -**distribu'tion** *n.* -**distrib'utor** *n.* [L. *distribuereé* cp. *tribute*]

dis'trict *n.* portion of territory; region. [F. = control, region controlled]

disturb' *v.t.* trouble, agitate; unsettle, derange. -**distur'bance** *n.* -**distur'ber** *n.* [L. *disturbare*, disorder]

ditch *n.* long narrow hollow dug in the ground, usually for drainage. -*v.t.* and *i.* make or repair ditches; discard. [OE. *dic*]

dit'to same, aforesaid; (used to avoid repetition in lists, *etc.*). [It., fr. L. *dictus*, the said]

ditt'y *n.* simple song. [OF. *dite*, poem]

diuret'ic (di-fir-) *a.* exciting discharge of urine. -*n.* substance with this property. [G. *diouretikos*]

diur'nal *a.* daily; in, or of, daytime; taking a day. [L. *diurnalis*, fr. *dies*, day]

di'va *n.* distinguished female singer; primadonna. [L. = *divine*]

di'van *n.* low seat by a wall; smokingroom; oriental council. [Turk.]

dive *v.i.* plunge under the surface of water; descend suddenly; disappear; go deep down into. -*n.* an act of diving; (*sl.*) disreputable place of entertainment. -**di'ver** *n.* [OE. *dufan*, sink, and *dyfan*, dip]

diverge' *v.i.* get further apart, separate. -**diver'gent** *a.* -**diver'gence** *n.* [L. *di-*, apart, and *uergere*, turn]

di'vers (-z) *a.* sundry. -**diverse'** *a.* different, varied. **divers'ify** *v.t.* -**diverse'ly** *adv.* -diversifica'tion *n.* -**diversity** *n.* [*divert*]

divert' *v.t.* turn aside, ward off, cause to turn; amuse, entertain. -**diver'sion** *n.* a turning aside; that which diverts; amusement; entertainment. [L. *divertere*, turn aside]

divest' *v.t.* unclothe, strip, dispossess. [L. *devestire*, undress]

divide *v.t.* make into two or more parts, split up, separate; classify; cut off; deal out; take or have a share; part into two groups for voting; -divide a number by another, find out how many times the former contains the latter. -*v.i.* become divided. -**div'idend** *n.* number to be divided by another; share of profits, of money divided among creditors, *etc.* -**divi'ders** *n. pl.* measuring compasses. -**divis'ible** *a,* -divis'ion *n.* (-vizh-n). -**divis'ional** *a.* -**divi'sor** *n.* [L. *dividere, divis-*, to force asunder]

divine' *a.* of, pertaining to, proceeding from, God; sacred; godlike, heavenly. -*n.* theologian; clergyman. -*v.t.* and *i.* guess; predict, tell by inspiration or magic. -**divine'ly** *adv.* -**divin'ity** *n.* quality of being divine; god; theology, [L. *divinus*, of the gods]

divina'tion *n.* divining. -**divi'ner** *n.* -

divi'ning-rod n. switch for detecting underground water or minerals. [*divine*]

divorce' n. legal dissolution of marriage; complete separation, disunion. -v.t. dissolve a marriage; put away; separate. -**divorcee'** n. divorced person. [F.]

div'ot n. patch of turf, *esp.* as dislodged accidentally in the game of golf. [Scot.]

divulge' v.t. reveal, let out (a secret). [L. *divulgare*, spread among the people, *vulgus*]

dizz'y a. feeling dazed, unsteady; causing, or fit to cause, dizziness, as of speed, *etc.* v.t. to make dizzy. -**dizz'iness** n. -**dizz'ily** adv. [OE. *dysig*, foolish]

do v.t. perform, effect, transact, bring about, finish, prepare, cook; cheat. v.i. act, manage, work, fare, serve, suffice. -v.*aux.* makes negative and interrogative sentences and expresses emphasis. [OE. *don*]

do'cile a. willing to obey; easily taught. -**docil'ity** n. [L. *docilis-*, *docere*, teach]

dock n. basin with flood-gates for loading or repairing ships. -v.t. put in a dock. v. i. go into dock. -**dock'yard** n. enclosure with docks, for building or repairing ships. -**dock'er** n. dockworker or docklaborer. [O. Du. *dokke*]

dock n. enclosure in a criminal court in which the prisoner is placed. [Flem, *dok*, hutch, pen]

dock'et n. endorsement showing the contents of a document; memorandum; certificate of payment of customs. -v.t. make a memorandum, endorse with a summary. [earlier *dogget*, orig. uncertain]

doc'tor n. one holding a University's highest degree in any faculty; medical practitioner. -v.t. treat medically; adulterate, garble. -**doc'torate** n. -**doc'toral** a. [L. *doctrina*, fr. *docere*, teach]

doc'trine n. what is taught; teaching of a church, school, or person; belief, opinion, dogma; statement of official government policy. [L. fr. *docere*, teach]

doc'ument n. something written furnishing evidence or information. -v.t. furnish with proofs, illustrations, cer tificates. -**document'ary** a. -**document- a'tion** n. [L. *documentum*, example]

doddering a. trembling with ague or frailty; useless; pottering. [cp. *dither*]

dodec'agon n. twelve-sided, twelve angled plane figure, [G. *dodeka*, twelve, *gonia*, angle]

dodge v.i. swerve, make zig-zag movement, *esp.* to avoid a pursuer or gain an advantage; shuffle. play fast and loose. v.t. elude by dodging. -n. an act of dodging; trick, artifice; shift, ingenious method. -**dodg'er** n. [orig. unknown]

doe n. female of deer, hare, rabbit, antelope *etc.* [OE. *do*]

doff v.t. take off (hat, clothing). [do off]

dog n. familiar domestic quadruped; person (in contempt, abuse, or playfully). -v.t. follow steadily or closely. [OE, *docga*]

dogg'erel n. slipshod, unpoetic or trivial verse. [orig. uncertain]

dog'ma n. article of belief, *esp.* one laid down authoritatively by a church; body of beliefs.

-dogmat'ic a. relating to dogma or dogmas; asserting opinions with arrogance. -**dogmat'ically** adv. -**dog'matism** n. arrogant assertion of opinion. **dog'matist** n. -**dog'matize** v.i. [G. *dokeiro*, to seem]

doi'ly n. small cloth, paper, piece of lace to place under a cake, finger-bowl, *etc.* [fr. *Doily*, 17th c. shopkeeper]

dol'drums n. pl. region of light winds and calms near the equator; state of depression, dumps. [*dull*]

dole n. charitable gift; (*sl.*) a payment from government funds to the unemployed. -v.t. (usually dole out) deal out, *esp.* in niggardly quantities. [OE. *dal*]

dole n. woe. -**dole'ful** a. full of grief; dismal. -**dole'fully** adv. [OF. *duel*]

doll, dolly n. child's toy image of a human being. [short for *Dorothy*]

doll'ar n. coin of Canada, U.S., and other countries. [Ger. *thaler*]

dol'or (-er) n. grief, sadness. -**dol'orous** a. -**dol'orously** adv. [L. *dolor*]

dol'phin a. sea mammal like a porpoise; figure of a curved, large-headed fish common in decoration and heraldry; buoy for mooring. -**dolphinar'ium**. n. a pool or aquarium for dolphins, *esp.* one in which they give public displays. [OF. *dalfin*, fr. L. *delphinus*]

dolt n. stupid fellow. [*dull*]

domain' n. lands held or ruled over; sphere, field of influence, province. [F. *domaine*, fr. L. *dorninium*]

dome n. rounded vault forming a roof, large cupola. -**domed** a. [F. *dome*]

domes'tic a. of or in the home; of the home country, not foreign; home-keeping; of animals, tamed, kept by man. -**domes'ticate** v.t. -**domestica'tion** n. -**domesti'city** n. [L. *domesticus*]

dom'icile n. person's regular place of living (usually legal). -**domicil'iary** a. pert. to the domicile. [F.]

dom'inate v.t. rule, control, sway; of heights, to overlook. -v.i. control, be the most powerful or influential member or part of something. [L. *dominus*, lord]

Domin'ican a. pert. to order of monks of St. Dominic. -n. Dominican monk. [*St. Dominic*]

dominion n. sovereignty, rule; territory of a government. [L. *dominio*]

dom'ino n. cloak with a half-mask for masquerading. -pl. game played with small flat pieces, marked on one side with 0 to 6 spots on each half of the face. -sing. one of these pieces. [It.]

don v.t. put on (clothes). [do on]

don n. (don'na *fem.*) Spanish (courtesy) title = English air; fellow of a college; (*sl.*) expert. [Sp., fr. L. *dominus*]

donate' v.t. give. -**dona'tion** n. donor n. [L. *donare*, give]

don'gle n. in computer technology, an electronic device that accompanies a software item to prevent the unauthorized copying of programs. [orig. uncertain]

donk'ey n. ass. -**donk'ey-engine** n. small hauling or hoisting engine on a ship. [orig.

uncertain]

doom n. fate, destiny; ruin; judicial sentence, condemnation; Last Judgment. -v.t. sentence, condemn; destine to destruction or suffering. **-dooms'day** n. day of the Last Judgment. [OE. dom]

door n. hinged, sliding, or revolving barrier to close the entrance to a room, carriage, etc. **-door-to-door** a. going from one building or destination to the next, usu. selling. - **door'way** n. entrance provided, or capable of being provided, with a door. [OE. dor, duru]

dopamine n. amine ($C_8H_{11}NO_2$) formed in the brain that is an essential neurotransmitter in the central nervous system's regulation of movement and emotions.

dope v.t. drug; stupefy with drugs. -n. narcotic drugs; stupid person. **-dope'y** a. dull-witted. [Du. doop, sauce]

dor'ic n. a Greek dialect. -a. simplest order of Greek architecture. [G. dorikos]

dor'mant a. not acting, in a state of suspension. **-dor'mancy** n. **-dorm'er** n. upright window set in a sloping roof **-dor'mitory** n. sleeping-room with a number of beds; building containing sleeping quarters. [L. dormire, sleep]

dor'sal a. of or on the back. **-dor'sally** adv. [L. dorsum, back]

do'ry n. a flat-bottomed boat. [Miskito, dori, dugout]

DOS n. (compute.) operating system for a computer. [disk operating system]

dose n. amount (of a drug, etc.) administered at one time. -v.t. give doses to. **-dos'age** n. [F.]

dossier (dos-ya) n. set of documents; record esp. of individual; brief. [F.]

dot n. small spot or mark. -v.t. mark with a dot or dots; place here and there. **dot ma'trix prin'ter** n. in computer technology, a printer in which each character is produced by a subset of an array of needles at the printhead. [OE. dott, speck]

dot (dot) n. dowry. [F.]

dote v.i. be silly or weak-minded; be passionately fond of. **-do'tage** n. feeble minded old age. **-do'tard** n. [AF. doter]

dou'ble (dub-) a. of two parts, layers etc.; folded; twice as much or many; of two kinds; ambiguous; deceitful. -adv. twice; to twice the amount or extent; in a pair. n. person or thing exactly like, or mistakable for, another; quantity twice as much as another; sharp turn; evasion or shift. v.t. and i. make or become double; increase twofold; fold in two; turn sharply; get round, sail round. [F. double, fr. L. duplus]

double team v.t. (sports) guard, defend against, or block an opposing player with two players.

doubt (dowt) v.t. hesitate to believe, call in question; suspect. -v.i. be wavering or uncertain in belief or opinion. -n. state of uncertainty, wavering in belief; state of affairs giving cause for uncertainty. **-doubt'er** n. **-doubt'ful** a. **-doubt'fully** adv. **doubt'lessly** adv. [L. dubitare]

douche n. jet or spray of water applied to the body or some part of it; shower. -v.t. give a douche to. [F.]

dough n. flour or meal kneaded with water. **-dough'y** a. [OE. dag]

dour a. grim, stubborn. [F. dur]

douse, dowse v.t. plunge into water; souse; strike; extinguish. -v.i. fall into water. [O. Du. doesen, beat]

dove (duv) n. bird of the pigeon family. [cp. Du. duif]

dowager (-j-) n. woman with title or property derived from her late husband. [OF. douagere, fr. L. dotare, endow]

dow'dy a. lacking smartness; unattractively or shabbily dressed. -n. woman so dressed. [ME. dowd]

dow'er n. widow's share for life of her husband's estate; dowry. -v.t. give dowry to; endow. **-dow'ry** n. property which a wife brings to her husband; talent. [F. douaire, -L. dotare, endow]

down n. open expanse of high land, esp. in England, e.g. the Sussex Downs. [OE. dun, hill]

down adv. to, or in, or towards, a lower position; with a current or wind; of paying, on the spot. -prep. from higher to lower part of; at a lower part of; along with. **-down'cast** a. looking down; dejected. **-down' link** n. communications path for transmission of information or signals from a spacecraft or satellite to earth. **-down'pour** n. heavy fall of rain. **-down'right** a. plain, straightforward. adv. quite, thoroughly. **-downsize** v.t. to make a smaller version. **-down'time** n. time during which a machine or plant is not working because it is incapable of production, as when under repair. [for adown, OE. of dune, off hill]

down n. fluff or fine hair of young birds; anything like this, soft and fluffy. **-down'y** a. [OE. dunn]

dow'ry. See **dower**.

dowse v.i. seek for water, minerals, with aid of divining-rod or **-dows'ing-rod** n. **-dows'er** n. water-diviner. [earlier dense, perh. conn. with Ger. deuter, indicate]

doze v.i. sleep drowsily, be half asleep. n. nap. [orig. uncertain]

doz'en twelve, a set of twelve. [F. douzaine, fr. L. duo, two, decem, ten]

drab a. of dull light brown; dull, monotonous. -n. drab color. [F. drop, cloth]

draft n. detachment of men, esp. troops, reinforcements; selection for compulsory military service; design, sketch; rough copy of a document; order for money; act of drinking, quantity drunk at once; one drawing of, or fish taken in, a net; dose; an inhaling; depth of water needed to float a ship; current of air between apertures in a room, etc. -a. constituting a preliminary version. -v.t. make an outline sketch or design of, make a preliminary version of something, esp. a piece of writing; to conscript for military service. **-drafts'man** n. one who draws plans and designs for buildings, ships etc., one skilled in drawing. [draw]

drag v.t. pull along with difficulty or friction; trail, go heavily; sweep with a net; protract.

-v.i. lag, trail; be tediously protracted. -n. check on progress; checked motion, iron shoe to check a wheel; vehicle; lure for hounds to hunt; kinds of harrow, sledge, net, grapnel, rake; (fig.) a tedious person or thing; (sl.) transvestite clothing. [var. of draw]

drag'on n. mythical fire-breathing monster, like a winged crocodile. -**drag'onfly** n. long-bodied insect with large gauzy wings. -**dragoon** n. cavalryman, usually of heavy cavalry. v.t. subject to military oppression; domineer over, persecute. [F.]

drain v.t. draw off (liquid) by pipes, ditches, etc.; dry; drink to the dregs; empty, exhaust. -v.i. flow off or away; become rid of liquid. -n. channel for removing liquid; constant outlet, expenditure, strain. **drain'age** n. [OE. dreahnian, strain a liquid]

drake n. male duck. [orig. uncertain]

dram n. small draught of strong drink; a drachm. [var of drachm, q.v.]

dra'ma (dra-) stage-play; art of literature of plays; play-like series of events. -**dramat'ic** a. of drama; vivid, arresting. -**dramatiza'tion** n. -**dram'atisperso'nae** n. characters of a play. [G. = action]

drape v.t. cover, adorn with cloth; arrange in graceful folds. -n. curtain **dra'per** n. dealer in cloth, linen, etc. -**dra'pery** n. [F. drop, cloth]

dras'tic a. strongly effective. [G. drastikos, active]

draw v.t. pull, pull along, haul; bend (a bow); inhale; entice, attract; bring (upon, out, etc.); get by lot; of a ship, require (depth of water); take from (a well, barrel, etc.); receive (money); delineate, portray with a pencil, etc.; -v.i. pull; shrink; attract; make or admit a current of air, etc.; write orders for money; come, approach (near). -n. act of drawing; casting of lots; unfinished game, a tie. -**draw'bridge** n . hinged bridge to pull up. -**draw'er** n. one who or that which draws; sliding box in a table or chest. -pl. two-legged undergarment. -**draw'ing** n.. action of the verb; art of depicting in line; sketch so done. [OE. dragon; drawn game, for withdrawn, the stakes being 'withdrawn' for lack of a decision; drawing-room for earlier withdrawing room]

drawl v.t. and i. speak slowly in indolence or affectation. -n. such speech. [Du. dralen]

dray n. low cart without sides. [OE. drege, see drag, draw]

dread (dred) v.t. fear greatly. -n. awe, terror. -a. feared, awful, revered. -**dread'ful** a. -**dreadlocks** n. pl. hair worn in the Rastafarian style of long matted or tightly curled strands. [OE. adrcovdan]

dream n. vision during sleep; fancy, reverie, vision of something ideal. v.i. have dreams. -v.t. see or imagine in dreams; think of as possible. [ME.]

drear'y a. dismal, dull; cheerless. [OE. dreorig, gory]

dredge n. machinery, appliance for bringing up mud, objects, etc., from the bottom of sea or river. -v.t. bring up, clean, deepen, with such appliance. -**dredg'er** n. ship for dredging. [cp. drag]

dredge v.t. sprinkle with flour. -**dredg'er** n. box with holes in the lid for dredging. [F. dragée, sweetmeat]

dregs n. pl. sediment, grounds, worthless part. [ON. dregg]

drench v.t. wet thoroughly, soak; make (an animal) take a dose of medicine. -n. dose for an animal; soaking. [OE. drencan, make drink]

dress v.t. clothe; array for show; trim, smooth, prepare surface of. draw up (troops) in proper line; prepare (food) for the table; put dressing on. -v.i. put on one's clothes; form in proper line. -n. clothing, clothing for ceremonial evening wear; frock. -**dress'er** n. one who dresses; surgeon's assistant; kitchen sideboard; chest of drawers, bureau with a mirror. -**dress'ing** n. esp. something applied to something else, as ointment to a wound, manure to land, stiffening to linen, sauce to food, etc. [F. dresser]

drib'ble v.i. flow in drops, trickle, run at the mouth; work a ball forward with small touches of the feet. -v.t. let trickle: work (ball) forward. -n. trickle, drop. -**dribblet** n. small installment. [drip]

drift n. being driven by a current; slow current or course; deviation from a course; (also **drift'age**); tendency; speaker's meaning; wind-heaped mass of snow, sand, etc.; material driven or carried by water; (in S. Africa) ford. -v.i. be carried as by current of air, water; move aimlessly or passively. [drive]

drill n. boring tool or machine; exercise of soldiers or others in handling of arms and maneuvers; routine teaching. -v.t. bore; exercise in military movements or other routine. -v.i. practice a routine. [Du. dril]

drink v.t. and i. swallow liquid; absorb; take intoxicating liquor, esp. to excess. n. liquid for drinking; portion of this; act of drinking; intoxicating liquor; excessive use of it. -**drink'er** n. -**drink'able** a. [OE. drincan]

drip v.t. and i. or let fall in drops. -n. process of dripping; that which falls by dripping. **drip'stone** n. projection over round window or door to stop dripping of water. **dripp'ing** n. act of dripping; melted fat that drips from roasting meat. [Scand.]

drive v.t. force to move in some direction; make move and steer (a vehicle, animal, etc.); chase; convey in a vehicle, fix by blows, as a nail; urge, impel. [OE. drijan]

drivel v.i. run at the mouth or nose; talk nonsense. -n. silly nonsense. driv'eller n. [OE. dreflian, slobber]

drive train n. system in a vehicle which delivers power from the transmission to the wheel axles, via the universal joint, drive shaft, and clutch.

driz'zle v.i. rain in fine drops -n. fine rain. [OE. dreosan, fall in drops]

drogue n. drag or brake; funnel-shaped device on the end of a feed-hose to facilitate mid-air refuelling of airplanes; small parachute which, when deployed, causes a larger parachute to open, or which is used as a brake. [*drag*]

droll *a.* funny, odd, queer. -*n.* funny fellow. [F. *drole*, amusing rascal]

drone *n.* male of the honey-bee; lazy idler; deep humming; bass pipe of bagpipe, or its note. -*v.t.* and *i.* hum; talk in a monotone. [OE. *dran*, bee]

droop *v.i.* hang down as in weariness, languish, flag. -*v.t.* let hang down. -*n.* drooping condition. [ON. *drupa*]

drop *n.* globule of liquid; very small quantity; fall, descent; thing that falls, as a gallows platform; distance through which a thing falls. -*v.t.* let fall; let fall in drops; utter casually; discontinue. -*v.i.* fall; fall in drops; lapse; come or go casually. [OE. *dropa*]

dross *n.* scum of molten metal, impurity, refuse; small coal. [OE. *dros*]

drought (-owt) *n.* long-continued dry weather; thirst. [OE. *drugoth*]

drove *n.* a herd, flock, crowd, *esp.* in motion. -**dro'ver** *n.* a driver of, or dealer in, cattle. [OE. *draft*]

drown *v.t.* suffocate in water; of sound, *etc.*, to overpower. -*v.i.* be suffocated in water. [OE. *druncnian*, to be drunk, get drowned]

drow'sy (-z-) *a.* half-asleep; lulling; dull, lacking life. -**drow'sily** *adv.* -**drow'si-ness** *n.* -**drowse** *v.i.* [obs. Du. *droosen*, become sleepy]

drudge *v.i.* work hard at mean or distasteful tasks. -*n.* one who drudges. -**drudg'ery** *n.* [orig. obscure]

drug *n.* medicinal substance; commodity not wanted (usually within the market). *v.t.* mix drugs with; administer a drug to, *esp.* one inducing sleep or unconsciousness. -**drug'store** *n.* retail store which sells medicines and a variety of other articles, such as food, film, household utensils, cosmetics. **drugg'ist** *n.* dealer in drugs, chemist. [F. *drogue*]

drum *n.* musical instrument, made of skin stretched over a round hollow frame or hemisphere, and played by beating with sticks; various things shaped like a drum; part of the ear. -*v.t.* and *i.* play a drum; tap or thump continuously. [imit. orig.]

drunk *a.* overcome by strong drink; fig. under the influence of strong emotion. -**drunk'en** *a.* drunk; often drunk; caused by or showing intoxication. -**drunk'ard** *n.* one given to excessive drinking. -**drunk'enness** *n.* [drink]

dry *a.* without moisture; rainless; not yielding milk, or other liquid; not in or under water; cold, unfriendly; caustically witty; having prohibition of alcoholic drink; uninteresting, needing effort to study; lacking sweetness. -*v.t.* remove water, moisture. -*v.i.* become dry, evaporate. -**dri'ly** *adv.* -**dry'ness** *n.* -**dry'goods** *n. pl.* drapery, textiles. -**dry'point** *n.* needle for engraving without acid; an engraving so made. [OE. *dryge*]

dry'ad *n.* wood-nymph. [G. *Dryas*]

du'al *a.* twofold; of two, forming a pair. -**dual'ity** *n.* -**du'alism** *n.* recognition of two independent powers or principles, as good and evil, mind and matter. -**dualis'tica.** [L. *dualis*]

dub *v.t.* confer knighthood on; give a title to; give fresh sound-track to (film); smear with grease, dubbin. -**dubb'in, dubbing** *n.* grease for making leather supple. [late OE. *dubbian*]

du'bious *a.* causing doubt, not clear or decided; of suspected character; hesitating. **dubi'ety** *n.* [L. *dubiosus*]

duch'ess *n.* the wife or widow of a duke. -**duch'y** *n.* territory of a duke. [F. *duchesse, ducho*]

duck *n.* familiar swimming bird; amphibious motor vehicle. drake *n. masc.* -**duck'ling** *n.* duck *v.i.* plunge under water; bend or bob down. -*v.t.* plunge someone under water. [OE. *duce*, diver]

duck *n.* strong linen or cotton fabric. -*pl.* trousers of it. [Du. *doek*, linen]

duct *n.* channel or tube. -**duct'less** *a.* (of giands) secreting directly certain substances essential to health. [L. *ductus*]

ductile *a.* capable of being drawn into wire; flexible and tough; docile. -**ductil'ity** *n.* [L. *ducere*, lead]

dud *n.* (*sl.*) shell that fails to explode; futile person or project or thing. *a.* [orig. uncertain]

dude *n.* someone from the city, *esp.* an Easterner in the West; dandy; guy. [orig. uncertain]

due *a.* that is owing; proper to be given, inflicted, *etc.*; adequate, fitting; usual, ascribable; under engagement to arrive, be present. -*adv.* (with points of the compass), exactly. -*n.* person's fair share; charge fee, *etc.* (*usu.* in *pl.*)-**du'ly** *adv.* [F. *du*, fr. *devoir*, L. *debere*, owe]

du'el *n.* fight with deadly weapons between two persons; keen two-sided contest. -*v.i.* fight in a dual or duels. -**du'ellist** *n.* [F.]

duet' *n.* piece of music for two performers. [It. *duetto*, fr. L. *duo*, two]

duff'el, duffle *n.* coarse woolen cloth; coat of this. [*Duffel*, in Brabant]

dug'out *n.* shelter for troops, civilians, in trenches, *etc.*, at any depth underground; hollowed-out tree canoe. [*dig*]

du jour *a.* available or served on that particular day; of the day. [F.]

duke *n.* peer of rank next below a prince; sovereign of a small state called a duchy. -**duke'dom** *n.* [L. *dux*, leader]

dul'cet (-set) *a.* (of sounds) sweet, harmonious, melodious. [L. *dulcis*]

dul'cimer (-sim-) *n.* stringed instrument played with hammers, an ancestor of the piano. [L. *dulce melos*, sweet tune]

dull *a.* stupid; sluggish; tedious; not keen or clear or bright or sharp or defined; lacking liveliness or variety; gloomy, overcast. -*v.t.* and *i.* make or become dull. —**dul'ly** *adv.* -**dull'ard** *n.* -**dull'ness** *n.* [OE. *dol*, foolish]

du'ly. See **due.**

dumb *a.* incapable of speech; silent; (*sl.*) stupid. -**dumb'bell** *n.* weight for exercises. -**dumbfound'**, **dumbfound'er** *v.t.* confound into silence. -**dumb'show** *n.* acting without words. -**dumb'ly** adv. -**dumb'ness** *n.* [OE.]

dumm'y *n.* imaginary card-player; imitation

object. (OE.]

dump *v.t.* throw down in a mass; send low-priced goods for sale abroad. -*n.* rubbish-heap; temporary depot of stores or munitions. [orig. uncertain]

dun *a.* of a dull grayish brown. -*n.* this color; horse of dun color. [OE. *dunn*]

dun *v.t.* to make persistent demands, *esp.* for payment of debts. -*n.* one who duns. [orig. uncertain]

dunce *n.* a dullard, slow learner, blockhead. [earlier *dunsman,* fr. *Duns* Scotus (d. 1308) whose followers were regarded as dull pedants, foes of enlightenment]

dune *n.* mound of dry shifting sand on a coast or desert. -**dune buggy** *n.* lightweight vehicle with oversize, low-pressure tires used mainly for driving on sand dunes and beaches. [F.]

dung *n.* excrement of animals; manure. *v.t.* to manure. -**dung'hill** *n.* manure heap. [OE.]

dung'eon (dunjn) *n.* underground cell or vault for prisoners; formerly a tower or keep of a castle. [F. *donion*]

dunk shot *n.* (*sports*) basketball shot in which the player jumps high enough to slam the ball down through the basket with one or both hands.

duodenum *n.* upper part of small intestine, 12 in. long. [L. *duodeni,* twelve]

dupe *n.* victim of delusion or sharp practice. -*v.t.* deceive for an advantage. [F.]

du'plex *a.* two-fold -*n.* apartment having rooms on two floors; a house consisting of two family units. duplicate *v.t.* make an exact copy of; double. *a.* double; twofold. -*n.* exact copy. [L.]

du'rable *a.* lasting, resisting wear. -durabil'ity *a.* -**dura'tion** *n.* time a thing lasts. -du'rably *adv.* [L. *durare,* last]

du'ress *n.* restraint, coercion, imprisonment; (*law*) illegal compulsion. [L. *durus,* hard]

du'ring *prep.* throughout, in the time of. [L. *durare,* last]

dusk *n.* darker stage of twilight; partial darkness. -**dusk'y** *a.* dark; dark colored. -**dusk'ily** *adv.* [OE. *dor*]

dust *n.* fine particles, powder, of earth or other matter, lying on a surface or blown along by the wind. -*v.t.* sprinkle with powder; rid of dust. -**dust'-cov'er** *n.* book-jacket. [OE.]

du'ty *n.* what one ought to do, moral or legal obligation; office, function, being occupied in these; tax on goods for the public revenue; respect. -**du'ty-free** *a.* (of goods) free from duty, tax. [AF. *duet,* what is due]

duvet' *n.* down-quilt. [F.]

dwarf *n.* very undersized person. -*a.* unusually small, stunted. -*v.t.* make stunted; make seem small by contrast.[OE. *dweorg*]

dwell *v.i.* live, make one's abode (in); fix one's attention, write or speak at length (on). -**dwell'ing** *n.* house. -**dwell'er** *n.* [OE. *dwellan,* linger]

dwindle *v.i.* grow less, waste away, to grow feeble. [OE. *dwinan*]

dye (di) *v.t.* impregnate (cloth, *etc.*) with coloring matter; color thus. -*n.* coloring matter in solution which may be dissolved for

dyeing; tinge, color. -**dy'er** *n.* [OE. *deagian,* v.; *deag,* n.]

dyke. *See* **dike.**

dynam'ics (di) *n. pl.* branch of physics dealing with force as producing or affecting motion; physical or moral forces. -**dynam'ic** *a.* of or relating to motive power, force in operation. -**dynam'ical** *a.* -**dynam'ically** *adv.* -**dy'namite** *n.* high explosive of nitroglycerin. -*v.t.* blow up with this. -**dy'namiter** *n.* -**dy'namo** *n.* machine to convert mechanical into electrical energy, generator of electricity. -**dyne** *n.* unit of force. [G. *dynamis,* power]

dynasty (din-) *n.* line or family of hereditary rulers. -**dyn'ast** *n.* -**dynast'ic** *a.* [G. *dynastes,* prince]

dysentery (dis-) *n.* inflammatory disease of the bowels. [G. *dusenteria*]

dyspepsia *n.* indigestion. -**dyspep'tic** *a.* and *n.* [G. *dyspepsia*]

dyspnoe'a *n.* difficulty in breathing. [G. *dys-, ill, pnoe,* breathing]

dystoc'ia *n.* abnormal, slow, or difficult childbirth, usually because of disordered or ineffective contractions of the uterus. [G. *dys-, ill, tokos,* childbirth]

E

each *a.* and *pron.* every one taken separately. [OE. *ælc*]

ea'ger (eg -) *a.* full of keen desire; keen, impatient. -**eag'erly** *adv.* -**eag'ernessn.** [F. *aigre,* sour, keen]

ea'gle (eegl) *n.* large bird of prey with keen sight and strong flight; (golf) hole played in two under par. -**ea'glet** n. young eagle. [F. *aigle*]

ear *n.* organ of hearing, *esp.* external part, sensitiveness to musical sounds; attention. -**ear'drum** *n.* tympanum. -**ear'mark** *n.* owner's mark on ear of sheep, *etc.* -*v.t.* mark thus; assign or reserve for a definite purpose. -**ear'** piercing *a.* shrill. -**ear'shot** *n.* hearing distance. -**ear'wig** *n.* insect formerly thought to enter the head through the ear. [OE. *eare*]

ear *n.* spike or head of corn. [OE.]

earl (erl) *n.* peer of rank next below a marquis. -**earl'dom** *n.* [OE. *eorl,* nobleman, warrior]

earl'y (erl -) *a.* and *adv.* in the first part, or near or nearer the beginning, of some portion of time. [OE. *ærlice*]

earn (ern) *v.t.* get for labor, merit, *etc.* -**earn'ings** *n. pl.* what has been earned. [OE. *earnian*]

earnest (ern -) *a.* serious, ardent, sincere. -**earn'estnessn.** -**earn'estly** *adv.* [OE. *eornost,* eagerness]

earth (er-) *n.* ground, soil: dry land; planet or world we live on; mold, soil, mineral; fox's hole. -*v.t.* cover with earth; connect electrically with the earth. -**earth'en** (-th-) *a.* -**earth'ly** *a.* -**earth'y** *a.* -**earth'enware** (-th-) *n.* vessels of baked clay. -**earth'quake** *n.* volcanic convulsion of the surface of the earth. [OE. *eorthe*]

ease (ez) *n.* comfort; freedom from constraint or annoyance or awkwardness or pain or

trouble; idleness; informal position or step;
relief, alleviation. -v.t. and i. to relieve of pain;
reduce burden; give bodily or mental ease to;
slacken, relax. -ease'ful a. -ease'ment n. (law)
right over another's property, as right of way.
-eas'y a. not difficult; free from bodily or mental pain, complaint; not in much demand; fitting loosely. [F. aise]

eas'el (ez-) n. frame to support a picture,
blackboard. etc. [Du. ezel, ass]

east n. part of the horizon where the sun rises;
regions towards that. -a. on or in or near the
east; coming from the east. -adv. from, or to,
the east. -east'erly a. and adv. from or to the
east. -east'ern a. of or dwelling in the east.
-east'erner n. east'ward a. and n. -
east'ward(s) adv. [OE. easte]

East'er n. Christian festival of the resurrec-
tion of Christ. [OE. Eastre, goddess of spring
festival]

eas'y. See ease.

eat v.t. and i. chew and swallow; swallow;
consume, destroy; gnaw; wear away. -n. pl.
(sl.) food ready for consumption, usu. of small
quantity. -eat'able a. [OE. etan]

eaves (evz) n. pl. overhanging edges of a roof.
-eaves'dropper n. one who stands under
eaves or elsewhere to overhear. -
eaves'dropping n. [OE. efes]

ebb n. flowing back of the tide; decline. -v.i.
flow back; decline. [OE. ebba]

EBCDIC n. a computer coding system that
can represent 256 different characters. [Ex-
tended Binary Coded Decimal Interchange
Code]

eb'ony n. hard black wood. -a. made of or
black as ebony. -eb'onite n. vulcanite. [L.
ebenus]

ebullient a. boiling; exuberant. [L. ebullire,
boil out]

eccentric a. not placed, or not having the
axis placed, centrally; not circular (in orbit);
irregular; odd, whimsical. -n. mechanical
contrivance to change circular into to-and-fro
movement, whimsical person [G. ekkentros,
out of center]

ecclesiastic a. of or belonging to the church-
clergyman. -ecclesias'tical a. [G. ekklesias-
tikos, ekklesia, church]

ech'elon n. formation of troops or warships
in parallel divisions each with its front clear of
the one in front. [F. echelon, rung of ladder]

ech'o (ek -) n. repetition of sounds by reflection; close imitation. -v.i. resound or be
repeated by echo. -v.t. repeat as an echo; imitate opinions. [G.]

éclair (dk -) n. cake finger filled with cream
and iced. [F.]

eclec'tic a. borrowing one's
philosophy from various sources; catholic in
views or taste. -n. eclectic person. -
eclec'ticism n. [G. eklektikos, selective]

eclipse' n. blotting out of the sun, moon, etc.,
by another body coming between it and the
eye or between it and the source of its light;
loss of light or brilliance; obscurity. -v.t. cause
to suffer eclipse; outshine, surpass. -eclip'tic
a. of an eclipse. -n. apparent path of the sun.

[G. ekleipsis, leave out]

ecol'ogy n. the science devoted to the system
of interrelationships between organisms and
their environments; the totality of these interrelationships; activity undertaken to maintain
or restore the balance of nature. -e'cological
a. relating to ecology; benefiting the balance
of nature. [G. oikos, house]

econ'omy n. management, administration;
thrift, frugal use, structure, organization. -
econom'ic a. on business lines. econom'ics
n. pl. political economy, the science of the
production and distribution of wealth.
econom'ical a. saving, frugal; of economics.
econom'ically adv. -econ'omist n. -
econ'omize v.t. and i. [G. oikonomia, house
-law]

ecru' n. and a. color of unbleached linen. [F.]

ec'stasy n. exalted state of feeling, rapture;
trance; frenzy. [G. ekstasis]

ectoplasm n. in spiritualism, a semi-
luminous plastic substance which exudes
from the body of the medium. [G. ektos, outside, and plasma, mold]

ecumen'ic(al) a. pert. to the universe of the
Christian world or church. -ecumeni'city n.
[G. oiken, inhabit]

ec'zema n. skin disease. [G. ekzema]

edd'y n. small whirl in water, smoke, etc. -v.
i. move in whirls. [orig. uncertain]

Ed'en n. garden of Adam and Eve; ideal spot.
[Heb.]

edge n. cutting side of a blade; sharpness;
border, boundary. -v.t. sharpen give an edge
or border to; move gradually. -v.i. advance
sideways or gradually. -edge'ways,
edge'wise adv. -ed'gy a. irritable. -on edge,
nervous, excited. [OE. ecg]

ed'ible a. eatable. -edibil'ity n. [L. edibilis,
edere, eat]

e'dict n. order proclaimed by authority,
a decree. [L. edictum]

ed'ifice (-fis) building, esp. a big one. -ed'ify
v.t. improve morally. -edifica'tion n. [L.
edificare, build]

ed'it v.t. prepare for publication. -ed'ition n.
form in which a book is published; number of
copies of a book, newspaper, etc.; printed at
one time, issue. -ed'itor n. [L. edere, give out]

ed'ucate v.t. bring up; train mentally and
morally; provide schooling for; train. [L.
educare, educat -]

educe' v.t. bring out, develop; infer. -
edu'cible deduction n. -educ'tor n. [L.
educere, lead out]

eel n. snakelike fish. [OE. sæl]

ee'rie, ee'ry a. weird; superstitiously timid.
[OE. earg, cowardly]

efface' v.t. wipe or rub out. -effacement n.
[F. effacer]

effect' n. result, consequence; impression.
-pl. property. -v. t. bring about, accomplish.
-effect'ive a. -effect'ively adv. -effect'ual a.
-effect'ually adv. -effect'uate v.t. [L. efficere,
effect -, bring about]

effem'inate a. womanish, unmanly. -
effem'inacy n. [L. effeminate, fr. femina,
woman]

ef'ferent *a.* bearing outward, away. [L. *efferre*, fr. *ferre*, carry]

effervesce' (-es) *v.i* give off bubbles; issue in bubbles. -**efferves'cent** *a.* -**efferves'cence** *n.* [L. *effervescere*]

effete' *a.* worn -out, feeble. [L. *effetus*, exhausted by breeding]

efficacious *a.* producing or sure to produce a desired result. -**efficacy** *n.* [L. *efficere*, effect]

effi'cient *a.* capable, competent; producing effect. **effi'ciently** *adv.* -**effi'ciency** *n.* [L. *eficere*, effect]

eff'igy *n.* image, likeness. [L. *effigies*, fr. *fingere*, form]

eff'luent *n.* flowing out. -*n.* stream flowing from a larger stream, lake, *etc.* -**eff'luence** *n.* -**efflu'vium** *n.* (*pl.* -ia) invisible vapors, *esp.* those affecting lungs or sense of smell. -**eff'lux** *n.* -**efflux'ion** *n.* [L. *effluere*, flow out]

eff'ort *n.* exertion, endeavor. -**eff'ort-less** *a.* [F., fr. L. *fortis*, strong]

effront'ery (-un-) *n.* brazen impudence. [F. *effronto* *a. lit.* without brow (for blushing)]

effu'sion *n.* a pouring out; literary composition. -**effu'sive** *a.* gushing, demonstrative. -**effu'sively** *adv.* -**effu'siveness** *n.* -**effuse'** *v. t.* to pour out. [L. *effundere, effus -*, pour out]

eft *n.* newt. [OE. *efete*, cp. *newt*]

egg *n.* oval body produced by the female of birds, *etc.*, *esp.* of domestic fowl, and containing the germ of their young. -**egg'-plant** *n.* plant with an edible, purple skinned fruit of pearshaped form; the fruit of this plant, aubergine. [ON.]

egg *v.t.* egg on, encourage, urge. [ON. *eggia*, fr. *egg*, edge]

ego *n.* the self, the conscious thinking subject. -**egocen'tric** *a.* selfcentered. -**eg'oism** *n.* systematic selfishness; theory that bases morality on self-interest. -**eg'oist** *n.* -**egois'tic**, **egois'tical** *a.* -**eg'otism** *n.* talking habitually about oneself -, self -conceit. -**eg'otist** *n.* -**egotis'tic, egotistical** *a.* [L. = 1]

e'gret *n.* lesser white heron. [F. *aigrette*]

ei'der (-i-) *n.* Arctic duck. -**ei'derdown** *n.* breast feathers of the eider; quilt stuffed with eiderdown. [ON. *æther*]

eight (at) *a.* and *n.* cardinal number, one above seven. **eighth** (at -th) *a.* ordinal number. -**eighth'ly** *adv.* -**eighteen** *a.* and *n.* eight more than ten. -**fig'ure-of-eight** *n.* skating figure; any figure shaped as 8. [OE. *eahta*]

eith'er (-TH-) *a.* and *pron.* one or theother; one of two; each. -*adv.* or *conj.* bringing in first of alternatives or strengthening an added negation. [OE. *æther*]

ejaculate *v.t.* and *i.* exclaim, utter suddenly. [L. *ejaculari*, shoot forth]

eject' *v.t.* throw out; expel, drive out. [L. *ejicere, eject-*, throw out]

eke *v.t.* eke out, supply deficiencies of, make with difficulty (a living, *etc.*). [OE. *ecan*, increase]

elaborate *v.t.* work out in detail; produce by labor. -*a.* worked out in detail; highly finished; complicated. -**elaboration** *n.* [L. *elaborate*]

elapse' *v.i.* of time, to pass by. [L. *elabi*, *elaps-*, slip away]

elas'tic *a.* resuming normal shape after distortion; springy; not unalterable or inflexible. -*n.* cord, fabric, made elastic with interwoven rubber. -**elasti'city** *n.* [G. *elastikos*]

ela'tion *n.* high spirits; pride. -**elate'** *v.t.* [L. *elatus, pp.* of *efferre*, bring out]

el'bow *n.* outer part of the joint between the upper arm and the forearm. -*v.t.* thrust, jostle with the elbows. [OE. *elnboga*]

el'der *n.* a white -flowered tree with much pith. [OE. *ellern*]

el'der *a.* older. -*n.* person of greater age; old person; official of certain churches. -**el'derly** *a.* growing old. -**elédest** *a.* oldest. [*old*]

elect *v.t.* choose; choose by vote. -*a.* chosen; select, choice. -**elec'tion** *n.* choosing, *esp.* by voting -**electioneer'** to busy oneself in political elections. -**elect'ive** *a*, appointed, filled, chosen by election. -**elect'or** *n.* -**elect'oral** *a.* -**elect'orate** *n.* body of electors. [L. *eligere, elect-*, fr. *legere*, choose]

electricity (-is'-) *n.* active condition of the molecules of a body or of the etherround it, produced by friction, magnetism, *etc.*; force which shows itself in lightning, *etc.*; study of this. -**elec'tric** *a.* of, charged with, worked by, producing, electricity. [G. *elektron*, amber]

elec'tro- *prefix* makes compounds meaning of, by, caused by, electricity, as. **elec'tro-biol'ogy** *n.* science of electrical phenomena in living creatures. -**elec'tro-mag'net** *n.* -**electrol'ysis** *n.* electrical decomposition of a chemical compound. -**elec'troscope** *n.* instrument to show the presence or kind of electricity. -**elec'trocute** *v. t.* cause death by electric shock; execute (criminals) by electricity. [G. *electron*, amber]

electrode *n.* terminal of electric circuit; conductor leading current into, out of, water or gas. [G. *hodos*, way]

elec'tron *n.* one of fundamental particles of matter identified with unit of charge of negative electricity and essential component of the atom. -**electron'ic** *a.* of electrons or electronics; using devices, such as semiconductors, transistors or valves, dependent on action of electrons. -**electron'ics** *pl. n.* technology concerned with development of electronic devices and circuits; science of behavior and control of electrons. **electron'ic brain** *n.* (*sl.*) electronic computer. -**electron'ic da'ta processing** *n.* data processing largely performed by electronic equipment. -**elec'tronmicroscope** *n.* microscope that uses electrons and electron lenses to produce magnified image. [G. *electron*, amber]

el'egant *a.* graceful, tasteful; refined. -**el'egance** *n.* [L. *elegans*]

el'egy *n.* lament for the dead; sad poem. -**elegi'ac** *a.* plaintive. -*n. pl.* elegiac verses. [G. *elegeia*]

el'ement *n.* component part; substance which cannot be chemically analyzed; proper abode or sphere; resistance wire of electric heater. -*pl.* powers of the atmosphere; rudiments, first principles. -**elemental** *a.* of the powers of nature; tremendous; not compounded. -element'ary a. rudimentary, simple; primary. [L. *elementum*]

el'ephant n. very big four-footed, thick-skinned animal with ivory tusks and a long trunk. -elephant'ine a. unwieldy, clumsy, heavily big. -elephanti'asis n. a skin disease. -ele'phant seal n. largest of the seals. [L. *elephas*]

el'evate v.t. raise, lift up. -eleva'tion n. raising; angle above the horizon, as of a gun; drawing of one side of a building, *etc.* -el'evator n. lift or hoist. [L. *elevare*]

elev'en a. and n. number next above ten, one added to ten; team of eleven persons. -elev'enth a. the ordinal number. [OE. *endleofan*]

elf n. fairy; small elemental being. -elf'in, elf'ish, elv'ish a. [OE. *ælf*]

elic'it (-a-) v.t. draw out. [L. *elicere*]

elide' v.t. omit in pronunciation (a vowel, syllable). -elis'ion n. [L. *elidere*, strike out]

el'igible a. fit or qualified to be chosen; suitable, desirable. eligibil'ity n. [L. *eligibilis* -*eligere*, fr. *legere*, choose]

eliminate v.t. remove, get rid of, set aside. -elimina'tion n. [E. *oliminare*, put out of doors]

elite' n. pick of (society, *etc.*).

elix'ir n. preparation sought by the alchemists to change base metals into gold, or to prolong life; sovereign remedy. [Arab. *al-iksiri*]

elk n. large deer. [OE. *eoth*]

ell n. measure of length. [OE. *eln*]

ellipse' n. an oval; figure made by a plane cutting a cone at a smaller angle with the side than the base makes; *gram.* omission of words needed to complete the grammatical construction or full sense. [L. *ellipsis*]

elm n. familiar tall tree with doubly-serrated leaves; its wood. [OE.]

elocution n. art of public speaking, recitation, voice, management. -elocu'tionist n. [L. *eloqui*, speak out]

e'longate v.t. lengthen. -elonga'tion n. [L. *e*, out, *longus*, long]

elope' v.i. run away with a lover; escape. -elope'ment n. [AF. *aloper*]

eloquence n. fluent and powerful use of language. -el'oquent a. el'oquently adv. [L. *eloqui*, speak out]

else adv. besides; otherwise. -pron. other. elsewhere' adv. in or to some other place. [OE. *elles*, otherwise]

elucidate v.t. throw light upon, explain. -elucida'tion n. -elu'cidatory a. [L. *lucidus*, bright]

elude' v.t. escape, slip away from, dodge. -elu'sion n. -elu'sive a. elusory a. elusively adv. [L. *eludere*, play off]

em n. (*printing*) the square of any size of type. [m.]

ema'ciate (shi-) v.t. to make lean. -emacia'tion n. [L. *emaciare*, emaciate, fr. *macies*, leanness]

em'anate v.i. issue from, originate. -emana'tion n. [L. *emanare*, flow out]

emancipate v.t. set free. -emancipa'tion n. -eman'cipator n. [L. *emancipate*, emancipate]

emasculate v.t. castrate; enfeeble, weaken. -emascula'tion n. -emas'cu-lative a. [L. *emasculate*]

embalm' (-bam) v.t. preserve (dead body) from decay with spices, *etc.*; perfume; reverently preserve (*e.g.*, a memory). [*balm*]

embar'go n. order stopping the movement of ships; suspension of commerce; ban. -v.t. put under an embargo. [Sp.]

embark' v.t. and i. put, go, on board ship; engage, involve (in). embarka'tion n. [F. *embarquer*, cp. bark]

embarrass v.t. perplex, put into difficulty; encumber. -embarr'assment n. [F. *embarrasser*, orig. put within 'bars']

em'bassy n. office or work or residence of an ambassador; deputation. [*ambassador*]

embatt'le v.t. provide with battlements. -embatt'led a. [*See* battlement]

embellish v.t. adorn. -embell'ishment n. [F. *embellir*]

em'ber n. glowing cinder. [OE. *æmerge*]

embezz'le v.t. divert fraudulently, misappropriate (money in trust, *etc.*). -embez'zler n. -embez'zlement n. [AF. *embesiler*, damage, steal]

embitter v.t. make bitter. [*bitter*]

emblazon v.t. depict in a coat-of-arms; deck in bright colors; praise widely. [F. *blason*, coat-of-arms]

em'blem n. symbol; heraldic device -emblemat'ic a. emblemat'icall y adv. [G. *emblems*, inlaid work]

embod'y v.t. give body, concrete expression, to; represent, be an expression of. embod'iment n. [*body*]

embold'en v.t. encourage. [*bold*]

em'bolism n. obstruction of artery by bloodclot. [G. *embolismos*, what is thrown in]

emboss' v.t. mold, stamp or carve in relief. [OF. *embosser*, cp. *boss*]

embrace' v.t. clasp in the arms; seize, avail oneself of, accept. -n. clasping in the arms. [F. *embrasser*]

embrasure (-zher) n. opening in a wall for a cannon; bevelling of a wall at the sides of a window. [F.]

embroider v.t. ornament with needlework; embellish, exaggerate (a story). -embroi'dery n. [F. *broder*]

embroil v.t. bring into confusion; involve in hostility. -embroil'ment n. [F. *embrouiller*, entangle]

em'bryo n. unborn or undeveloped offspring, germ; undeveloped thing. [G. *embryon*]

em'erald n. green precious stone. e. of the color of emerald. [F. *emeraude*]

emerge' v.i. come up, out; rise to notice; come out on inquiry. -emer'gence n. -emer'gent a. -emer'gency n. sudden unforeseen thing or event needing prompt action. [L. *emergere*]

em'ery n. hard mineral used for polishing. [F. *émeri*]

emet'ic *a.* causing vomiting. -*n.* medicine doing this. [G. *emetikos*]

em'igrate *v.t.* go and settle in another country. -**emigra'tion** *n.* **em'igrant** *n.* [L. *emigrare*]

em'inent *a.* distinguished, notable. - **em'inently** *adv.* -**em'inence** *n.* distinction; rising ground. -**Em'inence**, title of cardinal. [L. *eminere*, stand out]

emit' *v.t.* give out, put forth. -**emitt'er** *n.* - **emis'sion** *a.* -**em'issary** *n.* one sent out on a mission. -**emissiv'ity** *n.* power of emitting. [L. *emittere*]

emollient *a.* softening. -*n.* ointment or other softening application. [L. *emollire*, soften]

emo'tion *n.* mental agitation, excited state of feeling. -**emo'tional** *a.* given to emotion; appealing to the emotions. [L. *emotio*, fr. *emovere*, stir]

em'pathy *n.* ability to enter fully into another's feelings, experience. [G. *en*, in, *pathos*, feeling]

em'peror *n.* sovereign of an empire. - **em'press** *fem.* [L. *imperator*, fr. *imperare*, command]

em'phasis *n.* stress on words; vigor of speech, expression; importance attached. *n.* -**em'phasize** *v.t.* emphat'ic *a.* forcible; stressed. -**emphat'ically** *adv.* tG.]

em'pire *n.* large territory, *esp.* an aggregate of states under one supreme control. [F. fr. L. *imperium*]

empiric *a.* relying on experiment or experience, not on theory. -*n.* empiric scientist, physician. -**empir'ically** *adv.* -**empir'icism** *n.* [G. *empeirikos*, experienced]

employ' *n.* use; keep occupied; use the services of, keep in one's service. -**employ'er** *n.* -**employee'** *n.* -**employ'ment** *n.* [F. *employer*]

emporium *n.* center of commerce; (in affected language) store. [L. *mart*]

empow'er *v.t.* enable, authorize [*power*]

emp'ty *a.* containing nothing; unoccupied; senseless; vain, foolish. -*v.t.* and *i.* make or become empty. -*n.* empty box, basket, *etc.* -**emp'tiness** *n.* [OE. *æmeltig*]

e'mu *n.* large Australian bird like an ostrich. [Port. *ema*, ostrich]

em'ulate *v.t.* strive to equal or excel; imitate. -**em'utator** *n.* emula'tion *n.* competition, rivalry. -**em'ulative** *a.* -**em'ulous** *a.* [L. *æmulari*, rival]

emul'sion *n.* milky liquid mixture with oily or resinous particles in suspension. - **emul'sifier** *n.* an agent that forms or preserves an emulsion, *esp.* any food additive that prevents separation of sauces or other processed foods. -**emul'sive** *a.* -**emul'sify** *v.t.* [L. *mulgere*, milk]

en - *prefix* forms verbs with sense of put in, into, on; as: **engulf'** *v.t.* swallow up. -**enrage'** *v.t.* to put into a rage. Many such words are omitted and the meaning and derivation should be sought under the simple word. [F. *en*, L. *in*]

en (*typography*) half of an em (*q.v.*)

ena'ble *v.t.* make able, authorize; give power or strength. [*able*]

enact' *v.t.* make law; play, act. [act]

enam'el *n.* glasslike coating applied to metal, *etc.* to preserve the surface; coating of the teeth; any hard outer coating. -*v.t.* cover with enamel; adorn with colors. [*en*-, and obs. *amel*, F. *émail*, enamel]

enam'or (-er) *v.t.* inspire with love. [F. *enamourer*]

encamp' *v.t.* and *i* settle in a camp. - **encamp'ment** *n.* [*camp*]

encaustic *a.* burnt in. -*n.* art of burning colored designs into tiles *etc.* [G. *enkaustikos*, burnt in]

encephalitis *n.* inflammation of the brain. [G. *kephale*, head]

enchant' (-a-) *v.t.* bewitch, delight. - **enchant'ment** *n.* [F. *enchanter*]

encir'cle *v.t.* surround; embrace; go round. [*circle*]

enclave' *n.* portion of territory entirely surrounded by foreign land. [F.]

enclose' *v.t.* shut; place in with something else (in a letter, *etc.*); fence, *esp.* common land. -**enclo'sure** (-zher) *n.* [*close*]

enco'mium *n.* formal praise; eulogy. [L.]

encompas (-kum-) *v.t.* surround; include. [*compass*]

en'core *interj.* again, once more. -*n.* call for the repetition of a song, *etc.* ; the repetition. -*v.t.* call for repetition. [F.]

encounter *v.t.* meet in hostility; meet with. -*n.* hostile or casual meeting. [OF. *encontrer*]

encourage (-kur-) *v.t.* hearten, inspirit. -**encouragement** *n.* [*courage*]

encroach' *v.i* intrude (on) as a usurper. - **encroach'ment** *n.* [F. *accrocher*, hook on]

encrust' *v.i.* cover with hard coating crust. [L. *incrustare*]

encrypt' *v.t.* put (a message) into code; to put (computer data) into a coded form; to distort (a television or other signal) so that it cannot be understood without the appropriate decryption equipment. -**encrypted** *a.* - **en'cryption** *n.* [G. *kryptein*, hide]

encum'ber *v.t.* hamper; burden. - **encum'brance** *n.* [OF. *encombrer*]

encyclical *n.* circular letter from pope to bishops, on public affairs, *etc.* (G. *kyklos*, circle]

encyclopedia, encyclopae'dia *n.* book of information on all subjects, or on every branch of a subject, usually arranged alphabetically. [fr. G. *enkyklios paideia*, all-round education]

end *n.* limit; extremity; conclusion; fragment; latter part; death; event, issue; purpose, aim. -*v.t.* put an end to. -*v.i.* come to an end. [OE. *ende*]

endang'er *v.t.* expose to danger. -**endangered** *a.* in danger; used *esp.* of animals in danger of extinction. [F. fr. L. *dominium*, rule]

endeav'or (-dev-er) *v.i* try, attempt. -*n.* attempt, effort. [F. *devoir*, duty]

endemic *a.* regularly existing or found in a country or district. -*n.* -**endemic disease**. [G. *en*, in, *demos*, people]

en'dive *n.* curly leaved chicory. (F.]

en'docrine n. substance absorbed from the ductless glands into the bloodstream. a. -**endocrinol'ogy** n. [fr. G. *endon*, within, *krinein*, to separate]

endorse' v.t. write (*esp.* sign one's name) on the back of, ratify; confirm. -**endorse'ment** n. [F. *endosser*, fr. *dos*, back]

endow' v.t. provide a permanent income for; furnish. -**endow'ment** n. [OF. *endouer*]

endure' v.i last. -v.t. undergo; tolerate, put up with. -**endu'rance** n. power of enduring. -**endu'rable** a. [L. *indurate*, fr. *durus*, hard]

ene'ma, en'ema n. rectal injection; instrument for this. [G. *enienai*, send in]

en'emy n. hostile person, opponent; armed foe; hostile force or ship. (F. *ennemi*, fr. L. *inimicus*]

en'ergy n. vigor, force, activity. -**energet'ic** a. -**energet'ically** adv. -**en'ergize** v. t. give vigor to. [F. *Onergie*]

en'ervate v.t. weaken, deprive of vigor. -**enerva'tion** n. [L. *enervare*, deprive of sinew]

enfee'ble v.t. weaken. -**enfee'blement** n. [*feeble*]

enfold' v.t. enwrap; encompass. [*fold*]

enforce' v.t. compel obedience to; impose (action) upon; drive home. -**enforce'ment** n. -**enforce'able** a. [OF. *enforcier*, strengthen]

engage' v.t. bind by contract or promise; hire; order; pledge oneself, undertake; attract, occupy; bring into conflict; interlock. -v.i. begin to fight; employ oneself; promise. -**engage'ment** n. [F. *engager-gage*, pledge]

engen'der v.t. give rise to, beget; sow the seeds of. [F. *engendrer*]

en'gine n. complex mechanical contrivance; machine; instrument of war. -**engineer'** n. one who constructs or is in charge of engines, military works, or works of public utility (*e.g.* bridges, roads). -v.t. construct as an engineer; contrive. [F. *engin*, fr. L. *ingenium*, skill]

English (ing'gl-) a. of England. -n. language or people of England and of all peoples who have adopted this language. [OE. *Englise*]

engrave' v.t. and i. cut in lines on metal for printing; carve, incise; impress deeply. -**engra'ving** n. copy of a picture printed from an engraved plate. -**engra'ver** n. [*grave*]

engross' v.t. write out in large letters or in legal form; absorb (attention). -**engross'ment** n. [AF. *engrosser*, fr. *grosse*, large (letter)]

enhance' v.t. heighten, intensify, raise in price. -**enhance'ment** n. -**enhanc'ive** a. [F. *hausser*, rasie]

enig'ma n. riddle; puzzling thing or person. -**enigmat'ic**, **enigmatical** a. -**enigmat'ically** adv. [G. *ainigma*]

enjoin' v.t. command, impose, prescribe. [F. *enjoindre*]

enjoy' v.t. take pleasure in; have the use or benefit of. -v. *refl.* be happy.

enlarge' v.t. make bigger; set free. -v.i. grow bigger; talk at large (with on) -**enlarge'ment** n. [*large*]

enlighten (-lit-) v.t. instruct, inform. -**enlight'ened** a. factually well-informed, tolerant of alternative opinions, and guided by rational thought; privy to or claiming a sense of spiritual or religious revelation of truth. -**enlight'enment** n. [*light*]

enlist' v.t. and i. engage as a soldier or helper; gain (sympathies, *etc.*). -enlistment n. [*list*]

enli'ven v.t. brighten, make more lively or cheerful, [*life*]

enmesh' v.t. entangle; take in a net (*lit.* or *fig*). [*mesh*]

en'mity n. ill-will; hostility. [AF. *enimitg*]

ennui' n. boredom. [F.]

enor'mous a. very big, vast. -**enor'mity** n. gross offense; great wickedness. [L. *enormis*, abnormal]

enough' (e-nuf) a. as much or as many as need be, sufficient. -n. sufficient quantity. adv. sufficiently. -**enow'** a., n., and adv. enough. [OE. *genog*]

enrich' v.t. make rich; add to. -**enrich'ment** n. [*rich*]

enroll', **enrol'** (-ō-) v.t. write the name on a roll or list; engage, enlist, take in as a member; enter, record. -**enroll'ment** n. [F. *enrôler*]

ensconce' v.t. place snugly, comfortably in safety. [*sconce*]

ensem'ble (ong-song-bl) n. effect of any combination regarded as a whole; woman's matching dress; (*mus.*) concerted piece, passage. [F.]

en'sign (-sin) n. naval or military flag; badge, emblem; a commissioned officer of the lowest rank. [F, *enseigne*]

enslave' v.t. make into a slave. -**enslave'ment** n. -**ensla'ver** n. [*slave*]

ensue' v.i follow, happen, after; result from. -v.t. strive for. [F. *ensuivre*, fr. L. *insequi*, follow up]

ensure' v.t. make safe, certain to happen. [F. *assurer*, cp. *assure*]

entab'lature n. in architecture, part resting on capital of column. [L. *tabula*, table]

entail' v.t. settle (land, *etc.*) on persons in succession, none of whom can then dispose of it; involve as result. -n. such settlement. [F. *entailler*, cut into]

entan'gle (-ng-gi) v.t. entwine; involve; ensnare. -**entan'glement** n. [tangle]

entente' (ong-tongt) n. a friendly understanding between nations. [F.]

ent'er v.t. go or come into; join (a society, *etc.*); write in, register. -v.i. go or come in; join; begin: engage. -**en'trance** n. going or coming in; right to enter; fee paid for this; door or passage to enter. -**en'trant** n. one who enters, *esp.* a contest. -**en'try** n. entrance; an entering; item entered, *e.g.* in an account, list. [F. *entrer*]

enterprise n. design, undertaking, usually a bold or difficult one; -**enterprising** a. bold and active in spirit. [F.]

entertain' v.t. receive as guest; amuse; maintain; consider favorably, cherish. -**entertain'er** n. -**entertaining** a. amusing. -**entertain'ment** n. hospitality; amusement; public performance. [F. *entretenir*]

enthu'siasm n. ardent eagerness, zeal. -**enthu'siast** n. **enthusias'tic** a. -**enthusias'tically** adv. **enthuse'** v.i (colloq.) show enthusiasm. [G. *enthousiasmos*, inspiration]

entice' v.t. allure; attract or entrap adroitly. -**entice'ment** n. (OF. *enticier*, provoke]

entire' a. whole, complete, not broken. -**entire'ly** adv. -**entire'ty** n. [F. *entier*, fr. L. *integer*, whole]

enti'tle v.t. give a title or claim to. [*title*]

en'tity n. thing's being or existences thing having real existence. [Late L. *entitas*, fr. *esse*, be]

entomology n. study of insects, -**entomol'ogist** n. -**entomological** (-oj' -) a. [G. *entomon*, insect]

entourage' (ong-tōō-razh) n. retinue, suite; surroundings. [F.]

en'trails n. pl. bowels, intestines; inner parts. [F. *entrailles*]

entrain' v.t. and i. put, go, aboard a train. [*train*]

entrance. See enter.

entrap' v.t. catch in a trap; lure into atrap; lure into a position which compromises the victim. [*trap*]

entreat' v.t. ask earnestly, beg, implore. entreat'y n. [*treat*]

entrée' n. freedom of access; side dish served between courses; the main course itself. [F.]

entrust' v.t. confide (to); commit, put incharge. [*trust*]

entry. See enter.

enumerate v.t. count. -**enumera'tion** n. -**enumerator** n. one who enumerates. [L. *enumerate*, number of]

enunciate v.t. state clearly; pronounce. [L. *eauntiare*]

envel'op v.t. wrap up, enclose. -**envel'opment** n. **en'velope** n. folded, gummed cover of a letter; covering, wrapper. [F. *enveloper*]

envi'ron v.t. surround. -**envi'roriment** n. surroundings; conditions of life or growth. -**envi'rons** n. pl. districts round (a town, etc.). [F. *adv.*]

envisage v.t. view; look at. [*visage*]

en'voy n. messenger; diplomatic ministerof rank below an ambassador. (F. *envoyé*, one sent]

en'voy n. short concluding stanza of a poem. [F. *envoi*]

en'vy n. bitter or longing considerationof another's better fortune or success or qualities; object of this feeling. -v.t. feel envy of. —**en'vious** a. -**en'viable** a. [F. *envie*, L. *invidia*]

en'zyme n. digestive ferment; leaven. [G. *zyme*, leaven]

epaulette n. ornamental shoulder-piece of a uniform. [F. *Epaulette*]

ephemeral a. short-lived, lasting only for a day, or few days. -**ephem'eron, ephem'era** n. ephemeral insect or thing. [G. *ephemeros*]

ep'ic a. telling in continuous story the achievements of a hero or heroes. -n. epic poem. [G. *epikos*]

epicure n. one dainty in eating and drinking. -**epicure'an** a. of -Epicurus, who taught that pleasure, in the shape of practice of virtue,

was the highest good; given to refined sensuous enjoyment. -n. such a person or philosopher. -**epicure'anism** n. [*Epicurus*, of Athens (300 B.C.)]

epidemic a. prevalent for a time among a community. -n. -**epidemic disease.** [fr. G. *epi*, upon, *demos*, people]

epidermis n. outer skin. -**epidermic** a. [G.]

epiglott'is n. cartilage at root of tongue, closing larynx in swallowing. [G. *epi*, upon, *glotta*, tongue]

epigram n. short poem with a witty orsatirical ending; pointed saying. [G. *epigramma*, inscription]

epigraph n. inscription. [G. *epigrapheepi*, upon, *graphein*, write]

epilepsy n. disease in which the suffererfalls down in a fit, with foaming and spasms. **epilep'tic** a. subject to epilepsy. -n. person who suffers from epilepsy. [G. *epilepsia*, seizure]

ep'ilogue (-og) n. short speech or poemat the end of a play; the concluding part of a book. [G. *epilogos*, peroration]

Epiph'any n. festival of the appearance of Christ to the Magi. [G. *epiphania*, manifestation]

episcopal a. of a bishop; ruled bybishops. -**epis'capacy** n. government by bishops; body of bishops. -**episcopa'lian** a. of an episcopal system or churchman. member or adherent of an episcopal church. [*See* bishop]

episeotomy n. incision of the perineum to facilitate childbirth.

ep'isode n. incident; incidental narrativeor series of events; part of a Greek tragedy between choric songs. -**episod'ic, episod'ical** a. [G. *epeisodion*, coming inbesides]

epistemic a. of or pertaining to knowledge; cognitive. -**epistemology** n. study of the source, nature and limitations of knowledge. -**epist'emological** a. [G. *episteme*, knowledge]

epis'tle (-sl) n. letter, *esp*. of the apostles; poem in the form of a letter. -**epis'tolary** a. [G. *epistole*]

ep'itaph n. inscription on a tomb. [G. *epitaphion*, fr. *taphos*, tomb]

ep'ithet n. adjective expressing a quality or attribute; name full of meaning. -**epithet'ic** a. [G. *epitheton*]

epit'ome (-me) n. summary, abridgment. -**epitomize** v. t. **epit'omist** n. [G. , fr. *epitemnein*, cut into]

epizo'ic a. living or attached to the surface of an animal.

e'poch (-ok) n. beginning of a period; period, era, *esp*. one marked by notable events. -**e'pochal** a. [G. *epoche*, stoppage]

epon'ymous a. commemorated by the adoption of the name. [G. *eponymos*, giving name to]

e'qual a. same in number, size, merit, *etc*. ; fit or qualified; evenly balanced. -n. one equal to another. v.t. be equal to. [L. *æqualis*, fr. *æquus*, level]

e'qual opportu'nity n. theory and practice of employment opportunity unbiased because of race, color religion, gender, age, national origin, or mental or physical handicap.

equanim′ity *n.* calmness, evenness of mind or temper. [L. *æquanimitas*]

equate′ *v.t.* state or assume the quality of - **equa′tion** *n.* statement of equality between two mathematical expressions; balancing; compensation for inaccuracy. **-equa′tor** *n.* great circle of the earth eqidistant from the poles. **-equator′ial** *a.* [L. *æquare, equat-,* make equal]

equestrian *a.* of, skilled in, horseriding; mounted on a horse. *-n.* rider or performer on a horse. [L. *equestris*]

equi- *prefix,* equal, at equal. [L. *æqui-*] **-equiangular** (-ng-g-) *a.* having equal angles. [*angular*]. **-equidis′tant** *a.* at equal distances. [*distant*]. **-equilat′eral** *a.* having equal sides. [*lateral*] *etc.*

equilibrium *n.* state of balance; balanced mind. **-equili′brate** *v. t.* and *i.* **-equil′ibrist** *n.* **-equil′ibrator** *n.* stabilizing plane, fin, of airplane; acrobat, rope-walker. [L. *-equilibrium,* fr. *libra,* scales]

eq′uine *a.* of a horse. [L. *equinus,* fr. *equus,* horse]

e′quinox *n.* time at which the sun crosses the equator and day and night are equal. *-pl.* points at which the sun crosses the equator. - **equinoc′tial** *a.* [L. *æquinoctium,* fr. *nox,* night]

equip′ *v.t.* supply, fit out, array. **-equip′ment** *n.* **-eq′uipage** *n.* carriage, horses and attendants; retinue; outfit. [F. *équiper*]

eq′uity *n.* fairness; use of the principles of justice to supplement the law; system of law so made. **eq′uitable** *a.* fair, reasonable, just. **-eq′uitably** *adv.* [L. *æquitas,* fr. *æquus,* equal]

equivalent *a.* equal in value; having the same meaning or result; corresponding. *-n.* equivalent thing, amount, *etc.* **-equiv′alence, equivalency** *n.* [F. *equivalent,* L. *valens, ualentis,* worth]

equivocal *a.* ambiguous, of double or doubtful meaning; questionable, liable to suspicion. [Late L. *quivocare,* call alike]

e′ra *n.* system of time in which years are numbered from a particular event; time of the event; memorable date; period. [L. *æra,* brasses (as counters)]

eradicate *v.t.* root out. **-eradica′tion** *n.* **eradicator** *n.* (L. *eradicate*]

erase′ *v.t.* rub out; efface. **eraser** *n.* **-era′sure** *n.* [L. *eradere, eras-,* scrape out]

Er′ato *n.* muse of amatory poetry. [G.]

erect′ *a.* upright. *-v.t.* set up; build. **-erect′ile** *a.* **-erec′tion** *n.* **erect′or** *n.* [L. *erectus,* upright]

erg *n.* unit of work. [G. *ergon,* work]

er′go *adv.* therefore. [L.]

er′gonomics *n.* applied science, concerned with the nature and characteristics of people as they relate to design and activities with the intention of producing more effective results and greater safety.

er′got *n.* disease of rye and other plants; diseased seed used as a drug. **-er′gotism** *n.* ergot poisoning. [F.]

er′mine *n.* animal like a weasel with fur

brown in summer and white, except for black tail-tip, in winter; its fur *usu.* white. [OF.]

erne *n.* eagle, *esp.* sea-eagle. [OE. *earn*]

erode′ *v.t.* wear out, eat away. **-ero′sion** *n.* **-ero′sive** *a.* [L. *erodere, eros-*]

erot′ic *a.* relating to sexual love. [G. *erotikos,* fr. *Eros,* god of love]

err *v.i* make mistakes; be wrong; sin. - **errat′ic** *a.* irregular in movement, conduct, *etc.* **erra′tum (-a-)** *n.* **erra′ta** *pl.* mistake noted for correction. **-erroneous** *a.* mistaken, wrong. **-err′or** *n.* mistake; wrong opinion; sin. **-err′ant** *a.* wandering in search of adventure; erring. [F. *errer,* wander]

err′and *n.* short journey for a simple business; the business; purpose. **-err′and boy** *n.* [OE. *ærende,* message]

erratic *a.* odd, eccentric; following an irregular course. [*err*]

er′udite *a.* learned. **-erudi′tion** *n.* knowledge got by study. [L. *eruditas*]

erupt′ *v.i* burst out. **-erup′tion** *n.* bursting out, *esp.* a volcanic outbreak; rash. **-erupt′ive** *a.* [L. *erurnpere, erupt-*]

erythromycin *n.* antibiotic ($C_{37}H_{67}NO_{13}$) obtained from an actinomycete used in treating bacterial infactions.

escape′ *v.i* get free; get off safely; go unpunished; find a way out. *-v.t.* elude; come out unawares from. *-n.* an escaping; leakage. - **escapade′** *n.* flighty exploit. **-escap′ist** *n.* one who tries to escape from reality. [ONF. *escaper,* fr. L. *ex,* out of, *cappa,* cloak]

es′cort *n.* armed guard for a traveler, criminal, ships *etc.*; person or persons accompanying another for protection or courtesy. **-escort′** *v.t.* act as escort to. [F. *escorte*]

Es′kimo *n.* inhabitant of Arctic Amer., Greenland, *etc.*; Inuit; the language. *-a. pert.* to Eskimos and their language. [orig. uncertain]

ESL *abbr.* English as a second language.

esoteric *a.* secret; for the initiated. [G. *esoterikos,* fr. *eso,* within]

espionage *n.* spying; the use of spies [F. *espionnage*]

esplanade′ *n.* level space, *esp.* one used as a public promenade. [F.]

espouse (-z) *v.t.* marry; support, attach oneself to (a cause, *etc.*). **-espous′al** *n.* [OF. *espouser*]

esquire′ *n.* title of respect added to a gentleman's name, *esp.* on the address of a letter; formerly, a squire. [OF. *escuyer,* fr. L. *scutarius,* shield-bearer]

essay′ *v.t.* try, attempt; test. **-ess′ay** *n.* literary composition, usually short and in prose; attempt. **-ess′ayist** *n.* writer of essays. [F. *essayer*]

ess′ence *n.* existence, being; absolute being, reality; all that makes a thing what it is; extract got by distillation; perfume, scent. **-essen′tial** *a.* of, or constituting, the essence of a thing. *-n.* indispensable element; chief point. - **essential′ity** *n.* **-essen′tially** *adv.* [F.]

estab′lish *v.t.* set up; settle; found; prove. **-estab′lishment** *n.* establishing; church system established by law; permanent organized body; full number of a regiment, *etc.*; household; house of business; public institution. (L. *stabilire*, fr. *stare*, stand]

estate' *n.* landed property; person's property; a class as part of a nation; rank, state, condition. [OF. *estat*]

esteem' *v.t.* think highly of, consider; -*n.* favorable opinion, regard -esteemed' *a.* highly respected. [L. *æstimare*]

es'timate *v.t.* form an approximate idea of (amounts, measurements, *etc.*); form an opinion of, quote a probable price for. -*n.* approximate judgment of amounts, *etc.* ; the amount, *etc.*, arrived at; opinion; pricequoted by a contractor. -es'timable *a.* worthy of regard. -estima'tion *n.* opinion, judgment, esteem. [L. *stimare*]

estrange' *v.t.* make unfriendly, put astop to affection. -estrange'ment *n.* [OF. *estrangier*, make strange]

es'tuary *n.* tidal mouth of a river. [L. *æstuarium*, tidal]

etcet'era (abbrev. *etc.*), 'and the rest'. -*n. pl.* accessories, trimmings. [L.]

etch *v.t.* make an engraving by eating away the surface of a metal plate with acids, *etc.* -*v.i.* practice this art -etch'ing *n.* etch'er *n.* [Du. *etsen*]

eter'nal *a.* without beginning or end; everlasting; changeless. -eter'nally *adv.* eter'nity *n.* [L. *mternus*]

eth'ane *n.* gas without color or smell, burning with pale flame. [*ether*]

e'ther (-th-) *n.* substance or fluid supposed to fill all space; the clear sky, region above the clouds; colorless volatile liquid used as an anesthetic. -ethe'real *a.* light, airy; heavenly. -ethereal'ity *n.* [L. *ether*, upper air]

eth'ic, ethical *a.* relating to, or treating of, morals. -eth'ically *adv.* -eth'ics *n. pl.* science of morals; moral principles, rules of conduct. [G. *ethikos*, fr. *ethos*, character]

eth'nic *a.* of race. -ethnog'raphy *n.* description of races of men. -ethnograph'ic *a.* - ethnol'ogy *n.* science of races. ethnolo'gical *a.* [G. *ethnikos*, fr. *ethnos*, nation]

ethnobotany *n.* branch of botany concerned with the use of plants in the customs and folklore of a people.

e'thos *n.* distinctive character, genius, ethical make-up of an age, race, *etc.* [G.]

eth'yl *n.* base of alcohol, ether, *etc.* ; type of petrol. [*ether*]

etiol'ogy *n.* study of causes, *esp.* inquiry into the origin of disease. -etiol'ogical *a.* [G. *aitia*, cause]

etiquette *n.* conventional rules of manners; court ceremonial; code of conduct for a profession. [F. *Otiquette*]

etymology *n.* tracing, or an account of, a word's formation, origin, development; science of this. -etymolo'gical *a.* - etymolo'gically *adv.* -etymol'ogist *n.* - et'ymon *n.* primitive word from which a derivative comes. [G, *etymologia,* fr. *etymos,* true]

eucalyptus *n.* Australian gum-tree and allied plants. -eucalypt'us-oil *n.* disinfectant.

[fr. G. *eu*, well, and *kalyptos*, covered]

Eu'charist (-k-) *n.* sacrament of the Lord's Supper; consecrated elements. -eucharis'tic *a.* [G. *eucharistia,* thanksgiving]

Euclidian geometry *n.* theory based on the postulates of Euclid, including that only one line may be drawn through a given point parallel to a given line.

eugenic *a.* relating to, or tending towards, the production of fine offspring. -*n. pl.* science of this. -eugen'ist *n.* [G. *eu-*, well, and *root gen-*, bring forth]

eu'logy *n.* speech or writing in praise of a person; praise. -eu'logize *v.t.* -eu'logist *n.* eologistic *a.* -eulogis'tically *adv.* [G. *eulogia,* praise]

eu'nuch (-k) *n.* castrated man, *esp.* one employed in a harem. [G *eunouchos,* bedguard]

euphemism *n.* substitution of a mild word or expression for a blunt one; instance of this. [G. *euphemismos,* speaking fair]

eu'phony *n.* pleasantness of sound - euphon'ic *a.* -eupho'nious *a.* -eupho'nium *n.* bass saxhorn. [G. *euphonia,* fr. *phone,* voice]

Eura'sian *a.* of mixed European and Asiatic descent; of Europe and Asia as a single continent. -*n.* Eurasian person. [*European-Asian*]

Europe'an *a./n.* (native) of continent of Europe. [G. *Europe*]

euthanasia *n.* gentle, easy death; theory that incurables, *etc.* should be painlessly removed. [G.]

evac'uate *v.t.* empty; discharge; withdraw from; remove (people) from area. - evacua'tion *n.* -evacuee' *n.* evacuated person. [L. *vacuus*, empty]

evade' *v.t.* avoid, escape from; elude; frustrate. -eva'sion *n.* -eva'sive *a.* -eva'sively *adv.* [L. *euadere*, eva]

eval'uate *v.t.* find or state the value or number of. -evalua'tion *n.* [*value*]

evanesce' (-es) *v. i.* fade away. -evanes'cent *a.* -evanes'cence *n.* [L. *evanescere*, vanish]

evan'gel *n.* gospel. -evangel'ical *a.* of or according to the gospel teaching; of the Protestant school which maintains salvation by faith. -evangel'icalism, evangelism *n.* -evan'gelist *n.* writer of one of the four Gospels; preacher of the gospel; revivalist. -evan'gelize *v.t.* preach to; convert. -evangeliza'tion *n.* [G. *evangelion,* good tidings]

evaporate *v.i* turn into vapor; pass off in vapor. -*v.t.* turn into vapor. [L. *eva'porare,* fr. *vapor,* vapour]

eve *n.* evening before (a festival, *etc.*); time just before (an event, *etc.*); evening. [*even*]

e'ven *n.* evening. -e'vensong *n.* evening prayer. [OE. *æfen*]

e'ven *a.* flat, smooth; uniform in quality; equal in amount, balanced; divisable by two; impartial. -*v.t.* make even. *adv.* invites comparison with something as trong included by implication in the statement. [OE. *efen*]

e'vening (-vn-) *n.* close of day; of one's life, old age. [OE. *zefnung*]

event *n.* occurrence of a thing; notable occurrence; issue; result. -event'ful . full of exciting events. -event'ual a. that will happen under certain conditions; resulting in the end. -event'ually adv. -eventual'ity n. possible event. -event'uate v.i. turn out; end. (L. evenire, event -, come out]

ev'er adv. always; constantly; at anytime; by any chance. ev'erglade n. swamp. - ev'ergreen n. non-deciduousplant, shrub. -a. [OE. æfre]

everlasting a. eternal. -n. eternity; plant with lasting flowers, immortal. [ever and lasting]

ev'ery (-vr-) a. each of all; all possible. - ev'erybody n. -ev'eryday a. usual, ordinary. ev'eryone n. -ev'erything n. ev'erywhere adv. in all places. [OE. æfre lis, ever each]

evict v.t. expel by legal process, turnout. [L. evincere, evict -, prove]

ev'ident a. plain, obvious -ev'idently adv. -ev'idence n. sign, indications ground for belief, testimony; in evidence, conspicuous. -v.t. indicate, prove. -evidential a. [L. videre, see]

e'vil a. bad, harmful. -n. what is bad or harmful; sin, -e'villy adv. [OE. yfel]

evince' v.t. show, indicate. -evinc'ible a. - evinc'ive a. [L. evincere, prove]

eviscerate (-vis-er-) v.t. disembowel. - eviscera'tion n. [L. eviscerate]

evoke' v.t. call up. -evoca'tion n. -evoc'ative a. [L. evocare]

evolve' v.t. develop; unfold, open out; produce. -v.i. develop, esp. by natural process; open out. evolu'tion n. an evolving; development of species from earlier forms; movement of troops or ships; movement in dancing, etc. [L. evolvere, evolut -, to roll out]

ex', formerly, as in ex-king, etc. [G.]

exacerbate v.t. aggravate, embitter. - exacerba'tion n. [L. exacerbare, cp. acerbity]

exact' (-gz-) a. precise, accurate, strictly correct. -v.t. demand, extort; insist upon; enforce. -exact'ly adv. [L. exigere, exact -, to weigh, prove, forceout]

exaggerate v.t. magnify beyond truth, overstate. [L. exaggerate, heap up]

exalt' (egz-awlt') v.t. raise up; praise; make noble. -exalta'tion n. an exalting; rapture. [L. exaltare, fr. altos, high]

exam'ine v.t. investigate; ask questions of, test the knowledge or proficiency of by oral or written questions; inquire into. [L. examinare, weigh accurately]

exam'ple n. thing illustrating a general rule; specimen; model, pattern; warning, precedent. [L. exemplum, sample]

exasperate (-gz-) v.t. irritate, enrage; intensify, make worse. -exaspera'tion n. [L. exasperate, fr. asper, rough]

ex'cavate v.t. hollow out; make a hole by digging; unearth. -excava'tion n. act of excavating; resulting cavity. -ex'cavator n. [L. excavare, fr. cavus, hollow]

exceed' v.t. be greater than; do more than authorized, go beyond; surpass. -exceed'ingly adv. very. -excess' n. an exceeding; amount by which a thing exceeds; too great an amount;

intemperance or immoderate conduct. [L. excedere, excess -, to go beyond]

excel' v.t. be very good, pre-eminent. -v.t. surpass, be better than. -ex'cellent a. very good. -ex'cellence n. -ex'cellency n. title of ambassadors, etc. [L. excellere, rise above]

excelsior interj. higher. [L. comp. of excelsis, high, lofty]

except' v.t. leave or take out; exclude. -v.i. raise objection. -prep. not including; but. conj. unless. -except'ing prep. not including. - excep'tion n. an excepting; thing excepted, not included in a rule; objection. -excep'tional a. unusual. -excep'tionally adv. - excep'tionable a. open to objection. [L. exceptus, taken out]

excerpt (ek'serpt) n. quotation; selected passage; extract. -v.t. take out; quote. lex, from, carpere, to pick]

excess'. See exceed.

exchange' v.t. give (something) in return for something else. -v.i. of an officer, change posts with another. -n. giving one thing and receiving another; giving or receiving coin, bills. etc. of one country for those of another; thing given for another; building where merchants meet for business. -exchange'able a. - exchangeabil'ity n. [change]

excise' (-z) n. duty charged on homegoods during manufacture or before sale. -exci'sable a. liable to excise. [Du. accijns]

excise' v.t. cut out, cut away. -excis'ion n. [L. excidere, ercis-]

excite' v.t. rouse up, set in motion; stimulate, move to strong emotion. -exci'table a. - exci'tably adv. -excitabil'ity n. -excite'ment n. [L. excitare]

exclaim' v.i and t. cry out. -exclamation n. -exclama'tion point or mark, n. punctuation mark (!) used to indicate an interjection or an element of surprise or stress in an utterance. -exclam'atory a. expressing exclamation. [L. exclamare, shout out]

exclude' v.t. shut out; debar from. - exclu'sion n. -exclu'sive a. excluding; inclined to keep out (from society, etc.); sole, only; different from all others. -exclu'sively adv. [L. excludere]

excommunicate v.t. shut off from the sacraments of the church. [Church L. excommunicare, expel from communion]

excrement n. waste matter discharged from the bowels, dung. [L. excernere, excret -, sift out]

excursion n. journey, ramble, trip, for pleasure; deviation from planned route. [L. excursiona, running out]

excuse' (-z) v.t. try to clear from blame; overlook, forgive, gain exemption; set free, remit. -excuse' (-a) n. that which serves to excuse; apology. -excu'sable (-z-) a. [L. excusare, fr. causa, cause]

ex'eat n. formal leave of absence, esp. for a college student. [L. = 'let him go out']

ex'ecrate v.t. feel or express abhorrence, hatred for; curse. -execra'tion n. -ex'ecrable a. abominable, hatefully bad. [L. exsecrari, curse]

ex'ecute v.t. carry out, perform; sign (a document); kill (criminals). **execu'tion** n. **execu'tioner** n. one employed to kill those sentenced to death by law. **-exec'utant** n. performer, esp. of music. **-exec'utive** a. carrying into effect, esp. of branch of a government enforcing laws. **-n.** committee carrying on the business of a society, etc.; the administrative branch of government; a person with administrative or managerial control, esp. in business. **exec'utor** n. person appointed by one making a will to carry out the provisions of the will. **exec'utrix** fem. executive **privilege** n. the right of the president to refuse to give confidential information requested by a legislative or judiciary body if the disclosure would adversely affect government functions of processes. [L. exsequi, exsecut -, follow out]

exem'plar n. model type. **-exemp'lary** a. fit to be imitated, serving as an example. **exemp'larily** adv. **-exemp'lify** v.t. serve as example of, make an attested copy of. **exemplifica'tion** n. [L. exemplum, sample]

exempt' (-gz-) a. freed from, not liable. **-v.t.** free from. **exemp'tion** n. [L. exemptus, taken out]

ex'ercise (-z) n. employment, use (of limbs, faculty, etc.); use of limbs for health; practice for the sake of training; task set for training. **-v.t.** use, employ; give (training, health) exercise to; carryout, discharge; trouble, harass. **-v.i.** take exercise. [L. exercere, keep at work]

exert' (-gz -) v.t. bring into active operation. **-exer'tion** n. [L. exserere, exsert -, put forth]

exhale' v.t. breathe out; give off as vapor. **-v. i.** breathe out; pass of as vapor. **-exhala'tion** n. [L. exhalare, breathe out]

exhaust' (igz -awst') v.t. draw off; use up; empty, treat, discuss, thoroughly; tire out. **-n.** used steam, fluid or gas from an engine; passage from, or coming out of, this. [L. exhaurire, exhaust -, drain out]

exhibit (-gz-) v.t. show, display; manifest; show publicly in competition. **-n.** thing shown, esp. in competition or as evidence in a court. **-exhibi'tion** n. display; act of displaying; public show (of works of art, etc.); allowance made to a student, scholarship. [L. exhibere, hold forth]

exhilarate (-gz-) v.t. enliven, gladden. **exhilara'tion** n. [L. exhilarate, fr. hilaris, happy, merry]

exhort' v.t. urge, admonish earnestly. **exhorta'tion** n. **-exhort'er** n. [L. hortari, encourage]

exhume' v.t. unearth; take out again what has been buried. **-exhuma'tion** n. [L. ex, out of, humus, ground]

exigent (-j-) a. exacting; urgent. **-ex'igence, exigency** n. pressing need; emergency. [L. exigere, force out]

ex'ile n. banishment, expulsion from one's own country; long absence abroad; one banished. **-v.t.** banish. [F. exil]

exist' (-gz-) v.i be, have being, continue to be. **-existen'tialism** n. theory of the fortuitous nature of the universe, in which we create our own values. [F. exister, fr. L. ex(s)istere, make to stand out]

ex'it n. actor's departure from the stage; a going out; way out; death. **-ex'it** v.i sing. 'goes out'. **ex'eunt** (-i unt) pl. 'go out' n. stage directions, to indicate the going off of a player or players. (L. exire, go out]

ex'odus n. departure, esp. of a crowd. **Ex'odus**, second book of Old Testament, relating the departure of the Israelites from Egypt. [G. exodus, way out]

exonerate v.t. free, declare free, from blame; exculpate; acquit. **-exonera'tion** n. **exon'erative** a. [L. exonerate, un burden]

exorbitant a. very excessive, immoderate. **-exorb'itantly** adv. **exorbitance** n. [L. exorbitare, go out of one's orbit]

ex'orcize, exorcise (-z) v.t. cast out (evil spirits) by invocation; free a person of evil spirits. **-ex'orcism** n. **-ex'orcist** n. [G. exorkizein, from ex, out, horkos, oath]

exoskeleton n. bony outer structure of, e. g. crab, turtle; any hard or horny outer casing. [G. exo, outside, and skeleton]

exoter'ic a. understandable by the many; ordinary, popular (opposite of esoteric). [G. exoterikos]

exot'ic a. brought in from abroad, not native. **-n.** exotic plant, etc. [G. exotikos, fr. exo, outside]

expand' v.t. and i. spread out; enlarge, increase in bulk, develop. **-expan'sion** n. **expan'sive** a. wide-spreading; effusive. [L. expanders]

expatriate v.t. banish. **expatria'tion** n. [L. patria, country]

expect' v.t. look on as likely to happen; look for as due. (L. exspectare, look out for]

expectorate v.t. and i. spit out (phlegm, etc.) **-expectora'tion** n. [L. expectorate, fr. pectus, breast]

expedient a. fitting, advisable; politic. **-n.** device, contrivance. [expedite]

ex'pedite (-lt) v.t. help on, hasten. **expedi'tion** n. promptness; journey for a definite purpose; warlike enterprise; body of men sent on such enterprise. **-expedi'tionary** a. **-expedi'tious** a. prompt, speedy. [L. expedite, free the foot, help on]

expel' v.t. drive, cast out. **-expul'sion** n. expulsive a. [L. expellere, expuls -]

expend' v.t. spend, pay out; use up. **expend'iture** n. **-expense'** n. spending; cost. **-pl.** charges, outlay incurred. **-expens'ive** a. costly. [L. expendere, fr. pendere, pens -, weigh]

experience n. observation of facts as a source of knowledge; a being affected consciously by an event; the event. [L. experiential fr. experire, test thoroughly]

experiment n. test, trial; something done in the hope that it may succeed, or to test a theory. **-v.i.** make an experiment. **-experiment'al** a. **-experiment'ally** adv. [L. experiri, test]

ex'pert a. practiced, skillful. **-n.** one expert in something; an authority. [L. experiri, test]

expire' v.t. breathe out. **-v.i.** give out breath; die; die away; come to an end. [L. ex(s)pirare]

explain' *v.t.* make clear, intelligible; give details of, account for. **-explana'tion** *n.* **explan'atory** *a.* [L. *explanare*, make smooth]

explic'it (-a-) *a.* stated in detail; stated, not merely implied; outspoken. [L. *explicare*, unfold]

explode' *v.i* go off with a bang; burst violently. **-v.t.** made explode; discredit, expose (a theory, *etc.*). **-explo'sion** *n.* **-explo'sive** *a.* and *n.* [L. *explodere, explos-*, clap out (of theater)]

ex'ploit *n.* brilliant feat, deed. **-v.t.** turn to advantage; make use of for one's own ends. **-exploita'tion** *n.* [F.]

explore' *v.t.* examine (a country, *etc.*) by going through it; investigate. **-explora'tion** *n.* **-explor'atory** *a.* **-explor'er** *n.* [L. *explorare*, announce discovery]

explosion. *See* explode.

ex'port *v.t.* send (goods) out of the country. **-n.** exported article. **-expor-ta'tion** *n.* **export'er** *n.* [L. *exportare*, carry out]

expose' (-z) *v.t.* leave unprotected; lay open (to); exhibit, put up for sale; unmask; disclose. **-expo'sure** *n.* act of exposing, being exposed; (*photo.* the exposing of the sensitive plate to light; duration of this. [F. *exposer*]

expostulate *v.i* make (*esp.* friendly) remonstrances. [L. *expostulate*, demand urgently]

expound' *v.t.* explain, interpret. **-expo'nent** *n.* one who expounds; executant; maths. index, symbol showing the power of a factor. **-exponen'tial** *a.* **-exposi'tion** *n.* explanation, description; exhibition of goods, *etc.* **-expos'itory** *a.* **-expos'itor** *n.* [L. *exponere*, put forth]

express' *v.t.* put into words; make known or understood by words; conduct, *etc.*; squeeze out; send by express. **-a.** definitely stated, specially designed; of a messenger, specially sent off, of a train, fast and making few stops. **-n.** express train or messenger. **-adv.** specially, on purpose; with speed. **-express'ly** *adv.* **-express'ible** *a.* **-expres'sion** *n.* a pressing out; phrase, saying; what the features convey of thought, feeling, *etc.* **-expres'sionism** *n.* theory that art, literature, should be primarily an expression of the artist's personality. [L. *expressus*, squeezed out, clearly stated]

expulsion. *See* expel.

expurgate *v.t.* remove objectionable parts (from a book, *etc.*). **-expurga'tion** *n.* **ex'purgator** *n.* **-expurg'atory** *a.* [L. *expurgale*, make pure]

exquisite (-iz-it) *a.* of extreme beauty or delicacy; keen, acute; keenly sensitive. **-n.** dandy. **-ex'quisitely** *adv.* [L. *exquisitus*, sought out]

extant' *a.* of a document, *etc.*, still existing. [L. *exstare*, stand forth]

extempore (-ri) *a.* and *adj.* without preparation, off-hand. **-extempora'neous** *a.* **-extemp'orary** *a.* **-extemp'orize** *v.t.* speak without preparation; devise for the occasion. **-extemporiza'tion.** [L. *ex tempore*, out of the time]

extend' *v.t.* stretch out, lengthen; prolong in duration; widen in area, scope; accord, grant.

-v.i. reach; cover an area; have a range or scope; become larger or wider. **-exten'sible** *a.* **-extensibil'ity** *n.* **-extension** *n.* **-extens'ive** *a.* wide, large, comprehensive. **-extent'** *n.* size, scope; space, area; degree. [L. *extenders, extens -*, stretch out]

extended family *n.* nuclear family and close relatives, often living under one roof.

extenuate *v.t.* make less blameworthy. **extenua'tion** *n.* [L. *extenuate*, make thin, fr. *tenuis*, thin]

exte'rior *a.* outer, outward. **-n.** outside; outward appearance. [L.]

exterminate *v.t.* root out, destroy utterly. **-extermina'tion** *n.* [L. *exterminare*, drive over the boundary]

extern'al *a.* outside. **extern'ally** *adv.* [L. *externus*]

extinct' *a.* quenched, no longer burning; having died out or come to an end. **-extinc'tion** *n.* **-exting'uish** *v.t.* put out, quench; wipe out. **-exting'uishable** *a.* **-exting'uisher** *n.* that which extinguishes; cap to put out a candle; apparatus for putting out a fire. [L. *extinguere, extinct -*, quench]

extol *v.t.* praise highly; exalt. [L. *extollere*, lift up]

extort' *v.t.* get by force or threats; extract illegally. [L. *extorquere*, extort -, wrench away]

ex'tra *a.* additional; larger, better than usual. **-adv.** additionally; more than usually. **-n.** extra thing; something charged as additional. **-extrajudi'cial** *a.* outside court or normal legal practice. [for *extraordinary*]

extract' *v.t.* take out, *esp.* by force; obtain against a person's will; get by pressure, distillation, *etc.*; deduce, derive; copy out, quote. **-ex'tract** *n.* matter got by distillation; concentrated juice; passage from a book. **extrac'tion** *n.* extracting; ancestry. **extract'or** *n.* [L. *extrahere, extract -*, draw out]

extradi'tion *n.* delivery, under a treaty, of a foreign fugitive from justice to the authorities concerned. **ex'tradite** *v.t.* give or obtain such delivery. **extradi'table** *a.* [L. *extradition*, handing over]

extramur'al *a.* outside the walls, boundaries; (of a university lecturer) one not of the faculty. [*mural*]

extra'neous *a.* added from without, not naturally belonging. [L. *extraneus*]

ex'traordinary *a.* out of the usual course; additional; unusual, surprising, exceptional. **-extraord'inarily** *adv.* [L. *extraordinarius*, fr. *extraordinem*, outside the order]

extraterrest'rial *a.* of, or from outside the earth's atmosphere. [L. *extra*, outside, *terra*, earth]

extra'vagant *a.* wild, absurd; wasteful; exorbitant. [L. *extrauagari*, wander outside the bounds]

extreme' *a.* at the end, outermost; of a high or the highest degree; severe; going beyond moderation. **-n.** thing at one end or the other, first and last of a series; utmost degree. **extreme'ly** *adv.* **-extre'mist** *n.* advocate of extreme measures. **extrem'ity** *n.* end. *-pl.*

hands and feet; utmost distress; extreme measures. [*extremus*]

ex'tricate *v.t.* disentangle, set free. -ex'tricable *a.* -extrica'tion *n.* [L. *extricare,* extricate]

ex'trovert *n.* (*psych.*) one whose mind is turned outward away from himself. usually a cheerful and uninhibited person. [L. *extra,* outside, *vertere,* turn]

exub'erant *a.* prolific, abundant, luxuriant; effusive, high-flown. -exu'berance *n.* -exu'berantly *adv.* [L. *uber,* fertile]

exude' *v.i* ooze out. -*v.t.* give off (moisture). -exuda'tion *n.* [L. *exsudare,* sweat out]

exult' *v.i* rejoice, triumph. -exulta'tionn. exult'ant *a.* [L. *ex(s)ultare* leap for joy]

eye (i) *n.* organ of sight; look, glance; attention; various things resembling an eye. -*v.t.* look at; observe. -eye'-ball *n.* pupil. -eye'brow *n.* fringe of hair above the eye. -eye'lash *n.* hair fringing the eyelid. -eye'less *a.* -eye'let *n.* small hole for a rope, *etc.* to pass through. -eye'lid *n.* lid or cover of the eye. -eye'sore *n.* ugly mark, thing that annoys one to see. -eye'-witness *n.* one who saw something for himself. [OE. *eager*]

F

fable *n.* tale; legend; short story with a moral, *esp.* one with talking animals as characters. -*v.t.* invent, tell fables about. -fab'ulist *n.* writer of fables. -fab'ulous *a.* told of in fables; unhistorical; absurd, unbelievable. [L. *fabula,* fr. *fari,* speak]

fab'ric *n.* thing put together; building, frame, structure; woven stuff, texture. -fabri-cate *v.t.* invent (a lie, *etc.*); forge (a document). -fab'ricator *n.* -fabrica'- tion *n.* [L. *fabrica,* fr. *faber,* smith]

façade' *n.* front of a building. [F.]

face *n.* front of the head; front, surface, chief side of anything; outward appearance: look; coolness, impudence. *v.t.* meet boldly-. give or front towards; give a covering surface. -*v.i.* turn. -fa'cer *n.* blow in the face; sudden difficulty. [F.]

fac'et (fas'-) *n.* one side of a many-sided body, *esp.* of a cut gem. [F. *facette,* dim. of face]

facetious (fas-e-shus) *a.* waggish, jocose, given to jesting. -face'tiae (-se, 'shi) *n. pl.* pleasantries, witticisms. [L. *facetus,* graceful]

fac'ile *a.* easy; working easily; easygoing. -facil'itate (-sit-) *v.t.* make easy, help. -facil'ity *n.* easiness; dexterity. -*pl.* opportunities, good conditions. [F.]

facsimile (fak-sim'li) *n.* exact copy. fac-simile machine *n.* (FAX) device that scans a page of text or graphics and converts it into electronic pulses for tranmission to other locations via telephone lines. [L. *fac simile,* make like]

fact *n.* thing known to be true or to have occurred. [L. *factum,* thing done]

fac'tion *n.* political or other party (used always in a bad sense); misguided party spirit. -fac'tious *a.* [L. *factio*]

fac'tion *n.* a television program, film, or literary work comprising a dramatized presentation of actual events. [fr. *fact* and fiction]

fac'tor *n.* something contributing to a result; one of numbers that multiplied together give a given number; agent, one who buvs and sells for another. -fac'tory *n.* building where things are manufactured; trading station in a foreign country. [L. *facere,* to do]

fac'ulty *n.* ability, aptitude; inherent power; a power of the mind; department of a university; members of a profession; authorization. -fac'ultative *a.* optional. [L. *facultas,* power]

fad *n.* pet idea, craze. -fadd'y *a.* -fadd'ist *n.* [orig. uncertain]

fade *v.i.* wither; lose color; grow dim; disappear gradually. -fade in', -out', gradual appearance, disappearance, of a cinema scene; similar effect with sounds in radio. -fade'less *a.* [OF. *fader*]

Fah'renheit (-hit) *a.* of the thermometric scale on which the freezing point of water is 32° and the boiling point, 212° [*Fahrenheit,* Ger. inventor (d. 1736)]

fail *v.i.* be insufficient; run short; lose power; die away; be wanting at need; be unsuccessful; become bankrupt. -*v.t.* disappoint, give no help to. -fail'-safe *a.* designed to return to safe condition in the event of a failure or malfunction; (of a nuclear weapon) capable of being deactivated in the event of a failure or accident; unlikely to fail; foolproof. -fail'ure *n.* [L. *falterer,* to deceive]

fain *a.* glad, willing; inclined; constrained. -*adv.* gladly. [OE. *fægvgen,* glad]

faint *a.* feeble; dim; pale; weak; inclined to swoon. -*v.i.* swoon: to fade or decay; lose courage. -*n.* swoon. -faint'ly *adv.* [OF. *feint,* sluggish]

fair *n.* periodical gathering for trade, often with amusements added of shows and roundabouts. -fair'ing *n.* present from a fair; streamlining of an aircraft. [L. *feria,* holiday]

fair *a.* beautiful; ample; blond; unblemished; of moderate quality or amount; just, honest; of weather, favorable. -*adv.* honestly. [OE. *foeger*]

fair'way *n.* navigable channel in river; roadstead, *etc.*; (*golf*) main track from green to green, with 'rough' on either side. [*fair*]

fairy (fatr-) *n.* small elemental being with powers of magic. *a.* of fairies; like a fairy, beautiful and delicate. [OF. *faierie,* land of fays]

faith *n.* trust; belief; belief without proof; religion; promise; loyalty. [OF. feid fr. L. *fides,* cp. fidelity]

fake *v.t.* counterfeit; falsify; adulterate. -*n.* sham; counterfeit; dodge or trick. -*a.* [earlier *feak,* feague; Ger. *fegen,* furbish]

fal'con *n.* small bird of prey, *esp.* trained in hawking for sport. -fal'coner *n.* one who keeps, trains, or hunts with falcons. -fal'conry *n.* flow [L. *falcon-,* fr. *falx,* sickle (shape of wings, beak, claws)]

fall (-aw-) *v.i.* drop, come down freely; hang down; become lower; come to the ground; cease to stand; perish; collapse; be captured;

pass into a condition; become; happen. -n. a falling; amount that falls; amount of descent; yielding to temptation; autumn; rope of hoisting tackle. [OE. *feallan*]

fall'acy (fal'-a-si) n. misleading argument; flaw in logic; mistaken belief. -**falla'cious** (-a-) a. [L. *allere*, deceive]

fall'ible a. liable to error. -**fall'ibly** adv. -**fallibil'ity** n. [F. fr. *Low.* L. *fallibilis*]

fallow a. plowed and harrowed but left without crop; uncultivated. -n. fallow land. -v.t. break up (land). [OE. *fealg*, harrow]

fallow a. pale brown or reddish yellow. -**fall'ow-deer** n. [OE. *fealo*]

false (-aw-) a. wrong, erroneous; deceptive; faithless; sham; artificial; untrue. -**false'ly** adv. -**false'hood** n. lie. -**false'-ness**. -**fal'sity** n. -**fal'sify** v.t. to alter fraudulently; misrepresent; disappoint (hopes, etc.). -**falsification** n. [L. *falsus*, mistaken, fr. *fallere, fals-*, deceive]

falset'to n. forced voice above the natural range. [It. dim. of *falso*, false]

fal'ter (-aw-) v.i. stumble; speak hesitatingly; waver. -v.t. say hesitatingly. [orig. uncertain]

fame n. reputation; renown; rumor. [L. *fama*, report]

familiar a. intimate; closely acquainted; well-known, common; unceremonious. -n. familiar friend or demon. [L. *familiaris*, fr. *familia* household]

fam'ily n. household of parents and their children; group of parents and children, or near relatives; person's children; all descendants of a common ancestor; class, group of allied objects. -**fam'ily-tree** n. lineage of a person, family, in graphic form. [L. *familia*, household, fr. *famulus*, servant]

fam'ine (-in) n. extreme scarcity of food; starvation. -**fam'ish** v.t. starve. -v.i. be very hungry. [F. fr. L. *fames*, hunger]

fa'mous. See **fame**.

fan n. instrument for producing a current of air, esp. for cooling the face; winnowing machine; propellerblade; thing spread out as a bird's tail; ventilating machine. -v.t. winnow, blow, or cool with a fan. [OE. *fann*, fr. L. *vannus*]

fan n. enthusiastic follower (of a game, etc.), devotee (of a person). -**fan'mail** n. letters from one's fans. [for *fanatic*]

fanat'ic a. filled with mistaken enthusiasm, esp. in religion. -n. fanatic person; zealot. -**fanat'ical** a. -**fanat'ically** adv. -fanaticism n. [L. *fanaticus*]

fan'cy n. power of imagination; mental image; notion, whim, caprice; liking, inclination; followers of a hobby. a. ornamental, not plain; of whimsical or arbitrary kind. -v.t. imagine; be inclined to believe; have or take a liking for. -**fan'cier** n. one with liking and expert knowledge. [shortened fr. *fantasy*]

fan'fare n. flourish of trumpets. [F.]

fang n. long pointed tooth; snake's poison tooth; root of a tooth. [OE. *fang*, booty, fr. *fon*, seize]

fantasy n. power of imagination, esp. extravagant; mental image; fanciful invention

or design. -**fanta'sia** (-z-) n. fanciful musical composition. -**fantas'tic** a. quaint, grotesque, extremely fanciful. -**fantas'tically** adv. [G. *phantasia*]

far adv. at or to a great distance or advanced point; by very much. a. distant. -n. great distance or amount. -**far'-fetched** a. forced, not natural. -**far'sighted** a. able to see the future effects of present action; able to see objects clearly only when they are far from the eyes. [OE. *feorr*]

far'ad n. unit of electrical capacity. [Michael *Faraday*, 1791-1867]

farce n. play meant only to excite laughter; absurd and futile proceeding. [F.]

fare (fer) n. money paid by a passenger for conveyance; passenger; food. -v.i. happen; get on; travel. -**farewell'** interj. goodbye. -n. leave-taking. [OE. *faran*, travel]

fari'na n. meal; powder; starch; pollen. -**farina'ceous** a. mealy; starchy. [L.]

farm n. tract of cultivated land. -v.t. pay or take a fixed sum for the proceeds of (a tax, etc.); cultivate. [F. *ferme*]

fa'ro (fa-ro) n. a card-game not dependent on skill. [*Pharoah*]

far'ther (-TH-) a. more distant. -adv. to, at, greater distance. -**far'thest** a. most far. adv. to, at, greatest distance. [*far*]

fas'cia n. long flat surface of wood or stone in a building; part of shop-front bearing the merchant's name. [L.]

fascinate v.t. make powerless by look or presence; charm, attract. -**fascina'tion** n. -**fas'cinator** n. charmer; headscarf for evening wear. [L. *fascinate*, enchant]

Fas'cist n. member of Italian or similar political party aiming at the overthrow of communists, radicals, etc., by violence, and of strong rule by a dictator. [It. fascistic members of a *fascio*, union]

fash'ion (-shun) n. make, style; manner; custom, esp. in dress. -v.t. shape, make. -**fash'ionable** a. in the prevailing mode. -**fash'ionably** adv. [F. *faqon*]

fast (-a-) v.i. go without food or some kinds of food esp. as a religious exercise. -n. act or appointed time, of fasting. -**fast'day** n. [OE. *fæstan*]

fast (-a-) a. firm, fixed, steady, permanent; rapid; ahead of true time; dissipated. -adv. firmly, tightly; rapidly; in a dissipated way. -**fast'ness** n. fast state; fortress. [OE. *fæst*, firm]

fast'en (-sen) v.t. attach, fix, secure. -v.i. seize (upon) [*fast*]

fastidious a. hard to please; easily disgusted. [F. *fastidieux*, L. *fastidiosus*]

fat a. plump, thick, solid; containing much fat; fertile. -n. oily substance of animal bodies; fat part. -v.t. feed (animals) for slaughter. -**fatt'en** v.t. and i. -**fat'ness** n. -**fatt'y** a. [OE. *fætt*]

fate n. power supposed to predetermine events; goddess of destiny; destiny; person's appointed lot or condition; death or destruction. -v.t. preordain. -**fate'ful** a. prophetic, fraught with destiny. -**fa'tal** a. deadly, ending in death; destructive; very ill-advised, disastrous; inevitable. -**fa′tally** adj. -**fatal′ity** n. rule of fate; calamity; death by accident. -**fa′talism** n. belief that everything is predetermined; submission to fate. [L. fatum, decree of the gods]

fa′ther n. male parent; forefather, ancestor; originator, early leader; priest, confessor; oldest member of a society. -v.t. beget; originate; pass as father or author of, act as father to; fix the paternity of -**fa′therhood** n. -**fa′ther-in-law** n. father of one's husband or wife. -**fa′therly** a. -**fa′therless** a. -**fa′therland** n. one's country. -**Fa′ther's Day** n. day in which the father is honored by the family, usu. the third Sunday in June. [OE. fœder]

fath′om (-ia′TH-) n. (naut.) measure of six feet. -v.t. sound (water); get to the bottom of, understand. -**fath′omless** a. too deep to fathom. -**fath′omable** a. [OE. fœthm, two arms outstretched]

fatigue′ v.t. weary. -n. weariness of body or mind; toil; soldier's non-military duty-n. pl. informal army clothes. [F. fatiquer, L. fatigare].

fau′cet (-set) n. apparatus for controlling the flow of liquid from a pipe, esp. in a kitchen or bathroom; tap [F. fausseti]

fault n. defect; misdeed; blame, culpability; (tennis) ball wrongly served; (hunting) failure of scent; (geol.) a break in strata. -**fault′y** a. -**fault′less** a. -**fault′ily** adv. -**fault′lessly** adv. [F. faute]

faun′a n. animals of a region or period. [L. Fauna, sister of Faunus; v.s.]

faux′ pas (fo-pa) awkward blunder. [F. = false step]

favor (-ver) n. goodwill; approval; partiality; especial kindness; badge or knot of ribbons. -v.t. regard or treat with favor; oblige; treat with partiality; aid support. -**favorably** adv. -**fa′vorite** (-it) n. favored person or thing; horse, etc. expected to win race. a. chosen, preferred. -**fa′voritism** n. practice of showing undue preference. [L. favor]

fawn n. young fallow-deer. a. of a light yellowish-brown. [F. faon]

fawn v.i. of a dog, etc., show affection by wagging the tail and grovelling; of a person, cringe, court favor in a servile manner. [OE. fahnian]

faze v.t. (sl.) discomfit. [OE. fesiani]

fear n. dread, alarm; unpleasant emotion caused by coming evil or danger. -v.i. regard with fear; revere; hesitate, shrink from (doing something). [OE. fær, sudden peril]

feas′ible (-z-) a. practicable, that can be done. -**feas′ibly** adv. -**feasibil′ity** n. [F. faisable, fr. faire, do]

feast n. banquet, lavish meal; religious anniversary to be kept with joy; annual village festival. -v.i. partake of a banquet, fare sumptuously. -v.t. regale with a feast. [L. festa]

feat n. notable deed; surprising trick. [F. fait, fr. L. factum, deed]

feath′er (feTH′-) n. one of the barbed shafts which form the covering of birds. -v.t. provide

with feathers; turn (an oar) edgeways. -v.i. grow feathers; turn an oar. [OE. fether]

feat′ure n. part of the face (usu. pl.); characteristic or notable part of anything. -v.t. portray; give prominence to. -**feat′ureless** a. flat, undistinguished [OF. faiture, shape]

Feb′ruary n. second month of the year. [L. Februarius]

fe′ces n.pl. excrement, bodily waste matter. -**fe′cal** a. [L. faex, dregs]

fec′und a. fertile. [L. fecundus, fruitful]

fed′eral a. of, or like, the government of states which are united but retain more or less independence within themselves; pert. to the Union in the Civil War. [L. fœdus, foeder-, alliance]

fee n. payment for services, esp. one due to a public official or a professional man; entrance-money. -v.t. pay a fee to. [OE. feoh, cattle, money]

fee′ble a. weak; ineffective; insipid. -**fee′bly** adv. [F. faible]

feed v.t. give food to; supply, support. -v.i. take food. -n. a feeding; fodder, pasturage; allowance of fodder; material supplied to a machine; part of a machine taking in material. [OE. fedan]

feel v.t. examine, search, by touch; perceive, have knowledge of, by touch or in emotions. -v.i. use the sense of touch; grope; be conscious; have, be affected by (a sentiment); sympathize. -n. sense of touch; impression on it. -**feel′ing** n. sense of touch; physical sensation; emotion; sympathy, tenderness; conviction or opinion not solely based on reason. -pl. susceptibilities. a. sensitive, sympathetic. [OE. felan]

feign (fan) v.t. pretend, simulate. -v.i. pretend. [F. feindre, fr. L. fingere, invent]

feint (fant) n. sham attack or blow meant to deceive an opponent. -v.i. make such move. [F. feinte]

felic′ity (-is′-) n. great happiness, bliss; appropriateness of wording. -**felic′itous** a. apt, well-chosen; happy. -**felic′itate** v.t. congratulate. -**felicita′tion** n. (usu. in pl.), congratulations. [L. felix, felic-, happy]

fe′line a. of cats; catlike. -**felin′ity** n. [L. felinus, fr. felis, cat]

fell v.t. knock down; cut down (a tree). [OE. fellan]

fell′ow n. comrade, associate; counterpart, like thing; member (of certain learned societies, etc); person. -a. of the same class, associated. -**fell′owship** n. [ON. felagi, partner]

fel′on n. one who has committed a felony. a. cruel, fierce. -**fel′ony** n. crime more serious than a misdemeanor. -**felo′nious** a. [F. folon]

felt n. cloth made by rolling and pressing wool with size; thing made of this. -v.t. make into, or cover with, felt. [OE.]

fe′male a. of the sex which bears offspring; relating to this sex or to women. -n. one of this sex. -**fe′male screw**, screw cut on the inside surface of a screw-hole. [F. femelle]

fem′inine (-in) a. of women; womanly; (gram.) of the gender proper to women's names. -feminin'ity *n.* -fem'inism *n.* influence of women; advocacy of this, of women's political rights, *etc.* -fem'inist *n.* [L. *femininus*]

fem'oral *a.* of the thigh. [Late L. *femoralis,* fr. *femur,* thigh]

fence *n.* art of using a sword; hedge or railing; *(sl.)* receiver of stolen goods. -*v.t.* put a hedge round, enclose. -*v.i.* practice sword-play. - **fen'cing** *n.* [defence]

fend *v.t.* ward off, repel. -*v.i.* provide (for oneself, *etc*).. -fend'er *n.* bundle of rope, *etc.* hung over a ship's side to prevent chafing; frame round a hearth; guard of the wheel of an automobile. [*defend*]

fenn'el *n.* yellow-flowered fragrant herb. [OE. *finol,* fr. L. *feniculum*]

fe'ral **fe'rine** (fe-) *a.* of or like a wild beast. [L. *fera,* wild beast]

fer'ment *n.* leaven, substance causing a thing to ferment; excitement, tumult. - **ferment'** *v.i.* undergo a chemical change with effervescence, liberation of heat and alteration of properties, e. g. process set up in dough by yeast. -*v.t.* subject to this process; stir up, excite. -fermenta'tion *n.* [L. *fermentum*]

ferocious (-ō-shus) *a.* fierce, savage, cruel. -feroc'ity (-os'-) *n.* savage cruelty. [L. *ferax, feroc-*]

ferr'et *n.* half-tamed animal like a weasel used to catch rabbits, rats, *etc.* ; -*v.t.* take or clear with ferrets; search out. -*v.i.* search about, rummage. [F. *furet*]

ferr'ic *a.* ferr'ous *a.* containing iron. [L. *ferrum,* iron]

ferry *v.t.* and *i.* carry, pass, by boat across a river, strait, *etc.* -*n.* place or a boat for ferrying. -ferr'yman *n.* [OE. *ferian,* carry]

fer'tile *a.* fruitful, producing abundantly. - fertil'ity *n.* -fer'tilize *v.t.* make fertile. - fer'tilizer *n.* -fertiliza'tion *n.* [L. *fertilis,* fr. *ferre,* bear]

fer'ule *n.* flat stick, ruler, used for punishment. [L. *ferula,* giant fennel rod]

fer'vent *a.* hot, glowing; ardent, intense. - fer'vently adv, -fer'vency *n.* -fer'vor (-er) *n.* -fer'vid *a.* ardent, impassioned; zealous. - fer'vidly adv. [L. *fervere,* boil]

fes'tal *a.* of a feast; keeping holiday; gay. -fes'tive *a.* of a feast; joyous, gay; jovial. - **fes'tival** *n.* festal days; merrymaking; periodical musical celebration. -festiv'ity *n.* gaiety, mirth; occasion for rejoicing. -*pl.* festive proceedings. [L. *festum,* feast]

fes'ter *n.* suppurating condition, sore. -*v.i.* ulcerate, produce matter (in wound); rankle. -*v. t.* cause to fester. [OF. *festre*]

fetch *v.t.* go for and bring; draw forth; be sold for; charm. -*n.* trick. -fetch'ing *a.* attractive. [OE. *fetian*]

fetch *n.* wraith, double, of a living person, portending his death. [perh. fr. *fetch v.s.*]

fête, (feht) *n.* festival; saint's day. -*v.t.* hold festivities in honer of. [F.]

fet'id *a.* stinking. [L. *fetidus* from *fetere,* to stink]

fet'ish *n.* inanimate object worshipped by savages; as enshrining a spirit; anything

which is the object of irrational reverence. [F. *fetiche*]

falter *n.* chain or shackle for the feet; check, restraint. -*pl.* captivity. -*v.t.* chain up; restrain, hamper. [OE. *feter,* fr. *fet,* feet]

fet'tle *n.* condition, trim. [perh. fr. OE. *fetel,* belt, in sense of girding onself]

fe'tus *n.* fully-developed young in womb or egg. -fe'tal *a.* [L. = offspring]

feud (fud) *n.* bitter and lasting mutual hostility, *esp.* between two families or tribes. [OF. *faide*]

feud (fiad) *n.* fief. -feud'al *a.* of a fief. -feud'al system, medieval political system based on the holding of land from a superior in return for service. -feud'alism *n.* [Med. L. *feudum*]

fe'ver *n.* condition of illness with high temperature and waste of tissue; nervous excitement. -*v.t.* throw into fever. -fe'verish *a.* -fe'verishly adv. -fe'ver few *n.* herb formerly used as a febrifuge. [OE. *fefer,* fr. L. *febris*]

few *a.* not many. -*n.* small number. -few'ness *n.* [OE. *feawe*]

fiancé (fe-ong-sa,) *n.* , fiancee' *fem.* one betrothed. *a.* betrothed, engaged. [F.]

fias'co *n.* breakdown, ignominious failure. [It. = bottle]

fi'at *n.* decree; authorization; command. [L. = let it be done]

fib *n.* trivial lie. -*v.i.* tell a fib. -fibb'er *n.* [orig. uncertain]

fi'ber *n.* filament forming part of animal or plant tissue; substance that can be spun. - fi'brous *a.* -fi'berglass *n.* material made from glass fibers. -fiber optics *n.* cable consisting of glass or plastic fibers able to transmit data in the form of light. [L. *fibre*]

fibro'sis *n.* overgrowth of fibrous tissue. - fibrosi'tis (-i-) *n.* inflammation of fibrous tissue, kind of rheumatism. [*fibre*]

fib'ula *n.* outer leg-bone from knee to ankle; buckle; brooch, or clasp. [L.]

fic'kle *a.* changeable, inconstant. - fic'kleness *n.* [OE. *ficol,* tricky]

fic'tile *a.* plastic; molded, as pottery. [L. *fictilis*]

fic'tion *n.* invented statement or narrative; novels, stories collectively; conventionally accepted falsehood. -ficti'tious *a.* not genuine, imaginary; assumed. [L. *fictio,* fr. *fingere,* shape]

fid'dle *n.* violin; in a ship, a frame to stop things rolling off a table. -*v.i.* play the fiddle; make idle movements, trifle. -fid'dlestick *n.* bow. -*pl.* nonsense. -fid'dler *n.* [OE. *fithele*]

fidelity *n.* faithfulness. [L. *fidelitas*]

fidg'et *v.i.* move restlessly; be uneasy. -*n.* restless condition with aimless movements; restless mood; one who fidgets. -fidg'ety *a.* [orig. obscure]

fidu'ciary (-sh-) *a.* held or given in trust; relating to a trustee. -*n.* trustee. [L. *fiduciarius,* fr. *fides,* faith]

fief (fef) *n.* estate in land held of a superior in return for service. [F.]

field *n.* piece of land tilled or used as pasture; enclosed piece of land; battleground; tract of land rich in a specified product (*eg.* gold field); all the players in a game or sport; all competitors but the favorite; surface of a shield, coin, *etc.* ; range, area of operation or study. -*v. i.* and *t.* in certain sports, stop and return a ball. -*n.* (*compute.*) group of related characters (bytes) treated as a unit. -**field'-day** *n.* day of maneuvers; day of athletic contests; important occasion. -**field'glass** *n.* binoculars for outdoor use. -**field'er** *n.* one who fields at baseball, cricket *etc.* [OE. *feld*]

fiend *n.* devil. -**fiend'ish** *a.* fiend-like, devilish. [OE. *feond*, enemy]

fierce *a.* savage, wild, raging. -**fierce'ness** *n.* -**fierce'ly** *adv.* [L. *ferus*, wild]

fi'ery (fi-) *a.* consisting of fire; blazing, glowing; flashing; irritable; spirited; ardent, eager. [*fire*]

fife *n.* shrill flute played with drums in military music. -*v. i.* and *i.* play on a fife. -**fi'fer** *n.* [Ger. *pfeife*]

fifteen, fifty. *See* **five.**

fifth *See* **five.**

fifth col'umn *n.* body of potential collaborators, working secretly in enemy interest. [fr. 'fifth column' of General Franco's army] .

fig *n.* familiar soft round many-seeded fruit; tree bearing it. [F. *figue,* L. *ficus*]

fight (fit) *v.i.* contend in battle or in single combat. -*v.t.* contend with; maintain against an opponent; settle by combat; maneuver (ships, troops) in battle. -*n.* act of fighting, combat, battle; strife. -**fight'er** *n.* [OE. *feohtan*]

fig'ment *n.* invented statement purely imaginary thing. [L. *figmentum*]

fig'ure (-er) *n.* form, shape; bodily shape; appearance, *esp.* conspicuous appearance; space enclosed by lines or surfaces; diagram, illustration; likeness, image; pattern; movement in dancing, skating, *etc.*; numerical symbol; amount, number; abnormal form of expression for effect in speech, *e.g.* a metaphor. -*v.i.* use numbers; show, be conspicuous; be estimated; consider. -*v.t.* to calculate, estimate; represent by picture or diagram; to ornament. -**fig'urative** *a.* metaphorical; full of figures of speech. -**fig'uratively** *adv.* [F.]

fil'ament *n.* thread-like body; (*elec.*) wire in lamp. [Late L. *filamentum*]

file *n.* tool, usually of roughened steel, for smoothing or rubbing down metal or other material. -*v.t.* apply a file to, smooth, rub down, polish. -**fi'ling** *n.* action of using a file; scrap of metal removed by a file. [OE. *feol*]

file *n.* stiff wire on which papers are threaded; device for holding papers for reference; papers so arranged. -*v.t.* place in a file. [F. *fit,* thread]

file *n.* in formation of soldiers, a front-rank man and the man or men immediately behind him. -**in file,** arranged in two lines facing to one end of the rank.- **single,** or -**Indian file,** formation of a single line of men one behind the other. -*v.i.* march in file. [F. *file,* fr. *filer,* spin out]

fil'ial *a.* of, or befitting, a son or daughter.

-**fil'ially** *adv.* [L. *filius,* son]

filibuster *n.* one who deliberately obstructs the passage of legislation, *esp.* by making long speeches; adventurer in irregular warfare, privateer; pirate. -*v.i.* act as a filibuster. [F. *flibustier*]

fili'form *a.* thread-like, in form of fine thread. [L. *filum,* thread]

fil'igree *n.* fine tracery or open-work of metal, usually gold or silver wire. [F. *filigrane,* fr. L. *filum,* thread, *granum,* bead]

fill *v.t.* make full; occupy completely, hold, discharge duties of; stop up; satisfy; fulfill. -*v.i.* become full. -*n.* full supply; as much as desired. -**fill'er** *n.* -**fill'ing** *n.* what is used to pad, complete, stop a hole, *etc.* [OE. *fyllan*]

fill'et, fil'et *n.* head-band; strip of meat; piece of meat or fish boned, rolled and tied. -*v.t.* encircle with a fillet; make into fillets. [F. *filet*]

fill'y *n.* female foal. [ON. *fylja*]

film *n.* very thin skin or layer; thin sensitized sheet used in photography; sensitized celluloid roll used in cinema photography; cinematographic picture; dimness on the eyes; slight haze; thread. *v.t.* photograph or represent by moving pictures; cover with a film. -*v.i.* become covered with a film. -**film'y** *a.* -**film'star** *n.* popular actor or actress for films. [OE. *filmen*]

fil'ter *n.* cloth or other apparatus for straining liquids. -*v.t.* and *i.* pass through a filter. -*v.i.* make a way through. -**filtra'tion** *n.* (F. *filtre*]

filth (-th) *n.* loathsome dirt; garbage; vileness. [OE. *fylth*]

fin *n.* propelling or steering organ of a fish; erection on tail of an airplane. [OE. *finn*]

fi'nal *a.* coming at the end; conclusive. -*n.* game, heat, examination, *etc.* , coming at the end of a series. -**fi'nally** *adv.* -**final'ity** *n.* -**finalize** *v.t.* -**fina'le** *n.* closing part of a musical composition, opera, *etc.* [L. *finis,* end]

finance' *n.* management of money. -*pl.* money resources. -*v.t.* find capital for. -*v.i.* deal with money. -**finan'cial** *a.* -**finan'cially** *adv.* -**finan'cier** *n.* [F.]

find (fi-) *v.t.* come across, light upon, obtain; recognize; experience, discover; discover by searching; ascertain; declare on inquiry; supply. -*n.* a finding; something found. -**find'er** *n.* [OE. *findan*]

fine *n.* sum fixed as a penalty; sum paid in consideration of a low rent. -**in fine,** to sum up. -*v.t.* punish by a fine. [Low L. *finis,* fine]

fine *a.* choice, pure, of high quality, delicate, subtle; in small particles; slender; excellent; handsome; showy; free from rain; fastidious. -*n.* fine weather. -*adv.* in fine manner. -*v.t.* make clear or pure; thin; refine. -*v.i.* become clear or pure or thinned. -**fine'ly** *adv.* -**fine'ness** *n.* -**fi'nery** *n.* showy dress. -**finesse'** (fin-) *n.* artfulness; subtle management; at cards, the attempt to take a trick with the lower of two cards not having the intermediate one. -*v.t.* and *i.* to use finesse. [F. *fin*]

fin'ger (-ng-g-) *n.* one of the jointed branches of the hand; various things like this. -*v.t.* touch or handle with the fingers. [OE.]

fin'ial *n.* (*Gothic architecture*) ornament in

shape of bunch of foliage at top of pinnacles, gables, spires *etc.* [L. *finis*, end]

fi'nis (fi-) *n.* the end, conclusion. [L.]

fin'ish *v.t.* bring to an end, complete, perfect: kill. *-v.i.* come to an end. *-n.* end, last stage; decisive result: completed state; anything serving to complete or perfect-**fin'isher** *n.* [L. *finire*]

fi'nite (fi-nit) *a.* bounded, limited, conditioned. [L. *finitus*, fr. *finire*]

fiord', fjord (fyord') *n.* narrow inlet of the sea between cliffs. [*Norwegian*]

fir *n.* coniferious tree; its wood. [ON. *fyra*, cp. Dan. *fyr*, Ger. *föhre*]

fire *n.* state of burning, combustion, flame, glow; mass of burning fuel; destructive burning, conflagration; ardor, keenness, spirit; shooting of firearms. *-v.t.* make burn; supply with fuel; bake; inspire; explode; discharge (a firearm); propel from a firearm. *-v.i.* begin to burn; become excited; discharge a firearm; dismiss from employment. **-fire'arm** *n.* weapon shooting by explosion, a gun, pistol, cannon. **-fire department** *n.* organized body of men with appliances to put out fires and rescue those in danger from fire. **-fire-bug** *n.* incendiary, pyromaniac. **-fire'-engine** *n.* engine with apparatus for extinguishing fires. **-fire'-escape** *n.* apparatus for escaping from a burning house. **-fire'fly** *n.* insect giving out a glow of phosphorescent light. **-fire'irons** *n.pl.* tongs, poke, and shovel. **-fire'place** *n.* hearth in a room. **-fire'-plug** *n.* connection in a water main for a hose. **-fire'-proof** *a.* resistant to fire, incombustible. **-fire'work** *n.* device giving spectacular effects by explosions and colored flames. [OE. *fyr*]

firm *a.* solid, fixed, stable; steadfast; resolute; settled. *-v.t.* make firm; solidify. *-n.* commercial house. partners carrying on a business. [L. *firrnus*]

firmament *n.* vault of heaven. [L. *firmamentum*, fr. *firmare*, make firm]

first *a.* earliest in time or order; foremost in rank or position. *-adv.* before others in time, order, *etc.* **-first'-aid** *n.* help given to an injured person before the arrival of a doctor. **-first'ly** *adv.* **-first' strike** *a.* (of a nuclear missile) intended for use in an opening attack calculated to destroy the enemy's nuclear weapons. [OE. *fyrest*, fr. *fore*]

fis'cal *a.* of a state treasury; of public revenue, taxation. [L. *fiscus*, purse]

fish *n.* vertebrate cold-blooded animal with gills, living in water; flesh of fish. *-v.i.* try to catch fish; search for; try in a roundabout way to elicit information. *-v.t.* try to catch fish in; draw (up); produce. **-fish'er** *n.* **-fish'erman** *n.* one who lives by fishing. [OE. *fisc*]

fis'sure (-sh-) *n.* cleft, split. **-fis'sile** *a.* capable of splitting; tending to split. **-fis'sion** *n.* splitting; division of living cells into more cells. **-fissip'arous** *a.* reproducing by fission. [L. *fissura*]

fist *n.* clenched hand; handwriting. *-v.t.* strike with the clenched hand. **-fisticuffs** *n.pl.* fighting with fists. [OE. *fyst*]

fit *n.* sudden passing attack of illness; seizure with convulsions, spasms, loss of consciousness, *etc.*, as of epilepsy, hysteria, *etc.*; sudden and passing state, mood. **-fit'ful** *a.* spasmodic capricious. **-fit'fully** *adv.* [OE. *fitt*, conflict]

fit *a.* well-suited, worthy; proper, becoming; ready; in good condition. *-v.t.* be suited to; be properly adjusted to; arrange, adjust, apply, insert; supply, furnish. *-v.i.* be correctly adjusted or adapted, be of the right size. *-n.* way a garment fits; its style; adjustment. **-fit'ly** *-adv.* **-fit'ness** *n.* **-fitt'er** *n.* **-fit'ment** *n.* piece of furniture. **-fitt'ing** *n.* action of fitting; apparatus; fixture. *a.* that fits; becoming, proper. [orig. uncertain]

five *a.* and *n.* cardinal number next after four. **-fifth** *a.* ordinal number. **-fifth'genera'tion** *a.* denoting developments in computer design to produce machines with artifical intelligence. **-five'fold** *a.* and *adv.* **-fifteen'** *a.* and *n.* ten and five. **-fifteen'th** *a.* **-fifth'ly** *adv.* **-fifteenth'ly** *adv.* **-fif'ty** *a.* and *n.* five tens. **-fif'tieth** *a.* **-fives** *n.* ball-game played with the hand or a bat in a court. [OE. *fif*]

fix *v.t.* fasten, make firm or stable; set, establish; appoint, assign, determine; make fast, permanent. *-v.i.* become firm or solidified; determine. *-n.* difficult situation. **-fix'ity** *n.* **-fix'edly** *adv.* **-fixa'tion** *n.* fixing. (*psychoanalysis*) arrest in development. **-fix'ative** *a.* **-fix'ture** *n.* thing fixed in position; thing annexed to a house; date for a sporting event; the event. [L. *ligere, fix-*]

flabb'y *a.* hanging loose, limp; feeble. **-flabb'ily** *adv.* **-flabb'iness** *n.* [*flap*]

flac'cid (-ks-) flabby. **-flaccid'ity** *n.* [L. *flaccidus*, fr. *flaccus*, flabby]

flag *n.* water plant with sword-shaped leaves, *esp.* the iris. **-flagg'y** *a.* [ME. *flagge, flegge*]

flag *n.* flat slab of stone. *-pl.* pavement of flags. *-v.t.* pave with flags. **-flag'-stone** *n.* [ON. *flaga*]

flag *n.* banner, piece of bunting attached to a staff or halyard as a standard or signal. *-v.t.* inform by flag-signals. *-v.i.* droop, languish. **-flag'-day** *n.* day on which small flags or emblems are sold in the streets for charity. **-flag'-off'icer** *n.* admiral entitled to show a flag as an indication of his rank; commander of a fleet or squadron. **-flag'ship** *n.* ship with an admiral on board. **-flag'staff** *n.* pole on which flag is hoisted. [orig. uncertain]

flag *v.i.* droop, fade; lose vigor. [orig. uncertain]

flag'on *n.* vessel, usually with handle, spout and lid, to hold liquor for the table; large oval bottle. [F. *flacon*]

fla'grant *a.* glaring, scandalous; enormous. **-fla'grantly** *adv.* **-fla'grancy** *n.* [L. *flagrare*, burn]

flail *n.* instrument for threshing corn by hand, long handle with a short thick stick swinging at the end. *-v.t.* [OF. *flaiel*, fr. L. *flagellum*, scourge]

flair *n.* intuitive feeling or special aptitude (with for). [F. = scent]

flak *n.* opposition put up by anti-aircraft defences. [abbrev. of Ger. *fliegerab-wehrkanone*]

flake *n.* light fleecy piece, *esp.* of snow; thin broad piece, *esp.* split or peeled off, layer. -*v.i.* break flakes from. -*v.i.* come off in flakes. -**fla'ky** *a.* [orig. uncertain]

flamboyant *a.* marked by wavy lines; florid, gorgeous; showy. [F.]

flame *n.* burning gas; portion of burning gas, *esp.* above a fire; visible burning; passion, *esp.* love; sweetheart. -*v.i.* give out flames, blaze; burst out in anger, *etc.* **flame'-thrower** *n.* device for throwing jets of flame in battle. -**flam'mable** *a.* capable of being easily ignited and of burning quickly. [L. *flamma*]

flamin'go (-ng-g-) *n.* large, bright pink bird with very long neck and legs. [Port. *flainengo*, Fleming]

flan *n.* uncovered tart. [F.]

flange (-anj) *n.* projecting flat rim collar, or rib. -*v.t.* provide with a flange. [orig. uncertain]

flank *n.* fleshy part of the side between the hips and ribs; side of a building or body of troops. -*v.t.* guard or strengthen on the flank; attack or take in flank; be at, or move along, either side of. [F. *flanc*]

flann'el *n.* soft woolen cloth. -*pl.* garments of this, *esp.* trousers. *a.* made of flannel. -**flannelette'** *n.* cotton fabric imitating flannel. [Welsh *gwlanen*, fr. *gulan*, wool]

flap *v.t.* strike with something broad, flat and flexible; move (wings) up and down. -*v.i.* sway, swing, flutter. -*n.* act of flapping; broad piece of anything hanging from a hinge or loosely from one side. [imit. orig.]

flare (-ar) *v.i.* blaze with bright unsteady flame. -*n.* act of flaring; bright unsteady flame; signal light used at sea. [orig. uncertain]

flash *v.i.* break into sudden flame; gleam; burst into view; appear suddenly. -*v.t.* cause to gleam; emit (light, *etc.*) suddenly. -*n.* sudden burst of light or flame; sudden short access; ribbon or badge; display. *a.* showy; sham. -**flash'y** *a.* -**flash-back** *n.* break in book, play, film, to insert what has previously taken place. -**flash'light** *n.* small battery-operated portable light; apparatus for taking flash photographs. -**flash'point** *n.* temperature at which oil vapor ignites. [earlier meaning *dash*, *splash*; of imit. orig.]

flask (-a-) *n.* pocket-bottle; case for gunpowder; Italian bottle covered with wicker; long-necked bottle, *esp.* for scientific use. [F. *flasque*]

flat *a.* level; spread out; at full length; smooth; downright; dull, lifeless; below true pitch. -*n.* what is flat; simpleton; note half a tone below the natural pitch; punctured tire. -**flat'car** *n.* railroad freight vehicle with no raised sides and no roof. [ON. *flatr*]

flatt'er *v.t.* court, fawn on; praise insincerely; inspire a belief, *esp.* an unfounded one; gratify (senses); represent too favorably. -**flatt'erer** *n.* -**flatt'ery** *n.* [F. *flatter*, 'smooth']

flat'ulent *a.* generating gases in the intestines; caused by or attended by or troubled with such gases; vain, pretentious, turgid. -**flat'ulence** *n.* -**flat'ulency** *n.* [L. *flat-*, *flare*, blow]

flaunt *v.t.* and *i.* wave proudly; show off. [orig. uncertain]

flautist *n.* flute-player, flutist. [It. *flautista*]

fla'vor (-vvr) *n.* mixed sensation of smell and taste; distinctive taste; undefinable characteristic quality of anything. -*v. t.* give a flavor to; season. -**flavoring** *n.* [OF. *floor*, smell]

flaw *n.* crack; defect, blemish. -*v.t.* make a flaw in. -*v.i.* crack. -**flaw'less** *a.* [orig. uncertain]

flax *n.* plant grown for its textile fiber and seeds; its fibers; cloth of this, linen. -**flax'seed** *n.* linseed. -**flax'en** *a.* of flax; pale brown; blond. [OE. *fleax*]

flea (-e) *n.* small wingless jumping insect which feeds on human and other blood. -**flea'bane** *n.* wild plant. -**flea'-bite** *n.* the insect's bite; trifling injury; trifle; small red spot on a horse. -**flea'bitten** *a.* of a horse, with fleabites on a lighter ground. [OE.]

fleck *n.* spot on the skin, freckle; patch of color; speck. -*v.t.* mark with flecks, dapple, [ON. *flekkr*, spot]

fledge *v.t.* provide with feathers of down. -**fledge'ling** *n.* young bird just fledged [OE. *flycge*, fledged]

flee *v.i.* run away. -*v.t.* run away from; sbun. [OE. *fleon*]

fleece *n.* sheep's wool. -*v.t.* rob. -**flee'cy** *a.* [OE. *fleos*]

fleet *n.* naval force under an admiral; number of ships, *etc.*, sailing in company; number of automobiles, aircraft, *etc.*, owned by one company. [OE. *fleet*, ship]

fleet *a.* swift, nimble. [ON. *fljotr*]

flesh *n.* soft part, muscular substance, between skin and bone; this as food; of plants, the pulp; fat; sensual appetites. -**flesh'ings** *n. pl.* close-fitting flesh-colored theatrical garments. -**flesh-pots** *n. pl.* high living. -**flesh'ly** *a.* carnal, material. -**flesh'y** *a.* plump, pulpy. -**flesh'ily** *adv.* [OE. *flæsc*]

flex'ible *a.* that may be bent without breaking, pliable; manageable; supple. -**flexibil'ity** *n.* -**flex'ibly** *adv.* -**flex'ion**, **flec'tion** *n.* bending, bent state. -**flex'time**, **flex'itime** *n.* system permitting variation in starting and finishing times of work, providing an agreed number of hours is worked over a specified period. -**flexure** *n.* bend. [L. *flexibilis*]

flick'er *v.i.* burn or shine unsteadily; quiver. -*n.* flickering light or movement. [OE. *flicerian*]

flight (-it) *n.* act or manner of flying through the air; swift movement or passage; sally; distance flown; airplane journeys; stairs between two landings; number flying together, as birds. arrows. -**flight'y** *a.* light-headed, thoughtless, capricious. [*fly*]

flight (-It) *n.* a running away. [*floe*]

flim'sy (-zi) *a.* very thin; unsubstantial; fragile. -*n.* very thin paper. -**flim'sily** *adv.* [Welsh *llymsi*]

flinch *v.i.* shrink, draw back. [earlier *flench*, ME. *fleechen*]

fling *v.t.* throw. -*v.i.* rush, go hastily; kick, plunge. -*n.* throw; hasty attempt; spell of indulgence; vigorous dance. [orig. uncertain]

flint *n.* hard stone found in gray lumps with a white crust; piece of this. -flint'lock *n.* gun or its lock discharged by a spark struck from flint. [OE.]

flip *n.* flick or fillip, very light blow. -*v.t.* strike or move with a flick; turn over. -*v.i.* move in jerks; turn over; lose one's mind or composure. -flip'per *n.* limb or fin for swimming. [imit. orig.]

flip *n.* sweet drink of spirits, *etc.*; as egg flip. [orig. uncertain]

flirt *v.t.* throw with a jerk, give a brisk motion to. -*v.i.* play at courtship. -*n.* jerk, sudden throw; one who plays at courtship. -flirta'tion *n.* [imit. orig.]

flit *v.i.* go away; change dwelling; pass lightly and rapidly; make short flights. [ON. *flytja*]

flitt'er *v.i.* move lightly, uncertainly. [*flutter*]

float *v.i.* rest or drift on the surface of a liquid; be suspended freely (in a liquid). -*v.t.* of a liquid, support, bear along; commerce, get (a company) started. -*n.* anything small that floats (*esp.* to support something else, *e.g.*, a fishing net); lowbodied cart; footlight. -flota'tion *n.* act of floating, *esp.* floating of a company. [OE. *flotian*]

flock *n.* number of animals of one kind together; body of people, religious congregation. -*v.i.* gather in a crowd. [OE. *flocc*, herd]

floe (-ō) *n.* sheet of floating ice. [orig. uncertain]

flog *v.t.* beat with a whip, stick, *etc.* [orig, uncertain]

flood (flud) *n.* flowing in of the tide; flowing water; overflow of water, inundation. -*v.t.* inundate; cover or fill with water. -The Flood, great deluge of Noah's time. -flood'-gate *n.* gate for letting water in or out. -flood'-lighting *n.* illumination of, e. g. , exterior of a building, by distant projectors. -flood'lit *a.* -flood-tide *n.* rising tide. [OE. *flod*]

floor (flor) *n.* lower surface of a room; set of rooms on one level; flat space. -*v.t.* supply with a floor; knock down; confound. [OE. *flor*]

flop *v.i.* sway about heavily; move clumsily; sit or fall with a thump. -*v.t.* throw down with a thud. -*n.* flopping movement or sound. *adv.* with a flop. -flop'py *a.* -flop'py disk *n.* flexible magnetic disk that stores information and can be used to store data for use in a microprocessor. [imit. orig.]

flop *n.* (*sl.*) failure; something that falls flat. [*flop v. s.*]

flor'a (flaw'-) *n.* plants of a region; a list of them. -flo'ral *a.* of flowers, -flor'iculture *n.* cultivation of flowers. -flor'et *n.* small flower forming part of a composite flower. -flor'ist *n.* one who deals in, grows, or studies, flowers. [L. *flos, flor-*, flower]

flor'id *a.* flowery, ornate; ruddy, high-colored. -florid'ity *n.* [L. *flos*, flower]

floss *n.* rough silk on a cocoon; silk for embroidery; fluff. -floss'y *a.* light and downy. [OF. *flosche*, down]

flota'tion. See float.

flotill'a *n.* fleet of small vessels, *esp.* group of destroyers *etc.*, fleet. [Sp. dim of *flota*, fleet]

flot'sam *n.* floating wreckage. [F. *flottaison*, fr. *flotter*, float]

flounce *v.i.* go or move abruptly and impatiently. -*n.* fling, jerk of the body or a limb. [orig. uncertain]

flound'er *v.i.* plunge and struggle, *esp.* in water or mud; proceed in bungling or hesitating manner. -*n.* act of floundering. [orig. uncertain]

flour *n.* sifted finer part of meal; wheat meal; fine soft powder. -*v.t.* sprinkle with flour. -flour'y *a.* -flour'iness *n.* [flower of wheat]

flour'ish (flur-) *v.i.* thrive; be in the prime. -*v.t.* brandish, display; wave about. -*n.* ornamental curve in writing; florid expression; waving of hard, weapon, *etc.*; fanfare (of trumpets). [OF. *florir*, to bloom]

flow (flō) *v.i.* glide along as a stream; hang loose; move easily; move in waves; be ample in form; run full; abound. -*n.* act or fact of flowing; quantity that flows; rise of tide; ample supply; outpouring. [OE. *flowan*]

flow'er (flow-) *n.* colored (not green) part of a plant from which the fruit is developed, bloom, blossom; ornamen tation; choicest part, pick. -*v.i.* bloom, or blossom. -*v.t.* ornament with worked flowers. [F. *fleur*, fr. L. *flos*, *flor*-]

flu *abbrev.* of influenza, *q.v.* fluc'tuate *v. i.* vary irregularly, rise and fall; waver, be unstable. -fluctua'tion *n.* [L. *fluctuare*, fr. *fluctus*, wave]

flue *n.* passage for smoke or hot air, chimney. [orig. unknown]

flu'ent *a.* flowing, copious and ready (in words); graceful (in movement). -flu'ency *adv.* -flu'ency *n.* [L. *fluere*, flow]

fluff *n.* soft feathery stuff; down. -*v.t.* make into fluff. [orig. uncertain]

flu'id *a.* flowing easily, not solid. -*n.* fluid substance, gas or liquid. -fluid'ity *n.* [L. *fluidus*, fr. *fluere*, flow]

fluke *n.* flat triangular point of an anchor. [orig. uncertain fluke *n.* lucky stroke. -*v.i.* make a fluke. -flu'ky *a.* [orig. uncertain]

flume *n.* artificial water-course; steep narrow gorge. [L. *flumen*, river]

flunk *v.t.* fail someone in an examination or course. -*v.i.* fail in an examination or course. [orig. uncertain]

flunk'y, flunk'ey *n.* footman in livery; toady, snob. [orig. uncertain]

flu'or *n.* mineral containing fluorine. -fluores'cence *n.* luminous state produced in a transparent body by direct action of light, *esp.* violet and ultra-violet rays; power of rendering ultra-violet rays visible. -fluores'cent *a.* -fluores'cent lighting, lighting by electric discharge acting on fluorescent coating of tube, lamp. -fluoresce' *v.i.* -flu'orine *n.* nonmetallic element of the chlorine group. [L. fr. *fluere*, flow]

flurry *n.* squall, gust; nervous haste; death-agony of whale. -*v. t.* agitate, bewilder. [imit. orig.]

flush *v.i.* take wing and fly away. -*v.t.* cause to do this. -*n.* number of birds flushed at once. [orig. uncertain]

flush *n.* set of cards all of one suit. [L. *fluxus*, flow]

flush *v.i.* become suffused with blood; turn suddenly red in the face; blush. *-v.t.* cleanse by rush of water; cause to glow or redden. [orig. uncertain]

flus′ter *v.t.* flurry, bustle; confuse with drink. *-v.i.* be in a flurry. *-n.* flurry. [orig. uncertain]

flute *n.* musical wind instrument, wooden pipe with holes stopped by the fingers or keys and a blow-hole in the side; flute player in a band; groove or channel. *-v.i.* play on a flute. *-v.t.* make grooves in. *-*flut′ist, flautist *n.* one who plays the flute. [F. *flute*]

flutt′er *v.i.* flap wings rapidly without flight or in short flights; move, come down, quiveringly; be excited, agitated. *-v. t.* flap quickly; agitate. *-n.* fluttering, occasional bet, speculation. [OE. *floterian*]

flux *n.* morbid discharge, as of blood; a flowing; flow of the tide; constant succession of changes; substance mixed with metal to help melting. [L. *fluxus*]

fly *n.* two-winged insect; artificial fly of silk, *etc.* , used in angling. [OE. *fleoge*]

fly *v.i.* move through the air on wings or in aircraft; pass quickly through the air; float loosely, wave; spring, rush; flee, run away. *-v.t.* cause to fly; set flying; run from. *-n.* a flying; one-horse vehicle for hire; flap on a garment or tent; speed regulator in a machine. *-*fly′-wheel *n.* heavy wheel regulating a machine. *-*fly′ing-boat *n.* airplane fitted with floats instead of landing wheels. [OE. *fleogan*]

foal *n.* young of the horse, ass, or other equine animal. *-v. t.* bear (a foal). *-v.i.* bear a foal. [OE. *fola*]

foam *n.* collection of small bubbles in a liquid; froth; froth of saliva or perspiration. *-v.i.* give out, or form into, foam. *-*foam′y *a.* [OE. *fam*]

fo′cus *n.* point at which rays meet after being reflected or refracted; point of convergence; principal seat or centre. *-v. t.* bring to a focus. *-v.i.* come to a focus. *-*fo′cal *a.* [L. = *hearth*]

fodd′er *n.* dried food for horses, cattle, *etc.* *-v. t.* feed with fodder. [OE. *fodor*]

foe *n.* enemy. [OE. *fah*]

fog *n.* thick mist; unusually dark atmosphere. *-v.t.* cover in fog; puzzle. *-*fogg′y *a.* *-*fog′horn *n.* instrument to warn ships in fog. [orig. uncertain]

foi′ble *n.* weak point in character; quality a person prides himself on mistakenly. [OF. = weak]

foil *n.* small arc or space in the tracery of a window; thin layer; metal in a thin sheet; leaf of metal set under a gem; anything which sets off another thing to advantage; light blunt sword for fencing. [L. *folium*, leaf]

foil *v.t.* baffle, defeat; frustrate. [F. *fouler*, trample]

fold *v.t.* double up; bend part of; clasp (in the arms); interlace (the arms); wrap up. *-v.i.* become folded; be or admit of being folded. *-n.* a folding; space between two thicknesses; coil; winding; line, made by folding, a crease.

-fold′er *n.* [OE. *fealdan*]

fo′liage *n.* leaves collectively. [F. *feuillage*, fr. *feuille*, (L. *fola*), leaf]

fo′lio *n.* piece of paper numbered only on the front; two pages, or a page, with the opposite side of an account in a ledger; number of words as a unit of length; sheet of printing paper folded once into two leaves or four pages; book of such sheets. in folio, made of folios. *a.* made thus. [L. *folirim*, leaf]

folk (fōk) *n.* race of people; people in general. *-*folk′-song *n.* music originating among a people. *-*folk′-lore *n.* traditions, beliefs popularly held; study of these. *-*folk′-dance *n.* traditional dance among the people. [OE. *foic*]

foll′icle *n.* small sac; gland. *-*follic′ular *a.* [L. *folliculus*, dim. *offollis*, bag]

foll′ow *v.t.* go or come after; keep to (a path, *etc.*); accompany, attend on; take as a guide, conform to; engage in; be consequent on; grasp the meaning of. *-v.i.* go or come after; come next; result. *-*foll′ower *n.* *-*foll′ow through *n-* in ball games continuation of stroke after ball is struck. *-*foll′ow up *n.* deepening of impression, pursuing of advantage gained. [OE. *folgian*]

foll′y *n.* foolishness; foolish action, idea, enterprise, *etc.* [F. *folie*]

fond *a.* tender, loving; credulous; foolish. *-* fond of, having love or liking for. *-*fon′ dle *v.t.* caress. [ME. *fonnen*, be foolish]

font *n.* bowl for baptismal water. [L. *fons*, *font-*, fountain]

fontanelle′ *n.* gap between parietal bones of young child, animal. [F.]

food (′-ōō-) *n.* that which is eaten or meant to be; nourishment. [OE. *foda*]

fool (-ōō-) *n.* silly or empty-headed person; simpleton; jester, clown; dupe. *-v.i.* act as a fool. *-v.t.* delude; dupe; make a fool of, mock. *a.* foolish. *-*fool′ish *a.* *-*fool′ishly *adv.* *-*fool′ery *n.* *-*fool′hardy *a.* foolishly venturesome. *-*foolhard′iness *n.* *-*fool-proof *a.* able to withstand careless or inexpert handling. [F. *fol (fou)*]

fool *n.* dish of fruit stewed, crushed, and mixed with milk, *etc.* [orig. uncertain]

foot (-oo-) *n.* lowest part of the leg, from the ankle down; lowest part of anything, base, stand; end of a bed, *etc.*; infantry: measure of length of twelve inches; division of a verse. *-v.t.* set foot to; put a foot on (a stocking, *etc.*). *-v. i.* step, tread, dance. *-*foot′ing *n.* firm standing; relations, conditions. *-*foot′lights *n. pl.* row of lights at outer edge of stage. *-*foot′man *n.* liveried servant. *-*foot′note *n.* note at foot of page. [OE. *fot*]

for *prep.* because of, instead of; toward; on account of, , to prevent or heal; in favor of, respecting; during, in search of, in payment of; in the character of. *-conj.* because. [OE.]

for′age (-ij) *n.* food for cattle and horses, *esp.* of an army. *-v.i.* collect forage, make a roving search. *-*for′age cap *n.* undress cap in army. [F. *fourrage*]

for′ay *n.* raid. *-v.i.* make a raid. [OF. *forreor*, forager]

forbear' (-bar) *v.i.* refrain; be patient. *v.t.* refrain from; cease. -**forbear'ance** *n.* [OE. *forberan*]

forbid' *v.t.* order not to; refuse to allow. -**forbidden** *ptp.* prohibited, unlawful. -**forbidd'ing** *a.* uninviting. [OE. *forbeodan*]

force *n.* strength, power; body of troops; body of police; compulsion; mental or moral strength; measurable influence inclining a body to motion. -*v.t.* constrain, compel; break open; urge, strain; drive; produce by effort; hasten the maturity of. -**for'cible** *a.* -**for'cibly** *adv.* -**force'ful** *a.* [F.]

for'ceps *n.* surgical pincers. [L.]

ford. *n.* place where a river may be crossed by wading. -**ford'able** *a.* [OE.]

fore- *prefix* meaning previous, before, front. [OE.]

fore *a.* in front. -*n.* front part. -**fore-and-aft** *a.* placed in the line from bow to stern of a ship. -**fore'arm** *n.* arm from wrist to elbow. -**forearm'** *v.t.* arm beforehand. -**fore'bear,** **for'bear** *n.* ancestor. -**forebode'** *v.t.* betoken. foreboding *n.* presentiment. -**forecast'** *v.t.* estimate beforehand, prophesy. -**fore-cast** *n.* conjecture, guess at a future event. -**fore'castle** (*abbrev.* **fo'c'sle**) (fo'ksl) *n.* forward raised part of a ship; sailors' quarter. -**fore'father** *n.* ancestor. -**fore'finger** *n.* finger next the thumb. -**fore'front** *n.* the very front, foremost part. -**fore'ground** *n.* part of a view, *esp.* in a picture, nearest the spectator. -**fore'head** (for'hed) *n.* part of the face above the eyebrows and between the temples. -**fore'man** *n.* one in charge of work; leader of a jury. -**fore'runner** *n.* one who goes before, a precursor. -**foresee'** *v. t.* see beforehand. -**foreshad'ow** *v.t.* figure beforehand, be a type of. -**fore'sight** *n.* foreseeing; care for the future; front sight of a gun. -**forestall'** *v.t.* be beforehand with. -**fore-tell'** *v.t.* prophesy. -**forewarn'** *v.t.* warn beforehand. -**fore'word** *n.* preface. [fore-]

foreclose' *v.t.* take away the power of redeeming (a mortgage); shut out, bar. -**foreclo'sure** *n.* [F. *forclore*]

forego'ing *a.* preceding. -**foregone'** *a.* inevitable; predetermined, as in foregone conclusion. [go]

fore'most *a.* most advanced, chief *adv.* in the first place. [OE. *formest*]

foren'sic *a.* of courts of law. [L. *forensis,* fr. *forum,* market-place]

foren'sics *n.* study and practice of debate and formal argument.

for'est *n.* large wood; the trees in it; tract of land mainly occupied by trees; region kept waste for hunting. -**for'ester** *n.* one who lives in a forest or is employed in charge of one. -**for'estry** *n.* management of forests. [Med. L. *forestis,* unfenced]

forev'er *adv.* constantly; eternally. [*for* and *ever*]

for'feit (-fit) *n.* thing lost by crime or fault; penalty, fine. -*pl.* game. *a.* lost by crime or fault. -*v.t.* lose, have to pay or give up. -**for'feiture** *n.* [F. *forfait,* crime, wrong]

forge *v. t.* shape (metal) by heating in a fire

and hammering; invent; make in fraudulent imitation of a thing, to counterfeit. -*n.* smithy; gmith's hearth; workshop for melting or refining metal for'ger *n.* -**for'gery** *n.* forged document; the making of it. [F. *forger,* fr. L. *fabricate*]

forge *v.i.* advance, make headway, *esp.* of a boat, usually slowly or with effort. **forge ahead.** [corrupt. of *force*]

forget' *v.t.* lose memory of, not to remember. -**forget'ful** *a.* -**forget'fully** *adv.* -**forget'-me-not** *n.* plant with a small blue flower. [OE. *forgietan*]

forgive' (giv) *v.t.* pardon, remit. -**forgive'ness** *n.* [OE. *forgiefan*]

forgo', **forego'** *v. t.* go without; give up. [OE. *forgan,* pass over]

fork *n.* pronged farm tool for digging or lifting; pronged instrument for holding food in eating or cooking; division into branches; point of this division; one of the branches. -*v.i.* branch. -*v. t.* make forkshaped; dig, lift, or throw with a fork. forked *a.* [L. *urca*]

form *n.* shape, visible appearance; visible person or animal; structure; nature; species, kind; class in a school; customary way of doing a thing; set order of words; regularly drawn up document, *esp.* a printed one with blanks for particulars; behavior according to rule; condition, good condition; long seat without a back, a bench; hare's nest; frame for type (more often *forme*). -*v.t.* put into shape, mold, arrange, organize; train; shape in the mind, conceive; go to make up, make part of. -*v.i.* come into existence or shape. -**for'mal** *a.* ceremonial, according to rule; explicit; of outward form or routine; according to a rule that does not matter; precise; stiff. -**for'ma tive** *a.* serving or tending to form; used in forming. [L. *forma,* shape]

formal'dehyde *n.* colorless pungent gas used in solution in water or absorbed into porous materials as antiseptic and disinfectant. [L. *formica,* ant]

form at (-ma) *n.* size and shape of an object. [F.]

for'mer *a.* earlier in time; of past times; first-named. -*pron.* first-named thing or person or fact. -**for'merly** *adv.* [fr. OE. *superl. formest,* foremost]

for'mic *a.* of or derived from ants. -**for'mic a'cid,** acid originally got from ants. -**for'micant** *a.* with ant-like motion. -**for'micary** *n.* anthill. -**formi-ca'tion** *n.* feeling as of ants crawling on one's skin. [L. *formica,* ant]

formid'able *a'* to be feared; likely to cause difficulty serious. -**for'midably** *adv.* [L. *formido:r,* dread]

for'mula (-a-) *n.* set form of words setting forth a principle, or prescribed for an occasion; recipe; in science, a rule or fact expressed in symbols and figures. -**for'mulary** *n.* collection of formulas. -**for'mulate** *v.t.* express in a formula, or systematically. -**formula'tion** *n.* -**for'-mulator** *n.* -*pl.* **form'ulae, form'ulas.** [L., dim. of *forma,* form]

fornica'tion *n.* sexual intercourse between

man and woman. -**for'nicate** v.i. [L. *fornix*, brothel]

forsake' v.t. abandon, desert; give up. p.t. forsook. -forsaken a. [OE. *forsacan*]

forswear' v.t. renounce. -v. refl. perjure. [OE. *forswerian*, renounce an oath]

forsyth'ia n. shrub with jasmine-like yellow flowers. [W. *Forsyth*]

fort n. fortified place. [L. *fortis*, strong]

forte n. one's strong point. [F.*fort*, upper half of sword-blade]

forte (-ti) adv. in music, loudly. -**fortiss'imo** adv. very loud. [It.]

forth (-ith) adv. onwards, into view; onwards in time. -**forthcom'ing** a. about to come; ready when wanted. -**forth'right** n. straightforward; straightway. -**forthwith'** adv. at once, immediately. [OE.]

FORT'RAN n. high-level computer programming language for mathematical and scientific purposes. [fr. *formula translation*]

forthright a. candid, straightforward, blunt. [*forth* and *right*]

for'tify v.t. strengthen; provide with defensive works. -**fortifica'tion** n. [L.*fortis*, strong]

fortitude n. courage in adversity or pain. [L. *fortitude*, fr. *fortis*, strong]

fortnight (-nit) n. two weeks. -**fortnight'ly** adv. [*fourteen nights*]

fort'ress n. fortified place, military stronghold. [F. *forteresse*]

fortuitous a. accidental, due to chance. -**fortu'itously** adv. [L. *fortuitus*]

for'tune n. chance; luck, good luck, prosperity; wealth, stock of wealth. -**for'tunate** a. lucky, favorable. -**for'tunately** adv. -**for'tune-teller** n. one who predicts a person's future, usually for money. [L. *fortune*]

fo'rum n. market-place, esp. of ancient Rome; law-courts; tribunal; any place of judicature. [L.]

for'ward a. lying in front of one, onward; prompt; precocious; pert. -n. in football, a player in the first line. -adv. towards the future; towards the front; to the front, into view; at or in the fore part of a ship; onward, so as to make progress. -v.t. help forward; send, dispatch. -**for'wards** adv. forward. -**for'wardly** adv. pertly. forwardness n. [OE. *foreweard*]

foss'il a. petrified in the earth and recognizable as the remains of animals or plants, esp. prehistoric ones; (of persons) antiquated. -n. fossilized thing. -**foss'ilize** v.t. and i. turn into a fossil. [L. *fossilis*, fr. *fodere, foss-*, to dig]

foster v.t. encourage; be favorable to; formerly, to tend, cherish. -**fos'terbrother** n. one related by upbringing not by blood. [OE. *fostor*, feeding, food]

foul a. loathsome, offensive; dirty; charged with harmful matter; clogged, choked; unfair; wet, rough; obscene, disgustingly abusive. -n. collision; (in games) act of unfair play. -adv. unfairly. -v.i. become foul. -v.t. make foul; jam; collide with. -**foul'ly** adv. [OE. *ful*]

found v.t. establish, institute; lay the base of; base, ground. -**founda'tion** n. a founding; base, lowest part of a building; endowed institution. -**found'er** n. -**found'ress** fem. -Founding Fathers n. pl. American leaders who were members of the American Constitutional Convention of 1787. [F. *fonder*, fr. L. *fundus*, bottom]

found v.t. (of metals), melt and run into a mold. -**found'er** n. -**found'ry** n. workshop for founding. [F. *fondre*, fr. L. *fundare*, pour]

found'er v.i. of a horse, to fall lame, collapse. -v-t. cause to do this. [F. *effondrer*, knock out the bottom] **found'er** v.i. of a ship, to sink. [OF. *enfondrir*, engulf]

fount n. set of printer's type. [F.]

fount'ain (-in) n. spring; source; jet of water, esp. an ornamental one. [F.*fontaine*, fr. L.*fons, fontis*, spring]

four (for) n. and a. cardinal number next after three. -**fourth** a. ordinal number. -**fourth'ly** adv. -Fourth of July n. U.S. public holiday celebrating the Declaration of Independence; Independence Day. -**four'teen'** n. and a. four and ten. -**four-post'er** (-ō-) n. bed with four posts for curtains, etc. -**four'some** n. (golf) game for four players, two against two. **fourstar** a. of the highest military rank; highest quality. **fourth class** a. lowest rate and method of parcel post mailing. [OE. *feower*]

fowl n. domestic cock or hen; bird. -v.i. hunt wild birds. -**fowl'er** n. -**fowl'ing-piece** n. light gun. [OE. *fugol*]

fox n. red bushy-tailed animal, in many places preserved for hunting; cunning person. -v.t. discolor (paper) with brown spots. -v.i. act craftily; sham. -**fox-hole** n. (sl.) orig. in World War II small trench for one or two giving protection against snipers or divebombers. -**fox'trot** n. dance. [OE.]

frac'tion n. numerical quantity not an integer; fragment, piece, small part. -**frac'tional** a. [*fracture*]

frac'tious a. unruly, cross, fretful. [mixture of *factious* and *refractory*]

frac'ture n. breakage. -v.t. and i. break. [L. *frangere, fract-*, break]

frag'ile (-j-) a. breakable. -**fragility** n. [L. *fragilis*, fr. *frangere*, break]

frag'ment n. piece broken off, small portion; incomplete part. -**frag'mentary** a. [L. *fragmentum*]

fra'grant (-ag-) a. sweet-smelling. -**fra'grance** n. -**fra'grantly** adv. [L. *fragrans, fragrant-* fr. *fragrare*, smell]

frail a. easily broken, delicate; morally weak, unchaste. -**frail'ty** n. -**frail'ly** adv. [F. *fraiel*, fr. L. *fragilis*]

frail n. rush basket. [F. *fraiel*]

frame v.t. put together, make; adapt; put into words; put into a frame; trump-up a charge against. -n. that in which a thing is set or inserted, as a square of wood round a picture, etc.; structure; constitution; mood. -**frame-up** n. plot, manufactured evidence. -**frame'work** n. light wooden or other structure; structure into which completing parts can be fitted. [OE. *ramian*, avail]

fran'chise n. person or company granted a license to operate a store, hotel, etc., using the name of the parent company, but operating in an independent manner. **franchisee** *n.* person or company granted a franchise. -**franchise** *n.* right of voting; citizenship. [F. = *freedom*]

frank *a.* candid, outspoken, sincere. -*n.* signature on a letter of a person entitled to send it free of postage charges; letter with this. -*v.t.* mark a letter thus. [F. *franc*, Frank, conqueror, 'free man.' (conquest of Gaul)]

fran'tic *a.* mad with rage, grief, joy, *etc.* **fran'tically** *adv.* [F. *frénétique*]

fraternal *a.* of a brother; brotherly. -**frater'nally** *adv.* -**frater'nity** *n.* brotherliness; a brotherhood; club of male students *usu.* living in the same house. -**frat'ernize** *v. i.* associate, make friends. -**frat'ricide** *n.* killing of a brother or sister; the killer. -**frat'ricidal** *a.* [L. *frater*, brother]

fraud *n.* criminal deception; dishonest trick. -**fraud'ulence** *n.* -**fraud'ulent** *a.* [L. *fraus*, *fraud*-]

fray *v.t.* and *i.* wear through by rubbing, make or become ragged at the edge. [F. *frover*, fr. L. *fricare*, rub] -**fray** *n.* fight. [for *affray*]

freak *n.* caprice; prank; monstrosity. -**freak'ish** *a.* [*orig.* uncertain]

freck'le *n.* light brown spot on the skin. -*v.t.* and *i.* mark or become marked with such spots. [ON. *freknur*]

free *a.* having liberty; not in bondage; not restricted or impeded; released from strict law, literality, tax, obligation, *etc.* ; disengaged; spontaneous; liberal; frank; familiar. -*v.t.* set at liberty, disengage. -**free'fall** *n.* unchecked motion of a body in flight. -**free'ly** *adv.* -**free'lance** *n.* medieval mercenary; unattached journalist, artist, *etc.* ; politician independent of party. -**free'load** *v.i.* live off money and gifts provided by others without giving anything in return. -**free market** *n.* market in which prices are not government-regulated but are based on supply and demand. -**free'-will** *n.* spontaneity; freedom of choice. *a.* unrestrained, voluntary. [OE. *freo*, not in bondage]

freeze *v.i.* become ice; become rigid with cold; feel very cold. -*v.t.* turn solid by cold; chill; affect with frost. -*v.t.* and *i.* stop *esp.* if then held in a static position. -**freez'ing-point** *n.* temperature at which water becomes solid. -**freeze'-frame** *n.* single frame of a film repeated to give an effect like a still photograph; single frame of a video recording viewed as a still by stopping the tape. [OE. *freosan*]

freight (-at) *n.* hire of a ship; cargo; a load which is being transported; charge for the conveyance of goods. -*v.t.* hire or load (a ship). -**freighter** *n.* -**freight'age** *n.* [earlier *fraught*, *q. v.*]

French *a.* of France. -**french doors** *n. pl.* door mostly of glass, opening from a room to the outdoors, and serving also as a window. [OE. *Frencise*]

fren'zy *n.* fury, delirious excitement. -**fren'zied** *a.* [F. *frénésie*]

fre'quent *a.* happening often; common, habitual; numerous. [L. *frequens*]

fres'co *n.* method of painting in water color

on the plaster of a wall before it dries; painting done thus. -*v. t.* -**fres'coed** *a.* . [It.]

fresh *a.* new; additional; different; recent; inexperienced; pure; not pickled, salted, *etc.*; not stale; not faded or dimmed; not tired; of wind, strong. -**fresh'ly** *adv.* -**fresh'ness** *n.* -**fresh'en** *v.t.* and *i.* -**fresh'et** *n.* rush of water at a river mouth; flood of river water. -**fresh'man** *n.* member of a college in his first year. [OE. *fersc*, not salt]

fret *n.* pattern of straight lines intersecting; bar to aid the fingering of a stringed instrument. -*v.t.* ornament with carved pattern. -**fret'-saw** *n.* narrowbladed saw for fretwork. -**fret'-work** *n.* thin board with cut out pattern. [*orig.* uncertain] -**fret** *v.t.* and *i.* chafe, worry. -*n.* irritation. -**fret'ful** *a.* irritable, easily vexed. [OE. *fretan*, gnaw]

fri'ar *n.* member of a mendicant religious order. -**fri'ary** *n.* convent of friars. [F. *frère*, brother]

fric'tion *n.* rubbing; resistance met with by a body moving over another; unpleasantness, ill-feeling. -**fric'tional** *a.* [L. *fricare*, *frict*-, rub]

Fri'day *n.* sixth day of the week. -**Good Friday**, Friday before Easter. [OE. *frigedæg*, day of *Freyja*, Norse goddess of love]

friend (frend) *n.* one attached to another by affection and esteem; intimate associate; supporter; Quaker. [OE. *freond*]

frieze (frcz) *n.* band of decoration on wall of building. [F. *frise*]

frig'ate *n.* warship formerly next in size to a ship of the line; now smaller than a destroyer. [F. , formerly *frégate*]

fright *n.* sudden fear, grotesque person or thing. -*v.t.* terrify. -**fright'en** *v.t.* terrify. -**fright'ful** *a.* -**fright'ful-ness** *n.* [OE. *fyrhto*]

frig'id (ii-) *a.* cold; formal; dull. -**fri'gidly** *adv.* -**fridid'ity** *n.* [L. *frigidus*]

fringe *n.* ornamental border of threads, tassels, anything resembling this; border, outskirts. -*v.t.* adorn with, serve as, a fringe. [F. *frange*]

frisk *v.i.* frolic. -*n.* frolic. -**frisk'y** *a.* -**frisk'ily** *adv.* [OF. *frisque*, lively]

fritt'er *v.t.* fritter away, throw away, waste. [OE. *freture*, fragment]

frivolous *a.* silly, trifling; given to trifling. -**frivol'ity** *n.* [L. *frivolus*]

fro *adv.* away, from; (only in *to* and *fro*). [ON. *fra*, from]

frock *n.* woman's dress; monk's gown. -*v.t.* invest with the office of priest. -**frock coat** *n.* man's long coat not cut away in front. [F. *froc*]

frog *n.* tailless amphibious animal developed from a tadpole. [OE. *frogga*]

frol'ic *a.* sportive. -*v.i.* gambol, play pranks. -*n.* prank, merry-making. -**frolicsome** *a.* [Du. *vroolijk*]

from *prep.* expressing departure, moving away, source, distance, cause, change of state, *etc.* [OE. *from*]

frond *n.* plant organ consisting of stem and foliage, usually with fruit forms, *esp.* in ferns. [L. *frons*, *frond*-, leaf]

front (-unt) *n.* fore part; forehead. -*v.i.* look,

face. -v.t. face; oppose. a. of or at the front. [L. frons, front-, forehead]

front'ier n. part of a country which borders on another. [F. frontiers]

frontis'piece n. illustration facing the title-page of a book; principal face of a building. [F. frontispice]

frost n. act or state of freezing; weather in which the temperature falls below the point at which water turns to ice; frozen dew or mist. -v.t. injure by frost; cover with rime; powder with sugar, etc. ; give a slightly roughened surface; turn (hair) white. -frost'y a. -frost'ily adv. -frost'.bite n. inflammation of the skin due to cold. [OE.]

froth (-th) n. collection of small bubbles, foam; scum; idle talk. -v.i. and t. throw up, or cause to throw up, froth. -froth'y a. foamy; empty, light. -froth'ily adv. [ON. frotha]

frown v.i. knit the brows, esp. in anger or deep thought. -n. a knitting of the brows. [OF. froignier]

fru'gal a. sparing, economical, esp. in use of food. -fru'gally adv. -frugal'ity n. [L. frugalis, fr. frux, frug-, fruit]

fruit (frōōt) n. seed and its envelope, esp. an eatable one; vegetable products (usu. in pl.); produce; result, benefit. -v.i. bear fruit. -fruit'ful a. -fruit'less a. -frui'tion n. enjoyment; realization of hopes. -fruit'y a. [L. fructus, fr. frui, fruct-, enjoy]

frump n. dowdy woman. -frump'ish a. dowdy, plain. [orig. uncertain]

frustrate v.t. baffle, disappoint. frustration n. [L. frustrari]

fry n. young fishes. -small fry young or insignificant beings. [F. frai]

fry v.t. cook with fat in a shallow pan. internal parts of animals usually eaten ied. -fry'ing pan n. [F. frire]

fudge v.t. bungle; fake. -n. makeshift kind of candy. [orig. uncertain]

fudge interj. nonsense, rubbish. -n. [cp. Ger. futsch, no good]

fuel (ffi-) n. material for burning. -v.t. rovide fuel for; take in fuel; provide a ource of energy for. [ME. fewel, fr. L. cus, hearth]

fu'gitive (fa-) a. that runs, or has run, ay; fleeting, transient. -n. one who flees; exile, refugee. [L. fugitivus, fr. fugere, fugit-, flee]

fugue (f-ag) n. musical piece in which the emes seem to answer each other; loss of emory. [F.]

Führer (fur-) n. leader, title of German dictator, esp. Hitler. [Ger. leader]

fulcrum n. (ful'cra pl.) point on which lever is placed for support. [L.]

fulfill' (fool-) v. t. satisfy; carry out; obey; satisfy the requirements of. -fulfill'ment n. [OE. fullfyllan]

full (fool) a. holding all it can; containing abundance; ample; complete; plump. -adv. very; quite; exactly. -fully adv. -ful'ness, full'ness n. -full-blown a. of flowers, completely open. [OE.]

fulminate v.i. explode. -v.t. and i. thunder out (blame, etc.). -n. chemical compound exploding readily. -fulmina'tion n. [L. fulmen, thunderbolt]

ful'some a. offending by excess, cloying; fawning. [OE.]

fum'ble v.i. and t. handle awkwardly, grope about. [lorig, uncertain]

fume n. smoke; vapor; exhalation. -v.i. emit fumes; give way to anger, chafe. [L. lumare, smoke]

fum'et (ffima) n. strong-flavored liquid made from cooking fish. meat, or game, used to flavor sauces, [F. aroma]

fu'migate v.t. apply fumes or smoke to, esp. to disinfect. -fumiga'tion n. [fume]

fun n. sport, amusement, jest, diversion. -v.i. joke, -funn'y a. [ME, fonnen, be foolish]

func'tion n. work a thing is designed to do; official duty; profession; public occasion or ceremony. -v.i. operate, work. -func'tional a. -func'tionary n. official. [L. functio]

fund n. permanent stock; stock or sum of money. -pl. money resources. -v.t. convert (debt) into permanent form; invest money permanently. -fund'ament n. buttocks. -fundament'al a. essential, primary; of, affecting, or serving as, the base. -n. one laying stress on belief in literal and verbal inspiration of the Bible or other traditional creeds. -fundament'alism n. [L. fundus, bottom]

fu'neral a. of, or relating to, the burial of the dead. -n. ceremonies at a burial. -fune'real a. fit for a funeral, dismal. [L. funus, funer-, burial]

fun'gus (-ng-g-) n. fun'gi (-ji) fun'-guses pl. mushroom or allied plant; spongy morbid growth. -fun'gous a. -fun'gicide n. substance used to destroy fungus. [L.]

funic'ular a. of or worked by a rope. -funic'ular railways mountain or other cable-railway. [L. funiculus, dim. of funis, rope]

funn'el n. cone-shaped vessel or tube; chimney of locomotive or ship; ventilating shaft. [L. fundere, pour]

funn'y. See fun.

fur n. short soft hair of certain animals; lining or trimming or garment of dressed skins with such hair; crust or coating resembling this. -v.t. provide with fur. - furr'ier n. one who deals in furs. -furr'y a. [F. v. fourrer, fr. OF. fourre, sheath, cover]

furl v.t. roll up and bind (a sail, an umbrella. etc,). [F. ferier]

fur'longn eighth of a mile. [OE. furlang, length of a furrow, furh]

fur'lough n. leave of absence, esp. of soldier. [Du. verlol]

fur'nace n. apparatus for applying great heat to metals; hot place; closed fireplace for heating a boiler, etc. [F. fournaise]

fur'nish v.t. supply, fit up with; fit up a house with furniture; yield. -fur'niture n. movable contents of a house or room. [F. fournir]

furor' n. burst of enthusiastic popular admiration. [It.]

furr'ow (-a) n. trench made by a plow ship's track; rut, groove. -v.t. make furrows in. [OE. furh]

fur'ther (-TH-) adv. more; in addition; at or to a greater extent. a. additional; -v.t. help forward. [OE. *furthra a.; furthor adv.*]

fur'tive *a.* stealthy, sly. -**fur'tively** *adv.* [L. *furtivus,* fr. *fur,* thief]

fu'ry *n.* wild anger, rage; fierce passion; violence of storm, *etc.*; snakehaired avenging deity (*usu. pl.*). -**fu'rious** *a.* -**fu'riously** *adv.* [L. *furia*]

fuse *n.* tube containing material for setting light to a bomb, firework, *etc.*; device used as a safety measure which interrupts an electric circuit. [L. *fusus,* spindle]

fuse *v.t.* and *i.* melt with heat; blend by melting. -**fu'sible** *a.* -**fu'sion** *n.* [L. *fundere, fus-,* pour]

fu'selage *n.* spindle-shaped body of an airplane. [L. *fusus,* spindle]

fuss *n.* needless bustle or concern. -*v.i* make a fuss. -*v.t.* hustle. -**fuss'y** *a.* **fuss'ily** *adv.* -**fuss'iness** *n.* [orig. uncertain]

fu'tile *a.* useless, ineffectual, frivolous. -**futil'ity** *n.* [L. *futilis,* leaky]

fu'ture *a.* that will be; of, or relating to, time to come. -*n.* time to come; what will happen; tense of a verb indicating this. -**futu'rity** *n.* -**fu'turism** *n.* movement in art marked by complete abandonment of tradition. -**fu'turist** *n.* and *a.* [L. *futurus,* about to be]

fuzz *n.* fluff. -**fuzz'y** *a.* -**fuzz box** *n.* an electronic device that breaks up the sound passing through it, used *esp.* by guitarists. [imit. of blowing away light particles]

G

gab *n.* talk, chatter; gift of the gab, eloquence. -**gab'ble** *v. i.* and *t.* talk, utter inarticulately or too fast. -*n.* such talk. [imit. orig.]

ga'ble *n.* triangular upper part of the wall at the end of a ridged roof. [OF.]

gad *v. i.* go about idly. -**gad'about** *n.* gadding person. [fr. obs. *gadling*-OE. g, ædeling, comrade]

gad'fly *n.* cattle-biting fly. [obs. gad, spike, fr. ON. gaddr]

gadg'et *n.* small fitting or contrivance. [orig. uncertain]

Gael (gāl) *n.* Scottish Highlander, Celt. -**Gael'ic** *a.* of Gael or his language. [Gael, *Gaidheal*]

gaff *n.* barbed fishing spear; stick with an iron hook for landing fish; spar for the top of a fore-and-aft sail. -*v. t.* seize (a fish) with a gaff. [F. *gaffe*]

gaffe *n.* tactless or embarrassing blunder. [F.]

gag *n.* thing thrust into the mouth to prevent speech or hold it open for operation; closure in a debate. -*v. t.* apply a gag to; silence. [orig. *v.* strangle; imit. of victim's noises]

gag *n.* words inserted by an actor in his part. -*v. i.* of an actor, to put in words not in his part. [orig. uncertain]

gage *n.* pledge, thing given as security; challenge, or something symbolizing one. -*v. t.* pledge, stake. *See also* **gauge**. [F.]

gain *v.t.* obtain, secure; obtain as profit; win; earn; persuade; reach. -*v. i.* increase, improve. -*n.* profit, increase, improvement. [F. *gagner*]

gait *n.* manner of walking. [same as gate, street, way]

gala (gā-) *n.* festive occasion. [It.]

gal'axy *n.* Milky Way; any other of the stellar universes; brilliant company. **galac'tic** *a.* [G. *gala, galakt-,* milk]

gale *n.* strong wind. [orig. uncertain]

gall (gawl) *n.* bile of animals; bitterness, rancour. [OE. *gealla*]

gall (gawl) *n.* growth caused by insects on trees; oak-apple. [L. *galla*]

gall'ant *a.* fine, stately, brave; chivalrous; very attentive to women, amatory. *n.* man of fashion; lover, paramour. [F. *galant*]

gall'ery *n.* raised floor over part of the area of a building, *esp.* a church; top floor of seats in a theatre; its occupants; long narrow platform on the outside of a building; passage in a wall, open to the interior of a building; covered walk with side openings, a colonnade; room or rooms for showing works of art; horizontal passage in mining. [F. *galerie*]

gall'ey *n.* one-decked vessel with sails and oars, usually rowed by slaves or criminals; large rowing-boat, *esp.* that used by the captain of a warship; ship's kitchen; printer's tray for set-up type. -**gall'ey-proof** *n.* printer's proof in long slip form. [OF. *galee*]

gall'on *n.* liquid measure of eight pints or four quarts. [ONF. *galon*]

gall'op *v.i.* go at a gallop. -*v.t.* cause to move at a gallop. -*n.* horse's, or other quadruped's, fastest pace, with all four feet off the ground together in each stride; ride at this pace. -**gall'oper** *n.* [F. *galoper*]

gall'ows *n.* structure, usually of two upright beams and a cross-bar, *esp.* for hanging criminals on. [OE. gealga]

galore' *adv.* in plenty; in profusion. [Ir. *go leor,* in sufficiency]

galvanism *n.* electricity produced by chemical action. -**galvan'ic** *a.* -**galvan'ic batt'ery** *n.* -**gal'vanize** *v.t.* apply galvanism to; stimulate thus; rouse by shock; coat with metal by galvanism. -**galvaniza'tion** *n.* -**galvanom'eter** *n.* instrument for measuring galvanism. (Galvani, It. physicist, (d. 1798)]

gam'bit *n.* chess opening involving the sacrifice of a piece. [It. *gambetto,* wrestler's trip, fr. *gamba,* leg]

gam'ble *v.i.* play games of chance for money stakes; speculate wildly; risk much for great gain. -*n.* risky undertaking. -**gam'bler** *n.* [fr. *game n.*]

game *n.* diversion, pastime, jest; contest for amusement; scheme, plan of action; animals or birds hunted; their flesh, *a.* plucky, spirited. -*v. i.* gamble. -**game'ly** *a.* -**game'ster** *n.* gambler. -**game'cock** *n.* fowl bred for fighting. -**game'keeper** *n.* man employed to breed game, prevent poaching, *etc.* -**gam'y** *a.* having the flavor of hung game; spirited. [OE. gamen]

gamete' *n.* sexual reproductive cell. [G. *gamos,* marriage]

gamm'a-rays *n. pl.* rays given off by radioactive substances, e. g. , radium. [G. letter *gamma*]

gam'ut n. whole series of musical notes; scale; compass of a voice. [Med. L. *gamma*, and *ut*, names of notes]

gan'der n. male goose. [OE. gandra]

gang n. company, band. -**gang'er** n. foreman over a gang of workmen. -**gang'way** n. bridge from a ship to the shore; anything similar; passage between rows of seats. [OE. = going, way]

gang'lion (-ng-gl-) n. knot on a nerve from which nerve fibers spread out; nerve nucleus. [G. ganglion]

gang'rene n. mortification, decomposition of a part of the body. -v.t. affect with this. -v.i. be affected with this. -**gang'renous** a. [L. gangraena, G. gangraina]

gang'ster n. member of a gang of criminals, toughs. [gang]

gape v.i. open the mouth wide; stare; yawn. -n. yawn; wide opening of the mouth. [ON. gapa]

gar n. fish with slender body and pointed head, kind of pike. [OF. = dart]

gar'age n. building to house automobiles. -**gar'age sale** n. sale of personal belongings or household effects held at a person's home, usually in the garage. [F., fr. garer, make safe]

garb n. dress, fashion of dress. -v.t. dress, clothe. [OF. garbe, contour]

garb'age (-ij) n. offal; refuse; anything worthless; originally, giblets. [orig. uncertain]

gar'ble v.t. make selections from unfairly, so as to misrepresent. -**gar'bled** a. [arab. ghirbal, sieve]

gar'den n. ground for growing flowers, fruit, or vegetables. -v. i. cultivate a garden. -**gar'dener** n. -**gar'den ci'ty**, planned town with parks and planted areas. -**gar'dening** n. the planning and cultivation of a garden. [ONF. gardin]

garde'nia (-d-) n. tropical, subtropical shrub with fragrant white flowers. [Dr. A. Garden (d. 1791)]

gar a. huge, prodigious. [Gargantua, character of Rabelais]

gar'gle v.i. and i. wash the throat with liquid kept moving by the breath. -n. liquid used for this. [F. gargouiller]

gar'goyle n. grotesque water-spout. [F. gargouille, fr. L. gargulio, throat]

gar'ish a. showy; glaring; tawdry. [orig. uncertain]

gar'land n. wreath of flowers worn or hung as a decoration. -v.t. decorate with garlands. [OF. garlandle]

gar'lic n. plant with a strong smell and taste, used in cooking. [OE. garleac, spear leek]

gar'ment n. article of dress. -pl. clothes. fF. garniment, equipment]

gar'nish v.t. adorn, decorate (esp. food or literary matter). -n. material for this. [F. garnir]

garr'et n. room on the top floor, an attic. [orig. turret, OF. garite, refuge]

garrison n. troops stationed in a town, fort, etc. -v. t. furnish, or occupy, with a garrison; defend by this means. [OF. garison, fr. garir, protect]

garrotte' n. Spanish capital punishment by strangling; apparatus for this; robbery by throttling the victim. -v.t. execute, or rob, thus. [Sp. garrote, tourniquet]

garr'ulous a. talkative. -**garrul'ity** n. [L. garrulus -garrire, chatter]

gar'ter n. band worn near the knee to keep a stocking up. [ONF. gartier, fr. garet, bend of the knee]

gas n. elastic fluid such as air, esp. one not liquid or solid at ordinary temperature; such fluid, esp. coal-gas used for heating or lighting; such fluid or a mixture used as poison in warfare, or found as an explosive in mines, or employed as an anesthetic, etc.; gasoline. -v.t. project gas over; poison with gas. -**gas'eous** a. -**gaselier'** n. lamp of several burners for gas.

gash a. long deep cut, slash. -v.t. make a gash in. [earlier garshe, F. gercer, chap]

gas'oline, gas'olene n. liquid from petroleum, used as fuel. [gas]

gasp (-a-) v.i. catch the breath with open mouth, as in exhaustion or surprise. -n. convulsive catching of the breath. [ON, geispa, yawn]

gas'tric a. of the stomach. -**gastron'omy** n. art of good eating. -**gastro-** nom'ical a. -**gastron'omer**, **gas'tronome** n. judge of cooking. -**gas'teropod** n. mollusk, e. g. a snail, with organ of locomotion placed ventrally. [G. gaster, belly]

gate n. opening in a wall which may be closed by a barrier; barrier for closing it; device for regulating the flow of water; any entrance or way out; entrance-money at, e.g. a football-game -**gate'crasher** n. one who attends a party, etc. without being invited. [OE. geat]

gate n. (compute) electronic circuit which performs logical or mathematical calculations or operations.

gath'er (-TH-) v.t. bring together; collect; draw together, pucker; deduce. -v. i. come together; collect; form a swelling full of pus. -**gathers** n. pl. puckered part of a dress. [OE. gadrian]

gauche (gosh) a. awkward, clumsy. [F. left-handed]

gaud (gawd) n. showy ornament. -**gaud'y** a. showy without taste. [orig. uncertain]

gauge, **gage** (aj) n. standard measure, as of diameter of wire, etc. ; distance between rails of a railway; capacity; extent; instruments for measuring such things as size of wire, rainfall, height of water in a boiler, etc. -v.t. measure, test, estimate. [ONF.]

gaunt (gaw-) a. lean, haggard, starved-looking. [orig. uncertain]

gaunt'let (gaw-) n. armored glove; glove covering part of the arm. [F. gantelet, dim. of gant, glove]

gaunt'let (gaw-) n. run the gauntlet, punishment in which the victim had to run between two lines of men who struck at him with sticks, etc. to brave criticism. [Se. gatlopp, 'gate run']

gauze (gawz) n. thin transparent fabric of silk, wire, etc. -**gauz'y** a. [F. gaze]

gav'el n. a mallet; chairman's or auctioneer's hammer. [orig. unknown]

gay *a.* light-hearted; showy; dissolute; homosexual. **-gai'ly** *adv.* **-gai'ety** *n.* [F. *gai*]

gaze *v.i.* look fixedly. *-n.* long intent look. [orig. uncertain]

gaze'bo *n.* outlook turret on roof or wall; summer-house with wide prospect; belvedere. [orig. unknown]

gazelle' *n.* small soft-eyed antelope. [Arab. *ghazal*, wild goat]

gazette' *n.* official newspaper for announcements of government appointments, bankruptcies, *etc.*; title for a newspaper. *-v.t.* publish in the official gazette. **-gazetteer'** *n.* geographical dictionary. [It. *gazzetta*]

gear *n.* apparatus, tackle, tools; set of wheels working together, *esp.* by engaging cogs; rigging; harness; equipment; clothing; goods, utensils. *-v.t.* provide with gear; put in gear. **-gear'-box,-case** *n.* box, case protecting gearing of bicycle, car. **-gear'-wheel** *n.* wheel with cogs *etc.* for transmitting motion in cycle. **-in gear**, connected and in working order. **-out of gear**, disconnected, out of sorts. [ME. *gere*, fr. ON.]

Gei'ger counter *n.* instrument for measuring density of radio-active field. [Geiger, German physicist]

gei'sha *n.* Japanese dancing girl. [Chin. *i-che*, artistic ones]

gelatin gel'atine *n.* transparent substance made by stewing skin, tendons, *etc.* [It. *gelatins*, fr. *gelata*, jelly]

geld (g-) *v.i.* castrate. **-geld'ing** *n.* castrated horse. [ON. *geldr*, barren]

gel'ignite (jel'-ig-nit) *n.* high explosive. [gelatin and ignite]

gem *n.* precious stone; thing of great beauty or worth. *-v. t.* adorn with gems. [L. *gemma*, bud, gem]

gem'ini (jem'-i-ni) *n.* constellation containing Castor and Pollux; third sign of the zodiac (the twins) which sun enters c. May 21st. [L. *pl.* of *geminus*, twin]

gen'der *n.* sex, male or female; classification of nouns, corresponding roughly to sexes and sexlessness (in English). [F, *genre*, fr. L. *genus*, gener-, kind]

gene (jen) *n.* one of the biological factors determining heredity. [G. *genos*, race]

genealogy (je) *n.* account of descent from an ancestor or ancestors; pedigree; study of pedigrees. **-genealog'ical** *a.* **-geneal'ogize** *v.i.* **-geneal'ogist** *n.* [G. *geneaolgia*, fr. *genea*, race]

gen'eral *a.* not particular or partial; including or affecting or applicable to all or most; not restricted to one department; usual; prevalent; miscellaneous; dealing with main elements only. *-n.* officer in the armed forces of rank above lieutenant general. **-general'ity** *n.* **-gen'eral ize** *v.t.* reduce to general laws. *-v.i.* draw general conclusions. **-generaliza'tion** *n.* **-gen'erally** *adv.* **-gen'eralship** *n.* military skill; management. [L. *generalis*, fr. *genus*, gener-, kind]

gen'erate *v.t.* bring into being; produce. **-genera'tion** *n.* bringing into being; step in a pedigree; all persons born about the same time; average time in which children are ready to replace their parents (about 30 years). **-gen'erative** *a.* **-gen'erator** *n.* a begetter; apparatus for producing (steam, *etc.*). **-gen'erating-sta'tion** *n.* place where electricity is generated. [L. *generare*, procreate]

generic *a.* belonging to, characteristic of, a class or genus. **-gener'ically** *adv.* [L. *genus*, gener-, race]

gen'erous *a.* noble-minded; liberal, free in giving; copious; of wine, rich. **-gen'erously** *adv.* **-generos'ity** *n.* [L. *generosus*, of noble birth]

gen'esis *n.* origin; mode of formation. **-Genesis** *n.* first book of the Old Testament. [G.]

genetics *n.* science dealing with heredity, variation, reproduction. **-genet'ic** *a.* [G. *genesis*]

ge'nial *a.* kindly, jovial; sympathetic; mild, conducive to growth. [L. *genialis*]

ge'nie *n.* (ge'nii *pl.*) a demon. [F. *genie*, used for Arab. *jinni*]

gen'ital *a.* of generation. *-n. pl.* external generative organs. [L. *gignere*, genit-, beget]

ge'nius *n.* with high power of mind; person with this; tutelary spirit; prevalent feeling, taste; character, spirit. [L. = a spirit watching over a person from birth, fr. *gignere*, gen-, beget]

genre' (zhong'r) *n.* kind, variety; style of painting homely scenes. [F.]

genteel' *a.* elegant (usually ironical). [F. *gentil*, gentle]

gen'tian *n.* plant, usually with blue flowers. [L. *gentiana*]

gen'tile *a.* of race other than Jewish; *-n.* gentile person. [L. *gens, gent-*, race, translating G. *ta ethne*, the nations]

gen'tle *a.* mild, quiet, not rough or severe; courteous; noble; well-born. **-gentil'ity** *n.* social superiority. **-gen'tleman** *n.* chivalrous well-bred man; man of good social position; man of noble birth; man (used as a mark of politeness). **-gent'ry** *n.* people next below the nobility. [F. *gentil*]

gen'uflect *v.i.* bend the knee, *esp.* in worship. [fr. L. *genu*, knee, and *flectere*, flex, bend]

gen'uine *a.* real, true, not sham, properly so called. [L. *genuinus*, native]

ge'nus *n.* race, tribe, kind, class. [L.]

geode' *n.* rock cavity lined with crystals; stone containing this. [G. *geodes*, earth]

geography *n.* science of the earth's form, physical features, climate, population, *etc.*; book on this. **-geog'rapher** *n.* **-geograph'ical** *a.* **-geograph'ically** *adv.* [G. *ge*, earth, *graphein*, write]

geol'ogy *n.* science of the earth's crust, the rocks, their strata, *etc.* **-geol'ogist** *n.* **-geolog'ical** *a.* **-geolog'ically** *adv.* **-geol'ogize** *v.i.* practice geology. [G. *ge*, earth, *logia*, discourse]

geom'etry *n.* science of the properties and relations of magnitudes in space, as lines, surfaces, *etc.* [G. *ge*, earth, *metron*, measure]

gera'nium *n.* genus of plants with fruit resembling a crane's bill. [L., G. *geranos*, crane]

germ *n.* rudiment of a new organism, of an animal or plant; microbe; elementary thing. **-germ'icide** *n.* substance for destroying disease-germs. **-ger'mici'dal** *a.* **-ger'mina'te** *v.i.* sprout. *-v. t.* cause to sprout. **-germina'tion** *n.*

germ warfare *n.* warring method in which the weapons are germs released to produce disease among the enemy. [L. *gerrnen*, seed]

germane *a.* relevant, belonging to a subject. [L. *germanus, v. s.*]

gerrymander *v.t.* arrange matters for an election, manipulate an electoral district, so as to give undue influence to one side. [fr. Governor Gerry of Mass. and salamander]

Gesta'po *n.* secret state police of Nazi Germany. [*Geheime Stoats Polizei*]

gestation *n.* carrying of young in the womb between conception and birth; period of gestation. [L. *gestatio*]

gesticulate *v.i.* use expressive or lively movements accompanying, or instead of, speech. **-gesticula'tion** *n.* [L. *gestus*, action]

ges'ture *n.* movement to convey some meaning. [Low L. *gestura*]

get (g-) *v.t.* obtain, procure, earn; cause to go or come; bring into a position or state; induce; (in *perf. tense*) be in possession of, have (to do). *-v.i.* reach, attain; become. **get'-away** *n.* escape. [ON. *geta*]

gey'ser (giz-, gez-) *n.* hot spring spouting at intervals; apparatus for heating water and delivering it from a tap. [Ice. *geysir*]

ghast'ly (ga-) *a.* horrible, shocking; death-like, pallid; grim. *-adv.* horribly. [obs. gast, terrify. cp. aghast]

gher'kin (g-)*n.*kind of small cucumber. [Old Du. dim. of gurk, for *agurk*, cucumber]

ghett'o (g-, *n.* part of a city where members of a particular national or racial group predominate, or are restricted. [it.]

ghost *n.* spirit, dead person appearing again, specter; semblance. **ghost'ly** *a.* [OE. *gast*, spirit]

ghoul *n.* in Eastern tales, a spirit preying on corpses. **-ghoul'ish** *a.* revelling in the gruesome. [Arab. *ghul*]

gi'ant *n.* human being of superhuman size; very tall person, plant, *etc.* **-a.** huge. **-gigant'ic** *a.* enormous, huge [F. *goant*, fr. L. *gigas, giganti*]

gibb'on (g-) *n.* long-armed ape. [F.]

gibe, jibe *v.i.* utter taunts. *-v.t.* taunt. *n.* jeer. [orig. uncertain]

gib'let *n.* (in *pl.*) edible internal portion of a fowl, goose, *etc.*, removed before cooking. [orig. unknown]

gidd'y (g-) *a.* dizzy, feeling a swimming in the head; liable to cause this feeling; flighty, frivolous. [Oe. *gydig*, insane]

gift (g-) *n.* thing given, present; faculty, power. *-v.t.* endow or present (with). **gift'ed** *a.* talented. [give]

gift wrap *v.t.* to wrap a present in decorative paper and trimmings. - **gift wrap** *n.* - **gift wrapping** *n.* **gift wrapper** *n.*

gigabit *n.* (*comp. sci.*) unit of information equal to one billion bits or binary digits

gigahertz *n. pl.* gigahertz unit of frequency equal to one billion hertz; formerly gigacycle. [abbr. *GHz*]

gig'gle (g-) *v.i.* laugh in a half-suppressed way, foolishly or uncontrollably. *-n.* such a laugh. [limit. orig.]

GIGO (*compu. sci.*) term used to stress the fact the computer results are dependant upon the quality of the computer input. [Garbage In/Garbage Out]

gig'olo *n.* male professional dancing partner. [F.]

gi'la mon'ster *n.* black-and-yellow poisonous lizard of Arizona. [Gila River]

gild (g-) *v.t.* put a thin layer of gold on. **gilt** *a.* **gilded**-*n.* layer of gold put on. [OE. *gyldan*, fr. gold]

gill (g-) *n.* breathing organ in fishes; flesh below a person's jaws and ears. [orig. unknown. cp, Sw. *gill*, Dan. *giaelle*]

gim'let *n.* boring tool, usually with a screw point. [OF. *guimbelet*]

gimp *n.* kind of trimming, of silk covered cord. [F. *guimpe*]

gin *n.* snare, trap; kind of crane; machine for separating cotton from seeds. *-v.t.* snare; treat (cotton) in a gin. [F. *engin*, L. *ingenium*, skill]

gin *n.* spirit flavored with juniper. [short for *geneva*, F. *genievre*, fr. L. *juniperus*, juniper]

gin'ger *n.* plant with a hot-tasting spicy root used in cooking, *etc.*; the root; spirit, mettle; light reddish yellow color. **-gin'ger-bread** *n.* cake flavored with ginger. **-gin'gery** *a.* [Late L. *gingiber*, of Eastern orig.]

gin'gerly *a.* such as to avoid noise or injury; cautious. *-adv.* in a gingerly manner. [orig. uncertain]

giraffe' *n.* African ruminant animal, with spotted coat and very long neck and legs. [F. *girafe*, fr. Arab.]

gird (g-) *v.t.* put a belt round; fasten clothes thus; equip with or belt on a sword; encircle. **-gird'er** *n.* beam supporting joists; iron or steel beam. **-gir'dle** *n.* belt. *-v.t.* surround. **-gird** *v.i.* gibe. *-n.* gibe. [OE. *gyrdan*]

girl female child; young unmarried woman; woman. [ME. *gurie*; of unknown orig.]

girth (g-) *n.* band put round a horse to hold the saddle, *etc.*; measurement round a thing. *-v. t.* surround, secure, with a girth. [ON. *gjdrth*]

gist *n.* substance, essential point (of remarks, *etc.*). [OF. *gist* 'it lies']

give (g-) *v.t.* bestow, confer ownership of, make a present of, deliver, impart; assign; yield, supply; make over, cause to have. *v.i.* yield, give way. *-n.* yielding, elasticity. (gave *p. t.* -given *p.p.*)-**giv'er** *n.* [OE. *giefan*]

gizz'ard (g-) *n.* bird's second stomach for grinding food. [F. *gésier*]

glac'é- (glass) *a.* of cakes, fruit; smoothly iced, sugared. [F.]

gla'cier *n.* river of ice, a slow-moving mass of ice formed by accumulated snow in mountain valleys. **-gla'cia** (-shal) *a.* of ice, or of glaciers; crystallized. **-glacia'tion** *n.* **-gla'cis**

(-se) n outer sloping bank of a fortification. [F. , fr. glace, ice]

glad a. pleased; happy, joyous; giving joy. -v.t. make glad. [OE. glæd]

glade n. clear space in a wood or forest. [orig. uncertain **gladiator** n. trained fighter in ancient Roman shows. [L. fr. gladius, sword]

glam'or n. magic, enchantment. - **glam'orous** a. -**glamorize** v.t. make seem glamorous, esp. deceptively. [corrupt. of grammar, gramarye, magic]

glance v.i. glide off something struck; pass quickly; allude, touch; look rapidly. v.t. direct (the eyes) rapidly. -n. brief look; flash; sudden oblique movement or blow. [F. glacer, (formerly) slide]

gland n. organ separating constituents of the blood, for use or ejection. -**gland'ular** a. [L. glans, gland-, acorn]

glare (-ar) v.t. shine with oppressive brightness; look fiercely. -n. dazzling brightness; fierce look. [ME. glareni]

glass (-i-) n. hard transparent substance made by fusing sand with; a potash, etc. ; things made of it collectively; glass drinking vessel; contents of this; lens; telescope, barometer, or other instrument. pl. spectacles. -**glaze** v.t. furnish with glass; cover with glassy substance or glaze. -v. i. become glassy. -n. transparent coating; substance used to give this; glossy surface. -**gla'zier** n. one whose trade is to glaze windows. [OE. glæs]

glauco'ma n. eye disease. [G.]

gleam n. slight or passing beam of light; faint or momentary show. -v.i. give out gleams. [OE. glaees]

glean v.t. and i. gather, pick up, after reapers in a cornfield; pick up (facts, etc.). -**glean'er** n. [F. glaner]

glee n. mirth, merriment; musical composition for three or more voices, a catch. **glee'ful** a. -**glee'fully** adv. -**glee'man** n. minstrel. [OE. gliw, minstrelsy]

glen n. narrow valley, usually wooded and with a stream. [Gael. gleann]

glib a. fluent; more voluble than sincere. - **glib'ly** adv. -**glib'ness** n. [orig. uncertain. cp. Du. glibberig, slippery]

glide v.i. pass smoothly and continuously; go stealthily or gradually; of an airplane, move with engines shut off. -n. smooth, silent movement; in music, sounds made in passing from tone to tone. [OE. glidani]

glimm'er v.i. shine faintly or with flickering. -n. such light. [ME. glimeren]

glimpse n. momentary view; passing flash or appearance. -v.t. catch a glimpse of -v. i. glimmer. [gleam]

glint v.i. and t. flash, glitter; reflect. -n. glitter; glancing reflection. [ME. glent]

glis'ten (-is'n) v.i. glitter, sparkle, shine. [OE. glisnian, shine]

glitt'er v.i. shine with bright quivering light, sparkle. -n. [ON. glitra]

glitz n. (sl.) showy or flash appearance or display; ostentatious glamor; gaudiness v.i. -**glitzy** a.

gloat v.i. feast the eyes, usually with unholy joy. [orig. uncertain]

globe n. round body, sphere; heavenly sphere, esp. the earth; sphere with a map of the earth or the stars; anything of about this shape, as a lampshade, fish-bowl, etc. -**glob'al** a. -**globe'-trotter** n. hasty, sight-seeing traveller. -**glob'ule** n. small round body; drop. -**glob'ular** a. globe-shaped. [L. globus, round mass]

gloom n. darkness; melancholy, depression. -v. i. look sullen, or dark. -v.t. make dark or dismal. -**gloom'y** a. -**gloom'ily** adv. - **gloom'iness** n. [cp. glum]

glor'y n. renown, honorable fame; splendor; heavenly bliss; exalted or prosperous state. -v.i. take pride (in). **glor'ify** v.t. make glorious, invest with glory. -**glorifica'tion** n. -**glor'ious** a. **glor'iously** adv. [fL. gloria]

gloss n. surface shine. -v. t. put a gloss on. -**gloss'y** a. smooth and shining **gloss'iness** n. [orig. uncertain]

gloss n. marginal interpretation of a word; comment, explanation. -v.t. interpret; comment; explain away. -**gloss'ary** n. collection of glosses; dictionary or vocabulary of special words. [F. glose, fr. G. glossa, tongue]

glove (-uv) n. covering for the hand. -v. t. provide with, or put on, gloves. -**glo'ver** n. dealer in gloves. [OE. glof]

glow (-o) v.i. give out light and heat without flames; shine; be, or look, very hot, burn with emotion. -n. shining heat; feeling of bodily heat; warmth of color; ardor. -**glow'worm** n. small luminous insect. [OE. glowan]

glower v.i. scowl. [orig. uncertain]

glu'cose n. grape-sugar, dextrose. [G. glykys, sweet]

glue (-oo) n. hard substance made from horns, hoofs, etc. , and used warm as a cement. -v. t. fasten with glue. -**glu'ey** a. [F. glu, bird-lime]

glum a. sullen, frowning, dejected. [orig. uncertain] [gloom]

glut v.t. feed, gratify to the full or to excess; overstock. -n. excessive supply. [OF. gloutir, swallow]

glutinous a. sticky; tenacious. [gluten]

glutt'on n. one who eats too much, a greedy person; one eagerly devouring (books, work, etc.). -**glutt'onous** a. **glutt'ony** n. [F. glouton]

glutt'on n. carnivorous animal, the wolverine. [glution]

glycerine, glycerine (glis'er-in) n. colorless, sweet liquid obtained from oils and used in medicine and the making of explosives. [G. glykeros, sweet]

gnarled (narld) a. of a tree, knobby, rugged, twisted. [var. of knurled]

gnat (n-) n. small two-winged fly; mosquito. [OE. gnæt]

gnaw (n-) v.t. bite steadily, wear away by biting; corrode. [O. E. gnagan]

gnome (n-) n. goblin, a fairy living underground. [Mod. L. gnomus]

gnos'tic (n-) a. of knowledge; having mystical knowledge; pert. to the Gnostics. [G. gnostikos]

gnu (nu-) n. S. African antelope somewhat like an ox. [Kaffir nqu] **go** v.i. move along, make way; be moving; depart; elapse; be kept, put, be able to be put; result; contribute to a result; tend to; become. -n. energy, vigor. -go'er n. go'gett'er n. pushful, assertive person. [OE. gan]

goad n. spiked stick for driving cattle. v.t. drive with a goad; urge on: irritate. [OE. gad]

goal n. end of a race; object of effort; posts through which the ball or disk is to be driven in football, soccer, hockey etc. ; act of doing this. [orig. uncertain]

goat n. four-footed animal with long hair and horns, and a beard. -goat'herd n. one who tends goats. -goat'ee n. beard like a goat's. [OE. gat]

gob n. lump, mouthful. -gobb'et n. lump of food. -gob'ble v.t. eat hastily and noisily. [orig. uncertain]

gob'ble v.i. of a turkey, to make a gurg ling noise in the throat. [imit.]

gob'let n. drinking cup. [F. gobelet]

gob'lin n. mischievous and ugly demon. [F. gobelin]

god n. superhuman being worshipped as having supernatural power; object of worship, idol. -God n. Supreme Being. godd'ess fem. -God'speed, may God speed (you) and bring (you) success. [OE.]

gog'gle v.i. roll the eyes. -v.t. roll about (the eyes), -a. rolling, sticking out (only of eyes). -n. in pl. large spectacles to protect the eyes from glare, dust, etc. [orig. uncertain]

goi'ter n. enlargement of the thyroid gland. -goi'tered a. -goi'trous a. [F.]

gold n. yellow precious metal; coins of this, wealth; fig. beautiful or precious material or thing; color of gold. -a. of like, or having the color of, gold. -gold'en a. -gold'smith n. worker in gold. -gold-standard n. financial arrangement whereby currencies are expressed in fixed terms of gold. [OE.]

golf n. game in which a small hard ball is struck with clubs. -v.i. play this game. golf'er n. -golf course n. , place where golf is played, consisting of tees, greens and fairway. [Du. kilf, club]

go'nad n. sex gland. [G. gone, generation]

gon'dola n. Venetian canal-boat; car suspended from an airship. -gondolier' n. [It.]

gong n. metal disk with turned rim which resounds as a bell when struck with a soft mallet; anything used in the same way. [Malay]

gonorrhea n. venereal disease. [G. gonor-roia]

gonopore n. reproductive opening of certain worms and insects through which the egg or sperm is released.

good a. right; proper; excellent; virtuous; kind; safe; adequate; sound; valid. -n. that which is good; well-being; profit. -pl. property, wares. -good'-breeding n. politeness. -good-day, a greeting. -good fellowship n. sociability, merry company. Good Friday, Friday before Easter commemorating Christ's crucifixion. -good' will n. kindly feeling; heartiness; right of trading as a recognized successor. [OE. god]

good-bye' interj. farewell. [earlier godbwye, for God be with you]

goose n. large web-footed bird; its flesh; simpleton; tailor's smoothing iron. goose'flesh n. bristling state of the skin due to cold or fright [OE. gosi]

gooseberry (-z-) n. thorny shrub; its eatable berry; chaperon to lovers. [orig. uncertain]

gore n. clotted shed blood. -gor'y a. gor'ily adv. [OE. gor, blood, filth]

gorge n. inside of the throat; surfeit; narrow opening between hills. -v. i. feed greedily. -v.t. stuff with food; devour greedily. -gorg'et n. piece of armor for the throat. [F.]

gorge'ous (-jus) a. splendid, showy, dazzling. [OF. gorgias, swaggering]

gor'gon n. hideous mythical female creature, believed to turn beholder to stone; ugly woman. -gorgo'nian a. [G. gorgo]

Gorgonzo'la n. rich cheese. [It. town]

goril'a n. anthropoid ape of the largest kind. [orig. unknown]

gormandize v.t. eat like a glutton. [fr. gor-mand, old form of gourmand]

gorse n. prickly shrub with fragrant yellow flowers, furze, whin. [OE. gorst]

gos'ling (-z-) n. young goose. [dim. of goose]

gos'pel n. tidings preached by Jesus; record of his life; any of the four books by the evangelists. [OE. godspel, god spel, good tidings]

goss'amer n. filmy substance of spiders' web floating in calm air or spread on grass; filmy thing; delicate gauze. light, flimsy. [goose summer]

goss'ip n. idle talk about other persons, esp. regardless of fact; idle talk or writing; one who talks thus; formerly, a familiar friend. -v. i. talk gossip. [OE. godsibb, God akin, sponsor]

Goth'ic a. of Goths; barbarous; in architecture, of the pointed arch style common in Europe 12th-16th cent. ; a printing type. [L. Gothi, Goths]

gouge n. chisel with a curved cutting edge. -v. i. cut with a gouge, hollow (out). [F.]

gou'lash n. well-seasoned stew of beef and vegetables. [Hung. gulyas]

gourd (gord, goord) n. trailing or climbing plant; its large fleshy fruit; rind of this as a vessel. [F. gourde]

gour'mand a. greedy. -n. love of good fare. -gourmandize' (-dez) n. greediness for food. [F.]

gour'met (-ma) n. connoisseur of wine or food. [F.]

gout (gowt) n. disease with inflammation, esp. of the smaller joints; drop, splash. gout'y a. [F. goutte, drop]

govern (guv-) v.t. rule, direct, guide, control; serve as a precedent for; be followed by (a grammatical case, etc.). -gov'erness n. woman teacher esp. in a private household. gov'ernment n. rule; control; ruling body of a state; the state. -gov'ernmental a. [F. gouverner, fr. L. gubernare, steer]

gown n. loose flowing upper garment; woman's frock; official robe, as in a university, etc. [OF. gonne]

grab v.t. grasp suddenly, snatch. -n. sudden

clutch; greedy proceedings. grab'bing a. greedy. [orig. uncertain]

grace n. charm, attractiveness; easy and refined motion, manners, etc. ; ornament, accomplishment; favor; divine favor; short thanksgiving before or after a meal; title of a duke or archbishop. -v. t. add grace to honor. -grace'ful a. -grace'less a. shameless, depraved. -gra'cious a. indulgent, beneficent, condescending. grace'fully adv. -gra'ciously adv. [F. grace, fr. L. gratia, pleasing quality, favor]

grade n. step or stage; degree of rank, etc. ; class; slope; gradient. -v. t. arrange in classes. -grada'tion n. series of degrees or steps; each of them; arrangement in steps; insensible passing from one shade, etc. , to another. - grade school n. elementary school. - gra'dient n. degree of slope. -grad'ual a. taking place by es; moving step by step; slow and steady; not steep. -grad'ually adv. grad'uate v.i. receive a university degree diploma; one who has received a university degree or diploma. -gradua'tion n. [L. gradus, step]

graft n. shoot of a plant set in a stock of another plant; the process; (SL.) work. v.t. insert (a shoot) in another stock; transplant (living tissue in surgery). [earlier graffe, F. greefe]

graft n. bribery, corruption; profit or advancement obtained by corrupt means. [orig. uncertain]

grail n. Holy Grail, platter or cup used by Christ at the Last Supper. [OF. graal]

grain n. seed or fruit of a cereal plant; wheat and allied plants; small hard particle; unit of weight, 1/7000th of the pound avoirdupois; texture; arrangement of fibers; formerly cochineal, scarlet dye, dye in general. -v. i. paint in imitation of wood grain. -grainy a. [F. , cp. granary]

gram, gramme n. unit of weight in the metric system. [F. , fr. G. gramma letter, small weight]

gramm'ar n. science of the structure and usages of a language; book on this; correct use of words. grammar'ian (-ar-) n. -gramm'ar school n. elementary school. [G. gramma, letter]

gram'ophone n. an instrument for recording and reproducing sounds; phonograph. [phonogram reversed; (a trade name)]

gran'ary n. storehouse for grain. [L. granarium, fr. granum, grain]

grand a. chief, of chief importance; splendid, magnificent; lofty; imposing; final. - grand'child n. child of children. grand'daughter fem. , child of children. grandee' n. Spanish or Portuguese nobleman. -grand'eur n. nobility; magnificence; dignity. -grand'father n. parent of parents. - grandil'oquence n. -grandil'oquent a. pompous in speech. -grand-master n. head of order of knights or freemasons. - grand'mother fem, parent of parents. - grand-slam' n. (cards) taking of every trick in bridge. -grand'son n. child of children. -grand'stand n. raised seats for spectators at races, etc. [L. grandis, great]

grange n. granary; country-house with farm buildings. [F.]

granite (-it) n. hard crystalline rock, used for building. [It. granito]

grant v.t. consent to fulfill (a request); permit; bestow, give formally; admit. -n. a granting; thing granted. -grant'or n. grant'ee n. [AF. graanter]

gran'ule n. small grain. -granular a. of, or like, grains. -gran'ulate v.t. form into grains. -v. i. take the form of grains; of a wound, to begin to grow in small prominences like grains. -granula'tion n. [L. granum, grain]

grape n. fruit of the vine. -grape'fruit n. large citrus fruit, kind of shaddock. grape'shot n. bullets as scattering charge for a cannon. -grape'-sugar n. dextrose. -grape'-vine n. circulation of news, etc. , esp. among natives, without obvious means of communication. [F. grappe (de raisin), bunch (of grapes)]

grapheme n. smallest unit of a writing system or language; letter or combination of letters that represent a speech sound or phoneme; a letter of an alphabet.

graphic a. of, in, or relating to writing, drawing, painting, etc. ; vividly descriptive. -graph n. graphic formula, diagram showing symbolically a series of connections. - graph'ically adv. -graph'ite n. form of carbon (used in pencils). graphol'ogy n. study of handwriting. [G. graphein, write]

grap'nel n. iron instrument of hooks for seizing, as an enemy ship; small anchor with several flukes. [dim. fr. F. grappin, dim. of OF. grappe, hook]

grap'ple n. grapnel; grip; contest at close quarters. -v. t. seize with a grapnel; seize firmly. -v. i. contend (with), come to grips. [See grapnel]

grasp v.t. seize firmly, clutch; understand. -v.i. clutch (at). -n. firm hold; mastery. (ME. graspen)

grass n. herbage, plants grown for cattle to eat, to cover lawns, etc. ; plant of this kind. -v.t. cover with turf, put down on grass. - grass'hopper n. jumping, chirping insect. [OE. gærs]

grate n. fireplace, frame of bars for holding fuel; framework of crossed bars (also grating n.). [L. cratis, hurdle]

grate v.t. rub into small bits with something rough. -v.i. rub with harsh noise; have an irritating effect. -gra'ter n. [F. gratter, scratch]

grate'ful a. thankful; pleasing. -grate'fully adv. -grat'itude n. sense of being thankful for something received. [L. gratus, pleasing]

grat'ify v.t. do a favor to; indulge. gratifica'tion n. [L. gratificare, fr. gratus, pleasing]

gra'tis adv. and a. free, for nothing. [L. gratiis-gratia, favor]

gratu'ity n. gift of money. -gratu'itous a. given free, done for nothing; uncalled for. -gratu'itously adv. [Low L. gratuitat-, fr. gratus, pleasing]

grave n. hole dug for a dead body; monument on this; death. [OE. graf]

grave v.t. carve, engrave. -**gra'ven** a. [OE. grafan, dig]

grave a. serious, weighty; dignified, solemn; plain, dark in color, deep in note. -**grave'ly** adv. [L. gravis, heavy]

grav'el n. small stones, coarse sand; aggregation of urinary crystals; disease due to this. -v.t. cover with gravel; puzzle. -**grav'elly** a. [F. gravelle]

grav'ity n. importance; seriousness, heaviness; force of attraction of one body for another, esp. of objects to the earth. **grav'itate** v.i. move by gravity; sink, settle. -**gravita'tion** n. [L. gravitate, fr. gravis, heavy]

gra'vy n. juices from meat in cooking; dressing or sauce for food made from these juices. [orig. uncertain]

gray, grey a. between black and white in color, as ashes or lead; clouded; dismal; turning white; aged. -n. gray color; gray horse. -**gray'ling** n. gray fish. [OE. græg]

graze v.t. and t. feed on grass. [OE. grasiani]

graze v.t. touch lightly in passing; abrade the skin thus. -v.i. move so as to touch lightly. -n. [orig. uncertain]

grease n. soft melted fat of animals; thick oil as a lubricant. -v.t. apply grease to. [F. graisse]

great (-at) a. large, big; important; preeminent, distinguished. -as prefix, indicates a degree further removed in relationship, e.g. **great-grand'father** n. father of a grandfather or grandmother. **great'uncle** n. uncle of a parent. **great'ly** adv. -**great'ness** n. -**great'**- coat n. overcoat, esp. military. [OE.]

greed'y a. gluttonous, over-eager for food, wealth, etc. -**greed** n. -**greed'ily** adv. -**greed'iness** n. [OE. graedig]

Greek n. native of Greece. -a. of Greece. [G. Graikoi, Greeks]

green a. of color between blue and yellow, colored like growing grass; emerald, etc.; unripe; inexperienced; easily deceived. n. the color; piece of grass-covered land. (golf) putting-green, ground about each hole. -**green'ery** n. vegetation. [OE. grene]

Green'wich time British standard time; basis for calculating time throughout the world. [reckoned from the sun's passage over Greenwich meridian]

greet v.t. accost or salute; receive; meet. **greet'ing** n. [OE. gretan]

gregarious (-ar-) a. living or gathering in flocks; fond of company. [L. gregarius, fr. grex, greg-, herd]

grenade n. explosive shell or bomb, thrown by hand or shot from a rifle. **grenadier'** n. soldier of the Grenadier Guards; formerly, a soldier who threw grenades. [F. = pomegranate]

greyhound n. swift slender dog used in racing. [OE. grighund]

grid n. frame of bars; grating; grid-iron. [gridiron]

grid n. (elec.) system of power transmission lines; (radio) perforated screen as part of amplifying mechanism. [gridiron]

grid'iron n. cooking utensil of metal bars for broiling; football field. -**gridd'le** n. flat round iron plate for cooking. [AF. gridil]

grief (-ef) n. deep sorrow. -**griev'ance** n. real or imaginary ground of complaint. **grieve** v.i. feel grief. -v. t. cause grief to. **griev'ous** a. painful, oppressive. [F. grever, afflict]

grill n. gridiron; food cooked on one. -v.t. and t. broil on a gridiron. [F. gril]

grille n. lattice; grating; openwork metal screen. [grill]

grim a. stem; of stem or harsh aspect; joyless. -**grim'ly** adv. [OE. grimm, fierce]

grimace' n. wry face. -v.i. make one. [F. further orig. uncertain]

grime n. soot, dirt. -v.t. soil; befoul. **gri'my** a. -**gri'miness** n. [orig. uncertain]

grin v.i. show the teeth. -n. act of grinning; impish smile. [OE. grennian]

grind v.t. crush to powder between hard surfaces; oppress; make sharp or smooth; grate. -v.i. perform the action of grinding; work (esp. study) hard; -n. action of grinding; hard work. -**grind'stone** n. revolving disk of stone for grinding, etc. -**grind'er** n. [OE. grindan]

grip n. firm hold, grasp; grasping power; mastery; handle; bag. -v. t. grasp or hold tightly. [OE. gripa]

gripe v.t. grip; oppress; afflict with pains of colic. -n. grip. -pl. colic pains. **gri'ping** a. [OE. gripan]

gris'ly (-z) a. grim, horrible, causing terror. [OE. grislic, terrible]

grist n. corn to be ground. [OE.]

gris'tle (grist) n. cartilage, tough flexible tissue. -**gris'tly** a. [OE.]

grit n. particles of sand; coarse sandstone; courage. -v.i. make a grinding sound. v.t. grind (teeth). -**gritt'y** a. -**gritt'iness** n. [OE. greot, sand]

grizz'ly a. gray-haired, gray. -**grizz'ly bear** n. large N. Amer. bear. -**griz'zled** a. grizzly. [F. gris, gray; the bear's name is perhaps from grisly]

groan v.i. make a low deep sound of grief, pain or displeasure; be in pain or overburdened. -n. the sound. [OE. granian]

gro'cer n. dealer in, tea, spices, domestic stores; storekeeper. -**gro'cery** n. his trade, or, pl. wares. [OF. grossier, wholesaler]

grog n. spirit (esp. rum) and water. **grogg'y** a. unsteady, shaky, weak. [Old Grog, nickname, fr. grogram cloak of Admiral Vernon, who first ordered watering of sailors' rum (1740)]

groin n. depression between belly and thigh; edge made by intersection of two vaults; structure of timber, etc. to stop shifting of sand on sea beach. -v.t. build with groins. [orig. uncertain]

groom n. servant in charge of horses; bridegroom; officer in a royal household. v.t. tend, curry (a horse); neaten, smarten [orig. obscure]

groove n. channel, hollow, esp. cut by a tool as a guide, or to receive a ridge; rut, routine. -v. t. cut a groove in. [Du. groef, trench]

grope v.i. feel about, search blindly. **gro'pingly** adv. [OE. grapian]

gross *a.* rank; overfed; flagrant; total, not net; thick, solid; coarse; indecent. *-n.* twelve dozen. **-gross'ly** *adv.* **-gross out** *v.t.* (*sl.*) to cause (a person) to feel distaste or strong dislike for (something). [F. *gros*, fr. L. *grossus*, thick]

grotesque' (-esk) *n.* fantastic decorative painting; comically distorted figure. *-a.* in grotesque style; distorted; absurd. grotesquely *adv.* [F.]

grott'o *n.* cave; *esp.* artificial cave as garden retreat. [It. *grotta*]

ground (-ow-) *n.* bottom of the sea; surface of the earth; position, area, on this; soil; special area; reason, motive; surface or coating to work on with paint. -pl. dregs; enclosed land round a house. *-v.t.* establish; instruct (in elementary principles); place on the ground. *-v. i.* run ashore. [OE. *grund*]

group *n.* number of persons or things near together, or placed or classified together; class; two or more figures forming one artistic design. *-v. t.* arrange in a group. *-v. i.* fall into a group. [P. *groppo*, bunch]

group therapy *n.* (*psych.*) therapeutic technique in which patients are treated as a group, includes supervised, interactive discussion in an attempt to find solutions for problems.

grouse (-ows) *n.* game-bird, the moor fowl; its flesh. [orig. uncertain]

grouse, *v.i.* (*mil. sl.*) grumble. *-n.* grumble. **-grous'er** *n.* [origin unknown]

grout (-owt) *n.* thin fluid mortar. *-v.t.* fill with this. [OE. *grut*, coarse meal]

grove *n.* small wood. [OE. *graf*]

grov'el *v.i.* lie face down; abase oneself. [ON. *grufa*]

grow *v.i.* develop naturally; increase in size, height, *etc.*; be produced; become by degrees. *-v. t.* produce by cultivation. **-growth** *n.* growing; increase; what has grown or is growing. [OE, *growan*]

growl *v.i.* make a low guttural sound of anger, as of dog; murmur, complain. *-n.* such sound. **-growl'er** *n.* one who growls. limit. orig.]

grudge *v.t.* be unwilling to give or allow. *-n.* feeling of ill-will; earlier *grutch*, grumble. [OF. *groucier*]

gru'el *n.* food of oatmeal, *etc.*, boiled in milk or water. **-gru'eling** *a.* exhausting. [OF. = *crushed grain*]

grue'some *a.* fearful, horrible, disgusting. [ME. *grue*, shudder]

gruff *a.* surly, rough in manner or voice. - **gruff'ly** *adv.* [Du. *grof*]

grum'ble *v.i.* make growling sounds; murmur, complain. *-n.* low growl; complaint. - **grum'bler** *n.* [imit. orig.]

grump'y *a.* ill-tempered, surly. **-grump'ily** *adv.* **-grump'iness** *n.* [limit. orig.]

grunt *v.i.* of a hog, to make its characteristic sound; utter a sound like this, grumble. *-n.* hog's sound; noise like this. [OE. *grunnettan*]

Gruyère *n.* Swiss whole-milk cheese. [name of town]

guarantee' (ga-) *n.* giver of guaranty of

security; guaranty. *-v.t.* answer for the fulfillment, or genuineness or permanence of. secure (to) a person; secure (against risk, *etc.*). **-guar'anty** *n.* written or other undertaking to answer for performance of obligation; ground or basis of security. [F. *garantir*, protect]

guard (ga-) *n.* posture of defense; watch; protector; sentry; soldiers protecting anything; official in charge of a train; protection; defense. *-v. t.* protect, defend. *-v. i.* be careful. **-guard'ian** *n.* keeper, protector; person having custody of an infant, *etc.* guard'ianship *n.* [F. *garde*]

guerill'a (g-) *n.* irregular war; one engaged in it. [Sp. *guerrilla*, dim. of *guerra*, war]

guess (ges) *v.t.* estimate without calculation or measurement; conjecture, think likely. *-v.i.* form conjectures. *-n.* rough estimate. [ME. *gessen*]

guest (gest) *n.* one entertained at another's house; one living in a hotel. **pay'ing guest'**, *n.* boarder. [ON. *gestr*]

guide (gid) *n.* one who shows the way; adviser; book of instruction or infor. mation; contrivance for directing motion. *-v. t.* lead, act as guide to; arrange. **guid'ance** *n.* **-guide'-book** *n.* manual for travellers. **-guide'-post** *n.* signpost. **-guid'ed missile** *n.* projectile, rocket *etc.* directed by remote control. [F.]

guild, **gild** (g-) *n.* society for mutual help, or with common object. [OE. *gield*, payment]

guile *n.* cunning, treachery, deceit. **guile'ful** *a.* **-guile'less** *a.* [OF.]

guillotine *n.* machine for beheading; machine for cutting paper; drastic curtailment of parliamentary debate. *-v. t.* use a guillotine upon. [F. , Dr. Guillotin suggested its use (1789)]

guilt (gilt) *n.* fact or state of having offended; culpability. **-guilt'y** *a.* having committed an offence. **-guilt'ily** *adv.* **guilt'less** *a.* **-guilt'iness** *n.* [OE. *gylt*]

guin'ea *n.* in Britain, formerly, sum of 21 shillings; a gold coin of this value. **-guin'ea-fowl** *n.* fowl allied to the pheasant. [Guinea, in W. Africa]

guin'ea-pig *n.* S. American rodent brought home by the *Guineamen*, slavers.

guise (giz) *n.* external appearance, *esp.* one assumed. [F. *guise*, manner]

guitar' (git-) *n.* musical instrument with six strings. [F. *guitare*, L. *cithara*]

gulch *n.* gully. [orig. uncertain]

gulf *n.* partly enclosed portion of the sea; chasm, abyss. **-gulf stream** *n.* current of warm water moving from Gulf of Mexico to *n.* Atlantic and Europe. [F. *golfer*]

gull *n.* long-winged web-footed seabird. [Celtic orig.]

gull *n.* dupe, fool. *-v.t.* dupe, cheat. **gull'ible** *a.* easily deceived. **-gullibi'lity** *n.* [orig. uncertain]

gull'et *n.* food-passage from throat to stomach. [F. *goulet*, *gueule*, throat]

gull'y *n.* channel or ravine worn by water; a groove. [F. *goulet*]

gulp *v.t.* swallow. *-v. i.* gasp, choke. *-n.* act of gulping; effort to swallow; large mouthful.

[imit.]

gum *n.* firm flesh in which the teeth are set. **-gum'boil** *n.* abscess in the gum. [OE. *goma*]

gum *n.* sticky substance issuing from certain trees; this prepared for use to stick papers, *etc.*, together. *-v. t.* stick with gum. **-chew'ing gum** *n.* sticky substance for chewing. [F. *gomme*]

gum'bo *n.* okra plant, pods; dishes made from these. [Creole]

gun *n.* weapon consisting mainly of a metal tube from which missiles are thrown by explosion; cannon, pistol, *etc.* [short for *Gunhilda*, name of a medieval war-engine]

gunn'y n. jute-cloth used for seeking. **gunn'y-sack** *n.* (Hind. *gon*, sacking]

gu'ru (goo-roo) *n.* spiritual teacher, esp. in India; a venerable person. [Hind.]

gush *v.i.* flow out suddenly and copiously. *-n.* sudden copious flow; effusiveness. *-* **gush'er** *n.* gushing person or oil-well. [orig. uncertain]

guss'et *n.* triangle of material let into a garment. **-guss'etted** *a.* [F. *gousset*]

gust *n.* sudden blast of wind; burst of rain, anger, *etc.* **-gust'y** *a.* **-gust'ily** *adv.* [ON. *gustr*, blast]

gust'o *n.* enjoyment in doing a thing, zest. [It. = *taste*]

gut *n.* in *pl.* entrails, intestines; (*sl.*) courage, spirit. *-sing.* material made from guts of animals, as for violin strings, *etc.* ; narrow passage, strait. *-v.t.* remove the guts from (fish); remove or destroy the contents of (a house). [OE. *guttas* (pi.)]

gutt'er *n.* channel for carrying off water from a roof, from the side of a street. *-v. t.* make channels in. *-v. i.* flow in streams; of a candle, melt away by the wax forming channels and running down. **-gutt'er press** *n.* sensational newspapers. **gutt'er-snipe** *n.* child homeless or living mainly in the streets. [F. *gouttiere*, fr. *goutte*, drop]

gutt'ural *a.* of, relating to, or produced in, the throat. *-n.* guttural sound or letter. [L. *guttur*, throat]

guy (gi) *n.* rope or chain to steady or secure something. *-v. t.* to secure with a guy. **-guy'-rope** *n.* [OF. *guier*, guide]

guz'zle *v.t.* and *i.* eat or drink greedily. **guzz'ler** ri. [imit.]

gymna'sium *n.* place fitted up for muscular exercises, athletic training. **gymnast'ic** *a.* of exercise. *-n.* (in *pl*) muscular exercises, with or without apparatus such as parallel bars. **gym'nast** *n.* expert in gymnastics. [G. *gymnasion*, fr. *gymnos*, naked]

gynecology *n.* part of medicine dealing with functions and diseases of women. [G. *gyne*, woman]

gypsoph'ila *n.* small-flowered plant allied to pinks, gypsy grass. [G. *gypsos*, chalk, *phuleein*, love]

gyp'sum (jip-) *n.* mineral, source of plaster of Paris. [G. *gypsos*, chalk]

gypsy *n.* one of a wandering race of people, orig. from India, *usu.* maintaining a migratory way of life; one who lives in a way that resembles the life of a gypsy. [fr. Egyptian]

gyro *n. pl.* **gyros** a gyroscope. (*sl*) Greek sandwich of roasted lamb or beef stuffed in pita bread with vegetables. **-gyroscope** *n.* instrument consisting of a heavy wheel mounted on a set of rings so that its axis can turn freely in any direction.

H

ha *interj.* exclamation of surprise, pleasure, *etc.* [imit.]

hab'eas cor'pus *n.* writ issued to produce prisoner in court. [L. = *have the body*]

haberdasher *n.* dealer in men's clothing. **-hab'erdashery** *n.* [orig. uncertain]

hab'it *n.* settled tendency or practice; constitution; dress (esp. riding-habit). *v. t.* dress. **-habit'ual** *a.* that is a habit, customary. **-habit'ually** *adv.* **-habit'uate,** *v.t.* accustom. **-habitua'tion** *n.* habit'ué *n.* constant visitor; resident. **-hab'itude** *n.* customary manner of action. [F.]

hab'itable *a.* fit to live in **-habitation-** *n.* dwelling. **-hab'itat** *n.* natural home of an animal. [L. *habitare*, dwell]

hack *v. t.* cut, mangle, gash. *-n.* notch; bruise. **-hack'er** *n.* person that hacks; (*sl.*) a computer fanatic. [OE. *haccian*]

hack *n.* hired horse; horse for ordinary riding; literary drudge. *-v. t.* **hackney.** [short for *hackney*]

hack'le *n.* comb for flax; neck feathers of a cock, [cp. Ger. *hechel*]

hack'ney *n.* horse for ordinary riding; carriage kept for hire. *-v. t.* make trite or common. [Hackney, Middlesex]

Ha'des *n.* abode of the dead; lower world, hell. [G.]

hagg'ard *a.* lean; wild-looking. *-n.* untamed hawk. [F. *hagard*]

hag'gle *v. i.* dispute terms, chaffer. *-n.* chaffering. [ON. *hoggva*, chop]

hail *n.* frozen vapor falling in pellets. *v. i.* it hails, hail falls. *-v. t.* pour down. **hailstone** *n.* [OE. *hagol*]

hail *interj.* greeting. *-v. t.* greet; call. *-v. i.* hail from, be arrived from. *-n.* call, shout. [obs. *n.* hail health; ON. *heill*]

hair *n.* filament growing from the skin of an animal, as the covering of a man's head; such filaments collectively. **hair'y** *a.* **-hair'iness** *n.* **-hair'breadth** *n.* breadth of a hair; infinitesimal breadth. **-hair'pin** *n.* pin to secure hair in place. **-hair'pin curve** *n.* v-shaped bend on road. **-hair'-splitting** *a.* drawing over-fine distinctions. [OE. *hær*]

hal'cyon *n.* bird fabled to calm the sea to breed on a floating nest. **-halcyon days,** calm, happy days. [L. = *kingfisher*]

hale *a.* robust, healthy, *esp.* in old age. [OE. *hal*, whole]

half (haf) *n.* **halves** (havz) *pl.* either of two equal parts of a thing. *-a.* forming a half *-adv.* the extent of half **-half'-blood** *n.* relationship of persons with one common parent. **-half'breed** *n.* one of mixed parentage. **-half'-brother, -sister** *n.* brother (sister) by one parent only. **half'caste** *n.* half-breed *esp.* of

European and Asiatic parents. -half'-pay, (*esp.* in army) reduced salary to one not on active service. -halfpenny *n.* British bronze coin worth half a penny. -half' title *n.* (shortened) title of book printed on page before title page. [OE. *healf*]

hal'ibut *n.* large flat edible fish. [ME *haly*, holy, and *butt*, flatfish]

halitosis *n.* bad breath. -hal'itous *a.* [L. *halitus*, breath]

hall (hawl) *n.* large room; house of a landed proprietor; building belonging to a guild; entrance passage. -hall'mark *n.* mark used to indicate standard of tested gold and silver. -*v.t.* stamp with this. [OE. *heall*]

hallelujah *n.* and *interj.* 'Praise ye Jehovah'; hymn, song of praise. Also alleluia. [Heb. *halelu*, praise ye, *Jah*, Jehovah]

hall'ow *v. t.* make, or honor as, holy. [OE. *halgian*, fr. *halig*, holy]

Hallowe'en' *n.* All Hallows Eve, (Oct. 31) [OE. *halgian.* hallow]

hallucinate *v. t.* produce illusion in the mind of. -hallucina'tion *n.* illusion; see, hear, something that is not present. [L. *hallucinari*, wander in mind]

ha'lo *n.* circle of light round the moon, sun, *etc.*; disk of light round a saint's head in a picture; ideal glory attaching to a person. -*v.t.* surround with a halo. [G. *halos*, threshing-floor, disk]

halt (hawlt) *a.* lame. -*v. i.* limp; proceed hesitatingly. -halt'ing *a.* [OE. *healt*]

halt (hawlt) *n.* stoppage on a march or journey. -*v.i.* make a halt. -*v.t.* bring to a halt. [Ger.]

halt'er *n.* rope or strap with headstall to fasten horses or cattle; noose for hanging criminals. -*v. t.* fasten with a halter. [OE. *hælfter*]

ham *n.* hollow of the knee; back of the thigh; hog's thigh salted and dried. ham'string *n.* tendon at the back of the knee. -*v. t.* cripple by cutting this. [OE. *hamm*]

hamburger *n.* ground beef formed into cakes, fried or broiled and *usu.* served in a bun. [Hamburg, Germany]

ham'let *n.* small village. [OF. *hamelet*]

hamm'er *n.* tool, usually with a heavy head at the end of a handle, for beating, driving nails, *etc.*; machine for the same purposes; contrivance for exploding the charge of a gun; auctioneer's mallet. -*v. t.* and *i.* beat with, or as with, a hammer. [OE. *hamor*]

hammerhead *n.* kind of shark. [fr. shape of head]

hamm'ock *n.* bed of canvas, *etc.*, hung on ropes. [F. *hamac* (Carib. word)]

hamp'er *n.* large covered basket. [OF. *hanapier*, case for *hanaps*, goblets]

hamp'er *v. t.* impede, obstruct the movements of. -*n.* in a ship, cumbrous equipment. [orig. uncertain]

ham'ster *n.* rodent mammal with large cheek-pouches. [Ger.]

hamstring. *See* ham.

hand *n.* extremity of the arm beyond the wrist; side, quarter, direction; style of writing; cards dealt to a player; measure of four inches;

manual worker; person as a source. -*v. t.* lead or help with the hand; deliver; pass; hold out. -hand'bag *n.* bag for carrying in the hand. -hand'bill *n.* small printed notice for distribution by hand. -hand'book *n.* short treatise. -hand(s)'breadth *n.* breadth of hand, about 4 inches. -hand'cuff *n.* fetter for the wrist, usually joined in a pair. -*v. t.* secure with these. hand'ful *n.* small quantity. hand'icraft *n.* manual occupation or skill. -hand'ily *adv.* -hand'iwork *n.* thing done by any one in person. hand'kerchief *n.* small square of fabric carried in the pocket for wiping the nose, *etc.*, or worn round the neck. [OE.]

handicap *n.* race or contest in which the competitors' chances are equalized by starts, weights carried, *etc.*; condition so imposed; disability. -*v.t.* impose such conditions. -handicapper *n.* [*hand* in *cap*; orig. lottery game]

han'dle *n.* part of a thing made to hold it by; fact that may be taken advantage of -*v. t.* touch, feel, with the hands; manage, deal with; deal in. [OE. *handle n. handlian v. t.*]

hand'some (-ns-) *a.* of fine appearance; generous. -hand'somely *adv.* [*hand*; orig. pleasant to handle]

hang *v. t.* fasten to an object above, suspend; kill by suspending from gallows; attach or set up (wallpaper, doors, *etc.*). *v. i.* be suspended; cling. -hangdog *a.* of sneaking aspect. -hangman *n.* executioner. [OE. *hangian*]

hang'ar (-ng-) *n.* shed for aircraft. [F.]

hang'er *n.* that by which a thing is suspended *e.g.* coat-hanger. [*hang*]

hank *n.* coil, esp. as a measure of yarn. [ON. *hönk*, skein]

hank'er *v.i.* crave. [orig. uncertain]

hanky-panky *n.* trickery, sleight of hand. [orig. uncertain]

han'som *n.* two-wheeled cab for two to ride inside with the driver mounted up behind. [Hansom, inventor, 1834]

Han'ukkah, Chan'ukah *n.* eight-day Jewish festival of lights beginning on the 25th of Kislev and commemorating the rededication of the temple by Judas Maccabeus in 165 B.C. [fr. Heb. literally: a dedication]

hap *n.* chance. -*y. i.* happen. -hap'less *a.* unlucky. -haphaz'ard *a.* random, without design, -*adv.* by chance. -hap'ly *adv.* perhaps. -happ'en *v. i.* come about, occur. [ON. *happ*, luck]

happ'y *a.* glad, content; lucky, fortunate; apt. [*hap*]

harangue' (-ang) *n.* vehement speech. *v. i.* make one. -*v. t.* speak vehemently to, [F.]

har'ass *v. t.* worry, trouble; attack repeatedly. -har'assed *a.* [F. *harasser*]

harbinger (-j-) *n.* one who announces another's approach; forerunner. [ME. *herbegeur*, one sent on to get lodgings]

har'bor (-ber) *n.* place of shelter for ships; shelter, -*v. t.* give shelter to. -*v. i.* take shelter. [ME. *herberwe*]

hard *a.* firm, resisting pressure, solid; difficult to understand; harsh, unfeeling; difficult to bear; stingy; heavy; strenuous; of water, not making lather well with soap. -adv. vigorously; with difficulty; close. -hard-bitt'en a. tough in a fight. hard'-boiled a. (sl.) tough thick-skinned. -hard'en v. t. and i. -hard up , short of cash. -hard'ware n. small ware of metal. -hardware (compute.) computer equipment used to process data; physical equipment, e.g. printer, disk drive, etc. [OE. heard]

hard copy n. (compute.) paper printout of data from computer; physical form of data originating from the computer, originally viewed on the monitor.

hard'y a. robust, vigorous; able to endure hardship; bold; of plants, able to grow in the open all the year round. [F. hardi, bold]

hare n. rodent with long ears, short tail, and divided upper lip, noted for its speed. - hare'bell n. plant with delicate blue bell-shaped flowers. -hare'brained a. rash, wild. -hare'lip n. fissure of the upper lip. [OE. hara]

ha'rem n. women's part of a Muslim dwelling; a group of wives or concubines. [Arab. haram]

harlequin n. in pantomime, a mute character supposed to be invisible to the clown and pantaloon. [It. arlecchino]

harm n. damage, hurt. [OE. hearm]

har'mony n. agreement; combination of musical notes to make chords; melodious sound. -harmo'nious a. -harmo'niously adv. -harmon'ic a. of harmony. -n. tone got by vibration of an aliquot part of a string, etc. -harmo'nium n. small organ. -harmon'ica n. various musical intruments. -har'monize v. t. bring into harmony. -v. i. be in harmony. -har'monist n. -harmoniza'tion n. [G. harmonia]

har'ness n. gear of a draught horse; armor. -v. t. put harness on. -in har'ness, at work. [F. harnais]

harp n. musical instrument of strings played by the hand. -v. i. play on a harp; dwell on continuously. -harp'er n. harp'ist n. - harp'sichord n. stringed instrument with keyboard, an ancestor of the piano. [OE. hearpe]

harpoon' n. barbed dart with a line attached for catching whales, etc. -v. t. strike with a harpoon. -harpoon'er n. harpoon'-gun n. [F. harpon]

harridan n. haggard old woman; shrewish woman. [corrupt. of F. haridelle, wornout horse]

harrier n. hound used in hunting hares; cross-country runner. [harry]

harr'ow n. frame with iron teeth for breaking up clods. -v. t. draw a harrow over; distress greatly. -harr'owing a. [ME. harwe]

harsh a. rough, bitter, unpleasing to the touch or taste: severe; unfeeling. -harshly adv. [ME. harsk]

hart n. male deer. -harts'horn n. material made from harts' horns, formerly the chief source of ammonia. -hart's'-tongue n. fern with long tongue-like fronds. [OE. heort]

har'vest n. season for gathering in grain; the gathering; the crop; product of an action. -v.t. gather in. -har'vester n. har'vest home n. festival at end of harvest. -harvest-queen n. image of Ceres. [OE. hærfest]

hash v.t. cut up small. -n. dish of hashed meat. [F. hacher, chop]

hashish n. narcotic drug prepared from Indian hemp. [Arab.]

Ha'sid n. , Ha'sidim n. pl. sect of Jewish mystics characterized by religious zeal and a spirit of prayer, joy, and charity; Jewish sect of the 2nd century B.C., formed to combat Hellenistic influences. -Ha'sidic a. -Ha'sidism n. [Heb.]

hasp n. clasp passing over a staple for fastening a door, -v. t. fasten with a hasp. [OE. hasp]

has'sle v. t. and i. annoy persistently; insist repeatedly; argue-n. troublesome concern; argument. [fr. harass and hustler]

hass'ock n. kneeling-cushion; tuft of grass. [OE. hassuc, coarse grass]

haste n. speed, quickness; hurry. v. i. hasten. -hast'en (-sen) v. i. come or go quickly or hurriedly. -v. t. hurry; accelerate. -ha'sty a. quick; impetuous. ha'stily adv. [OF.]

hat n. covering for the head, usually with a brim. -hatt'er n. dealer in, or maker of, hats. [OE. hætt]

hatch n. lower half of a divided door; hatchway; trapdoor over it. -hatch'way n. opening in the deck of a ship for cargo, etc. [OE. hæc]

hatch v. t. bring forth young birds from the shell; incubate. -v. i. come forth from the shell. -n. a hatching; the brood hatched. -hatch'ery n. hatching place for fish. [ME. hacchen]

hate v. t. dislike strongly; bear malice to. -n. hatred. -hate'ful a. -hate'fully adv. -ha'tred n. emotion of extreme dislike. active ill-will. [OE. hatian, hate]

haughty (hawt'i) a. proud, arrogant. haught'ily adv. [F. haut, high]

haul v.t. pull, drag. -v. i. of wind, to shift. -n. a hauling; draught of fishes; acquisition. - haul'age n. carrying of loads; charge of this. [hale]

haunch (hawnsh) n. part of the body between ribs and thighs; leg and loin of venison, etc. [F. hanche]

haunt v.t. resort to habitually; of ghosts, visit regularly. -n. place of frequent resort. [F. hanter, frequent]

have (hav) v. t. hold or possess; be possessed or affected with; be obliged (to do); engage in, carry on; obtain; (as auxiliary forms perfect and other tenses). [OE. habban]

ha'ven n. harbor; refuge. [OE. hæfn]

hav'oc n. pillage, devastation, ruin. [orig. to cry havoc, gave the signal for pillage; OF. havo]

hawk n. bird of prey-v. t. and i. hunt with hawks. [OE. hafoc]

hawk v.i. clear throat noisily. [imit.]

hawk'er n. one who carries wares for sale. -hawk v.t. [Du. heuker, huckster]

haw'ser (-z-) n. large rope or small cable, often of steel. [orig. uncertain]

hay *n.* grass mown and dried. -**hay'box** *n.* box filled with hay in which heated food is left to finish cooking. -**hay'cock** *n.* conical heap of hay. -**hay'seed** *n.* grass seed. -**hay'stack, hay'rick** *n.* large pile of hay with ridged or pointed top. **hay wire** *a.* (*sl.*) disordered, crazy. [OE. *hieg*]

haz'ard *n.* game at dice; chance, a chance; risk, danger; (*golf*) bunker or other hindrance. -*v.t.* expose to risk; run the risk of. -**haz'ardous** *a.* risky, perilous. [F. *hasard*]

haze *n.* misty appearance in the air, often due to heat; mental obscurity. -**ha'zy** *a.* misty. [orig. uncertain]

haze *v. t.* bully; tease with practical jokes, rag. [OF, *haser*, annoy]

hazer *n.* bush bearing nuts; reddish-brown color of the nuts. *v.* of this color. [OE. *hæsel*]

he *pron.* male person or animal already referred to. -*n.* a male. [OE.]

head (hed) *n.* upper part of a man's or animal's body, containing mouth, sense organs and brain; upper part of anything; chief part; leader; progress; title, heading; headland. -*v. t.* provide with a head; get the lead of. -*v. i.* face, front. -**head'ache** (-ak) *n.* continuous pain in the head. **head'dress** *n.* covering, often ornamental, for head. -**head'-gear** *n.* hat, head covering. -**head'ing** *n.* a title. -**head'-land** *n.* promontory. **headlight** *n.* front light of automobile or other vehicle. -**head'-lines** *n. pl.* headings in newspaper. -**headquar'ters** *n. pl.* residence of commander-in-chief, center of operations. -**head'stone** *n.* tombstone. -**head'strong** *a.* self-willed. **head'way** *n.* progress. [OE. *heafod*]

heal *v. t.* restore to health, make well, cure. -*v. i.* become sound. -**health** *n.* soundness of body; condition of body; toast drunk in a person's honor. **health'ful** *a.* health-giving. -**health'y** *a.* having, or tending to give, health. **health'ily** *adv.* [OE. *hælan*]

heap *n.* number of things lying one on another; great quantity. -*v. t.* pile up; load (with gifts, *etc.*). [OE.]

hear *v. t.* perceive with the ear; listen to; try (a case); get to know. -*v. i.* perceive sound; learn. -**hear'er** *n.* -**hear'say** *n.* rumor. *a.* not based on personal knowledge. [OE. *hieran*]

hearse *n.* carriage for a coffin. [F. *herse*, harrow; orig. a frame for candles over coffin]

heart (hart) *n.* hollow organ which makes the blood circulate; seat of the emotions and affections; mind, soul; courage; middle of anything; playing card marked with a figure of a heart, one of these marks. -**heartache** *n.* grief, anguish. **heart'broken** *a.* crushed by grief. **heart'burn** *n.* sharp, burning feeling at heart, caused by gastric acidity. -**heart'felt** *a.* very sincere. -**heart'less** *a.* unfeeling. -**heart'rending** *a.* extremely sad, agonizing. **heart'y** *a.* friendly; vigorous; in good health; satisfying the appetite. -**heart'ily** *adj.* [OE. *heorth*]

hearth (harth) *n.* place where a fire is made in a house. -**hearth'stone** *n.* stone forming fireplace; soft whitening stone for hearths. [OE. *heorth*]

heat *n.* hotness; sensation of this; hot weather or climate; warmth of feeling, anger, *etc.*; sexual excitement in animals; race (one of several) to decide the persons to compete in a deciding course. -*v. t.* make hot. -*v. i.* become hot. -**heat'edly** *adv.* [OE. *hæte*]

heathen (-TH-) *n.* one who is an adherent of a lower form of religion, or who has no religion; a pagan. [OE, *hæthen*]

heath'er (heTH'er) *n.* shrub growing on heaths and mountains; heath. [orig. uncertain]

heave *v.t.* lift with effort; throw something heavy), utter (a sigh). -*v.i.* swell, rise. -*n.* a heaving. -**heave to** *.* (of a ship) come to a stop. [OE. *hebban*]

heav'en *n.* sky; abode of God; God; place of bliss. -**heav'enly** *a.* of, like heaven; divine. [OE. *hæfon*]

heav'y (hev-) *a.* of great weight; striking or failing with force; sluggish; difficult; severe; sorrowful; serious; dull; over compact. -**heav'ily** *adv.* -**heav'iness** *n.* **heav'y wat'er,** water in which hydrogen is replaced by deuterium. [OE. *hefig*]

He'brew *n.* Jew, Jewish language. **hebra'ic** *a.* [I. *Hebraeus*]

heck'le *n.* hackle. -*v.t.* comb with a hackle; question severely, tease with questions.

hec'tic *a.* constitutional; (*sl.*) exciting. **hec'tic flush',** feverish, consumptive, flush. [G. *hektikos*, habitual]

hedge *n.* fence of bushes. -*v. t.* surround with a hedge. -*v. i.* make or trim hedges; bet on both sides; secure against loss; shift, shuffle. -**hedge'hog** *n.* small animal covered with spines. -**hedge'row** *n.* bushes forming a hedge. -**hedge' sparrow** *n.* small bird. [OE. *hecg*]

hed'onism *n.* doctrine that pleasure is the chief good. -**hed'onist** *n.* -**hedonist'ic** *a.* [G. *hedone,* pleasure]

heed *v. t.* take notice of, care for. **heed'ful** *a.* -**heed'less** *a.* [OE. *hedan]*

heel *n.* hinder part of the foot; part of a shoe supporting this; (*colloq*) unpleasant person. -*v. t.* supply with a heel; touch ground or a ball, with the heel. -**heel'ball** *a.* cobbler's wax. -**heel'-tap** *n.* drop of liquor left in glass. [OE. *hela*]

heel *v. i.* of a ship, to lean to one side. *v. t.* cause to do this. -*n.* a heeling. [OE. *hieldan,* incline]

heft'y *a.* brawny; sturdy; muscular, strong. [*heft* obs. p. p. of *heave*]

hegem'ony *n.* leadership. political domination. -**hegemon'ic** *a.* [G. *hegemon,* leader]

heif'er *n.* young cow that has not had a calf. [OE. *heahfore*]

height *n.* measure from base to top; quality of being high; high position, highest degree; hill-top. -**height'en** *v.t.* make higher; intensity. [OE. *hiehthu*]

hei'nous *a.* atrocious, very bad. [F. *hanieux.* fr. *hair,* hate]

heir *n.* person legally entitled to succeed to property or rank. -**heir'ess** *fem.* -**heir'loom** *n.* chattel that goes with real estate; thing that has been in a family for generations. [L. *heres*]

hel'ical *a.* spiral. **-helicop'ter** *n.* aircraft made to rise vertically by the pull of an airscrew or screws, revolving horizontally. **-heli'port, heli'pad** *n.* a place for helicopters to land and take off. [G. *helix*, spiral; *pteron*, wing]

he'lium *n.* gaseous element, first discovered in the sun's atmosphere by Lockyer in 1868. [G. *helios*, sun]

he'lix *n.* coil, spiral; snail; outer rim of ear. [G. *helix*, spiral]

hell *n.* abode of the damned; place or state of wickedness, or misery, or torture; abode of the dead generally; gambling resort. **hell'ish** *a.* [OE.]

Hellen'ic *a.* relating to the Hellenes or Greeks, period 776-323 B. C. **-Grecian**; Hellenism *n.* [G. *Hellenes*, the Greeks]

helm *n.* tiller or wheel for turning the rudder of a ship. [OE. *helma*]

helm *n.* helmet. **-helm'et** *n.* defensive covering for the head. [OE.]

help *v.t.* aid, assist; serve (food, with food); remedy, prevent. **-n.** aid, assistance; an aid, support. **-help'er** *n.* [OE. *helpan*]

Helvet'ic, Helve'tian *a.* Swiss. [L. *Helvetia*, Switzerland]

hem *n.* border of a piece of cloth, esp. one made by turning over the edge and sewing it down. **-v. t.** sew thus; confine, shut in. **hem'stitch** *n.* ornamental stitch. **-v.t.** sew with this. [OE.]

hemisphere *n.* half sphere; half of the celestial sphere; half of the earth. **hemispher'ical** *a.* [G. *hemi-*, half]

hem'lock *n.* poisonous plant; coniferous tree. [OE. *hymlice*]

hemoglobin *n.* red coloring matter of the blood. [G. *haima*, blood, *globus*, ball]

hemophilia *n.* tendency to excessive bleeding from slight injuries. **hemophil'iac** *n.* [G. *haima*, blood]

hemorrhage *n.* bleeding. [G. *haumorragia*, fr. *haima*, blood]

hemorrhoids *n.* piles. [G. *haimorrois*, *haimorroid-*, *v.s.*]

hemp *n.* Indian plant of which the fiber is used to make rope; the fiber. **-hemp'en** *a.* [OE. *henep*]

hen *n.* female of the domestic fowl and other birds. **-hen'bane** *n.* poisonous plant allied to nightshade. **-hen'pecked** *a.* domineered over by a wife. [OE. *henn*]

hench'man *n.* squire; servant; supporter. [ME. *henxt-man*, groom]

henn'a *n.* Egyptian privet; dye made from it. [Arab. *hinna*]

hepat'ic *a.* pert. to the liver. **-hepatit'is** *n.* disease or condition relating to inflammation of the liver. [L. *hepar*, liver]

hep'tagon *n.* plane figure with seven sides, angles. **-heptag'onal** *a.* **-hep'tarchy** (-ki) *n.* rule by seven. **-hep'tateuch** (-tuk) *n.* first seven books of the Old Testament. [G. *hepta*, seven]

her *pron.obj.,possess.,* of *she.* **-herself'**, emphatic, reflex, of *she, her;* in her proper character. [OE. *hire*, fr. *heo* she]

herb *n.* plant with a soft stem which dies down after flowering; plant of which parts are used for medicine, food or scent. **herba'ceous** (-shus) *a.* of or like a herb. **herb'age** *n.* herbs; grass, pasture. **herb'al** *a.* of herbs. **-n.** book on herbs. **herb'alist** *n.* writer on herbs; dealer in medicinal herbs. **-herbar'ium** *n.* collection of dried plants. **-herb'y** *a.* of herbs. [L. *herba*, grass]

Hercu'lean *a.* very strong; very difficult. [Hercules, Greek hero; his twelve labors]

herd *n.* number of animals feeding or traveling together; large number of people (*in contempt*); herdsman. **-v. i.** go to a herd. **-v. t.** tend (a herd); crowd together. **herds'man** *n.* [OE. *heord*]

here *adv.* in this place; at or to this point. [OE. *her*]

heredity *n.* tendency of an organism to transmit its nature to its descendants. **-hereditary** *a.* descending by inheritance; holding office by inheritance; that can be transmitted from one generation to another. [L. *heres, hered-*, heir]

her'esy *n.* opinion contrary to the orthodox opinion. **-here'siarch** originator or leader of a heresy. **-her'etic** *n.* holder of a heresy. **-heret'ical** *a.* **heret'ically** *adv.* [G. *hairesis*, sect, school of thought]

hermaphrodite *n.* person or animal with the characteristics of both sexes. [G. *Hermaphroditos*, in G. myth.]

hermet'ic *a.* of alchemy; sealed. [G. *Hermes, Mercury*, regarded as the patron of alchemy]

her'mit *n.* person living in solitude, *esp.* from religious motives. **-her'mitage** *n.* his abode. **-her'mit-crab** *n.* kind of crab living in discarded mollusk shells. [G. *eremites*, fr. *eremia*, desert]

hern'ia *n.* protrusion of an internal organ through the wall of tissue that encloses it; rupture. [L.]

he'ro *n.* illustrious warrior; one greatly regarded for achievements or qualities chief man in a poem, play, or story; demigod. [G. *heros*, demigod, hero]

her'oin *n.* strongly addictive narcotic drug derived from morphine. [Ger. trade-name]

her'on *n.* long-legged, long-necked wading bird. **-her'onry** *n.* place where herons breed. [F. *héron*]

her'pes *n.* any of several skin diseases, including shingles (herpes zoster) and cold sores (herpes simplex). [G. *herpein*, creep.]

herr'ing *n.* familiar sea-fish. **-herr'ing-bone** *n.* stitch or pattern of zigzag lines. [OE. *hæring*]

hertz *n.* (*radio*) unit of frequency. [H. Hertz, 1857-94]

hes'itate *v.i.* hold back, feel, show, indecision; be reluctant. **-hes'itant** *a.* **hes'itantly** *adv.* **-hes'itancy** *n.* indecision, doubt. **-hesita'tion** *n.* [L. *hæsitare*, fr. *hærere, hæs-*, stick fast]

heteroge'neous *a.* composed of diverse elements. **-heterogene'ity** *n.* [G. *heteros*, other, *genos*, kind]

hew *v.t.* and *i.* chop or cut with ax or sword. -**hew′er** *n.* [OE. *heawan*]

hexagon *n.* figure with six sides, angles. -**hexag′onal** *a.* -**hexam′eter** *n.* verse line of six feet. [G. *hex*, six]

hia′tus *n.* gap in a series; break between two vowels, *esp.* in consecutive words. [L. fr. *hiare*, *hiat-*, gape]

hibernate *v.i.* pass the winter, *esp.* in torpor. -**hiberna′tion** *n.* [L. *hibernare* hibernat, fr. *heims* winter]

hiccup *n.* spasm of the breathing organs with an abrupt sound. -*v. i.* have this. [imit.]

hick *n.* farmer; unsophisticated country person. -*a.* [fr. Richard]

hick′ory *n.* N. Amer. tree like walnut with tough wood and edible nuts. [*pohickery*, native name]

hide *n.* skin, raw or dressed. -**hide′bound** *a.* with skin tight to body as cattle. (*sl.*) prejudiced, narrow-minded. IOE. *hyd*]

hide *n.* old measure of land. [OE. *hid*]

hide *v.t.* put or keep out of sight; conceal, keep secret. -*v. i.* conceal oneself. **hid′den** *a.* [OE. *hydan*]

hid′eous *a.* repulsive, revolting. hideously *adv.* IF. *hideux*]

hie *v.i.* and *refl.* go quickly; betake (oneself). [OE. *higian*, strive]

hierarch (-k) *n.* chief priest. -**hi′erarchy** *n.* graded priesthood or other organization. -**hierarch′ical** *a.* -**hierat′ic** *a.* of the priests (*esp.* of old Egyptian writing). -**hi′eroglyph** *n.* figure of an object standing for a word or sound as in ancient Egyptian writing. -**hieroglyph′ic** *a.* -**hieroglyph′ics** *n. pl.* **hi′erograph** *n.* sacred writing. -**hi′erophant** *n.* expounder of sacred mysteries. [C *hieros*, holy]

high *a.* of great or specified extent upwards; far up; of great rank, quality or importance; of roads, main; of meat, tainted; of a season, well advanced; of sound, acute in pitch. -*adv.* far up; strongly, to a great extent; at or to a high pitch; at a high rate. -**high-born** *a.* of noble birth. -**high′brow** *a.* intellectual-*n.* -**high′-explosive** *n.* powerful explosive as lyddite, t. n. t. -*a.* -**high′lands** *n. pl.* mountainous country. -**high′ly** *adv.* -**high′-minded** *a.* -**high′ness** *n.* quality of being high; title of princes. -**high′seas** *n.* ocean. -**high-spirited** *a.* courageous, daring. **high′strung** *a.* supersensitive. -**highwater** *n.* high tide. -**high′way** *n.* main road; ordinary route. -**high′wayman** *n.* robber on the road, *esp.* a mounted one. [OE. *heah*]

hi′jack -*v.t.* divert criminally, *esp.* means of transport and for purposes of extortion. -*n.* -**hi′jacker** *n.* one who carries out a hijack. [orig. uncertain]

hike *v.t.* hoist, shoulder. -*v. i.* tramp, camp out, *esp.* carrying one's equipment. -*n.* ramble, walking-tour. -**hi′ker** *n.* [orig. uncertain]

hilar′ity *n.* cheerfulness, boisterous joy. -**hilar′ious** *a.* [G. *hilaros*, cheerful]

hill *n.* natural elevation, small mountain; mound. -**hill′ock** *n.* little hillbilly *a.* -**hill′iness**

n. [OE. *hyll*]

hillbilly *n.* backwoodsman. -*a.* [*hill*]

hilt *n.* handle of a sword, *etc.* [OE.]

him *pron.* , *obj.* of *he.* -**himself′**, emphatic and reflex. of *he*, *him*; in his proper character, sane. -**his**, *possess.* of *he.* [OE.]

hind, **hind′er** *a.* at the back. **hind′most**, **hind′ermost** *a.* farthest behind. [OE. *hinder*, backwards]

hind′er *v.t.* obstruct, bamper. -**hind′rance** *n.* obstacle. [OE. *hinder*, behind]

Hindu′ *n.* Indian, devotee of Hinduism. **Hindu′ism** *n.* religion and philosophy of Hindus. [Hind. Hindu, India]

hinge (-j) *n.* movable joint, as that on which a door bangs. -*v. t.* attach with, or as with, a hinge. -*v. i.* turn on, depend on. [ME. *heng*]

hint *n.* slight indication, covert suggestion. -*v. t.* give a hint of. -*v. i.* make a hint. [OE. *hentan*, pursue]

hip *n.* projecting part of thigh; the hip joint. [OE. *hype*]

hipped *a.* depressed. [*hypochondria*]

hippo′drome *n.* race-course; circus. [G. *hippos*, horse]

hippo′potamus *n.* large African animal living in rivers. [G. *hippos*, horse, *potamus*, river]

hire *n.* payment for the use of a thing; wages; a hiring or being hired. -*v. t.* take or give on hire. -**hire′ling** n, one who serves for wages (usually in contempt). **hi′rer** *n.* [OE. *hyr*, wages]

hir′sute *a.* hairy. [L. *hirsutus*, shaggy]

his *See* him.

hiss *v. i.* make a sharp sound of the letter S, *esp.* in disapproval. -*v.t.* express disapproval of, with hissing. -*n.* the sound. [imit.]

histology *n.* science dealing with minute structure of organic tissues. [G. *histos*, web]

his′tory *n.* study of past events; record of these; past events; train of events, public or private; course of life or existence; systematic account of phenomena. **histor′ian** *n.* writer of history. -**histor′ic** *a.* noted in history. -**histor′ical** *a.* of, or based on history; belonging to the past. -**histor′ically** *adv.* [G. *historia* narrative]

histrionic *a.* of acting, affected. -*n. pl.* theatricals. [L. *histrio*, actor]

hit *v.t.* strike with a blow or missile; affect injuriously; find; suit. -*v. i.* strike; light (upon). -*n.* blow; success, *esp.* relating to music, theater *etc.* -**hitt′er** *n.* -**hit list** *n.* list of people to be murdered; list of targets to be eliminated in some way. [ON. *hitta*, meet with]

hitch *v. t.* raise or move with a jerk; fasten with a loop, *etc.* -*v. i.* be caught or fastened. -*n.* jerk; fastening, loop or knot; difficulty, obstruction. -**hitch′hike** *v.i.* progress by hiking and by getting free rides from vehicles. (hitch and hike). [orig. uncertain]

hive *n.* box in which bees are housed. *v.t.* gather or place (bees) in a hive. -*v. i.* enter a hive. [OE. *kyf*]

hives *n. pl.* skin disease, *e.g.* nettle rash; laryngitis. [unknown]

hoard *n.* stock, store, *esp.* hidden away. -*v.t.* amass and hide away; store. [OE, *hord*, treasure]

hoard'ing *n.* temporary board fence round a building or piece of ground, *esp.* when used for posting bills. [F. *hourd*, palisade]

hoarse *a.* rough and harsh sounding, husky; having a hoarse voice. **hoarsely** *adv.* - **hoarse'ness** *n.* [OE. *has*]

hoax *v. t.* deceive by an amusing or mischievous story. -*n.* such deception. [contr. of *hocus*]

hob *n.* rustic; clown. -**hob-gob'lin** *n.* mischievous imp. [*Hob*, for Robert]

hobble *v. i.* walk lamely. -*v. t.* tie the legs together of (horse, *etc.*). -*n.* limping gait; rope for hobbling. [orig. uncertain]

hobb'y *n.* formerly a small horse; favorite occupation as a pastime. **hobb'yhorse** *n.* wicker horse fastened round a dancer's waist; stick with a horse's head as a toy; rocking-horse; roundabout horse. [*Hob*, for Robert]

ho'bo *n.* tramp. [orig. unknown]

hock *n.* joint of a quadruped's hind leg between knee and fetlock. -*v. t.* disable by cutting the tendons of the hock. [OE. *hoh*, heel]

hock'ey *n.* game played with a ball or disk and curved sticks. -**field hock'ey** *n.* -**ice hock'ey** *n.* [OF. *hoquet*, crook]

hoe *n.* tool for scraping up weeds, breaking ground, etc.—*v. t.* break up or weed with a hoe. [F. *houe*]

hoe *n.* promontory [OE. *hoh*]

hog *n.* pig, *esp.* one required for fattening; greedy or dirty person. -**hogs'head** *n.* large cask; liquid measure of 52½ gallons. [OE. *hogg*]

hoist *v.t.* raise aloft, raise with tackle, *etc.* -*n.* a hoisting; lift, elevator. [earlier *hysse*, Du. *hijschen*]

hold *v.t.* keep fast, grasp; support in or with the hands, *etc.*; maintain in a position; have capacity for: own, occupy; carry on; detain; celebrate; keep back; believe. -*v. i.* cling; not give way; abide (by), keep (to); last, proceed, be in force; occur. -*n.* grasp; fortress. -**hold'er** *n.* **hold'-all** *n.* portable wrapping as baggage. -**hold'fast** *n.* clamp. -**hold'ing** *n.* thing held, *e.g.* stocks, land, *etc.* **hold'up** *n.* armed robbery. [OE. *healdan*]

hold *n.* space below deck of a ship for cargo. [earlier *hole*]

hole *n.* hollow place, cavity; perforation, opening. -*v.t.* perforate, make a hole in. [OE. *hol*, *a.* hollow]

Holerith card *n.* (*compute.*) card containing data represented by 12 rows and 80 columns of punch positions.

holiday *n.* day or period of rest from work, or of recreation; originally a religious festival. [*holy day*]

holl'ow *n.* cavity, hole, valley. -*a.* having a cavity, not solid; empty; false; not full-toned. -*v. t.* make a hollow in; bend hollow. [OE *holh*]

holl'y *n.* evergreen shrub with prickly leaves and red berries. [OE. *holegn*]

holocaust *n.* burnt sacrifice; great slaughter or sacrifice. [G. *holos*, whole]

holograph *n.* document wholly written by the signer. -**holog'raphy** *n.* science of using lasers to produce a photographic record. - **hol'ogram** *n.* photographic record produced by illuminating the object with light (as from a laser), *esp.* in order to produce a three-dimensional image. [G. *holos*, whole]

hol'ster *n.* leather case for a pistol fixed to a saddle or belt. [Du.]

ho'ly *a.* belonging to, or devoted to, God; free from sin, divine. -**ho'lily** *adv.* **ho'liness** *n.* quality of being holy; title of the Pope. [OE. *halig*]

hom'age *n.* formal acknowledgment of allegiance; tribute, respect paid. [F. *hommage*, fr. *homme*, man]

home *n.* dwelling-place; fixed residence; native place; institution for the infirm, *etc.* -*a.* of or connected with home; not foreign. -*adv.* to or at one's home: to the point aimed at. -**home'less** *a.* -**home'-sick** *a.* depressed by absence from home. -**home'spun** *a.* spun or made at home. -*n.* cloth made of home-spun yarn: anything plain or homely. -**home'stead** *n.* house with outbuildings, farm. - **home'ward** *a.* and *adv.* -**home'wards** *adv.* [OE. *ham*]

homeopathy *n.* treatment of disease by small doses of what would produce the symptoms in a healthy person. - **homeopath'ic** *a.* [fr. G. *homoios*, of the same kind, and *pathos*, suffering]

Homer'ic *a.* of Homer, Greek poet, or his poems.

homicide *n.* killing of a human being; the killer. -**hom'icidal** *a.* [L. *homicide*, man slayer]

hom'ily *n.* sermon. -**homilet'ic** *a.* of sermons. -*n. pl.* art of preaching. [G. *homilia*, converse]

homogeneous *a.* of the same nature: formed of uniform parts. -**homogene'ity** *n.* -**homog'enize** *v. t.* make uniform, blend. [G. *homos*, same, *genos*, kind]

hom'onym *n.* word of the same form as another but of different sense. [G. *homos*, same, *onoma*, name]

homosexuality *n.* sexuality between members of same sex. [G. *homos*, same]

hone *n.* whetstone. -*v.t.* sharpen on one. [OE. *han.* stone]

hon'est (on-) *a.* upright, just; free from fraud; unadulterated. -**hon'estly** *adv.* **hon'esty** *n.* uprightness; plant with semitransparent pods. [L. *honestus*]

hon'ey *n.* sweet fluid collected by bees. - **hon'eycomb** *n.* structure of wax in hexagonal cells in which bees place honey, eggs, *etc.* -*v. t.* fill with cells of perforations. -**hon'eydew** *n.* sweet sticky substance found on plants. -**hon'eymoon** *n.* month after marriage; holiday taken by a newly-wedded pair. - **hon'eysuckle** *n.* climbing plant, woodbine. [OE. *hunig*]

honk *n.* cry of wild geese; any sound resembling this. -*v. i.* [imit.]

hon'or (on-er) *n.* high respect; renown; reputation; sense of what is right or due; chastity; high rank or position; source or cause of honor; court-card. -pt. mark of respect; distinction in examination. -v. t. respect highly; confer honor on; accept or pay (a bill, *etc.*) when due. -hon'orable *a* -hon'orably *adv.* -hon'orary *a.* conferred for the sake of honor only; holding a position without pay or usual requirements; giving services without pay. – honorif'ic *a.* conferring honor. honorarium *n.* fee. [F. *honneur*, fr. L. *honos*, honor-]

hood (hood) *n.* cover for the head and neck, often part of a cloak; cover for the engine of an automobile. -*v.t.* put a hood on. -hood'wink *v. t.* deceive. [OE. *hod*]

hoodlum *n.* ruffian, hooligan. [orig. uncertain]

hoof *n.* horny casing of the foot of a horse, *etc.* [OE. *hof*]

hook (hook) *n.* bent piece of metal, *etc.* for catching hold, hanging up, *etc.*; curved cutting tool. -*v. t.* catch or secure with a hook. [OE. *hoe*]

hook'ah *n.* pipe in which the smoke is drawn through water and a long tube. [Arab. *huqqah*, vessel]

hoop *n.* band of metal, *etc.* for binding a cask; circle of wood or metal for trundling as a toy; circle of flexible material for expanding a woman's skirt. *v. t.* bind with a hoop. [OE. *hop*]

hoot *n.* cry of an owl; cry of disapproval. -*v.t.* assail with hoots. -*v. i.* utter hoots. -hoot'er *n.* siren. [imit.]

hop *n.* climbing plant with bitter cones used to flavor beer, *etc.* -*pl.* the cones. hopping *n.* gathering hops. -hop'garden *n.* field of hops. [Du.]

hop *v.i.* spring (of person on one foot; of animals, on all feet at once). -*n.* act or the action of hopping. -(*sl.*) dance. -hopp'er *n.* one who hops; device for feeding material into a mill or machine; boat which takes away dredged matter. hop'scotch *n.* game played by hopping in an arrangement of squares. [OE. *hopian*]

hope *n.* expectation of something desired; thing that gives, or an object of, this feeling. -*v.i.* feel hope. -*v.t.* expect and desire. - hope'ful *a.* optimistic. -hope'fully *adv.* - hope'less *a.* [OE. *hopian*]

horde *n.* troop of nomads; gang, rabble. [Turk. *orda*, *urdu*, camp]

horizon *n.* boundary of the part of the earth seen from any given point; line where earth (or sea) and sky seem to meet; boundary of mental outlook. -horizon'tal *a.* parallel with the horizon, level. horizon'tally *adv.* [G. = bounding]

hor'mone *n.* internal glandular secretion stimulating growth, action of organs, *etc.* [G *hormaein*, stir up]

horn *n.* hard projection on the heads of certain animals, *e.g.* , cows; substance of it; various things made of it, or resembling a horn; wind instrument originally made of a horn. -horn'ed (-nd) *a.* having horns. horn'y *a.* -horn'beam *n.* tree like a beech. -horn'-book *n.* old primer in frame and covered with

thin layer of horn. -horn'pipe *n.* lively dance, *esp.* with sailors. [OE.]

horn'et *n.* large insect of the wasp family. [OE. *hyrnet*]

horoscope *n.* observation of, or a scheme showing the disposition of the planets, *etc.* [G. *horoskopos*, fr. *hora*, time]

horr'or *n.* terror; intense dislike or fear; something causing this. -horr'ible *a.* exciting horror, hideous, shocking. horr'ibly *adv.* - horr'id *a.* horrible. horr'idly *adv.* -horr'ify *v. t.* move to horror. -horrif'ic *a.* [L. *horrere*, bristle]

hors-d'oeuvres' *n. pl.* dish served at the start of a meal as appetizer. [F.]

horse *n.* familiar four-footed animal used for riding and draught; cavalry; vaulting-block; frame for support. -*v. t.* provide with a horse or horses; carry or support on the back. - horse'-lat'itudes *n. pl.* regions of calm in the Atlantic Ocean. -horse laugh *n.* rough boisterous laugh. -horse'man *n.* (skilled) rider. -horse'-play *n.* rough play. -horse'-power *n.* unit of rate of work of an engine, *etc.*; 550 foot-pounds per second. - horse'radish *n.* plant with a pungent root. -horse'shoe *n.* iron shoe for a horse; thing so shaped. [OE. *hors*]

horticulture *n.* gardening. -horticult'ural *a.* -horticult'urist *n.* [L. *hortus*, garden *cultura-colere*, cultivate]

hose *n.* stockings; flexible tube for conveying water. -*v. t.* water with a hose. -ho'siery *n.* his goods. [OE. *hosa*]

hos'pice (-is) *it.* travellers' house of rest kept by a religious order; hospital for the terminally ill. [*host*]

hos'pital *n.* institution for the care of the sick; charitable institution. [OF.]

hospitality *n.* friendly and liberal reception of strangers or guests. hospitable *a.* - hos'pitably *adv.* -hos'pitaller *n.* one of charitable religious order. -hospitalize *v.t.* place in a hospital as a patient. [*host*]

host *n.* one who entertains another; the keeper of an inn. -hostess *fem.* [L. *hospes*, *hospit*-, host, guest]

host *n.* army; large crowd. hostil'ity *n.* [*host*]

host *n.* bread consecrated in the Eucharist. [L. *hostia*, victim]

hos'tage *n.* person taken or given as a pledge; person seized for the purposes of extortion. [OE. *ostage*]

hos'tel *n.* a house of residence for students; an inn. -hos'telry *n.* an inn. [host]

hos'tile *a.* of an enemy; opposed. [L. *hostis*, *hostil*-, enemy]

hot *a.* of high temperature, very warm, giving or feeling heat; pungent; angry; severe. -hot air *n.* (*sl.*) nonsense. empty talk. -hot'-bed *n.* glass-covered bed for forcing plants; atmosphere favorable to growth. -hot'-blooded *a.* ardent, passionate; irritable. -hot'-dog *n.* hot sausage in a long roll. -hot'-head *n.* a hasty person. -hot-headed *a.* rash, impetuous. hot'house *n.* glass-house for rearing of delicate plants. -hotly *adv.* -hot'ness *n.* -hot'-pot *n.* stew of mutton and potatoes. [OE. *hat*]

hotel' *n.* large or superior inn. **hotel'-keeper** *n.* **-hotel'ier** *n.* [F. *hotel*]

hound *n.* hunting dog; runner following scent in a paperchase; despicable man. *v. t.* chase (as) with hounds. [OE. *hund*]

hour (owr) *n.* twenty-fourth part of a day; time of day; appointed time *-pl.* fixed times for prayer; the prayers; book of them. **-hour'ly** *adv.* every hour; frequently. *-a.* frequent; happening every hour. **-hour'-glass** *n.* sand-glass running an hour. [F, *heure.* Tr. L. *hora*]

house *n.* building for human habitation; building for other specified purpose; inn; legislative or other assembly; family: business firm; school boarding-house. *-v. t.* receive, store in a house; furnish with houses. *-v. i.* dwell, take shelter. **-house'boat** *n.* boat fitted for living in on a river, *etc.*. **house'keeper** *n.* woman managing the affairs of a household. **-house'-party** *n.* company of guests staying at a country house. **house'warming** *n.* party to celebrate the entry into a new house. **-house'wife** *n.* mistress of a household; case for needles, thread, *etc.* [OE. *hus*]

housing *n.* horse-cloth (*usu. pl.*). [F. *housse*]

hov'el *n.* mean dwelling; open shed. [orig. uncertain]

hov'er *v. i.* hang in the air (or bird, *etc.*); be undecided. [orig. uncertain]

how *adv.* in what way; by what means; in what condition; to what degree; (in direct or dependent question). **-how-be'it** *adv.* nevertheless. **-howev'er** *adv.* in whatever manner, to whatever extent; all the same. [OE. *hu*]

howl *v.i.* utter long, loud cry. *-n.* such cry. **-how'ler** *n.* loud-voiced S. Amer. monkey; (*sl.*) comical error. [imit.]

hub *n.* middle part of a wheel, from which the spokes radiate; central point of activity. [orig. uncertain]

huckleberry *n.* N. Amer. shrub; its fruit, a blueberry. [orig. uncertain]

huck'ster *n.* hawker; mercenary person. *-v.i.* haggle. *-v. t.* deal in a small scale. [obs. Du. *hoekster*]

hud'dle *v.t.* and *i.* heap, crowd together confusedly. *-n.* confused heap. [orig. uncertain]

hue *n.* color, complexion. [OE. *hiw*]

hue *n.* hue and cry, outcry after a criminal. [F. *huer*, hoot]

huff *v.t.* bully; offend. *-v. i.* take offence. *n.* fit of petulance. **-huff'y** *a.* **-huff'ily** *adv.* [imit.]

hug *v.t.* clasp tightly in the arms; cling; keep close to. *-n.* strong clasp. [orig. uncertain]

huge *a.* very big. **-huge'ly** *adv.* very much. [OF. *ahuge*]

hulk *n.* hull; dismantled ship; this used as a prison; big person or mass. **-hulk'ing** *a.* big, unwieldy; ungainly, bulky. [OE. *hule*, ship]

hull *n.* shell, husk; body of a ship. *-v.t.* remove shell or husk; send a shot into the hull of (a ship). [OE. *hulu*, husk]

hum *v.i.* make a low continuous sound as a bee or top. *-v. t.* sing with closed lips. *n.* humming sound. **-humm'ing bird** *n.* very small bird whose wings hum. [imit.]

hu'man *a.* of man, relating to, or characteristic of the nature of man. **-hu'manly** *adv.* **-humane'** *a.* benevolent, kind; tending to refine. **-hu'manize** *v.t.* make human; civilize. **-hu'manism** *n.* literary culture; devotion to human interests. **hu'manist** *n.* classical scholar. **-humanitar'ian** *n.* philanthropist. *-a.* of, or holding the views of a humanitarian. **human'ity** *n.* human nature; human race. **-human'ities** *n. pl.* polite learning *esp.* Latin and Greek. [L. *humanus*]

hum'ble *a.* not proud, lowly, modest. *v.t.* bring low, abase. **-hum'bly** *adv.* [L. *humilis*, fr. *humus*, ground]

hu'merus *n.* bone of upper arm. [L.]

hu'mid *a.* moist, damp. **-humid'ity** *n.* [L. *humidus*, fr. *humere*. be moist]

humiliate *v.t.* lower the dignity of, abase, mortify. **-humilia'tion** *n.* [L. *humiliare*, *humiliat-*]

humil'ity *n.* state of being humble, meekness. [L. *humilis*, low. cp. humble]

humm'ock *n.* low knoll, hillock. **humm'ocky** *a.* [orig. uncertain]

hu'mor *n.* state of mind, mood; temperment; faculty of saying, or perceiving what excites amusement; transparent fluid of an animal or plant. *-v. t.* gratify, indulge. **-humoresque'** (-esk) *n.* musical caprice. **-hu'morist** *n.* **-hu'morous** *a.* witty; facetious. **-hu'morously** *adv.* [L. *humor*, moisture]

hump *n.* normal or deforming lump, *esp.* on the back. *-v.t.* make hump-shaped. **hump'back** *n.* person with a hump. **hump'backed** *a.* having a hump. [orig. uncertain]

hu'mus *n.* decomposed vegetable matter, garden mold. [L. *humus*, ground]

Hun *n.* one of savage nomadic race which overran Europe in 4th and 5th cents.; barbarian. [OE.]

hunch *v. t.* thrust or bend into a hump. *n.* hump, lump; (*sl.*) idea. **-hunch'back** *n.* humpback. [orig. uncertain]

hun'dred *n.* and *a.* cardinal number, ten times ten; subdivision of a county. **hun'dredth** *a.* ordinal number. **hun'dredfold** *a.* and *adv.* **-hun'dredweight** *n.* weight of 112 lbs., twentieth part of a ton. [OE.]

hun'ger *n.* discomfort or exhaustion caused by lack of food; strong desire. *-v.i.* feel hunger. **-hung'ry** *a.* **hung'rily** *adv.* [OE. *hungor*]

hunk *n.* thick piece. [orig. uncertain]

hunt *v.i.* go in pursuit of wild animals or game. *-v. t.* pursue (game, *etc.*); do this over (a district); use (dogs, horses) in hunting; search for. *-n.* hunting; hunting district or society. **-hunts'man** *n.* man in charge of a pack of hounds. **-hunt'er** *n.* **hunt'ress** *fem.* [OE. *huntian*]

hur'dle *n.* portable frame of bars to make temporary fences or as obstacles in a hurdle-race *n.* **-hurd'ler** *n.* **-one** who makes, or races over, hurdles. [OE. *hurdel*]

hurl *v.t.* throw with violence. *-n.* violent throw. **-hur'ly-bur'ly** *n.* tumult, [orig. uncertain]

hurrah' *interj.* of acclamation, joy, *etc.* [fr. earlier *huzza*]

hurricane *n.* violent storm, tempest. **hurr'icane-lamp** *n.* lamp made to be carried in wind. [Sp. *huracan*]

hurr'y *n.* undue haste; eagerness. -*v. t.* move or act in great haste. -*v.i.* cause to act with haste; urge to haste. -**hurr'iedly** *adv.* [orig. uncertain]

hurt *v.t.* injure, damage, give pain to, wound -*n.* wound, injury, harm. **hurt'ful** *a.* [F. *heurter*, dash against]

hus'band (-z-) *n.* man married to a woman. -*v. t.* economize. -**hus'bandman** *n.* farmer. -**hus'bandry** *n.* farming. [OE. *husbonda*, master of the house]

hush *v. t.* silence. -*v. i.* be silent. -*n.* silence. -also *interj.* [imit.]

husk *n.* dry covering of certain seeds and fruits; worthless outside part. -*v. t.* remove the husk from. [orig. uncertain]

husk'y *a.* of, or full of, husks; dry as a husk, dry in the throat; hefty, powerful, vigorous. -*n.* Eskimo dog. [orig. uncertain]

huss'y *n.* pert girl; woman of bad behavior. [for *housewife*]

hustle *v.t.* push about, jostle. -*v. i.* push one's way, bustle. -*n.* bustle. [Du. *hutselen*, shake up]

hut *n.* small mean dwelling; temporary wooden house. -**hut'ment** *n.* camp of huts. [F. *huttle*]

hutch *n.* pen for rabbits; coal wagon used in pits, *etc.* [F. *huche*, coffer]

hy'acinth *n.* bulbous plant with bell-shaped flowers, *esp.* blue; this blue; orange precious stone. [G. *hyakinthos*]

hy'brid *n.* offspring of two plants or animals of different species; mongrel. -*a.* cross-bred. -**hy'bridize** *v.t.* and *i.* -**hy'-bridism** *n.* [L. *hybrida*]

hy'dra (hi-) *n.* mythical, many-headed water serpent; fresh-water polyp. -**hydra-headed** *a.* many headed, difficult to root out. [G. *hudra*]

hydro- *prefix.* [G. *hydor*, water] in **hydrant** *n.* water-pipe with a nozzle for a hose. -**hydraul'ic** *a.* relating to the conveyance of water; worked by water power. -*n.* (in *pl.*) science of water conveyance or water-power. -**hydrocar'bon** *n.* compound of hydrogen and carbon. **hydrochlor'ic** *a.* of acid containing hydrogen and carbon. -**hydroelec'tric** *a.* of electricity obtained from water power or steam. **hy'drogen** *n.* colorless gas which combines with oxygen to form water. -**hy'drophone** *n.* instrument for detecting sound through water. -**hy'droplane** *n.* light skimming motor-boat. -**hydropon'ics** *n. pl.* science of cultivating plants in water without using soil. -**hydrostat'ic** *a.* of hydrostatics. **hydrostat'ics** *n. pl.* science of fluids at rest. Also many other compounds.

hy'ena *n.* wild animal related to the dog. [G. *hyaina*, swine]

hy'giene *n.* principles of health; sanitary science. -**hygien'ic** *a.* -**hygien'-ically** *adv.* -**hy'gienist** *n.* [G. *hygies*, healthy]

hygrometer *n.* instrument for measuring the amount of moisture in air. [G. *hygros*, fluid]

hymn (him) *n.* song of praise, *esp.* to God. -*v.t.* praise in song. -**hym'nal** *a.* of hymns. -*n.* book of hymns. [G. *hymnos*]

hyperbola *n.* curve produced when a cone is cut by a plane making a larger angle with the base than the side makes. [G. *hyperbole*, hyper, beyond, *ballein*, throw]

hyperbole (-li) *n.* rhetorical exaggeration. -**hyperbol'ical** *a.* [*hyperbola*]

hy'phen *n.* a short stroke joining two words or syllables. **hyphenate** *v. t.* to connect by a hyphen. [G. *hypo-*, under, *hen*, one]

hypno'sis (hip-) *n.* state like deep sleep in which the subject acts on external suggestion. -**hypnot'ic** *a.* of hypnosis. *n.* person under hypnosis; thing producing it. -**hyp'notism** *n.* production of hypnosis. -**hyp'notist** *n.* -**hyp'notize** *v.t.* [G. *hypnos*, sleep]

hypochon'dria *n.* morbid depression. -**hypochon'driac** *a.* affected by this. -*n.* sufferer from it. -**hypochrondri'acal** *a.* [G. *hypochondria*, parts below the costal cartilages (as the seat of melancholy)]

hypoc'risy *n.* assuming of a false appearance of virtue; insincerity **hypocrite** *n.* -**hypocrit'ical** *a.* -**hypocrit'ically** *adv.* [G. *hypokrisis*, acting a part]

hypoderm'ic *a.* introduced beneath the skin. [G. *hypo*, under, *derma*, skin]

hypot'enuse *n.* side of a right-angled triangle opposite the right angle. [G. *hypoteinousa*, 'subtending']

hypoth'ecate *v.t.* pledge, mortgage. -**hypotheca'tion** *n.* [G. *hypotheke*]

hypoth'esis *n.* supposition as a basis for reasoning; assumption. -**hypothet'ical** *a.* -**hypothet'ically** *adv.* [fr. G. *hypo*, under, and *tithenai*, place]

hyste'ria (his-) *n.* disturbance of (a woman's) nervous system with convulsions, disturbance of mental faculties, *etc.*; morbid excitement. -**hyster'ical** *a.* -**hyster'ically** *adv.* -**hyster'ics** *n. pl.* fits of hysteria. [G. *hystera*, womb]

I

I *pron.* pronoun of the first person singular. [OE. *ic*]

iamb'us, i'amb *n.* metrical foot of a short followed by a long syllable. -**iamb'ic** *a.* [G. *iambos*]

Ibe'rian *a.* of Spain and Portugal. [*Iberia*]

i'bex *n.* wild goat with large horns. [L.]

i'bis *n.* stork-like wading bird. [G.]

ice *n.* frozen water; frozen confection. -*v.t.* cover with ice; cool with ice; cover with sugar. -**ice'-age** *n.* glacial period. -**ice'ax** *n.* climber's ax for ice. -**ice'berg** *n.* large floating mass of ice. -**ice'-blink** *n.* reflection in air of distant ice. -**ice'-bound** *a.* bound, surrounded by ice. -**icecap** *n.* frozen region at N., S. Pole. -**ice'-cream** *a.* frozen flavored cream or similar substance. -**ice'field** *n.* large expanse of ice. -**ice'-floe** *n.* floating icefield. -**ice'-rink** *n.*, sheet of ice for skating. -**i'cy** *a.* -**i'cily** *adv.*

[OE. *is*]

ichthyol'ogy (ikth-) *n.* branch of zoology treating of fishes. -**ichthyosaur'us** *n.* prehistoric marine animal. [G. *ichthys*, fish, *sauros*, lizard]

icicle. *See* ice.

i'con, ikon *n.* image; sacred picture. -**icon'oclast** *n.* breaker of images. -**iconoclas'tic** *a.* [G, *eikon*, likeness]

id *n.* (*psych.*) instinctive impulses of the individual. [L. = it]

ide'a *n.* notion in the mind; way of thinking; vague belief, plan, aim. -**ide'al** *a.* existing only in idea; visionary; perfect. -*n.* perfect type. -**ide'ally** *adv.* **ide'alism** *n.* imaginative treatment; philosophy that the object of external perception consists of ideas. -**ide'alist** *n.* -**ide'alize** *v.t.* represent or look upon as ideal. -idealization *n.* [G. = *look*; semblance]

ident'ity *n.* absolute sameness; individuality. -**ident'ical** *a.* the very same. -**ident'ically** *adv.* -**ident'ify** *v.t.* establish the identity of; associate (oneself) within, separately; treat as identical. -**identifica'tion** *n.* [L. *idem*, same]

Ides *n. pl.* in Ancient Roman Calendar 15th March, May, July and Oct. and 13th of other months. [L. *idus*]

ideol'ogy *n.* science of ideas; system of ideas; abstract speculation. -**ideol'ogist** *n.* [*idea* and G. *logia*, discourse]

id'iom *n.* one's language; way of expression natural to a language; expression peculiar to it. -**idiomat'ic** *a.* characteristic of a language; marked by the use of idioms, colloquial. -**idiomat'ically** *adv.* [*See* **idiot**]

idiosyn'crasy *n.* feeling or view peculiar to a person. [G. *idios*, one's own, *synkrasis*, mixture]

id'iot *n.* mentally deficient person. -**id'iocy** *n.* state of being an idiot. -**idiot'ic** *a.* -**idiot'ically** *adv.* [G. *idios*, own, peculiar]

i'dle *a.* doing nothing; lazy; useless, vain, groundless. -*v.i.* be idle. -*v.t.* pass time in idleness. -**i'dleness** *n.* -**i'dly** *adv.* -**i'dler** *n.* [OE. *idel*, useless]

i'dol *n.* image of a deity as an object of worship; false god; object of excessive devotion. -**idol'ator** *n.* worshipper of idols. -**i'dolize** *v.i.* make an idol of; love or venerate to excess. [G. *eidolon*, image]

i'dyll *n.* short description, usually in verse, of a picturesque scene or incident, *esp.* of rustic life. -**idyll'ic** *a.* [G. *eidyllion*, dim. of *eidos*, picture]

if *conj.* on the condition or supposition that; whether. [OE. *gif*]

ig'loo *n.* Eskimo snow-hut. [Eskimo]

ig'neous *a.* fiery; resulting from fire. -**ignite'** *v.t.* set on fire. -*v.i.* take fire. -**igni'tion** *n.* device for igniting explosive mixture in internal-combustion engine.[L. *ignis*, fire]

ig'nominy *n.* dishonor, disgrace; infamous-conduct. [L. *ignominia*]

ignore' *v.t.* disregard, leave out of account. -**ignora'mus** *n.* ignorant person. -**ig'norance** *n.* lack of knowledge. [L. *ignorare*, not to know]

igua'na (igwä-) *n.* large tree lizard of tropical America; S. African monitor lizard. -**igua'nodon** *n.* extinct giant lizard. [Sp. fr. Carib.]

Il'iad *n.* epic poem by Homer on siege of Troy. [G. *Ilias*, Troy]

il- *prefix*, for in- before '*l*', negatives the idea of the simple word: e.g. **ille'gal** *a.* not legal. -**illeg'ible** *a.* not legible; *etc. etc.* Such words are not given where the meaning and derivation are clear from the simple word.

ill *a.* out of health; bad, evil; faulty. -*n.* evil, harm; *adv.* not well; faultily, unfavorably. -**ill'-bred** *a.* bad-mannered. -**ill'favored** *a.* ugly. -**ill'-feeling** *a.* resentment, unpleasantness. -**ill-natured** *a.* bad-tempered. -**ill'ness** *n.* -**ill-timed** *a.* inopportune. -**ill-will** *n.* enmity. [ON. *illr*]

illegiti'mate *a.* illegal; born out of wedlock. -*n.* bastard. -**illegit'imacy** *n.* [L. *illegitirnus*]

illic'it *a.* unlawful; forbidden. [L. *il*, (*in*), not-*licere*, to be lawful]

illit'erate *a.* unable to read or write. -**illit'eracy** *n.* [L. *il-*, not, -*litteratus*]

illu'minate *v.t.* light up; decorate with lights; decorate with gold and colors. [L. *il-luminare*, throw into light, *lumen*]

illu'sion *n.* deceptive appearance, belief, or statement. -**illu'sionist** *n.* conjuror. -**illu'sive** *a.* -**illu'sory** *a.* [L. *illudere*, *illus-*, mock]

ill'ustrate *v.t.* make clear, *esp.* by examples or drawings; adorn with pictures. -**illus'trious** *a.* famous. [L. *illustrare*, throw into brightness]

im'age *n.* statue; semblance; type; simile, metaphor; counterpart; optical counterpart, as in a mirror. -*v. t.* make an image of, reflect. -**im'agery** *n.* images; use of rhetorical figures. [L. *imago*, *imagin-*, image]

imag'ine (-j-) *v. t.* picture to oneself; conjecture; think. -**imag'inable** *a.* -**imag'-inary** *a.* existing only in fancy. -**imagina'tion** *n.* faculty of making mental images; fancy. -**imag'inative** *a.* -**imag'inatively** *adv.* [image]

im'becile *a.* mentally weak. -*n.* person of weak mind. -**imbecil'ity** *n.* [L. *imbe cillus*, weak in body or mind]

im'itate *v.t.* take as model; mimic, copy. -**im'itable** *a.* -**imita'tion** *n.* -**im'itative** *a.* -**im'itator** *n.* [L. *imitari*]

im- *prefix*, for in- before '*m*', negatives the idea of the simple word: *e.g.*, **imm'ature** *a.* not mature. -**immo'bile** *a.* not mobile, *etc.*, *etc.* Such words are not given where the meaning and derivation are clear from the simple word.

immac'ulate *a.* spotless; pure. -**immac'ulately** *adv.* [L. *macula*, spot]

immate'rial *a.* not composed of matter; unimportant. [L. *im-* and *materialis*]

imme'diate *a.* occurring at once; direct, not separated by others. -**imme'diately** *adv.* -**imme'diacy** *n.* [Med. L. *immediatus*]

immense' *a.* huge, vast, immeasurable. -**immen'sity** *n.* -**immense'ly** *adv.* [L. *immen-sus*, unmeasured]

immerse' *v.t.* dip, plunge, into a liquid. [L. *immergere*, *immers-*]

imm'igrate *v.i.* come into a country as a settler. -immigra'tion *n.* -imm'igrant *n.* -a. [L. *immigrate, immigrat-*]

imm'inent *a.* close at hand. imminently *adv.* -imm'inence *n.* [L. *imminere, imminent-*, overhang]

immob'ilize *v.t.* put out of action; deprive of mobility. [*mobile*]

imm'olate *v.t.* sacrifice. -immola'tion *n.* [L. *immolare, immolate-*]

immor'tal *a.* not mortal, undying, everlasting. -immor'talize *v.t.* render immortal; make famous for ever. [L. *immortalis*]

immune' *a.* secure, exempt; proof (against a disease, *etc.*). -immunize *v.t.* -immu'nity *n.* [L. *immunis*, exempt, orig, from public service, *munus*]

im- *prefix*, for *in-* before 'p', negatives the idea of the simple word: *e.g.*, impal'pable *a.* not palpable, untouchable. -impar'tial *a.* not partial, fair; *etc.*, *etc.* Such words are not given where the meaning and derivation are clear from the simple word.

im'pact *n.* collision, or the impulse resulting therefrom. [L. *impingere, impact-*, dash against]

impair' *v.t.* weaken, damage. -impair'ment *n.* [F. *empirer*, make worse]

impale' *v.t.* transfix, *esp.* on a stake, to put to death; combine (two coats of arms) by placing them side by side with a line between. -impale'ment *n.* [F. *empaler*, fr. *pal*, stake]

impart' *v.t.* give a share of; communicate. [L. *impartire*, fr. *pars*, part]

impar'tial *a.* unbiased. [L. *im-*, and *pars, partis*]

im'passe *n.* position, situation from which there is no escape; deadlock. [F.]

impass'ible *a.* not liable to pain or suffering. [L. *pati, pass-*, suffer]

impas'sioned *a.* deeply moved; showing deep feeling. [*passion*]

impeach' *v.t.* call in question; accuse; accuse of treason. [orig. hinder, F. *empecher*, prevent]

impecc'able *a.* incapable of sin or error. [L. *impeccabilis*, fr. *peccare*, sin]

impecu'nious *a.* having no money. -impecunios'ity *n.* [L. *pecuniosus*, rich]

impede' *v.t.* hinder. -imped'iment *n.* -impediment'a *n. pl.* baggage, *esp.* of an army. [L. *impedire*, shackle]

impel' *v.t.* drive, force. [L. *pellere*]

impend' *v.i.* be imminent; threaten. [L. *impendere*, hang over]

imper'ative *a.* expressing command; obligatory. -*n.* imperative mood. -imper'atively *adv.* [L. *imperare*, command]

imper'fect *a.* not perfect, having flaws; (*Gram.*) of tense denoting continuous action in the past [L *imperfectus*]

impe'rial *a.* of an empire; of an emperor; majestic. [L. *imperium*, rule, empire]

imper'sonate *v.t.* play the part of. -impersona'tion *n* -imper'sonator *n.* one who impersonates another, *esp.* on the stage. [*person*]

impert'inent *a.* insolent, saucy, irrelevant.

-impert'inence *n.* -impert'inently *adv.* [*pertinent*]

imper'vious *a.* unable to be penetrated or affected. [L. *imperuius*]

im'petus *n.* force with which a body moves; impulse. -impet'uous *a.* ardent, vehement; acting or moving with a rush. -impet'uously *adv.* -impetuos'ity *n.* ardor; rashness [L. = attack]

impinge' *v.i.* dash, strike; touch (with, on, upon). [L. *impingere*]

implac'able *a.* not to be appeased, inexorable. [L. *implacabilis*]

implant' *v.t.* insert, fix. [*plant*]

im'plement *n.* tool, instrument, utensil. -*v.t.* (im-ple-ment') carry (a contract, *etc.*) into effect. [L. *implore*, fill up]

im'plicate *v.t.* involve, include; entangle; imply. -implica'tion *n.* -implic'it (-s-) *a.* implied but not expressed; involved in a general principle, exclusive of individual judgment. -implic'itly (-s-) *adv.* -imply' *v.t.* involve the truth of, mean. [L. *implicare*, entangle]

implore' *v.t.* entreat earnestly. [L. *implorare*, fr. *plorare*, weep]

impon'derable *a.* without perceptible weight, as electricity, light. -*n.* [L. *pondus, ponder-*, weight]

import' *v.t.* bring in, introduce (*esp.* goods from a foreign country); imply; mean; express; be of consequence to. -im'port *n.* thing imported; meaning; importance. [L. *importare*, fr. *portare*, carry]

importune' *v.t.* solicit pressingly. -impor'tunate *a.* persistent in soliciting. [L. *importunus*, troublesome]

impose' *v.t.* lay (a tax, duty, *etc.*) upon. *v.i.* be impressive take advantage, practice deceit (on). -imposi'tion *n.* -impos'ter *n.* deceiver, one who assumes a false character. [F. *imposer*]

im'potent *a.* powerless, ineffective. im'potence *n.* -im'potently *adj.* [*potent*]

impound' *v.t.* shut up (cattle, *etc.*) in a pound; confiscate. [*pound*]

impov'erish *v.t.* make poor or weak. -impov'erishment *n.* [OF. *enipourir*]

impreg'nable *a.* proof against attack. -impregnabil'ity *n.* -impreg'nably *adv.* [F. *imprenable*, fr. *prendre*, take]

impreg'nate *v.t.* make pregnant; saturate. -impregna'tion *n.* [*pregnant*]

impresa'rio *n.* organizer of a public entertainment; operatic manager. [It.]

impress' *v.t.* imprint, stamp; fix; affect deeply. -im'press *n.* act of impressing; mark impressed. -impres'sion *n.* impress; printed copy; total of copies printed at once; effect produced, *esp.* on mind or feelings; notion, belief. -impres'sionism *n.* method of painting or writing to give general effect without detail. [L. *imprimere, irnpress-*, fr. *premere*, press]

impress' *v.t.* press into service. impress'ment *n.* [*press*]

imprint' *v.t.* impress; stamp; publisher's name on the title page of a book. -im'print *n.* impression, stamp. [*print*]

impris'on (-z-) *v.t.* put in prison. -

imprison'onment n. [prison]

impromp'tu adv. and a. extempore. -n. something composed or said extempore. [F., fr. L. promptus, readiness]

improve' v.t. make better; make good use of. -v.i. become better. [A.F. emprower, turn to profit, OF. prou, profit]

im'provise v.t. compose or utter extempore; get up, arrange, extempore. -improvisa'tion n. [F. improviser]

im'pudent a. pert, insolent, saucy. [L. impudens, impudent-, shameless]

impugn' v.t. call in question, challenge. [L. impugnare, assail]

im'pulse n. sudden application of force; motion caused by it; sudden inclination to act; incitement. -impul'sion n. impulse, usually in the first sense. -impul'sive a. given to acting without reflection. -impul'sively adv. [L. impellere, impuls-, cp. impel]

impu'nity n. freedom from injurious consequences. [L. impunitas]

impute' v.t. set to the account of, ascribe. -imputabil'ity n. -imputa'tion n. [L. imputare, fr. putare, reckon]

in prep. expresses inclusion within limits of space, time, circumstances, etc. -adv. in or into some state, place, etc. [OE.]

in- prefix negatives the idea of the simple word; e.g., inact'ive a. not active; incapable a. not capable, etc., etc. Such words are omitted where the meaning and derivation may easily be inferred from the simple word. [L. in-, not]

inadvert'ent a. failing to pay attention; unintentional. [obs. advertent; L. advertere, turn to]

inane' a. empty, void; foolish, silly. -inan'ity n. -inani'tion n. being empty, exhaustion. [L. inanis, empty]

inaug'urate v.t. admit to office; begin, initiate, esp. with ceremony. [L. inaugurate, take auguries before action]

in'born a. born with. [born]

inbred' a. inherent, innate. [bred]

incandes'cent a. glowing with heat, shining; of artificial light; produced by glowing filament. -incandes'cence n. -incandesce' v.i. and t. [L. candescere, begin to glow, candere]

incapac'itate (-as-) v.t. make unable; disqualify. -incapac'ity n. inability; disability. [L. capere, hold]

incar'cerate v.t. imprison, shut up. -incarcera'tion n. -incar'cerator n. [L. in, in, carcer, prison]

incen'diary a. of the malicious setting on fire of property; guilty of this; inflammatory. -n. one guilty of arson, incendiary person. -incen'diarism n. [L. incendere, set on fire]

incense' v.t. enrage; incite, urge. [L. incendere, incens-]

in'cense n. gum or spice giving a sweet smell when burned; its smoke; flattery. v.t. burn incense to; perfume with incense. [L. incendere, incens-, kindle]

incen'tive a. arousing. -n. something that arouses to feeling or action. [L. incentivus, setting the tune]

incep'tion n. beginning. -incep'tive a. initial. [L. incipere, incept-, begin]

incess'ant a. unceasing; continual; without intermission. -incessantly adv. [L. cessare, cease]

in'cest n. sexual intercourse of kindred within forbidden degrees. -incest'uous a. [L. incestus, impure, unchaste]

inch (-sh) n. one-twelfth of a foot. [OE. ynce, L. uncia, twelfth part]

inch (-sh) n. island. [Gael. innis]

in'cident n. event, occurrence. -a. naturally attaching to; striking, falling (upon). -in'cidence n. failing on, or affecting. -incident'al a. casual, not essential. -incident'ally adv. [L. incidere, fall in]

incin'erate v.t. consume by fire. -incin'erator n. -incinera'tion n. [Med. L. incinerare, reduce to ashes]

incip'ient a. beginning. -incip'ience n. -incip'iently a. [L. incipere, begin]

incise' v.t. cut into; engrave. -inci'sion (-sizh-) n. -inci'sive a. sharp; pointed, trenchant. -inci'sor n. cutting tooth. [L. incidere, incis-, cut into]

incite' v.t. urge, stir up. -incite'ment n. [L. incitare, rouse]

inclem'ent a. of weather, stormy, severe, cold. -inclem'ency n. [clement]

incline' v.t. bend, turn from the vertical; dispose. -v.i. slope; be disposed. -in'cline n. slope. -inclina'tion n. [F. incliner, cp. decline]

include' v.t. reckon in; comprise. -inclu'sion n. -inclu'sive a. -inclu'sively adv. [L. includere, shut in]

incog'nito adv. with identity concealed or not avowed. -a. concealing or not avowing identity. -n. this condition. [It., fr. L. incognitus, unknown]

incohe'rent a. unable to be understood. [in- and L. cohaerere]

in'come n. receipts, esp. annual, from work, investments, etc. -in'come-tax n. direct tax on income. [in and come]

incong'ruous a. not accordant, absurd. -incongru'ity n. -incong'ru-ously adv. [See congruent]

increase' v.i. become greater in size, number, etc. -v.t. make greater. -in'crease n. growth, enlargement, multiplication. -in'crement n. increase; profit. [L. increscere, fr. crescere, grow]

incrim'inate v.t. charge with crime; involve in an accusation. -incrim'in-atory a. [L. crimen, crime]

in'cubate v.t. hatch (eggs). -v.i. sit on eggs; of disease germs, pass through the stage between infection and appearance of symptoms. -incuba'tion n. -in'cubator n. apparatus for artificially hatching eggs. [L. incubare]

incumb'ent a. lying, resting on, -n. present holder of an office. -incumb'ency n. office or tenure of an incumbent. [L. incumbere, lie upon]

incunab'ula n. pl. early printed books. as from the cradle of printing. [L. in, in, cunabula, cradle]

incur' v.t. fall into, bring upon oneself [L.

incurrere, run into]

incur'sion *n.* invasion, inroad. [*incur*]

indebt'ed *a.* owing; under an obligation. -indebt'edness *n.* [*debt*]

indeed' *adv.* in truth, really. [*in deed*]

indefat'igable *v.* untiring. -indefat'-igably *adv.* [L. *defatigare*, tire out]

indel'ible *a.* that cannot be blotted out, or effaced; permanent. -indel'ibly *adv.* - indelibil'ity *n.* [L. *delere*, wipe out]

indem'nity *n.* security against loss; compensation, *esp.* exacted by a victorious country after war. -indem'nify *v.t.* compensate. -indemnifica'tion *n.* [L. *indemnis*, unharmed]

indent' *v.t.* make notches or holes in; draw up a document in duplicate; make an order (upon some one *for*); requisition, order by indent; (*print.*) give relatively wider margin to (line, passage). -in'dent *n.* notch; an order, requisition. -indenta'tion *n.* -indent'ure *n.* indented document 'sealed agreement, *esp.* one binding apprentice to master. *v.t.* bind by indenture. [Med. L. *iridetitare*, give a serrated edge]

indepen'dent *a.* not subject to others; self-reliant; free; valid in itself; politically of no party. -inde'pen'dence or indepen'dency *n.* being independent; self-reliance; self-support. [L. *depinigere*, depend]

in'dex *n.* (in'dexes, in'dices *pl.*) forefinger, anything that points out. an indicator; alphabetical list of references, usually at the end of a book. -*v.t.* provide a book with an index; insert in an index. -in'dicate *v.t.* point out, state briefly. -indica'tion *n.* -indic'ative *a.* that indicates; *gram.* stating as a fact. -in'dicator *n.* [L. *indicare*, fr. *dicare*, make known]

In'dian *a.* of India, the Indies; or the aborigines of America. -in'dia-rub'ber *n.* natural rubber made from latex. -In'dian corn', maize. -In'dian file, single file. - In'dian sum'mer, period of summer weather in late autumn. [L. *India - Indus*, the Indus]

in'dicate. *See* index.

indict' *v.t.* accuse, *esp.* by legal process. - indict'ment *n.* -indict'able *a.* [OF. *enditer*, fr. L. *dictare*, proclaim]

indiff'erent *a,* impartial; careless; unimportant neither good nor bad, tolerable; having no inclination for or against. -indiff'erently *adv.* -indiff'erence *n.* [*different*]

indi'genous *a.* born in or natural to a country. [L. *indigena*, native]

in'digent (-j-) *a.* poor, needy. -in'digence *n.* [L. *indigere*, lack]

indig'nant *a.* moved by anger and scorn; angered by injury. -indig'nantly *adv.* - indigna'tion *n.* contemptuous resentment. - indig'nity *n.* unworthy treatment; insult. [L. *indignari*, be angry at something unworthy, *indignus*]

in'digo it. blue dye obtained from a plant; the plant. [earlier *indico*, fr. L. *Indicus*, of India]

indite' *v.t.* write, put into words. [ME. *enditen*, OF. *enditer*, cp. *indict*]

individ'ual *a.* single; characteristic of a single person or thing. -*n.* single person. -

individ'ually *adv.* -individual'ity *n.* individual existence or character. - **individ'ualism** *n.* social theory of free action of individuals. -individ'ualist *n.* [L. *iridividuus.* undivided, single]

in'dolent *a.* lazy. -in'dolence *n.* - in'dolently *adv.* [F.]

indom'itable *a.* unsubduable. - indom'itably *adv.* [L. *domare, domit-*, tame]

in'door *a.* within, used within, *etc.*, a house. -indoors' *adv.* [*door*]

induce' *v.t.* persuade; bring about; infer; produce (electricity) by induction. - induce'ment *n.* incentive, attraction. induct' *v.t.* instal in office. -induc'tion *n.* inducting; general inference from particular instances; production of electric or magnetic state in a body by its being near (not touching) an electrified or magnetized body. -induc'tive *a.* -induc'tively *adv.* -induc'tor *n.* [L. *inducere, induct-*, lead in]

indulge' *v.t.* gratify; give free course to; take pleasure in freely. -indul'gent *a.* -indul'gence *n.* -indul'gently *adv.* [L. *indulgere*, be courteous]

in'dustry *n.* diligence; habitual hard work; branch of manufacture or trade. -indus'trious *a.* diligent. -indus'trial *a.* of industries, trades. -indus'trialism *n.* factory system. - indus'trialize *v.t.* [L. *industria*]

ine'briate *v.t.* make drunk. -*a.* drunken. -*n.* drunkard. [L. *ebrius*, drunk]

inept' *a.* absurd, out of place, irrelevant; fatuous. -inept'itude *n.* [L. *ineptus*, fr. *aptus*, cp. *apt*]

inert' *a.* without power of action or resistance; slow, sluggish. -iner'tia (-shya) *n.* property by which matter continues in its existing state of rest or motion in a straight line unless that state is changed by external force; inability to exert oneself. -inert'ly *adv.* - inert'ness *n.* [L. *iners, inert-*, sluggish]

inev'itable *a.* unavoidable, not to be escaped. -inev'itably *adv.* -inevitabil'ity *n.* [L. *inevitabilis*, fr. *euitare*, avoid]

inex'orable *a.* unrelenting. -inex'orably *adv.* [L. *exorare*, entreat]

infall'ible *a.* never wrong, certain, unfailing. [*in-*, and Low L. *fallibilis*]

in'famous *a.* of ill fame, shameless, bad. -in'famy *n.* ill repute; vileness. -in'famously *adv.* [*fame*]

in'fant *n.* small child; person under the age of one, a minor. -in'fancy *n.* -infant'icide *n.* murder of new-born child; person guilty of this. -in'fantile *a.* childish. [L. *infans, infant-*, unable to speak]

in'fantry *n.* foot soldier. [It. *infanteria*]

infat'uate *v.t.* affect to folly or foolish passion. -infatua'tion *n.* [L. *infatuare*, fr. *fatuus*, foolish]

infect' *v.t.* make noxious; affect (with disease). -infec'tion *n.* -infec'tious *a.* catching. [L. *inficere, infect-*, dip in]

infer' *v.t.* deduce by reasoning, conclude. -inference *n.* -inferen'tial *a.* -infer'-able *a.* [L. *inferre*, bring in]

infe'rior *a.* lower; of poor quality. -*n.* one

lower (in rank, *etc.*). -inferior'ity *n.* -inferior'ity complex (*psych.*) suppressed sense of inferiority. resulting in undue self-assertion; (*colloq.*) sense of inferiority. [L. comp. of *inferus*, low]

in'fidel *n.* unbeliever. -*a.* unbelieving. -infidel'ity *n.* disbelief (in religion); disloyalty. [L. *infidelis*, fr. *fides*, faith]

infil'trate *v.i.* percolate, trickle through. -*v.t.* cause to pass through pores. -infiltra'tion *n.* [*See* filter]

in'finite (-it) *a.* boundless. -infinites'imal *a.* extremely or infinitely small. -in'finitely *adv.* -infin'ity *n.* -infin'itive *a. gram.* in the mood expressing the notion of the verb without limitation by any particular subject. -*n.* verb in this mood; the mood, [L. *infinitus*, unbounded]

infirm' *a.* physically, mentally, weak, irresolute. -infirm'ity *n.* -infirm'ary *n* hospital. [L. *infirm us*, cp. *firm*]

inflame' *v.t.* set alight, raise to heat or excitement. -*v.i.* catch fire; become excited. -inflamm'able *a.* easily set on fire; excitable; flammable. -inflammabil'ity *n.* -inflamma'tion *n.* morbid process affecting part of the body with heat, swelling and redness. -inflamm'atory *a.* [L. *inflammare*, set on fire]

inflate' *v.t.* blow up with air or gas; raise (price) artificially; increase (currency of a state) abnormally. -infla'tion *n.* [L. *flare, flat-*, blow]

inflect' *v.t.* bend; modify (words) to show grammatical relationships. -inflec'tion, inflex'ion *n.* [L. *inflectere*]

inflex'ible *a.* unbending, unyielding; stern. [L. *in-, flexibilis*, yielding]

inflict' *v.t.* impose, deliver forcibly, cause to be borne. -inflic'tion *n.* inflicting; boring experience. [L. *infligere, inflict-*.]

in'fluence *n.* agent or action working invisibly (upon); moral power (over, with); thing or person exercising this. -*v.t.* exert influence upon. -influen'tial *a.* -influen'tially *adv.* [L. *fluere*, flow]

influen'za *n.* contagious feverish illness; severe catarrh. [It.]

in'flux *n.* a flowing in. [L. *influxus*]

inform' *v.t.* tell; inspire. -*v.i.* bring a charge against. -inform'ant *n.* one who tells. -informa'tion *n.* telling; what is told, knowledge. -informa'tion techno'logy *n.* the technology of the production, storage, and communication of information using computers and microelectronics. -inform'ative *a.* -inform'er *n.* one who brings a charge. [L. *informare*, give form to]

in'fra-red *a.* beyond the red end of the spectrum, as in infra-red rays. [L. *infra*, below, and *red*]

infringe' *v.t.* transgress, break. -infringe'ment *n.* -infrac'tion *n.* (L. *infringere*, fr., *frangere, fract-*, break]

infuriate *v.t.* fill with fury. [*fury*]

infuse' *v.t.* pour in, instil; steep in order to extract soluble properties. -infu'sion *n.* infusing; liquid extracts obtained. [L, *fundere, fus-*, pour]

ingem'inate (-jem-) *v.t.* repeat. -ingemina'tion *n.* [L. *ingeminare*, fr. *geminus*, twin]

inge'nious *a.* clever at contriving; cleverly contrived. -ingenu'ity *n.* skill in planning, invention. -inge'niously *adv.* [L. *ingenium*, natural ability]

in'génue *n.* artless young girl, *esp.* as a stage type. [F.]

ingen'uous *a.* frank, artless, innocent. -ingen'uously *adv.* -ingen'uousness *n.* [L. *ingenuus*, free-born, frank]

inges'tion *n.* taking into the body. [L. *in*, in, and *gerere*, carry]

in'got (ing-g-) *n.* brick or cast metal, *esp.* gold or silver. [OE. *geotan*, pour]

ingra'tiate *v. refl.* work oneself into a position of favor. [L. *in gratiam*, into favor]

ingre'dient *n.* component part of a mixture. [L. *ingredi*, step in]

in'gress *n.* entry; right, means, of entry. [L. *ingressus*]

ingui'nal (ing-gwi-) *a.* of the groin. [L. *inguinus*, groin]

inhab'it *v.t.* dwell in. -inhab'itable *a.* -inhab'itant *n.* [L. *habitare*, dwell]

inhale' *v.t.* breathe in. -*v. i.* breathe in air. -inhala'tion *n.* [L. *inhalare*]

inher'it *v.t.* take as heir; derive from parents. -*v. i.* succeed as heir. [L. *heres*, heir]

inhib'it *v.t.* forbid; forbid to exercise clerical functions; hinder (action). [L. *inhibere, inhibit-*, hold in]

inim'itable *a.* defying imitation. -inim'itably *adv.* [*imitate*]

iniq'uity *n.* wickedness; gross injustice. -iniquitous *a.* -iniq'uitously *adv.* [L. *iniquitas, æquus*, fair, even]

ini'tial (-ish-) *a.* of the beginning, occurring at the beginning. -*n.* initial letter. *v. t.* mark, sign, with one's initials. -ini'tiate *v.t.* set on foot, begin; admit, *esp.* into a secret society. -*n.* initiated person. -initia'tion *n.* -ini'tiative *n.* first step, lead; power of acting independently. -*a.* originating. -ini'tiatory *a.* [L. *initialis*, fr. *initium*, beginning]

inject *v.t.* force in (fluid, medicine, *etc.*), as with a syringe; fill thus. -injec'tion *n.* [L. *injicere, inject-*, throw in]

injunc'tion *n.* judicial order to restrain; authoritative order; exhortation. [Late L. *injunctio*, cp. *enjoin*]

in'jury *n.* wrong, damage, harm. -in'jure *v.t.* do wrong to, damage. -injurious *a.* harmful. -inju'riously *adv.* [L. *injuria*, fr. *jus, jur-*, law]

ink *a.* fluid used for writing; paste used for printing. -*v. t.* mark with ink; cover or smear with it. -ink'bottle *n.* [ME. *enke*. G. *enkhaustos*, burnt in]

ink'ling *n.* hint, slight knowledge or suspicion. [ME. *inklen*, whisper]

in'land *n.* interior of a country. -*a.* in this; away from the sea; within a country. *adv.* in or towards the inland. [*in* and *land*]

in-law *n.* relative by marriage as mother-in-law. [*in* and *law*]

in'lay *v.t.* embed; decorate thus. -*n.* inlaid

work. [*in* and *lay*]

in'let *n.* entrance; creek; piece inserted. [*in* and *let*]

in'mate *n.* occupant, inhabitant *esp.* in institution. [*in* and *mate*]

inn *n.* public house for the lodging or refreshment of travelers. -inn'keeper *n.* [OE.]

innate' *a.* inborn. [L. *innatus*]

inn'er *a.* lying within. [compar. of *in*]

inn'ings *n. pl.* in games, batsman's turn of play, side's turn of batting. [*in*]

inn'ocent *a.* free from guilt; guileless; harmless. -*n.* innocent person, *esp.* a young child; idiot. [L. *nocere*, harm]

innoc'uous *a.* harmless. [*See* innocent]

inn'ovate *v.t.* bring in changes, new things. -inn'ovator *n.* -innova'tion *n.* [L. *innocare*, fr. *novus*, new]

innuen'do *n.* allusive remark, hint (usually depreciatory). [L. = by nodding to, fr. *nuere*, nod]

inoc'ulate *v.t.* treat with disease germs, *esp.* as a protection; implant (disease germs). -inocula'tion *n.* [orig. graft, L. *inoculate*, fr. *oculus*, eye, bud]

inord'inate *a.* excessive. [L. *inordinatus*, unordered, cp. *order*]

inorgan'ic *a.* not organic or organized; of substance without carbon. [*in*-, and L. *organcus*]

in'put *n.* power or information supplied to machine; work or money put into an enterprise. [*in* and *put*]

in'quest *n.* legal or judicial inquiry, *esp.* into cause of sudden, violent, death. [OF. *enqueste*, inquiry]

inquire', enquire' *v. t.* seek information. -*v.t.* ask to be told. -inqui'rer, enqui'rer *n.* -inqui'ry, enqui'ry *n.* -inquisi'tion *n.* investigation, official inquiry. Inquisition *n.* tribunal for the suppression of heresy. [L. *inquirere, inquis-*]

in'road *n.* incursion; encroachment. [*road* in sense of riding]

insane' *a.* mad. -insan'ity *n.* [L. *insanus*]

inscribe' *v.t.* write (in or on something); mark; trace (figure) within another; dedicate. -inscrip'tion *n.* inscribing, words inscribed on a monument, coin, *etc.* [L. *inscribere, inscript-*]

inscru'table *a.* mysterious, impenetrable. -inscru'tably *adv.* -inscrutabil'ity *n.* [*See* scrutiny]

in'sect *n.* small invertebrate animal with six legs, body divided into segments and two or four wings. -insect'icide *n.* prep aration for killing insects. -insectiv'orous *a.* insect-eating. [L. *insectum*, cut into (from the segments)]

insem'inate *v.t.* sow; impregnate. -insemina'tion *n.* [*in*-, and L. *seminare*, to sow]

insert' *v.t.* place or put (in, into, between); introduce (into written matter, *etc.*). -inser'tion *n.* [L. *inserere*, fr. *serere, sert-*, join]

in'set *n.* something extra inserted; picture set into a larger one. [*in* and *set*]

in'side *n.* inner side, surface, or part. -*a.* of,

in, or on, the inside. -*adv.* in or into the inside. -prep. within, on the inner side. [*in* and *side*]

insid'ious *a.* stealthy, treacherous. -insid'iously *adv.* [L. *insidiosus*, fr. *insidere*, lie in wait]

in'sight *n.* mental penetration. [*sight*]

insig'nia *n. pl.* badges or emblems of an honor or office. [L. = distinguished things; fr. *signum*, sign]

insin'uate *v.t.* bring or get (something into something) gradually or subtly; hint. -insinua'tion *n.* [L. *insinuate*, introduce tortuously. cp. *sinuous*]

insip'id *a.* dull, tasteless. -insipid'ity *n.* [L. *insipidus*, fr. *sapidus*, tasty]

insist' *v. i.* dwell on, maintain, demand persistently. [L. *insistere*, fr. *sistere*, stand]

in'solent *a.* insulting, offensively contemptuous. -in'solently *adv.* -in'solence *n.* [L. *insolens*; orig. unaccustomed]

insom'nia *n.* sleeplessness. [L.]

inspect' *v.t.* examine closely or officially. -inspec'tion *n.* -inspec'tor *n.* [L. *inspicere, inspect-*, look into]

inspire' *v.t.* breathe in; infuse thought or feeling into; arouse, to create. -inspira'tion *n.* breath; influence, *esp.* divine influence. [L. *inspirare*]

install' *v.t.* place (person in an office, *etc.*) with ceremony; establish, have put in. installa'tion *n.* [F. *installer*, put in a stall]

install'ment (-awl-) *n.* payment of part of a debt; any of parts of a whole delivered in succession; installation. [earlier *estallment*, fr. OF. *estaler*, fix]

in'stance *n.* example; particular case; request; place in a series. -*v. t.* cite. -in'stant *a.* urgent; belonging to the current month; immediate. -*n.* moment, point of time. -in'stantly *adv.* at once. -instanta'neous *a.* happening in an instant. [L. *instantia*, fr. *instare*, be present, urge]

instead' (-ed) *adv.* in place (of). [*stead*]

in'step *n.* top of the foot between toes and ankle. [orig. uncertain]

in'stigate *v.t.* incite. -instiga'tion *n.* -in'stigator *n.* [L. *instigate*]

instill' *v. t.* put in by drops; drop slowly (into the mind). [L. *stillare*, drop]

in'stinct *n.* inborn impulse or propensity; unconscious skill; intuition; involuntary impulse. -instinct' *a.* charged, full. -instinct'ive *a.* -instinct'ively *adv.* [L. *instinctus*, fr. *instinguere*, urge]

in'stitute *v.t.* establish, found; appoint; set going. -*n.* society for promoting some public object, *esp.* scientific; its building. -institu'tion *n.* instituting; established custom or law; institute. -institu'tional *a.* -in'stitutor *n.* [L. *instituere, institute*, set up]

instruct' *v.t.* teach, inform, give directions to. -instruc'tion *n.* [L. *instruere, instruct-*, build]

in'strument *n.* tool or implement, *esp.* for scientific purposes; person or thing made use of; contrivance for producing music; legal document. -instrument'al *a.* -instrument'alist *n.* player of musical instrument. [L. *instrumentum*, fr. *instruere*, build]

insubor'dinate *a.* disobedient. - insubor'dination *n.* [*in*-, and Med. L. *subordinatus*]

in'sular *a.* of an island; of islanders. - insular'ity *n.* -in'sulate *v. t.* make into an island; isolate, *esp.* by materials not conducting electricity or beat. insulation *n.* - in'sulator *n.* [L. *insula*, island]

in'sulin (-sōi-) *n.* extract used in the treatment of diabetes and mental diseases. [L. *insula*, island]

insult' *v.t.* assail with abuse in act or word. -in'sult *n.* scornful abuse, affront. [L. *insultare*, jump at]

insu'perable *a.* not to be got over. - insu'perably *adv.* -insuperabil'ity *n.* [L. *superare*, overcome, fr. *super*, over]

insure' *v.t.* secure the payment of a sum in event of loss, death, *etc.*, by a contract and payment of sums called premiums; make such contract about; make safe (against); make certain. [var. of *ensure*]

insur'gent *a.* in revolt. -*n.* one in revolt. - insurrec'tion *n.* revolt. [L. insurgere, insurrect-, rise upon]

intact' *a.* untouched; whole, uninjured. [L. *tangere, tact-,* touch]

intang'ible *a.* not perceptible to touch, elusive. -intangibil'ity *n.* [*in*-, and L. *tangibilis*]

in'teger (-j-) *n.* whole number. -in'tegral (-g-) *a.* -in'tegrate *v. t.* combine into a whole. -integra'tion *n.* -integ'rity *n.* original perfect state; honesty, uprightness. [L. = *untouched*]

in'tellect *n.* faculty of thinking and reasoning. -intellec'tual *a.* of, or appealing to, the intellect; having good intellect.-*n.* intellectual person, high-brow. -intellectuality *n.* [L. *intellegere*, intellect, understand,

intell'igent *a.* having or showing good intellect; quick at understanding. -intelligently *adv.* -intell'igence *n.* intellect; quickness of understanding; information. news. - intell'igible *a.* that can be understood. - intell'igence quo'tient (-shent'),ratio indicated in percentages) of one's mental age to one's actual age (*abbrev.* IQ). [L. *intelligens, intelligent*-]

intem'perate *a.* not temperate, immoderate in drinking; passionate. [L. *intemperatus*]

intend' *v.t.* design, purpose, mean. [L. *intenders, intens-, intent-,* bend the mind on, fr. *tendere,* stretch]

intense' *a.* very strong or acute -intens'ify *v.t.* -intens'ive *a.* giving emphasis; aiming at increased productiveness. -intens'ively *adv.* [See intend]

intent' *n.* purpose. -*a.* eager; resolved, bent. -intent'ly *adv.* -inten'tion *n.* purpose, aim. -inten'tional *a.* -intent'ness *n.* [*See* intend]

inter' *v. t.* bury. -inter'ment *n.* [F. *enterrer,* fr. *terre,* earth]

inter' *prefix* meaning between, among, mutually; forms compounds, *e.g.,* intercolo'nial *a.* between colonies. [L. *inter,* between]

interactive language *n.* (*compute.*) means or method by which programmers communicate while executing a program.

intercede' *v.i.* plead. -intercession *n.* - intercess'or *n.* [L. *cedere, cess*-, go]

intercept' *v.t.* cut off, seize in transit. - intercep'tion *n.* [L. *capere, capt*-, take]

in'tercourse *n.* mutual dealings; communication; connection. [OF. *entrecours,* fr. *entrecourre,* run between]

in'terdict *n.* prohibition; prohibitory decree. -interdict' *v. t.* prohibit; restrain. -interdiction *n.* -interdict'ory *a.* [L. *interdicere, interdict*-, decree]

in'terest *n.* concern, curiosity; thing exciting this; money paid for use of borrowed money; legal concern; right; advantage; personal influence. -*v. t.* excite interest; cause to feel interest. -interesting *a.* - in'terestingly *adv.* [L. *interesse*, be a concern to]

interfere' *v.i.* meddle; clash; of rays, *etc.*, strike together. -interfe'rence *n,* in telecommunications, spoiling of reception by other signals on similar wave-lengths, or by atmospheric conditions. -interfe'ringly *adv.* [L. *ferire,* strike]

in'terim *n.* meantime. -*a.* temporary, intervening. [L. = meanwhile]

inte'rior *a.* situated within; inland. -*n.* inside, inland. [L. comp. of *interns,* fr. L. *intra,* within]

interjec'tion *n.* word thrown in, or uttered abruptly. -interject' *v.t.* [L. *interjectio,* fr. *jicere, ject*-, throw]

in'terlude *n.* intermission in a play; something filling it, as music, intermezzo; interval. [L. *ludus,* play]

interme'diate *a.* coming between two; interposed. -interme'diary *n.* one acting between two parties, go-between. [L. *medius,* middle]

interm'inable *a.* endless. -interm'inably *adv.* [*terminable*]

intermit' *v.t.* and *i.* stop for a time. - intermis'sion *n.* -intermitt'ent *a.* ceasing at intervals. [L. *mittere,* put, send]

intern' *v.t.* oblige to live within prescribed limits. -*n.* resident assistant surgeon, physician, in hospital-also **interne'**, - intern'ment *n.* [F. *interner,* fr. *interne,* resident within]

inter'nal *a.* in, of, the interior; of home (as opposed to foreign) affairs. -inter'nal-combus'tion en'gine, engine driven by explosions of gas within its cylinder. [L. *internus*]

interna'tional (-nash-) *a.* between nations. -*n.* international (games, *etc.*) contest; one taking part in such. [*nationa*]

inter'polate *v.t.* put in new (*esp.* misleading) matter (in book, *etc.*). -interpola'tion *n.* -inter'polative a.* [L. *interpolale,* furbish up]

interpose' *v.t.* insert; say as interruption; put in the way. -*v.i.* intervene; obstruct, mediate. -interposi'tion *n.* [F. *interposer*]

inter'pret *v.t.* explain; explain to oneself; translate for another's benefit; in art, render, represent. -inter'preter n. - interpretation n. [L. interpretari]

inter'preter n. (compute.) computer program which converts information from progamming language into machine language.

interr'ogate v.t. question esp. closely or officially. -interroga'tion n. -interrog'ative a. questioning; used in asking a question. [L. rogare, ask]

interrupt' v.t. break in upon; stop the course of. -interrup'tion n. [L. rumpere, rapt-, break]

intersect' v.t. cut into or through; divide; cross (each other). -intersec'tion n. -intersec'tional a. [L. secare, sect-, cut]

intersperse' v.t. scatter; diversify. -interspers'ion n. [L. spargere, spars-, scatter]

in'terval n. pause, break, intervening time or space; difference of pitch between any two musical tones. [L. intervallum, orig. space between ramparts]

intervene' v.i. happen in the meantime; be placed, come in, between others; interfere. -interven'tion n. interference; mediation. [L. venire, come]

in'terview n. meeting, esp. formally arranged; meeting of a journalist and person whose views he wishes to publish.-v.t. have an interview with. -in'terviewer n. [F. entrevue, fr. voir, see]

intest'ate a. not having made a will. -n. intestate person. [L. testari, testat-, make a will]

in'timate a. familiar, closely acquainted; close. -n. intimate friend. -in'timacy n. -in'timate v.t. make known; announce. -intima'tion v.i. [L. intimatus]

in'timidate v.t. force or deter by threats. -intimida'tion n. -intim'idator n. [Late L. intimidate, fr. timidus, timid]

in'to prep. expresses motion to a point within. [in to]

intone' v.t. recite in monotone or singing voice. -intona'tion n. modulation of voice; intoning. [Church L. intoniare, fr. tonus, tone]

intox'icate v.t. make drunk; excite beyond self-control. -intox'icant a. intoxicating. -n. intoxicating liquor. intoxication n. [G. toxicon, arrow poison]

intran'sigent a. refusing to come to terms. -n. politically irreconcilable. [F. intransigeant, fr. Sp. in transigentes, extreme Republican party]

intrep'id a. fearless. -intrepid'ity n. [L. trepidus, alarmed]

in'tricate a. involved, puzzlingly entangled. [L. intricatus, entangled]

intrigue' n. underhand plotting or plot; secret love affair. -v.i. carry on an intrigue. -v.t. whet the interest of, fascinate. -intri'guer n. [F., fr. L. intricare, entangle, v.s.]

intrin'sic a. inherent, essential. -intrin'sically adv. -intrinsical'ity n. [L. intrinsecus, adv. inwardly]

introduce' v.t. bring in, forward; make known formally; bring to notice; insert. -introduc'tion n. preface to a book. -introduc'tory a. [L. introducere, lead in]

introspec'tion n. examination of one's own thoughts. [L. introspicere, introspect-, look within]

introvert' v.t. turn inwards. -n. (in'-) (psych.) introspective person, one whose mind is turned within. -introversion n. [L. vertere, turn]

intrude' v.i. thrust in without invitation or right. -v. t. force in. -intru'sion n. -intru'sive a. [L, intruders, intrus-, thrust in]

intui'tion (-ish-) n. immediate or direct apprehension by the mind without reasoning; immediate insight. -intu'itive a. -intu'itively adv. [Med. L. intuitio, fr. intueri, intuit-, look upon]

in'undate v. t. flood. -inunda'tion n. [L. inundate, fr. unda, wave]

invade' v.t. enter with hostile intent; assail; encroach on. -inva'der n. -inva'sion n. [L. invadere, invas, go in]

inval'id a. not valid, of no legal force. -inval'idate v. t. -invalid'ity n. -in'valid a. ill, enfeebled by sickness or injury. -n. person so disabled. [L, invalidus fr. validus, strong]

inval'uable a. above price. [valuable]

invent' v.t. devise, originate. -inven'tion n. -invent'ive a. -invent'ively adv. -invent'or n. [L. invenire, invent-, come upon, discover]

in'ventory n. list of goods, etc. -v.t. enter in an inventory. [L. inventarium]

invert' v. t. turn upside down; reverse the position or relations of. -in'verse a. inverted. -n. opposite. -inverse ratio, the ratio of reciprocals. [L. invertere, invers-.]

inver'tebrate a/n. (animal) with no backbone; spineless, weak. [L. in-, and vertebra]

invest' v.t. lay out (money); clothe; endue; cover as a garment; lay siege to. -invest'iture n. formal installation of person in office or rank. -invest'ment n. investing; money invested; stocks and shares bought. -invest'or n. [L. inuestire, clothe]

invest'igate v.t. inquire into. -investiga'tion n. -invest'igator n. [L. investgare, fr. vestigare, track]

invet'erate a. deep-rooted, long established. -invet'eracy n. [L. inveterate, make old, vetus, veter-]

invig'orate v. t. give vigor to. -invig'orating a. strengthening. [See vigorous]

invin'cible a. unconquerable. -invincibil'ity n. [L. vincere, conquer]

invite' v. t. request courteously; attract, tend to call forth. -invita'tion n. -invi'ting a. enticing, attractive. invitingly adv. [L. invitare]

in'voice n. list of goods sent, with prices. -v.t. make an invoice of. [pl. of obs, invoy, F. envoi, sending]

invoke' v.t. call on; appeal to; ask earnestly for. -invoca'tion n. [L. invocare, fr. vocare, call]

invol'untary a. without power of will or choice; unintentional. [L. involuntarius]

involve' v. t. wrap up, entangle, implicate; imply, entail. -in'volute a. intricate; rolled spirally. -involu'tion n. [L. involvere, fr. volvere, volut-, roll]

in'ward adv. towards the inside, centre. -a.

internal; in the heart, mind. -in'wardly *adv.*
-in'wardness *n.* inner meaning. [OE. *innan-weard*]

I/O *n.* equipment or data used to communicate with a computer [*I*nput/*O*utput]

i'odine *n.* non-metallic element of the chlorine group, used in medicine. [G. *iodes*, violet-colored, fr. color of its vapor]

i'on *n.* electrically charged atom or group of atoms. [G. = *going*]

ion'ic *a.* of Iona in Greece, pert. to style of architecture characterized by column with ramshorn volute at top. [Ionia]

io'ta *n.* Greek letter *i;* an atom, jot, insignificant particle. [G.]

ire *n.* anger, wrath. -irate *a.* angry. -iras'cible *a.* hot-tempered. -irascibil'ity *n.* -iras'cibly *adv.* [L. *ira*]

i'ris *n.* genus of plants with sword-shaped leaves and showy flowers: circular membrane of the eye containing the pupil; formerly, rainbow. -irides'cent *a.* showing colors like a rainbow; changing color with change of position. -irides'cence *n.* [G. = rainbow]

I'rish *a.* of Ireland. -I'rish bull', laughable contradiction in speech. [OE. *Irise*]

irk *v.t.* weary, trouble. -irk'some *a.* [ME. irken, weary, disgust]

i'ron *n.* metal, much used for tools, utensils, *etc.*, and the raw material of steel: tool, *etc.*, of this metal; smoothing iron; (*golf*) iron-headed club. [OE. *iren*]

i'rony *n.* speech in which the meaning is the opposite of that actually expressed; words used with an inner meaning. -iron'ical *a.* -iron'ically *adv.* [G. *eironeia*, dissimulation, affected ignorance]

ir- *prefix* for *in*- before 'r'. Many words are omitted in which the prefix simply negatives the idea of the simple word, as in *irregular a.* not regular, *etc.* irra'diate *v.t.* shine upon, throw light upon. -irradia'tion *n.* [L. *radius*, ray]

irrespec'tive *a.* without taking account (of), without regard (to). [*respect*]

irr'igate *v.t.* water by channels or streams. -irriga'tion *n.* -irr'igator *n.* [L. *irrigare*, irrigate, fr. *rigare*, moisten]

irri'tate *v.t.* excite to anger; excite, inflame, stimulate. -irrita'tion *n.* -irritant *a.* causing irritation. -*n.* thing doing this. -irr'itable *a.* easily annoyed. -irr'itably *adv.* [L. *irritare, irritat*]

is *v.* 3rd. pers. sing. pres. of *be.* [OE.]

Is'lam, Is'lamism *n.* the Muslim religion; the entire Muslim world. -Is'lamic *a.* [Ar., *slam -salama*, to submit to God]

i'sland (-il-) *n.* piece of land surrounded by water; anything like this. -i'slander *n.* dweller on an island. [earlier *iland*, OE. *iegland*]

isle (-il) *n.* island, little island. [OF. *isle*, L. *insula*]

ism *n.* doctrine, theory, practice, *esp.* of a faddy or extravagant nature. [Suffix -*ism*, G. -*ismos*]

i'so *pref.* equal. [G. *isos*]

i'sobar *n.* line (on chart *etc.*) connecting places of equal barometric pressure. [G. *baros*, weight]

i'solate *v.t.* place apart or alone. -isola'tion *n.* -isola'tionism *n.* political doctrine of (national) isolation. [L. *insula*, island]

isos'celes *a.* of a triangle, having two of its sides equal. [G. *isosceles*, fr. *isos*, equal, and *skelos*, leg]

i'sotope (-tōp) *n.* element chemically identical with others, but having a different nuclear mass, hence atomic weight. [G. *topos*, place]

iss'ue *n.* going or passing out; outlet; offspring, children; outcome, result; question, dispute; a sending or giving out officially or publicly; number or amount so given out. -*v.i.* go out; result in; arise (from). -*v.t.* emit, give out, send out. [OF. *issir*, go out, L. *exire*]

isth'mus *n.* a narrow neck of land connecting two larger areas. [G. *isthmos*]

it *pron.* neuter pronoun of the third person. -itself' *pron.* reflex and emphatic of it. [OE. *hit*]

ital'ic *a.* of type, sloping. -ital'ics *n. pl.* this type, now used for emphasis, foreign words, *etc.* -ital'icize *v. t.* put in italics. [L. *Italicus*, Italian]

itch *v.i.* feel an irritation in the skin; be anxious or keen to. -*n.* irritation in the skin; impatient desire. -itch'y *a.* [OE. *giccan*]

i'tem *n.* any of a list of things; detail; entry in an account or list. -*adv.*, also. -itemize *v.i.* list item by item; give particulars. [L. *adv* = in like manner; formerly used in inventories to introduce entries]

it'erate *v. t.* repeat. -itera'tion *n.* -it'erative *a.* [L. *iterare-iterum*, again]

itin'erant *a.* travelling from place to place; travelling on circuit. -itin'eracy *n.* -itin'erary *n.* record of travel; route, line of travel; guidebook. [L. *iter, itiner-*, journey]

i'vory *n.* hard white substance of the tusks of elephants, *etc.* [F. *iuoire*]

i'vy *n.* climbing evergreen plant. -i'vied *a.* overgrown with ivy. [OE. *ifig*]

J

jab *v.t.* poke roughly, thrust abruptly. -*n.* poke. [var. of job]

jack *n.* sailor; boy, servant; knave in a pack of cards; various mechanical appliances, *esp.* for raising heavy weights; flag or ensign; various small things; added to names of animals. [F., Jacques, James, but in E. a pet form of John]

jack *n.* leather coat; leather bottle for liquor. [F. *Jacque*]

jack'al *n.* wild animal closely allied to the dog. [Pers. *shagal*]

jack'ass *n.* male donkey; stupid fellow [Jack = the *male*, and *ass*]

jack'et *n.* sleeved outer garment, a short coat; outer casing. [F. *jaquette*]

jacu'zzi *n.* system of underwater jets that keep the water in a bath or pool constantly agitated; a bath or pool equipped with this. [Trademark]

jade *n.* sorry nag, worn-out horse; in contempt, a woman. -*v.t.* tire out; weary. [orig. uncertain]

jade *n.* ornamental stone, usually green. [Sp. (*piedra de*) *ijada*, *colie* (stone), as supposed to cure pain]

jag *n.* sharp projection, *e. g.*, point of rock. -**jagg'ed** *a.* [orig. unknown]

jag'uar *n.* large spotted, wild animal of the cat tribe. [Braz. *jaguara*]

jail *n.* building for confinement of criminals or suspects; -*v.t.* send to, confine in prison. [OF. *gaole*, prison]

jalousie' *n.* outside slatted shutters. [F. = *jealousy*]

jam *v. t.* squeeze; cause to stick and become unworkable; pack together; interfere with. - *v.i.* stick and become unworkable. -*n.* fruit preserved by boiling with sugar; blockage, *esp.* traffic; musical improvisation by a group of musicians. [orig. uncertain]

jamb (jam) *n.* door-post. [F. *jambe*, leg]

jang'le (-ng-gl) *v.i.* sound harshly, as a bell. -*v.t.* make do this. -*n.* harsh metallic sound; wrangle. [OF. *jangler*]

jan'itor *n.* caretaker, doorkeeper. [L.]

Jan'uary *n.* first month of the year. [L. *januarius*, of Janus]

jar *n.* vessel of glass, earthenware, *etc.* [Arab. *, iarrah*, earthen vessel]

jar *v.i.* make a grating noise; vibrate gratingly, wrangle *v.t.* cause to vibrate. -*n.* jarring sound; shock, *etc.* [imit.]

jar'gon *n.* barbarous or distorted language; gibberish; excessively technical language. [F.]

jaundice (-dis) *n.* disease marked by yellowness of the skin. -**jaun'diced** *a.* jealous, of soured outlook. [F. *jaunisse*, fr. *jaune*, yellow]

jaunt *n.* short pleasure excursion. -*v.i.* make one. [orig. uncertain]

jaunt'y *a.* sprightly; briskly pleased with life. -**jaunt'ily** *adv.* [F. *gentil*]

jav'elin *n.* light spear for throwing. [F. *javelins*]

jaw *n.* one of the bones in which the teeth are set. -*pl.* mouth; gripping part of vice, *etc.* [F. *joue*, cheek]

jay *n.* noisy bird of brilliant plumage; chatterer. -**jay'walk'er**, careless pedestrian, *esp.* one who ignores traffic rules. [F. *geai*]

jazz *n.* syncopated music and dance. -*v.i.* indulge in jazz. -*a.* discordant or bizarre in color, *etc.* -**jazz up'** (*sl.*) liven. [orig. unknown]

jeal'ous *a.* suspiciously watchful; distrustful of the faithfulness (of); envious; anxiously solicitous (for). -**jeal'ousy** *n.* **jeal'ously** *adv.* [F. *jaloux*]

jean *n.* twilled cotton cloth. -*n. pl.* overalls; trousers. [Genoa]

jeep' *n.* small high-powered open car first used in U.S. army. [G. P., for 'general purposes']

jeer *v. t.* and *i.* scoff, deride. -*n.* scoff, mocking taunt. [orig. uncertain]

Jeho'vah *n.* Hebrew name for God. [Heb. *Yahweh*]

jell'y *n.* semi-transparent food made with gelatin, becoming stiff as it cools; anything of the consistency of this. **jell'y-fish** *n.* jelly-like small sea-animal. [F. *gelée*, fr. *geler*, freeze]

jeop'ardy *n.* danger. -**jeop'ardize** *v.t.* endanger. [F. *jeu parti*, even game]

jerk *n.* sharp, abruptly stopped movement, twitch, start, sharp pull. -*v.t.* and *i.* move, or throw, with a jerk; sneer. -**jerk'y** *a.* spasmodic. -**jerk'ily** *adv.* **jerk'iness** *n.* [orig. unknown]

jerk *v. t.* cut (beef) in strips and dry. **jerked'beef** *n.* beef so treated, charqui. [Peruv. *echarqui*]

jerry-built *a.* of flimsy construction with bad materials. [orig. uncertain]

jer'sey (-z-) *n.* close-fitted knitted jacket. [Jersey, in Channel Islands]

jest *n.* joke. -*v.i.* joke. -**jest'er** *n.* joker, *esp.* professional fool of a court. [F. *geste*, exploit]

Jes'uit *n.* member of the Society of Jesus, an Order founded by Ignatius Loyola in 1533. -**Jesuit'ical** *a.* [Jesus]

jet *n.* hard black mineral capable of a brilliant polish. [G. *gagates*]

jet *n.* stream of liquid, gas, *etc.*, *esp.* shot from a small hole; the small hole; spout, nozzle; aircraft driven by jet propulsion. -*v.t.* and *i.* spurt out in jets. -**jet lag** *n.* fatigue caused by crossing time zones in jet aircraft. -**jet'propul'sion** *n.* mode of propulsion with jet (of air, gas, fluid) as motive power. -**jet set** *n.* rich, fashionable social set, members of which travel widely for pleasure. [F. , fr. *jeter*, to throw]

jet'sam *n.* goods thrown out to lighten a ship and later washed ashore. -**jett'ison** *v.t.* throw overboard thus. [OF. *jetaison*, fr. *jeter*, throw]

jett'y *n.* small pier or landing-place. [F. *jetge*, fr. *jeter*, throw]

jew'el *n.* precious stone; personal ornament containing one; precious thing. **jew'eler**, *n.* dealer in jewels. -**jew'elry** *n.* [OF. *goiel*]

jib *n.* ship's triangular staysail. -*v.t.* pull over (a sail) to the other side; of a horse or person, to stop and refuse to go on, object to precede. [var. of *gybe*]

jibe *v.i.* of the boom of a for-and-aft sail, to swing over to the other side with following wind. -*v.t.* cause this; change course thus. [Du. *gijpen*]

jig *n.* lively dance; music for it; various mechanisms or fittings. -*v.i.* dance a jig; make jerky up-and-down movements. -**jig'saw** *n.* machine fretsaw. -**jig'saw** puzzle picture cut into irregular pieces to be fitted together again. -**jigg'er** *n.* [orig. uncertain]

jilt *v.t.* cast off (a over) after encouraging. -*n.* one who does this. [earlier *jillet*, dim. of Jill]

jing'le *n.* metallic noise. as of shaken chain; repetition of same sounds in words. -*v.i.* make the sound. -*v. t.* cause to make it. [imit.]

jing'o (-ng-g-) warmonger. -**jingo'ism** *n.* -by Jingo, a form of asseveration. [orig. uncertain; political sense due to use of *by Jingo* in music-hall song (1878)]

jinx' *n.* unlucky thing, person; hoodoo. [L. *iynx*]

jitt'ers *n. pl.* state of nerves, trepidation. -**jitt'ery** *a.* -**jitt'erbug** *n.* jazz dance, dancer; alarmist. [prob. imit.]

jive *n.* swing music. [orig. unknown]

job *n.* piece of work; employment; un-scrupulous transaction. -*v.i.* do odd jobs: deal in stocks. [orig. uncertain]

job *n.* prod, jab. [imit.]

jock'ey *a.* professional rider in horseraces. -*v.t.* cheat; maneuver. [dim. of Jock, var. of Jack]

joc'und *a.* merry. -**jocund'ity** *n.* [L. *jucun-dus,* pleasant]

jog *v.t.* move or push with a jerk. -*v.i.* walk or ride with jolting pace; take exercise. -*n.* a jog-ging. -**jog'ger** *n.* person who runs at a jog trot over some distance for exercise, usually regularly. [orig. uncertain]

join *v.t.* put together. fasten, unite. -*v.i.* be-come united or connected. -*n.* a joining; place of joining. -**join'er** *n.* one who joins; maker of furniture and light woodwork. -**join'ery** *n.* his work. -**joint** *n.* arrangement by which two things fit or are joined together, rigidly or loosely: bone with meat on, as food, low-class public house.-*a.* common: share of or by two or more. -*v.i.* connect by joints: divide at the joints.-**joint'ly** *adv.* [F. *joindre,* fr. L., *jungere, junct-,* join]

joist *n.* parallel beam stretched from wall to wall on which to fix floor or ceiling. [OF. *giste,* fr. L. *jacere,* lie]

joke *n.* thing said or done to cause laughter, something not in earnest. *v.i.* make jokes. *v.t.* banter. -**jo'ker** *n.* [L. *jocus,* jest]

joll'y *a.* festive, merry. -**joll'ity** *n.* -**jollifica'tion** *n.* merrymaking. [F. *joli*]

joll'y-boat *n.* small ship's boat. [orig. un-certain]

Jolly Roger *n.* pirate's flag: black with white skull and cross-bones. [*jolly* and Roger, name]

jolt n. jerk; throwing up or forwards. as from a seat-*v.t.* and *i.* move or shake with jolts. [orig. uncertain]

jos'tle *v.t.* and *i.* knock or push against. -*n.* a jostling. -**joust** *n.* encounter with lances be-tween two mounted knights. -*v.i.* take part in a joust. [OF, jouster]

jot *n.* small amount.-*v.t.* write (down) briefly. -**jott'er** *n.* book for rough notes; one who jots. [G. *iota*]

joule *n.* unit of electrical energy; unit of heat. [J. P, Joule, 1818-1891]

jour'nal *n.* daily record; logbook; daily newspaper or other periodical; part of an axle or shaft resting on the bearings. -**journalese'** *n.* jargon of journalists. -**jour'nalism** *n.* edit-ing, or writing in, periodicals. -**jour'nalist** *n.* **journalis'tic** *a.* [F. *journal,* fr. L. *diurnalis*]

jour'ney (jur-) *n.* a going to a place; distance traveled. -t. *t.* travel. -**jour'neyman** *n.* one who has learned a trade and works as an artisan paid by the day: hireling. [*See* journal]

joust. *See* jostle.

jo'vial *a.* jolly, convivial. [Jove]

jowl *n.* cheek, jaw; outside of the throat when prominent. [orig. obscure]

joy *n.* gladness, pleasure; cause of this. -**joy'-ride** *n.* (*sl.*) pleasurable, reckless (and often unlawful) drive in a vehicle.-**joy'stick** *n.* con-trol-lever, *esp.* of an airplane or computer game control. [F. *joie*]

ju'bilee *n.* fiftieth anniversary; time of rejoicing. [Heb. *joebl,* horn, trumpet]

Juda'ic(al) *a.* of Jews. **Ju'daism** *n.* doctrine of Jews. [G, *Joudaios,* Jew]

judge (juj) *n.* officer appointed to try and decide cases in law court; one who decides a dispute, question. contest; -**judg'ment** *n.* sen-tence of a court; opinion; faculty of judging: misfortune regarded as a sign of divine dis-pleasure. -**judi'cious** *a.* sensible, prudent. -**judi'ciously** *adv,* . - **judi'ciary** *n.* courts of law, system of courts and judges. [L. *judex, n. judicare, v. ,* fr. *jus,* law]

ju'do *n.* variation on *ju-jitsu.* [Jap.]

jug *n.* deep vessel for liquids; contents of one. -*v.t.* stew (*esp.* a hare) in a jug or jar (**jugged** *p.t./p.p.* **jugg'ing** *pres. p.*); (*sl.*) imprison. [orig. uncertain]

jug'gle *v.i.* play conjuring tricks, amuse by sleight of hand; practice deceit. -*v.t.* trick or cheat (out of). -*n.* a juggling. **jug'gler** *n.* -**jug'gler** *n.* -**jug'glery** *n.* [OF. *joglere,* L. *joculari,* jest]

jug'ular *a.* of or in the neck or throat. [L. *jugulum,* collar-bone]

juice *n.* liquid part of vegetable, fruit, meat; (coll.) gasoline or other source of power. -**juic'y** *a.* [L. *jus,* broth]

ju-jit'su, ju'jutsu *n.* Japanese art of wres-tling and self-defense. [Jap. fr. Chin. *jou-shu,* 'gentle art']

juke-box *n.* automatic slot-machine play-ing records. [orig. unknown]

ju'lep *n.* sweet drink; medicated drink. [Pers. *gul-ab,* rose-water]

July' *n.* seventh month of the year. [L. birth-month of Julius Caesar]

jum'ble *v.t.* mingle, mix in confusion. -*v.i.* move about in disorder. -*n.* a confused heap, muddle. [imit. orig.]

jump *v.i.* spring from the ground. -*v.t.* pass by jumping. -*n.* leap, sudden upward move-ment. -**jump'er** *n.* -**jump'y** *a.* nervous. [of It. orig,]

jum'per *n.* sailor's loose jacket; woman's loose outer garment slipped over the head and reaching to the hips. [earlier *jump* fr. F. *jupe,* petticoat]

junc'tion *n.* joining; place of joining; rail-way station where lines join. -**junc'ture** *n.* state of affairs; critical point. [L. *jungere, junct-,* join]

June *n.* sixth month of the year. [L. *Junius*]

jung'le (-ng-gl) *n.* tangled vegetation; land covered with it, *esp.* in India and the tropics; tangled mass. -**jung'ly** *a.* [Hind. *jangal,* Sans. *jangala,* desert]

jun'ior *a.* young person. -**junior'ity** *n.* [L. , comp, of *juuenis,* young]

juniper *n.* evergreen shrub with berries yielding oil of juniper, used for medicine and gin. [L. *juniperus*]

junk *n.* old rope; saltmeat; old odds and ends. -**jun'k food** *n.* food that is low in nutritional value, often highly processed or ready-prepared, and eaten instead of or in addition to well-balanced meals. [orig. unknown]

junk *n.* sailing vessel of the Chinese seas. [Port. *junco*]

junk'et *n.* curdled milk flavored and sweetened. *-v.i.* feast, picnic. [orig. a basket, fr. L. *juncus*, reed]

junt'a *n.* council in Spain, Italy; group of persons, *esp.* military, holding power after a revolution. [Sp.]

Ju'piter *n.* Roman chief of gods; largest of the planets. [L.]

jurid'ical *a.* relating to the administration of law, legal. **-jurisconsult'** *n.* one learned in law. **-jurisdic'tion** *n.* administration of justice; authority; territory covered by a court or authority. **-jurispru'dence** *n.* science of, and skill in, law. **-jurist** *n.* one skilled in law. **juris'tic** *a.* [L. *jus, jur-*, law]

jur'y *n.* body of persons sworn to render a verdict in a court of law; body of judges in a competition. **-jur'or** *n.* one who serves on a jury. [L. *jurare*, swear, fr. *jus*, law]

just *a.* upright, fair; proper, right, equitable. *-adv.* exactly, barely. **-just'ly** *adv.* **-justice** (-is) *n.* quality of being just. fairness; judicial proceedings; judge, magistrate. **-just'ify** *v.t.* show to be right or true or innocent; be sufficient grounds for. [L. *justus*, fr. *jus*, law, right]

jut *v.i.* project. *-n.* projection. [*jet*]

ju'venile *a.* young; of, or for, the youthful. *-n.* young person, child. **juvenil'ia** *n. pl.* early, youthful, writings. [L. *juvenilis-juvenis*, young]

juxtapose' (-z) *v.t.* put side by side. **-juxtaposi'tion** *n.* [L. *juxta*, beside]

K

Kai'ser *n.* emperor, *esp.* of Germany. [L. Caesar]

kale, kail *n.* cabbage, cole; (Scot.) broth. **kail'yard** *n.* kitchen garden. [L. *caulis*]

kaleid'oscope *n.* tube in which patterns are produced by reflection of pieces of colored glass as tube is rotated. **-kaleidoscop'ic** *a.* swiftly changing. [G. *kalos*, beautiful. *eidos*, shape]

kangaroo' *n.* Australian pouched mammal with very strong hind legs for jumping. [orig. uncertain]

kar'ma *n.* physical action; the law of cause and effect or ethical causation; self-created destiny. [Sans. = *action*]

kay'ak (ki-) *n.* skin-covered Eskimo canoe. [Eskimo]

keel *n.* lowest longitudinal timber, or steel substitute, on which a ship is built up. *-v.t.* turn keel up. capsize. [ON. *kjölr*]

keen *a.* sharp, vivid, acute, eager, strong. **-keenly** *adv.* [OE. *cene*]

keen *n.* funeral lament. *-v.i.* wail over the dead. [Ir. *caoine*]

keep *v.t.* observe, carry out; retain possession of, not lose; maintain; detain; cause to continue; reserve; manage. *-v.i.* remain good; remain; continue. *-n.* maintenance, food; central tower of a castle, a stronghold. **-keep'er** *n.* **-keep'ing** *n.* care, charge. posses-sion; harmony, agreement. **-keep'sake** *n.* thing treasured for giver's sake. [OE. *cepan*]

keg *n.* small cask. [ON. *kaggi*, cask]

kelp *n.* large seaweed; ashes of it for extraction of iodine. [ME. *culp*]

kenn'el *n.* house of shelter for dogs; place where dogs are bred or lodged; hovel. *-v.t.* put into a kennel. [F. *chenit*, fr. L. *canis*, dog]

ker'chief (-if) *n.* headcloth. [F. *couvrechef*, cover-head]

ker'osene *n.* lamp-oil or burning oil from petroleum or coal and shale. [G. *keros*, wax]

kes'trel *n.* small hawk. [F. *crécerelle*]

ketch *n.* two-masted or cutter-rigged sailing vessel. [earlier catch, of uncertain orig.]

ketch'up. *See* catsup.

ket'tle *n.* metal vessel with spout and handle, for boiling liquids. **-ket'tledrum** *n.* drum of parchment stretched over a metal hemisphere. [ON. ketill]

key *n.* instrument for moving the bolt of a lock; *fig.* anything that 'unlocks'; music, a set of related notes, fever to play a note of piano, organ, *etc.* **-key'board** *n.* set of keys on a piano, *etc.* **-key'-hole** *n.* hole into which key is inserted. **-key'light** *n.* in photography *etc.*. the main stage or studio light that gives the required overall intensity of illumination. **-key'note** *n.* note on which a musical key is based; dominant idea. **-key'pad** *n.* small keyboard with push buttons, as on a pocket calculator, remote control unit for a television, *etc.*; a data input device consisting of a limited number of keys, each with nominated functions. [OE. *caeg*]

kha'ki *a.* dull yellowish-brown. *-n.* khaki cloth, military uniform, [Pers. *khak*, dust]

kick *v.i.* strike out with the foot; be recalcitrant; recoil. *-v.t.* strike with the feet. *-n.* blow with the foot; recoil. [ME. *kiken*, of unknown orig.]

kid *n.* young goat; leather of its skin; (*sl.*) child. *v.t.* (*sl.*) to hoax. [ON. *kith*]

kid'nap *v.t.* steal (a child), abduct (a person). **-kid'naper** *n.* [*kid*, child, *nap*, nab]

kid'ney *n.* either of the pair of organs which secretes the urine; nature, kind. [orig. uncertain]

kill *v. t.* deprive of life, slay. [ME. *kellen*]

kiln *n.* furnace, oven. [OE. *cylen*, L. *culina*, kitchen]

kil'ogram *n.* weight of 1,000 grams. **-kil'ometer** *n.* **-kil'oliter** *n.* **-kil'owatt** *n.* electrical power of 1,000 watts. [G. *chilioi*, thousand]

kimo'no *n.* loose outer robe. [Jap.]

kin *n.* family, relatives. *-a.* related by blood. **-kin'dred** *n.* relatives. *-a.* related. **-kin'ship** *n.* **-kins'man** *n.*; **kins'woman** *fem.*; **kins'folk** *n.* [OE. cynn]

kind (kind) *n.* genus, sort, variety, class. *-a.* having a sympathetic nature, considerate, good, benevolent. **-kind'ly** *a.* kind, genial. **-kind'liness** *n.* **-kind'ly** *adj.* [OE. *gecynd*, nature]

kin'dergarten *n.* school for teaching young children by games, *etc.* [Ger. = children's garden; (coined by Froebel)]

kin'dle v.t. set on fire. -v.i. catch fire. -**kind'ling** n. act of lighting; small wood to kindle fires. [ON. kynda]

kinemat'ic (ki-) a. relating to pure motion. -n. pl. science of this. -**kinemat'ograph** see **cinematograph.** -**kinet'ic** a. of motion in relation to force. -n. pl. science of this, [G. kinein, move]

king n. male sovereign ruler of an independent state; piece in the game of chess; card in each suit with a picture of a king. -**king'dom** n. state ruled by a king. realm, sphere. [OE. ying]

kiosk n. small open pavilion; covered stall. [Turk. kioshk]

kis'met n. fate, destiny. [Turk. qismat]

kiss n. caress with the lips. -v. t. -v.i. exchange kisses. [OE. cyssan]

kit n. wooden tub; outfit; personal effects, esp. of traveller. -**kit'-bag** n. bag for soldier's or traveler's kit. [orig. uncertain]

kitch'en n. room used for cooking. -**kitch'en-garden** n. garden for vegetables, fruit. -**kitch'enmaid** n. **kitch'ener** n. cooking-range. **kitchenette** n. small compact kitchen. [OE. cycene]

kite n. bird of prey; light frame flown in wind. [OE. cyta]

kitt'en n. young cat. [var. of F. chaton, dim. of chat, cat]

ki'wi n. New Zealand wingless bird, the Apteryx. [Maori]

kleptoma'nia n. morbid tendency to steal for the sake of theft. -**kleptomaniac** n. [G. kleptes, thief]

knack (n-) toy, trifle; acquired faculty for doing something adroitly; trick. [orig. uncertain]

knap (nap) v.t. break off with snapping sound; hammer to pieces; rap. [Du. knappen, crack]

knap'sack (n-) n. soldier's, traveler's, bag to strap to back. [Du. knapzak]

knave (na-) n. rogue; at cards, lowest court card, jack. -**kna'very** n. -**kna'vish** a. [orig. boy, OE. cnafa]

knead v.t. work up into dough; work, massage. [OE. enedan]

knee (n-) n. joint between the thigh and lower leg; corresponding joint in animals; part of a garment covering the knee. -**knee'cap** n. (also **kneepan** n.) knee, protective covering for a bone in the front of the knee. [OE. cneow]

kneel (n-) v.i. fall or rest on the knees. [OE. cneowlian. cp. knee]

knell (-n-) n. sound of a bell, esp. at a funeral or after a death. [OE. cynll]

knife (n-) n. (knives pl.) cutting blade in a handle. -v.t. cut or stab with a knife. **knife'board** n. board for cleaning knives [OE. cnif]

knight (nit) n. person of a rank below baronet, given the right to prefix Sir to his name; military follower, a champion; piece in the game of chess. -v. t. make (person) a knight. -**knight er'rant** n. knight wandering in search of adventure. -**knighthood** n. -**knight'age** n. the knights; list of them. -**knight'ly** a. [OE.

cniht, youth]

knit (n-) v.t. form a fabric by putting together a series of loops in wool, or other yarn; make close or compact. -v.i. unite. [OE cyntian]

knob (n-) n. rounded lump, esp. at the end or on the surface of anything. -**knobb'y** a. [of Teutonic origin; cp. Ger. knopf, button]

knock (n-) v.t. strike, hit. -n. blow, rap. -**knock'er** n. who or what knocks; metal appliance for knocking on a door. -**knock'-kneed** a. having incurved legs. -**knock-'out** n. boxer's finishing blow. [OE. cnocian]

knot (n-) n. twisting together of parts of two or more strings, ropes, etc. , to fasten them together; cockade, cluster; hard lump, esp. of wood where a branch joins or has joined in; measure of speed of ships, e.g. , ten knots means ten nautical miles per hour; difficulty. -v. t. tie with or in knots. [OE. enotta]

know v.t. be aware of, have information about, be acquainted with, recognize, have experience, understand. -v.i. have information or understanding. -**know'able** a. -**know'ing** a. that knows; cunning, shrewd. -**know'ingly** adv. -**knowledge** (nol-) n. knowing; what one knows; all that is or may be known. -**knowl'edgeable** (nolij-) a. intelligent, well-informed. [OE. cnawan]

knuc'kle (nuc-kl) n. bone at a finger joint. -v.i. knuckle down, to put the knuckles on the ground in playing marbles; yield -v. t. strike with the knuckles. [ME. knokel]

Koran (kor'an, koran') n. sacred book of Islam. [Arab. qur'an, reading]

ko'sher a. of food, etc.. fulfilling the Jewish law. -n. kosher food or shop. [Heb. kosher, right]

Krem'lin n. citadel esp. in Moscow; government of Russia. [Russ. kreml]

ku'dos n. credit, prestige. [G.]

kyr'ie (kir-ie. kir'i) n. form of Greek prayer; part of Mass in R. C. church. [G. kyrie, eleison, Lord, have pity]

L

la'bel n. slip of paper, metal. etc., fixed to an object to give some information about it. -v.t. affix a label to; (fig.) a descriptive phrase associated with a person. [OF, narrow strip]

la'bial a. of the lips; pronounced with the lips. -n. sound so pronounced: letter representing it. [L. labium, lip]

la'bile a. likely to slip, err, lapse; unstable (chem) [L. labilis, labi]

la'bor (-her) n. exertion of the body or mind; task; pains of childbirth workmen collectively. -v.i. work hard; strive; maintain normal motion with difficulty; esp. of a ship, be tossed heavily. -v.t. elaborate; stress to excess. -**La'bor Day** n. (in the U.S. and Canada) a public holiday in honor of labor, held on the first Monday in September. -**la'borer** n. one who labors, esp. a man doing manual work for wages. -**laborious** a. hard-working: toilsome. **labor'iously** adv. -**lab'oratory** n. place set apart for scientific investigations or for manufacture of chemicals. [L. labor, toil]

Lab'rador n. breed of large, smooth-coated retriever dog. also **Labrador retriever** n. [Labrador]

labyrinth v.i. network of passages in which it is hard to find the way, a maze. **labyrin'thine** a. [G. labyrinthos]

lace n. cord to draw edges together, e. g., to tighten shoes, stays, etc.; ornamental braid; fine open work fabric, often of elaborate pattern. -v.t. fasten with laces: intertwine; flavor with spirit. [L. laqueus, noose]

lack n. deficiency, want. -v.t. be without, or poorly supplied with, [of Teutonic original]

lack'ey n. footman; menial attendant; obsequious person. -v.t. be, or play the, lackey to. [F. laquais]

laconic a. using, or expressed in, few words. **-lacon'ically** adv. **-lacon'icism** n. [G. Lakonikos, Spartan]

lac'quer n. hard varnish made from lac. -v. t. coat with lacquer. [Port. lacre, sealing-wax, fr. lac, q.v.]

lacrosse' n. ball-game played with long-handled rackets. [F. (jeu de) la crosse, the crook]

lac'tic a. of milk. **-lacta'tion** n. secreting of milk. **-lae'teal** a. of milk. **-lac'tose** n. milk sugar. **-lac'tic a'cid**, acid got from sour milk, [L. lac, lact-, milk]

lad n. boy, young fellow; stripling. [ME., servant]

ladd'er n. appliance consisting of two poles connected by cross-bars (rungs) used as means of ascent. [OE. hlaeder]

la'dle n. spoon with a long handle and large bowl. -v.t. lift out with a ladle. **la'dleful** n. [OE. hladan]

la'dy n. woman of good breeding or social position; title of woman of rank; formerly, mistress, wife, love; polite term for any woman. **-our Lady**, Virgin Mary. **la'dylike** a. **-la'dyship** n. [OE. hloefdige, loaf-kneader]

lag v.i. go too slow, fall, behind. -n. (sl.) convict. **-lagg'ard** n. one who lags. -a. loitering, slow. [orig. obscure]

lagoon' n. salt-water lake, often one enclosed by a reef or an atoll. [F. lagu ne, fr. L. locus. lake]

lair (lar) n. resting-place of a wild animal. [OE. leger, couch]

laissez-faire (les-a-fer) n. leaving alone; principle of non-intervention. [F.]

lake n. large body of water surrounded by land. **-lake'let** n. small lake. **-lake'-dwelling**, n. prehistoric dwelling built on piles in a lake. [OE. lac, L. locus]

lamb (lam) n. young of the sheep; its meat; innocent or helpless creature. -v. i. of a sheep, to give birth to a lamb. **lambing** n. birth of lambs; shepherd's work tending the ewes and newborn lambs at this time. **-lamb'like** a. meek. [OE.]

lambaste' v.t. thrash; criticize, scold severely. [lanz and baste]

lame a. crippled in a limb, esp. leg or foot; limping; of an excuse, etc., unconvincing. v.t. make lame. **-lame duck** n. disabled person; useless political official. [OE. lama]

lament' n. passionate expression of grief, song of grief. -v.t. and i. feel or express sorrow (for). **-lamenta'tion** n. **-lam'entable** a. deplorable. [L. lamentum, cry of mourning]

lamp n. vessel holding oil to be burnt at a wick for lighting; various other appliances as sources of light. **lamp'black** n. pigment made from soot. [G. lampas]

lampoon' n. venomous satire on an individual, -v.t. write lampoons against. [F. lampon, fr. lampons, 'let us guzzle' refrain to scurrilous songs]

lamp'rey n. fish like an eel with a sucker mouth. [F. lamproie]

lance (-a-) n. horseman's spear. -v.t. pierce with a lance or lancet. **-lan'cet** n. pointed two-edged surgical knife. **lan'cer** n. cavalry soldier armed with a lance. [F.]

land n. solid part of the earth's surface; ground, soil; country; property consisting of land. -pl. estates. -v.i- come to land, disembark. -v. t. bring to land. **-land'ing** n. act of landing; platform between flights of stairs. **-land'locked** a. enclosed by land. **-land'lord** n. **-land'lady** fem. person who lets land or houses, etc.; master or mistress of an inn, boarding house, etc. **-land'lubber** n. person ignorant of the sea and ships. [OE.]

landscape n. piece of inland scenery; picture of it, **-land'scape-painter** n. **land'scape-gard'ening** n. laying out of grounds picturesquely. [Du. landschap]

lane n. narrow road or street; passage in a crowd of people. [OE.]

lang'uage (-ng-gw-) n. speech; words used by a people; words used in a branch of learning; style of speech. [F. langage, fr. L. lingua, tongue]

lang'uish (ng-gw-) v. i. be or become weak or faint; be in depressing or painful conditions; droop, pine. **-lang'uid** a. weak, faint, spiritless, dull. **-lang'uidly** adv. **-lang'uor** (-gur) n. faintness; want of energy or interest; tender mood; softness of atmosphere. **-lang'uorous** a. [F. languir]

lant'ern n. transparent case for a lamp or candle; erection on a dome or roof to admit light. **-lant'horn** n. lantern. **lant'ern-jaws** n. pl. long thin jaws, giving concave effect. [L. lanterns]

lap n. fold, flap; front of a woman's skirt as used to hold anything; seat or receptacle made by a sitting person's thighs; single turn of wound thread, etc.; round of a racecourse. -v.t. enfold, wrap round. **lap'dog** n. small pet dog. [OE. lappa]

lap v. t. drink by scooping up with the tongue; of waves, etc., to make a sound like an animal lapping. [OE. lapian]

lapa'roscope n. medical instrument consisting of a tube that is inserted through the abdominal wall and illuminated to enable a doctor to view the internal organs. **-lapa'roscopy** n. [G. lapara, flank]

lapel' n. part of the front of a coat folded back toward the shoulders. [lap]

lapse n. slip; mistake; fall from virtue; passing (of time, etc.). -v.i. fall away; come to an end, *esp.* through some failure. [L. *lapsus, slip*]

lap'wing *n.* plover. [OE. *hleapewince*]

lard *n.* prepared pig's fat. -*v.t.* insert strips of bacon; intersperse or decorate (speech with strange words, *etc.*) [F. = *bacon*]

lard'er *n.* store-room for meat and other food. [OF. *lardier*, bacon-tub]

large *a.* broad in range or area; great in size, number, *etc.*; liberal; generous. **large'ly** *adv.* [L. *largus*, copious]

lark *n.* frolic, spree. -*v.i.* indulge in one. **lark'y** *a.* [ME. *laik*, sport; ON. *leikr*]

lar'va *n.* (**lar'vae** *pl.*) insect in the stage between grub and caterpillar. -**lar'val** *a.* [L. = *ghost, mask*]

lar'ynx *n.* part of the throat containing the vocal chords. -**laryngi'tis** *n-* inflammation of this. [G.]

la'ser *n.* device for concentrating electromagnetic radiation or light of mixed frequencies into an intense, narrow concentrated beam. [fr. *light amplication by stimulaued emission of radiation*]

lash *n.* stroke with a whip; flexible part of a whip. -*v. t.* strike with a whip thong, *etc.* -t). *i.* aim a violent blow of a whip, *etc.* [orig. uncertain]

lash *v.t.* fasten or bind with cord, *etc.* [OF. *lachier*, lace]

lass'o *n.* rope with a noose for catching cattle, *etc.*, by throwing the noose over the head. -*v.t.* catch with a lasso. [Sp. *lazo*, fr. L. *laqueus*, noose]

last *n.* model of foot on which shoemaker shapes boots, *etc.* [OE. *loeste*]

last *a.* and *adv.* last person or thing. **last'ly** *adv.* -**last'post** (*mil.*) bugle call at retiring hour, sounded also at military funerals. [OE. *latost*, fr. late]

last *v. i.* continue, hold out, remain alive or unexhausted. [OE. *loestan*, follow, continue]

latch *v.t.* fasten with a latch. -*n.* fastening for a door, consisting of a bar, a catch for it. and a lever to lift it, small lock with spring action. -**latch'key** *n.* [OE. *loeccan*, catch]

late *a.* after the proper time, backward; far on in a period of time; that was recently but now is not; recently dead; recent in date; of a late stage of development. -*adv.* after the proper time; recently; at or till a late hour. -**late'ly** *adv.* not long since. [OE. *loet*, tardy]

lat'eral *a.* of or at the side. -**lat'erally** *adv.* [L. *lateralis*, fr. *latus*, later-, side]

la'tex (la-) *n.* milky plant-juice. [L.]

lath (lath) *n.* strip of wood. -**lath'y** *a.* like a lath; tall and thin. [OE. *loett*]

lathe *n.* machine for spinning an object while it is being cut or shaped. [orig. uncertain]

lath'er (-TH-) *n.* froth of soap and water; frothy sweat. -*v.t.* cover (chin) with lather. -*v.i.* form a lather. [OE. leather, foam, washing-soda]

Lat'in *a.* of the ancient Romans; of or in their language; speaking a language descended from theirs; of such people. -*n.* language of the ancient Romans. **latin'ity** *n.* manner of writing Latin; Latin style. -**lat'inism** *n.* word

of idiom imitating Latin. [L. *Latinus*, of Latium (the part of Italy which included Rome)]

lat'itude *n.* freedom from restriction; scope. (*geog.*) angular distance on a meridian reckoned North or South from the equator. -*pl.* regions, climes. [L. *latus*, wide]

latrine (-en) *n.* camp or barracks substitute for a toilet; any such toilet. [L. *latrina*, for *lavatrina*, lavatory]

laud *n.* praise, song of praise. -*v. t.* **laud'able** *a.* -**laud'ably** *adv.* -**lauda'tion** *n.* [L. *laus*, laud-]

laugh *v. i.* make the sounds instinctively expressing amusement or merri ment or scorn. -*n.* sound or act of laughing. -**laugh'able** *a.* funny. **laugh'ter** *n.* laughing. [OE. hliehhan]

launch *v.t.* hurl; set going; set afloat. *v. i.* enter on a course. -*n.* the setting afloat of a vessel. [F. *lancer*]

launch *n.* largest boat carried by a warship; large power-driven boat. [Sp. *lancha*]

laundress *n.* washerwoman. -**laun'dry** *n.* place for washing clothes, *esp.* as a business. -**laun'der** *v. t.* wash and iron, *etc.* -**launderette, laundromat** *n.* self-service laundry. [ME. *lavander*, L. *lavare*, wash]

la'va (la-) *n.* matter thrown out by volcanoes in fluid form and solidifying as it cools. [It., fr. L. *lavare*, wash]

lav'ender *n.* shrub with fragrant flowers; color of the flowers, a pale blue tinged with lilac. [Med. L. *livendula*]

lav'ish *a.* giving or spending profusely; very or too abundant. -*v.t.* spend, give, profusely. [OE. *lavasse*, deluge of rain]

law *n.* rule binding on a community; system of such rules; branch of this system; knowledge of it, administration of it; general principle deduced from facts; invariable sequence of events in nature. **law'ful** *a.* allowed by the law. -**law'yer** *n.* professional expert in law. -**law'-abiding** *a.* obedient to the laws. -**law'suit** *n.* carrying on of a claim in a court. [OE. *lagu*]

lawn *n.* fine linen. [*laon*, in France]

lawn *n.* stretch of carefully tended turf in a garden, *etc.* -**lawn'-mower** *n.* machine for cutting grass. -**lawn'-tennis** *n.* game played on a flat ground with a net across the middle. [earlier, *launde*, glade, fr. F. *lande*, moor]

lawyer. See law.

lay *v.t.* deposit on a surface, cause to lie; produce eggs. -**lay'er** *n.* one who lays; thickness of matter spread on a surface; one of several such; shoot fastened down to take root. -*v. t.* propagate plants by making layers. -**lay off**, cease; discontinue or suspend. [OE. *lecgan*]

lay *n.* minstrel's song, ballad. [F. *lai*]

lay *a.* not clerical; of or done by persons not clergymen; non-professional. -**lay'man** *n.* [G. *laikos*, of the people]

layette (-et) *n.* clothes needed for a newborn child. [F. dim. of *laie*, box]

la'zy *a.* averse to work, indolent. -**la'zily** *adv.* -**la'ziness** *n.* -**laze** *v.i.* indulge in laziness. [orig. uncertain]

lea *n.* piece of meadow or open ground. [OE. *leah*, track of ground]

leach *v.t.* and *i.* remove or be removed from substance by percolating liquid; lose soluble substances by action of percolating liquid. -*n.* act or process of leaching; substance that is leached or constituents removed by leaching; porous vessel for leaching. [perh. *retch*, muddy ditch]

lead (led) *n.* soft, heavy grey metal; plummet or lump of this used for sounding depths of water; graphite in a pencil. -*pl.* piece of roof covered with the metal; strips of it used to widen spaces in printing, *etc.* -*v. t.* cover, weight or space with lead. -**lead'en** *a.* of or resembling lead. -**lead'-pencil** *n.* drawing, writing, implement of graphite enclosed in wood. [OE.]

lead (led) *v.t.* guide, conduct; persuade; serve as a way, conduct people. -*v. i.* be or go or play the first. -*n.* leading; example; front place. -**lead'er** *n.* one who leads; article in a newspaper expressing editorial views. -also reading artéicle. -**lead'ership** *n.* -**lead'ing question** *n.* question worded to prompt the answer desired; question which demands exploration of considerations not yet taken into account. [OE. *lcedan*]

leaf *n.* (**leaves** *pl.*) part of a plant's foliage consisting usually of a green blade on a stem; two pages of a book, *etc.*; thin sheet; flap or movable part of a table, *etc.* -**leaf'let** *n.* small leaf; single sheet, often folded, of printed matter for distribution, a hand-bill. [OE.]

league *n.* measure of road distance, about three miles. [OF. *legue*]

league (leg) *n.* agreement for mutual help; parties to it; federation of clubs, *etc.* -*v. t.* and *i.* combine in a league. **leag'uer** *n.* member of a league.

leak *n.* hole or break through which a liquid undesirably passes in or out. -*v. i.* let liquid in or out of; of a liquid, to find its way through a leak. [cp. Ger. *lech*]

lean *a.* not fat; thin. -*n.* lean part of meat, mainly muscular tissue. -**lean'ness** *n.* [OE. *hloene*]

lean *v.i.* bend or incline; tend (toward). *v.t.* cause to lean, prop (against). [OE. hliniani

leap *v.i.* spring from the ground. -*v. t.* spring over. -*n.* jump. -**leap'-frog** *n.* game in which a player vaults over another bending down. -**leap'-year** *n.* year with February 29th as an extra day. [OE. *hleapan*]

learn *v. t.* gain skill or knowledge by study, practice or being taught. -*v. i.* gain knowledge; be taught; find out. **learn'ed** *a.* showing or requiring learning. [OE. *leornian*]

lease *n.* a contract by which land or property is given for a stated time by an owner to a tenant, usually for a rent. -*v. t.* take or give the use of by a lease. -**lease'hold** *n.* -**less'or** *n.* granter of a lease. -**less'ee** *n.* one to whom a lease is granted. [OF. *lais*, fr. *laisser*, leave]

leash *n.* thong for holding dogs; set of three animals. [F. *laisse*]

least *a.* smallest. -*n.* smallest one. -*adv*, in smallest degree. [OE. *læst*]

leath'er (leTH'-) *n.* skin of an animal prepared for use. -**leath'ern** *a.* of leather. -**leath'ery** *a.* tough. [OE. *lether*]

leave *v.t.* go away from; deposit; allow to remain; depart without taking; bequeath. -*v.i.* go away, set out. (left, p.t./p.p. - leaving, press). [OE. *loefan*]

leave *n.* permission; permission to be absent from duty. [OE. *leaf*]

lec'tern *n.* reading-desk in church. [OF. *letrin*, fr. L. *legere*, to read]

lect'ure *n.* discourse for the instruction of an audience; speech of reproof. -*v.t.* reprove. -*v.i.* deliver a discourse. **lect'urer** *n.* -**lect'ureship** *n.* appointment as lecturer. [L. *lecture*, reading]

ledge *n.* narrow flat surface projecting from a wall, cliff, *etc.*; ridge or rock below the surface of the sea. [ME. *legge*]

ledg'er *n.* book of debit and credit accounts, chief account book of a firm. [orig. a (church) book lying permanently in one place, fr. ME. *liggen*, lie]

lee *n.* shelter; side of anything, *esp.* a ship, away from the wind. -**lee'-shore** *n.* shore on lee-side of ship. -**lee-side** *n.* sheltered side (of ships, *etc.*). [OE. *hleo*]

leech *n.* blood-sucking worm; (formerly) physician. [OE. *loece*]

leer *v.i.* glance with malign, sly, or immodest expression. -*n.* such glance. [orig. uncertain]

lees *n. pl.* sediment of wine, *etc.* [F. *lie*]

left *a.* denotes the side, limb, *etc.*, opposite to the right; (seeright). -*n.* left hand or part. -(pol.) Socialist, democratic, party; their more extreme sections. -**left'ist** *n. adj.* on or towards the left. -**left'-handed** *a.* having more power, skill, in the left hand. [OE. *lyft*, weak]

leg *n.* one of the limbs on which a person or animal walks, runs, or stands; support resembling this; part of a garment covering a leg. -**legg'ing** *n.* (usu. in *pl.*) covering of leather or other material for the leg. [ON. *leggr*]

leg'acy *n.* anything left by a will; thing handed down to a successor. [L. *legare*, bequeath, fr. *lex, leg-,* law]

le'gal *a.* of, appointed or permitted by, or based on, law. -**le'gally** *adv.* -**legal'ity** *n.* -**le'galize** *v.t.* to make legal. **legalization** *n.* -**le'gal ten'der**, money which can legally be used in paying a debt. [L. *legalis*, fr. *lex,* law]

legatee' *n.* one who receives a legacy. [irregularly fr. *legacy*]

leg'end *n.* traditional story or myth; traditional literature; inscription. **legendary** *a.* [L. *legenda*, be read]

legible (-j-) *a.* easily read. -**legibil'ity** *n.* -**leg'ibly** *adv.* [L. *legere*, read]

le'gion *n.* body of infantry in the Roman army; various modern military bodies; association of veterans; large number. -**le'gionary** *a.* and *n.* [L. *legio*, fr. *legere*, levy]

leg'islator (-j-) *n.* maker of laws. -**leg'islature** *n.* body that makes laws. [L. *legislator*, proposer of laws]

legit'imate (-j-) *a.* lawful, proper, regular; born in wedlock. [L. *legitimus*, fr. *lex, leg-,* law]

lei'sure *n.* freedom from occupation, spare time. [F. *loisir*, fr. L. *licere*, be lawful]

lem'on *n.* pale-yellow fruit with acid juice; tree bearing it; its color. **lemonade'** *n.* drink made from lemon juice. **-lem'on y** *a.* [F. *limon*, lime]

lend *v. t.* give the temporary use of, let out for hire or interest; give, bestow. **-lends** itself to, is adapted to. **-lend'er** *n.* [OE. *laenan*]

length (-th) *n.* quality of being long; measurement from end to end; long stretch; piece of a certain length. **length'en** *v.t.* and *i.* - **length'wise** *a.* and *adv.* **-length'y** *a.* - **length'ily** *adv.* -at length, at last. [OE. *lengthu*]

le'nient *a.* mild, being without severity. [L. *lenis*, mild]

lens (-z) it. **len'ses** *pl.* piece of glass with one or both sides curved, used for concentrating or dispersing light in cameras, spectacles, telescopes, *etc.*; combination of such glasses in an instrument. **-lentic'ula** *n.* small lens; freckle. **-lentic'ular** *a.* like a lens; double-convex. **-also len'tiform** *a.* **-len'toid** *a.* lens-shaped. [L. *lentil* (fr. its shape)]

Lent *n.* period of fasting from Ash Wednesday to Easter-Eve (40 days). [OE. *lencten*, Spring]

lent'il *n.* eatable seed of a leguminous plant. **-leintic'ular** *a.* like lentil. [F. *lentille*, dim. fr. L. *lens*, lentil]

Le'o *n.* the lion, 5th sign of Zodiac, which sun enters c. 22nd July; constellation. **le'onine** *a.* like a lion. [L. *leo*, lion]

leop'ard (lep') *n.* large carnivorous animal with spotted coat. **-leop'ardess** fem. [G. *leopardos*, lionpard]

lep'er *n.* one suffering from leprosy; outcast. **-lep'rosy** *n.* disease forming silvery scales on the skin and eating away parts affected. **-lep'rous** *a.* [G. *lepis*, scale]

les'bian *a.* homosexual (of women). **lesbianism** *n.* [island of Lesbos]

le'sion *n.* wound, injury. [L. *laedere*, hurt]

less *a.* comp. of little; not so much. **-adv.** to smaller extent or degree. **-pron.** less amount or number. **-prep.** after deductions, minus. **-less'en** *v. t.* make less, diminish. **-less'er** *a.* [OE. *laessa*, less]

less'on *n.* portion of Scripture read in church; something to be learnt by a pupil; part of a course of teaching; experience that teaches. **-v. t.** teach, discipline. [F. *lecon*, L. *lectio*, reading]

let *v.t.* allow, enable, cause to; allow to escape; grant use of for rent, lease. **-v. i.** be leased. [OE. *loetan*]

let *v.t.* hinder. **-n.** hindrance; in games, an obstruction of a ball or player cancelling the stroke. **-let alone'**, not to mention; not interfere with. **-let down'**, disappoint, desert, fail. **-let go'**, cease to hold. **-let off**, withhold punishment. **-let on'** (*sl.*) pretend; disclose (secret, *etc.*; let out', make a way of escape for. [OE. *lettan*]

le'thal *a.* deadly, fatal. [L. *lethalis*]

leth'argy *n.* drowsiness, apathy, want of energy or interest. **-lethar'gic** *a.* lethargically *adv.* [G. *lethargia*]

lett'er *n.* one of the symbols with which words are written; a written message. **-pl.** literature, knowledge of books. *v.t.* mark with letters. **-lett'ered** *a.* learned. **lett'erpress** *n.* matter printed from type [F. *lettre*, fr. L. *littera*]

lett'uce (-tis) *n.* salad plant with milky juice. [L. *lactuca*, fr. *lac*, milk]

leu'cocyte *n.* white corpuscle of blood or lymph. [G. *leukos*, whiter]

leukemia, leukaem'ia *n.* a progressive blood disease characterized by an excessive number of white corpuscles. [G. *leukos*, white]

Levant' *n.* eastern part of the Mediterranean and the adjoining countries; wind of those regions. **-Levant'ine** *n.* [F. *levant*, rising, east]

lev'el *n.* instrument for showing or testing a horizontal line or surface; horizontal passage in a mine; social or moral standard. **-a.** horizontal; even in surface; even in style, quality, *etc.* **-v.t.** make level, bring to the same level; lay low; aim (a gun). **-level-head'ed** *a.* not apt to be carried away by emotion or excitement. [L. *libella*, dim. of *libra*, balance]

le'ver *n.* bar used to apply force at one end by pressure exerted at the other, a point in between resting against a fixed support. **-le'verage** *n.* action or power of a lever. [L. *levare*, raise]

levitation *n.* power of raising a solid body into the air by annulling gravitational pull. **-lev'itate** *v. t.* and *i.* to make lighter. [L. *levis*, light]

lev'y *n.* act of collecting taxes or enrolling troops; amount or number levied. **-v. t.** raise or impose by compulsion. [F. *lever*, raise]

lewd *a.* indecent. [OE. *loewede*, lay, layman]

lex'icon *n.* dictionary. **-lexicog'raphy** *n.* compiling of dictionaries. **-lexicog'rapher** *n.* [G. *lexikon* (*biblion*), word (book)]

li'able *a.* subject (to), exposed (to), answerable. **-liabil'ity** *n.* state of being liable. **-pl.** debts. [F. *lier*, bind]

liai'son *n.* connecting link; illicit love. [F.]

liar. *See* lie.

li'bel *n.* written, published, statement damaging to a person's reputation. **-v.t.** write, publish, a libel against. [L. *libellus*, dim. of *liber*, book]

lib'eral *a.* generous; open-minded; of a political party, favoring changes making towards democracy. **-n.** one of such a party. [L. *liber*, free]

lib'erty *n.* freedom. **-lib'erate** *v.t.* set free. [L. *liber*]

libidinous *a.* lustful. **-libi'do** *n.* (*psych.*) emotional urge behind human activities, *e. g.*, sex. [L. *libido*, lust]

Li'bra *n.* the Balance 7th. sign of zodiac, which sun enters c. Sept. 22nd, zodiacal constellation; pound weight. [L.]

li'brary *n.* collection of books; place where the books are kept; reading or writing room in a house. **-librar'ian** *n.* keeper of a library. **-librar'ianship** *n.* [L. *liber*, book]

librett'o *n.* book of words of an opera. **librett'ist** *n.* [It. = little book]

li'cense *n.* leave, permission; formal permission; document giving it; excessive liberty; dissoluteness; writer's or artist's transgression of the rules of his art (often poetic license). -li'cense *v. t.* grant a license to. -licen'tious *a.* sexually immoral. [L. *licentia*, fr. *licere*, be allowed]

lice *See* louse.

lick *v.t.* pass the tongue over; (*sl.*) beat. *n.* act of licking. [OE. *liccian*]

lid *n.* movable cover; cover of the eye, the eyelid. -lidd'ed *a.* [OE. *hlid*]

lie *v.i.* be horizontal or at rest; be situated; recline. -*n.* direction; state (of affairs, *etc.*). [OE. *licgan*]

lie *v.i.* make a false statement. -*n.* untrue statement. -li'ar *n.* [OE, *leogan*]

lien *n.* right to hold property until a claim is met. [F. = *bond*]

lieu *n.* in lieu of, instead of. lieuten'ant *n.* substitute; junior army or navy officer. [F. fr. L. *locus*, place]

life *n.* lives *pl.* active principle of the existence of animals and plants, animate existence; time of its lasting; history of such an existence; manner of living; vigor, vivacity. -life'-belt *n.* -life'-jacket *n.* life'-preserv'er *n.* devices to keep one afloat in water. -life'-blood *n.* blood on which life depends. -life'boat *n.* boat for rescuing shipwrecked persons. -life'buoy *n.* buoy to support a person in water. -life'-class *n.* art class with living models. -life'-cycle *n.* successive stages of an organism through a complete generation. -life-guard *n.* bodyguard. rescuer of bathers in difficulties. life'less *a.* [OE. *lif*]

lift *v.t.* raise to a higher position. -*v.i.* rise. -*n.* act of lifting; journey as a passenger in someone else's vehicle, given free of charge; in Britain, elevator. [ON. *lypta*]

lig'ament *n.* band of tissue joining bones. -lig'ature *n.* thread for tying up an artery. [L. *ligare*, bind]

light *a.* of, or bearing, little weight; gentle; easy, requiring little effort; trivial. -*adv.* in a light manner. -light'*v.i.* get down from a horse or vehicle; come by chance (upon). -light'en *v.t.* reduce or remove a load, *etc.* -light'-fing'ered *a.* thievish. -light'-hand'ed *a.* having a light touch. —light'-headed *a.* delirious, giddy. [OE. *leoht*]

light *n.* natural agent by which things are visible; source of this; window; mental vision; light part of anything. -*a.* bright; pale, not dark-*v.t.* set burning; give light to. -*v.i.* take fire; brighten. light'en *v.t.* give light to. -light'ning *n.* visible discharge of electricity in the atmosphere. -light'house *n.* tower with a light to guide ships. [OE. *leoht*]

lighter *n.* large boat used for loading and unloading ships. [*light*]

like *a.* similar, resembling. -*adv.* in the manner of. -*pron.* similar thing. -like'ly *a.* probably true; hopeful, promising. *adv.* probably. -like'ness *n.* quality of being like: portrait. -like'wise *adv.* in like manner. [OE. *gelic*, similar]

like *v.t.* to find agreeable. -*v.i.* to be pleasing. -like'able *a.* [OE. *lician*, please]

li'lac *n.* shrub bearing pale violet flowers; their color. -*a.* of this color. [OF. Pers. *lilak*, blue]

lilt *v.t.* and *i.* sing merrily. -*n.* rhythmical effect in music. [ME. *lulten*, strike up loudly]

lil'y *n.* bulbous flowering plant. lilia'ceous *a.* -li'ly of the valley, plant with fragrant small white bells. [L. *liliurn*]

limb *n.* arm or leg; branch of a tree. [OE. *tim*]

limb *n.* edge of the sun or moon. [L. *limbus*, edge]

lim'ber *n.* detachable front part of a guncarriage. -*v.t.* attach the limber to (a gun). [orig. uncertain]

limber *a.* lithe, supple. [orig. uncertain]

lime *n.* sticky substance used for catching birds; alkaline earth from which mortar is made. -*v.t.* smear, or catch, with lime. treat (land) with lime. [OE. *lim*]

lime *n.* acid fruit like a lemon. [F.]

limit *n.* boundary; utmost extent or duration. -*v.t.* restrict, bound. -limita'tion *n.* -lim'itable *a.* [L. *limes*, *limit*-, boundary]

limousine' (-zen) *n.* closed type of automobile with the top projecting over the driver's seat. [F. fr. hood worn by natives of province of Limousin]

limp *a.* without firmness or stiffness. [orig. uncertain]

limp *v.i.* walk lamely. -*n.* limping gait. [orig. uncertain]

line *n.* linen thread; any cord or string; wire; stroke made with a pen, *etc.*; long narrow mark; continuous length without breadth; row; series; course; province of activity; trade or business. -*v. t.* cover inside; mark with a line or lines; bring into line. -li'ning *n.* covering for the inside of a garment, *etc.* -lin'eage *n.* descent from, or the descendants of an ancestor. [OE.]

lin'en *a.* made of flax. -*n.* cloth made of flax; linen articles collectively. [L. *linum*, flax]

li'ner *n.* large passenger ship or airplane. [*line*]

ling'er (-ng-g) *v.i.* tarry, loiter; remain long. [OE. *lengan*, prolong]

linge'rie *n.* linen goods, *esp.* women's underwear. [F.]

liniment *n.* embrocation. [L. *linimentum*, fr. *linere*, smear]

link *n.* ring of a chain; connection. -*v.t*, join with, or as with, a link. -*v.i.* be so joined. -link'up *n.* establishing of a connection or union between objects, groups, organizations, *etc.*; connection or union established. [of ON. orig.]

link *n.* torch. [orig. uncertain]

links *n. pl.* undulating ground near sea; golfcourse. [OE. *hlinc*]

lino'leum *n.* floorcloth surfaced with hardened linseed oil. -linocut *n.* engraving on linoleum instead of wood; print from this. [L. *linum*, flax, *oleum*, oil]

li'notype *n.* machine for producing lines of words cast in one piece; line of type so cast. [line-of-type]

lin'seed *n.* flax seed. [L. *linum*, flax]

lint *n.* soft material of fluffed-up linen; fluff; scraps of thread. [ME. *linnet*]

lint'el *n.* top piece of a door or window. [OF.]

li'on *n.* large animal of the cat tribe; person of importance. -**li'oness** *fem.* **li'onize** *v.t.* treat as a celebrity. [F., fr. L. *leo, leon-*]

lip *n.* either edge of the mouth; edge or margin; (*sl.*) insolence. -**lipp'ed** *a.* -**lip'-service** *n.* insincere devotion. -**lip'stick** *n.* cosmetic in stick form for coloring lips. [OE. *lippa*]

lipo- *prefix* fat, as in **lipoid** *a.* fat-like. [G. *lipos*, fat]

liq'uid *a.* fluid, not solid or gaseous: bright, clear. -*n.* a liquid substance. **liq'uefy** *v. t.* and *i.* [L. *liquere*, be clear]

liquidate *v. t.* pay (debt); arrange the affairs of, and dissolve (a company *sl.*) put out of action, wipe out. [L. *liquere*, be clear]

liq'uor (lik'er) *n.* liquid, *esp.* alcoholic one for drinking. -**liqueur** (likur) *n.* alcoholic liquor flavored and sweetened. [L. *liquere*, be clear]

liq'uorice, licorice (-kur-is) *n.* black substance used in medicine and as a sweet-meat; plant or its root, from which the substance is obtained. [fr. G. *glykus*, sweet, and *rhiza*, root]

lisp *v.t.* and *i.* speak with faulty pronunciation of the sibilants; speak falteringly. *n.* a lisping. [OE. *awlyspian*] **list** *n.* border or edge of cloth; strips of cloth, *esp.* used as material for slippers. *pl.* space for tilting. [OE. *lisle*]

list *n.* roll or catalogue. -*v. t.* write down in a list. [list, *v.s.*] **list** *v. t.* desire; of a ship, incline, lean to one side. -*n.* desire; inclination of a ship. -**list'less** *a.* indifferent, languid. **list'lessly** *adv.* (OE. *lystan*, please]

list'en (lis'en) *v. i.* try to hear, give attention in order to hear. -**listen-in** *v. i.* listen to a radio broadcast. -**list'ener** *n.* (OE. *hlystan*]

lit'any *n.* form of prayer. [G. *litaneia*]

lit'er *n.* measure of capacity in the French decimal system, equal to 2. 11 pints. [F.]

lit'eral *a.* of letters; exact as to words; according to the sense of actual words, not figurative or metaphorical. -**lit'erally** *adv.* [L. *litera*, letter]

lit'erary *a.* of, or learned in, literature. **li'terate** *a.* educated. -**lit'eracy** *n.* -**litera'tim** *adv.* letter for letter. -**lit'erature** *n.* books and writings of artistic value; production of these; profession of writers. [L. *litera*, letter]

lith'o- *prefix* pertaining to stone, as in **lith'ocarp** *n.* fossil fruit. -**lith'oglyph** *n.* engraving on stone, *esp.* on a gem. -**lith'ophyl** *n.* fossil leaf -**lith'ophyte** *n.* coral polyp. [G. *lithos*, stone]

lithog'raphy *n.* the making of drawings on stone for printing. -**lith'ograph** *n.* print so produced. -*v.t.* print thus. [G. *lithos*, stone, *graphein*, write]

lit'igate *v. i.* go to law. -**lit'igant** *a.* and *n.* -**litiga'tion** *n.* -**litig'ious** (-j-) *a.* fond of going to law. -**litig'iousness** *n.* [L. *litigare*, fr. lis, lit-, lawsuit]

lit'mus *n.* blue coloring-matter turned red by acids. -**lit'mus-paper** *n.* (ON. *litmose*, lichen (used in dyeing)]

litt'er *n.* portable couch; kind of stretcher for the wounded; straw, *etc.*, as bedding for animals; fragments lying about, untidy refuse of paper, *etc.*; young of an animal produced at a birth. -*v.t.* strew (a place) with litter; bring forth. [F. *litiere*, fr. *lit*, bed]

lit'tle *a.* small, not much. -*n.* small quantity. -*adv.* slightly. [OE. *lytel*]

lit'urgy *n.* form of public worship. **litur'gical** *a.* -**lit'urgist** *n.* state. [G. *leitourgia*, public worship]

live (liv) *v.i.* have life; pass one's life, continue in life; dwell; feed. -**liv'ing** *n.* state of being in life; means of earning livelihood; church benefice. [OE. *lifian*]

live (liv) *a.* living; flaming. -**live-stock** domestic animals *esp.* horses, cattle, pigs. -**live'-wire** *n.* wire carrying an electric current; (*sl.*) energetic person. [from alive) **livelihood** *n.* means of living. [OE. *liflad*, life-course]

live'ly *a.* brisk, active, vivid. -**live'liness** *n.* [OE. *liflic*, like life]

liv'er *n.* organ which secretes bile. *a.* liver-colored, reddish-brown. -**liv'erish** *a.* of liver; irritable. [OE. *lifer*]

liv'ery *n.* allowance of food for horses; distinctive dress of a person's servants. [F. *livrée*, handed over (orig. of any allowance)]

liz'ard *n.* four-footed, five-toed reptile with scaly body; saurian. [L. *lacertus*]

lla'ma *n.* Peruvian animal used as a beast of burden; its wool. (Peruv.)

load *n.* burden; amount usually carried at once. -*v. i.* put a load on or into; charge (a gun); weigh down. [OE. *lad*, way, journey]

loaf *n.* loaves *pl.* mass of bread as baked; cone of sugar. [OE. *hlaf*] **loaf** *v. i.* idle. -**loaf'er** *n.* [orig. uncertain **loam** *n.* fertile soil. [OE. *lam*]

loan *n.* thing lent; an act of lending. -*v.t.* lend. [ON. *lan*]

loath, loth (-th) *a.* unwilling. -**loath'ly** *a.* -**loath'some** *a.* disgusting. -**loathe** (-TH) *v. t.* abhor. [OE. *lath*, repulsive]

lobb'y *n.* corridor into which rooms open; pressure group, *esp.* one seeking influence on government. -*v. t.* and *i.* exert pressure in this way. [med. L. *lobium*]

lobe *n.* soft hanging part of the ear; any similar flap. [G. *lobos*, lobe of ear]

lob'ster *n.* shellfish with long tail and claws, which turns scarlet when boiled. [OE. *loppestre*]

lo'cal *a.* relating to place; of or existing in a particular place. -**local'ity** *n.* place, situation; district. -**lo'cally** *adv.* -**lo'calize** *v.t.* -**locate'** *v.t.* attribute to a place; find the place of. -**loca'tion** *n.* a placing; situation. [L. *locus*. place]

lock *n.* tress of hair. [OE. *loc*]

lock *n.* appliance for fastening a door, lid, *etc.*; mechanism for discharging a firearm; enclosure in a river or canal for moving boats from one level to another; close crowd of vehicles. -*v. t.* fasten with a lock; join firmly; embrace closely-*v. i.* become fixed or united. -**lock'er** *n.* small cup board with a lock. -**lock'jaw** *n.* tetanus. -**lookout** *n.* exclusion of workmen by employers as a means of coercion. -**lock'smith** *n.* one who makes and mends locks. -**lock'et** *n.* small pendant of precious metal for a portrait, *etc*. -lock-up *n*. place for housing prisoners, cars, *etc*. [OE. *loc*]

locomo'tive *a*. having the power of moving from place to place. -*n*. engine moving from place to place by its own power; railway engine. -locomo'tion *n*. action or power of moving from place to place. [fr. L. *loco*, from a place, and *moveri*, be moved]

lo'cust *n*. destructive winged insect; carobtree; its fruit, resembling a bean in shape. [L. *locusta*, lobster]

lode *n*. vein of ore. [*See* load]

lodge *n*. house for a shooting or hunting party; house at the gate of an estate; meeting-place of a branch of freemasons, *etc*.; the branch. -*v. t*. house; deposit. -*v. i*. live in another's house at a fixed charge; become fixed after being thrown. [F. *loge*]

loft *n*. attic; room over a stable; gallery in a church. -*v. t*. send (a golf-ball) high. -loft'y *a*. of great height; elevated. loft'ily *adv*. [ON. *lopt*, sky]

log *n*. unhewn portion of a felled tree; apparatus for measuring the speed of a ship; journal kept on board ship, *etc*., a log'-book *n*. -*v. t*. record, *usu*. as written data on a regular basis. -log'ger *n*. a lumberjack. [orig. uncertain]

log'arithm *n*. one of a series of arithmetical functions tabulated for use in calculation. -logarith'mic *a*. [G. *logos*, word, ratio, *arithmos*, number]

log'ic *n*. art of reasoning. -log'ical *a*. relating to logic; according to reason; able to reason well. [G. *logos*, word]

loin *n*. part of the body on either side between ribs and hip. [OF. *loigne*, fr. L. *lumlus*]

loi'ter *v.i*. waste time on the way, hang about. -loi'terer *n*. [Du. *leuteren*]

loll *v.i*. sit or lie lazily; of the tongue, hang out. -*v.t*. hang out (the tongue). [imit. orig.]

lollipop *n*. a sweet. [child language]

lone *a*. solitary. -lone'ly *a*. alone; feeling sad because alone. -lone'liness *n*. lone'some *a*. [for *alone*]

long *a*. having length, *esp*. great length. *adv*. for a long time. -long-headed *a*. shrewd, intelligent. -long-run *n*. outcome, result. -longshoreman *n*. dock laborer. [OE. *long*]

long *v.i*. have a keen desire. -long'ing *n*. [OE. *langian*, grow long]

longevity (-j-) *n*. long existence of life. longe'vial *a*. [L. *longaevus-aevum*, age]

longitude *n*. distance of a place east or west from a standard meridian. longitu'dinal *a*. of length or longitude. [L. *longus*, long]

look *v. i*. direct or use the eyes; face; take care; seem; hope. -*n*. a looking; expression; aspect. -look'alike *n*. a person, *esp*. a celebrity, or thing that is the double of another. -look'ing glass *n*. mirror. -look af'ter, take care of. -look alive', hasten. -look'-out *n*. watch; place for watching; watchman. [OE. *locian*]

loom *n*. machine for weaving. [OE. *geloma*, tool] loom *v.i*. appear dimly, *esp*. with vague or enlarged appearance, or (fig.) out of the future. [orig. unknown]

loop *n*. figure made by a curved line crossing itself; similar rounded shape in a cord or rope,

etc., crossed on itself. *v.t*. form into a loop. -*v.i*. form a loop. [orig. uncertain]

loose *a*. not tight or fastened or fixed or exact or tense; slack; vague; dissolute. *v. t*. set free; unfasten; make slack. -*v.i*. shoot, let fly. -loose'ly *adv*. -loos'en *v.t*. make loose. -loose'ness *n*. [ON. *lauss*]

loot *n*. and *v.t*. plunder. [Hind. *lut*]

lop *v.t*. cut away twigs and branches; chop off. [OE. *loppian*] lop *v.i*. hang; imply. -lop'-ear *n*. drooping ear; rabbit with such ears. lopsi'ded *a*. with one side lower than the other, badly balanced. [orig. uncertain]

lord *n*. feudal superior; one ruling others; owner; God; title of peers of the realm. *v.i*. domineer. [OE. *hlafweard*, loaf-ward]

lore *n*. learning; body of facts and traditions. [OE. *lar*]

lose *v.t*. be deprived of, fail to retain; let slip; fail to get; be late for; be defeated in. -*v.i*. suffer loss. -loss *n*. a losing; what is lost; harm or damage resulting from losing. -los'er *n*. -lost *a*. [OE. *losian*, be lost]

lot *n*. one of a set of objects used to decide something by chance (to cast lots); fate, destiny; item at an auction; collection; large quantity. [OE. *hlot*]

lo'tion *n*. liquid for washing wounds, improving the skin, *etc*. [L. *lotio*]

lott'ery *n*- gamble in which part of the money paid for tickets is distributed to some owners of tickets selected by chance. [*lot*]

lott'o *n*. game of chance. [*lot*]

loud *a*. strongly audible; noisy; obtrusive. -loud'ly *adv*. -loud'speak'er *n*. device for magnifying sound. [OE. *hlud*]

lounge *v.i*. loll; move lazily. -*n*. place for, or a spell of, lounging; deep chair or sofa. [orig. uncertain]

louse *n*. lice *pl*. parasitic insect. -lous'y *a*. infested with lice; (fig.) bad, mean. [OE. *lus*]

lou'ver, **lou'vre** *n*. set of boards or slats set parallel and slanting to admit air without rain; ventilating structure of these. [OF. *lover*]

love (luv) *n*. warm affection; sexual passion; sweetheart; score of nothing. -*v. t*. have love for. -*v.i*. be in love. -lov'able *a*. -love'less *a*. -love'lorn *a*. forsaken by, or pining for, a lover. -love'ly *a*. beautiful, delightful. -lov'er *n*. -love'-apple *n*. tomato. -love'-bird *n*. small green parrot. [OE. *lufu*]

low *a*. not tall or high or elevated; humble; commonplace; vulgar; dejected; not loud. -low'er *v.t*. cause or allow to descend; diminish; degrade. -low'land *n*. low-lying country. -low'ly *a*. modest, humble. -low'liness *n*. -low'brow *n*. person not an intellectual. -*a*. -low'down *a*. mean, despicable. -*n*. inside information. [OE. *lah*]

loy'al *a*. faithful; true to allegiance. [F., fr. L. *legalis*, legal]

loz'enge *n*. diamond figure; small sweetmeat or tablet of medicine, formerly of this shape. [F. *losange*]

lub'ricate *v.t*. oil or grease; make slippery. -lu'bricant *n*. substance used for this. -lubrica'tion *n*. [L. *lubricate*, fr. *lubricus*, slippery]

lu'cid a. clear; easily understood. **lucid'ity** n. **-lu'cidly** adv. **-lu'cifer** n. morning star; Satan; match. [L. lucidus, fr. lux, light]

luck n. fortune, good or ill; chance. **luck'y** a. having good luck. **-luck'less** a. **-luck'ily** adv. fortunately. [Du. luk]

luge n. light Alpine sleigh for one. **-v.i.** [F.]

lugg'age n. traveler's baggage. [orig. uncertain]

lug'sail n. oblong sail fixed on a yard which hangs slanting on a mast. **-lugg'er** n. vessel with such sails. [orig. uncertain]

lull v.t. soothe with sounds, sing to sleep; make quiet. **-v.i.** become quiet. **-n.** brief time of quiet in storm or pain. **-lull'aby** (-bi) n. lulling song or sounds. [imit. origin]

lum'bar a. relating to the loins. **lumba'go** n. rheumatism in the loins. [L. lumbus, loin]

lum'ber v.i. move heavily; obstruct. **-n.** disused articles, useless rubbish; timber, esp. in planks. [orig. obscure]

lu'minous a. bright, shedding light. **-lu'minary** n. heavenly body giving light; person noted for learning. **luminos'ity** n. [L. lumen, lumin-, light]

lump n. shapeless piece, mass; swelling; sum covering various items. **-v.t.** throw together in one mass or sum. **-v.i.** move heavily. **-lump'ish** a. clumsy; stupid. **lump'y** a. [orig. uncertain]

lu'nar a. of the moon. **-lunar caustic**, nitrate of silver. [L. luna, moon]

lu'natic a. insane. **-n.** insane person. **lu'nacy** n. [L. luna, moon]

lunch n. meal taken in the middle of the day. **-lunch'eon** (-shn) n. lunch; midday banquet. [orig. uncertain]

lung n. light, spongy air-breathing organ. [OE. lungen]

lunge v.i. thrust with a sword, etc. **-n.** such thrust, or thrusting movement. [F. allonger, lengthen, stretch out]

lurch n. leave in the lurch, leave in difficulties, abandon (a comrade) [obs. card game of lurch]

lurch n. sudden roll to one side. **-v.i.** make a lurch. [orig. uncertain]

lure n. falconer's apparatus for recalling a hawk; something which entices, a bait. **-v.i.** recall (a hawk); entice. [F. leurre]

lu'rid a. ghastly, pale, glaring. **-lu'ridly** adv. [L. luridus, yellowish]

lurk v.i. lie hidden; be latent. **-lurk'er** n. **-lurk'ing** a. [orig. uncertain]

lush a. of grass, etc., luxuriant and juicy. **-n.** (sl.) habitually drunken person. [orig. uncertain]

lust n. sensual desire; passionate desire, v.i. have passionate desire. **-lust'ful** a. lust'y a. healthy, vigorous. **-lust'ily** adv. [OE. = pleasure]

lus'ter n. gloss, shine; splendid reputation, glory; glossy material. **-lus'trous** a. [L. lustrare, shine]

lux'ury n. possession and use of costly and choice things for enjoyment; enjoyable but not necessary thing; comfortable surroundings. **-luxu'rious** a. **-luxu'riously** adv. **-luxu'riate** v.i. indulge in luxury; grow rank; take delight (in). **-luxu'riant** a. growing profusely; abundant. **-luxu'riantly** adv. **-luxu'riance** n. [L. luxuria]

lye n. water made alkali with wood ashes, etc., for washing. [OE. leag]

lymph n. colorless animal fluid; matter from cowpox used in vaccination. **-lymphat'ic** a. of lymph; flabby, sluggish. **-n.** vessel in the body conveying lymph. [L. lympha, water]

lynch n. lynch law, procedure of a self appointed court trying and executing an accused person. **-v.t.** put to death without proper trial. [orig. uncertain]

lynx n. animal of cat tribe noted for keen sight. **-lynx-eyed** a. quick-sighted. [G.]

lyre n. instrument like a harp. **-lyr'ic, lyr'ical** a. relating to the lyre; meant to be sung; of short poems, expressing the poet's own thoughts and feelings; describing a poet who writes such poems. **-lyr'ic** n. **lyric poem.** **-lyricist** n. lyric poet. [G. lyra]

M

maca'bre (-a-ber) a. gruesomely imaginative. [F.]

macaro'ni n. Italian paste of wheat in long tubes. [It. maccheroni]

macaroon' n. small cake containing ground almonds. [It. maccherone]

mache'te n. W. Indian cutlass. [Sp.]

Machiavell'ian (mak-i-a-vell'-yan) a. crafty, unprincipled, in politics; dictated by expediency. [Machiavelli, It. statesman (d. 1527)]

machination (-kin-) n. plotting, intrigue. **-mac'hinate** v.i. lay plots.

machine' (-shen) n. apparatus combining the action of several parts, to apply mechanical force for some purpose; person like a machine from regulation or sensibility; controlling organization; bicycle, vehicle, automobile. **-v.t.** sew, print with a machine. **-machi'nery** n. parts of a machine collectively; machines. **-machi'nist** n. one who makes or works machines. **-machine'-gun** n. gun firing repeatedly and continuously by means of a loading and firing mechanisms [G. mechane]

mach'o (-ch-) a. denoting or exhibiting pride in characteristics believed to be typically masculine, as physical strength, sexual appetite, etc. **-n.** man who displays such characteristics. [Sp. = male]

mack'erel n. sea-fish with blue and silver barred skin. [F. maquereau]

macro- prefix great, long, as in **macrobiot'ic** a. long-lived. **-macrop'terous** a. long-winged. **-macru'rous** a. long-tailed. [G. makros, long, large]

macroscopic a. visible to the naked eye, opp. to microscopic. [G. makros, large, skopeein, to look at]

mad a. suffering from mental disease, insane; wildly foolish; excited; angry. [OE.]

mad'am n. polite form of address to a woman. [F. madame, my lady]

madd'er n. climbing plant; its root; dyestuff made from this. [OE. mædere]

madonn'a n. Virgin Mary; picture or statue of the Virgin Mary. (It.)

Maf'ia n. international secret criminal organization. [it.]

magazine' n. storehouse for explosives and the military stores; a periodical with stories and articles by different writers; an appliance for supplying cartridges automatically to a gun. [F. magasn, store, shop]

mag'ic (-j-) art of influencing events by controlling nature or spirits, any mysterious agency of power; witchcraft, conjuring. [G. magos]

magistrate (-j-) n. civil officer administering the law. -magiste'rial a. at or referring to a magistrate or master; dictatorial. -mag'istracy n. office of a magistrate; magistrates collectively. [L. magister, master]

magnanimous a. great souled, above resentment, etc. -magnanim'ity n. [fr. L. magnus, great, animus, soul]

magne'sium n. metallic chemical element. -magne'sia n. white powder compound of this used in medicine. [Magnesia, in Greece]

mag'net n. piece of iron having the properties of attracting iron and pointing north and south when suspended; lodestone. -magnet'ic a. -magnet'ically adv. -mag'netism n. magnetic phenomena; the science of this; personal chann or power of attracting others. [G. magnes, Magnesian stone. (u.s.)]

magnificent a. splendid, stately, imposing, excellent. -magnif'icently a. -magnificence n. [magnify]

mag'nify v.t. exaggerate; make greater; increase the apparent size, as with a lens; praise. [L. magnus, great, facere, make]

magnitude n. size; extent; amount; importance. [L. magnitudae]

mag'num n. wine bottle holding two quarts. [L. magnus, great]

mahog'any n. tropical American tree; its reddish-brown wood. [W. Ind.]

maid'en n. young unmarried woman. -a. unmarried; of, or suited to, a maiden; having a blank record. -maid n. young unmarried woman; woman servant. [OE. mægden, girl]

mail n. armor made of interlaced rings or overlapping plates. -mail'ed a. covered with mail. [L. macula, mesh]

mail n. bag of letters; letters conveyed at one time; official despatch of letters. -v.t. send by mail. -mail'box n. public box for depositing mail that is being sent out; box at a house or business to which mail is delivered for the occupier. -mail'man n. one who delivers mail. [OF. male, leather bag]

maim v.t. cripple, mutilate. [OF. mahaignier, mutilate]

main n. open sea, chief matter; strength, power. -a. chief, principal, leading. -maindeck n. ship's chief deck. -main'land n. stretch of land which forms the main part of the country. -main'ly adv. -main'mast n. chief mast in a ship. -main'sail n. lowest sail of a mainmast. -main'spring n. chief spring of a watch or clock. -main'stay n. rope from top of mainmast to deck; chief support. -main'-yard n. lower yard on main-mast. [OE. mægen, strength]

mainframe n. in a large computer, the central processing unit.

maintain' v.t. carry on; preserve; support, sustain, keep up; keep supplied; affirm. -maintain'able a. -main'tenance n. [L. manu tenere, hold with the hand]

maize n. Indian corn, a cereal. [Sp. maiz, fr. Cuban]

maj'esty n. stateliness; kingship or queenship. -majes'tic a. -majes'tically adv. [L. majestas]

major a. greater; out of minority. -n. one out of minority; officer in the army, ranking below lieutenant-colonel. -major'ity n. state of having reached the full legal age; the greater number; the larger party voting together; excess of the vote on one side. [L. = greater]

make v.t. construct; produce; bring into being-, establish; appoint; amount to; cause to do something; accomplish; reach; earn. -v.i. tend; contribute, of the tide, to raise. -n. style of construction, form, manufacture. -make-up n. constituents; style; cosmetics. make'-believe v.i. pretend. -n. -a. [OE. macian]

mal- prefix ill, badly, miss; not [L. male, ill] . -maladjust'ment n. faulty adjustment. -maladministra'tion n. faulty administration. -maladroit' a. clumsy, not dexterous. -mal'content a. actively discontented. -n. malcontent person. -malev'olent a. full of ill-will. -malev'olence n. -malforma'tion n. faulty information. -malnutri'tion n. faulty, inadequate. nutrition. -malprac'tice n. wrongdoing. -mal'treat v. t. treat ill, handle roughly. -maltreat'ment a.

mal'ady n. disease. [F. maladie]

malaise' n. vague discomfort, uneasiness. as in fever. [OF.]

mal'apropism n. laughable misuse of words, (Mrs. Malaprop, char. in play)

malar'ia (-Ar-) n. fever due to mosquito bites. -malar'ial n. -malar'ious n. [It. maléaria, bad air]

male a. of the begetting sex; of man or male animals. -n. male person or animal. [F. mdle, fr. L. masculus]

mal'ice n. action of ill-will. [L. malitia]

malign (-lin) a. hurtful. -v.t. slander, misrepresent. -malig'nant a. feeling extreme ill-will; of a disease, very virulent. [L. malignus]

maling'erer n. one who pretends illness to escape duty. -maling'er v.i. [OF. malingreux, beggar with artificial sores]

mall (mawl, mal) n. level shaded walk or avenue; urban shopping area with a variety of shops. [L. malleus, hammer]

mall'eable a. capable of being hammered into shape. -malleabil'ity n. [L. malleus, hammer]

mall'et n. hammer, usually of wood. [F. maillet, malleus, hammer]

malt n. grain used for brewing. -v. t. make into malt. [OE. mealt]

mamm'al a. animal of the type feeding their

young with their milk. -**mamma'lian** a. [L. *mamma*, breast]

mamm'oth n. extinct animal like an elephant. [Russ. *mamont*]

man n. (men *pl.*) human being; person: humanrace; adulthumanmale; man-servant; piece used in a game, *e.g.*, chess. -*v.t.* supply (a ship, *etc.*), with necessary men. -**man'ful** a. brave, resolute. -**man'fully** adv. -**man'hole** n. opening through which a man may pass. -**man'hood** n. -**mankind'** n. human beings in general. -**man'like** a. **man'ly** a. -**man'liness** n. -**mann'ish** a. manlike. -**man'hand'le** v.t. move by man-power; (*sl.*) knock about. [OE. *mann*]

man'acle n. fetter for the hand. -*v. t.* handcuff. [L. *manicula*, small sleeve]

man'age v.t. carry on, conduct; succeed in doing; handle; persuade. -*v.i.* conduct affairs. [It. *maneggiare*, train horses]

mandarin n. Chinese official; small sweet orange. [Port. *mandarim*]

man'date a. command of, or commission to act for another. **man'datary** n. holder of a mandate. **man'datory** a. [L. *mandatum*]

man'dible n. lower jaw bone; either part of a bird's beak. [OF. fr. L. *mandere*, chew]

man'dolin(e) n. stringed musical instrument like a lute. [F.]

mane n. long hair at the back of the neck of a horse, lion, *etc.* [OE. *manu*]

maneuv'er n. movement of troops or ships in war, stratagem. -*v.t.* cause to perform maneuvers. -*v.i.* perform maneuvers; employ stratagems, to work adroitly. [F.]

mange n. skin disease of dogs, *etc.* -**ma'ngy** a. [OF. *manjue*, itch]

man'ger (manjer) n. eating trough in a stable or byre. [F. *mangeoire*]

mang'le (mang'gl) v. t. hack, mutilate, spoil. (AF. *mahangler*]

man'grove n. swamp-growing tropical tree whose drooping shoots take root. [orig. uncertain]

ma'nia n. madness; prevailing craze. -**ma'niac** a. affected by mania. -n. mad person. -**mani'acal** a, [G.]

man'icure n. treatment of the nails and hands; person doing this professionally. -*v.t.* apply such treatment to. [L. *manus* hand, *cura*, care]

manifest a. clearly revealed, visible, undoubted. -*v.t.* make manifest. -n. list of cargo for the Customs. -**manifesta'tion** n. -**manifes'to** n. declaration of policy by a sovereign or commander or body of persons; any formal declaration of overall political intent. [L. *manifestos*]

man'ifold a. numerous, varied. -n. pipe with several outlets. -*v.t.* make copies of (a document). [*many* and *fold*]

manipulate v. t. handle; deal with skillfully; manage craftily. [L. *manipulus*, handful]

mannequin (or mann'ekin) n. live model employed by dressmakers, *etc.* [F.]

mann'er n. way a thing happens or is done; sort or kind; custom; style. -*pl.* social behavior. [F. *manière*]

man'or n. unit of land in the feudal period. -**man'or-house** n. residence of the lord of the manor. -**manor'ial** a. [F. *manoir*, L. *manere*, dwell]

man'sion n. large dwelling-house. [L. *mansio*]

man'tel n. structure enclosing a fireplace. -**man'telpiece** n. mantel or mantel-shelf. [var. of *mantle*]

man'tis n. locustlike insect. -**praying man'tis** n. mantis that crosses its forelegs as if in prayer. [G.]

man'tle n. loose cloak; covering; hood fixed round a gas jet for incandescent light. -*v.t.* cover; conceal. -*v.i.* become covered with scum; of the blood, rush to the checks; of the face, blush. -**mant'let** n. short mantle; moveable bullet-proof screen. [L. *mantellum*, cloak]

man'ual a. of or done with the hands. -n. handbook, text book; organ keyboard. [L. *manualis-manus*, hand]

manufacture n. making of articles or materials, *esp.* in large quantities for sale. -*v.t.* produce (articles), work up (materials) into finished articles. -**manufac'turer** n. owner of a factory. [F. fr. L. *manu facere*, make by hand]

manure' v.t. enrich land. -n. dung or other substances used for fertilizing land. [F. *manceuvrer*]

manuscript a. written by hand. -n. book, document, *etc.*, written by hand; copy of matter to be printed. [Med. L. *manuscriptum*]

man'y (men'i) a. numerous. -n. large number. [OE. *manig*]

map n. flat representation of the earth or some part of it, or of the heavens. -*v.t.* make a map of. [L. *mappa*, cloth]

ma'ple n. tree of the sycamore family, one kind yielding sugar. [OE. *mapel*]

mar v.t. spoil, impair. [OE. *mierran*]

mar'athon n. long-distance race. [*Marathon*, Greece]

maraud' v.t. and i. make a raid for plunder. -maraud'er n. [F. *marauder*]

mar'ble n. kind of lime stone capable of taking a polish; slab of this; small ball used in a game called marbles. -*v.t.* color so as to resemble veined marble. [L. *marmor*]

March n. third month of the year. [L. *martius* (*mensis*), (month) of Mars]

march n. border or frontier. -v. i. border. [F. *marche*] march v.i. walk with a military step; start on a march; go. -*v.t.* cause to march or go. -n. action of marching; distance marched in a day; tune to accompany marching. IF. *marcher*, walk]

mare n. female of the horse or other equine animal. -**mare's nest** n. fancied discovery. [OE. *mere*]

margarine (-g-) n. vegetable substance imitating butter, and containing vegetable and animal oils. [F.]

mar'gin (-j-) n. border or edge; amount allowed beyond what is absolutely necessary; blank space round a printed page. [L. *margo, margin-*]

marinade' v.t. soak (meat, fish) in wine

spices, etc., before cooking. -n. the marinading liquor. [F.]

marine' a. of the sea or shipping; used at sea. -n. shipping collectively; soldier serving on board a ship. -mar'iner n. sailor. [L. mare, sea]

marionette' n. puppet worked with strings. [F.]

mar'ital a. relating to a husband or marriage. [L. maritus, husband]

mar'itime a. bordering on the sea; connected with seafaring or navigation. [L. maritimus, fr. mare, sea]

mark n. something set up to be aimed at; sign or token; inscription; line, dot, scar, or any visible trace or impression. -v.t. make a mark on; indicate, be a distinguishing mark of, watch. -v.i. take notice. marks'man n. one skilled in shooting. -mark'er n. [OE. mearc]

mark n. German coin; various old coins. [orig. uncertain]

mark'et n. place or assembly for buying and selling; demand for goods; place or center for trade. -v.t. bring to or sell in a market. -mark'etable a. [L. mercari, mercat-, trade]

marl'ine (-in) n. two-strand cord. [Du. marlijn, fr. marren, bind]

marmalade n. orange preserve. [F. marmalade]

maroon' n. fugitive slave in the West Indies; marooned person. -v.t. leave on a desert island. [Sp, cimarron, wild]

marquee' (-ke) n. roof-like structure or awning, usu. at the entrance of a building; large tent. [F. marquise, lit. marchioness]

marquetry (-ket-) n. inlaid work of wood, ivory etc. [F. marqueterie]

marquise, mar'quess n. nobleman of rank next below a duke. -mar'quisate n. [OF. marchis, L. marca, boundary]

ma'rrow n. fatty substance inside bones. [OE. me rg]

ma'rry v.t. join as husband and wife; take as husband or wife. -v. i. take a husband or wife. -mar'riage (-rij) n. state of being married: act of marrying. [F. marier, L. maritare]

Mars' n. Roman god of war; 2nd nearest planet to earth. -martian a. of Mars. -n. supposed dweller in Mars. [L. Mars, Mart-]

marsh n. low-lying wet land. -marshmall'ow n. herb growing near marshes; soft candy orig. made from this. [OE. mersc]

marsh'al n. high officer of state; military rank; chief officer of a district. -v. t. arrange in due order; conduct with ceremony. [F. maréchal, orig. a horse-servant]

marsupial n. animal that carries its young in a pouch, e. g. the kangaroo. [G. marsupion, small bag]

mart n. market place or market hall; auction room. [Du. markt, market]

mar'tial (-shal) a. relating to war; warlike. [L. Mars, god of war]

martinet' n. strict disciplinarian. [orig. uncertain]

mar'tyr (-ter) n. one put to death for refusing to give up a belief or cause, esp. the Christian faith; one who suffers in some cause; one in constant suffering. -v.t. make a martyr of. [G. = witness]

mar'vel n. wonderful thing. -v.i. wonder. -mar'velous a. [F. merueille]

Marx'ist (-ks-) a. of Karl Marx, Socialist (d. 1883) of his works or doctrine. -Marxism n. Marx's doctrine of materialist conception of history.

marzipan' n. paste of sugar and ground almonds, [Ger.]

masca'ra n. eyelash cosmetic. [Sp.]

mas'cot n. thing supposed to bring good luck. [F. mascotte]

masculine (-lin) a. of males; manly, vigorous; (gram.) of the gender to which names of males belong. [L. masculinus]

mask (-d-) n. covering for the face; disguise or pretense. -v.t. cover with mask; hide, disguise. -masque n. form of amateur theatrical performance; masquerade. -masquerade n. masked ball. -v. i. go about in disguise. [F. masque]

masochism n. form of sexual perversion which delights in endurance of pain. -mas'ochist n. [Sacher-Masoch, novelist]

ma'son n. worker in stone; freemason. [F. macon]

mass n. service of the Eucharist. [L. missa, fr. mittere, send]

mass n. quantity of matter; dense collection of this; large quantity. -the mass'es, the populace. -v.t. and i. form into a mass. -mass'ive a. having great size and weight. -mass' production, large-scale production. [G. maza, barley cake]

mass'acre (-ker) n. general slaughter; indiscriminate killing, esp. of unresisting people. -v.t. make a massacre of. [F.]

mass'age a. rubbing and kneading the muscles, etc., as curative treatment. v.t. apply this treatment to. -mass'eur n. -mass'euse fem., one who practises massage. [F. fr. G. massein, knead]

mast n. (naut.) of timber, steel etc., pole for supporting sails, derricks etc. [OE. mcest]

mast n. fruit of beech, oak, etc., used as food for pigs. [OE. mæst]

mast'er (ma-) n. one who employs another; head of a household; owner; one in control: captain of a merchant ship; teacher; artist of great reputation. -v.t. overcome; acquire knowledge of, or skill in. -mast'erful a. imperious, self- willed. -mast'erly a. skillfully done. -mast'ery n. victory, authority. -mast'erpiece n. finest work of artist or craftsman. [L. magister]

masticate v.t. chew. -mastica'tion n. [L. masticate, chew gum]

mastiff n. large dog used as watch-dog. [OF. mastin (a.), domestic]

mast'odon n. extinct elephant. [G. mastos, breast, odous, odon-, tooth]

mast'oid a. breast-shaped, esp. of the bone behind the ear. -n. this bone; sinusitis of the mastoid. [G. mastos, breast]

mat n. small carpet or strip of plaited rushes, etc.;thick tangled mass. -v.t. and i. form into such a mass. -matt'ing n. fabric of mats. [L. matta]

mat'ador n. man who kills the bull in a bull fight. [Sp. fr. L. mactare, to kill]

match n. person or thing exactly corresponding to another; one able to contend equally with another; trial of skill; marriage; person regarded as eligible for marriage. -v.t. join in marriage; meet equally in contest; place in contest with; get something corresponding to (a color, pattern, etc.). -v.i. correspond. -match'less a. unequalled. [OE. gernæcca]

match n. small stick with a head of combustible material, which bursts into flame when rubbed; fuse. [F. meche, wick]

mate n. comrade, husband or wife; officer in a merchant ship immediately below the captain. -v.t. marry. -v. i. keep company. [Du. maat]

mate'rial a. of matter or body; unspiritual; essential, important. -n. stuff from which anything is made; stuff or fabric. -materialism n. opinion that nothing exists except matter. -mate'rialist a. and n. -materialis'tic a. -mate'rialize v.t. make material. -v.i. come into existence. -materially adv. [L.materia, matter]

mater'nal a. of or related through a mother. -matern'ity n. motherhood. [L. mater, mother]

mathematics n. pl. science of space and number. [mathernatike, fr. G. manthanein, learn]

mat'inee n. morning and afternoon performance. [F. matins, morning]

matriarch n. mother as ruler of family. [L. mater, mother]

matricide n. killing of one's own mother; the killer. [L. mater, mother]

matriculate v.t. enter on a college or university register. -v.i. enter one's name on such register; pass an examination entitling one to do this. [Med. L. matricula, register of numbers]

matrimony n. marriage. -matrimo'nial a. [L. matrimoniurn, mater, mother]

mat'rix n. mold for casting. [L.]

ma'tron n. married woman; woman superintendent of a hospital, school, etc. ma'tronly a. [L. matrona]

matt'er n. substance of which a thing is made up; physical or bodily substance in general; pus; substance of a book, etc.; affair; reason, cause of trouble. -v.i. be of importance. [F. matiere fr. L. materia]

matt'ress n. stuffed flat case used as or under a bed; a frame with stretched wires for supporting a bed. [OF. materas]

mature' a. ripe, completely developed, grown. -v.t. bring to maturity. - v.i. come to maturity; of a bill, become due. matu'rity n. [L. maturus, ripe]

maud'lin a. weakly sentimental. [L. magdalena, Mary Magdalen, fr. pictures showing her weeping]

maul, mawl n. heavy wooden hammer, - maul v.t. beat or bruise; handle roughly. [L. mialleus, hammer]

mausole'um n. stately building as a tomb. [L. fr. Mausolus, King of Caria]

maxill'a n. jawbone. -maxill'ary a. of the jaw or jawbone. [L.]

max'im n. short pithy saying; axiom; rule of conduct. [F. maxime]

max'im n. a machine-gun. [Sir H. Vaxitn, inventor]

max'imum n. greatest possible size or number. -a. greatest. -maximize v.t. [L. = greatest]

May n. fifth month of the year; hawthorn; its flowers. -v. i. take part in May-day festivities. [L. Maius, fr. Maia, goddess of growth]

may v. aux. express possibility, permission, opportunity, etc. -may'be adv. possibly, perhaps. [OE. mæg]

mayonnaise' n. sauce of egg-yolk, olive-oil, lemon-juice, etc. [F.]

may'or n. head of a municipality. -may'oral a. -may'oralty n. office or time of office, of a mayor. [L. major, greater]

maze n. labyrinth; network of paths or lines. -v. t. stupefy. [cp. amaze]

me pron. objective case singular of the 1st personal pronoun I. [OE.]

mead n. alcoholic drink made from honey. [OE, meodu]

mea'ger a. lean, thin, scanty. [F.maigre, thin]

meal n. grain ground to powder. -meal'y a. [OE. melo]

meal n. occasion of taking food; food taken. [OE. mael, time fixed]

mean a. inferior, shabby; small-minded; niggardly, miserly; bad-tempered. mean'ly adv. -mean'ness. (OE. gemaene]

mean a. intermediate in time; quality, etc. -n. anything which is intermediate. pl. that by which something is done; money resources. -mean'time n. meanwhile n. time between one happening and another. -adv. during this time. [OF. meien]

mean v.t. intend, design; signify; import. -mean'ing n. sense, significance. -a. expressive. [OE. mænan]

meas'les (mez'ls) n.pl. infectious disease with red spots. -meas'ly a. of measles; poor, wretched. [ME. maseles]

meas'ure (mezh-er) n. size or quantity; vessel, rod, line, etc., for ascertaining size or quantity; unit of size or quantity; poetical rhythm; order or tune; musical time; slow dance; course or plan of action; law. -v.t. ascertain size or quantity of-, estimate; bring into competition (with). v.i. be (so much) in size or quantity. [F. mesure]

meat n. food; flesh of animals used as food. -meat'y a. [OE. mete]

mechan'ic (-k-) a. relating to a machine. -n. one employed in working with machinery; skilled workman. -pl. branch of science dealing with motion and tendency of motion. -mechan'ical a. concerned with machines or manual operation; worked or produced by, or as though by, a machine; like a machine; relating to mechanics. -mechan'ically adv. [G. mechane, machine]

med'al n. piece of metal usually round or star-shaped with an inscription, used as a reward or memento. -medall'ion n. large medal; various things like this in decorative work. -med'alist *n.* winner of a medal; maker of medals. [L. *metallum*, metal]

med'dle *v.i.* interfere, busy one's self with unnecessarily. -meddlesome *a.* [AF. *medlar*, OF. *mesler* (mod. *méler*) mix]

me'dial *a.* middle; average. -me'dian *a.* [L. *medius*, middle]

me'diate *v.i.* go between in order to reconcile. -*v.t.* bring about by mediation. -*a.* not immediate, depending on something intermediate. -media'tion *a.* me'diator *a.* [Late L. *mediare*]

medicine *n.* art of healing by remedies and the regulation of diet: remedy or mixture of drugs. -med'ical *a.* -med'ically *adv.* - med'icament *n.* remedy. med'icate *v.t.* impregnate with medicinal substances. - medic'inal *a.* having healing properties, curative. [L. *medicinal* fr. *medicus*, physician]

Medieval *a.* relating to the Middle Ages. [fr. L. *medius*, middle, and *aevum*, age]

me'diocre *a.* neither bad nor good, ordinary. -medioc'rity *n.* [L. *mediocris*]

meditate *v. t.* think about; plan. -*v.i.* be occupied in thought. -medita'tion *n.* - med'itative *a.* reflective. -med'itatively *adv.* [L. *meditari*]

Meditera'nean *n.* the sea between Europe and Africa. [L. *medius*, middle, *terra*, earth]

me'dium *n.* (me'diums, me'dia *pl.*) middle quality or degree; intermediate substance conveying force; surroundings; environment; means, agency; (spirit.) person as medium for spirit manifestations. -*a.* between two qualities, degrees, moderate, *etc.* [L.]

med'ley *n.* miscellaneous mixture; jumble. [OF. *mesler*, mix]

meek *a.* submissive, humble. -meek'ly *adv.* -meek'ness *n.* [ON. *miukr*, soft]

meet *a.* fit, suitable. -meet'ly *adv.* meet'ness *n.* IOE. *gemæte*]

meet *v.t.* come face to face with; encounter; satisfy, pay. -*v.i.* come face to face; assemble; come into contact. -*n.* meeting for a hunt. -meet'ing *n.* assembly. [OE. *metan*]

meg'a- *prefix* great. [G. *mesas*, *mesa*-, great] -meg'afog *n.* fog-signal fitted with-megaphones. -megalith'ic *a.* consisting of great stones. -megaloma'nia *n.* a passion for great things. -meg'aphone *n.* an instrument for carrying the sound of the voice to a distance. -meg'astar *n.* a very well-known personality in the entertainment business.

meio'sis *n.* rhetorical understatement opposite of hyperbole. [G.*meiosiss*, diminution]

megabyte *n.* (*compute.*) about 1 million bytes; 1,024 Kbytes

melancholy (-k-) *n.* sadness, dejection, gloom. -*a.* gloomy, dejected. -melancho'lia *n.* mental disease accompanied by depression. -melanchol'ic *a.* [G. *melangcholia*, black bile]

mell'ow *a.* ripe; juicy; (*colloq.*) partly drunk. -*v.t.* and *i.* make or become mellow. [ME. *melwe*, ripe]

melodrama *n.* play full of sensational happenings and ending happily. melodramatic *a.* [F. *mélodrame*]

mel'ody *n.* sweet sound; series of musical notes arranged to make a tune. [G. *melos*, song]

mel'on *n.* various gourds eaten as fruit, *esp.* watermelon. [G. *melon*, apple]

melt *v.i.* become liquid by heat; be dissolved; become softened; waste away. -*v.t.* cause to soften or dissolve or become liquid by heat. -melt'down *n.* (in nuclear reactor) the melting of the fuel rods as a result of a defect in the cooling system, with the possible escape of radiation into the environment. [OE. *meltan*]

mem'ber *n.* limb; any part of a complicated structure; any of the individuals making up a body or society. -mem' bership *n.* [L. *membrum*, limb]

mem'brane *n.* thin flexible tissue in a plant or animal body. [L. *membrane*]

mem'oir *a.* record of events; autobiography or biography. [F. *mémoire*, memory]

mem'ory *n.* faculty of recollecting or recalling to mind; recollection; length of time one can remember. -memor'ial *a.* of or preserving memory. -*n.* something which serves to keep in memory; statement in a petition. - memor'ialize *v.t.* commemorate; petition. - memor'ialist *n.* -mem'orize *v.t.* commit to memory. mem'orable *a.* worthy of being remembered. -mem'orably *adv.* - memoran'dum, mem'o *n.* note to help the memory; note of a contract; informal letter. [L. *memor*, mindful]

men'ace *n.* threat. -*v.t.* threaten. [F., fr. L. *minari*, threaten

mend *v.t.* repair, correct, put right. -*v.i.* improve, *esp.* in health. -*n.* [*amend*]

menial *a.* relating to a servant in a house; servile. -*n.* household servant. [ME. *meinie*, household]

meningi'tis *n.* inflammation of membranes of brain. [G. *méninx*, membrane]

menopause *n.* cessation of menstruation. [G. *men*, month, *pausis*, cessation]

men'sal *a.* monthly. -men'ses *n, pl.* monthly discharge from uterus. -men'strual *a.* - menstrua'tion *n.* approximately monthly discharge of blood and cellular debris from womb of nonpregnant woman. -men'struate *v.i.* [L. mensis, month]

menstruation. *See* mensal.

ment'al *a.* relating to or done by the mind. -ment'ally *adv.* -mental'ity *n.* quality of mind. [L. *mens*, *ment*-, mind]

mentation *n.* activities of the mind; thinking.

men'thol *n.* kind of camphor extracted from peppermint. [L. *mentha*, mint]

men'tion (-shun) *n.* reference to or remark about (person or thing). -*v.t.* refer to, speak of. [L. *mentio*]

men'tor *n.* wise and trusted adviser. [G. *Mentor*, counselor of the son of Ulysses]

men'u *n.* bill of fare. [F. = detailed]

mercenary *n.* (-s-)*a.* hired; working simply for reward. -*n.* hired soldier in foreign service. [L. *merces*, reward]

mer'chant *n.* wholesale trader. mer'chandise *n.* things in which he deals. -mer'chantman *n.* trading ship. [F. *Mar-*

chand]

mer'cury *n.* liquid white metal, quicksilver. -**Mercury**, Roman god of eloquence, messenger of the gods; planet nearest to the sun. -**mercu'rial** *a.* lively, sprightly of, or containing mercury. [L. *Mercurius*, orig. god of merchandiser]

mer'cy *n.* quality of compassion, clemency; a refraining from the infliction of suffering by one who has the right or power to inflict it. -**mer'ciful** *a.* **mer'ciless** *a.* [L. *merces*, reward]

mere *a.* only; not of more value or size, *etc.*, than name implies. -**mere'ly** *adv.* [L. *merus*, unmixed]

merge *v.i.* lose identity, mix in. -*v. t.* cause to lose identity or to be absorbed. -**mer'ger** (-j-) *n.* a being absorbed into something greater; a combining of business firms. [L. *mergere*, dip]

merid'ian *a.* relating to noon, or the position of the sun at noon. -*n.* noon; highest point reached by a star, *etc.*; period of greatest splendor; imaginary circle in the sky passing through the celestial poles: circle of the earth passing through the poles and a place stated. [L. *meridies*, mid-day]

mer'it *n.* excellence, worth; quality of deserving well. -*pl.* excellences or defects. -*v.t.* deserve. -**merito'rious** *a.* deserving well. [L. *meritum*]

mer'maid *n.* imaginary sea creature having the upper part of a woman and the tail of a fish. [obs. *mere*, sea]

mer'ry *a.* joyous, cheerful. -**merr'ily** *adv.* -**merr'iment** *n.* -**merr'ythought** *n.* forked bone between the head and breast of a bird. -**merr'y-go-round** *n.* revolving machine with wooden horses, model automobiles *etc.* [OE. *myrge*]

mesh *n.* one of the open spaces of a net. -*v.t.* catch in meshes. [OE. *masc*]

mess *n.* portion of food; state of untidy confusion; company of people who regularly eat together; place where they do this. -*v.i.* take one's meals thus; busy one's self untidily. -*v.t.* make a mess of, to muddle. [OF. *mes*, fr. *mettre*, put]

message *n.* communication from one person to another. -**mess'enger** *n.* message-bearer. [F. fr. L. *mittere, miss-*, send]

Messi'ah *n.* promised deliverer of the Jews; Christ. -**Messian'ic** *a.* [Heb. *mashiah*, anointed

meta- *prefix* over, beyond; also expressing change. [G.]

metabolism *n.* process of chemical change in a living organism. -**metabol'ic** *a.* [G. *metabole*, change]

met'al *n.* any of a number of chemical elements usually bright and easy to melt, *e.g.* gold, iron, *etc.*, broken stone used for macadam roads. -**metall'ic** *a.* -**met'allurgy** *n.* art of refining metals. -**met'allurgist** *n.* [G. *metallon*, mine]

metamer *n.* (*chem.*) compound that has the same molecular weight and same elements in the same proportion as another compound, but differs in structure.

metamorphosis *n.* change of shape, substance, character, *etc.* [G. *morphe*, form]

metaphor *n.* (*rhet.*) transference of a term to something it does not literally apply to; substance of this. -**metaphor'ical** *a.* [G. *pherein*, carry]

metaphysics *n.pl.* theory of being and knowing. -**metaphys'ical** *a.* [fr. books of Aristotle, called in G. *ta meta ta physika*, 'the (works) after the physics,' referring to position but later mistaken for 'Works beyond or above physics']

me'teor *n.* shining body appearing temporarily in the sky; shooting star. -**meteor'ic** *a.* -**me'teorite** *n.* fallen meteor. -**meteor'ogy** *n.* science of weather. -**meteorolog'ical** *a.* -**meteorol'ogist** *n.* [G. *meteoros* *a.*, lofty]

me'ter *n.* instrument for measuring, *esp.* gas or electricity consumption; verse, rhythm; unit of length in the French decimal system, 39.37 inches. -**met'ric** *a.* of this system. -**met'rical** *a.* of measurement or of poetic meter. [G. *metron*, measurer]

methane *n.* a light colorless gas, marsh-gas. [G. *methan*]

meth'od *n.* a way of doing something; orderliness, system. -**method'ical** *a.* -**Meth'odist** *n.* member of any of the churches originated by John Wesley and G. Whitefield. -**Meth'odism** *n.* -**meth'od-ize** *v.t.* reduce to order. [G. *methodos*, investigation]

meth'yl *n.* base of wood spirit; many other organic compounds. -**meth'ylate** *v.t.* mix with methyl. [fr. G. *methy*, wine, *hyle*, wood]

meticulous *a.* (over) particular about details. [L. *meticulosus*, timid]

met'ric. *See* meter.

metronome *n.* (*music*) device for beating time at the required tempo. [F. *metronome*]

metropolis *n.* (metropolises) *pl.* chief city of a state. [G. *meter*, mother, *polis*, city]

mezzanine *n.* (*archit.*) in a building, low story between two higher ones. [It. *mezzanine*]

mi'ca *n.* mineral found in glittering scales or plates. [L. = crumb]

micro- *prefix* small. [G. *mikros*] -**mi'crochip** *n.* a small piece of semiconductor material carrying many integrated circuits. -**mi'crocomputer** *n.* a small computer in which the central processing unit is contained in one or more silicon chips. -**mi'crocosm** *n.* world of man; man as an epitome of the universe. -**microcos'mic** *a.* -**mi'crofilm** *n.* minute film of book or manuscript. -**micro'meter** *n.* instrument for making very small measurements. -**mi'crophone** *n.* instrument for recording or making sounds louder, *e.g.*, as part of a telephone or of broadcasting apparatus. **micropro'cessor** *n.* integrated circuit acting as central processing unit in a small computer. -**mi'croscope** *n.* instrument by which a very small body is magnified and made, visible. -**microscop'ic** *a.* relating to a microscope; so small as to be only visible through a microscope. -**mi'crosurgery** *n.* intricate surgery performed on cells, tissues, *etc.*, using a specially designed operating microscope and miniature precision instruments. -mi'crobe *n.* minute plant or animal, *esp.* one causing disease or fermentation. [F., fr. G. *mikros*, small *bios*, life]

mid- *prefix* intermediate, that is in the middle. -mid'day *n.* noon or about then. -midd'ling *a.* medium, mediocre, fair. -mid'land *n.* middle part of a country. -mid'night *n.* twelve o'clock at night. -mid'rib *n.* rib along center of leaf. -mid'ship *n.* middle part of ship. -mid'shipman *n.* junior naval officer attending service academy. -mid'summer *n.* summer solstice; middle part of the summer. -Mid'summer Day *n.* June 24th. -mid'way *a.* and *adv.* half-way. [OE. *midd*]

mid'dle *a.* equal distance from, or between, two extremes; medium, intermediate. -*n.* middle point or part. -mid'dleman *n.* trader handling goods between producer and consumer. -Mid'dle A'ges, roughly, period from 5th to 15th c. -mid'dle weight *n.* and *a.* (jockey, boxer) between light and heavy weight. [OE. *middel*]

midst *n.* in the midst of, surrounded by, among. -*prep.* among. [ME. *middes*]

mid'wife *n.* woman who assists others in childbirth. [OE. *mid*, with, *wif*, woman]

might (mit) *n.* power, strength. -might'y *a.* -might'ily *adv.* [OE. *miht*]

mi'graine (me-) *n.* severe sick headache, often affecting one side of head. [F., fr. G. *hemi*, half, *kranion*, skull]

mi'grate *v.i.* move from one place to another. -mi'grant *a.* and *n.* -migra'tion *n.* -mi'gratorya. [L. *migrare*]

mild (-i-) *a.* gentle, merciful, indulgent; not strongly flavored. -mild'ly *a.* -mild'ness *n.* [OE. *milde*]

mil'dew *n.* destructive fungus on plants or things exposed to damp. -*v.i.* become tainted with mildew. -*v.t.* affect with mildew. IOE. *meledeaw*, honey dew]

mile *n.* measure of length, 1760 yards. -mi'leage *n.* distance in miles. -mile'stone *n.* stone at mile intervals to mark distances. [L. *mille* (passuum) thousand (paces)]

mil'itary *a.* of, or for, soldiers or armies or warfare. -*n.* soldiers. -mil'itant *a.* engaged in warfare; combative. -*n.* militant person. -mili'tia (-ish-a) *n.* force of citizens, not professional soldiers, which may be called on at need for military service. [L. *miles*, *milit-*, soldier]

milk *n.* white fluid with which animals feed their young. -*v.t.* draw milk from. -milk'maid *n.* woman working with cows or in a dairy. -milk'-teeth *n.* first set of animal teeth. -milk'weed, milk'wort *n.* plants producing milky juice. -milk'y *a.* containing or like milk. -Milk'y Way, the galaxy. [OE. *meolc*]

mill *n.* machinery for grinding corn, *etc.*; building containing this; various manufacturing machines; factory. -*v.t.* put through a mill; pound. -mill'er *n.* -mill'race *n.* stream of water driving a mill wheel. -mill'stone *n.* one of a pair of flat circular stones used for grinding. -mill'wright *n.* builder and repairer of mills. [OE. *myln*]

millennium *n.* period of a thousand years; period of Christ's reign on earth at his Second Coming. -millenn'ial *a.* [L. *mille*, thousand]

mill'epede, millipede *n.* many-legged wormlike insect. [L. *mille*, thousand, *ped*, foot]

mill'et *n.* small grain of an Indian cereal plant: the plant. [F.]

milligram *n.* thousandth part of a gram. -mill'imeter *n.* -mill'iliter *n.* [L. *mille*, thousand]

mill'iner *n.* one who makes up or deals in women's hats, ribbons, *etc.* -mill'inery *n.* [for *Milaner*, orig. a dealer in articles of *Milan* (Italy)]

mill'ion *n.* thousand thousands. [L. *mille*, thousand]

millisecond *n.* one thousandth of a second (*abbr.* ms, msec)

mime *n.* jester; old form of dramatic representation, *esp.* one not using words. -mim'eograph *n.* form of duplicating machine. -mim'ic a. imitated, feigned, esp. to amuse. -*n.* one skilled in amusing imitation. -*v.t.* imitate, ludicrously or closely. -mim'icry *n.* [G. *mimos*, buffoon]

mince *v.t.* cut or chop small; utter with affected carefulness. -*v.i.* walk in an affected manner. -*n.* minced-meat. [OF. *mincier*, small]

mind (-i-) *n.* thinking faculties as distinguished from the body, intellectual faculties; memory; attention; intentions taste. -*v. t.* attend to; care for; keep in memory. -mind'ed *a.* disposed. -mind'ful *a.* taking thought; keeping in memory. [OE. *gemynd*]

mine *pron.* that belonging to me. [OE. *min*, gen. of *I*, *me*]

mine *n.* deep hole for digging out coal, metals, *etc.*; underground gallery with a charge of explosive; large shell or canister of explosive placed in the sea to destroy ships. -*v.t.* dig from a mine; make a mine in or under. -*v.i.* make or work in a mine. -mine'-field *n.* area of sea sown with mines. -mine'-layer *n.* ship used for laying mines. -mine'-sweeper *n.* ship used to clear away mines. [F.]

min'eral *a.* got by mining; inorganic. -*n.* mineral substance. -min'eral-water *n.* water containing some mineral, *etc.*, natural or artificial kinds used for drinking. [F.]

mini *n.* anything that is very short or small; a miniature. -*n.* garment *usu.* a skirt, that is very short and falls well above the knees.

min'iature *n.* small painted portrait; book or model on a small scale. -*a.* small scale. -min'iaturist *n.* painter of miniatures. [It. *miniatura*, fr. *miniare*, paint in red lead]

min'imize *v.t.* bring to, estimate at, the smallest possible amount. -min'imum *n.* lowest size, quantity. -*a.* smallest in size, quantity. [L.*minimus*, smallest]

min'ister *n.* person in charge of a department of the State; diplomatic representative; clergyman. -*v.t.* supply. -*v.i.* serve; contribute; be serviceable or helpful. [L. = *servant*]

mink (-ngk) *n.* weasellike animal; its valuable fur. [cp. Low Ger. *mink*, otter]

minn'ow *n.* small freshwater fish. [F. *menuise*, small fish]

mi'nor *a.* lesser; smaller; underage. *-n.* person under the legal age. **-minor'ity** *n.* state of being a minor; lesser number; smaller party voting together. [L.]

Min'otaur *n.* mythical monster, half bull, half-man. [G. *Minos*, in Crete, and *tauros*. bull]

mint *n.* place where money is coined. *-v.t.* to coin money. [L. *moneta*]

mint *n.* aromatic plant used in cooking. [G. *mintha*]

min'uend *n.* number from which another is to be subtracted. [L. *minure*, lessen]

mi'nus *prep.* less, with the deduction of. *-a.* quantities, negative. [L.]

minute' (mi-nfit) *a.* very small; very precise. **-minute'ly** *adv.* - **minu'tiae** *n. pl.* trifles, precise details. [L. *minutus*, small]

min'ute *n.* 60th part of an hour or of a degree or angle; moment; memorandum. *-pl.* record of the proceedings of a meeting, *etc.* *-v.t.* make a minute of, record in minutes. [*minute* (v.s.)]

miracle *n.* supernatural event; marvel. [F., fr. L. *mirus*, wonderful]

mirage' *n.* deceptive image in the atmosphere, *e.g.* of a lake in the desert. [F. fr. *se mirer*, be reflected]

mire *n.* bog, deep mud—*v.t.* stick in, dirty with mud. [ON. *myrr*]

mirr'or *n.* polished surface for reflecting images. *-v.t.* reflect an image of [OF. *mireor*, L. *mirari*, contemplate]

mirth *n.* merriment. **-mirth'ful** *a.* [OE. *myrgth-merg*, merry]

mis- *prefix* meaning amiss, wrongly; makes compounds, *e.g.* **misapply'** *v.t.* apply wrongly. **-misman'agement** *n.* bad management. Such words are not given where the meaning and derivation may easily be found from the simple word.

misadventure *n.* mishap, accident, bad luck. [OF. *mesaventure*]

misalliance *n.* improper or degrading marriage. [*alliance*]

misanthrope *n.* hater of mankind. [G. *misein*, hate, *anthropos*, man]

misappropriate *v.t.* embezzle, put to wrong use. [*mis-* and Low L. *appropriare*]

misbehave *v.i.* to behave improperly. **-misbehavior** *n.* [*mis-* and *behave*]

miscegenation *n.* interbreeding of races; marriage or sexual relations between two people of different race. [L. *miscue*, mix, *genus*, race]

miscellaneous *a.* mixed, assorted. - **miscell'any** *n.* collection of assorted writings in one book, literary medley. [L. *miscellaneous*, fr. *miscere*, mix]

mis'chief (-chif) *n.* source of harm or annoyance; annoying conduct. **-mis'chievous** *a.* having harmful effect; disposed to or full of mischief. [OF. *meschief*, fr. *meschever*, come to grief]

misconduct *n.* bad behavior; wrong management. [*mis-* and *conduct*]

misconstrue' *v.t.* to interpret wrongly. **-misconstruction** *n.* [*mis-* and *construe*]

mis'deed *n.* evil deed; crime. [OE. *misdaed*]

misdemeanor *n.* (law) offense less than a felony. [*demeanor*]

mi'ser (-z-) *n.* one who hoards instead of using money; stingy person. **-mi'serly** *a.* [L. = wretched]

miserable *a.* very unhappy, wretched; mean; disappointing. **-mis'ery** *n.* great unhappiness; distress, poverty. [L. *miser*]

misfire' *v.i.* to fail to explode; (*fig.*) to produce no effect. [*mis-* and *fire*]

mis'fit *n.* a bad fit; a person unable to adapt himself to his surroundings. [*mis* and *fit*]

misfortune *n.* bad luck; calamity. [*mis* and *fortune*]

misgiving *n.* doubt, mistrust. **-misgive'** *v.t.* [ME. give = suggest]

mis'hap *n.* accident, calamity. [*hap*]

mislead' *v.t.* to lead astray; to deceive *-p.p.* misled'**-mislead'ing** *a.* deceptive, [*mis-* and *lead*]

misno'mer *n.* wrong name; use of one. [OF. *mesnorner*, fr. L. *norninare*, name]

misog'amy *n.* hatred of marriage. - **misog'amist** *n.* [G. *misein, gamos*, marriage]

misog'yny (-j-) *n.* hatred of women. - **misog'ynist** *n.* [G. *misein, gyne*, woman]

misquote' *v.t.* to quote wrongly. - **misquota'tion** *n.* an incorrect quotation. [*mis-* and *quotation*]

misrepresent' *v.t.* to give a false description on account of **-misrepresenta'tion** *n.* [*mis-* and *represent*]

Miss *n.* title of an unmarried woman or girl; girl. [short for mistress]

miss *v.t.* fail to hit, reach, find, catch, notice; not be in time for; omit, notice, regret absence of. *-n.* fact of missing. **-miss'ing** *a.* lost, absent, [OE. *missan*]

miss'al *n.* mass-book. [Church L. *missale*, fr. *missa*, mass]

miss'ile (-il) that which may be thrown or shot to do damage. **-guid'ed miss'ile** *n.* air rocket or other explosive weapon which is guided to the target either from the ground, or by its own internal mechanism. [L. *missiles*, fr. *mittere miss-*, send]

mis'sion (mish'un) *n.* sending or being sent on some service; party of persons sent; person's calling in life. **missionary** *n.* of religious missions. *-n.* one who goes on religious missions. [L. *mission*]

mist *n.* water vapor in fine drops. [OE. = *darkness*]

mistake' *v.t.* not to understand; form a wrong opinion about; take (a person or thing) for another. *-v. i.* be in error. *-n.* error in thought or action. [*take*]

mis'ter *n.* courteous form of address to a man (written *Mr.*). [*master*]

mis'tress *n.* woman who employs other persons; woman with mastery or control; woman teacher; object of a man's illicit love; mode of address to a woman (written *Mrs.*, pron. *miséiz*). [OF. maistresse, fem. of maistre, master]

mistrust' v.t. to feel no confidence in; to look on with suspicion. -n. want of trust. [mis- and trust]

misunderstand' v.t. to take a wrong meaning from. [mis and understand]

mitt'en n. glove without separate fingers. [F. mitaine]

mix v.t. put together or combine or blend, mingle. -v.i. be mixed; associate. -mix'er n. one that mixes; person at ease in any society. -mix'ture n. [L. mixtus, mixed, fr. miscere, mix]

mnemon'ic (n-) a. helping the memory. -n. something intended to help the memory. -pl. art of improving the memory. [G. mnēmon, mindful]

moan n. low murmur, usually indicating pain. -v.t. bewail. -v.i. utter a moan. [OE. muan]

moat n. deep wide ditch round a town or building. -v.t. surround with a moat. [ME. mote, mound]

mob n. disorderly crowd of people; mixed assembly. -v.t. attack in a mob, hustle or ill-treat. [abbrev. fr. L. mobile (vulgus), fickle (crowd)]

mo'bile (-bil) a. capable of movement; easily moved or changed. -mobil'ity n. mo'bilize v.t. prepare (forces) for active service. -v.i. an army, prepare for active service. - mobiliza'tion n. [L. mobilis]

mocc'asin n. Native Amer. soft shoe, usually of deerskin; shoe or slipper of similar shape; poisonous water snake. [Native American]

mock v.t. make fun of, hold up to ridicule; disappoint. -v.i. scoff. -n. act of mocking. -a. sham, imitation. - mock'ing-bird n. N. Amer. bird which mimics other birds' notes. [F. moquer]

mode n. method, manner, fashion. -mo'dish a. in the fashion. [F.]

mod'el n. representation of an object made to scale; pattern; person or thing worthy of imitation; person employed by an artist to pose, or by a dressmaker to show off clothes. -v.t. work into shape; make according to a model. [F. modèle]

modem n. (compute.) device used to connect computer terminals to telephone transmission lines. [modulator/demodulator]

mod'erate (-it) a. not going to extremes, not excessive. medium. -n. person of moderate views. -v.t. and i. make or become less violent or excessive. -modera'tion n. -mod'erator n. go-between or mediator; president of a Presbyterian body. [L. moderatus]

mod'ern a. of present or recent times; new fashioned. -n. person living in modern times. -mod'ernism n. of modern character or views. [F. moderne, Late L. modernus]

mod'est a. unassuming, retiring, not over-rating one's qualities or achievements. - mod'esty n. [L. modestus]

mod'ify (fi) v.t. make small changes in, tone down. -modifica'tion n. [L. modificare, limit]

mod'ulate v.t. regulate; vary in tone. -v.i. change the key of music. modulation n. [L. modulari, measure]

mo'hair n. fine cloth of goat's hair. [Arab. mukhayyar]

Mohamm'edan, Muhammadan a. of Mohammed or his religion; Muslim; Islamic. -n. believer in Mohammed. [Mohammed]

moist a. damp, slightly wet. -moist'en v.t. -mois'ture n. liquid, esp. diffused or in drops. [OF. moiste]

mo'lar a. of teeth, serving to grind. -n. molar tooth. [L. molaris, fr. mola, millstone]

molass'es (-ez) n. drainings of raw sugar, treacle. [L. mel, honey]

mold (mold) n. pattern for shaping; hollow object in which metal is cast; character, form. -v.i. shape or pattern. mold'er v.i. crumble, decay, rot. -mold'ing n. molded object; decoration, esp. a long strip of ornamental section. [F. moule]

mold n. growth caused by dampness. - mold'y a. [ME. moulen, become mildewed]

mole n. small burrowing animal. [earlier mouldwarp, 'earth-thrower']

mol'ecule n. one of the uniform small particles, composed of atoms, of which a homogeneous substance is made up. - molec'ular a. [F., fr. L. moles, mass]

molest' v.t. interfere with, meddle with so as to annoy or injure. -molesta'tion n. [L. molestare]

mortify v.t. calm down. [L. mollificare, make soft]

mollusks, moll'usc n. soft-bodied and usually hard-shelled animal. [L. molluscus- mollis, soft]

molt v.i. change feathers. -v.t. shed (feathers). -n. action of molting. [OE. mutian, fr. L. mutare, change]

molt'en a. melted. [old pp. of melt]

moment n. very short space of time. - mo'mentary a. lasting a moment. - mo'mentarily adv. -moment'ous a. important. -moment'um n. force of moving body. [L. momentum, movement]

mon'arch (-k) n. sovereign ruler of a state. -mon'archy n. state ruled by a sovereigns his rule. [G. monos, alone, archein, ruler]

monastery n. house occupied by a religious order. -monast'ic a. relating to monks, nuns, or monasteries. -monast'icism n. [Late G. monasterion, fr. monazein, live alone]

Mon'day (mun'da) n. second day of the week. [OE. monandæg, moon day]

mon'ey (mun'-) n. current coin; medium of exchange. -mon'etary a. -mon'etar-ism n. theory that inflation is caused by an excess quantity of money in an economy; economic policy based on this theory and on a belief in the efficiency of free market forces. -money market n. financial system for the trade of low-risk, short-term securigites. [F. monnaie. See mint]

mon'itor n. one who gives warning or advice; senior pupil in a school charged with special duties and authority; small warship with heavy guns; kind of lizard. [L. fr. monere, monit-, admonish]

monk (monk) n. one of a religious community of men living apart under vows. -

monk'ish *a.* -monk's-hood *n.* poisonous plant, the aconite. [OE. *munic*, Late G. *monachos*, solitary]

monk'ey (munk'i) *n.* animal closely allied to man; imitative or mischievous child. -*v.i.* play tricks. -monk'ey-wrench *n.* wrench with movable jaw. [G. *Moneke*, son of Martin the Ape, in 15th c. version of Reynard the Fox]

mono- *prefix.* [G. *monos*, alone, single] -monochrome *n.* representation in one color. -*a.* of only one color. -monochromatic *a.* -mon'ocle *n.* single eyeglass. -monog'amy *n.* custom of being married to only one person at a time. -mon'ogram *n.* two or more letters interwoven. -mon'ograph *n.* short book on a single subject. -mon'olith *n.* prehistoric monument, a single large stone. - mon'ologue, mon'olog *n.* dramatic composition with only one speaker. -monop'oly *n.* exclusive possession of a trade, privilege, *etc.* -monop'olize *v.t.* -monop'olist *n.* -mon'orail *n.* railway having cars running on or suspended from a single rail. -mon'osyllable *n.* word of one syllable. -monosyllab'ic *a.* -mon'otheism *n.* belief that there is only one God. mon'otheist *n.* -mon'otone *n.* continuing on one note. -monot'onous *a.* lacking in variety, wearisome. -monot'ony *n.* - mon'otype *n.* machine for casting and setting printing type in individual letters.

monsoon' *n.* seasonal wind of the Indian Ocean; other periodical winds. [Arab. *mausim*, lit. season]

mon'ster *n.* misshapen animal or plant; person of great wickedness huge animal or thing. -*a.* huge. [L. *monstrum*, marvel]

month (munth) *n.* one of the twelve periods into which a year is divided; period of the revolution of the moon. -month'ly *a.* happening, payable, *etc.*, once a month. -*adv.* once a month. -*n.* monthly magazine. [OE. *monath*; fr. *moon*]

mon'ument *n.* anything that commemorates; written record. -monument'al *a.* of or serving as a monument; vast, stupendous. [L. *monumentum*]

mood *n.* state of mind and feelings. -mood'y *a.* changeable in mood; gloomy. -mood'ily *adv.* -mood'iness *n.* [OE. *mod*]

mood *n.* (*gram.*) group of forms indicating function of verb. [var. of *mode*]

moon *n.* satellite revolving round the earth; satellite of a planet. -*v. i.* go about dreamily. -moon'light *n.* -moon'shine *n.* nonsense; smuggled liquor. -moon'stone *n.* precious stone. -moon'-struck *a.* lunatic. [OE. *mona*]

moor *n.* tract of waste land, often hilly and heath-clad; land preserved for grouse shooting. [OE. *mor*]

moor *v.t.* fasten (a ship) with chains, ropes or cable and anchor. -*v.i.* secure a ship thus. - moorings *n.* [orig. uncertain]

moose *n.* Amer. elk. [Algonkin, *mus*]

moot *v.t.* bring for discussion. -*a.* open to argument. -*n.* (*hist.-v.*) meeting, as town-*moot*. folk-*moot*. [OE. *mot*]

mop *n.* bundle of yarn, cloth, *etc.*, fastened to the end of a stick and used for cleaning. -*v.t.*

clean or wipe with a mop or with any absorbent stuff. [OF. *mappe*, L. *mappa*, napkin]

mope *v.i.* be depressed, dull or dispirited. [Du. *moppen*, sulk]

mor'al *a.* concerned with right and wrong conduct; of good conduct. -moral victory *n.* failure or defeat that inspirits instead of crushing the loser. -morale' *n.* discipline and spirit of an army or other body of persons. -mor'alist *n.* teacher of morals. -moral'ity *n.* good moral conduct; moral goodness or badness; kind of medieval drama, containing a moral lesson. -mor'alize *v.t.* interpret morally. -*v.i.* write or think on moral aspects of things. -mor'ally *adv.* [L. *moralis*]

morass' *n.* marsh, bog. [Du. *moeras*]

moratorium *n.* government's authority to delay payment of debts during national emergency; suspension of activity, *esp.* during a period of reconsideration. [L. *mora*, delay]

mor'bid *a.* unwholesome, sickly. - mor'bidly *adv.* -morbid'ity *n.* [L. *morbidus*, from *morbus*, disease]

more *a.* greater in quantity or number. -*adv.* to a greater extent; in addition. -*pron.* greater or additional amount or number. -moreo'ver *adv.* besides. [OE. *mora*]

morgue' (morg) *n.* mortuary in which dead bodies are placed for identification, *etc.* [F.]

moribund *a.* dying. [L. *moribundus*]

Mor'mon *n.* member of the Church of Jesus Christ of Latter-Day Saints, founded in U.S.A. by Joseph Smith (1805-1844) in 1830. [fr. *Mormon*, alleged author of *The Book of Mormon*]

morn *n.* morning. -morn'ing *n.* early part of the day. -morn'ing glo'ry *n.* convolvulus. [OE. *morgen*]

mo'ron *n.* adult with mental capacity of a child. [G. *moros*, foolish]

morose' *a.* sullen, unsociable. [L. *morosus*, moody]

morph'ia, morph'ine *n.* narcotic part of opium. [G. *Morpheus*, god of sleep]

morphology *n.* science of the forms of living organisms. [G. *morphe*, form]

Morse *a.* Morse-code *n.* system of signalling in which the letters of the alphabet are represented by various combinations of dots and dashes, short and long flashes, *etc.* [*Morse*, inventor (d. 1872)]

mor'sel *n.* mouthful; fragment. [L. *morsus*, bite]

mort'al *a.* subject to death; fatal. -*n.* mortal creature. -mortal'ity *n.* being mortal; great loss of life; death rate. -mort'ally *adv.* [L. *mors*, *mort-*, death]

mort'ar *n.* vessel in which substances are pounded; short gun throwing at high angles; mixture of lime, sand, and water for holding bricks and stones together. [L. *mortarium*]

mort'gage (morg-aj) *n.* conveyance of property as security for debt with provision that the property be reconveyed at payment within an agreed time. -*v.t.* convey by mortgage. [OF. = dead pledger]

morti'cian (-ish-) *n.* funeral undertaker. [L. *mors*, *mort-*, death]

mort'ify *v.i.* subdue by self-denial; humiliate. [L. *mortificare*, make dead]

mort'ise (-is) *n.* hole made in a piece of wood, *etc.*, to receive the tongue at the end of another piece called a tenon. -*v.t.* make a mortise in; fasten by mortise and tenon. [F. *mortaise*]

mort'uary *a.* of or for burial. -*n.* building where dead bodies are kept for a time. [L. *mortuarius-mors*, death]

mosa'ic *n.* picture or pattern made by fixing side by side small bits of colored stone, glass, *etc.*; this process of decoration. [F. *mosaique*]

Mos'lem. See Mus'lim.

mosque (mosk) *n.* Islamic place of worship. [Arab. *masjid*]

mosqui'to (-ke-to) *n.* various kinds of gnat. [Sp., fr. L. *musca*, fly]

moss *n.* swamp; small plant growing in masses on a surface. -*v.t.* cover with moss. [OE. *mos*]

most *a.* greatest in size, number, degree. -*n.* greatest amount, degree. -*adv.* in the greatest degree. -**most'ly** *adv.* for the most part. [OE. *moest*]

mot (mo) *n.* pithy or witty saying. -**mot juste**, right word. [F.]

mote *n.* speck of dust. [OE. *mot*]

moth *n.* nocturnal insect of butterfly family. -**moth'eaten** *a.* [OE. *moththe*]

moth'er (muTH-) *n.* female parent; head of a religious community of women. -*a.* inborn. -*v.t.* act as a mother to. -**moth'erhood** *n.* -**moth'erly** *a.* -**moth'er-in-law** *n.* mother of one's wife or husband. -**moth'erboard** *n.* (in an electronic system) a printed circuit board through which signals between all other boards are routed. -**moth'er of pearl'** *n.* iridescent substance forming the lining of certain shells. -**Moth'er's Day** *n.* day in which the mother is honored by the family, *usu.* the second Sunday in May. [OE. *moder*]

mo'tion *n.* process or action or way of moving; proposal in a meeting; application to a judge. -*v.t.* direct by a sign. -**mo'tionless** *a.* [L. *motio*, fr. *movere, mot-*, move]

mot'tle *n.* blotch on a surface; arrangement of blotches. -*v.t.* mark with blotches. -**mott'led** *a.* blotchy. [prob. from *motley*, (*v.s.*)]

mo'tor *n.* that which imparts movement; machine to supply motive power. **mo'torize** *v.t.* mechanize. -**mo'tor-boat** (-bus, -launch, *etc.*) *n.* one moved by an engine carried inside it. -**mo'torcade** *n.* formal procession of motor vehicles. -**mo'torist** *n.* user of an automobile. [*motion*]

mott'o *n.* (mott'oes *pl.*) saying adopted as a rule of conduct; short inscribed sentence; word or sentence accompanying a heraldic crest. [It.]

mound *n.* heap of earth or stones; small hill. [orig. uncertain]

mount *n.* hill; that on which anything is supported or fitted; horse. -*v.i.* go up; get on horseback; rise. -*v.t.* go up; get on the back of, set on a mount; furnish with a horse. -**mount'ain** *n.* hill of great size. -**mountaineer'** *n.* one who lives among or climbs mountains. [L. *mons, mont-*, hill]

mourn -*v.i.* feel or show sorrow. -*v.t.* grieve for. -**mourn'ing** *n.* act of mourning; conventional signs of grief for a death; clothes of a mourner. [OE. *murnan*]

mouse *n.* (mice *pl.*) small rodent animal. -*v.i.* catch mice. [OE. *mus*]

mouse *n.* (*compute.*) input device that is moved about on a tabletop or pad and directs a pointer (cursor) on a video screen

mousse *n.* dish of frozen whipped cream; similar cold dishes. [F.]

mouth (-th; *pl.* -THz) *n.* opening in the head, used for eating, speaking, *etc.*; opening into anything hollow; outfall of a river, entrance to harbor, *etc.* -(-TH) *v.t.* take into the mouth; declaim. -*v.i.* declaim. [OE. *muth*]

move -*v.t.* change the position of-, stir; propose. -*v. i.* change places; take action. -*n.* a moving; motion making towards some goal. -**mov'able** *a.* and *n.* **move'ment** *n.* process or action of moving; moving parts of a machine; main division of a piece of music. -**mov'ie** *n.* (*sl.*) motion picture, film. [L. *movere*]

mow *v.t.* cut (grass, *etc.*); cut down, kill. -*v.i.* cut grass. [OE. *mawan*]

much *a.* in quantity. -*n.* large amount; important matter. -*adv.* in a great degree, nearly. [ME. *muche*]

mu'cus *n.* viscous secretion of the mucous membrane. -**mu'cous** *a.* -**mu'cous membrane**, lining of body cavities, canals. [L.]

mud *a.* wet and soft earth. -**mud'dle** *v.t.* confuse; bewilder; mismanage. -*v. i.* be busy in a fumbling way. -*n.* confusion. -**mudd'y** *a.* [of Teutonic orig.]

muff'in *n.* light round flat cake, toasted and buttered. [orig. uncertain]

muffle *v.t.* wrap up; of sound, deaden. -**muff'ler** *n.* scarf to cover neck and throat; device which deadens sound, esp. as attached to the exhaust system of an automobile, *etc.* [F. *emmoufler*, swathe]

mug *n.* drinking cup. -(*sl.*) face; fool. -*v. i.* study hard; to attack or threaten with the intention of robbing, *usu.* in the street. -**mugg'er** *n.* one who robs in this way. [fr. *mugan*]

mugg'y *a.* damp and stifling. [dial. *mug*, mist, fr. ON. *mugga*]

Muhammadan. See Mohammedan.

mulch *n.* straw, leaves, *etc.*, spread as a protection for the roots of plants. -*v.t.* protect in this way. [orig. uncertain]

mule *n.* cross between horse and ass; obstinate person. -**muleteer'** *n.* mule driver. -**mu'lish** *a.* [L. *mulus*]

mule *n.* heelless slipper. [F.]

mull *v.t.* heat (wine or ale) with sugar and spices. [orig. uncertain]

mult-, multi- *prefix* much, many. [L. *multus*, much] -**multian'gular** (-ng-g-) *a.* many-angled. -**multicult'ural** *a.* consisting of, relating to, or designed for the cultures of several different races. -**multidisciplinary** *a.* of, or relating to, or involving many disciplines or branches of learning. **multieth'nic** *a.* consisting of, relating to, or designed for various different races. -**multifa'rious** *a.* manifold, varied. -mul'tiform a. many forms. -multilat'eral a. many-sided. -mul'tiple!a. having many parts. -n. quantity which contains another an exact number of times. -mul'tiplicand n. number to be multiplied by another. -multiplica'tion n. -multiplicity, variety, greatness in number. -mul'tiply v.t. make many; find the sum of a given number taken a stated number of times. -v. i. increase in number or amount. -mul'titude n. great number; great crowd. -multitu'dinous a. very numerous.

mum' a. silent. [imit.]

mum'ble v. i. and t. speak indistinctly. [ME. momelen]

mumm'y n. embalmed body. -munim'ify v.t. [Arab. mumiyah]

mumps n. pl. contagious disease marked by swelling in the glands of the neck. [obs. mump, grimace]

mundane a. worldly; ordinary. [L. mundanus]

municipal (-is'-) a. belonging to the affairs of a city or town. -municipal'ity n. city or town with local self-government; its governing body. [L. municipium, town with rights of Roman citizenship]

muni'tion (-ish'-) n. (usually pt.) military stores. [L. munitio]

mu'ral a. of or on a wall. -n. wall painting. [L. murus, wall]

mur'der n. the unlawful and deliberate killing of a human being. -v.t. to kill thus. [OE. morthor]

mur'mur v. i. make a low continuous sound; complain. -v. t. utter in a low voice. -n. sound or act of murmuring. [L. murmurare]

mus'cle (mus'l) n. part of the body which produces movement by contracting; part of the body made up of muscles. -mus'cular a. [F.]

Muse (-z) n. one of the nine goddesses inspiring learning and the arts. [L. musa]

muse (-z) v.i. be lost in thought. -n. state of musing. [F. muser]

muse'um n. place to show objects illustrating the arts, history, etc. [L.]

mush n. pulp; boiled corn meal; (fig.) sentimentality. [mash]

mush'room n. kind of edible fungus. -a. of rapid growth. [F. mousseron]

mu'sic (-z-) n. art of expressing or causing an emotion by melodious and harmonious combination of notes; the laws of this; composition in this art; such composition represented on paper. -mu'sical a. -mu'sically adv. -musi'cian n. -mu'sical n. colorful light drama with songs, music. [G. mousike (techne), (art of the) muses]

musk n. a scent obtained from a gland of the musk-deer; various plants with a similar scent. [F. musc]

musk'et n. infantryman's gun, esp. unrifled. -musketeer' n. -musk'etry n. use of firearms. [F. mousquet]

Mus'lim, Mos'lem n. follower of Mohammed. -a. of the Islamic religion. [Arab. salama, submit to God]

mus'lin (-z-) n. fine cotton fabric. [orig. fr. Mosul, in Mesopotamia]

muss'el n. bivalve shellfish. [L. musculus, little mouse]

must n. unfermented wine. [L. mustum]

must v. aux. be obliged to, or certain to. [OE. moste]

mustache (mus-tash) n. hair on the upper lip. [F.]

mus'tang n. wild horse of American prairies. [Sp. mestengo]

mustard n. powdered seeds of a plant used in paste as a condiment; the plant. [OF. moustarde]

must'er v.t. and i. assemble. -n. assembly, esp. for exercise, inspection. [L. monstrare, show]

must'y a. moldy. [orig. uncertain]

mute a. dumb; silent. -n. dumb person; hired mourner; clip, etc. to deaden sound of musical instruments. [L. mutus]

mu'tilate v.t. deprive of a limb or other part; damage. -mutila'tion n. -mu'til- ator n. [L. mutilare]

mu'tiny n. rebellion against authority, esp. against the officers of a disciplined body. -v.i. commit mutiny. -mu'tinous a. -mutineer' n. [F. mutiner]

mutt'er v.i. speak with the mouth nearly closed, indistinctly. -v.t. utter in such tones. -n. act of muttering. [imit.]

mu'tual a. done, possessed, etc., by each of two with respect to the other. mu'tually adv. common to both. [L. mutuus]

muz'zle n. projecting mouth and nose of an animal; thing put over these to prevent biting; end of a firearm by which the projectile leaves. -v.t. put a muzzle on. [OF. musel, snout]

my poss. a. belonging to me. -myself' pron. emphatic and reflex, of I, me. [for mine]

myeli'tis n. inflammation of the spinal cord. [G. myelos. marrow]

myo'pia n. short-sightedness. -my'opic a. [G. myein, close, ops, eye]

myeso'tis n. various small flowering plants including the forget-me-not. (myosote). [G. mys., mouse, ous, ot-, ear]

myr'iad (mir-) n. ten thousand; endless number. -a. innumerable. [G. myrias, myriad-]

myrrh (mer) n. aromatic gum of the balsamodendron. [G. myrrha]

myrtle n. evergreen shrub. [OF. myrtille, myrtle-berry]

mys'tery (mis-) n. obscure or secret thing; state of being obscure; religious rite; miracle-play. -myst'ic a. of hidden meaning, esp. in a religious sense. -n. one who seeks direct communication with God by self-surrender or contemplation. -myst'ify v.t. bewilder. [G. mysterion, secret]

myth (mith) n. tale with supernatural characters or events; imaginary person or object. -myth'ical a. -mythol'ogy n. myths collectively; study of these. [G. mythos, fable]

N

nab *v.t.* (*sl.*) seize, catch, [orig. uncertain. *cp. nap*]

nacelle' (-sel') *n.* streamlined part of an aircraft that houses engine, crew, passengers, and cargo. [L. *navicella*, little ship]

na'cre (na-ker) *n.* mother-of-pearl. [F.]

na'dir *n.* point opposite the zenith. [Arab. *niazir*, opposite]

nag *n.* small horse for riding; horse. [orig. uncertain]

nag *v.t.* and *i.* worry, be worrying, by constant fault-finding. [Sw. *nagga*, peck]

nail *n.* horny shield of the ends of the fingers; claw; small metal spike for fixing wood, *etc.* -*v.t.* fix with a nail. [OE. *nægel*]

naïve *a.* simple, unaffected. [F.]

na'ked *a.* bare, unclothed. -na'kedness *n.* -na'kedly *adv.* [OE. *nacod*]

name *n.* word by which a person, thing. *etc.* is denoted; reputation. -*v. t.* give a name to; call by a name; appoint; mention. -name'less *a.* -name'ly *adj.*, that is to say. -name'sake *n.* person having the same name as another. [OE. *nama*]

nann'y *n.* female goat (also nann'ygoat); children's nurse. [*name*]

nap *n.* roughish surface cloth made by projecting fibers. [Du. *nop*]

nap *v.i.* take a short sleep. -*n.* short sleep. [OE. *knappian*]

nape *n.* back of the neck; hollow there. [OE. *hnoepp*, bowl]

naph'tha *n.* flammable oil distilled from coal, *etc.* -naph'thalene *n.* disinfectant. [G.]

nap'kin *n.* square piece of linen for wiping fingers or lips at table; similar such pieces of cloth or absorbent material. [F. *nappe*, cloth]

narcissus *n.* bulbous plant with a white scented flower; (*psychoanalysis*) one who loves himself. [G. *narkissos*]

narcotic *n.* drug causing sleep, insensibility or hallucination. -*a.* -narco'sis *n.* stupefying effect of narcotic. [G. *narkotikos*]

narrate' *v. t.* relate, tell (story). -narration *n.* -narr'ative *n.* account or story. [L. *narrare*]

narr'ow *a.* of little breadth. -*n. pl.* narrow part of a strait. -*v. t.* and *i.* make, become, narrow. -narr'owly *adv.* -narr'ow-minded *a.* bigoted. -narr'owness *n.* [OE. *nearu*]

na'sal (-z-) *a.* of the nose. -*n.* sound uttered through the nose. -na'salize *v.t.* make nasal in sound. [L. *nasus*, nose]

nas'ty *a.* foul, disagreeable. -nast'ily *adv.* -nas'tiness *n.* [orig. uncertain]

na'tal *a.* relating to birth. [L. *natalis*]

na'tion (-shun) *n.* people or race organized as a state. -na'tional(nash-) *a.* nationally *adv.* -national'ity *n.* national quality or feeling; facts of belonging to a particular nation. -nat'ionalist *n.* one who supports national rights. -nat'ionalize *v. t.* convert into the property of a nation. [L. *natio*]

na'tive (-tiv) *a.* born in a particular place; originating from that country; found in a pure state; of one's birth. -*n.* one born in a place;

oyster reared in an artificial bed. -nativ'ity *n.* -Nativ'ity *n.* birth of Christ; Christmas. [L. *natiuus- nasci, nāt-*, be born]

na'ture *n.* innate or essential qualities of a thing; class, sort; life force; disposition; power underlying all phenomena in the material world; material world as a whole. -nat'ural *a.* of, according to, occurring in, provided by, nature. -*n.* half-witted person; (*music*) sign restoring sharp or flat note to its natural pitch. **nat'urally** *adv.* -nat'uralist *n.* one who studies plants and animals. -nat'uralize *v. t.* admit to citizenship; accustom to a new climate. -naturaliza'tion *n.* [L. *aatura*, fr. *nasci, not-*, to be born]

naught (nawt) *n.* nothing, zero. *a.* bad, useless. -naught'y *a.* wayward, not behaving well. -naught'ily *adv.* [OE. *nawiht*, no whit]

nau'sea *n.* sickness. -nau'seate *v.t.* affect with sickness; reject with loathing. -nau'seous *a.* [L. = seasickness]

nautical *a.* of seamen or ships. [G. *nautes*, sailor]

nautilus *n.* shellfish with a membrane which acts as a sail. [G. *nautilos*, sailor]

naval. See navy.

nave *n.* main body of a church building. [L. *nauis*, ship]

na'vel *n.* small pit on the abdomen. [OE. *nafela*, dim. of *nafu*, nave, hub]

navigate *v. i.* sail. -*v.t.* sail over; direct the steering of a ship. -nav'igator *n.* one who navigates; worker digging a canal. -navv'y *n.* laborer (navigator in second sense). [L. *navigare*, fr. *nauis*, ship]

na'vy *n.* fleet; warships of a country with their crews and organization. -na'val *a.* [OF. *navie- navis*, ship]

Nazi *n.* German National Socialist Party; member of this; one holding views similar to this. *a.* [contr. of Ger. *National sozialist*]

Nean'derthal man (ne-an'-der-tal), primitive type of prehistoric man. [fr. skull found in the *Neanderthal*, valley near Dusseldorf]

near *adv.* at or to a short distance. -*prep.* close to. -*a.* close at hand, close; closely related; stingy; of horses, vehicles, *etc.*, left. -*v.t.* and *i.* approach. -near'ly *adv.* closely; almost. -near'ness *n.* -near'sighted *a.* able to see objects clearly only if they are near to the eyes.

neat *a.* pure, undiluted; simple and elegant; cleverly worded; deft. -neat'ly *adv.* -neat'ness *n.* [F. *net*, clean]

neb'ula *n.* star-cluster. -neb'ular *a.* -neb'ulous *a.* cloudy; vague. [L. = *mist*]

necessary (nes'-) *a.* needful, requisite, that must be done. -*n.* needful thing. nec'essarily *adv.* -necess'ity *n.* compel, give power or state of affairs; a being needful; needful thing; poverty. **necessitate** *v. t.* make necessary. [L. *aecessarius*]

neck *n.* part of the body joining the head to the shoulders; narrower part of a bottle, *etc.*; narrow piece of anything between wider parts. -neck'erchief (chif) *n.* kerchief for the neck. -neck'lace *n.* ornament round the neck. -neck'tie *n.* narrow strip of tailored material worn about the neck and tied at the front. [OE.

hnecca, nape of neck]

necrol'ogy n. list of deaths, obituaries. [G. nekros, dead body]

nec'tar n. drink of the gods; the honey of flowers. **-nect'arine** a. -n. variety of peach. [G. nektar]

née (nā) a. born, preceding maiden surname of a married woman. [F.]

need n. want, requirement; necessity; poverty. -v.t. want, require. [OE. nied]

need'le n. pointed pin with an eye and no head, for passing thread through cloth, etc.; knitting pin; magnetized bar of a compass; obelisk. [OE. ntdl]

neg'ative a. expressing denial or refusal; wanting in positive qualities; not positive. -n. negative word or statement; in photography, a picture made by the action of light on chemicals in which the lights and shades are reversed. -v.t. disprove, reject. **-negate'** v. t. deny. **-nega'tion** n. [L. negativus, negare, deny]

neglect' v.t. disregard, take no care of; fail to do; omit through carelessness. -n. fact of neglecting or being neglected. **neglect'ful** a. [L. neglegere, neglect-, not to pick up]

negotiate v.i. discuss with a view to finding terms of agreement. -v.t. arrange by conference; transfer (bill, etc.); get over (an obstacle). [L. negotiari, negotium, business]

Ne'gro n. member of the black African race. [Sp., fr. L. niger, negr-, black]

neigh v.i. of a horse, to utter its cry. -n. the cry. [OE. hnægan]

neigh'bor (nq'bur) n. one who lives, stands, etc. near another. **-neigh'boring** a. situated near by. **-neigh'borhood** n. district; people of a district; region round about. [OE. neah-gebur, 'nigh boor', near by farmer]

nei'ther a. and pron. not either. -adv. not on the one hand; not either. -conj. nor yet. [OE. nahwæther, not whether]

neo- pref. new. [G. neos, new]

neolith'ic a. of the later stone age. **-neol'ogism** n. new coined word or phrase. **-neontol'ogy** n. study of still-existing races of animals. **-neoter'ic** a. modern. **-ne'ophyte** n. new convert; beginner.

ne'on n. rare atmospheric gas. **-ne'on lighting**, produced by passing an electric current through a tube containing neon. [G. neos, new]

neph'ew n. brother's or sister's son, [F. neveu, fr. L. nepos]

ne'potism n. favoritism. [It. nepotismo, fr. nepote, nephew. (orig. because of favors bestowed by a pope on his nephews)]

Nep'tune n. Roman god of the sea; one of the outermost planets of the Solar system. [G. Neptunus]

nerve n. sinew, tendon; fiber or bundle of fibers conveying feeling, impulses to motion, etc., between the brain and other parts of the body; assurance, coolness in danger. (sl.) impudence. -pl. irritability, unusual sensitiveness to fear, annoyance, etc. -v. t. give courage or strength to. **-nerve'less** a. **-nerv'ous** a. of the nerves; vigorous; excitable; timid. -

nerv'ously adv. **-nerv'ousness** n. **-nerv'y** a. brash; courageous. [L. nervus, sinew]

nest n. place in which a bird lays and hatches its eggs; animal's breeding place; any snug retreat. -v. i. make or have a nest. **-nes'tle** (-sl) v. i. settle comfortably, usually pressing in or close to something. **-nest'ling** n. bird too young to leave the nest. [OE.]

net n. open-work fabric of meshes of cord, etc.; piece of it used to catch fish, etc. -v. t. to cover with, or catch in, a net. -v. i. make net. **-net'ting** n. string or wire net. **-net'work** n. intricate system-e.g., of transport systems. **-network** (compute.) system of computers or terminals interconnected by communication circuits. [OE. nett]

net, nett a. left after all deductions; clear profit. -v.t. gain as clear profit. [F. clean]

nett'le n. plant with stinging hairs on the leaves. -v.t. irritate, provoke. [OE. netele]

neuralgia n. pain in the nerves, esp. of face and head. **-neural'gic** a. **-neurasthe'nia** n. nervous debility. **-neurasthen'ic** a. **-neuri'tis** n. inflammation of nerves. **-neuro'sis** n. nervous disorder. **-neurot'ic** a. suffering from neurosis; abnormally sensitive. -n. neurotic person. [G. neuron, nerve]

neut'er a. neither masculine nor feminine. -n. neuter word; neuter gender. [L. = neither]

neut'ral a. taking neither side in a war; dispute, etc.; without marked qualities; belonging to neither of two classes. -n. neutral state, or a subject of one. **neutral'ity** n. impartiality. **-neut'ralize** v. t. make ineffective; counterbalance. [L. = neither]

neut'ron n. electrically uncharged particle of the atom. **-neut'ron bomb** n. nuclear bomb designed to destroy people but not buildings. [L. neuter, neither]

nev'er adv. at no time. **-nevertheless'** adv. for all that. [OE. næfre]

new a. not existing before, fresh; lately come into some state or existence. adv. (usually new-) recently, fresh. **-newfang'led** (-ng-gid) a. of new fashion. **new'ly** adv. **-new'ness** n. **-news** n. report of recent happenings, fresh information. **-news'-dealer** n. one who deals in newspaper, magazines etc. **-news'paper** n. periodical publication containing news. [OE. niave, new; cp. F. nouvelles]

next a. nearest; immediately following.-adv. on the first future occasion. [OE. niehst, superl. of neah, high]

nex'us n. connecting link. [L.]

nib n. pen-point. -pl. crushed cocoa beans. [earlier neb, beak, OE. nebb]

nib'ble v.t. take little bites of. -v.i. take little bites. -n. little bite. [fr. nip]

nice a. hard to please; careful, exact; difficult to decide; minute; subtle, fine; (sl.) pleasant, friendly, kind, agreeable, etc. **-nice'ly** adv. **-ni'cety** n. precision; minute distinction or detail. [OF. nice, foolish]

nick v. t. make a notch in, indent; just catch in time. -n. notch; exact point of time. [orig. uncertain]

nick'el n. silver-white metal much used in alloys and plating; five cent piece. [Sw. abbrev. fr. Ger. *kupfernickel*, copper nickel (ore)]

nick'name *n.* name added to or replacing an ordinary name. -*v.t.* give a nickname to. [earlier, a *nickname* was an *eke-name*; fr. *eke*, also, [OE. *ecan*, cp. *newt*]

nic'otine- *n.* poisonous oily liquid in tobacco. [F. fr. J. *Nicot*, who sent tobacco plants to France (1560)]

niece *n.* brother's or sister's daughter. [F. niece, fr. L. neptis]

night (nit) *n.* time of darkness between day and day; end of daylight; dark. **night'-blind'ness** *n.* inability to see in a dim light. -**night'-club** *n.* club open at night for dancing, entertainment. -**night'fall** *n.* end of day. -**night'ingale** *n.* small bird which sings usually at night. -**night'ly** *a.* happening or done every night; of the night. -**night'ly** *adj.* every night, by night. -**night'mare** *n.* feeling of distress during sleep; bad dream. -**night'shade** *n.* various plants of the potato family, some of them with very poisonous berries. -**night'-shift** *n.* night duty; relay of workmen on night duty. -**night'stick** *n.* policeman's club. [OE. *nihl*]

ni'hilism *n.* denial of all reality; rejection of all religious and moral principles; opposition to all constituted authority or government. -**ni'hilist** *n.* [L. *nihil*, nothing]

nil *n.* nothing, zero. [contr. of L. *nihil*]

nim'ble *a.* active, quick. [OE. *niman*, take, capture]

nim'bus *n.* cloud of glory, halo; raincloud or storm-cloud. [L. = cloud]

nine *a.* and *n.* cardinal number next above eight. -**ninth** (-i-) *a.* -**ninth'ly** *adv.* -**nine'teen** *a.* and *n.* nine and ten. -**nine'teenth** *a.* -**nine'ty** *a.* and *n.* nine tens. -**nine'tieth** *a.* [OE. *nigon*]

ninja *n.* member of secret Japanese feudal organization.

nip *v. t.* pinch sharply; detach by pinching; check growth (of plants) thus. -*n.* pinch; check to growth; sharp coldness of weather. [orig. uncertain]

nipp'le *n.* point of a breast, teat. [orig. uncertain]

Nirva'na *n.* in Buddhism, attainment of union with the divine by the conquest of personal desires and passions. [Sanskrit = extinction]

ni'trogen *n.* colorless, tasteless gaseous element forming four-fifths of the atmosphere. -**nitrog'enous** (-j-) *a.* of or containing nitrogen. [G. *nitron*]

nitroglycerin *n.* high explosive produced by interaction of glycerin and nitric or sulfuric acids. [G. *nitron*]

no *a.* not any. -*adv.* expresses a negative reply to question or request. -**no'body** *n.* no person; person of no importance. -**noth'ing** (nuth'-) *n.* not anything. *a.* for earlier none; *adv.* [OE. *na*]

no'ble *a.* distinguished by deeds, character, rank or birth; of lofty characters impressive; excellent. -*n.* member of the nobility. -**nobil'ity** *n.* class holding special rank, usually hereditary, in a state; a noble being. -**no'bly** *adv.* **no'bleman** *n.* [L. *nobilis*]

nocturnal *a.* of, in, or by night; active by night. -**noc'tule** *n.* night-flying list. -**noc'turne** *n.* dreamy piece of music; night scene. [L. *nocturnus*, fr. *nox, noct-,* night]

nod *v. i.* bow the head slightly and quickly in assent, command, *etc.*; let the head droop with sleep, err through carelessness or inattention. -*v.t.* incline (the head) thus. -*n.* an act of nodding. [orig. uncertain]

Noël *n.* Christmas; Christmas carol. [F.]

no-fault *a.* of or pertaining to, automobile insurance which guarantees that an accident victim is compensated for damages by their insurance company without determination of blame.

no-frills *a.* (*sl.*) basic; plain; reduced to the essentials; without extras or special features.

noise *n.* clamor, din; any sound. -*v. t.* rumor. -**noise'less** *a.* -**nois'y** *a.* -**nois'ily** *adv.* (F.)

nom'ad *a.* roaming from pasture to pasture; not having a fixed place of dwelling. -*n.* member of a nomad tribe; wanderer. -**nomad'ic** *a.* [G. *nomas, nomad-*]

nomenclature *n.* system of names or naming. [L. *nomen*, name]

nom'inal *a.* of a name or names; existing only in name. -**nom'inally** *adv.* **nom'inate** *v.t.* propose as a candidate appoint to an office. -**nom'inator** *n.* **nomina'tion** *n.* -**nominee'** *n.* [L. *nominalis,* fr. *nomen,* name]

non- *prefix* makes compounds that negative the idea of the simple word, *e.g.,* -**noncom'batant** *n.* one who does not fight. The meaning and derivation of those not given should be sought by reference to the simple word. [L. = note]

nonagenarian (-är-) *a.* between ninety and a hundred years old. -*n.* person of such age. [L. *nonagenarius,* fr. *nonageni,* ninety each]

nonchalant (-sh-) *a.* unconcerned. **non'chalantly** *adv.* -**non'chalance** *n.* [F.]

noncommittal *a.* not committing or pledging oneself to opinion, *etc.* [*non-,* and L. *committere*]

nonconformist *n.* one who does not conform to the established church. **nonconform'ity** *n.* [*conform*]

non'descript *a.* not easily described. indeterminate. [*describe*]

none (nun) *pron.* no one. -*a.* no. -*adv.* in no way. [OE. *nan* for *ne an,* not one]

nonentity *n.* non-existence; nonexistent thing; person of no importance [*entity*]

noninvasive *a.* not entering the body by penetration, *esp.* surgery and diagnostic procedures.

nonplus' *n.* state of perplexity, deadlock. -*v.t.* bring to a nonplus. [L. *non plus,* not more]

non'sense *n.* words or actions that are foolish or meaningless; -**nonsen'sical** *a.* [*non-* and *sense*]

non violence *n.* the belief or practice of peaceful methods in pursuit of any goal; lack or absence of violence.

nood'le *n.* (*cookery*) hardened paste of flour and eggs, used in soup. [Ger. *nudel*]

nook *n.* sheltered corner. [cp. Gael. *niue*]

noon *n.* midday. [L. *nona* (*hora*), ninth

(hour)]

noose *n.* running loop; snare. -*v.t.* to catch in a noose. [L. *nodus*, knot]

nor *conj.* and not. [ME. *nother*]

norm *n.* rule; pattern; type. -**nor'mal** *a.* perpendicular; conforming to type, ordinary. -**normal'ity** *n.* -**nor'mally** *adv.* -**normal'ize** *v.t.* to render normal; bring into conformity with standard; heat (steel) above critical temperature and allow it to cool in air to relieve internal stresses. -**normal'ization** *n.* [L. *norma*, carpenter's square]

Norse *a.* of Norway. -*n.* Norwegian people or language.

north (-th) *n.* region or cardinal point opposite to the midday sun; part of the world, of a country, *etc.* , towards this point. -*adv.* towards or in the north. -*a.* to, from, or in the north. -**nor'therly** (-TH-) *a.* -**nor'thern** *a.* -**nor'therner** *n.* -**northwards** *adv.* [OE.]

Norwe'gian *a.* of, *pert.* to Norway. -*n.* [OE. *Northweg*]

nose *n.* organ of smell, used also in breathing. -*v. t.* detect by smell. -*v. i.* smell. [OE. *nosu*]

nostal'gia *n.* home-sickness. [G. *nostos*, return home, *algos*, pain]

nos'tril *n.* one of the openings of the nose. [OE. noshvri, nose-hole]

not *adv.* expressing negation. [*nought*]

no'table *a.* worthy of note, remarkable. -**no'tably** *adv.* -**notabil'ity** *n.* eminent person. [*note*]

nota'tion *n.* representing of numbers, quantities, *etc.* , by symbols; set of such symbols. [L. *notare*, *notat-*, note]

notch *n.* small V-shaped cut or indention. -*v.t.* make a notch in; score. [F. *oche*]

note *n.* symbol standing for a musical sound; single tone; mark, sign; brief written message, memorandum, letter; fame, regard. -*v. t.* observe; set down. -**no'ted** *a.* well known. [L. *nota*, mark; *notare*, note]

nothing (nuth'-) *n.* no thing; not anything. *adv.* not at all. [*no thing*]

no'tice (-tis) *n.* warning, intimation, announcement; bill, *etc.* , with an announcement. -*v.t.* mention; observe; give attention to. -**no'ticeable** *a.* [L. *notus*, known]

no'tify (-i) *v.t.* report, give notice of or to. -**notifica'tion** *n.* [L. *notificare*]

no'tion *n.* idea, opinion, belief-, fancy. (*colloq.*) desire, whim. [F. fr. L. *notio*]

notorious *a.* known for something bad; well known. -**notori'ety** *n.* [Low L. *notorius*]

nought (nawt) *n.* nothing; cipher (0) [OE. *nowiht*]

noun (nown) *n.* word used as a name of person, or thing. [L. *nomen*, name]

nourish (nur'-) *v. t.* supply with food; keep up. -**nour'ishment** *n.* [F. *nourrir*, fr. L. *nutrire*, feed]

no'va *n.* (novae *pl.*) new star. [L.]

nov'el *a.* new, strange. -*n.* fictitious tale published as a book. -**nov'elist** *n.* writer of novels. [L. *novus*, new]

November *n.* eleventh month of the year. [L. *novem*, nine]

nov'ice *n.* candidate for admission to a religious order; one new to anything. -**novi'tiate**, **novi'ciate** (-vish-) [L. *novitius*, fr. *novus*, new]

now *adv.* at the present time. **now'adays** *adv.* in these times. [OE. *nu*]

no'where *adv.* not anywhere; (*sl.*) far behind; defeated. [*no* and *where*]

nox'ious (-ksh) *a.* hurtful, harmful, dangerous. [L. *noxa*, harm]

noz'zle *n.* pointed spout, *esp.* at the end of a hose. [dim. of *nose*]

nu'ance (-ong-s) shade of difference. [F.]

nu'bile *a.* marriageable. [L. *nubere*, marry]

nu'cleus *n.* center, kernel; beginning meant to receive additions; head of a comet; central part of an atom. -**nu'clear** *a.* of, pert. to atomic nucleus. -**nu'clear bomb** *n.* bomb whose force is due to uncontrolled nuclear fusion or nuclear fission. -**nu'clear disarmament** *n.* elimination of nuclear weapons from country's armament. -**nu'clear en'ergy** *n.* energy released by nuclear fission. -**nu'clear fam'ily** *n.* primary social unit consisting of parents and their offspring. -**nu'clear fis'sion** *n.* disintegration of the atom. -**nu'clear fu'sion** *n.* reaction in which two nuclei combine to form nucleus with release of energy (also **fu'sion**). -**nu'clear phy'sics** *n.* branch of physics concerned with structure of nucleus and particles of which it consists. -**nu'clear reac'tion** *n.* change in structure and energy content of atomic nucleus by interaction with another nucleus, particle. [L. = *kernel*]

nude *a.* naked. -**nu'dity** *n.* [L. *nudus*]

nudge *v. t.* touch with the elbow. -*n.* such touch. [orig. uncertain]

nugg'et *n.* rough lump of native gold. [orig. uncertain]

nuisance *n.* something offensive or annoying. [F. *noire*, *nuis-*, harm]

null *a.* of no effect, void. [L. *nullus*, none]

numb (num) *a.* deprived of feeling, *esp.* by cold. -*v. t.* [OE. *numen*]

num'ber *n.* sum or aggregate; word or symbol saying how many; single issue of a paper, *etc.*, issued in regular series; classification as to singular or plural; rhythm; metrical feet or verses; company or collection. -*v.t.* count; class, reckon; give a number to; amount to. -**nu'meral** *a.* of or expressing number. -*n.* sign or word denoting a number. -**nu'merate** *v.t.* count. -*a.* able to count. -**numera'tion** *n.* -**nu'merator** *n.* top part of a fraction, figure showing how many of the fractional units are taken. -**numer'ical** *a.* of, or in respect of, number, or numbers. -**nu'merous** *a.* many. [L. *numerus*]

numismatic *a.* of coins. -*n.* in *pl.* study of coins. -**numis'matist** *n.* [L. *numisma*, current coin]

nun *n.* woman living in a convent under religious vows. -**nunn'ery** *n.* convent of nuns. [Church L. *nonna*, *fem.* of *nonnus*, monk]

nup'tial *a.* of or relating to marriage or a marriage. -*n.* in *pl.* marriage. [L. *nupti*—, wedding]

nurse *n.* person trained for the care of the sick or injured; woman tending another's child.

-v.t. act as a nurse to. -nurs'ery n. room for children; rearing place for plants. -nurs'ing-home n. private hospital. [L. nutrix, foster-mother]

nur'ture n. bringing-up. -v.t. bring up. [F. nourriture, nourishment]

nut n. fruit consisting of a hard shell and ker-nel: small block with a hole to be screwed on a bolt. -v. i. gather nuts. [OE. hnutu]

nutriment n. food. -nutri'tion (-trish'n) n. the receiving or supply of food; food. -nutri'tious a. good in effects as food. -nu'tritive a. [L. nutrire, nourish]

ny'lon n. synthetic filament of great strength and fineness, made into fabrics, etc. -pl. nylon stockings. (New York, London)

nymph n. legendary semi-divine maiden living in the sea, woods, mountains, etc. [G. nymphe, bride]

O

oaf n. changeling; dolt. [ON. a!fr, elf]

oak n. familiar forest tree. -oak'en a. -oak-apple n. insect-gall on the oak. [OE. ac]

oar n. wooden lever with a broad blade worked by the hands to propel a boat. [OE. ar]

oa'sis n. fertile spot in the desert. [G. of Egypt, orig.]

oat n. grain of a common cereal plant (usu. pl.); the plant. [OE. ate]

oath n. confirmation of the truth of a state-ment by the naming of something sacred; act of swearing. [OE. ath]

ob'durate a. stubborn. -ob'duracy n. [L. ob-duratus-durare, durat-, harden]

obedient. See obey.

obeis'ance n. bow, curtsy. [F. obéissance, obedience]

obese' a. very fat. -obe'sity n. corpulence. [L. obesus]

obey v.t. do the bidding of-, be moved by. [L. oboedire]

obit'uscate v.t. confuse; make dark or obscure. [L. obfuscare, darken]

obit'uary n. notice or record of a death or deaths. [Med. L. obituarius, fr. obitus, depar-ture]

ob'ject n. material thing; that to which feeling or action is directed; end or aim; word depend-ent on a verb or preposition. -object' v.i. state in opposition. -v.i. feel dislike or reluctance to something. -objective a. external to the mind. -n. thing or place aimed at. [Med, L. objectum, thrown in the way]

oblige' v.t. bind morally or legally to do a service to; compel. -obliga'tion n. binding promise; debt of gratitude; indebtedness for a favor; duty. [L. obligare, fr. ligare, bind]

oblique' a. slanting; indirect. -obliq'uity n. -oblique'ly adv. [F., fr. L obliquus-liquis, slanting]

oblit'erate v.t. blot out. -oblitera'tion n. [L. obliterare, fr. litera, letter]

obliv'ion n. forgetting or being forgotten. -obliv'ious a. [L. oblivio]

ob'long a. rectangular with adjacent sides unequal. -n. oblong figure. [L. oblongus]

obnox'ious (-okshus) a. offensive, disliked. [L. obnoxius, exposed to harm]

o'boe n. wood wind instrument. o'boist n. [F. hautbois, hautboy]

obscene' a. indecent; offensive. -obscen'ity n. [L. obscœnus]

obscure' a. dark, dim; indistinct; unex-plained; humble. -v.t. dim; conceal; make unintelligible. [L. obscurus]

obse'quious a. servile, fawning. [L. obse-quiosus, compliant]

observe' (-z-) v.t. keep, follow; watch; note systematically; notice; remark. v.i. make a remark. -observ'able a. -observ'ance n. paying attention; keeping. -observa'tion n. action or habit of observing; noticing; remark. -observ'atory n. a building scientifically equipped for the observation of stars, etc. [L. observare, fr. servare, guard]

obsess' v.t. haunt, fill the mind.-obses'sion n. -obsess'ional a. [L. obsidere, obsess, besiege]

ob'solete a. no longer in use, out of date. -obsoles'cent a. going out of use. [L. obsoles-cere, grow out of use]

ob'stacle n. thing in the way; hindrance to progress. [L. obstaculum]

obstet'ric a. of midwifery. -n. in pl. mid-wifery. [L. obstetrix, midwife]

ob'stinate a. stubborn. [L. obstinatus]

obstruct' v.t. hinder; block up. -obstruc'tion n. [L. obstruere, obstruct-, build up against]

obtain v.t. get. -v.i. be customary. -obtain'able a. [L. obtinere]

obtuse' a. not sharp or pointed; greater than a right angle; stupid. -obtuse'ly adv. [L. ob-tusus, blunt]

ob'verse n. side of a coin or medal with the chief design. -a. turned towards one. [L. ob-versus, turned towards]

ob'vious a. clear, evident. [L. obvius, what meets one in the way]

occa'sion n. opportunity; reason, need; im-mediate but subsidiary cause; time when a thing happens. -v.t. cause. -occa'sional a. hap-pening or found now and then. -occa'sionally adv. sometimes, now and then. [L. occasio]

occult' a. secret, mysterious. -v.t. hide from view. [L. occultus, fr. occulere, hide]

occ'upy v.t. take possession of; inhabit; fill; employ. -occ'upancy n. fact of occupying; residing. -occ'upant n. -occupa'tion n. seizure; possession; employment. -occ'upier n. [L. occupare, take possession of]

occur' v.i. happen; come to mind. -occurr'ence n. [L. occurrere, run against]

o'cean n. great body of water surrounding the land of the globe; large division of this; sea. -ocean'ic a. [G. okeanos, stream encircling the world]

OCR n. (compute.) ability of certain light sen-sitive machines to recognize printed letters, numbers, and special characters, and translate them into computer terms. [optical character recognition]

oct-', oc'ta-, oc'to- prefix eight. -oc'tagon n. figure with eight angles. -octag'onal a. -octang'ular a. having eight angles. -oc'tave *n.* group of eight days; eight lines of verse; note eight degrees above or below a given note; this space. **-Octo′ber** *n.* tenth month of the year. (Roman eighth.) **-octogena′rian** *a.* of an age between eighty and ninety. *-n.* a person of such age. **-oc′topus** *n.* a mollusk with eight arms covered with suckers. **-octet** *n.* group of eight. [G. and L. *okto,* eight]

oc′ular *a.* of the eye or sight. **-oc′ularly** *adv.* **-oc′ulate** *a.* **-oc′ulist** *n.* eye surgeon. [L. *oculus,* eye]

odd *a.* that is one in addition when the rest have been divided into two equal groups; not even; not part of a set; strange, queer. **-odd′ity** *n.* quality of being odd; odd person or thing. **-odd′ments** *n. pl.* odd things. **-odds** *n. pl.* difference, balance; advantage to one of two competitors; advantage conceded in betting; likelihood. [ON. *odda(tala),* odd (number)]

ode *n.* lyric poem of lofty style. [G.]

o′dor *n.* smell. **-o′dorize** *v.t.* fill with scent. [L. *odor*]

oen′ophile *n.* lover or connoisseur of wines. [G. *oinos,* wine, *philos,* loving]

of *prep.* denotes removal, separation, ownership, attribute, material, quality, *etc.* [OE.]

off *adv.* away. *-prep.* away from. *-a.* distant; of horses, vehicles, *etc.* , right. **off′chance** *n.* remote possibility. **off′col′or,** indisposed, not at one's best. **-off′shoot** *n.* branch from main stem. **off′spring** *n.* children, issue. **-off′ing** *n.* more distant part of the sea visible to an observer. [var. of *of*]

off′al *n.* parts cut out in preparing a carcase for food; refuse. [= *off-fall*]

offend′ *v.t.* displease. *-v.i.* do wrong. **-offense′** *n.* **-offend′er** *n.* **-offen′sive** *a.* causing displeasure. *-n.* position or movement of attack. [L. *offendere,* strike against]

off′er *v.t.* present for acceptance or refusal; propose; attempt. *-v. i.* present itself.*-n.* offering, bid. [L. *offerre*]

off′ice *n.* service; duty; official position; form of worship; place for doing business; corporation carrying on business. **-off′icer** *n.* one in command in an army, navy, air force, *etc. -v.t.* supply with officers. **-offi′cial** (fish′-) *a.* having or by authority. *-n.* one holding an office, *esp.* in a public body. **-offi′cialism** *n.* undue official authority or routine. **-offi′cialdom** *n.* officials collectively; their work, usually in a contemptuous sense. **-offi′ciate** *v.i.* to perform the duties of an office; perform a service. **-offi′cious** (-ish′us) *a.* meddlesome, importunate in offering service. **-offi′ciousness** *n.* [L. *officium,* duty]

o′gle *v. i.* make eyes. *-v. t.* make eyes at. *n.* amorous glance. [Low Ger. *oegeln,* eye]

ohm *n.* unit of electrical resistance. [*Ohm,* Ger. physicist (d. 1854)]

oil *n.* light flammable viscous liquid, obtained from various plants, animal substances, and minerals. *-v. t.* apply oil to. *-v.i.* of a ship *etc.* take in oil fuel. **oil′-cake** *n.* cattle food made from linseed *etc.* **-oil′-cloth** *n.* oil-coated canvas, linoleum. **-oil′skin** *n.* material made waterproof with oil. **-oil′y** *a.* [L. *oleum*]

oint′ment *n.* greasy preparation for healing the skin. [OF. *oignement*]

okay′, OK *adv.* and *a.* all right. *-v.t.* pass as correct. [perh. abbrev. for *orl korrekt*]

old *a.* advanced in age, having lived or existed long; belonging to an earlier period. **-old′en** *a.* old. **-old-fash′ioned** *a.* in the style of an earlier period, out of date; fond of old ways. [OE. *eald*]

olfac′tory *a.* of smell. **-olfac′tion** *n.* [L. *olfacere,* cause to smell]

ol′igarchy (-ki) *n.* government by a few. [G. *oligarchia,* fr. *oligos,* few]

ol′ive (-iv) *n.* evergreen tree; its oil-yielding fruit. *-a.* gray-green in color. [L. *oliva*]

Olym′pic *a.* of Olympus. **-Olym′pic Games,** great athletic festival of ancient Greece; (*mod.*) international sports meeting held every four years. [G.]

o′mega *n.* last letter of Greek alphabet; end. [G.]

om′elet, om′elette *n.* dish of fried eggs with seasoning, *etc.* [F. *omelette*]

o′men *n.* prophetic object or happening. **-om′inous** *a.* portending evil. [L.]

omit′ *v.t.* leave out, neglect. **-omis′sion** *n.* [L. *omittere*]

omni- all. [L. *omnis,* all] **-om′nibus** *n.* road vehicle travelling on a fixed route and taking passengers at any stage; several books bound in one volume. *-a.* serving or containing several objects. [L. = for all] **-omnip′otent** *a.* all powerful. **-omnip′otence** *n.* **-omnipres′ent** *a.* everywhere at the same time. **-omnipres′cence** *n.* **-omnis′cient** (shient) *a.* knowing everything. **-omnis′cience** *n.* **-omniv′orous** *a.* devouring all foods. [L. *ominis,* all]

on *prep.* above and touching, at, near, towards, *etc.* *-adv* . so as to be on, forwards, continuously, *etc.* **-on′ward** *a.* and *adv.* **-on′wards** *adv.* [OE.]

once (wuns) *adv.* one time; ever; formerly. [ME. *ones,* fr. *one*]

one (wun) *a.* lowest cardinal number; single; united; only, without others; identical. *-n.* number or figure 1; unity; single specimen. *-pron.* particular but not stated person; any person. **-oneself′** *pron.* **-one′-sided** *a.* lopsided; biased. **-one-sidedness** *n.* **-one′ness** *n.* [OE. *an*]

on′erous *a.* burdensome. [L. *onerosus*]

on′ion (un′yun) *n.* plant with a bulb of pungent flavor. [L. *unio*]

on′ly *a.* that is the one specimen. *adv.* solely, merely, exclusively. *conj.* but, excepting that. [OE. *anlic,* one like]

onomatopoe′ia *n.* formation of a word by using sounds that resemble or suggest the object or action to be named. [G. *onomatopoiia*]

on′set set *n.* assault, attack; start. [*on. set*]

ontol′ogy *n.* science of being, of the real nature of things. [G. *on,* being]

o′nus *n.* responsibility. [L. = *burden*]

ooze *n.* wet mud, slime; sluggish flow. *v.i.* pass slowly through, exude. [OE. *was,* juice; *wase,* mud]

o′pal *n.* white or bluish stone with iridescent reflections. **-opales′cent** *a.* showing changing colors. [G. *oppallios*]

opaque' *a.* not transparent. **-opa'city** *n.* [L. *opacus*]

o'pen *a.* not shut or blocked up; without lid or door; bare; undisguised; not enclosed or covered or limited or exclusive; frank; free. *-v.t.* set open, uncover, give access to; disclose, lay bare; make a hole in. *-v.i.* become open. *-n.* clear space, unenclosed country. [OE.]

op'era *n.* musical drama. **-operat'ic** *a.* - **op'era-glass** *n.* binoculars for viewing stage performance. [It. L. = work]

opera'ting system *n.* (*compute.*) software that controls the execution of computer programs.

opera'tion *n.* working, way a thing works; scope; act of surgery. **-op'erate** *v.i.* - **op'erative** *a.* workingman. *n.* mechanic. - **op'erator** *n.* [L. *operation* fr. *opus*, work]

ophthal'mia *n.* inflammation of the eye. - **ophthal'mic** *n.* **-ophthalmol'ogist** *n.* specialist in eye infections. [G.]

opin'ion *n.* what one thinks about some thing; belief; judgment. **-opine'** *v.t.* think; utter an opinion. **-opin'ionated**, opinionative *a.* stubborn in holding an opinion. [L. *opinio*]

o'pium *n.* sedative and narcotic drug made from the poppy. **-o'piate** *v.t.* mix with opium. *-n.* opiated drug. [L.]

oppo'nent *n.* adversary. *a.*. opposed, adverse. [L. *opponere*, place against]

opportune' *a.* seasonable, well timed. - **opportu'nity** *n.* favorable time or condition. [L. *opportunus*]

oppose' (-z) *v.t.* set against; contrast; resist, withstand. *-past p.* adverse. **-oppo'ser** *n.* - **opp'osite** (-zit) *a.* contrary facing, diametrically different. **-opposi'tion** (-ish) *n.* a being opposite; resistance; party opposed to that in power. [F. *opposer*]

oppress' *v.t.* govern with tyranny; weigh down. [L. *opprimere*, *oppress-*, press down]

op'tic *a.* of the eye or sight. *-n.* eye; in *pl.* science of sight or light. **-op'tical** *a.* opti'cian (-ish-) *n.* maker of, dealer in, optical instruments. [G. *optikos*]

op'timism *n.* belief that the world is the best possible world; doctrine that good must prevail in the end; disposition to look on the bright side. [L. *optimus*, best]

op'tion *n.* choice. **-op'tional** *a.* [L. *optio*, fr. *optare*, choose]

op'ulent *a.* rich; profuse. **-op'ulence** *n.* [L. *opulentus*, wealthy]

o'pus *n.* (op'era *pl.*) musical composition of a particular composer, usually numbered in sequence. [L.]

or *conj.* introduces alternatives; if not. [ME. *other*, (mod. *either*)]

or'acle *n.* place where divine utterances were supposed to be given; answer there given, often ambiguous; wise or mysterious adviser. [L. *oraculum*, orate, speak]

or'al *a.* by mouth; spoken. **-or'ally** *adv.* [L. *os, or-*, mouth]

or'ange (-inj) *n.* familiar bright reddish-yellow round fruit; tree bearing it; color of the fruit. *-a.* of the color of an orange. [Pers. *narang*]

or'ator *n.* maker of a speech, skillful speaker. **-ora'tion** *n.* formal speech. **-orator'ical** *a.* of an orator or oration. **-or'atory** *n.* speeches; eloquent language; small chapel. **-orator'io** *n.* semi-dramatic composition of sacred music. [L. *orare*, speak]

orb *n.* globe, sphere. **orbed'**, **orbic'ular**, **orbic'ulate(d)** *a.* spherical. **-orb'it** *n.* cavity holding the eye; track of a heavenly body. **-or'bital** *a.* pert. to orbit. [L. *orbis*, circle]

orch'ard *n.* enclosure containing fruit trees. [OE. *ortgeard*]

or'chestra *n.* band of musicians; place occupied by such band in a theater, *etc.*; the forward section of seats on the main floor of a theater. **-or'chestrate**, *v.t.* compose or arrange music for an orchestra. **-orchestra'tion** *n.* [G. = dancing space for chorus]

or'chid, (-k-) *n.* various flowering plants. [Med. L. *orchideæ*]

ordain' *v.t.* admit to Christian ministry; confer holy orders upon; decree, destine. [OF. *ordener*, fr. L. *ordo*, order]

ord'inance *n.* decree, rule, municipal regulation; ceremony. [L. *ordinare*]

or'deal *n.* method of trial by requiring the accused to undergo a dangerous physical test; trying experience. [OE. *ordal*, judicial test]

or'der *n.* rank, class, group; monastic society; sequence, succession, arrangement; command, pass, instruction. *-v.i.* arrange; command; require. **-or'derly** *a.* methodical. *-n.* soldier following an officer to carry orders; soldier in a military hospital acting as attendant. - **or'derliness** *n.* [F. *ordre-*L. *ordo, ordin-*]

or'dinal *a.* showing number or position in a series, as first, second *etc.* [*order*]

or'dinary *a.* usually commonplace. *-n.* bishop in his province; public meal supplied at a fixed time and price. [L. *ordo, ordin-*, order]

ore *n.* native mineral from which metal is extracted. [OE. *ora*]

oreg'ano *n.* herb, variety of marjoram. [G. *origanon*, wild marjoram]

or'gan *n.* musical instrument of pipes worked by bellows and played by keys; member of an animal or plant carrying out a particular function; means of action; newspaper. **-organ'ic** *a.* of the bodily organs; affecting bodily organs; having vital organs; organized, systematic. **-organ'ically** *adv.* **-or'ganism** *n.* organized body or system. **-or'ganist** *n.* one who plays an organ. **-or'ganize** *v.t.* furnish with news; give a definite structure; get up, arrange, put into working order. [G. *organon*, instrument]

or'gasm *n.* paroxysm of emotion, *esp.* sexual; climax of sexual arousal. [G. *orgasmos*, swelling]

or'gy (-ji) *n.* drunken or licentious revel. - **orgias'tic** *a.* [G. *orgia*, pl. , secret rites]

or'ient *n.* the East; luster of the best pearls. *-a.* rising; Eastern; of pearls, from the Indian seas. *-v.t.* place so as to face the east; find one's bearings. **-orien'tal** *a.* and *n.* **-orienta'tion** *n.*

-orien'talist *n.* expert in Eastern languages and history. **-ori'entate** *v.t.* relate to the points of the compass; take bearings of. [L. *oriens, orient-*, rising]

or'ifice *n.* opening, mouth of a cavity. [Late L. *orifium*]

or'igin *n.* beginning, source, parentage. **-original** (-ij-) *a.* primitive, earliest; new, not copied or derived; thinking or acting for oneself, eccentric. **-***n.* pattern, thing from which another is copied; eccentric person. **-ori'ginally** *adv.* **-original'ity** *n.* **-ori'ginate** *v. t.* bring into existence. [L. *origo, origin-*, fr. *oriri*, rise]

Ori'on *n.* constellation containing seven very bright stars, three of which form Orion's belt. [Orion, a hunter placed among the stars at his death]

or'nament *n.* decoration. **-***v.t.* adorn. **-ornate'** *a.* highly decorated, elaborate. [L. *orna mentum*]

ornithol'ogy *n.* science of birds. **-ornitholo'gical** *a.* **-ornithol'ogist** *n.* [G *ornis, ornith-*, bird]

or'phan *n.* child bereaved of one or both of its parents. **-or'phanage** *n.* institution for the care of orphans. **-or'phanhood** *n.* [G. *orphanos*, bereaved]

ortho- *prefix* right. [G. *orthos*, right] **-or'thodox** *a.* holding accepted views or doctrine; conventional. **-or'thodoxy** *n.* **-orthog'raphy** *n.* correct spelling. **-orthopedic, -orthopaed'ic** *a.* for curing deformity.

or'yx *n.* kind of straight-horned antelope. [G. =*pickax*]

os'cillate *v. i.* swing to and fro; vary between extremes; set up wave motion in wireless apparatus. **-oscilla'tion** *n.* **-os'cillator** *n.* one that oscillates, *esp.* a person setting up unauthorized wireless waves from a radio receiving set. [L. *oscillare*, swing]

os'culate *v.t.* and *i.* kiss. **-oscula'tion** *n.* **-oscula'tory** *a.* [L. *osculari*, fr. *as*, mouth]

osmo'sis *n.* intermixing of fluids by percolation through a dividing membrane. [G. *osmos*, impulse]

os'prey *n.* fishing eagle; egret plume. [L. *ossifraga*, 'bone-breaker']

osten'sible *n.* professed, used as a blind. **-osten'sibly** *adv.* **-ostenta'tion** *n.* show, display. [L. *ostendere*, show]

osteop'athy *n.* art of treating diseases by removing structural derangement by manipulation, *esp.* of spine. **-os'teopath** *n.* one skilled in this art. [G. *osteon*, bone, and *patheia*, suffering]

os'tracize *v. t.* exclude from society, exile. **-os'tracism** *n.* [G. *ostrakizein*]

os'trich *n.* large swift-running flightless African bird. [OF. *austruche*]

oth'er (uTH'-) *a.* not this, not the same; alternative, different. **-***pron.* other person or thing. **-oth'erwise** (-iz) *adv.* differently, [OE.]

ott'er *n.* furry aquatic fish-eating animal. [OE. *otor*]

ott'oman *n.* cushioned seat without back or arms. [*Othman*, founder of a Turk. dynasty]

ought (awt) *v. aux.* expressing duty or obligation or advisability. [*owe*]

ounce *n.* weight, twelfth of the Troy pound, sixteenth of the avoirdupois pound. [L. *uncia*]

ounce *n.* snow-leopard. [F. *once*]

our *pron.* belonging to us. [OE. *ure*]

out *adv.* from within, from among, away, not in the usual or right state. **-out'ing** *n.* pleasure excursion. **-out'side** *n.* outer side, exterior. *n*, exterior; external. *adv.* on the outer side. *-prep.* beyond. **-out'ward** *a.* and *adv.* **-out'wards** *adv.* **-out'wardly** *adv.* [OE. *ut*]

out- as *prefix* makes many compounds with the sense of beyond, in excess, *etc., e.g.* **outflank'** *v.t.* get beyond the flank. **-out'put** *n.* quantity put out, *etc.* These are not given where the meaning and derivation may easily be found from the simple word.

out'age *n.* quantity of something lost during storage or transportation; failure, interruption, esp. in the supply of electric current; period or time during such a failure. [*out*]

out'back *n.* (Australia) remote open country. [*out* and *back*]

out'cast *n.* homeless person; vagabond, pariah. [ME.]

outclass' *v.t.* excel, surpass. [*out* and *class*]

out'come *n.* result, consequence. [ME.]

out'law *n.* one placed beyond the protection of the law, an exile. **-out'lawry** *n.* [ON. *utlagi*]

out'post *n.* post, station beyond main company. [*out* and *post*]

out'rage *n.* violation of others' rights; gross or violent offense or indignity. *-v.t.* injure, violate, ravish, insult. [F.]

out'rigger *n.* frame outside a ship's gunwale; frame on the side of a rowing boat with a rowlock at the outer edge. [earlier *outlegger*, Du. *uitlegger*, 'outlyer']

outskirts' *n. pl.* environs; parts farthest from the center. [*out* and *skirts*]

out'set *n.* beginning, start. [*out* and *set*]

out'take *n.* unreleased take from a recording session, film, or television program. [*out* and *take*]

o'val *a.* egg-shaped, elliptical. **-***n.* oval figure or thing. **-o'vary** *n.* egg-producing organ. [L. *ovum*, egg]

ova'tion *n.* enthusiastic burst of applause. [L. *ovatio*]

ov'en (uv-) *n.* heated iron box or other receptacle for baking in. [OE. *ofn*]

o'ver *adv.* above, above and beyond, going beyond in excess, too much, past, finished, in repetition, across, *etc. -prep.* above, on, upon, more than, in excess of, along, across, *etc. a.*upper, outer. [OE. *ofer*]

o'ver- as *prefix* makes compounds with meaning of too, too much, in excess, above, *e.g.* **o'verdo** *v.t.* do too much. These words are not given where the meaning and derivation may be found from the simple word.

overbear' *v. t.* bear down, dominate, overwhelm. **-overbear'ing** *a.* domineering, haughty. [*over* and *bear*]

overboard' *adv.* over ship's side into water. [*over* and *board*]

overcast' *a.* dull and heavy, (of sky) clouded. [*over* and *cast*]

overhaul' *v.t.* come up with in pursuit; examine and set in order. -*n.* thorough examination, *esp.* for repairs. [*haul*]

o'verhead *a.* over one's head, above. *adv.* above. -**o'verhead charg'es,** costs, business expenses apart from cost of production. [*over* and *head*]

o'verpass *n.* elevated level to allow free flow of traffic over traffic moving in another direction.

oversee' *v. t.* look, see over. -**over-seer'** *n.* supervisor of work. [OE. *oferseon*]

o'versight *n.* error, *esp.* of omission. [ME.]

o'vert *a.* open, unconcealed. -**o'vertly** *adv.* [OF. = opened]

overthrow' *v.t.* vanquish; overturn; remove from office; throw too far. -*n.* ruin, disaster; defeat.

overtime *adv./n.* (work) done after regular hours. [*over* and *time*]

o'verture *n.* opening of negotiations; proposal; introduction of an opera, *etc.* [OF. = opening]

overwhelm' *v.t.* flow over, submerge, overbear. -**overwhelm'ing** *a.* resistless. [*over* and *whelm*]

oviparous *a.* egg-laying. [L. *ovum, parere,* bring forth]

o'void *a.* egg-shaped. [L. *ovum,* egg, G. *cidos,* form]

owe *v. t.* be bound to repay, be indebted for. -**ow'ing** *a.* owed, due. -**owing to,** caused by. [OE. *agan,* own]

owl *n.* night bird of prey. -**owl'et** *n.* young owl. -**owl'ish** *a.* solemn and dull. [OE. *ule*]

own *a.* emphasizes possession. -*v. t.* possess; acknowledge. -*v.i.* confess. [OE. *agen, a. ,* one's own, *agnian, v.*]

ox *n.* **ox'en** *pl.* large cloven-footed and usually horned animal used for draft, milk, and meat, a bull or cow. [OE. *oxa*]

ox'ygen *n.* gas in the atmosphere which is essential to life, burning; *etc.* -**ox'ide** *n.* compound of oxygen. -**ox'idize** *v.t.* cause to combine with oxygen; cover with oxide, make rusty. -*v. i.* combine with oxygen, rust. -**ox'yacet'ylene** *a.* involving, using mixture of oxygen and acetylene. [G. *oxys,* sour]

oxymoron *n.* (*rhet.*) figure of speech combining incongruous terms. [G. *oxys,* sharp, *moros,* foolish]

oy'ster *n.* bivalve mollusk or shellfish, usually eaten alive. [G. *ostreon*]

o'zone *n.* condensed form of oxygen with a pungent odor; refreshing influence. [G. *ozein,* smell]

P

pab'ulum *n.* food, nourishment. [L.]

pace *n.* step; length of a step; walk or speed of stepping; speed. -*v.i.* step. -*v.t.* cross or measure with steps; set the speed for. -**pa'cer** *n.* -**pace'maker** *n.* one that sets the pace at which something happens or should happen; electronic device surgically implanted in those with heart disease. [L. *passus*]

pach'yderm (-k-) *n.* thick-skinned animal, *e.g.* an elephant. [G. *pachydermos*]

pacif'ic *a.* quiet; tending to peace. -**pac'ify** (-s-) *v.t.* calm; establish peace. -**pacif'icist, pa'cifist** *n.* advocate of the abolition of war; one who refuses to help in war. -**pac'ificism** *n.* (L. *pacifus,* peacemaking, fr. *pax, pac-,* peace]

pack *n.* bundle; company of animals, large set of people or things; set of playing cards; packet; mass of floating ice. -*v.t.* make into a bundle; put together in a box, *etc.*; arrange one's luggage for traveling; fill with things; order off. -**pack'age** *n.* parcel. -**pack'et** *n.* small parcel. -**pack'-horse** *n.* horse for carrying bundles of goods. [Du. *pak*]

pact *n.* covenant of agreement. -also **pac'tion.** [L. *pactus,* contract]

pad *n.* piece of soft stuff used as a cushion; shin-guard; sheets of paper fastened together in a block; foot or sole of various animals. -*v.t.* make soft, fill in, protect, *etc.*, with a pad or padding. -**padd'ing** *n.* stuffing; literary matter put in simply to increase quantity. [*orig.* uncertain]

pad'dle *n.* short oar with a broad blade at one or each end; blade of a paddle wheel. -*v.i.* move by paddles; roll gently. -*v.t.* propel by paddles. -**pad'dle-wheel** *n.* wheel with crosswise blades which strike the water successively to propel a ship. [*orig.* unknown]

pad'dle *v.i.* walk with bare feet in shallow water. [*orig.* uncertain]

pad'lock *n.* detachable lock with a hinged hoop to go through a staple or ring. -*v.t.* fasten with padlock. [*orig.* uncertain]

pa'gan *a.* heathen. -*n.* heathen. -**pa'ganism** *n.* [L. *paganus,* rustic]

page *n.* boy servant, attendant. [F.]

page *n.* one side of a leaf of a book. -*v.t.* number the pages of. -**pa'ginate** *v.t.* number the pages of. -**pagina'tion** *n.* [L. *pagina-pangere,* fasten]

pa'geant (paj'-ent) *n.* procession, dramatic show, of persons in costume, usually illustrating history, brilliant show. -**pa'geantry** *n.* [*orig.* uncertain]

pail *n.* large round open vessel for carrying liquids *etc.*; bucket. -**pail'ful** *n.* [*orig.* uncertain]

pain *n.* bodily or mental suffering; penalty. -*v.t.* inflict pain upon. [L. *poena,* penalty]

paint *n.* coloring matter prepared for putting on a surface with brushes. -*v.t.* portray, color, coat, or make a picture of, with paint; describe. [F. *peint,* p.p- of *peindre*]

paint'er *n.* rope for fastening bow of a boat to a ship, *etc.* [L. *pendere,* hang]

pair (por) *n.* set of two, *esp.* existing or generally used together. -*v.t.* arrange in a pair or pairs. -*v.i.* come together in pair or pairs. [L. *par,* equal]

paja'mas *n. pl.* sleeping suit of loose trousers and jacket. [Pers. *pae, jamah,* leg garment]

pal'ace *n.* official residence of a king, bishop, *etc.*; stately mansion. [L. *palatium*]

pal'ate *n.* roof of the mouth; sense of taste.

-pal'atable *a.* agreeable to eat. [L. *palatum*]

pale *a.* faint in color, dim, whitish. *-v.i.* grow white. [L. *pallidus*]

paleo- *prefix* ancient. [G. *palaios*).- paleolith'ic *a.* of the early part of the Stone Age. -paleontol'ogy *n.* study of ancient life (through fossils, *etc.*). paleozool'ogy *n.* study of fossil animals.

pal'ette *n.* artist's flat board for mixing colors on. -palette-knife *n.* [F.]

palisade' *n.* fence of pointed stakes. *esp.* for defense. *-v.t.* enclose with one. [F. *palissade*, fr. *pal*, stake]

pall (pawl) *i.* become tasteless or tiresome. *-v.t.* to cloy, dull. [for appal]

pall'et *n.* straw bed, small bed, portable platform for storing or moving goods. [A. F. *paillette*, fr. *paille*, straw]

pall'id *a.* pale. -pall'or *n.* paleness. [L. *pallidus*, pale]

palm (pim) *n.* flat of the hand: tropical tree; leaf of the tree as a symbol of victory. *-v.t.* conceal in the palm of the hand; pass off by trickery. -palm'istry *n.* fortune-telling from the lines on the palm of the hand. [L. *palma*]

pal'pitate *v.t.* throb. -palpita'tion *n.* [L. *palpare*, *palpitarè*, freq. of feel]

pam'pas *n. pl.* vast grassy plains of S. America. [Sp.]

pam'per *v.t.* over-indulge. [orig. uncertain]

pamph'let *n.* thin paper cover book, stitched but not bound. -pamphleteer' *n.* writer of pamphlets. [OF. *Pamphilet*, title of a medieval poem (taken as type of a small book)]

pan *n.* broad, shallow vessel. -pan'cake *n.* thin cake of fried batter. -pan'cake landing, awkward flat landing of aircraft. -pan'handle *v.i.* beg for food or money in the street. [OE. *panne*]

panace'a *n.* universal remedy. [G. *panakeia*, all-healing]

pan'creas *n.* large gland secreting a digestive fluid, sweetbread. -pancreat'ic *a.* -pan'creatin *n.* pancreatic secretion. [G. *pan*, all, *kreas*, flesh]

pandem'ic *a.* universal. *-n.* widespread epidemic disease. [G. *pas, pan*, all, *demos*, people]

pan'der *n.* go-between in illicit love affair; procurer. *v.t.* minister basely. [fr. *Pandarus*, prince who acted as agent between Troilus and Cressida]

pane *n.* piece of glass in a window. [F *pan*. flat section]

pan'el *n.* compartment of a surface, usually raised or sunk, *e.g.* in a door; strip of different material in a dress; thin board with a picture on it; list of jurors, doctors, *etc.* *-v.t.* decorate with panels. -pan'eling *n.* paneled work. [OF. = *small pane*]

pan'ic *n.* sudden and infectious fear. *-a.* of such fear; due to uncontrollable general impulse. [G. *panikos*, of Pan]

pan'oply *n.* full suit of armor; complete, magnificent array. [G. *panoplia-pan-*, all, *hoplon*, weapon]

panoram'a *n.* picture arranged round a spectator or unrolled before him; wide or complete view. -panoram'ic *a.* (G. *pan-*, all, *horama*, view]

pan'sy (-zi) *n.* flowering plant; a species of violet. [F. *pensèe*, thought]

pant *v.i.* gasp for breath. *-n.* gasp. -pant'ing *adv.* [orig. uncertain]

pan'theism *n.* identification of God with the universe. -pan'theist *n.* -pan'theon *n.* temple of all the gods; building for memorials of a nation's great dead. [G. *pan-*, all, *theos*, a god]

pan'tomime *n.* dramatic entertainment in dumb show; Christmas-time dramatic entertainment. -pantomim'ic *a.* [G. *pantomimos*, all mimic]

pan'try *n.* room for storing food or utensils. [F. *paneterie*- L. *panis*, bread]

pants *n. pl.* trousers. [*pantaloons*]

pa'pacy *n.* office of the Pope; papal system. -pa'pist *a.* of, or relating to, the Pope. -pa'pist *n.* -papist'ic *a.* [Med. L. *papatia*, see pope]

pa'per *n.* material made by pressing pulp of rags, straw, wood, *etc.*, into thin flat sheets; sheet of paper written or printed on; newspaper; article or essay. *-pl.* documents, *etc.* *-v.t.* cover with paper. -pap'ier mâché *n.* paper pulp shaped by molding and dried hard. [G. *papyros*, Nile rush from which paper was made]

papoose' *n.* N. Amer. Indian child. [native]

par *n.* equality of value or standing; equality between market and nominal value. -par'ity *n.* equality. [L. = equal]

par'able *n.* allegory, story pointing a moral. [G. *parabole*, comparison]

parab'ola *n.* curve formed by cutting cone with plane parallel to its slope. [G. *para*, beside, *ballein*, throw]

parab'ole *n.* parable, sustained simile. [*See* parabola]

parachute' (-sh-) *n.* apparatus extending like an umbrella to enable a person to come safely to earth from a great height. [L. *parare*, ward off, and chute]

parade' *n.* display; muster of troops; parade ground. *-v.t.* muster; display. *-v.i.* march with display. [F.]

par'adigm (-dim) *n.* model, example. [G. *paradeigma*]

par'adise *n.* garden of Eden; Heaven; state of bliss. [G. *paradeisos*, pleasureground]

par'adox *n.* statement that seems absurd but may be true. -paradox'ical *a.* [G. *paradoxos*, contrary to opinion]

par'affin *n.* wax or oil distilled from shale, wood, *etc.* [fr. L. *parum*, little, and affinis, related (because of its lack of affinity with other bodies)]

par'agon *n.* pattern or model. [OF.]

par'agraph *n.* section of a chapter or book; short record. *-v.t.* arrange in para graphs. [G. *paragraphos*, written beside (orig. of the sign indicating the new section)]

par'allel *a.* continuously at equal distances; precisely corresponding. *-n.* line of latitude; thing exactly like another; comparison. *-v.t.* represent as similar, compare. -par'allelism *n.* [G. *parallelos*, beside one another]

parallel'ogram *n.* four-sided plane figure

with opposite sides equal and parallel. [L.]

par'allel out'put n. (*compute*.) form of computer output in which all characters on a line are transmitted at the same instant.

paral'ysis n. incapacity to move or feel, due to damage to the nerve system. **-par'alyze** v.t. [G. *paralysis*, cp. **palsy**]

paramed'ical a. of persons working in various capacities in support of medical profession. [G. *para*, beside, L. *medicus*, physician]

par'amount a. supreme. [F. *par amont*, upwards]

par'anoia n. kind of mental disease. **-parano'ic** n. [G. *para*, beside, *noein*, to think]

parapherna'lia n.pl. personal belongings, trappings, odds and ends of equipment. [Med. L.]

paraphrase n. expression of a meaning of a passage in other words. -v.t. put the meaning of in other words. [G. *paraphrases*, beside phrase]

par'asite n. self-interested hanger-on; animal or plant living in or on another. [G. *parasitos*]

par'atroops n. pl. airborne troops to be dropped by parachute. **-par'atrooper** n. [*parachute* and *troops*]

par'boil v.i. scald the surface in boiling water, boil partly; scorch. [OF. *parboillir*, boil thoroughly]

par'buckle n. rope for raising or lowering round objects, the middle being secured at the higher level and the ends passed under and round the object. -v.t. raise or lower in this way. [orig. uncertain]

par'cel n. packet of goods, specially one enclosed in paper; quantity dealt with at one time; piece of land. -v.t. divide into parts; make up in a parcel. [F. *parcelle*, small part]

parch v.t. and i. dry by exposure to heat, roast slightly, make or become hot and dry. [ME. *perché*, contr. of perish]

parch'ment n. skin prepared for writing; manuscript of this. [*pergamum*, in Asia Minor (where first used)]

par'don v.t. forgive. -n. forgiveness. [F. *pardonner*]

pare (pār) v.t. trim by cutting away the edge or surface of [F. *parer*, make ready]

paregor'ic a. soothing. -n. soothing medicine; tincture of opium. [G. *paregorikos*, comforting]

par'ent n. father or mother. [L. *parere*, bring forth]

paren'thesis n. **paren'theses** pl. n. word, phrase, or sentence inserted in a passage independently of the grammatical sequence and usually marked off by brackets, dashes, or commas. -pl. round brackets, ( ), used for this. **-parenthet'ic** a. [G.]

par'iah (pā-ri-a) n. Indian of no caste; social outcast. [Tamil, *parairyar*]

par'ish n. district under a priest; subdivision of a county. **-parish'ioner** n. inhabitant of a parish. [F. *paroisse*]

parity check n. (*compute*.) system for detecting errors during transmission between computers, checking whether the number of bit (0s or 1s) is odd or even.

park n. large enclosed piece of ground, usually with grass or woodland, attached to a country house or set aside for public use. [F. *parc*]

parl'ance n. way of speaking. **-parl'ey** n. meeting between leaders or representatives of opposing forces to discuss terms. v.i. hold a discussion about terms. [F. *parler*, speak]

parl'iament n. legislature of the United Kingdom; any legislative assembly. [F. *parlement-parler*, speak]

parl'or n. sitting-room or room for receiving company in a small house; private room in an inn; store selling some special service or goods. [F. *parloir* fr. *parler*, speak]

paro'chial (-k-) a. of a parish; narrow, provincial. **-paro'chialism** n. concentration on the local interests. (Late L. *parochial* parish]

par'ody n. composition in which author's characteristics are made fun of by imitation; burlesque; feeble imitation. -v.t. write a parody of. **-par'odist** n. [G. *parodia*]

parole' n. early freeing of prisoner on condition he is of good behavior; word of honor. -v.t. place on parole. [F.]

par'onym n. word with same derivation; word with same sound but differing spelling and meaning, e.g., moat, mote. [G. *para*, beside, *onoma*, name]

par'oxysm n. sudden violent attack of pain, rage, laughter, etc. [G. *paroxysmos para*, beyond, *oxys*, sharp]

par'quet (-ka) n. flooring of wooden blocks. -v.t. lay a parquet. [F.]

parr'icide n. murder or murderer of one's own parent. [L. *parricida*]

parr'ot n. bird with short hooked beak, some varieties of which can be taught to imitate speech; unintelligent imitator. [dim. of F. *Pierre*, Peter]

parr'y v.t. ward off. -n. act of parrying, *esp*. in fencing. [F. *parer*]

parse (-z) v.t. describe (a word) or analyze (a sentence) in terms of grammar. [fr. school question, L. *quæ pars orationis?* What part of speech?]

par'simony n. stinginess; undue economy. **-parsimo'nious** a. [L. *parsimonia*, fr. *parcere*, spare]

par'sley n. herb used for seasoning, etc. [G. *petroselinon*, rock parsley]

par'snip n. plant with a yellow root cooked as a vegetable. [L. *pastinaca*, fr. *pastinare*, dig up]

par'son n. clergyman of a parish or church; clergyman. **-par'sonage** n. parson's house. [*person*]

part n. portion, section, share; duty; character given to an actor to play; interest. -v.t. divide; separate; distribute. -v.i. separate from. [L. *pars, part-*, part]

par'tial a. prejudiced; fond of; being only in part. **-partial'ity** n. **-par'tially** adv. [L. *partialis*]

partic'ipate (-is-) v.t. and i. share in. -

partic'ipant n. -partic'ipator n. -participa'tion n. -part'iciple n. adjective made by inflection from a verb and keeping the verb's relation to dependent words. -particip'ial a. [L. participate, fr. pars, part, and capere, take]

part'icle n. minute portion of matter; least possible amount; minor part of speech. [L. particular dim. of pars, part]

partic'ular a. relating to one, not general; considered apart from others; minute; exact, fastidious. -n. detail or item. -pl. details. [L. particularist]

partisan' (-z-) n. adherent of a party. -a. adherent to a faction. [F.]

parti'tion n. division; dividing wall. -v.t. divide. [L. partition]

part'ner n. member of a partnership; one that dances with another; husband or wife. -part'nership n. association of persons for business, etc. [OF. parconier]

part'ridge n. small game bird of the grouse family. [G. perdix]

part'y n. number of persons united in opinion; side; social assembly. -a. of, or belonging to, a faction. -part'y col'ored a. differently colored in different parts, variegated. [F. parti]

pass (-ki-) v.t. go by, beyond, through, etc.; exceed; be accepted by. -v.i. go; be transferred from one state to another; elapse; undergo examination successfully. -n. way, esp. a narrow and difficult way; passport; condition; successful result from a test. -pass'able a. -past a. ended. -n. bygone times. -adv. by; along. -prep. beyond; after. [L. passus, step]

pass'age n. journey; voyage; fare; part of a book, etc.; encounter. -pass'enger n. traveler, etc. by some conveyance. -pass'port n. document granting permission to pass. -pass'word n. in warfare, secret word to distinguish friend from foe. [F.]

pas'sion n. suffering; strong feeling; wrath; object of ardent desire. passionate a. easily moved to anger; moved by strong emotions. [L. passio]

pass'ive a- suffering; submissive; denoting the grammatical mood of a verb in which the action is suffered by the subject. [L. pati, pass, suffer]

Pass'over n. feast of the Jews to commemorate the time when God, smiting the first-born of the Egyptians, passed over the houses of Israel. [pass over]

paste n. soft composition, as of flour and water; fine glass to imitate gems. -v.t. fasten with paste. -past'y n. pie enclosed in paste. -a. like paste. -pa'stry n. articles of food made chiefly of paste. paste'board n. stiff, thick paper. [G. barley porridge]

pas'tel n. crayon; art of crayon-drawing; a drawing in this medium. -pas'tellist n. -pas'tel-shades n. pl. delicate colors. [F.]

pasteurize v.t. sterilize (milk etc.) by heating, [Louis Pasteur d. 1895]

pas'time (-ā-) n. that which serves to make time pass agreeably, recreation. [pass and time]

pas'tor n. minister of the gospel. -past'oral a. relating to shepherds or rural life; relating to the office of pastor. -n. poem describing rural life. -past'orate n. office or jurisdiction of a spiritual pastor. [L. = shepherd]

past'ure (-ā-) n. grass for food of cattle; ground on which cattle graze. -v.t. feed on grass. -v.i. graze. -past'urage n. business of grazing cattle; pasture. [L. pascere, past-, feed]

pat n. light, quick blow; small mass as of butternut. tap. [imit. orig.]

patch n. piece of cloth sewed on a garment; spot or plot; plot of ground. -v.t. mend; repair clumsily. -patch'y a. full of patches. [OF. pieche, piece]

pa'tent n. open; evident; manifest; open to public perusal, as letters patent. -n. deed securing to a person the exclusive right to an invention. -v.t. secure a patent. [L. patens, patent-, fr. patere, lie open]

pater'nal a. of a father; fatherly. [L. pater, father]

path (-ā-) n. way or track; course of action. [OE. pæth]

pathol'ogy n. science of the causes and nature of diseases. -patholog'ical a. pert. to science of disease; due to disease, morbid, unhealthy, diseased. [G. = suffering]

pa'thos n. power of exciting tender emotions. -pathet'ic, pathet'ical a. affecting or moving such emotions. (G. = feeling]

pa'tient (-shent) a. bearing trials without murmuring. -n. person under medical treatment. -pa'tience n. quality of enduring. [L. pati, suffer]

pa'triarch (-k) n. father and ruler of a family, esp. in Biblical history; venerable old man. -patriarch'al a. [G. patriarches, head of a family]

patri'cian (-shan) n. noble of ancient Rome; person of noble birth. [fr. L. patricius, one sprung from the patres conscripti, or senators]

pat'riot n. one that loves and serves his country. -a. patriotic. -patriot'ic a. inspired by love of one's country. [G. patriotes, fellow-countryman]

patrol' n. marching round as a guard; small body patroling. -v.i. go round on guard, or reconnoitering. [F. patrouiller]

pa'tron n. man under whose protection another has placed himself, guardian saint; one that has the disposition of a church-living, etc. -pat'ronage n. special countenance or support; right of presentation to a church-living, etc. -pat'ronize v.t. assume the air of a superior towards; frequent as a customer. [L. patronus]

patt'er v.i. tap in quick succession; make a noise, as the sound of quick, short steps; pray or talk rapidly. -n. quick succession of small sounds. [frequentative of pat]

patt'ern n. model for imitation; specimen. [L. patronus]

pau'per n. poor person, esp. one supported by the public. -pau'perism n. state of being destitute of the means of support. [L. = poor]

pause n. stop or rest. -v.i. cease for a time. [G.

pausis]

pave *v.t.* form a surface with stone or brick. -**pave'ment** *n.* paved floor or footpath; material for paving. [L. *pavire*, ram down]

pawn *n.* goods deposited as security for money borrowed. -*v.t.* pledge. -**pawn'-broker** *n.* one that lends money on goods pledged. [OF. *pan*]

pawn *n.* piece in a game, *esp.*chess. [OF. *paon*, fr. L. *pedo, pedon-*, footsoldier]

pay *v.t.* give money, *etc.*, for goods received or services rendered; compensate. -*v.i.* be remunerative. -*n.* wages. -**pay'able** *a.* justly due. -**pay'ment** *n.* discharge of a debt. [F. *payer*]

pea *n.*fruit, growing in pods, of a leguminous plant; the plant. -**pea'nut** *n.* groundnut. [G. *pison*]

peace *n.* calm; repose; freedom from war; quietness of mind. -**peace'keeping** *n.* a maintenance of peace, *esp.* the prevention of further fighting between hostile forces in an area. [L. *pax, pac-*]

peach *a.* stone-fruit of delicate flavor; tree which bears this. [F. *pêche*]

pea'cock *n.* bird, remarkable for the beauty of its plumage and fan-like spotted tail. [L. *pavo* and *cock*]

peak *n.* pointed end of anything, *esp.* the sharp top of a hill; maximum point in a curve or record. [var. of *pike*]

peal *n.* loud sound, or succession of loud sounds; chime; set of bells. -*v.i.* sound loudly. [for *appeal*]

pear *n.* tree yielding sweet, juicy fruit; the fruit. [L. *pirum*]

peas'ant (pez'-) *n.* rural laborer; rustic. -*a.* rural. [F. *paysan-pays*, country]

peat *n.* decomposed vegetable substance, dried and used for fuel. [Celt. orig.]

peb'ble *n.* small, roundish stone; transparent and colorless rock-crystal. [OE. *popelstan*]

pecan' *n.* N. American tree; its nut-also **pecan'-nut.** [Chin.]

peck *n.*fourth part of a bushel; great deal. [AF. *pek*]

peck *v.t.* and *i.* pick or strike with the beak; eat with beak. [var. of *pick*]

pec'toral *a.* of the chest. -*n.* medicine for chest ailments; breast-plate; cross worn over chest. [L. *pectoralis*]

pecu'liar *a.* one's own; particular; strange. -**peculiar'ity** *n.* something that belongs to, or is found in, one person or thing only. [L. *peculiaris*]

ped'agogue (-gog) *n.* schoolmaster; pedantic or narrow-minded teacher. [G. *paidogogos,* 'boy-leader']

ped'al *a.* of a foot. -*n.* something to transmit motion from the foot. -*v.i.* use a pedal. [L. *pedalis,* fr. *pes,* foot]

ped'ant *n.* one who overvalues, or insists unreasonably on, petty details of booklearning, grammatical rules, *etc.* -**pedant'ic** *a.* [F. *pédant*]

ped'estal *n.* base of a column, pillar, *etc.* [F. *pédestal;* L. *pes, pedis,* foot]

pedes'trian *a.* going on foot. -*n.* one that walks on foot. -**pedes'trianism** *n.* the practice of walking. [L. *pedester, pedestr-,* fr. *pes,* foot]

pediat'rics *n.* treatment of children's diseases. -**pedia'trician** *n.* [G. *paidos,* child]

ped'igree *n.* register of ancestors; genealogy. [AF. *pe de gru,* crane's foot]

ped'lar, pedd'ler *n.* one who travels about hawking small commodities. -**ped'dle** *v.t.* and *i.* [OE. *ped,* basket]

pedom'eter *n.* instrument which records the distance walked by a person. [L. *pes, pedis,* a foot, [G. *metron,* a measure]

pe'dophilia *n.* sexual perversion of which children are the object of desire. [G. *paidos,* child, *philos,* loving]

peel *v.t.* strip off the skin, bark or rind. -*v.i.* come off, as the skin or rind. -*n.* rind, skin. [F. *peler*]

peep *v.i.* cry, as a chick; chirp. -*n.* cry of a young chicken. [imit. orig.]

peer *n.* one of the same rank; nobleman. -**peer'less** *a.* unequaled; matchless. -**peer'age** *n.* rank of a peer; body of peers. [L. *par,* equal]

peer *v.i.* peep; look narrowly, as with shortsighted eyes. [Teutonic orig.]

peev'ish *a.* fretful; querulous. [orig. uncertain]

peg *n.* wooden nail or pin. -*v.t.* fasten with pegs. [orig. uncertain]

pel'ican *n.* large water-fowl, remarkable for the enormous pouch beneath its bill. [G. *pelekan*]

pell'et *n.* little ball. [F. *pelote*]

pelt *v.t.* strike with missiles. -*v.i.* throw missiles; fall persistently, as rain. [orig. uncertain]

pelt *n.* hide or skin. [L. *pellis*]

pel'vis *n.* bony cavity at lower end of the body. [L. = *basin*]

pen *n.* instrument for writing. -*v.t.* compose and commit to paper; write. **pen-knife** *n.* pocket-knife. -**pen'name** *n.* one skilled in hand-writing, author. **pen'manship** *n.* [L. *penna,* feather]

pen *n.* small enclosure, as for sheep. -*v.t.* shut up. -**pent** *a.* closely confined; shut up. [OE. *penn*]

pe'nal *a.* relating to, incurring, or inflicting punishment. -**pen'alty** *n.* punishment for a crime or offense. -**pe'nalize** *v.t.* lay under penalty. [L. *penalis, poena,* punishment]

pen'ance *n.* suffering submitted to as an expression of penitence. [OF. *penëance,* L. *pœnitentia*]

pen'cil *n.* small brush used by painters; instrument, as of graphite, for writing, *etc.* -*v.t.* paint or draw; mark with a pencil. [L. *penicillum,* little tail]

pend'ant *n.* hanging ornament. -*a.* suspended; hanging; projecting. -**pend'-ing** *prep.* during. -*a.* awaiting decision. [L. *pendere,* hang]

pen'dent *a.* pendant, hanging. [L. *pendere,* hang]

pend'ulum *n.* suspended weight swinging to and fro, *esp.* as a regulator for a clock. [L. *pendulus,* hanging]

pen'etrate *v.t.* enter into; pierce; arrive at the

meaning of. -pen'etrable a. capable of being pierced. [L. penetrare]

pen'guin n. swimming bird, unable to fly. [Welsh pen gwyn, white head]

penicill'in n. extract of the mold penicillium notatum, used to prevent growth of bacteria. [L. penicillus, little tail]

penin'sula n. land nearly surrounded by water. [L. paene, almost, insula, island]

pe'nis n. male organ of generation. [L.]

pen'itent a. affected by a sense of guilt. -n. one that repents of sin. -pen'itence n. sorrow for sin; repentance. -peniten'tiary -n. prison. [L. pænitere, repent]

penn'ant n. narrow piece of bunting, esp. a long narrow flag, on a lance, etc. -also pen-non. [L. penna, plume]

penn'y n. penn'ies pl. (denoting the number of coins). -pence pl. (amount of pennies in value), copper coin; cent; 100th part of a pound. -penn'iless a. having no money. [OE. pennig]

pen'sion n. allowance for past services; annuity paid to retired public officers, soldiers, etc. -v.t. grant a pension to. -pen'sioner n. [L. pensio-pendere, pens, weigh]

pen'sive a. thoughtful with sadness, wistful. [F. pensif, L. pensare, weigh]

pent'agon n. plane figure having five sides and five angles. -Pent'agon n. headquarters of the Department of Defense; the U.S. military leadership. -pentag'onal a. -pent'ateuch (-k) n. the first five books of the Old Testament. [G. pente, five]

pent'house n. shed standing with its roof sloping against a higher wall; structure or dwelling built on the roof of a building. [F. appentis, L. appendicium, appendage]

penulti'mate n. second last. [L. paene, almost, ultimus, last]

penum'bra n. imperfect shadow; partial shade between shadow and full light. -penum'bral a. [L. paene, almost, umbra, shadow]

pen'ury n. want; extreme poverty. penu'rious a. niggardly. [L. penuria]

peo'ple n. body of persons that compose a community; nation; persons generally. -v.t. stock with inhabitants. [F. peuple, nation; L. populus]

pepp'er n. fruit of a climbing plant, which yields a pungent aromatic spice. -v.t. sprinkle with pepper; pelt with shot. -pepp'ery a. having the qualities of pepper; irritable. -pepp'ermint n. aromatic plant. [G. peperi]

peram'bulate v.t. walk through or over, traverse. -v.i. walk about. [L. perambulare, per, through, ambulare, walk]

perceive' v.t. obtain knowledge of through the senses; observe; understand. -perceiv'able a. -percep'tible a. discernible. [L. percipere]

percent'age n. proportion or rate per hundred. -per cent, in each hundred. [L. per centum, by the hundred]

percen'tile n. one of 99 actual or notional values of a variable dividing its distribution into 100 groups with equal frequencies; cen-

tile. [L. per centum, by the hundred]

per'colate v.t. and i. pass through small interstices, as a liquor; filter. -percola'tion n. [L. percolate]

percus'sion n. collision; vibratory shock. -percus'sion instrument, musical instrument played by striking, e. g. drum or cymbal. [L. percussio]

per'egrinate v.i. travel from place to place. [L. peregrinus, foreigner]

perempt'ory a. authoritative; forbidding debate; final; absolute. [L. peremptorius, destructive]

perenn'ial a. lasting through the years; perpetual; (bot.) continuing more than two years. [L. perennis]

per'fect a. complete; finished. -n. tense denoting a complete act. -v.t. finish; make skillful. -perfec'tion n. state of being perfect. [L. perfectus, done thoroughly]

per'fidy n. treachery. [L. perfidia, faithlessness]

per'forate v.t. pierce. -perfora'tion n. hole bored through anything. [L. perforare-per, through, forare, bore]

perform' v.t. bring to completion; fulfill; represent on the stage. -v.i. act a part; play, as on a musical instrument. perform'ance n. -perform'er n. one who performs, esp. actor or other entertainer. [OF. par-fournir, furnish through]

per'fume n. agreeable scent; fragrance. -v.t. scent. [L. perfumare, perfume]

perfunct'ory a. done indifferently, careless. -perfunct'orily adv. [L. perfungi, perfunct-, get done with]

perhaps' adv. it may be; possibly. [E. hap, chance]

pericard'ium n. membrane, enclosing heart. [G. peri, around, kardia, heart]

perigee' n. point on moon or planet's orbit, at which it is nearest earth. [G. peri, around, ge, earth]

per'il n. danger; exposure to injury. -per'ilous a. full of peril. [L. periculum]

perim'eter n. outer boundary of a plane figure. [G. perimetros]

pe'riod n. time in which a heavenly body makes a revolution; particular portion of time; complete sentence. punctuation mark at the end of a sentence (.). -period'ic a. recurring at regular intervals. -period'ical a. relating to a period; periodic. -n. publication issued at regular intervals. [G. periodos, circuit]

peripatet'ic a. walking about. [G. peripatetikos]

periph'ery n. circumference; surface; outside. [G. peri, around, pherein, carry]

periph'erals n. pl. (compute.) any hardware device separate and distinct from the main computer. also periph'eral equipment.

per'iscope n. an instrument, used esp. in submarines, for giving a view of objects that are on a different level. [G. peri-, round, and skopein, to look]

per'ish v.i. die, waste away. per'ishable a. [L. perire]

peritoni'tis n. inflammation of the

peritoneum. [G. *peritoneion*]

per'jure (-jer) *v.t.* forswear. -*v.i.* bear false witness. [L. *perjurare*]

perk *v.t.* and *i.* smarten; become cheerful; toss head. **-perky** *a.* smart, cheeky. [orig. uncertain]

per'manent *a.* continuing in the same state; lasting. **-per'manent wave**, lasting artificial hair-wave. [L. *permanere*]

per'meate *v.t.* pass through the pores of, saturate. **-per'meable** *a.* admitting of the passage of fluids. [L. *permeate, permeate*, pass through]

permit' *v.t.* allow; give leave to; give leave. -(per'-) *n.* written permission. **-permis'sion** *n.* leave; liberty. - [L. *permittere, permiss-*]

permute' *v.t.* interchange. **-permuta'tion** *n.* mutual transference; (*alg.*) change in the arrangement of a number of quantities. [L. *permutare*, change thoroughly]

perni'cious (-nish'-) *a.* having the quality of destroying or injuring; hurtful. [L. *perniciosus*]

perox'ide *n.* oxide with largest proportion of oxygen. [L. *per*, intens., and *oxide*]

perpendic'ular *a.* exactly upright; at right angles to the plane of the horizon; at right angles to a given line or surface. [L. *perpendicularis*]

per'petrate *v.t.* commit (something bad). [L. *perpetrare*, accomplish]

perpet'ual *a.* continuous, lasting for ever. **-perpet'ually** *adv.* **-perpet'uate** *v.t.* make perpetual; not to allow to be forgotten. [L. *perpetualis*]

perplex' *v.t.* puzzle; complicate. **perplex'ity** *n.* puzzled or tangled state. [L. *perplexus*, entangled]

per'quisite (-it) *n.* casual payment in addition to salary belonging to an employment. [L. *perquisitum*, thing eagerly sought]

per'secute *v.t.* oppress for the holding of an opinion; subject to persistent ill treatment. [L. *persequi, persecute*, pursue]

persevere' *v.i.* persist, maintain an effort. **-persevere'rance** *n,* [L. *perseverare*]

persimm'on *n.* N. American tree bearing edible plum-like fruit; the fruit. [*Algonkin*]

persist' *v.i.* continue in a state or action in spite of obstacles or objections. **persist'ent** *a.* **-persist'ence** *n.* [L. *persistere*, fr. *sistere*, stand]

per'son *n.* individual human being; individual divine being; character in a play, *etc.*; in grammar a classification, or one of the classes, of pronouns, and verb-forms according to the person speaking, spoken to, or spoken of. **-per'sonable** *a.* good-looking. **-per'sonal** *a.* individual, private, of one's own; of or relating to grammatical person. **-personal'ity** *n.* distinctive character. **-per'sonally** *adv.* in person. **-per'sonalty** *n.* personal property. **-person'ify** *v.t.* represent as a person; typify. **personifica'tion** *n.* **-personnel'** *n.* staff employed in a service or institution. [L. *persona*, char. in a play]

perspec'tive (-iv) *n.* art of drawing on a flat surface to give the effect of solidity and relative distances and sizes; drawing in perspective; mental view. **-in perspective**, in due proportion. [L. *perspicere, perspect-*, look through]

perspire' *v.i.* sweat. **-perspira'tion** *n.* [L. *perspirare*, breathe through]

persuade' (-sw-) *v.t.* convince; bring (any one to do something) by argument, *etc.* **-persuasion** *n.* **-persua'sive** *a.* [L. *persuadere, persuas-*]

pertain' *v.i.* belong, relate. **-pert'inent** *a.* to the point. [L. *pertinere*, belong]

pertinacity (-as'-) *n.* **-pertina'cious** *a.* obstinate, persistent. [L. *pertinax*]

perturb' *v.t.* disturb gradually; alarm. [L. *perturbare*]

peruse' *v.t.* read, *esp.* in a slow or careful manner. **-peru'sal** *n.* [orig. uncertain]

pervade' *v.t.* spread through. **-perva'sion** *n.* **-perva'sive** *a.* [L. *pervadere, pervas*, go through]

pervert' *v.t.* turn to a wrong use; lead astray. **-per'vert** *a.* one who has turned to error, *esp.* in religion, morals *etc.*; abnormal person in matters of sex. **-perverse'** *a.* obstinately or unreasonably wrong, wayward, *etc.* **-perver'sity** *n.* [L. *pervertere, perverse*, turn away]

pess'imism *n.* theory that everything turns to evil; tendency to see the worst side of things. [L. *pessimus*, worst]

pest *n.* troublesome or harmful thing or person; plague. **-pestif'erous** *a.* bringing plague; harmful, deadly. **-pest'ilent** *a.* troublesome; deadly. **-pest'ilence** *n.* deadly plague. [L. *pestis*]

pest'er *v.t.* annoy, trouble or vex persistently. [OF. *empestrer*]

pet *n.* animal or person kept or regarded with affection. -*v.t.* make a pet of. **pet** *n.* fit of ill-temper or sulking. **-pett'ish** *a.* [orig. uncertain]

pet'al *n.* colored flower leaf. [G. *petalon*, thin plate]

petit' *a.* petité, *fem.*, small, dainty. [F.]

peti'tion (-ish'-) *n.* request, *esp.* one presented to a sovereign or government. *v.t.* present a petition to. [L. *petitio*]

pet'rify *v.t.* turn into stone; paralyze with fear, *etc.* **-petrifac'tion** *n.* [L. *petra*, rock]

petro'leum *n.* mineral oil. **-pet'rol** *n.* refined petroleum; gasoline. **-petro'leum jelly**, soft paraffin, vaseline. [fr. L. *petra*, rock, and *oleum*, oil]

petti'coat *n.* woman's underskirt. [orig. *petty coat*, small coat]

pett'y *a.* unimportant, trivial; on a small scale. **-pett'y offi'cer** *n.* non-commissioned naval officer. [F. *petit*, small]

pet'ulant *a.* given to small fits of temper. **-pet'ulance**. [L. *petulans, petulant-*, pert, wanton]

petu'nia *n.* plant with funnel-shaped flowers allied to tobacco. -*a.* purplish pink. [Amer. Ind. *petun*, tobacco]

pew *n.* fixed seat in a church. [OF. *puie*, fr. G. *podium*, pedestal]

pew'ter *n.* alloy of tin and lead; ware made

of this. [OF. *peutre*]

phag'ocyte (fag'o-sit) *n.* white blood corpuscle, leucocyte, devouring microbes. [G. *phagein*, eat, *kytos*, cell]

pharmaceut'ic *a.* relating to pharmacy. -*n.* in *pl.* science of pharmacy. -**pharmaceut'ical** *a.* -**pharmaco-poe'ia** *n.* official book with a list and directions for the use of drugs. -**phar'macy** *n.* preparation and dispensing of drugs; drugstore. -**phar'macist** *n.* [G. *pharmakon*, poison, drug]

pharynx (far'ingks) *n.* tube or cavity that connects the mouth with the gullet. [E. *pharynx*. -*yngos*]

phase (-z) *n.* aspect of the moon or a planet; stage of development. -**pha'sic** *a.* [G. *phasis*]

phase. See faze.

pheas'ant (fez'-) *n.* game-bird. [G. Phasis, river in Colchis (where the bird first came from)]

phenomenon *n.* **phenomena** *pl.* anything appearing or observed; remarkable person or thing. -**phenom'enal** *a.* (*colloq.*) exceptional. [G. *phainein*, show]

phil- prefix loving. [G. *philein*, love]; **philan'der** *v.i.* amuse oneself with lovemaking. -**philan'thropy** *n.* love of mankind; practise of doing good to one's fellow men. -**philanthrop'ic** *a.* -**philan'thropist** *n.* -**philat'ely** *n.* stamp collecting. -**philat'elist** *n.* -**philatel'ic** *a.* -**philol'ogy** *n.* science of the structure and development of languages. -**philos'ophy** *n.* pursuit of wisdom; study of realities and general principles; system of theories on the nature of things or on conduct. -**philos'opher** *n.* one who studies, or possesses, or originates, philosophy.

phlebitis *n.* inflammation of a vein. [G. *phleps, phlep-*, vein]

phlebotomy *n.* bleeding, blood-letting. -**phlebot'omist** *n.* [G. *phleps*, vein]

phlegm (flem) *n.* viscid secretion of the mucus membrane, ejected by coughing, *etc.*; calmness, sluggishness. [G. *phlegma*, inflammation]

pho'bia *n.* morbid fear, dislike. [G. *Phobos*, fear]

phoenix *n.* legendary bird supposed to be only one of its kind and after living for centuries to burn (fire) and rise renewed from the ashes; unique thing. [G. *Phoiinix*, purple red.]

phone *n.* , *a.* , and *v.i.* abbrev. of telephone. [G. *phone*, voice, sound]

pho'ney *a.* not genuine. [orig. uncertain]

phon'ic(al) *a.* of sound, phonetic. [G. *phone*, voice, sound]

phono- prefix. [G. *phone*, voice]. **phonet'ic** *a.* of, or relating to, vocal sounds. -*n.* in *pl.* the science of vocal sounds. -**phoneti'cian** *n.* -**pho'nograph** *n.* instrument recording and reproducing sounds.

phosphorus *n.* non-metallic element which appears luminous in the dark. -**phosphores'cence** *n.* faint glow in the dark. [G. *phos*, light]

pho'to- prefix light. [G. *phos*, phot-, light]. -**pho'to-electri'city** *n.* electricity produced or affected by the action of light. -**pho'tograph**

n. picture made by the chemical action of light on a sensitive film. -*v.t.* take a photograph of. -**photog'rapher** *n.* -**photographic** *a.* -**photog'raphy** *a.* -**pho'tostat** *n.* photographic apparatus for obtaining exact copies of manuscript, drawing, *etc.* **photosyn'thesis** *n.* (*bot.*) formation of complex compounds by the action of light on chlorophyll. -**photogenic** *a.* able to photograph well and attractively. [G. *phos. phot-*, light, and *gignesthai*]

phrase (-z) *n.* mode of expression; small group of words; pithy expression. -*v.t.* express in words. -**phraseology** (-i-ol'-) *n.* manner of expression, choice of words. [G. *phrasis*]

phrenol'ogy *n.* study of the shape of the skull; theory that mental powers are indicated by the shape of the skull. -**phrenol'ogist** *n.* [G. *phren*, mind]

phys'ics (-iz'-) *n.* medicine. -*pl.* science of the properties of matter and energy. -*v.t.* dose with medicine. -**phys'ical** *a.* relating to physic, or physics, or the body. -**physically** *adv.* -**physi'cian** *n.* qualified medical practitioner. -**phys'icist** *n.* student of physics. -**physiog'nomy** *n.* judging character by face; the face. -**physique'** (-ek) *n.* bodily structure and development. [G. *physis*, nature]

pian'o *a.* and *adv.* in a low tone or voice. -*n.* pianoforte. -**pian'oforte** (-ta) *n.* musical instrument with strings which are struck by hammers worked by a keyboard. -**pi'anist** *n.* performer on the pianoforte. [It. *piano*, soft, *forte*, loud]

pic'ador *n.* mounted bull-fighter armed with a lance, who excites the bull. [Sp. *pica*, a pike]

picc'olo *n.* small flute. [IT. = little]

pick *n.* tool consisting of a curved iron crossbar and a wooden shaft for breaking up hard ground or masonry. -**pick'ax** *n.* pick. [orig. *piker*]

pick *v.t.* break the surface of, skin with something pointed; gather; choose, select carefully; find an occasion for. -*n.* act of picking; choicest part. -**pick'ings** *n. pl.* odds and ends of profit. [OE. *pycan*]

pick'et *n.* prong or pointed stake: small body of soldiers on police duty; party of trade unionists posted to deter would-be workers during a strike. -*v.t.* tether to a peg; post as a picket; beset with pickets. [F. *piquet*]

pic'kle (pik'l) *n.* brine or other liquid for preserving food; sorry plight; troublesome child. -*pl.* pickled vegetables. -*v.t.* preserve in pickle. [Du. *pekel*]

pic'nic *n.* pleasure excursion including a meal out of doors. -*v.i.* take part in a picnic. [F. *pique-nique*]

pic'ture *n.* drawing or painting or photograph; representation; image. -*v.t.* represent in, or as in, a picture. -**pictor'ial** *a.* of, in, with, painting or pictures; graphic. -*n.* newspaper with many pictures. -**pictor'ially** *adv.* -**picturesque'** (-ésk) *a.* such as would be effective in a picture; striking, vivid. [L. *pictura-pingere, pict-*, paint]

pie *n.* a magpie, wood-pecker; dish of meat, fruit, *etc.*, covered with pastry; mass of printer's type in confusion, *etc*. [L. *pica*]

piece *n*. separate part or fragment; single object; literary or musical composition, *etc*. -*v.t*. mend, put together. -**piece'work** *n*. work paid by amount done regardless of time taken. [F. *piece*]

pier *n*. piece of solid upright masonry, *esp*. supporting a bridge or between two windows; structure running into the sea as a landing stage, *etc*. -**pier-** glass *n*. tall mirror. [Med. L. *pera*]

pierce *v.t*. make a hole in; make a way through. [F. *percer*]

pi'ety *n*. godliness, devoutness; dutifulness. -**pi'etism** *n*. affected or exaggerated piety. [L. *pietas*]

pig *n*. swine; oblong mass of smelted metal. -*v.i*. of a sow, to produce a litter; herded together in a dirty untidy way.-**pig'tail** *n*. plait of hair hanging from the back of the head. [of Teut. orig.]

pi'geon *n*. bird of many wild and domesticated varieties, often trained to carry messages, *etc*. -**pi'geon'hole** *n*. compartment for papers. [F.]

pig'ment *n*. coloring matter, paint or dye. [L. *pigmentum*]

pike *n*. spear formerly used by infantry; peaked hill; large freshwater fish; turnpike or tollgate. [OE. *pic*]

pile *n*. beam driven into the ground, *esp*. as a foundation for building in water or wet ground. [L. *pilum*, dart]

pile *n*. nap of cloth, *esp*. of velvet, carpet. [L. *pilus*, hair]

piles *n*. (in *pl*.) tumors of veins of rectum; hemorrhoids. [L. *pila*, ball]

pil'fer *v.t*. steal in small quantities. -**pil'ferage** *n*. [OF. *pelfrer*]

pil'grim *n*. one who walks to sacred place; wanderer. -**pil'grimage** *n*. [L. *peregrinus*]

pill *n*. pellet of medicine. [L. *pila*, ball]

pill'age *n*. seizing goods by force; *esp*. in war; plunder. -*v.t*. and *i*. plunder. [F.]

pill'box *n*. (mil. *sl*.) small concrete fort or blockhouse. [*pill* and *box*]

pill'ory *n*. frame with holes for head and hands in which an offender was confined and exposed to pelting and ridicule. -*v.t*. set in pillory; expose to ridicule and abuse. [F. *pilori*]

pill'ow *n*. cushion for the head, especially in bed. -*v.t*. lay on a pillow. [L. *pulvinus*]

pi'lot *n*. person qualified to take charge of a ship entering or leaving a harbor, or where knowledge of local waters is needed; steersman; navigator of an airplane; guide. -*v.t*. act as pilot to. -**pi'lot stud'y** *n*. a small-scale experiment or set of observations undertaken to decide how and whether to launch a full-scale project. [F. *pilote*]

pimp *n*. procurer; pander. -*v.i*. pander. [orig. unknown]

pimpernel *n*. plant with small scarlet or blue or white flowers closing in dull weather. [F. *pirnprenelle*]

pim'ple *n*. small pustular spot on the skin. -**pim'ply** *a*. [orig. uncertain]

pin *n*. short thin piece of stiff wire with a point and head for fastening soft materials together; wooden or metal peg or rivet. -*v.t*. fasten with a pin or pins; seize and hold fast. -**pin'-cushion** *n*. pad into which pins are stuck. - [OE. *pinn*, peg]

pin'afore *n*. washing apron or overall. [because pinned afore the dress]

piñata *n*. papier-maché or clay form filled with candy or toys, hung at parties and festivities to be broken open with a stick.

pince'-nez *n*. eye-glasses held on the nose by a spring catch. [F.]

pincers *n. pl*. tool for gripping, composed of two limbs crossed and pivoted. [F. *pincer*]

pinch *v.t*. nip, squeeze. -*n*. nip; stress: as much as can be taken up between finger and thumb. [ONF. *pinchier*]

pine *n*. evergreen coniferous tree. -**pine'apple** *n*. tropical fruit. [L. *pinus*]

pine *v.i*. waste away with grief, want, *etc*. [OE, *pinian*, fr. *pin*, pain]

ping'-pong *n*. table-tennis. [imit.]

pin'ion *n*. wing. -*v.t*. disable by binding wings, arms. [L. *penna*, feather]

pinn'acle *n*. pointed turret on a buttress or roof; mountain peak; highest pitch or point. [L. *pinna*, point]

pint (pint) *n*. liquid and dry measure, half a quart. [F, pinte]

pioneer *n*. one of an advanced body preparing a road for troops; explorer; one who first originates. -*v.i*. act as pioneer or leader. [F. *pionier*, fr. *pion*, foot soldier]

pi'ous *n*. devout. [L. *pius*]

pip *n*. seed in a fruit. [short for *pippin*]

pipe *n*. tube of metal or other material; musical instrument, a whistle; shrill voice, or bird's note; tube with a small bowl at the end for smoking tobacco; wine cask. -*v.i*. and *t*. play on a pipe. [OE.]

pipp'in *n*. various sorts of apples. [F. *pepin*, seed]

pi'quant *a*. pungent; stimulating. [F. *piquer*, string, prick]

pique *v.t*. irritate; hurt the pride of; stimulate. -*n*. feeling of injury or baffled curiosity. [F.]

pi'qué *n*. stiff ribbed cotton fabric. [F.]

pi'rate *n*. sea-robber; publisher, *etc*., who infringes copyright. -*v.t*. publish or reproduce regardless of copyright. [G. *peirates*, fr. *peiran*, attack]

pirouette' *n*. spinning round on the toe. -*v.i*. do this. [F.]

Pisc'es *n. pl*. the Fishes, 12th sign of the zodiac, which the sun enters c. Feb. 19. -**pis'cine** *a*. of or like a fish. [L. *piscis*, fish]

pist'il *n*. female organ of a flower consisting of ovary, style, stigma. [L. *pistillum*, pestle]

pist'ol *n*. small gun used with one hand. -*v.t*. shoot with a pistol. [F. *pistolet*]

pist'on *n*. plug fitting a cylinder and working up and down, *e.g*. as in a steam engine, *etc*. -**piston-rod** *n*. rod connecting piston with other parts of machinery. [F.]

pit *n*. deep hole in the ground; coal mine or its shaft; depression in any surface; in a theater, section for musicians in front of the stage; enclosure in which animals were set to fight. -v.t. set to fight; mark with small scars. -pit'fall n. covered pit for catching animals or men; concealed danger. [L. puteus, well]

pit n. stone of a fruit. [OE. pitha]

pitch n. dark sticky substance obtained from tar or turpentine. -v.t. coat with this. -pitch'-blende n. an oxide of uranium. [L. pix, pic-]

pitch v.t. set up; cast or throw. -v.i. fix upon; fall headlong; of a ship to plunge lengthwise. -n. act of pitching; degree height, station; slope; degree of acuteness of sounds. - pitch'er n. -pitch'fork n. fork for lifting and pitching hay, etc. -v.t. throw with, or as with, a pitchfork. [orig. uncertain]

pitch'er n. large jug. [OF. pichier]

pith n. tissue in the stems and branches of certain plants; essential substance, most important part. -pith'y a. consisting of pith; terse, concise. -pith'ily adv. [OE. pitha]

pitt'ance n. small allowance; inadequate wages. [F. pitance, orig. = pity]

pituitary a. mucous. -pitu'itary gland, small ductless gland situated beneath the brain. [L. pituitarius]

pit'y n. sympathy or sorrow for others' suffering; regrettable fact. -v.t. feel pity for. - pit'iful a. full of pity; contemptible. [F. pitie fr. L. pietas, piety]

piv'ot n. shaft or pin on which something turns; central fact; important factor. -v.t. furnish with a pivot. -v.i. to turn on one. [F.]

pix'el n. any of a number of very small picture elements that make up a picture, as on a visual display unit. [fr. pix (pictures) and elements]

pix'y, pix'ie n. fairy. [orig. uncertain]

placate v.t. conciliate, pacify. -plac'able a. [L. placare]

place n. particular part of space, spot; position; town, village, residence, buildings; office or employment. -v.t. put in a particular place. [F.]

placenta (pla-sen'ta) n. organ connecting the parent with the unborn mammal; that portion of a plant to which the seeds are attached. [L. placenta, a flat cake]

pla'cer n. deposit yielding gold after washing. [Sp.]

pla'cid (-as'-) a. calm; not easily agitated. -placid'ity n. [L. placidus]

pla'giary n. one who publishes borrowed or copied literary work as original; act of so doing. [L. plagiarius, kidnapper]

plague (plāg) n. pestilence; affliction. -v.t. trouble or annoy. -pla'guy a. -pla'guily adv. [L. plaga, stroke]

plaid n. long Scottish-Highland shawl. [Gael. plaide, blanket, fr. peallaid, sheepskin]

plain a. flat, level; unobstructed, not intricate; easily understood; simple, ordinary; unadorned; not beautiful. -n. tract of level country. adv. clearly. -plain'ly adv. -plain'-dealing n. honesty, candidness. -plain'-speaking n. outspokenness, frankness. [L. planus, smooth]

plait (plat) n. fold; braid of hair, straw, etc. -v.t. form into plaits. [OF. pleit]

plan n. drawing representing a thing's horizontal section; diagram, map; project, design; way of proceeding. -v.t. make a plan of; make a design; arrange beforehand. [F. fr. L. planus, level]

plane n. carpenter's tool for smoothing wood. -v.t. make smooth with one. [L. planus, level]

plane a. perfect, flat, or level; smooth surface. [var. of plain]

plane n. abbrev. of airplane; wing of an airplane or glider. -v.t. glide in an airplane. [F. planer, hover]

plan'et n. heavenly body revolving round the sun. -plan'etary a. [G. planetes, wanderer]

planeta'rian n. apparatus showing movement of sun, moon, stars and planets by projecting lights on inside of dome; building in which the apparatus is housed. [G. planetes, wanderer]

plank n. long flat piece of sawn timber. [Late L. planca]

plank'ton n. general term for free-floating organisms in sea or lake, etc. [G. plangktos, wandering]

plant n. member of the vegetable kingdom, living organism feeding on inorganic substances; equipment or machinery needed for a manufacture. -v.t. set in the ground. - planta'tion n. wood of planted trees; estate for cultivation of tea, tobacco, etc.; formerly, a colony. [L. planta]

plant'ain n. tropical tree like a banana; its fruit. [Sp. plantano]

plaque (plak) n. ornamental plate or tablet; plate of clasp or brooch. [F.]

plast'er n. mixture of lime, sand, etc., to spread on walls, etc.; piece of fabric spread with a medicinal or adhesive substance for application to the body. -v.t. apply plaster to. -plast'erer n. [G. plassein, mold]

plast'ic a. produced by molding; easily molded; molding shapeless matter. [G. plas-tikos-plassein, mold]

plas'tics n. pl. name for various synthetic or natural substances capable of being molded into shape, e.g., casein, bitumen, resins. [plas-tic]

plate n. flat thin sheet of metal, glass, etc.; utensils of gold or silver; shallow round dish from which food is eaten. -v.t. cover with a thin coating of gold, silver, or other metal. [G. platus, broad, flat]

plat'eau n. level high land. [F.]

plat'en n. plate by which paper is pressed against type in a printing press; roller in a typewriter. [G. platus, broad, flat]

plat'form n. raised level surface or floor. [F. plate-forme, flat form]

platitude n. commonplace remark. [F. -plat, flat]

platinum n. white heavy malleable metal. -plat'inotype n. photographic process or print in which platinum is used. [Sp. platina, dim. of plate, silver]

Platon'ic a. of, pert. to Plato and his philosophy; (of love) spiritual, friendly. [Plato]

platoon' n. small body of soldiers employed as a unit; sub-division of an infantry company. [F. *peloton*]

platt'er n. a flat dish. [AF. *plater*]

plaud'it n. act of applause. [L. *plaudere*, clap the hands]

plausible a. something fair or reasonable; fair-spoken. -plausibil'ity n. [L. *plausibilis*]

play (plā) v.i. move with light or irregular motion, flicker, etc.; amuse oneself; take part in a game; perform on a musical instrument. -v.t. use or work (an instrument); take part in (a game); contend with in a game; perform (music), perform on (an instrument); act; act the part of -n. brisk or free movement; activity; sport; amusement; gambling; dramatic piece or performance. -play'er n. -play'fellow, play'mate n. friend, companion in play.-play'thing n. toy. -play'wright n. author of plays. [OE. *plegian*]

plea n. that is pleaded; excuse; statement of a prisoner or defendant. -plead v.i. address a court of law; make an earnest appeal. -v.t. bring forward as an excuse or plea. [F. *plaid*]

pleach' v.t. interweave the branches of (a hedge, etc.). [OF. *presser*]

please v.t. be agreeable to. -v.i. like; be willing. -pleas'ance (plez'-) n. delight; pleasure-ground. -pleas'ure n. enjoy ment; satisfaction; will, choice. -pleas'urable a. giving pleasure.-pleas'ant a. pleasing, agreeable.[F. *plaire, plais-* fr. L. *placere*]

pleat n. three-fold band on a garment etc., made by folding the material on itself. v.i. make a pleat in. [*plait*]

plebeian a. belonging to the common people; low or rough. -n. one of the common people. [L. *plebs*, common people]

plebiscite n. a decision by direct voting of a whole people. [F.]

pledge n. thing given as security; toast; promise. -v.t. give over as security; engage; drink the health of. [OF. *plege*]

Plei'stocene a. of Glacial period or formation. [G. *pleistos*, most, *kainos*, new]

plent'y n. quite enough; abundance. -plent'eous a. -plent'iful a. abundant. [OF. *plente*-L. *plenus*, full]

pleth'ora n. excess of red corpuscles in the blood; oversupply. -plethor'ic a. [G. *plethein*, become full]

pleu'ra n. membrane enclosing lung. -pleu'ral a. [G. *pleura*, side]

pleur'isy n. inflammation of membrane round the lungs. [G. *pleura*, side]

pli'able a. easily bent or influenced. -pliabil'ity n. -pli'ant a. pliable. -pli'ancy n. [F.]

pli'ers n.pl. small pincers with a flat grip. [L. *plicare*, bend]

plight n. state (usually of a distressing kind); predicament. [OE. *plit*, fold or plait]

plinth n. square slab as the base of a column, etc. [G. *plinthos*, brick]

plod v.i. walk or work doggedly. [imit. orig.]

plot n. small piece of land; plan or essential facts of a story, play, etc.; secret design, conspiracy. -v.t. make a map of; devise secretly.

-v.i. take part in conspiracy. [OE.]

plotter n. (*compute.*) output device that converts electronic signals into figures, lines, or curves; printing device.

plow n. implement for turning up the soil. -v.i. turn up with a plow, furrow. -plow'share n. cutting blade of plow. [ON. *plogr*]

pluck v.i. pull or pick off, strip the feathers from; reject in an examination. -n. plucking; beast's heart, lungs, etc.; courage. [OE. *pluecian*]

plug n. something fitting into and filling a hole; tobacco pressed hard; piece of this for chewing. -v.t. stop with a plug. -(*sl.*) push; advertise persistently. [Du. = *bung*]

plum n. stone fruit; tree bearing it. plum-cake, plum-pudding n. rich cake, pudding full of raisins, other fruits and spices. [OE. *plume*, L. *prune*]

plumb (-m) n. ball of lead attached to a string and used for sounding, finding the perpendicular, etc. -a. perpendicular. -adv. perpendicularly; exactly. -v.t. find the depth of, set exactly upright. -plumb'er (-mer) n. one who works in lead, etc. and repairs water pipes etc. [L. *plumbuimi*, lead]

plume n. feather; ornament consisting of feathers or horse-hair. -v.t. furnish with plumes; strip of feathers; boast. -plu'mage n. feathers of a bird. [L. *pluma*, feather]

plump a. of rounded form, moderately fat. [Du. *plomp*, blunt]

plun'der v.t. rob systematically; take by open force. -v.i. rob. -n. violent robbery; property so obtained, spoils. [Ger. *plundern*, pillage]

plunge v.t. put forcibly (into). -v.i. throw oneself (into); enter or move forward with violence. -n. plunge, dive. -plun'ger n. [F. *plonger*]

pluperfect a. of a tense, expressing action completed before a past point of time. [L. *plus quam perfectum*, more than perfect]

plus prep. with addition of (usually indicated by the sign +). -a. to be added; positive. [L. *plus*, more]

plur'al a. more than one; denoting more than one person or thing. -n. word in its plural form. -plu'ralism n. holding more than one appointment, vote, etc. [L. *plus, plur-*, more]

plush n. fabric like velvet, but with a long soft nap. [F. *peluche*]

Plu'to n. outermost of the planets so far discovered. -Pluto'nian a. pert. to Pluto; dark subterranean; igneous. [G. *Plouton*, god of the underworld]

plutocracy n. government by the rich, wealthy class. -plu'tocrat n. wealthy person. -plutocrat'ic a. [G. *ploutokratia*, power by wealth]

plutonium n. element produced by radioactive decay of neptunium. [*Pluto*]

ply n. fold, thickness. [L. *plicare*, fold]

ply v.t. wield, work at; supply pressingly. -v.i. go to and fro. [*apply*]

pneumatic a. of, or coated by, or inflated with, wind or air. -pneumo'nia n. inflammation of the lungs. [G. *pneuma*, breath]

poach v.i. cook (an egg) by dropping without

the shell into boiling water. [F. *pocher*, pocket]

poach *v.t.* hunt (game) illegally. -*v.i.* trespass for this purpose. -**poach′er** *n.* [orig. uncertain]

pock *n.* pustule as in smallpox, *etc.* **pock-marks, pock′pit** *n.* mark or small hole left on skin after smallpox *etc.* [OE. *poc*]

pock′et *n.* small bag inserted in a garment; cavity filled with ore, *etc.*; mass of water or air differing in some way from that surrounding it. -*v.t.* put into one's pocket; appropriate. -**pock′etbook** *n.* small bag or case for holding money, papers *etc.* [F. *poche*, cp. *poke*]

pod *n.* long seed-vessel, as of peas, beans, *etc.* -*v.i.* form pods. -*v.t.* shell. [orig. uncertain]

po′em *n.* imaginative composition in verse. -**po′et** *n.* writer of poems. -**po′etess** *fem.* -**po′etry** *n.* art or work of a poet. -**po′esy** *n.* poetry. [G. *poiein*, make]

pog′ram *n.* concerted rising (against, *e.g.*, the Jews), with massacre and pillage. [Russ.]

poign′ant (poin′-) *a.* pungent, stinging, moving, vivid. -**poign′ancy** *n.* [F. *poindre*, *poign-*, fr. L. *pungere*, prick]

point *n.* dot or mark; punctuation mark; item, detail; unit of value; position, degree, stage; moment; essential object or thing; sharp end; headland; movable rail, changing a train to other rails; one of the direction marks of a compass; striking or effective part or quality; act of pointing. -*v.t.* sharpen; give value to (words, *etc.*); fill up joints with mortar; aim or direct. -*v.i.* show direction or position by extending a finger, stick, *etc.*; direct attention; of a dog, to indicate the position of game by standing facing it.-**point′-blank′** *a.* aimed horizontally; at short range. *adv.* with level aim (there being no necessity to elevate for distances), at short range. [L. *puncture*, fr. *pungere*, prick]

poise *v.t.* place or hold in a balanced or steady position. -*v.i.* be so held; hover. -*n.* balance, equilibrium, carriage (of body, *etc.*). [OF. *pois*, weight]

poi′son (-z-) *n.* substance which kills or injures when introduced into living organism. -*v.t.* give poison to; infect; pervert, spoil. -**poi′soner** *n.* -**poi′sonous** *a.* [F.]

poke *v.t.* push or thrust with a finger, stick, *etc.*; thrust forward. -*v.i.* make thrusts; to pry. -*n.* act of poking. -**po′ker** *n.* metal rod for poking a fire. -**po′ky** *n.* bag; pouch. [ONF. *paque*; F. *poche*, obteut. orig.]

po′ker *n.* card game. [orig. uncertain]

pol′aroid *n.* type of plastic which polarizes light; camera that develops print very quickly inside itself. [Trademark]

pole *n.* long rounded piece of wood; measure of length, 5½ yards; measure of area, 30¼ square yards. -*v.t.* propel with a pole. [OE. *pal*, fr. L. *palus*]

pole *n.* each of the two points about which the stars appear to revolve; each of the ends of the axis of the earth; each of the opposite ends of a magnet, electric cell, *etc.* -**po′lar** *a.* -**polar′ity** *n.* -**po′larize** *v.t.* give magnetic polarity to; affect light so that its vibrations are kept to one plane. -**polariza′tion** *n.* -**pole′-star** *n.* north star; guide, lodestar. [G. *polos*,

pivot]

pole′cat *n.* small animal of the weasel family; skunk. [F. *poule*, hen (fr. its preying on *poultry*)]

polem′ic *a.* controversial. -*n. pl.* war of words; art of controversy; branch of theology dealing with differences in doctrines. -**polem′ical** *a.* [G. *polemos*, war]

police′ *n.* public order; civil force which maintains public order. -*v.t.* keep in order. -**police′man** *n.* [G. *polis*, city]

pol′icy *n.* a contract of insurance. [It. *polizza*, invoice]

pol′icy *n.* political wisdom; course of action adopted, *e.g.* in state affairs; prudent procedure. [OF. *policie* fr. G. *politeia*, government]

poliomyelitis, polio *n.* inflammation of the spinal cord; infantile paralysis. [G. *polios*, gray, *myelos*, marrow]

pol′ish *v.t.* make smooth and glossy; refine. -*n.* act of polishing; gloss; refinement of manners; substance used in polishing. [L. *polire*, make to shine]

polite′ *a.* refined; having refined manners, courteous. -**polite′ly** *adv.* -**polite′ness** *n.* [L. *politus*]

pol′itic (pol′-it-ic) *a.* wise, shrewd, expedient, cunning. -*n.* in *pl.* art of government; political affairs or life. -**polit′ical** *a.* of the state or its affairs. -**politi′cian** *n.* one engaged in politics. [fr. G. *polites*, a citizen]

pol′itics *n.* science and art of civil government; political principles or opinions; political methods. -**pol′itic** *a.* prudent; crafty, scheming. -**political** *a.* [v.s.]

pol′ka *n.* quick, round dance; music for it. -*v.i.* dance a polka. [Polish]

poll *n.* head or top of the head, counting of voters; voting; number of votes recorded. -*v.t.* cut off the top of; take the votes of, receive (votes). *v.i.* to vote. -**poll′-tax** *n.* tax on each head, or person. [of Teut. orig.]

poll′en *n.* fertilizing dust of a flower. -**pollina′tion** *n.* transferring of pollen to stigma by insects, *etc.* [L. = fine dust]

pollute′ *v.t.* make foul; desecrate. -**pollu′tion** *n.* [L. *polluere, pollut-*]

po′lo *n.* game like hockey played by men on ponies, four-a-side. -**wa′ter po′lo,** ballgame played in water. [Balti = ball]

polonaise′ *n.* Polish dance; music for it; gown looped up over hooped petticoat, [F. = Polish]

poltergeist *n.* (*psych. research*) spirit, ghost, throwing things about and causing unexplained noises. [Ger.]

poly- *prefix.* many. [G. *polus*, many] -**polyan′dry** *n.* polygamy in which one woman has more than one husband. -**pol′ychrome** *a.* many colors. -*n.* work of art in many colors. -**polychromat′ic** *a.* -**polyeth′ylene** *n.* tough thermoplastic material. -**polyg′amy** *n.* custom of being married to several persons at a time. -**polyg′amist** *n.* -**pol′yglot** *a.* speaking, writing, or written in several languages. -**pol′ygon** *n.* figure with many angles or sides. -**polyg′onal** *a.* -**polygynyn.** polygamy in which one man has more than one wife. -

polyhe'dron n. solid figure contained by many faces. **-pol'ytheism** n. belief in many gods. **-pol'ytheist** n. **-polytheist'ic** a.

pom'egranate n. large fruit with thick rind containing many seeds in a red pulp; the tree. [OF. *pome grenade*]

pomp n. splendid display or ceremony. **-pomp'ous** a. self-important; puffed up; of language, inflated. **-pompos'ity** n. [G. *pompe*, solemn procession]

pon'cho n. blanket worn orig. by S. American Indians. [Sp.]

pond n. small body of still water, *esp.* for watering cattle, *etc.* [same as *pound*]

pon'der v.t. and i. meditate, think over; **-pond'erable** a. capable of being weighed. **-pond'erous** a. heavy, unwieldy. [L. *pondus*, *ponder-*, weight]

pon'tiff n. Pope; high priest. **pontifical** a. pompous and dogmatic. **-pontif'icate** v.i.. [L. *pontifex*, high priest]

pontoon' flat bottomed boat or metal drum for use in supporting a temporary bridge. [L. *ponto*, punt]

po'ny n. horse of a small breed. [Gael. *poniadh*]

poo'dle n. variety of pet dog with long curly hair often clipped fancifully. [Ger. *pudel*, orig. water dog]

pool n. small body of still water (*esp.* of natural formation); deep place in a river. [OE. *pol*]

pool n. collective stakes in various games; variety of billiards; combination of capitalists to fix prices and divide business; common fund. *-v.t.* throw into a common fund. [F. *poule*, hen]

poor a. having little money; unproductive, inadequate, insignificant, unfortunate. **-poor'ly** a. not in good health. [L. *pauper*]

pop n. abrupt small explosive sound. *v.i.* make such sound; go or come unexpectedly or suddenly. *-v.t.* put or place suddenly. **pop-corn** n. Indian corn puffed up through exposure to heat. [imit. orig.]

pop n. music of general appeal, *esp.* to young people. *-a.* popular. [fr. *popular*]

Pope n. bishop of Rome as head of the Roman Catholic Church. [G. *pappas*, father]

pop'lar n. tree noted for slender tallness and tremulous leaves. [L. *populus*]

pop'lin n. corded fabric of silk and worsted. [It. *papalina* (*fem.*), papal, because made at Avignon (seat of the Pope, 1309-1408)]

popp'y n. bright flowered plant which yields opium. [OE. *popig*, L. *papaver*]

pop'ulace n. common people. **-pop'ular** a. of or by the people; finding general favor. **-popular'ity** n. being generally liked. **-pop'ularize** v.t. make popular. **-populate** v.t. fill with inhabitants. **-population** n. inhabitants; the number of them. **-pop'ulous** a. thickly populated. [L. *populus*]

porcelain n. fine earthenware, china. [F. *porcelaine*]

porch n. covered approach to the entrance of a building; a veranda. [F. *porche*, fr. L. *porticos*, colonnade]

porcupine n. rodent animal covered with long pointed quills. [OF. *porc esp in*, "Spiny pig"]

pore n. minute opening, *esp.* in the skin. **-por'ous** a. full of pores; allowing a liquid to soak through. **-poros'ity, porousness** n. [G. *poros*]

pore v.i. fix the eyes or mind upon; study attentively. [ME. *pouren*]

pork n. pig's flesh as food. **-pork'er** n. pig raised for food. **-pork'y** a. fleshy; fat. [L. *porcus*, pig]

pornography n. indecent art, literature. [G. *porne*, whore, *graphein*, write, draw]

por'poise (-pus) n. blunt-nosed sea animal about five feet long. [OF. *porpeis*, pig-fish]

porridge n. soft food of oatmeal or other meal boiled in water. [var. of *pottage*]

port n. harbor or haven; town with a harbor. [L. *portus*]

port n. city gate; opening in the side of a ship. [L. *porta*, a gate]

port n. strong red wine. [*Oporto*]

port n. bearing. *-v.t.* carry (a rifle) slanting upwards in front of the body. **-port'able** a. easily carried. **-port'age** n. carrying or transporting. **-port'ly** a. large and dignified in appearance. [L. *portare*, carry]

port'al n. large door or gate. [OF.]

portend' v.t. foretell; be an omen of. **port'ent** n. omen, marvel. **-portent'ous** a. [L. *portendere*, foretell]

port'er n. door keeper. [L. *porta*, gate]

port'er n. person employed to carry burdens, *esp.* at airports *etc.*; railway sleeping-car attendant; a dark beer. [L. *portare*, carry]

portfolio n. case for papers, *etc.*; office of a minister of state. [corrupt. of It. *portafogli*, carry leaves]

port'hole n. small opening in the side or superstructure of a ship for light and air. [L. *porta*, a gate]

por'tion n. part or share; destiny, lot; dowry. *-v.t.* divide into shares; give dowry to. **-por'tionless** a. [L. *portio*]

portray' v.t. make a picture of, describe. **port'rait** n. likeness. [L. *protrahere*, draw forth]

pose v.t. lay down; place in an attitude. *-v.i.* assume an attitude, give oneself out as. *-n.* attitude, *esp.* one assumed for effect. **-poseur** (-ur) n. one who poses for effect. [F. *poser*]

posh a. (*sl.*) stylish, smart. *-v.t.* spruce up. [perh. *port out, starboard home*, the fashionable sides of the ship to travel to India during the British Raj]

position n. way a thing is placed; situation, attitude; state of affairs; office for employment; strategic point. [L. *ponere, posit-*, lay down]

positive a. firmly laid down; definite; absolute, unquestionable; confident; overconfident; not negative; greater than zero. *-n.* positive degree; in photography, print in which the lights and shadows are not reversed. [L. *positivus, posit-*]

poss'e n. a force, body (of police or others with legal authority). [L. *posse*, be able]

possess' (-zes')v.t. own; of an evil spirit, have the mastery of. **-posses'sion** n. **-possess'ive** a. of or indicating possession n. possessive case in grammar. **-possessor** n. [L. possidere, possess-]

possible a. that can or may be, exist, happen, be done. **-possibil'ity** n. **- poss'ibly** adv. [L. possibilis]

post n. upright pole of timber or metal fixed firmly, usually as a support for something. -v.t. display; stick up (on a post, notice board, etc.). **-post'er** n. placard; advertising bill. [L. postis]

post (pōst) n. official carrying of letters or parcels; collection or delivery of these; point, station or place of duty; place where a soldier is stationed; place held by a body of troops, fort; office or situation. -v.t. put into the official box for carriage by post; transfer (entries) to a ledger; supply with latest information; station (soldiers, etc.) in a particular spot. v.i. travel with post horses. -adv. in haste. **-post'age** n. charge for carrying a letter, etc. **-post'al** a. **-post'card** n. card with message sent by post. **-post'man** n. man who collects or delivers the post. **post'mark** n. official mark with the name of the office, etc., stamped on letters. **-post'-master** n. official in charge of a post office. **post-office** n. office which receives and transmits mail; government department in charge of conveying of mail. **-postproduction** n. editing of a film or recording that takes place after the artists' taping is complete. [L. ponere, posit-, place]

post-, later, after. [L. post, after]. **-postdate'** v. t. give a date later than the actual date. **-post-grad'uate** a. carried on after graduation. **-poste'rior** (post-)a. later; hinder. **-poster'ity** n. descendants; later generations. **-post'ern** n. back or private door. **-post'humous** a. born after the father's death; published after the author's death; occurring, conferred, etc. , after death. **-postmortem** a. taking place after death. -n. medical examination of a dead body. **-postpone'** v.t. put off to a later time. **-postpone'ment** n. **-post'script** n. addition to a letter or book.

postmerid'ian a. of the afternoon. -n. afternoon, cont. p. m. [L. post, after]

post o'bit a. taking effect after death. -n. bond given by borrower securing repayment on death of one from whom he has expectations. [L. post, after, obitus, death]

postulate v.t. claim, demand, take for granted. -n. something taken for granted. [L. postulare, demand]

pos'ture n. attitude, position. [L. positura, fr. ponere, place]

po'sy n. bunch of flowers; verse accompanying it. [shortened fr. poesy]

pot n. round vessel; cooking vessel. -v.t. put into or preserve in a pot. [OE. pott]

po'table a. drinkable. [L. potare, drink]

pot'ash n. alkali used in soap, etc.; crude potassium carbonate. **-potass'ium** n. white metal. [orig. pot ashes]

pota'to n. plant with tubers grown for food. -(pl.) potatoes. **-pota'to-bug** n. Colorado beetle. [Sp. patata]

po'tent a. powerful. **-po'tency** n. **-po'tentate** a. ruler. **-poten'tial** a. latent, may or might but does not now exist or act. -n. amount of potential energy or work. [L. potens, pres. p. of posse, be able]

po'tion n. a draught; dose of medicine or poison. [L. potio-potare, drink]

potpourri n. mixture of rose petals, spices, etc.; musical or literary medley. [F.]

pott'er n. maker of earthenware vessels. **-pott'ery** n. place where earthenware is made; earthenware; art of making it. [pot]

pouch n. small bag. -v.t. put into one. [F. poche, pocket]

poult n. chicken. **-poult'erer** n. dealer in poultry. **-poult'ry** n. domestic fowls. [F. poulet, dim. of poule, hen]

pounce v.i. spring upon suddenly, swoop. -n. swoop or sudden descent upon something. [orig. uncertain]

pound n. weight, 12 oz. troy, 16 ozs. avoirdupois; unit of money, 100 pence. **pound'age** n. payment or commission of so much per pound (money); charge of so much per pound (weight). [OE. pund, L. pondus, weight]

pound n. enclosure for stray cattle. -v.t. shut up in one. [OE. pund]

pound v.t. crush to pieces or powder; thump; cannonade. [OE. púnian]

pour (pawr) v.i. come out in a stream, crowd, etc. -v.t. give out thus; cause to run out. [orig. unknown]

pout v.i. thrust out the lips. -v.t. thrust out (the lips). -n. act of pouting. **-pout'er** n. pigeon with the power of inflating its crop. [orig. uncertain]

pov'erty n. the condition of being poor; poorness, lack. [F. pauvreté]

pow'der n. solid matter in fine dry particles; medicine in this form; gunpowder. -v.t. apply powder to, reduce to powder. **-pow'dery** a. [F. poudre]

pow'er n. ability to do or act; authority; person or thing having authority. **-pow'erful** a. **-pow'erless** a. **-pow'erhouse**; power station n. building where electrical power is generated. [OF. poeir]

pox n. one of several diseases marked by pustular eruptions of skin, e.g. chickenpox, smallpox. [pl. of pock]

prac'tice v.t. do habitually; put into action; work at; exercise oneself in. -v.i. exercise oneself, exercise a profession. -n. habitual doing; action as distinguished from theory; habit; exercise in an art or profession. **-prac'tical** a. relating to action or real existence; given to action rather than theory; that is (something) in effect though not in name. **-prac'tically** adv. virtually, almost; in actuality, rather than in theory. **-practi'tioner** n. one engaged in a profession. [G. praktikos, concerned with action]

practicum n. educational course based on the practical application of theory through field work or research; course offering supervised practical experience.

pragmat'ic a. of the affairs of a state; concerned with practical consequences; officious, dogmatic. [G. *pragmatikos*, skilled in business]

prair'ie *n.* large tract of grass-land without trees. [F. = meadow]

praise *v.t.* express approval or admiration of, glorify. -*n.* commendation; fact or state of being praised. -**praise'worthy** *a.* [OF. *preisier*]

prance *v.i.* walk with bounds; strut about. -*n.* a prancing. [orig. uncertain]

prank *n.* frolicsome trick or escapade. [orig. uncertain]

prank *v.t.* adorn, rig out showily. -*v.i.* make a great display. [orig. uncertain]

prate *v.i.* talk idly, chatter; give away a secret. -*n.* chatter. -**prat'tle** *v.i.* and *v.t.* utter childishly. -*n.* childish chatter. -**pratt'ler** *n.* [Du. *praten*]

prawn *n.* edible sea crustacean like a shrimp. [orig. unknown]

pray *v.t.* ask earnestly. -*v.i.* offer prayers, especially to God. -**pray'er** *n.* earnest entreaty; action or practice of praying to God. -**pray'erful** *a.* [OF. *preier* fr. L. *precari*]

pre- *prefix*, makes compounds with the meaning of before, or beforehand; *e.g.* **predeter'mine** *v.t.* determine beforehand. [L. *prae-, pre-*, before]

preach *v.i.* deliver a sermon. -*v.t.* set forth in religious discourse. -**preach'er** *n.* [F. *precher*, fr. L. *praedicare*, fr. *dicare*, to proclaim]

pream'ble *n.* introductory part; preface. [L. *proeambulus*, going before]

precarious *a.* insecure, unstable, perilous. [L. *precarius*, uncertainly possessed]

precaution *n.* preventive measure; cautious foresight. -**precautionary** *a.*

precede' *v.t.* go or come before in rank, order, time, *etc.* -*v.i.* go or come before. -**pre'cedence** *n.* higher or more honorable place; right to this. -**prec'edent** (pres'-) *n.* previous case or occurrence taken as a rule. [L. *praecedere*, go before]

pre'cept *n.* rule for conduct; maxim. -**precept'or** *n.* teacher. [L. *praecipere*, *praecept-*, take before, order]

pre'cinct *n.* ground attached to a sacred or official building; limit or boundary; division of a city as relates to policing, voting *etc.* [Med. L. *præcinctum*, enclosure]

prec'ious (presh'us) *a.* of great value, highly valued; affected, overrefined. **prec'iously** *adv.* -**prec'iousness** *n.* **precios'ity** *n.* overrefinement in art or literature. [L. *pretiosus*, valuable]

precipice (pres'-) *n.* very steep cliff or rock-face. [L. *prxicipitium*, fr. *praeceps*, head first]

precipitate *v.t.* throw headlong; hasten the happening of; in chemistry, cause to be deposited in solid form from a solution. -*a.* over-sudden, rash. -*n.* substance chemically precipitated. [L. *praecipitare*]

precise' *a.* exact, strictly; worded; particular; careful in observance. [L. *praecisus*, cut off in front]

preclude' *v.t.* prevent. [L. *praecludere*]

precocious *a.* developed too soon, *esp.* mentally. -**preco'city** (-os-) *n.* [L. *praecox, precoc*, early ripe]

precognition *n.* knowledge beforehand. [pre-, and L. *cognoscere, cognit-*, know]

preconceive' *v.t.* conceive opinion or idea without previous knowledge. **preconcep'tion** *n.* [pre-, and F. *concevoir*]

preconcert' *v.t.* agree upon, settle before. [pre- and F. concerter]

precursor *n.* forerunner. [L.]

predatory *a.* relating to plunder; given to plundering; rapacious. -**preda'cious** *a.* of animals, living by capturing prey. [L. *praeda*, booty]

predecessor *n.* one who precedes another in an office, *etc.* [Late L. *praedecessor*, fr. *decessor*, one who withdraws]

predestine *v.t.* destine, ordain beforehand. -**predes'tinate** *v.t.* foreordain by unchangeable purpose. -**predes'tined** *a.* **predestina'tion** *n.* doctrine that man's fate is unalterably fixed. [pre-, and L. *destinare*, make fast]

predicate *v.t.* affirm or assert. -*n.* that which is predicated; in grammar, a statement made about a subject. [L. *praedicare*, proclaim]

predict' *v.t.* foretell. -**predic'tion** *n.* [L. *praedicere, predict-*, say before]

predilection *n.* preference or liking; predisposition in favor of. [F. *predilection*]

predominate *v.i.* be the main or controlling element. -**predom'inance** *n.* -**predom'inant** *a.* [*dominate*]

pre-eminent *a.* excelling all others. -**pre-em'inently** *adv.* outstandingly. **pre'em'inence** *n.* [*eminent*]

preen *v.t.* trim (feathers) with a beak; smarten oneself, [var. of *prune*]

prefab'ricate *v.t.* . make beforehand parts (of a house *etc.*) to be assembled at a chosen site. -**prefab** *n.* (*sl.*) prefabricated house. [L. *fabricari*, fabricate, construct]

pref'ace *n.* introduction to a book, *etc.* -*v.t.* introduce. -**prefatory** *a.* [L. *prae fatio*, speaking beforehand]

pre'fect *n.* person put in authority; Roman official; head of a department; schoolboy with responsibility for maintaining discipline. [L. *praefectus*]

prefer' *v.t.* like better; promote. **preferable** *a.* -**pref'erably** *adv.* - **preference** *n.* - **preferen'tial** *a.* giving or receiving a preference. [L. *praeferre*, bear before]

pre'fix *n.* preposition or particle put at the beginning of a word or title. -**prefix'** *v.t.* put as introduction; put before a word to make a compound. [*fix*]

preg'nant *a.* with child; full of meaning. -**preg'nancy** *n.* [L. *praegnans*]

prehensile *a.* capable of grasping. [L. *prehendre, prehens-*, seize]

prejudice (is) *n.* judgment or bias decided beforehand; harm likely to happen to a person or his rights as a result of others' action or judgment; prepossession (usually unfavorable). -*v.t.* influence unfairly; injure. -**prejudi'cial** *a.* harmful; detrimental. [L. *praejudicium*]

prel'ate *n.* bishop or other church dignitary of equal or higher rank. [L. *praelatus*, pp. of praeferre, put before]

prelim'inary a. preparatory, introductory. -n. introductory or preparatory statement or action. [F. préliminaire, fr. L. limen, threshold]

prel'ude n. performance, event, etc., serving as an introduction; in music, introductory movement. -v.i. and t. serve as prelude. [L. ludere, play]

premature a. happening or done before the proper time. [mature]

premeditate v.t. think out beforehand. [meditate]

premenstrual a. of or occurring before a menstrual period. -pre'menstrual ten'sion or syn'drome n. any of various symptoms, including esp.nervous tension, that may be experienced as a result of hormonal changes in the days before a menstrual period starts. [pre-, and L. menstruus, monthly]

prem'ier a. chief, foremost. -n. prime minister. [F. = first]

première' (-yer) n. first performance of a play or film. [F.]

prem'ise (prem'is) n. in logic, a proposition from which an inference is drawn. -pl. in law, beginning of a deed; house or buildings with its belongings. -premise' (-iz) v.t. state by way of introduction. -prem'iss n. (logical) premise. [L. praemittere, prerni, send in front]

premium n. reward; sum paid for insurance; bonus; excess over nominal value. [L. praemium, booty, reward]

preoccupy (-pi) v.t. occupy to the exclusion of other things. -preoccupa'tion n. mental concentration with the appearance of absentmindedness. [occupy]

prep n. (schoolboy sl.) preparation (of lessons). -prep school, contr. for preparatory school.

prepare' v.t. make ready; make. -v.i. get ready. -prepara'tion n. -prepar'atory a. [L. praeparare, make ready before]

preponderate v.i. be of greater weight, numbers, or power. -prepond'erance n. [L. pondus, weight]

preposition n. part of speech; a word marking the relation between two other words. -preposi'tional a. [L. praeponere, praeposit-, put before]

prepossess' v.t. impress, esp.favorably, beforehand. -prepossess'ing a. prepossess'ion n. [possess]

preposterous a. utterly absurd. [L. praeposterus, lit. 'before behind']

prep'py a. characteristic of or denoting a fashion style of neat, understated, and often expensive clothes, suggesting that the wearer is well off, upper class, and conservative. -n. a person exhibiting such style. [fr. preparatory school]

prequel n. book, film, play, or other work that is based on another but describes a time that preceded those in the original work, or the characters at an earlier stage.

prerogative n. peculiar power or right, esp. as vested in a sovereign. [L. praerogative, right to vote first]

pres'age n. omen, indication of something to come. -presage' v.t. foretell. [L. praesagium]

prescience (pre'-shi-ens) n. foreknowledge. -pres'eient (pre'-shi-ent) a. [L. pre scientia, knowledge]

prescribe' v.t. and i. order, appoint; order the use of (a medicine). -prescription n. prescribing; thing prescribed; written statement of it; in law, uninterrupted use as the basis of a right or title; such title. -prescrip'tive a. [L. praescribere, praescript-, write before]

pres'ent a. that is here, now existing or happening. -n. -pres'ently adv. soon. -pres'ence n. a being present; personal appearance. [L. praesens, pres. p. of prae-esse, be before]

present v.t. introduce formally; show; point or aim; give, offer. -pres'ent n. gift. -present'able a. fit to be seen. -presenta'tion n. -present'ment n. [L. praesentare, place before]

presentiment (-z-) n. foreboding. [L. praesentire, feel before]

preserve' (-z-) v.t. keep from harm or injury or decay. -n. jam; place where game is kept for shooting. -preserva'tion n. -preserv'ative a. and n. [L. servare, protect]

preside' (-z-) v.i. be chairman; superintend. -pres'ident n. head of a society, company, republic. -pres'idency n. -presiden'tial a. [L. praesidere, fr. sedere, sit]

press v.t. subject to push or squeeze; urge steadily or earnestly. -v.i. bring weight to bear. -n. crowd; machine for pressing, esp. a printing machine; printing house; its work or art; newspapers collectively; large cupboard. -pressing a. urgent. -pres'sure n. and v.t. -press'urize v.t. apply pressure to; maintain normal atmospheric pressure inside the cabin during high-altitude flying, etc. -press'urized a. [L. pressare, frequent, of premere]

press v.t. force to serve in the navy or army; take for royal or public use. [earlier prest fr. L. praestare, furnish]

prestidigitator (-j-) n. magician, conjurer. [F. prestidigitateur]

prestige' n. reputation, or influence depending on it. [F. = magic]

presume' (-z-) v.t. take for granted. -v.i. take liberties. -presu'mable a. -presumably adv. -presump'tion n. -presump'tuous a. forward, taking liberties. [L. praesumere, praesumpt-, take before]

pretend v.t. feign, make believe. -v.i. layclaim, feign. -pretense' n. -pretend'er n. -preten'tion n. -preten'tious a. making claim to special (and usu. unjustified) merit or importance. [L. praetendere, hold before, put forward]

pre'text n. excuse; ostensible motive. [L. praetexere, weave in front]

prett'y (prit'-i) a. having beauty that is attractive rather than imposing; charming, etc. adv. fairly, moderately. -prett'ily adv. [OE. praet-tig, tricky]

prevail' v.i. gain the mastery; be in fashion or generally established. [L. praevalere-valere, be powerful]

prevar'icate v.i. make evasive or misleading statements. [L. *praevaricare*, walk crookedly]

prevent′ *v.t.* stop from happening. [L. *praevenire, praevent-*, come before]

pre′vious *a.* preceding; happening before. -**pre′viously** *adv.* [L. *praevius*, fr. *via*, way]

prey *n.* that is hunted and killed by carnivorous animals; victim. -*v.i.* prey upon; treat as prey, afflict. [OF. *preie*, fr. L. *praeda*, booty]

priapic *a.* overly concerned with masculinity or virility. [Greek god, *Priapus*, god of procreation]

price *n.* that for which a thing is bought or sold. -*v.t.* fix or ask a price of. -**price′less** *a.* invaluable. [F. *prix*, fr. L. *pretium*, reward, value]

prick *n.* slight hole made by pricking; a pricking or being pricked. -*v.t.* pierce slightly with a sharp point; mark by a prick; erect (the ears). [OE. *prica*, point]

pride *n.* too high an opinion of oneself, haughtiness; feeling of elation or great satisfaction; something causing this. -*v. refl.* take pride. [OE. *pryto*]

pride *n.* company (of lions). [*pride*]

priest *n.* official minister of a religion; clergyman. [OE. *preost*]

prig *n.* self-righteous person who professes superior culture, morality, *etc.* -**prigg′ish** *a.* [orig. uncertain]

prim *a.* very restrained, formally prudish. [orig. uncertain]

pri′ma don′na, leading woman singer in opera; (*fig.*) woman, *usu.* of some standing, who demands special treatment. [It.]

pri′mal *a.* of the earliest age; first, original. -**pri′mary** *a.* chief, of the first stage, decision, *etc.* [L. *primus*, first]

pri′mate *n.* archbishop. [*prime*]

pri′mates *n. pl.* first order of mammals, including man and the higher apes. [L. *primus*, first]

prime *a.* first in time, quality, *etc.* Prime Min′ister, the leader of a government. -*n.* office for the first canonical hour of the day; first or best part of anything. [L. *primus*, first]

prime *v.t.* fill up, *e.g.*, with information; prepare (a gun, explosive charge, *etc.*), for being let off by laying a trail of powder; prepare canvas for paint with preliminary coating of oil, *etc.* [orig. uncertain]

prim′er *n.* elementary school book. [*prime*]

prime′val *a.* of the earliest age of the world. [L. *primaevus*]

primitive *a.* of an early, undeveloped kind. [L. *primitivus*]

primordial *a.* existing at or from the beginning. [L. *primus*, first, *ordo*, order]

prince *n.* ruler or chief; son of a king or queen. -**prin′cess** *fem.* -**prince′ly** *a.* -**prince′ling** *n.* young prince; petty ruler. [L. *princess, princip-*, first, chief]

principal *a.* chief in importance. -*n.* head of certain institutes, *esp.* schools or colleges, person for whom another is agent or second; sum of money lent and yielding interest; chief actor. -**principal′ity** *n.* territory or dignity of a prince. [L. *principalis*]

principle *n.* fundamental truth or element; moral rule or settled reason of action; uprightness. [L. *principium*]

print *v.t.* impress; reproduce (words, pictures, *etc.*), by pressing inked types on blocks to paper, *etc.*, produce in this way; stamp (a fabric) with a colored design. -*n.* impression mark left on a surface by something that has pressed against it; printed cotton fabric, printed lettering; photograph; written imitation of printed type. -**print′er** *n.* one engaged in printing. [OF. *preinte* fr. L. *premere*, press]

pri′or *a.* earlier. -*adv.* prior to, before. -*n.* chief of a religious house or order. -**pri′oress** *fem.* -**prior′ity** *n.* precedence in time or importance. -**prior′itize** *v.t.* arrange (items to be attended to) in order of their relative importance; give priority to or establish as a priority. -**pri′ory** *n.* monastery or nunnery under a prior or prioress. [L. = superior, former]

prism *n.* solid whose two ends are similar, equal, of parallel rectilinear figures and whose sides are parallelograms; transparent body of this form usually with triangular ends by which light can be reflected [G. *prisma*, piece sawn off]

pris′on (-z-) *n.* jail. -**pris′oner** *n.* one kept in prison; one captured in war. [F. fr. *prehendere, prehens-*, seize]

prist′ine *a.* original, primitive, unspoiled. [L. *pristinus*]

pri′vate *a.* not public, reserved for or belonging to or concerning an individual only; of a soldier, not holding any rank. -*n.* private soldier. -**pri′vacy** *n.* **privately** *adv.* [L. *privatus*, set apart]

priv′et *n.* bushy evergreen shrub used for hedges. [orig. uncertain]

privilege *n.* right or advantage belonging to a person or class; an advantage or favor that only a few obtain. -*v.t.* give an advantage to. [L. *privilegium*, private law, fr. *lex*, law]

priv′y *a.* private, confidential. -*n.* latrine. - Privy Council, a body of persons appointed by the sovereign, *esp.* in recognition of great public services. -**priv′ily** *adv.* [F. *priue*, fr. L. *privatus*, private]

prize *n.* reward for success in competition; thing striven for; thing that is won, *e.g.*, in a lottery, *etc.* -**prize′-fight** *n.* boxing match with money prize. -**prize′-money** *n.* money from the sale of prizes. -**prize′-ring** *n.* arena in which prize fight takes place. -*v.t.* value highly. [OF. *pris*, fr. L. *pretium*]

prize *n.* ship or property captured in naval warfare. [F. *prise*, capture]

prob′able *a.* likely. [L. *probabilis-probare*, prove]

pro′bate *n.* a proving of a will; certificate of this. [L. *probare, probat-*, prove]

probation *n.* testing of a candidate before admission to full membership of some body; system of releasing offenders, *esp.* juvenile ones, or first offenders, so that their punishment may be canceled by a period of good behavior. [F.]

probe *n.* blunt rod for examining a wound. -*v.t.* explore with a probe; examine into. (L.

probare, prove]
pro'bity n. honesty, uprightness. [L. probitas-probus, good]
problems n. question or difficulty set for or needing a solution. [G. problema, thing thrown before]
proboscis (-sis) n. trunk or long snout, e.g., of an elephant. [G. proboskis, 'food instrument']
proceed' v.i. go forward; be carried on; go to law. -**proce'dure** n. act or manner of proceeding; method of conducting business proceedings; conduct. -**pro'ceeds** n.pl. price or profit. -**pro'cess** n. state of going on, series of actions or changes; method of operation; action of law; outgrowth. -**proces'sion** n. body of persons going along in a fixed or formal order. **processional** a. [L. procedere, process-, to go forward]
proclaim' v.t. announce, make public. proclama'tion n. [L. proclamare]
proclivity n. inclination; tendency. [L. proclivitas, downward slope]
procrastinate v.i. put off, delay. [L. procrastinate, fr. cras, to-morrow]
procreate v.t. beget; bring into being. -**procrea'tion** n. [L. procreare]
procure' v.t. obtain; bring about. -procu'rable a. -**procura'tor** n. Roman official in a province; one who manages another's affairs. -**procura'tion** n. appointment or hority of a procurator. -**procure'ment** n. act or an instance of procuring; act of buying. [L. procurare, bring about, get as agent]
prod v.t. poke with something pointed. -n. a prodding. [orig. uncertain]
prod'igal a. wasteful. -n. spendthrift. [L. prodigere, squander]
prod'igy (-ji) n. marvel; person with some marvellous gift. [L. prodigium]
produce' v.t. bring forward; bring into existence, make; stage, or prepare to stage (a play, etc.); extend in length. -**prod'uce** n. that which is yielded or made.-**produ'cer** n. one who grows or makes produce; one who produces plays. etc. -**produ'cer goods**, raw materials, etc. used in production. -**prod'uct** n. result of a process of manufacture; number resulting from a multiplication. -**produc'tion** n. producing; things produced. -**produc'tive** a. -**productiv'ity** n. [L. producere, product-, bring forth]
profane' a. not sacred; blasphemous, irreverent. -v.t. pollute, desecrate. profanation n. -**profan'ity** n. profane talk or behavior. [L. profanus]
profess' v.t. assert; lay claim to; have as one's profession or business; teach as a professor. -**profess'edly** adv. avowedly. -**profes'sion** n. a professing, vow of religious faith, entering a religious order; calling or occupation, esp. learned or scientific or artistic. -**profes'sional** a. of a profession. -n. paid player. -**profess'or** n. teacher of the highest rank in a university. -**professo'rial** adv. - professorship n. - **profess'orate** n, professorship. - **professor'iate** n. body of professors of a university. [L. profiteri, profess-, own or ac-

knowledge]
proficient (ish'-) a. skilled. -n. one who is skilled. -**profi'ciency** n. [L. proficere, be useful]
pro'file (-fil) n. outline of anything as seen from the side. [It. proffilo]
profit n. benefit obtained; money gains. -v.t. and i. benefit. -**profitable** a. yielding profit. -**profitless** a. [F. fr. L. profectus, progress, profit]
profligate a. dissolute; reckless; abandoned. -n. dissolute man. -**prof'ligacy** n. [L. profligatus, ruined, fr. fligare, strike down]
profound' a. deep; very learned. - profun'dity n. [L. profundus]
profuse' a. abundant, prodigal. -**profusion** n. [L. profusus, poured out]
pro'geny n. descendants. -**progenitor** n. ancestor. [L. progenies]
prognosis n. forecast, esp. of the course of a disease from observation of its symptoms. -prognost'icate v.t. foretell. [G.]
programs n. plan, detailed notes of intended proceedings; broadcast on radio or television; syllabus or curriculum; detailed instructions for computer. -v.t. feed program into (computer); arrange detailed instructions for (computer) **pro'grammer** n. [G. programma, public written notice]
pro'gress n. onward movement; development; state journey. -**progress'** v.i. go forward [L. progressus]
prohibit v.t. forbid. -**prohibi'tion** n. forbidding by law of the sale of intoxicants. -prohibi'tionist n. -**prohib'itive** a. tending to forbid. -**prohib'itory** a. [L. prohibere, prohibit-]
proj'ect n. plan. -**project'** v.t. throw; plan; cause to appear on a distant background. -v.i. stick out. -**project'ile** a. capable of being thrown. -n. heavy missile, esp. shell from big gun. -**projec'tion** n. -**project'or** n. machine which throws pictures on the cinema screen and reproduces sound from the sound-track. [L. projectum, thrown forward]
proletariat, proletariats (-tär-) n. lowest class of a community, common people. - **proletar'ian** a. [L. proles, offspring with which Roman proletarius served the state]
proliferate v.i. and t. reproduce by process of budding or cell division; increase in numbers in a similar way. -**prolif'eration** n. [L. proles, progeny, ferre, bear]
prolific a. fruitful; producing much, [L. proles, offspring, ferre, bear]
pro'logue, prolog n. preface, esp. to a lay. [G. prologos, 'fore-speech']
prolong' v.t. lengthen out. -**prolonga'tion** n. [L. longus, long]
promenade n. leisurely walk; lace made or used for this. -v.i. take a leisurely walk; go up and down. [F.]
prom'inent a. sticking out; distinguished; eminent. -**prom'inence** n. [L. prominere, jut out]
promis'cuous a. mixing without distinction, indiscriminate; having a number of sexual partners without formal attachment.

-promiscu'ity n. [L. *propiscuus*, fr. *miscere*, mix]

prom'ise (-is) n. undertaking to do or not do something. -v.t. make a promise -v.i. make a promise. -prom'issory a. containing a promise. [L. *promittere, promiss-*, send forth]

prom'ontory n. point of high land jutting out into the sea; headland. [Med. *promontoriurn*]

promote' v.t. move up to a higher rank or sition; help forward; begin the process of forming or making. -promo'ter n. -promo'tion n. [L. *promovere, promot-*, move forward]

prompt a. done at once; ready. -v.t. and i. suggest, help out (an actor or speaker) by reading his next words or suggesting words. -prompt'er n. [L. *promptus*, pp. of *promere*, put forth]

prone a. lying face or front downward; inclined to. [OF. fr. L. *pronus*]

prong n. one spike of a fork or similar instrument. [orig. uncertain]

pro'noun n. word used to represent a noun. -pronom'inal a. [L. *pronomen*]

pronounce' v.t. utter formally; form with the organs of speech. -v.i. give an opinion or decision. -pronounce'able a. -pronounced' a. strongly marked, decided. -pronounce'ment n. declaration. -pronuncia'tion n. way a word, *etc.*, is pronounced. [F. *prononcer*, L. *pronuntiare*, proclaim]

proof n. something which proves; test or demonstration; standard of strength of spirits; trial impression from type or an engraved plate. -a. of proved strength; giving impenetrable defense against. -proof mark n. mark on a proved, or tested, gun. -proof'-reader n. reader and corrector of printer's proofs. [F. *preuve. See* prove]

prop n. pole, beam, *etc.*, used as a support. -v.t. support, hold up. [Du.]

propaganda n. association or scheme for propagating a doctrine; attempt, or material used, to propagate a doctrine. -propagand'ist n. [L. *propagandus*]

propagate v.t. reproduce or breed; spread by sowing, breeding, example, instruction, persuasion. *etc.* -v.i. breed or multiply. -propaga'tion n. [L. *propagare*, propagate, fr. *propago*, slip for transplanting]

propel' v.t. cause to move forward. -propell'er n. revolving shaft with blades for driving a ship or airplane. propulsion n. [L. *propellers, propuls-*]

prop'er a. own, peculiar, individual; of a noun, denoting an individual person or place; fit, suitable; strict; conforming to etiquette, decorous. -prop'erly adv. [L. *proprius*, own]

prop'erty n. owning; being owned; that is owned; quality or attribute belonging to something; article used on the stage in a play, *etc.* [F. *propriété*]

proph'et n. inspired teacher or revealer of the Divine Will; one who foretells future events. -proph'etess *fem.* -proph'ecy (-si) n. prediction or prophetic utterance. -proph'esy (-si)

v.i. utter predictions. -v.t. foretell. -prophet'ic a. -prophet'ically adv. [G. *prophetes*, forespeaker]

prophylactic (pro-) a. done or used to ward off disease. -n. prophylactic medicine or measure. [G. *prophylaktikos*, guarding, before]

proportion n. share; relation; comparison; relative size or number; due relation between connected things or parts. -v.t. arrange proportions of. [L. *proportio-portio*, share]

propose' v.t. put forward for consideration; present (someone) for office, membership *etc.*; propose a toast to be drunk. -v.i. offer marriage. -propo'sal n. -propo'ser n. [L. *proporere, proposit-*]

proposition n. statement or assertion; suggestion of terms. [L. *propositio*]

proprietor n. owner. [F. *propriété*]

propriety n. fitness; properness; correct conduct. [L. *proprietarius*, fr. *proprietas*, property]

proscribe' v.t. outlaw, condemn. -proscrip'tion n. [L. *proscribere*]

prose n. speech or writing not verse. -v.t. talk or write prosily. -prosa'ic a. commonplace. -pro'sy a. tedious, dull. -pro'sily adv. -pro'siness n. [L. *prosus*, straightforward]

prosecute v.t. carry on, bring legal proceedings against. [L. *prosequi*, fr. *sequi, secut-*, to follow]

proselyte n. convert. -proselytize' v.t. [G. *proselytos*, having come]

pros'pect n. view; mental view; that is to be expected. -v.t. and i. explore, *esp.* for gold. -prospect'ive a. future. -prospect'ively adv. -prospect'or n. -prospec'tus n. circular describing a company, school, *etc.* [L. *prospicere, prospect-*, look forward]

pros'per v.i. do well. -v.t. cause to do well. -prosper'ity n. good fortune, well-being. -pros'perous a. flourishing; rich. -pros'perously adv. [L.]

prostitute n. woman who hires herself for sexual intercourse. -v.t. make a prostitute of; sell basely, put to an infamous use. -prostitu'tion n. [L. *prostituere, prostitut-*, offer for sale]

prostrate a. lying full length; overcome; exhausted. -v.t. throw down; overthrow; exhaust; lay flat; bow (oneself) to the ground. -prostra'tion n. [L. *pro*, forward, *sternere, strat-*, strew]

protagonist n. leading actor in a play; leading figure in a cause, debate, *etc.* [G. *protos*, first, *agonistes*, combatant]

protect' v.i. defend or guard. -protec'tion n. -protect'ive a. -protec'tionist n. one who advocates protecting industries by taxing competing imports. -protector n. one who protects; regent. -protect'orate n. office or period of a protector of a state; relation of a state to a territory that it protects and controls; such territory. [L. *protegere, protect-*, cover in front]

prot'égé (-āzha-) n. -pro'tégée *fem.* person who is under the care and protection of another. [F.]

pro'tein *n.* kinds of organic compound, which form the most essential part of the food of living creatures. **protein'ic** *a.* [G. *protos*, first]

protest' *v.i.* assert formally; make a declaration against. -**pro'test** *n.* declaration of objection. -**Prot'estant** *a.* belonging to any branch of the Western Church outside the Roman communion. -*n.* member of such church. -**Prot'estantism** *n.* -**protesta'tion** *n.* [L. *protestari*, testify]

pro'tocol *n.* draft of terms signed by the parties as the basis of a formal treaty; rules of diplomatic etiquette. [G. *protokollon*, first leaf]

pro'ton *n.* electrically positive nucleus containing same quantity of electricity, but greater mass, than the electron, [G. *proton*, first]

protoplasm *n.* physical basis of all living organisms, a colorless, formless substance resembling albumen. -**protoplas'mic** *a.* [G. *protos*, first, *plasma*, form]

prototype *n.* original type or model. [G. *protos*, first, and *type*]

protozo'a *n.* lowest class of animals. [G. *protos*, first, *zōon*, animal]

protract' *v.t.* lengthen; draw to scale. -**protrac'tion** *n.* -**protract'or** *n.* instrument for setting out angles on paper. [L. *protrahere*, *protract*-, draw forward]

protrude' *v.i.* and *t.* stick out. -**protru'sion** *n.* [L. *protudere*]

proud *a.* feeling or displaying pride, that is the cause of pride; stately. -**proud'ly** *adv.* [OE. *prud*]

prove *v.t.* demonstrate, test; establish the validity of (a will, *etc.*). -*v.i.* turn out (to be, *etc.*). [F. *prouver*, fr. L. *probare*]

provender *n.* fodder; food. [OF. *provendre*]

prov'erb *n.* short pithy saying in common use, *esp.* one with a moral. **proverb'ial** *a.* [L. *proverbium*]

provide' *v.i.* make preparation. -*v.t.* supply or equip, get in what will be required. -**provi'ded** (that) *conj.* on condition that. -**prov'ident** *a.* thrifty; showing foresight. -**prov'idence** *n.* foresight, economy; kindly care of God or nature. -**provi'sional** *a.* temporary. -**provi'so** *n.* condition. [L. *providere*, *provis*-, foresee]

prov'ince *n.* division of a country; a sphere of action. -*pl.* any part of the country outside the capital. -**provin'cial** *n.* one belonging to a province. -*a.* narrow, lacking in polish. -**provin'cialism** *n.* [L. *provincia*]

provoke' *v.t.* bring about, irritate. [L. *provocare*, call forth]

provolone *n.* hard, light-colored Italian cheese made of cow's milk.

prov'ost *n.* head of certain colleges, or administrative assistant to the president. [OF. fr. Late L. *propositus*, placed before]

prow *n.* bow of a ship. [F. *proue*]

prow'ess *n.* bravery, fighting capacity. [F. *prouesse*, gallantry]

prowl *v.i.* roam stealthily, *esp.* in search of prey, *etc.* [ME. *prollen*]

prox'y *n.* authorized agent or substitute; writing authorizing a substitute. [fr. *procuracy*.

See **procure**]

prude *n.* woman who affects excessive propriety with regard to relations of the sexes. [F.]

pru'dent *a.* careful, discreet, exercising forethought. -**pru'dence** *n.* -**pruden'-tial** *a.* [L. *prudens*, *prudent*-, far-seeing]

prune *n.* dried plum. [F.]

prune *v.t.* cut out dead parts, excessive branches, *etc.* [OF. *prooignier*]

pru'rient *a.* given to or springing from lewd thoughts. -**pru'rience** *n.* [L. *pruriens*, *pr. p.* of *prurire*, itch]

pry *v.i.* look curiously; make furtive or inquisitive enquiries. [ME. *prien*]

psalm *n.* sacred song. -**psalm'ist** *n.* writer of psalms. [G. *psalmos*, twanging of strings]

pseudo- *prefix*, sham. -**pseu'donym** *n.* false name. [G. *pseudes*, false]

psy'chic (si'kik) *a.* of the soul or mind; that appears to be outside the region of physical law. -**psychi'atrist** *n.* one who treats mental diseases. -**psy'chical** *a.* psychic. -**psy'choanal'ysis** *n.* theory that the mind can be divided into conscious and unconscious elements; medical practice based on this. -**psy'choan'alyst** *n.* -**psychol'ogy** *n.* study of the mind. -**psycholo'gical** *a.* -**psychol'ogist** *n.* -**psychosomat'ic** *a.* pert. to mind and body as one unit, of physical disease having emotion as origin. -**psy'chother'apy** *n.* treatment of disease by mental influence. [G. *psyche*, breath, soul]

psychobabble *n.* jargon of psychotherapy, psychology, or psychiatry, employed in speech or writing, *esp.* in a superficial or inaccurate way.

ptero- (ter-) *prefix*. winged. (G. *pteron*, wing] -**pterocar'pous** *a.* having winged seeds. -**pterodac'tyl** *n.* prehistoric large flying reptile with bat-like wings.

pto'maine (t-) *n.* poisonous alkaloid found in putrefying animal or vegetable matter. [G. *ptoma*, dead body]

pu'berty *n.* sexual maturity. [L. *pubertas*]

pub'lic *a.* of or concerning the public as a whole; not private; open to general observation or knowledge. -*n.* community or its members. -**publica'tion** *n.* -**pub'licist** *n.* writer on public concerns. -**publi'city** *n.* being generally known; notoriety. -**pub'licly** *adv.* [L. *publicus*, fr. *populus*, people]

pub'lish *v.t.* make generally known; prepare and issue for sale (books, music, *etc.*). -**pub'lisher** *n.* [*public*]

puc'ker *v.t.* and *i.* gather into wrinkles. -*n.* wrinkle. [fr. *poke*, bag]

pudding (pood-) *n.* form of cooked food usually in a soft mass. [F. *boudin*, black pudding]

pud'dle *n.* small muddy pool; rough cement for lining ponds, *etc.* -*v.t.* line with puddle; produce wrought iron. [OE. *pudd*, ditch]

pu'erile *a.* childish. [L. *puer*, boy]

puer'peral *a.* of, caused by childbirth. -**puerperium** *n.* state of a woman during and immediately after childbirth. [L. *puer*, child, *parere*, bear]

puff *n.* short blast of breath of wind, *etc.*; its sound; piece of pastry; laudatory notice, piece of advertisement. -*v.i.* blow abruptly; breathe hard. -*v.t.* send out in a puff, blow up; advertise; smoke hard. -**puff'y** *a.* -**puff'-add'er** *n.* poisonous African snake. [imit. orig.]

pug *n.* small snub-nosed dog. -**pug'-nose** *n.* snub nose. [orig. uncertain]

pu'gilist *n.* boxer. L. *pugil,* boxer]

pugna'cious *a.* given to fighting. **pugna'city** *n.* (L. *pugnax, pugnac-,*]

pulchritude *n.* beauty. [L. *pulchritude*]

pull (pool) *v.t.* pluck or tug at; draw or haul; propel by rowing. -*n.* an act of pulling; force exerted by it; draught of liquor. [OE. *pullian,* snatch]

pull'ey (poo-) *n.* wheel with a groove in the rim for a cord, used to raise weights by a downward pull. [F. *poulie*]

pul'monary *a.* of, or affecting the lungs. [L. *pulmo,* lung]

pulp *n.* soft moist vegetable or animal matter. -*v.t.* reduce to pulp. [L. *pulpa*]

pul'pit (poo-) *n.* erection or platform for a preacher. (L. *pulpitum,* a stage]

pulse *n.* throbbing of the arteries, *esp.* in the wrist; vibration. -**pulsate'** *v.i.* throb, quiver. -**pulsa'tion** *n.* [L. *pulsus*]

pulverize *v.t.* reduce to powder. [L. *pulvis, pulver-,* powder]

pu'ma *n.* large American carnivorous animal of the cat family. [*Peruv.*]

pum'ice (-is) *n.* light porous variety of lava. [L. *pumex*]

pumm'el *v.t.* pommel, *q.v.*

pump *n.* appliance in which the piston and handle are used for raising water, or putting in or taking out air or liquid, *etc.* -*v.t.* raise, put in, take out, *etc.*, with a pump. -*v.i.* work a pump. [orig. uncertain]

pump *n.* light shoe. [Du. *pampoesje*]

pump'kin *n.* large gourd used as food. [OF. *pompon*]

pun *n.* play on words. -*v.i.* make one. -**pun'ster** *n.* [orig. uncertain]

punch *n.* tool for perforating or stamping; blow with the fist; (*sl.*) energy, drive. -*v.t.* stamp or perforate with a punch; strike with the fist; drive (of cattle). [F. *poincon,* awl, fr. *pungere,* pierce]

punch *n.* drink made of spirit, or wine with water or milk, lemon, spice, *etc.* -**punch-bowl** *n.* [Hindu *panch,* five (ingredients)]

punctilio *n.* minute detail of conduct; mere form. -**puncti'ious** *a.* making much of punctilios. [Sp. *puntillo*]

punc'tual *a.* in good time, not late. [L. *punctus,* point]

punctuate *v.t.* to put in punctuation marks. -**punctua'tion** *n.* putting in marks, *e.g.* commas, colons, *etc.*, in writing or printing to assist in making the sense clear. [L. *punctus,* point]

punc'ture *n.* an act of pricking; a hole made by pricking. -*v.t.* to prick a hole in. [L. *punctura*]

pun'dit *n.* one learned in Hindu philosophy;

any learned person. [Hind. *pandit*]

pungent *a.* biting; irritant. [L. *pungens, pungeni-,* fr. *pungere,* prick]

pun'ish *v.t.* cause to suffer for an offense, inflict a penalty on. -(*sl.*) treat roughly. -**pun'ishable** *a.* -**pun'ishment** *n.* -**pu'nitive** *a.* inflicting or intending to inflict punishment. [L. *punire*]

punk *a.* crumbling, decayed; worthless. -*n.* young, inexperienced person; petty gangster; style of rock music characterized by a savage rejection of convention; one who follows such a style. [orig. uncertain]

punt *n.* flat-bottomed, square-ended boat, propelled by pushing with a pole. -*v.t.* propel with a pole. [L. *ponto*]

puny *a.* small and feeble. [OF. *puisne,* fr. L. *post natus,* younger]

pup. See puppy.

pu'pa *n.* **pu'pae** *pl.* chrysalis. [L. = doll]

pu'pil *n.* person being taught; opening in the middle of the eye. -**pu'pillary** *a.* [L. *pupillus,* child]

pupp'et *n.* figure of a human being often with jointed limbs controlled by wire, a marionette. [OF. *poupette,* doll]

pupp'y *n.* young dog; conceited young man. -**pup** *n.* puppy. [F. *poupée,* doll]

pur'chase *v.t.* buy. -*n.* buying; what is bought; leverage, grip, good position for applying force. [F. *pourchasser,* to obtain by pursuit]

pure *a.* unmixed, untainted; simple; spotless; faultless; innocent. -**pure'ly** *adv.* **pu'rify** *v.t.* and *i.* -**purifica'tion** *n* **purifica'tory** *a.* -**pu'rism** *n.* excessive insistence on correctness of language. -**pu'rist** *n.* -**pu'rity** *n.* state of being pure. [L. *purus,* clean, pure]

purée *n.* fruit, vegetables, boiled to a pulp and sieved or blended. [F.]

purge *v.t.* make clean, clear out. -*n.* aperient. -**purg'atory** *n.* place for spiritual purging; state of pain or distress. [L. *purgare*]

purl *n.* edging of gold or silver wire or of small loops; stitch that forms a rib in knitting. -*v.t.* ornament with purls. -*v.i.* knit in purl. [It. *pirlare,* twirl]

purloin *v.t.* steal. [OF. *porloignier,* remove, fr. *loin,* far]

pur'ple *n.* color between crimson and violet. *a.* of this color. -*v.t.* make purple. [G. *Porphyra,* shell-fish that gave Tyrian purple]

purport *v.t.* mean; be intended to seem. -**pur'port** *n.* meaning, apparent meaning. [OF. *porporter,* embody]

pur'pose (-pos) *n.* intention, design, aim. -*v.t.* intend. -**pur'posely** *adv.* [OF. *porpos,* fr. *porposer,* propose]

purr *n.* noise a cat makes when pleased. -*v.i.* make this sound. [imit.]

purse *n.* small bag for money. -*v.t.* contract in wrinkles. -*v.i.* become wrinkled and drawn in. -**pur'ser** *n.* officer who keeps accounts, *etc.*, on a ship. [G. *pyrsa,* hide, leather]

pursue' *v.t.* run after; aim at; engage in. -*v.i.* go in pursuit; continue. **pursu'ance** *n.* carrying out. -**pursu'ant** *adv.* accordingly. -**pursu'er** *n.* -**pursuit'** *n.* running after, attempt to catch;

occupation. [F. *poursuivre*, fr. L. *prosequi*, follow]

purvey' *v.t.* to supply. **-purvey'or** *n.* [F. *pourvoir*, fr. L. *providere*, to provide]

pur'view *n.* scope or range. [AF. *purveu est*, it is provided (words used to introduce new enactment in a law)]

pus *n.* matter formed or discharged in a sore or inflammation. **-pu'rulent** *a.* forming pus. **-pu'rulence** *n.* [L.]

push (poosh) *v.t.* move or try to move away by pressure. **-v.i.** make one's way. **-n.** an act of pushing; persevering self assertion. **-push'ful** *a.* given to pushing oneself. [F. *pousser*]

pusillanimous *a.* cowardly. **pusillanim'ity** *n.* [fr. L. *pusillus*, very small, and *animus*, spirit]

puss (poos) *n.* cat; hare. **-puss'y** *n.* [orig. name to call a cat]

pus'tule *n.* small pimple containing pus. [L. *pustula*]

put (poot) *v.t.* place or set; express; put on, don (clothes); assume (airs) **-put out**, annoy; disconcert; eject. **-put-up** *a.* concocted. **-put up with**, tolerate. [Late OE. *putian*]

pu'tative *a.* supposed, reputed. putatively *adv.* [L, *putare*, think]

putsch *n.* sudden sharp revolt. [Ger.]

pu'trid *a.* rotten. **-pu'trefy** *v.t.* and *i.* make or become rotten. [L. *putrid us*]

putt (put) *v.t.* throw (a weight or shot) from the shoulder; strike (a golf ball) along the ground in the direction of the hole. **-putt'er** *n.* golf club for putting. [var. of *put*]

putt'er *v. i.* work or act in a feeble, unsystematic way. [OE. *potian*, poker]

putt'y *n.* paste of whiting and oil used by glaziers; polishing powder of calcined tin used by jewelers. **-v.t.** fix or fill with putty. [F. *potée*]

puz'zle *n.* bewildering or perplexing question, problem, or toy. **-v.t.** perplex. **-v.i.** think in perplexity. [fr. ME. *opposal*, question, interrogation]

pyg'my, pig'my *n.* dwarfed. dwarf. [G. *pygmaios*, fr. *pygme*, measure of length, 13½ inches]

py'lon *n.* gateway to Egyptian temple; steel erection to mark out an airfield or carry power cables etc. [G. = *gateway*]

pyr'amid *n.* solid figure with sloping sides meeting at an apex; solid structure of this shape, *esp.* the ancient Egyptian monuments (usually with a square base); group of persons or things highest in the middle. **-pyram'idal** *a.* [G. *pyramis, pyramid-*,]

pyre *n.* pile of wood for burning a dead body. **-pyrol'ogy** *n.* science of heat. [G. *pyr*, fire]

pyri'tes *n.* term for sulfides of various metals (*e.g.* iron) in gold-colored crystals. [L.]

pyromania n. uncontrollable impulse and practice of setting things on fire. **pyroman'iac** *n.* [G. *pyr*, fire, and *mania*]

pyrotechnics (-k-) *n.* art of making or using fireworks; firework display. [G. *pyr* and *technikos*, skilled]

Pythagore'an *a.* of, pert. to Pythagoras or his doctrine of transmigration of souls.

py'thon (-th-) *n.* large nonpoisonous snake that crushes its prey. **-py'thoness** *n.* Apollo's priestess at Delphi; witch. [G. *Python*, name of a serpent killed by Apollo]

Q

qua (qua) *conj.* as, in capacity of [L.]

quack *n.* harsh cry of the duck; pretender to medical or other skill. **-v.i.** of a duck, to utter its cry. [imit.]

quadr-, four. [L. *quattuor*]. **-quad'rangle** *n.* four-sided figure; four sided court in a building. *contr.* quad. **-quadrang'ular** *a.* **-**quad'rant *n.* quarter of a circle; instrument for taking angular measurements. **-quadrate** *v.t.* make square.

quaff *v.i.* drink deeply. **-v.t.** drink, drain. [orig. uncertain]

quag, quag'mire *n.* marshy tract with quaking surface. [*quake*]

quail *n.* small bird of the partridge family. [OF. *quaille*]

quaint *a.* interestingly old-fashioned or odd. **-quaint'ly** *adv.* [OF. *cointe*]

quake *v.i.* shake or tremble (from fear, apprehension). **-Qua'ker** *n.* member of the Society of Friends, a Christian religious sect. [OE. *cwacian*]

qual'ify (kwol'-) *v.t.* ascribe a quality to, describe; make competent; moderate. **-v.i.** make oneself competent, *esp.* by passing an examination. **-qualific'ation** *n.* qualifying, thing that qualifies. **-qual'ity** *n.* attribute, characteristic, property; degree of excellence; rank. **-qual'itative** *a.* relating to quality. [L. *qualis*, of what kind]

qualm (kwam) *n.* sudden feeling of sickness; misgiving; scruple. [Du.]

quandary state of perplexity, puzzling situation. [orig. uncertain]

quan'tity (kwon'-) *n.* size, number, amount; specified or considerable amount. **quan'titative** *a.* **-quan'tum** *n.* desired or required amount. [L. *quantus*, how much]

quarantine *n.* isolation to prevent infection. **-v.t.** put in quarantine. [L. *quadriginta*, forty (ref to days of isolation)]

quark *n.* in physics, any of several hypothetical particles thought to be fundamental units of matter. [word coined by Murray Gell-Mann, physicist]

quarr'el (kwor'-) *n.* angry dispute; break-up of friendship. **-v.i.** fall out with; find fault with. [F. *querelle* fr. L. *queri*, complain]

quarr'y *n.* object of a hunt. [F. *curée*]

quarr'y *n.* place where stone is got from the ground for building, *etc.* **-v.t.** and *i.* get from a quarry. [L. *quadrare*, square (stones)]

quart (kwort) *n.* quarter of a gallon, or two pints. [*quarter*]

quar'ter *n.* fourth part; region, district; mercy. **-***pl.* lodgings. **-v.t.** divide into quarters. **-quart'erdeck** *n.* part of upper deck used by officers. **-quartet'** *n.* music for four performers; group of four musicians. [L. *quartus*, fourth]

quartz (kworts) *n.* stone of silica, often containing gold. [Ger. quarz]

quasar *n.* extremely distant starlike object emitting powerful radio waves. [Fr. *quasi* stellar]

quash (kwosh) *v.t.* annul, *esp.* by legal procedure. [F. *casser*, break]

qua'si *conj.* and *adv.* almost; in a sense; in appearance. [L. *quam si*, as if]

quat'rain *n.* four-lined stanza, with alternate rhymes. [F.]

qua'ver *v.i.* tremble, shake, say or sing in quavering tones. -*n.* trill; musical note half the length of a crotchet. [orig. uncertain]

queas'y *a.* inclined to, or causing, sickness. [orig. uncertain]

queen *n.* wife of a king; female sovereign; piece of the game of chess; perfect female bee, wasp, *etc.*; court card. **-queen'ly** *a.* [OE. *cwen*]

queer *a.* odd, strange. **-queer'ly** *adv.* [Ger. quer, athwart, across]

quell *v.t.* crush, put down, suppress; allay. [OE. *cwellan*, kill]

quench *v.t.* extinguish, put out; slake. [OE. *cwencan*, quench]

que'ry *n.* question; mark of interrogation. -*v.t.* question, ask; mark with a query. [L. *quaere*, seek]

quest *n.* search. -*v.i.* search. [L. *qusit-*, to seek]

ques'tion (-chn) *n.* sentence seeking for an answer; problem; debate, strife. -*v.t.* ask questions of, interrogate; dispute. **ques'tionable** *a.* doubtful, *esp.* [F.]

quib'ble *n.* play on words; evasion, merely verbal point in argument. -*v.i.* evade a point by a quibble. [dim. of obs. *quib*]

quick *a.* rapid, swift, keen, brisk; living. -*n.* sensitive flesh. -*adv.* rapidly. **-quick'ly** *adv.* **-quick'en** *v.t.* give life to; make speedier, stir up. -*v.t., i.* become living; become faster. **-quick'sand** *n.* loose wet sand which swallows up animals, ships, *etc.* [OE. *cwic*, living]

qui'et *a.* undisturbed; with little or no motion or noise. -*n.* state of peacefulness, absence of noise or disturbance. -*v.t.* and *i.* make or become quiet. [L. *quies, quiet-, n.* quiet]

quill *n.* hollow stem of a large feather; spine of a porcupine; pen, fishing-float, *etc.*, made of a feather-quill. [orig. uncertain]

quilt *n.* padded coverlet. -*v. t.* stitch (two pieces of cloth) with padding between. [L. *culcita*, cushion]

quinine' *n.* bitter drug made from the bark of a tree and used to cure fever, *etc.* [Peruv. *kina*, bark]

quintes'sence *n.* purest form or essential feature. **-quintessen'tial** *a.* [Med. L. *quinta essentia*, substance of the heavenly bodies; (outside the 'four elements')]

quintet', **quintette'** *n.* musical piece for five singers, players; the singers, players. [It. *quintetto*]

quintuple *a.* multiplied by five, greater by five times, composed of five parts. [L. *quintus*, fifth]

quip *n.* smart saying, epigram. [L. *quippe*, forsooth (ironical)]

quirk *n.* fanciful turn; quibble; evasion. **-quirk'y** *a.* full of twists; peculiar. (orig. unknown]

quit *a.* free, rid. -*v.t.* leave, go away on equal or even terms by repayment, *etc.* **quitt'ance** *n.* receipt, discharge. **-quitt'er** *n.* shirker; deserter. [L. *quietus*, discharge]

quite *a.* wholly, completely. [*quit*]

quiv'er *n.* a carrying-case for arrows. (OF. *cuivre*, ult. of Teut. orig.]

quiv'er *v.i.* shake or tremble. -*n.* an act of quivering. [*quaver*]

quixot'ic *a.* showing enthusiasm for visionary ideals, generous, helpful, against one's own interests. [Don Quixote, hero of novel of Cervantes (d. 1616)]

quiz *v.t.* make fun of, look at curiously or critically. -*n.* entertainment in which general or specific knowledge of players is tested by questions; examination, interrogation. **-quizz'ical** *a.* questioning; mocking. [orig. uncertain]

quoin *n.* external corner-stone of wall or wedge-shaped piece of metal *etc.*, building. **-quoin post** *n.* the vertical post at the side of a lock gate, about which the gate swings. [*conj*]

quor'um *n.* number that must be present in a meeting to make its transactions valid. [L. = *of whom*]

quo'ta *n.* share to be contributed or received. [L. *quot*, how many]

quote *v. t.* copy or repeat passages from; refer to, *esp.* to confirm a view; state a price for. **-quota'tion** *n.* **-quota'tion mark** *n.* marks of punctuation ("-") indicating the beginning and end of quotation. **-quo'table** *a.* **-quo'tably** *adv.* [Med. L. *quotare*, distinguish by numbers]

quo'tient (-shent) *n.* number resulting from dividing one number by another. [L. *quotiens*, how many times]

R

rabb'et *n.* groove cut in edge of plank allowing another to fit into it. -*v. t.* cut rabbet in. [OF. *rabat*, abatement]

rabb'i *n.* Jewish teacher, doctor of law; pastor of congregation. **-rabbin'ic, rabbinical** *a.* **-rabbin'ics** *n.* the study of rabbinic literature of the post-Talmudic period.]

rabb'it *n.* small rodent animal which resembles the hare. -*v.i.* hunt rabbits. [orig. uncertain]

rab'ble *n.* crowd of vulgar, noisy people; mob. [orig. unknown]

rab'id *a.* raging; mad. **-ra'bies** *n.* canine madness. [L. *rabere*, to be mad]

rac(c)oon' *n.* climbing American animal of the bear family; its fur. [Algonkin]

race *n.* descendants of a common ancestor; one of the distinct varieties of the human species; peculiar breed, as of horses, *etc.* **-ra'cial** *a.* of race or lineage. **-ra'cialism, rac'ism** *n.* belief in innate superiority of particular race, antagonism towards members of different race based on this belief. [F.]

race n. running; act of running in competition for a prize; strong current of water, esp. leading to a water-wheel. -pl. meeting for the sport of horse-racing. -v.i. contend with in a race. -v.i. run swiftly. **ra′cer** n. **-race′course** n. ground on which horse races are run. **-race′horse** n. horse bred for racing only. [ON. ras]

rack v.t. stretch or strain; stretch on the rack or wheel; torture. -n. instrument for stretching anything. [Du. rak; n. fr. rekken, stretch]

rack′et n. bat used in tennis, badminton, etc. -pl. ball game played in a paved court surrounded by four walls. **-rack′et-court** n. [F. raquette]

rack′et n. loud noise, uproar; (sl.) dishonest enterprise; organized fraud or roguery. **-rack′eteer** n. gangster, swindler. -v.i. make a noise. [Gael. racaid]

ra′cy a. having a strong flavor; spicy; spirited; piquant. [F. race]

ra′dar n. device for finding range and direction by ultrahigh-frequency point-to-point radio waves, which reflect back to their source and reveal position and nature of objects sought [radio angle detection and ranging]

ra′diate v.t. emit rays. -v.t. emit in rays. **-radia′tion** n. transmission of heat, light etc. from one body to another; particles, rays emitted in nuclear decay; act of radiating. **-ra′diance** n. brightness. **-ra′diant** a. **-ra′diator** n. that which radiates, esp. heating apparatus for a room, or a part of an engine for cooling it. [L. radius, ray, wheel-spoke]

radical a. of a root; fundamental; thorough. -n. politician desiring thorough reforms. **-rad′icalism** n. [L. radix, radic-, root]

ra′dio n. use of electromagnetic waves for broadcasting, communication etc; device for receiving, amplifying radio signals; broadcasting, content of radio program. v.t. transmit (message etc.) by radio. **radioac′tive** a. emitting invisible rays that penetrate matter. **-radioactiv′ity** n. **-radiocar′bon da′ting** technique for determining age of organic materials based on their content of radioisotope ^{14}C acquired from atmosphere when they formed part of living plant. **ra′dio frequency** any frequency that lies in range 10 kilohertz to 300,000 megahertz and can be used for broadcasting; frequency transmitted by particular radio station. **-ra′diograph** n. image produced on sensitized film or plate by radiation. **-radiographer** n. radiography n. production of image on film or plate by radiation. **-radiois′otope** n. radioactive isotope. **-radiol′ogist** n. **radiol′ogy** n. science of use of rays in medicine **-radio ther′apy** n. diagnosis and treatment of disease by x-rays.

rad′ish n. pungent root. [L. radix]

ra′dium n. rare metal named from its radioactive power. [radiate]

ra′dius n. straight line from center to circumference of a circle or sphere. **ra′dial** a. of a ray or rays; of a radius; of radium. [radiate]

raf′fle n. lottery in which an article is assigned by lot to one of those buying tickets. -v.t. dispose of by raffle. [orig. dicing game, F. rafle]

raft n. number of logs or planks, etc., of wood tied together and floating. [ON. raptr, beam]

raft′er n. one of the main beams of a roof. [OE. roefter]

rag n. fragment of cloth; torn piece. **ragg′ed** a. shaggy; torn; clothed in frayed or torn clothes; wanting smoothness. **rag′time** n. music with strong syncopation. [OE. ragg]

rage n. violent anger or passion; fury. -v.i. speak or act with fury; be widely and violently prevalent. **-the rage**, the fashion. [F. fr. L. rabies, madness]

raid n. rush, attack; foray. -v.t. make a raid on. **-raid′er** n. [var. of road, cp. inroad]

rail n. horizontal bar, esp. as part of a fence, railway line, etc. -v.t. enclose with rails. **-rail′ing** n. fence of rails. **-rail** n. road with lines of iron rails on which trains run. **-rail** n. [OF. reille fr. L. regula, ruler]

rail v.i. utter abuse. **-raill′ery** n. light-hearted banter. [F. railler]

rai′ment n. clothing. [for arrayment]

rain n. moisture falling in drops from the clouds; fall of such drops. -v.i. fall as rain. -v.t. pour down like rain. **-rain′y** a. **-rain′bow** n. arch of prismatic colors formed in the sky by the sun's rays. **-rain check** n. ticket for a future performance, game etc. when one has been postponed by rain; agreement that one may claim later something that is being offered now. **rain′coat** n. light rainproof overcoat. **rain′fall** n. quantity of rain falling in given area. [OE. regn]

raise v.t. set up, rear; lift up; breed, bring into existence; levy, collect; end (a siege). -n. rise, esp. in salary. [ON. reisa]

rai′sin n. dried grape. [F. = grape]

rake n. tool consisting of a long handle with a cross-piece armed with teeth for drawing together hay, etc., or breaking the ground. -v.t. draw or break with a rake; sweep or search over; sweep with shot. [OE. raca]

rall′y v.t. bring together, esp. what has been scattered, as a routed army or dispersed troops. -v.i. come together; regain health or strength n. act of rallying. [F. rallier]

ram n. male sheep; swinging beam with metal head for battering hydraulic machine; beak projecting from bow of a warship. -v.t. beat down; stuff, strike with a ram. [OE. ramm]

Ram′adan n. ninth month of the Islamic (lunar) year during which fasting is observed from dawn until dusk. [Arab.]

ram′ble v.i. walk without definite route, wander; talk incoherently. -n. rambling walk. **-ram′bler** n. one who rambles; climbing rose. **-ram′bling** a. [ME. ramen, roam]

ramp v.i. stand on the hind legs. -n. slope. **-ramp′ant** a. rearing; violent. [F. ramper clamber]

ramp′art n. mound for defence, esp. of a fortification. [F. rempart]

ranch n. very large farm, esp. one where sheep, cattle or horses are produced. -v.i. conduct such a form. -v.i. conduct one. **ranch′er** n. [Sp. rancho, row (of huts, etc.)]

ran′cid a. smelling or tasting like stale fat. **-rancid′ity** n. [L. rancidus]

ran'cor *n.* bitter and inveterate illfeeling. -**ran'corous** *a.* [L. *rancor*]

ran'dom *n.* at random, haphazard. *a.* made or done at random. [OF. *randon*, headlong rush]

range *n.* rank; area, scope, sphere; distance a gun can reach; distance of a mark shot at; place for practicing shooting; kitchen stove. -*v.t.* set in a row; roam. -*v.i.* extend; roam. -**ran'ger** *n.* **range'-finder** *n.* instrument to determine distance of object. [F. *rang*]

ran'ger *n.* one who guards a tract of forest; armed patrol man. [fr. *range*, *v.*]

rank *n.* row or line; order; social position; high social position; relative place or position. -*v.t.* draw up in a rank, classify. -*v.i.* have rank or place. (F. *rang*). rank *a.* growing too thickly or coarsely; offensively strong; vile; flagrant. **rank'ly** *adv.* [OE. *ranc*, insolent]

ransack *v.t.* search thoroughly. [ON. *rann*, house, *soekaj*, seek]

ran'som *n.* release from captivity by payment; amount paid. -*v.t.* pay ransom for. -**ran'somer** *n.* [F. *rancon* fr. L. *redemptio*, buying back]

rant *v.i.* talk, preach, in a loud, bombastic way. -*n.* bombast. -**rant'er** *n.* [O. Du. *ranten*, rave]

rap *n.* smart slight blow. -*v.t.* give a rap to. -*v.i.* [imit. orig.]- **rap** *n.* talk, conversation. -*v.i.* [orig. uncertain]

rape *n.* plant with oil-yielding seeds; plant fed to sheep. [L. *rapum*, turnip]

rape *v.t.* violate; force a person to submit unwillingly to sexual intercourse. -*n.* act of raping. -**ra'pist** *n.* [ME. *rappen*, seize. L. *rapere*, seize]

rap'id *a.* quick, swift; speedy. -**rapid'ity** *n.* -**rap'idly** *adv.* [L. *rapidus*]

ra'pier *n.* light, pointed sword for thrusting only. [F. *rapière*]

rapport' *n.* rotation; harmony, sympathy. [F.]

rapproche'ment *n.* (re-)establishment or renewal of friendly relations. [F.]

rapt *a.* snatched away; lost in thought; intent. -**rap'ture** *n.* ecstasy. -**rap'turous** *a.* [L. *rapere*, snatch]

rare *a.* uncommon; of uncommon quality. -**rare'bit** *n.* Welsh rabbit, cheese sauce on toast. -**rar'efy** *v.t.* lessen the density of. -**rar'ity** *n.* anything rare. [L. *rarus*, thinly sown]

rare *a.* raw, underdone. [OE. *hrér*, half-cooked]

ras'cal *n.* rogue, knave. -**ras'cally** *a.* **rascal'ity** *n.* [OF. *rascaille*. rabble]

rash *n.* skin eruption. [OF. *rasche*]

rash *a.* hasty, reckless, without due caution. -**rash'ly** *adv.* [Du *rasch* quick]

rasp *n.* coarse file. -*v.t.* scrape with one. -*v.i.* scrape; make a scraping noise. [OF. *raspe*]

raspberry *n.* familiar soft fruit; the plant. [orig. uncertain]

rat *n.* small rodent animal; one who deserts his party. -**ratt'y** *a.* (*sl.*) riled. *v.i.* hunt rats; desert one's party. -**rat's-bane** *n.* poison for rats. [OE. *rcét*]

rat'chet *n.* set of teeth on a bar wheel allowing motion in one direction only. [F. *rochet*]

rate *n.* proportion between two things; charge; degree of speed, *etc.* -*v.t.* estimate the value of. -**rat'able** *a.* that can be rated; liable to pay rates. [Med. L. *rata*, fr. *reri*, *rat-*, think, judge]

rate *v.t.* scold. [OF. *reter*, accuse]

ra'ther *adv.* some extent; in preference. [OE. *hrathe*, quickly]

rat'ify *v.t.* confirm, make valid. **ratifica'tion** *n.* [F. *ratifier*]

ra'ting *n.* (*naut.*) grading of a seaman on ship's books; tonnage-class of racing yacht; amount fixed as a rate. [*rate*]

ra'tio *n.* relative magnitude; proportion. [L. = *reason*]

ra'tion (rash'un) *n.* fixed daily allowance. -*v.t.* supply with, or limit to, rations. [L. *ratio*]

ra'tional *a.* reasonable. -**ra'tionalism** *n.* philosophy which regards reason as the only guide or authority. -**ra'tionalist** *n.* -**ra'tionalize** *v.t.* explain away by reasoning. -**rational'ity** *n.* -**ra'tionally** *adv.* [L. , fr. *veri*, *rat-*, think, judge]

rat'tle *v.i.* give out a succession of short sharp sounds, as of shaking small stones in a box. -*v.t.* cause to sound thus; (*sl.*) irritate, make angry. -*n.* the sound; instrument for making it; set of horny rings in a rattlesnake's tail. -**rat'tle-snake** *n.* poisonous snake that makes a rattling noise with its tail. [imit. orig.]

rauc'ous *a.* hoarse; harsh-sounding. [L. *raucus*]

rav'age *v.t.* lay waste. -*n.* destruction and pillage; devastation. [F.]

rave *v.i.* talk in delirium or with great enthusiasm. [F. *rêver*, dream]

rave'lin *n.* detached work with two faces meeting in salient angle at front and open at rear. [F.]

ra'ven *n.* black bird of the crow family. [OE. *hroefn*]

rav'en *v.t.* and *i.* seek prey or plunder. -**rav'enous** *a.* very hungry. [OF. *ravine* -L. *rapina*, plunder]

ravine' *n.* narrow gorge worn by running water. [F. fr. L. *rapina*]

rav'ish *v. t.* carry off, sweep away; commit rape upon (a woman); enrapture. **rav'ishment** *n.* [F. *ravir* fr. L. *rapere*, snatch]

raw *a.* uncooked; not manufactured; crude, inexperienced, uncultivated; stripped of skin; sensitive; chilly. [OE. *hreaw*]

ray *n.* single line or narrow beam of light, heat, *etc.*; any of a set of radiating lines. *v. i.* radiate. (OF. *rai*, fr. L. *radius*]

raze *v.t.* destroy completely; level to the ground; wipe out, delete. [F. *raser*, fr. L. *radere*, *ras-*, scrape]

raz'or *n.* an instrument for shaving. -**razor-bill** *n.* bird, a kind of auk. [F. *raser*, fr. L. *radere*, *ras-*, scrape]

re, in re *prep.* in the matter of. [L.]

re- *prefix* makes compounds with meaning of, again, *e.g.* **readdress'** *v. t.* address afresh. -**recap'ture** *v. t.* capture again. These are not given where the meaning and derivation may easily be found from the simple word. [L.]

reach v.t. succeed in touching; arrive at. -v.i. stretch out the hand; extend. -n. act of reaching; grasp; scope; stretch of river between two bends, (OE. *roecan*, stretch out]

react v.i. act in return or opposition or towards a former state. -**reac'tion** n. **reac'tionary** n. one advocating backward movement, in politics, etc. -a. of or inclined to such reaction. -**rea'gent** n. chemical substance that reacts with another and is used to detect the presence of the other. [act]

read v.t. look at and understand written or printed matter; interpret mentally; learn by reading; read and utter. -v.i. be occupied in reading; find mentioned in reading. -**read'able** a. that can be read with pleasure. [OE. *roedan*, make out]

read'y (red'i) a. prepared, prompt. **read'iness** n. -**read'ily** adv. [OE. *gero-ode*]

re'al a. existing in fact; happening; actual; of property, consisting of land and houses. -**re'alism** n. regarding things as they are; artistic treatment with this outlook. -**re'alist** n. -**realist'ic** a. **real'ity** n. real existence. -**re'alize** v. t. make real; convert into money. **realiza'tion** n. -**re'ally** adv. -real estate' n. immovable property, as houses etc. -**real'tor** n. real estate agent. **re'alty** n. real estate. [F. *reel*, fr. L. *res*, thing]

realm (relm) n. kingdom, province, sphere. [OF. *reame*, fr. L. *regimen*]

reap v.i. cut grain. -v.t. cut (grain). **reap'er** n. [OE. *repan*]

rear n. back part. -**rear'-guard** n. troops protecting rear of an army. [arrear]

rear v. t. set on end; build up; breed, bring up. -v. i. rise on the hind feet. [OE. *roeran*, raise]

reas'on (-z-) n. ground or motive; faculty of thinking; sensible or logical view. -v.i. think logically in forming conclusions. v.t. persuade by logical argument (into doing, etc.). -**reas'onable** a. sensible, not excessive, suitable; marked by logic. [F. *raison*, fr. L. *ratio*]

reassure' v.t. calm, give confidence to. [assure]

re'bate n. discount. -v.t. diminish; allow as discount. [F. *rabattre*]

rebel' v. i. revolt, take arms against the ruling power. -**reb'el** n. one who rebels; one resisting authority. -a. in rebellion. **rebell'ion** n. organized open resistance to authority. [L. *rebellare*]

rebound' v.t. drive back. -v. i. spring back; re-echo; recoil. -n. [bound]

rebuke' v.t. reprove, reprimand, find fault with. -n. act of rebuking. [OF. *rebuchier*, repulse]

re'bus n. riddle in which words are represented by pictures standing for the syllables, etc. [L. = 'by things']

rebut' v.t. force back, refute evidence etc. -**rebutt'al** [F. *rebouter*]

recant' v.t. withdraw a statement, opinion, etc. -**recanta'tion** n. [L. *recantare*, fr. *cantare* sing]

recapitulate v.t. state again briefly. -

recapitula'tion n. (L. *recapitulare-capitulum*, chapter]

recast' v.t. remold; reshape. [cast]

recede' v.i. go back. -**rece'ding** a. going, sloping, backward. [L. *recedere*]

receipt' n. written acknowledgment of money received; fact of receiving or being received; recipe. -**receive'** v.t. take, accept, get; experience. [L. *recipere, recept-*, fr. *capere*, take]

re'cent a. that has lately happened, new, fresh. -**re'cently** adv. [L. *recens*]

receptacle n. containing vessel, place or space. -**recep'tion** n. receiving; manner of receiving; formal receiving of guests. -**recep'tionist** n. one who receives (hotel) guests or clients. **receptive** a. able or quick to receive, esp. impressions. -**receptiv'ity** n. [L. *recipere*, receive]

re'cess n. vacation or holiday; niche or alcove; secret hidden place. [recede]

recidivist n. one who relapses into crime. [L. *recidere*, fall back]

re'cipe (res'i-pe) n. directions for cooking a dish, prescription. [L. *recipere*, receive]

recipient a. that can or does receive. n. that which receives. [L. *recipere*, receive]

reciprocal a. in return, mutual. **recip'rocally** adv. -**recip'rocate** v.i. move backwards and forwards. -v.t. give in return, give and receive mutually. [L. *reciprocus*]

recite' v.t. repeat aloud, esp. to an audience. -**reci'tal** n. narrative; musical performance by one person. -**recita'tion** n. [L. *recitare*]

reck v.i. care, heed. -**reck'less** a. rash; heedless; careless. [OE. reccan]

reck'on v.t. count; include; consider. -v. i. make calculations, cast accounts. **reck'oner** n. [OE. *gerecenian*]

reclaim' v.t. bring back (from wrong); make fit for cultivation. -**reclaim'able** a. -**reclama'tion** n. reformation; regaining, as of land from the sea. [L. *reclamare*, call back]

recline' v.i. sit or lie with back supported on a slope; repose. [L. *reclinare*]

recluse' a. living in complete retirement. -n. hermit. [L. *reclusus*]

recognize v.t. know again; treat as valid; notice. -**recogni'tion** n. -**recogni'zable** a. [L. *recognoscere*]

recoil' n. rebound, esp. of a gun when fired; act of recoiling. -v. i. draw or spring back. [F. *reculer*]

recollect' v.t. call back to mind, remember. -**recollec'tion** n. [L. *recolligere, recollect-*, collect again]

recommend' v. t. entrust; present as worthy of favor or trial; make acceptable. -**recommenda'tion** n. [F. *recommander*. cp. command, commend]

reconcile v. t. bring back into friendship; adjust, settle, harmonize. [L. *reconciliare*]

reconnoiter (-ter) v.t. survey the position of an enemy, strange district, etc. -v. i. make a reconnaissance. **reconnaissance** n. such survey. [OF. *reconnoitre* (F. *reconnoitre*) recognize]

reconstruct' v.t. rebuild. -**reconstruc'tion**

n. a rebuilding; rebuilding of a country, its trade, *etc.*, after war. [*construct*]

record′ *v.t.* put down in writing. **rec′ord** *n.* a being recorded; document or other thing that records, *e.g.*, gramophone record; best recorded achievement. **record′er** *n.* a person or thing that records; type of flute. **record′ing** *n.* art of registering sounds for reproduction. [L. *recordari*, get by heart]

recount′ *v.t.* tell in detail. -*n.* second count (of votes, *etc.*) [OF, *reconter*]

recoup′ *v.t.* recompense; indemnify. [F. *recouper*, cut back]

recourse′ *n.* resorting to for help. [L, *recurrere*, *recurs-*, run back]

recov′er (-kuv) *v.t.* get back. -*v.i.* get back health. [F. *recouvrir*, fr. L. *recuperare*]

rec′reate *v.t.* restore. -*v.i.* take recreation. - **recrea′tion** *n.* agreeable or refreshing occupation. **-rec′reative** *a.* [L. *recreare*, make again]

recriminate *v.i.* make a counter charge or mutual accusation. [L. *crimen*, charge, crime]

recruit′ (-oot) *n.* newly-enlisted soldier; one newly joining a society. -*v. i.* enlist, *v.t.* enlist fresh soldiers, *etc.*; recover health. - **recruit′ment** *n.* [OF. *recrue*, reinforcement]

rectangle *n.* four-sided figure with four right-angles. **-rectang′ular** *a.* [L. *rectus*, right, straight]

rect′ify (-fi) *v.t.* put right, purify; (*elec.*) change from alternate to direct current. [L. *rectus*, right]

rec′to *n.* right hand page, front of a leaf. [L. *rectus*]

rec′tor *n.* clergyman of the Protestant Episcopal Church in charge of a parish; head of certain schools and colleges. **recto′rial** *a.* of a rector. **-rec′tory** *n.* house or province of a rector. [L. *regere*, *rect-*, rule]

rect′um *n.* the final section of the large intestine. [L. *rectus*]

recumbent *a.* lying down; reclining. [L. *recumbere*, to lie down]

recuperate *v.t.* and *i.* to restore, be restored from illness. losses, *etc.* [L. *recuperate*, to recover]

recur′ *v. i.* go or come back in mind; happen again. [L. *recurrere*, run back]

red *a.* of a color varying from crimson to orange and seen in blood, rubies, glowing fire, *etc.*; (politics) communist. -*n.* the color. [OE. *read*]

redeem′ *v.t.* ransom, atone for; save: fulfill (a promise); make good use of (time). - **redeem′er** *n.* -the Redeem′er Jesus Christ [L. *redimere*, *redempt-*]

red′olent *a.* scented with, diffusing the fragrance, odor of. **-red′olence** *n.* [F.]

redoub′le (-dub-) *v.t.* and *i.* to increase, multiply. [*doubler*]

redress *v.t.* set right. -*n.* compensation. [F. *redresser*, put right again]

reduce *v.t.* bring down, lower, lessen; bring by force or necessity to some state or action. -*v. i.* slim. [L. *reducere*, *reduct-*, lead back]

redundant *a.* superfluous, unnecesary; become deprived of a job. **-redundancy** *n.* [L.

redundare, overflow]

reduplicate *v.t.* double again. [*duplicate*]

reed *n.* various marsh or water plants; tall straight stem of one; vibrating part of certain musical instruments. **-reed′y** *a.* full of reeds; like a reed instrument in tone. [OE. *hreod*]

reef *n.* part of a sail which can be rolled up to reduce the area; ridge of rock near the surface of the sea; lodge of auriferous quartz. -*v.t.* take in a reef of. [ON. *rif*, reef, rib]

reek *n.* strong smell or smoke. -*v.i.* smoke, emit fumes. **-reek′y** *a.* smoky. [OE. *reocan*, to smoke]

reel *n.* winding apparatus; cylinder for winding cotton, *etc.*, on; act of staggering. -*v. t.* wind on a reel. -*v. i.* stagger away. [OE. *hreol*]

reel *n.* lively dance; music for it, [Gael. *righil*]

refer′ *v.t.* trace or ascribe to; submit for decision; send to for information. -*v. i.* have relation, allude. **-ref′erable** *a.* referee′ *n.* umpire; arbitrator. **-ref′erence** *n.* **-referen′dum** *n.* submitting of a question to a whole body of voters. [L. *referre*, carry back]

refine′ *v.t.* purify. **-refi′nery** *n.* place where sugar, *etc.*, is refined. [F. *raffiner*]

reflect′ *v.t.* throw back, *esp.* rays of light; cast (discredit, fame, etc.), upon. -*v.i.* meditate. **-reflec′tion, reflex′ion** *n.* **-reflect′ive** *a.* - **reflect′or** *n.* a polished surface for reflecting light, *etc.* **-re′flex** *a.* reflected, bent back; of muscular action, involuntary. **-reflex′ive** *a.* in grammar, describes a verb denoting the agent′s action on himself. [L. *reflectere*, bend back]

re′flux *n.* a flowing back. **-ref′luent** *a.* flowing back, ebbing. [L. *fluxus*, flow]

reform′ *v.t.* and *i.* amend, improve. -*n.* amendment, improvement. **-reforma′tion** *n.* - **reform′atory, reform′ school** *n.* institution for reforming juvenile offenders. **-a.** reforming, reform′er *n.* [L. *reformare*, reshape]

refract′ *v.t.* break the course of (light, *etc.*). **-refract′ive** *a.* **-refrac′tion** *n.* [L. *refringere*, break back]

refrain′ *n.* chorus of a song. [F.]

refrain′ *v.i.* abstain from. -*v.t.* check. [L. *refrenare*, bridle]

refresh′ *v.t.* give freshness to. **-refresher** *n.* **-refresh′ment** *n.* that which refreshes, *esp.* food or drink. [F. *rafraichir-frais*, fresh]

refrig′erate (-j-) freeze, cool. **-refrig′erator** *n.* apparatus for cooling or freezing. [L. *frigus*, *frigerare*, *frigeral-*, cold]

ref′uge *n.* shelter, protection. **-refugee′** *n.* one who seeks refuge, *esp.* in a foreign country. [L. *refugium*, fr. *fugere*, flee]

refund′ *v.t.* pay back: restore. -*n.* refunder *n.* [L. *refundere*, pour back]

refuse′ (-z) *v.t.* and *i.* decline. **-ref′use** (-s) *a.* discarded. -*n.* rubbish, useless matter. - **refu′sal** *n.* [L. *refusare*]

refute′ *v. t.* disprove. **-refu′table** *a.* refuta′tion *n.* [L. *refutare*, repel]

re′gal *a.* of, or like, a king. **-rega′lia** *n. pl.* insignia of royalty, as used at a coronation, *etc.* [L, *regales*, fr. *rex*, *reg-*, king]

regale′ *v.t.* and *i.* feast. [F. *régaler*]

regard′ *v. t.* look at; consider (as); heed; relate

to. -*n.* look; particular respect; esteem. -*pl.* expression of goodwill. **-regard'ing** *prep.* concerning. **-regard'less** *a.* [F. *regarder*]

regen'erate *v.t.* and *i.* cause spiritual rebirth, reform morally; reproduce, recreate, reorganize. [*generate*]

re'gent *a.* ruling. -*n.* one who rules a kingdom during the absence, minority, *etc.*, of its king. **-re'gency** *n.* [L. *regere*, rule]

régime *n.* system of government. [F.]

reg'imen *n.* prescribed system of diet. [L.]

regiment *n.* an organized body of troops as a unit of an army. **-regiment'al** *a.* of a regiment. -*n.* in *pl.* uniform. [F. *régiment*]

re'gion (-jun) *n.* area, district. [L. *regio, region-*, fr. *regere*, rule]

reg'ister (-j-) *n.* written record; compass of a voice; device for registering. -*v. t.* set down in writing; enter in a register; express. -*v. i.* make a visible impress. **- registrar'** *n.* keeper of a register. **- registra'tion** *n.* **-reg'istry** *n.* registering; place where registers are kept. [F. *registre*]

regress *n.* passage back; ability to pass back. **-regress'ive** *a.* passing back. salon *n.* returning, retrogression. [L. *re*, back, *gradi*, step]

regret' *v.t.* grieve for the loss of, or on account of-*n.* grief for something done or left undone or lost. **-regret'ful** *a.* **- regrett'able** *a.* (F. *regretter*]

reg'ular *a.* done according to rule; habitual; living under rule; belonging to the standing army. -*n.* regular soldier. **-regular'ity** *n.* **-reg'ulate** *v.t.* adjust; put under rule. **- regula'tion** *n.* rule; law; ordinance. **- reg'ulator** *n.* [L. *regularis*, fr. *regula*, rule]

rehabilitate *v.t.* restore to reputation or former physical state. **-rehabilita'tion** *n.* (L. *habilitare*, make fit]

rehearse' (-hers) *v.t.* repeat aloud; say over again; practice (a play, *etc.*). **rehears'al** *n.* [OF. *rehercier*, repeat (lit. rake over again)]

reign (rai)) *n.* royal power; dominion; supremacy; period of a sovereign's rule. -*v.i.* be sovereign. [L. *regnum*]

reimburse' *v. t.* pay back, refund (expenses, *etc.*). [F. *rembourser*, fr. *bourse*, purse]

rein *n.* narrow strap attached to the bit to check or guide a horse. -*v. t.* check or manage with reins. [OF. *reine*, fr. L. *retinere*, hold back]

reinforce' *v.t.* strengthen, *esp.* by sending fresh men. **-reinforce'ment** *n.* **reinforced' con'crete**, concrete strengthened with steel. [F. *reinforcer*]

reinstate' *v. t.* replace, restore. **reinstate'ment** *n.* [obs. *insate*]

reiterate *v.t.* repeat over and over again. **- reitera'tion** *n.* [*iterate*]

reject' *v.t.* refuse, put aside; decline. **rejec'tion** *n.* [L. *rejacere, reject-*, throw back]

rejoice' *v.t.* and *i.* make or be joyful. [F. *rejouir, rejouiss-*,]

rejoin' *v.i.* say in answer. **-rejoin'der** *n.* answer; response. [F. *réjoindre*]

rejuvenate *v. t.* restore to youth. [L. *juvenis*, young]

relapse' *v.i.* fall back, into evil, illness, *etc.* -*n.* [L. *relabi, relaps-*, slip back]

relate' *v.t.* narrate, recount; establish relation between; have reference or relation to. **- rela'tion** *n.* narration, narrative; correspondence, connection; connection by blood or marriage. **-rel'ative** *a.* dependent on relation to something else not absolute; have reference or relation to. -*n.* relative word or thing; one connected by blood or marriage. **-relativ'ity** *n.* Einstein's theory in physics that motion or velocity is relative, not absolute, and that time is a correlate of space. [F. *relater*]

relax' *v. t.* make loose or slack. -*v. i.* become loosened or slack; become more friendly. **-relaxa'tion** *n.* relaxing; recreation. [L. *laxus*, loose]

re'lay *n.* set of fresh horses to replace tired ones; gang of men, supply of material, *etc.*, used similarly; (radio) broadcast relayed from another station. *v.t.* pass on broadcast thus. [F. *relais*]

release' *v.t.* give up, surrender, set free. -*n.* a releasing; written discharge. [OF. *relaissier*]

relent' *v.i.* give up harsh intention, become less severe. [L. *lentus*, slow]

rel'evant *a.* having to do with the matter in hand; pertinent. **-rel'evance** *n.* [L. *relevare*, raise up]

rel'ic *n.* something remaining as a memorial of a saint, *etc.*; a thing kept as a memento. -*pl.* dead body; remains, surviving traces. **-rel'ict** *n.* a widow. [L. *relinquere, relict-*, to leave]

relief *n.* alleviation or end of pain, distress, *etc.*; money or food given to victims of a disaster, poverty, *etc.*; release from duty; one who relieves another; projection of a carved design from a surface; distinctness, prominence. [OF. *relief* fr. *relever*]

relieve' *v.t.* bring or give relief to; set free; free (a person or duty) by taking his place. [F. *relever*, raise up]

reli'gion (-ijun) *n.* system of faith and worship. [L. *religio*]

relinquish (-inkw-) *v.t.* give up. [L. *relinquere*]

rel'ish *n.* taste or flavor; savory taste; liking. -*v.t.* enjoy, like. [OF. *relaissier*, leave behind, (after-taste)]

reluctant *a.* unwilling. **-reluct'ance** *n.* [L. *reluctari*, struggle against]

rely' *v.i.* depend (on). **-reli'able** *a.* trustworthy. [L. *religare*, bind together]

remain' *v.i.* stay or be left behind; continue. **-remaind'er** *n.* rest, what is left after subtraction. [L. *remanere*]

remand' *v. t.* send back, *esp.* into custody. [L. *remandare*, order back]

remark' *v. t.* take notice of; say. -*v. i*, make a remark (on). -*n.* observation, comment. **- remark'able** *a.* noteworthy, unusual. [F. *remarquer*]

rem'edy *n.* means of curing, counteracting or relieving a disease, trouble, *etc.* -*v. t.* put right. [L. *remedium*]

remem'ber *v.t.* retain in or recall to the memory. -*v. i.* have in mind. **-remem'brance** *n.* [L. *memor*, mindful]

remind' (-mind) *v.t.* put in mind (of). **- remind'er** *n.* [mind]

reminisc'ence *n.* remembering; thing recollected. **-reminis'cent** *a.* reminding. [L. *reminisce*, remember]

remiss' *a.* negligent. **-remiss'ly** *adv.* **-remit'** *v.t.* forgive, not to exact, give up; slacken. *-v.i.* slacken, give up. **remissible** *a.* **-remis'sion** *n.* **-remit'tance** *n.* a sending of money; money sent. [L. *remittere, remiss-*, send back, slacken]

rem'nant *n.* fragment or small piece remaining. [OF. *remanant*, remaining]

remorse' *a.* regret and repentance. **-remorse'ful** *a.* **-remorse'fully** *adv.* **remorse'less** *a.* pitiless. [L. *remordere, remors-*, bite again]

remote' *a.* far away; distant in time or place. **-remote'ly** *adv.* [L. *removere, remot-*]

remove' *v.t.* take away or off. *-v.i.* go away; change residence. **-remo'val** *n.* removable *a.* [L.]

remunerate *v.t.* reward, pay. [L. *remunerare*]

renaissance *n.* revival, rebirth, *esp.* revival or learning in the 14th-16th centuries. [F. *renaissance*, fr. L. *nasci*, be born]

re'nal *a.* of the kidneys. [L. *renalis*]

renascent *a.* springing up again. [F. *renaissance*, fr. L. *nasci*, be born]

rend *v. t.* and *i.* tear. [OE. *rendan*]

rend'er *v.t.* give in return, deliver up; submit, present; portray, represent; melt down. **-rendi'tion** *n.* surrender; translation. [F. *rendre*]

rendezvous *n.* meeting; meeting-place. *-v.i.* meet, come together. [F.]

ren'egade *n.* deserter; outlaw; rebel. [L. *negare*, deny]

renege *v.i.* revoke at cards; back out; renounce. [L. *negare*, deny]

renounce *v.t.* give up, cast off. *-v. i.* in cards, fail to follow suit. **-renuncia'tion** *n.* [F. *renoncer*, fr. L. *renuntiare*, protest against]

ren'ovate *v.t.* restore, repair. [L. *renovare-novus*, new]

rent *n.* payment for the use of land or buildings. *-v. t.* hold as a tenant; lease; hire **-rent'al** *n.* sum payable as rent. [F. *rente*, income]

rent *n.* tear. [obs. *rent = rend*]

repair' *v.i.* resort, betake oneself (to). [OF. *repairier*, fr. Late L. *repatriare*, go home, return to one's country]

repair' *v.t.* mend. *-n.* mend. **-repair'able** *a.* **-repara'tion** *n.* a repairing; amends, compensation. [L. *reparare*, fr. *parare*, prepare]

repatriate *v.t.* restore to one's own country. [Late L. *repatriate*]

repay' *v.t.* pay back; make return for. [pay]

repeal' *v.t.* annul, cancel. *-n.* act of repealing, [appeal]

repeat' *v.t.* say or do again, reproduce. **repeat'edly** *adv.* **-repeat'er** *n.* **-repeti'-** tion *n.* [L. *repetere, repetit-*, try again]

repel' *v.t.* drive back, ward off, refuse. **repell'ent** *a.* [L. *repellere*]

repent' *v.i.* feel penitence; feel regret for a deed or omission. *-v.t.* feel regret for. [F. *se repentir*]

repercussion *n.* recoil; echo; indirect effect. [percussion]

repertoire (-twar) *n.* stock of plays, songs, *etc.*, that a player or company is prepared to give. [F.]

repertory *n.* store; repertoire. **repertory the'ater**, theater with a permanent company and a stock of plays. [L. *repertorium*]

replace' *v.t.* put back; fill up with a substitute for. **-replace'ment** *n.* [place]

replay *v.t.* to repeat an action or process, game or match; show a videotape of a portion of a televised event. *-n.* an act or instance or repeating an action.

replenish *v. t.* fill up again. [OF. *replenir*]

replete' *a.* filled; abounding in. [L. *repletus*]

rep'lica *n.* copy of a work of art made by the artist; reproduction. [It.]

reply' *v.t.* and *i.* answer. *-n.* answer. (F. *replier*, fold back]

report' *v.i.* relate; take down in writing; make or give an account of-, name as an offender. *-v. i.* make a report. *-n.* rumor; account or statement; repute; bang. **-report'er** *n.* one who reports, *esp.* for a newspaper. [L. *reportare*, bring back]

repose' *v.i.* take rest. *-v.t.* give rest to; put (trust, etc). *-n.* rest. **-repos'itory** *n.* store or shop. [F. *reposer*]

represent' *v.t.* call up by description or portrait; make out to be; act, play, symbolize; act as deputy for; stand for. [F. *reprosenter*]

repress' *v.t.* keep down or under. [L. *reprimere, repress-*, press back]

reprieve' *v.t.* suspend the execution of (condemned person); a reprieving or warrant for it. [for earlier *repry*, fr. F. *repris*, taken back]

rep'rimand *n.* sharp, rebuke. *-v. t.* rebuke sharply. [F. *reprimande*, fr. *réprimer*, repress]

reprint' *v.t.* print again. *-n.* book, publication reprinted. [print]

reproach' *v.t.* scold, rebuke. *-n.* scolding or upbraiding; expression of this; thing bringing discredit. **-reproach'ful** *a.* [F. *reprocher*]

rep'robate *v.t.* disapprove of, reject. *-a.* depraved, cast off by God. *-n.* reprobate person. **-reproba'tion** *n.* [L. *reprobare, reprobat-*, reprove, reject]

reproduce' *v.t.* produce anew; produce a copy of, bring new individuals into existence. **-reproduct'ive** *a.* [produce]

rep'tile *n.* cold-blooded air-breathing vertebrate with horny scales or plates, such as a snake, lizard, tortoise, *etc.* **-reptil'ian** *a.* [L. *reptiles- repere*, creep]

repub'lic *n.* state in which the supremacy of the people or its elected representatives is formally acknowledged. [L. *res publica*, common weal]

repudiate *v.t.* cast off, disown; disclaim. **-repudia'tion** *n.* [L. *repudiare*, fr. *repudium*, divorce]

repugnant *a.* contrary; distasteful; refractory. [L. *repugnare*, fight back]

repulse' *v.t.* drive back; rebuff. [L. *repellere, repuls-*,]

repute' *v.t.* reckon, consider. *-n.* reputation,

credit. **-reputa'tion** *n.* what is generally believed about a character; good fame. **-rep'utable** *a.* of good repute. [L. *reputare*, consider, weigh]

request' *n.* asking; thing asked for. *-v. t.* ask. [OF. *requester*]

require *v.t.* demand; want, need. **require'ment** *n.* **-req'uisite** (-zit) *a.* needed. *-n.* something necessary. **requisition** *n.* formal demand, usually for military supplies, etc-*v.t.* demand by an order of requisition; press into service. [L. *requirere*, requisite,]

requite' *v.t.* repay; make return for; retaliate on. **-requi'tal** *n.* [quit]

res'cue *v.t.* save, deliver. *-n.* rescuing. **res'cuer** *n.* [OF. *resourre*]

research' *n.* investigation, *esp.* scientific study to try to discover facts. **-research'er** *n.* [search]

resem'ble (-z-) *v.t.* be like. **-resem'blance** *n.* [F. *ressembler*]

resent' (-z-) *v.t.* show or feel indignation at, retain bitterness about. [F. *ressentir*]

reserve' (-z-) *v.t.* hold back, set apart, keep for future use. *-n.* something reserved; part of an army only called out in emergency; reticence, concealment of feelings or friendliness. *-pl.* troops in support. [L. *reservuare*, keep back]

reservoir *n.* receptacle for liquid, *esp.* a large one built for storing water. [F. *reservoir*]

reside' (-z-) *v.i.* dwell. **-res'idence** *n.* dwelling; house. **-res'idency** *n.* act or time of dwelling in a place. **-res'ident** *a.* and *n.* **-residen'tial** *a.* (L. *residere*, fr. *sedere*, sit]

res'idue (-z-) *n.* what is left. [L. *residuum*]

resign' (-zin) *v.t.* give up—*v.i.* give up an office, employment, *etc.* **-resigned'** *a.* content to endure. **-resigna'tion** *n.* resigning; being resigned. [L. *resignare*, unseal]

resilient (-z-) *a.* rebounding. **-resil'ience** *n.* [L. *resilire*, jump back]

res'in (-z-) *n.* sticky substance formed in and oozing from plants, *esp.* firs and pines. [L. *resina*]

resist' (-z-) *v.t.* withstand. *-v.i.* oppose. [L. *resistere*]

res'olute *a.* resolved; fixed in purpose. **res'olutely** *adv.* **-resolu'tion** *n.* a resolving; fixed determination; firmness; formal proposal put before a meeting. [resolve]

resolve' *v.t.* break up into parts, disintegrate; dissolve, disperse; solve (a problem); decide, determine; (*mus.*) follow a discord by a concord. **-resolved'** *a.* firm; set on a course of action. [F., L. *resolvers*, *resolut-*, loose]

res'onant (-z-) *a.* echoing, resounding. **res'onance** *n.* [L. *resonare*, resound]

resort' (-z-) *v. i.* have recourse; frequent. *-n.* recourse; frequented place. [F. *ressortir*, rebound, go back]

resource *n.* skill in devising means. *-pl.* means of supplying a want; stock that can be drawn on, means of support. **-resource'ful** *a.* **-resource'**- fully *adv.* [F. *ressource*]

respect' *v.t.* defer to, treat with esteem. esteem; point or aspect. **-respect'able** *a.* worthy of respect. **-respect'ive** *a.* several, separate.

-respect'ively *adv.* [L. *respi- cere*, respect-, look back at]

respire' *v.i.* breathe. **-respi'rable** *a.* **respira'tion** *n.* **-res'pirator** *n.* apparatus worn over the mouth and breathed through as a protection against dust, poison-gas, *etc.* [L. *respir- are*]

res'pite *n.* delay; breathing space; suspension of capital sentence; reprieve; suspension of labor. *-v. t.* grant respite to; reprieve; relieve by resting. [L. *respectus*, respect]

resplendent *a.* brilliant, shining. **resplend'ence** *n.* [L. *resplendere*, shine]

respond' *v.i.* answer; act in answer. **respond'ent** *a.* replying. *-n.* one who answers; defendant. **-response'** *n.* answer. **responsible** *a.* liable to answer for something; of good credit or position. **-responsibil'ity** *n.* **-respon'sive** *a.* [L. *responders*, response,]

rest *n.* repose; freedom from exertion or activity; pause; supporting appliance; *-v.i.* take rest; be supported. *-v. t.* give rest to; place on a support. **-rest'ful** *a.* **rest'less** *a.* [OE. *roest*]

rest *n.* remainder. *-v.i.* be left over. [F. *reste-* L. *restare*, remain]

restaurant *n.* eating-house. **restauranteur'** *n.* keeper of one. [F.]

restitution *n.* giving back or making up: indemnification. [L. *restitutio*]

restore' *v.t.* build up again, repair, renew; re-establish; give back. **restoration** *n.* **restor'ative** *a.* restoring. *-n.* medicine to strengthen, *etc.* [L, *restaurare*, *restaurat-*, repair]

restrain' *v.t.* check, hold back. **restraint'** *a.* restraining or means of restraining. [L. *restringere*, restrict-]

restrict' *v.t.* limit, bound. **-restric'tion** *n.* **restrict'ive** *a.* [L. *restringere*, restrict]

result' (-z-) *v.i.* follow as a consequence, end. *-n.* effect, outcome. **-result'ant** *a.* [L. *resultare*, leap back]

resume *v.t.* begin again; summarize. **ré'umé** *n.* summary. **-resump'tion** *n.* a resuming. **-resump'tive** *a.* [L. *resumere*, *resumpt-*, take back]

resurge' *v.i.* rise again. **-resur'gent** *a.* [L. *resurgere*]

resurrect' *v.t.* restore to life. **ressurec'tion** *n.* rising again; revival. [L. *resurrec resurgere*. resurrect-]

resuscitate *v.t.* revive, bring back from being nearly dead. **-resuscita'tion** *n.* [L. *resuscitare*, raise up again]

re'tail *n.* sale in small quantities. *-v.t.* sell in small quantities; recount. *-adv.* by retail. **re'tailer** *n.* [OF. *retailler*, cut up]

retain' *v. t.* keep; engage services of retain'er *n.* fee to retain a lawyer, or other professional person; follower of a nobleman, *etc.* [L. *retinere*, hold back]

retaliate *v.t.* and *i.* repay in kind. [L. *retaliare*, *retaliate*, fr. *talis*, like, such]

retard' *v.,t.* make slow or late. **retarda'tion** *n.* [I, . *retardate*, *tardus*, slow]

ret'icent *a.* reserved in speech, not communicative. **-ret'icence** *n.* [L. *reticere*, fr. *tacere*, be silent]

retic'ulation *n.* netlike or meshlike structure, arrangement, pattern or appearance; network.

ret'ina *n.* sensitive layer at the back of the eye. [Med. L.]

retire' *v. i.* withdraw; give up office or work; go away; go to bed. -*v.t.* cause to retire. -retired' *a.* that has retired from office, *etc.* - **retire'ment** *n.* -**reti'ring** *a.* unobtrusive, shy. [F. *retirer*, pull back]

retort' *v.t.* repay in kind; reply; hurl back (a charge, *etc.*). -*n.* thing done or said as vigorous reply or repartee; vessel with a bent neck used for distilling. [L. *retorquere*, retort-, twist back]

retract' *v. t.* draw back; recant. -*v. i.* recant. -**retracta'tion** *n.* [L. *retrahere. retract-*, draw back]

retreat' *n.* act of, or military signal for, retiring; sunset call on a bugle, *etc;* place of seclusion. -*v.i.* retire. [F. *retraite*, fr. *retraire*, draw back]

retribution *n.* recompense, *esp.* for evil deed; vengeance. -**retrib'utive** *a.* [L. *retributio* payment]

retrieve' *v. t.* bring in: regain; restore; rescue from a bad state. [F. *retrouver*, find again]

retro-, backward.[L.]. -**ret'rograde** *a.* going backwards, reverting reactionary. - **retrogres'sion** *n.* -**retrogress'ive** *a.* - **ret'rospect** *n.* a looking back, survey of the past.

retrovirus *n. pl* -**retroviruses** any of a group of viruses that use RNA and reverse transcriptase to encode information and which cause cancers, AIDS, leukemia, etc.

retsina *n.* strong Greek wine flavored with pine resin.

return *v.i.* go or come back. -*v.t.* give or send back report officially; report as being elected; elect. [F. *retourner.* -L. *tornare*, turn]

rev *n,* (*sl.*) abbrev. of **revolution** (of engine)- **rev up** *v.t.* and *i.* cause (engine) to quicken speed; speed up.

reveal' *v.t.* make known; disclose. **revela'tion** *n.* what is revealed. *esp.* by divine inspiration. [L. *revelare*, draw back the veil, *velum*]

rev'el *v.i.* make merry. -*n.* merrymaking. [OF. *reveler*, make tumult]

revenge' *v. refl.* avenge oneself-*v. t.* make retaliation for; avenge. -*n.* a revenging, desire for vengeance; act that satisfies this. [OF. *revengier*, fr. L. *revindicare*]

rev'enue *n.* income, *esp.* of a state or institution; receipts; profits. [L. *revenière*, come back]

reverberate *v.t.* and *i.* echo or throwback. -**reverbera'tion** *n.* [L. *reverberare*, beat back]

revere' *v.t.* hold in great regard or religious respect. -**rev'erence** *n.* revering; veneration; capacity for revering. [L. *revereri*, fr. *vereri*, fear]

reverse' *v.t.* turn upside down or the other way round; change completely. -*n.* opposite or contrary; side opposite the obverse; defeat. *a.* opposite, contrary, revers'al *n.* -revers'ible *a.* -**revert'** *v.i.* return to a former state; come

back to a subject. [L. *vertere*, *vers-*, turn]

review *n.* revision; survey, inspection, *esp.* of massed military forces; critical notice of a book, *etc.*; periodical with critical articles, discussion of current events, *etc.* -*v. t.* hold, make, or write, a review of -**review'er** *n.* writer of reviews. [F. *revue*, fr. *revoir*, see again, revise]

revile' *v.t.* abuse, reproach. [OF. *reviler*]

revise' *v.t.* look over and correct. **revi'ser** *n.* -revi'sion *n.* . [L. *revisere*]

revive' *v.i.* come back to life, vigor, *etc.* *v.t.* bring back to life, vigor, use *etc.* **revi'val** *n.* a reviving, *esp.* of religious fervor. [L. *viuere*, live]

revoke' *v.t.* annul. -*v.i.* at cards, to fail to follow suit though able to. -*n.* at cards, an act of revoking. [L. *revocare*, call back]

revolt' *v.i.* rise in rebellion; feel disgust. -*v.t.* affect with disgust. -*n.* rebellion. -**revolt'ing** *a.* disgusting, horrible. [F. *révolter*]

revolve' *v.i.* turn round, rotate. -*v.t.* rotate; meditate upon. -**revolu'tion** *n.* rotation or turning round; turning or spinning round; great change; the violent overthrow of a system of government. -**revolu'tionary** *a.* and *n.* -**revolu'tionize** *v.t.* -**revol'ver** *n.* repeating pistol with a revolving cartridge-magazine. [L. *revoluere*, *revolut-*]

revulsion *n.* sudden violent change of feeling; strong distaste. [L. *revulsio*]

reward' (-word) *v.t.* pay, or make return, for service, conduct, *etc-n.* recompense or return. [ONF. *rewarder*]

rhap'sody *n.* enthusiastic or highflown composition. -**rhapsod'ic** *a.* -**rhap'sodist** *n.* (G. *rhapsodia*, piece of epic verse for one recital]

rhe'ostat *n.* instrument for regulating electric current to constant degree of power. [G. *rheos*, stream]

rhetoric *n.* art of effective speaking or writing; artificial or exaggerated language. - **rhetor'ical** *a.* -**rhetori'cian** *n.* [G. *rhetor*, orator]

rhinoceros *n.* large thick-skinned animal with one or two horns on its nose. [G. *rhinokeros*, 'nosehorn']

rhinovirus *n. pl.* -**rhinoviruses** any of a large group of picornaviruses which are the cause of the common cold and other respiratory diseases.

rhizosphere *n.* The region of soil immediately surrounding and influenced by the roots of the plant. -**rhizospheric** *a.*

rhom'bus, rhomb *n.* equilateral but not right-angled parallelogram, diamond or lozenge. [G. *rhombus*, thing that can be twirled]

rhyme *n-* identity of sounds at ends of lines of verse, or in words, word or syllable identical in sound to another; verse marked by rhyme; *v.t.* use (word) to make rhymes. -**rhymester**, **rhym'er** *n.* poet, *esp.* one considered mediocre; poetaster, versifier. -**rhyme scheme** *n.* pattern of rhymes used in piece of verse, *usu.* indicated by letters. -**rhym'ing slang** *n.* slang in which word is replaced by word or phrase that rhymes with it. [F. *rime*, fr. G. *rhythmos*, rhythm]

rhythm (riTHm) *n.* measured beat or flow, *esp,* of words, music, *etc.* [G. *rhythmos*]

rib *n.* one of the curved bones springing from the spine and making the framework of the upper part of the body; curved timber of the framework of a boat. *-v.t.* furnish or mark with ribs. [OE. *ribb*]

ribb'on, rib'and *n.* narrow band of fine fabric. [OF. *riban*]

ribcage *n.* cagelike enclosure of the chest formed by the rigs and their connecting bones.

ribosomal RNA *n.* type of ribonucleic acid that is a basic, permanent component of the ribosomes and plays a major part in protein synthesis. [*abbr.* **rRNA**]

ricotta *n.* soft Italian cheese made from why, whole milk, or both.

rice *n.* white seeds of an Eastern plant, used as food; the plant. **-rice'-paper** *n.* fine Chinese paper. [F. *riz*]

rich *a.* wealthy; fertile; abounding in some product or material; valuable; of food, containing much fat or sugar; mellow; amusing. [OE. *rice,* powerful, rich]

rick *n.* stack of hay, *etc.* [OE. *hreac*]

rick'ets *n.* disease of children marked by softening of bones, bowlegs, *etc.* **-rick'ety** *a.* suffering from rickets; shaky, insecure. [orig. uncertain]

ric'ochet *n.* skipping on water or ground of a bullet or other projectile; hit made after it. *-v. i.* skip thus. *-v. t.* hit or aim with a ricochet. [F.]

rid *v.t.* clear, relieve of **-ridd'ance** *n.* [ON. *rythja,* to clear (land)]

rid'dle *n.* question made puzzling to test the ingenuity of the hearer, enigma; puzzling fact, thing, or person. *-v.i.* speak in or make riddles. [OE. roedels]

ride *v.i.* go on horseback or in a vehicle; lie at anchor; float lightly. *-n.* journey on a horse or other animal or in any vehicle; road for riding on horseback. **-ri'der** *n.* one who rides; supplementary clause; mathematical problem on a given proposition. **-ri'derless** *n.* [OE. *ridan*]

ridge *n.* line of meeting of two sloping surfaces; long narrow hill; long narrow elevation on a surface. *-v. t.* form into ridges. [OE. *hyrcg,* spine, back]

ridiculous *a.* deserving to be laughed at, absurd, foolish. **-rid'icule** *v.t.* laugh at, hold up as ridiculous. *-n.* treatment of a person or thing as ridiculous. [L. *ridiculus-ridere,* laugh]

rife *a.* prevalent; plentiful. [OE.]

ri'fle *v. t.* search and rob; make spiral grooves in (gun-barrel, *etc.*). *-n.* firearm with a long barrel. **-ri'fling** *n.* arrangement of grooves in a gun barrel. [F. *rifler*]

rift *n.* a crack, split. **-rift'-vall'ey** *n.* (geol.) subsistence between two faults. [ON. *ript*]

rig *v.t.* provide (a ship) with spars, ropes, *etc.*; equip; set up, *esp.* as a makeshift. *-n.* way a ship's masts and sails are arranged; costume; style of dress; apparatus for drilling oil and gas. **-rigg'ing** *n.* spars and ropes of a ship. [orig. uncertain]

rigatoni *n.* pasta in the form of short, curved, thick tubes with grooved sides.

right (rit) *a.* straight; just; proper; true; correct; genuine. **-right side,** side of a person which is to the east when he faces north, opposite of left. *-v.t.* bring back to a vertical position; do justice to. *-v.i.* come back to a vertical position-*n.* what is right, just, or due. *-adv.* straight; properly; very; on or to the right side. **-righteous** (ri-chus) *a.* just, upright. **-right'-hand man,** subordinate chiefly relied on. [OE. *riht*]

ri'gid *a.* stiff; harsh; unyielding. **rigid 'ity** *n.* **-ri'gidly** *adv.* [L. *rigidus*]

rig'or *n.* harshness, severity, strictness; sense of chill and shivering. **-rig'orous** *a.* [L. *rigor*]

rile *v.t.* make angry. [earlier *roil,* disturb, fr. OF. *rouil,* mud]

rim *n.* outer ring of a wheel; edge, border. **-rim'less** *a.* [OE. *rima*]

rime *n.* hoar-frost. [OE. *hrim*]

rind *n.* outer coating of trees, fruits, *etc.* [OE]

ring *n.* small circle of gold, *etc.,* *esp.* as worn on the finger; any circular appliance, band, coil, rim, *etc.*; circle of persons. *-v. t.* put a ring round. [OE. *hring*]

ring *v. i.* give out a clear resonant sound, as a bell; resound. *-v. t.* cause (a bell) to sound. *-n.* a ringing. [OE. *hringan*]

rink *n.* sheet of ice for skating; floor for roller-skating. [Sc.]

rinse (-s) *v. t.* clean by putting in and emptying out water; wash lightly. *-n.* a rinsing. [F. *rincer*]

ri'ot *n.* tumult, disorder; loud revelry; unrestrained indulgence or display. *-v. i.* make or engage in a riot; brawl. **-ri'otous** *a.* **-ri'otously** *adv.* [F. *riotte*]

rip *v.t.* cut or tear away, slash, rend. *-n.* rent or tear, broken water, as in tide-rip. [of Teutonic orig.]

ripe *a.* matured, ready to be reaped, eaten, *etc.* **-ri'pen** *v. i.* and *t.* [OE. *rip*]

rip'ple *v. i.* flow or form into little waves. *-v.t.* form ripples on. *-n.* slight wave or ruffling of surface. [rip]

rise *v.i.* get up; move upwards; reach a higher level; appear above the horizon; adjourn. *-n.* rising; upslope; increase; beginning. [OE. *risan*]

ri'sing *n.* revolt. [rise]

risk *n.* danger. *-v. t.* venture. [F. *risque*]

rite *n.* a formal practice or custom, *esp.* religious. **-rit'ual** *a.* concerning rites. *-n.* prescribed order or book of rites. [L. *ritus*]

ri'val *n.* one that competes with another for favor, success, *etc.* *-v. t.* vie with. *a.* in the position of a rival. **-ri'valry** *n.* emulation; competition. (L. *rivalis*]

riv'er *n.* large stream of water. **riv'erbead** *n.* spring, source, of a river. **riv'er basin** *n.* land that is drained by a river and its tributaries. **-riv'er-horse** *n.* hippopotamus. [F. *rivière*]

riv'et *n.* bolt for fastening plates of metal together, the end being put through the holes and then beaten flat. *-v. t.* fasten with rivets; clinch; *(fig.)* fascinate, enthrall. [F.]

riv'ulet *n.* small stream. [It. *rivoletto*]

road *n.* track or way prepared for passengers, vehicles, *etc.*; direction; way; roadstead. [OE.

rad, riding]

roam *v.i.* and *i.* wander about, rove. [orig. uncertain]

roan *a.* having a coat in which the main color is thickly interspersed with another, *esp.* bay or sorrel or chestnut mixed with white or gray. *-n.* animal with such a coat. [F. *rouan*]

roar *n.* loud deep hoarse sound as of a lion, thunder, voice in anger, *etc.* -make such sound. *-v. t.* utter in roaring voice, shout out. [OE. *rarian*]

roast *v.t.* cook by exposure to an open fire, achieve a similar effect by cooking in an oven. *-v.i.* be roasted. [OF. *rostir*]

rob *v.t.* plunder, steal from. -**robb'er** *n.* -**robb'ery** *n.* [OF. *rober*]

robe *n.* long outer garment. *-v. t.* dress. *v. i.* put on robes or vestments. [F.]

rob'in *n.* brown red-breasted bird of the thrush family. -**robin-red'-breast** *n.* [Robin]

ro'bot *n.* automated machine, *esp.* performing functions in a human manner; automaton, mechanical slave. -**ro'botics** *n.* science or technology of designing, building, and using robots; robot dancing. [Czech, fr. Karel Kapek's play, *R.U.R.* (Rossum's Universal Robots)]

robust *a.* sturdy. [L. *robustus*]

rock *n.* stone; large rugged mass of stone; hard toffee. -**rock'ery, rock-garden** *n.* mound or grotto of stones or rocks for plants in a garden. -**rock'y** *a.* [F. *roche*]

rock *v. i.* sway to and fro. *-v. t.* cause to do this. -**rock'er** *n.* curved piece of wood, *etc.* , on which a thing may rock; rocking chair. -**rock mus'ic** *n.* pop music developing from the rock-and-roll idiom. [OE. *rocoian*]

rock'et *n.* self-propelling device powered by burning of explosive contents, used as firework, for display, signalling, line carrying, weapon *etc.*; vehicle propelled by rocket engine, as weapon or carrying spacecraft. *-v. i.* move fast, *esp.* upwards, as rocket -**rock'etry** *n.* [It. *rocchetta,* dim. of *rocca,* distaff]

roco'co *a.* of furniture, architecture *etc.* , having much conventional decoration, tastelessly florid; antiquated. *-n.* rococo style. [F.]

rod *n.* slender, straight round bar, wand, stick or switch; birch or cane; measure a pole). [OE. *rood*]

ro'dent *a.* gnawing. *-n.* gnawing animal, *e.g.* rat, hare *etc.* [L. *rodere,* gnaw]

ro'deo *n.* gathering of cattle to be branded or marked; exhibition of skill in steer wrestling, and bronco riding *etc.* [Mex. -Sp.]

roe *n.* mass of eggs in a fish. [of Teutonic origin]

rogue *n.* rascal, knave; sturdy beggar; mischief-loving person or child wild beast of savage temper living apart from its herd. [orig. uncertain]

role *n.* actor's part; part played in real life. [F]

roll *n.* piece of paper, *etc.*, rolled up; list or catalogue; small loaf-*v.t.* move by turning over and over; wind round; smooth out with a roller. *-v.i.* move by turning over and over; move or sweep along; of a ship, swing from side to side. **roll'-call** *n.* calling out of a list of

names, *e.g.* as in schools, army. -**roll'er** *n.* cylinder used for pressing or smoothing, supporting something to be moved, winding something on *etc.* [F. *rouler,* fr. L. *rotula,* dim. of *rota,* wheel]

rollicking *a.* boisterously jovial. *-n.* jollity; frolic. [orig. unknown]

Ro'man *a.* of Rome or the Church of Rome. -**Roman type,** plain upright letters, ordinary script of printing. -**Roman figures, letters,** V, X, L, C, D, M, used to represent numbers in the manner of the Romans. [L. *Romanus,* fr. *Roma,* Rome]

Romance *n.* vernacular language of certain countries, developed from Latin and developing into French, Spanish, *etc.* -**romance** *n.* tale of chivalry; tale with scenes remote from ordinary life; love-affair or event suggesting it. [OF. *romanz*]

romp *v.i.* frolic. *-n.* spell of romping; child given to romping. [earlier *ramp*]

rood *n.* the Cross on which Christ died; crucifix; quarter of an acre. [OE. *rod,* gallows, measure of land]

roof *n.* outside upper covering of a building; (aircraft) flying height limit. *v. t.* put a roof on, be a roof over. -**roof-garden** *n.* garden on a flat roof. [OE. *hrol*]

rook (-oo) *n.* bird of the crow family. **rook'ery** *n.* colony of rooks; breeding-ground of seals. [OE. *hróc*]

rook *n.* piece at chess, also called a castle. [Pars. *rukh*]

rook'ie *n.* (*sl.*) raw recruit. [recruit]

room *n.* space; space enough; division of a house. -**room'ing house** *n.* building divided into separate rooms for rent. -**room'y** *a.* having plenty of space. [OE. *rum*]

roost *n.* perch for fowls; henhouse. *v.i.* perch. -**roost'er** *n.* barnyard cock. [OE. *hrost*]

root *n.* part of a plant that grows down into the earth and conveys nourishment to the plant; source, origin; original or vital part. *-v.t.* cause to take root; pull by the roots. *-v.i.* take root. [ON. *rot*]

rope *n.* thick cord. *-v.t.* secure or mark off with a rope. -**ro'py** *a.* sticky and stringy. -**ropedancer** *n.* tight-rope performer. -**rope'-trick** *n.*ndian vanishing trick. -**rope'-walk** *n,* long shed for rope-spinning. -**rope'-walk'er** *n.* walker on the tight rope, an acrobat. [OE. *rap*]

rose *n.* beautiful flower of many varieties rose-bush; perforated flat nozzle for a hose, *etc.*; pink color-a. of this color. -**rosa'ceous** *a.* like a rose, of rose family. **ro'sary** *n.* string of beads for keeping count of prayers, form of prayer. -**ro'sery** *n.* rose-garden. [L. *rose*]

rose'mary *n.* evergreen fragrant shrub. [L. *ros marinus,* 'sea-dew']

ros'in. See resin.

ros'ter *n.* list or plan showing turns of duty. [Du. *rooster,* list]

ros'trum *n.* platform for public speaking. [L. = *beak*]

rot *v.t.* and *i.* decompose naturally. *-n.* decay, putrefaction; disease of sheep; nonsense. -**rott'en** *a.* decomposed; corrupt. [OE, *rotian*]

ro'tary *a.* of movement, circular. **rotate'** *v.i.*

move round a center or on a pivot. -v.t. cause to do this. [L. rota, wheel]

rote n. by rote, by memory without understanding. [orig. uncertain]

ro'tor n. rotating part of machine or apparatus, e.g. dynamo, turbine, etc. [L. rota, wheel]

rotund' a. round; plump; rich sounding. [L. rotuitdas fr. rota, wheel]

rouge n. red powder used to color the cheeks or lips. -v. t. and i. color with rouge. [F. = red]

rough (ruf), a. not smooth, of irregular surface; violent, boisterous; lacking refinement; approximate; in a preliminary form. -v. t. make rough; plan out approximately. -n. disorderly ruffian; rough state; (golf) rough ground adjoining the fairway. -rough'age n. bulky, unassimilated portion of food promoting proper intestinal action. -rough'-house n. indoor brawl. [OE. ruh]

roulette n. game of chance played with a ball on a table with a revolving center. [F.]

round (rownd) a. spherical or cylindrical or circular or nearly so; roughly correct; large; plain. -adv with a circular or circuitous course. -n. something round in shape; rung; movement in a circle; recurrent duties; customary course, as of a postman or military patrol; cartridge for a firearm. -prep. about; on all sides of. v.t. make round; get round. -v. i. become round. -round-trip n. journey to a place and back again, usu. by the same route. round'-up n. driving of cattle together; arresting of criminals. [F. rond]

rouse (rowz) v.t. wake up, stir up, cause to rise. -v.i. waken. -rous'ing a. stirring. [orig. unknown]

rout (rowt) n. troop; disorderly crowd; large evening party; disorderly retreat. v.t. defeat decisively; throw into disarray. [L. rupta, broken]

route n. road, way. [F.]

routine' n. regular course; regularity of procedure. [F. fr. route]

rove v.i. wander without fixed destination. -v.t. wander over. -ro'ver n. one who roves; pirate. [orig. uncertain]

row n. number of things in a straight line. [OE. raw]

row v.i. propel a boat by oars. -v.t. propel by oars. -n. spell of rowing. [OE. rowan]

row n. uproar; dispute. [orig. uncertain]

row'an n. mountain ash. [Scand. orig.]

rowd'y n. rough. a. disorderly. [orig. uncertain]

row'el n. small wheel with points on a spur. [F. roue, wheel]

roy'al a. of, worthy of, befitting, patronzed by, a king or queen; splendid. -roy'alist n. supporter of monarchy. -roy'alty n. royal dignity or power; royal persons; payment to an owner of land for the right to work minerals, or to an inventor for use of his invention; payment to an author based on sales. [F. fr. L. regalia, fr. rex. reg-, king]

rub v.t. subject to friction; pass the hand over; abrade, chafe; remove by friction. v.i. come into contact accompanied by friction, become frayed or worn with friction. -rub'bing n. [orig. obscure]

rubb'er n. coagulated sap of rough, elastic consistency, of certain tropical trees; piece of rubber etc. used for erasing. -a. made of rubber; -rub'berize v.t. coat, impregnate, treat with rubber. -rub'bery a. -rub'berneck (sl.) n. person who gapes inquisitively; sightseer, tourist. -v.i. stare in naive or foolish manner. -rub'ber stamp n. device for imprinting dates, etc.; automatic authorization. [orig. obscure]

rubb'er n. series of three games at various card games; series of an odd number of games or contests at various games; two out of three games won. [orig. uncertain]

rubb'ish n. refuse, waste material; trash, nonsense. [orig. uncertain]

rub'ble n. irregular pieces of stone, brick, etc.; masonry made of this. [orig. uncertain. c.f. rubbish]

ru'by n. red precious stone; its color. -a. of this color. [L. ruber, red]

ruck n. a crease. -v.t. and i. to make or become wrinkled. [ON. hrukka]

ruck'sack n. pack carried on the back by hikers, climbers. [Ger. rüken. back, sack, bag]

rudd'er n. flat piece hinged to the stern of a ship, boat, airplane etc. to steer by. [OE. rothor, steering oar]

rudd'y a. of a fresh or healthy red; ruddyfaced. [OE. rudig]

rude a. primitive; roughly made; uneducated; uncivil. [L. rudis, rough]

ru'diment n. beginning, germ. -pl. elements, first principles. [L. rudis, rough]

rue v.t. and i. regret; repent; lament; suffer for. -n. repentance. [OE. hreowan]

ruff n. starched and frilled collar; bird with cuff of feathers. -(reeve fem.) -ruf'fle n. frilled cuff. -v.t. crumple, disorder; frill or pleat; annoy, put out. [orig. uncertain]

rug n. thick woolen wrap; floor-mat, of shaggy or thick-piled surface. -rugg'ed a. rough, broken; furrowed; unpolishable; harsh. [of Scand. orig.]

rug'by n. British football game, played with two teams of fifteen players each. -rugg'er n. (sl.) [Rugby school]

ru'in n. downfall; fallen or broken state; decay, destruction. -pl. ruined buildings, etc. -v.t. reduce to ruins; bring to decay or destruction, spoil; cause loss of fortune to. [L. ruina, fr. ruere, rush down]

rule n. a principle or precept; what is usual; government; strip of wood, etc., for measuring length. -v.t. govern, decide. -ru'ler n. one who governs; strip of wood, etc., for measuring or drawing straight lines. [OF. reule, fr. L. reguila-regere, govern]

rum n. spirit distilled from sugar cane. [orig. uncertain]

rum'ba n. Cuban dance. [Sp]

rum'ble v.i. make a noise as of distant thunder, a heavy cart moving along, etc. -n. such noise. [imit. orig.]

ru'minate v.i. chew and cud; meditate. -ru'minant a. cud-chewing. -n. cud-chewing animal. [L. ruminari, chew the cud]

ru'mor n. hearsay, common talk; current but unproved statement, usually rather vague. -v.t. put round as a rumor. [L. rumor, noise]

rump n. tail-end; buttocks. [ME. rumpe]

rum'ple v.t. crease or winkle. -n. crease. [of Teutonic orig.]

run v.i. move rapidly on the legs -n. act or spell of running, rush; tendency, course; space for keeping chickens. -runn'er n. -runner-up n. next after winner in a contest. -run'way n. pathway made by animals to and from feeding ground or water; level stretch of ground for aircraft landing and taking off. [OE. rinnan]

rung n. cross-bar or spoke, esp. in a ladder. [OE. hrung]

rup'ture n. breaking or breach; hernia. -v.t. and i. break or burst. [L. ruptura, fr. rumpere, break]

ru'ral a. of the country; rustic. -ru'rally adv. [L. ruralis, fr. rus, rur-, country]

ruse (-z-) n. stratagem, trick. [F.]

rush n. plant with a slender pithy stem growing in marshes, etc.; the stems as a material for baskets. [OE. rysc]

rush v.t. impel or carry along violently and rapidly; take by sudden assault. -v.i. move violently or rapidly. -n. a rushing; pressure of business affairs. [AF. russher, OF- ruser, drive back]

rusk n. piece of bread rebaked; various biscuits. (Sp. rosca, twist (of bread)]

rust n. reddish-brown coating formed on iron by oxidation and corrosion; disease of plants. -v.i. and v.t. contract or affect with rust. -rust'y a. -rust'less a. -rust'proof a, [OE.].

rust'ic a. of, or as of, country people; rural; of rude manufacture; made of untrimmed branches. -n. country-man, peasant. -rusti'city n. -rust'icate v.t. banish from a university. -v.i. live a country life. -rustica'tion n. [L. rusticus, fr. rus, country]

rus'tle (-sl-) v.i. make a sound as of brown dead leaves, etc.; steal, esp. cattle. -n. the sound. -rus'tler n. someone, something, that rustles; cattle thief. [imit. orig.]

rut n. periodical sexual excitement of the male deer and certain other animals. v.i. be under the influence of this. [F., fr. L. rugire, roar]

rut n. furrow made by a wheel; settled habit or way of living. -rutt'y a. [F. rotate, way, track, etc.]

ruth n. pity. -Ruth n. book of the Old Testament -ruth'less a. pitiless. -ruth'lessly adv. [rue]

rye n. grain used as fodder or for bread; plant bearing it.; whiskey made from it -rye-bread n. [OE. ryge]

S

Sabb'ath n. Jewish Sunday or seventh day, i.e. Christian Saturday. [Heb. shabbath]

sa'ber (-her) n. cavalry sword, slightly curved. -v.t. strike with one. [F.]

sa'ble n. small Arctic animal; its fur; black. -a. black. [OF.]

sab'ot n. wooden shoe worn by some European peasants. -sab'otage n. intentional damage done by workmen to their materials, etc -saboteur' n. [F.]

sac n. cavity in an animal or vegetable body. [F. = sack]

sacc'harin(e) a. pertaining to sugar. -n. extremely sweet substance from coal tar. [F., fr. G. sakcharon, sugar]

sa'chet n. small envelope or bag. [F.]

sack n. large bag, usually of some coarse textile material; (sl.) dismissal. -v.t. pillage (a captured town, etc.); (sl.) dismiss. -sack'-cloth n. coarse fabric used for sacks. -sacking n. material used for sacks. [Heb. saq]

sack n. dry wine; warmed and spiced drink. [F. vin sec, dry wine]

sacrament n. one of certain ceremonies of the Christian Church, esp. the Eucharist. -sacrament'al a. [L. sacramentum]

sa'cred a. dedicated, regarded as holy. -sa'credly adv. [OF. sacrer-, L. sacer, sacred]

sac'rifice n. making of an offering to a god; thing offered; giving something up for the sake of something else; act of giving up; thing so given up as a sacrifice. -v.t. offer as sacrifice. -sacrifi'cial a. pert. to sacrifice. [OF.]

sacrilege n. violation of something sacred. -sacrile'gious a. [F. fr. L. sacer, holy]

sac'rosanct a. secure by religious fear against desecration or violence. [L. sacrosametus fr. sacer, sacred]

sad a. sorrowful; deplorably bad; of color; dull, sober. -sad'ly adv. -sadd'en v.t. [OE. sced, sated]

sad'dle n. rider's seat to fasten on a horse, or form part of a bicycle, etc.; part of a shaft; joint of mutton or venison; ridge of a hill. -v.t. put a saddle on -sadd'le-back n. hill with saddle-shaped depression on top. -sadd'le-bag n. bag hung from horse's or bicycle saddle. -sadd'le-bow n. arched front of saddle. -sadd'le-cloth n. cloth placed on horse's back under saddle. -sadd'ler n. maker of saddles, etc. -sadd'lery n. -sad'dle-tree n. saddle frame. [OE. sadol]

sa'dism (-a-) n. psychological perversion involving delight in cruelty; (colloq.) love of cruelty. [Marquis de Sade, 1740-1814]

safa'ri n. (party) making overland (hunting) trip, esp. in Africa. [Swahili]

safe a. uninjured, out of danger; not involving risk; cautious; trustworthy. -n. strong box; ventilated cupboard for meat, etc. -safe'ly adv. -safe'ty n. -safecon'duct n. passport or permit to pass somewhere. -safe'-guard n. protection. -v.t. protect. -safety-curtain n. in theater, fire-proof curtain. -safe'ty-lamp n. miner's lamp constructed to prevent its flame igniting flammable gases. -safety-valve n. valve allowing escape of excess steam etc.; outlet for emotion. [F. sauf, fr. L salvos]

saff'ron n. orange-red coloring matter obtained from the crocus. -a. of this color.[F. safran]

sag v.i. sink in the middle, hang sideways or curve downwards under pressure. [of Teut. orig.]

sa′ga n. medieval tale of Norse heroes; any such long tale of events. [ON. cp. *saw*]

sage n. aromatic herb. [F. *sauge*, fr. L. *salvia*]

sage a. wise, discreet. -n. very wise man. -sage′ly adv. [F., fr. L. *sapere*, be wise]

Sagitta′rius n. (The Archer) 9th sign of Zodiac, operative Nov. 22-Dec. 20; southern constellation. [L. *Sagitta*, arrow]

sail n. piece of canvas stretched to catch the wind for propelling a ship; windcatching appliance forming the arm of a windmill; ships collectively; act of sailing. -v.i. travel by water; begin a voyage. -v.t. navigate. -sail′board n. craft used for windsurfing, consisting of a molded board like a surfboard, to which a mast bearing a single sail is attached by a swivel joint. -sail′or n. [OE. segl]

saint adj. holy; title of a canonized person. -n. one who has been canonized. -saint′ly adj. -saint′ed a. canonized; sacred. -saint′liness n. -St. Bernard n. kind of large dog used to rescue travellers in the snow. n. -St. Vitus's dance n. chores. [F., fr. L. *sanctus*, consecrated]

sake n. for the sake of, on behalf of, to please or benefit, or get, or keep. [OE. *sacu*, dispute at law]

sake′, saki′ n. Japanese alcoholic drink made from fermented rice. [*Jap.*]

sal′ad n. uncooked vegetables as food; lettuce or other plant suitable for this use. [F. *salade*]

sala′mi, n. highly-spiced sausage. [It.]

sal′ary n. fixed payment of persons employed in non-manual or non-mechanical work. -sal′aried a. [L. *solarium*, soldiers' pay]

sale n. a selling; special disposal of stock t low prices; auction. -sales′man n. shop assistant or traveler. -sales′manship n. -sale′price n. special price at a sale. [OE. *sala*]

sa′line n. fruit salt. -a. salty. [L. *salinus*]

sali′va n. liquid which forms in the mouth. -sali′vary a. [L.]

sall′ow n. kind of willow. [OE. *sealh*]

sall′ow a. of a sickly yellow or pale in color. [OE. *sato*]

sall′y v.i. rush; set out. -n. a rushing out, *esp*. from a fort; an outburst; witty remark. [F. *saillir*, rush]

salm′on (sam′-) n. large silvery-scaled fish with orange-pink flesh valued as food; color of its flesh. -a. of this color. [OF. *aulmon*, fr. L. *salmon*]

sal′on (-ong) n. drawing-room; reception graced by celebrities. [F.]

saloon′ n. large reception room; public dining-room; principal cabin or sitting-room in a passenger ship; Pullman car on a railway; public place where liquor is sold and consumed. [F. *salon*]

salt (solt) n. sodium chloride, a substance which gives sea-water its taste; chemical compound of an acid and a metal. -a. preserved with, or full of, or tasting like, salt. -v.i. preserved with salt; put salt on. -salt′ern n. salt works. -salt′ing n. area of low ground regularly inundated with salt water. -sailt′y

a. -salt′ness n. -salt′-cellar n. small vessel for salt on the table. -salt lake n. inland lake of high salinity resulting from inland drainage in an and area of high evaporation. -salt marsh n. area of marshy ground that is intermittently inundated with salt water or that retains pools or rivulets of salt or brackish. -salt′peter n. potassium nitrate used in gunpowder. [OE. *sealt*]

sal′utary n. wholesome, resulting in good. [L. *salutaris*]

salute′ v.t. greet with words or sign. -v.i. perform a military salute. -n. word or sign by which one greets another: prescribed motion of the arm as a mark of respect to a superior, *etc.*, in military usage. -saluta′tion n. [L. *salus, salut-*, health]

sal′vage n. payment for saving a ship from danger; act of saving a ship or other property from danger; property or materials so saved. [OF.]

salva′tion n. fact or state of being saved. -salva′tionist n. member of religious group, Salvation Army. -salve v. save from peril. [L. *salvus*, safe]

salve n. healing ointment. -v.i. anoint with such. [OE. *sealf*]

same a. identical, not different, unchanged, unvarying. -same′ness n. monotony. [ON. *samr*]

sa′mite (sa-) n. medieval heavy silk stuff. [OF. *samit*]

sam′pan n. Chinese boat, sculled from stern, *usu.* with a sail and a cabin made of mats. (Chin. *sam*, three, *pan*, board]

sam′phire n. herb found on rocky coasts; St. Peter's wort; sea-feud. [F. *Saint-Pierre*, St. Peter]

sam′ple n. specimen. -v.i. take or give a sample of. -sam′pler a. beginner's exercise in embroidery. [for ME. *essample*, See **example**]

sanatoriums n. establishment for the treatment of invalids, *esp*, by therapy and diet; health resort. [L.]

sanc′tify v.t. set apart as holy; free from sin. -sanctifica′tion n. -sanctimo′nious a. making a show of piety. -sanc′tity n. saintliness, sacredness; inviolability. -sanc′tuary n. holy place; place where a fugitive was safe from arrest or violence. -sanc′tum n. sacred place or shrine; person's private room. [L. *sanctus*, holy]

sanc′tion n. penalty or reward following the breaking or observing of a law; treaty; permission with authority; countenance given by custom. -n.pl. boycott or other coercive measure, *esp*. by one state against another regarded as having violated a law, right *etc*. -v.i. allow or authorize. [L. *sanctus*, holy]

sand n. powdery substance made by the wearing down of rock. -pl. stretches or banks of this, usually forming a seashore. -v.t. cover or mix with sand. -sand′stone n. rock composed of sand. -sand′bag n. bag filled with sand or earth and used in fortification. -sand′paper n. paper with sand stuck on it for scraping or polishing wood, *etc.* -sand′piper *n.* longlegged wading bird. *etc.* -sand'y *a.* [OE.]

san'dal *n.* shoe consisting of a sole attached by straps. [G. *sandalon*]

sand'wich *n.* two slices of bread with meat or other substance between. *-v.t.* insert between two other different things. [Earl of *Sandwich* (d. 1792)]

sane *a.* of sound mind, sensible. -san'ity *n.* [L. *sanus*, healthy]

san'guine (sang-gwin) *a.* hopeful or confident; florid. [L. *sanguis, sanguin-*, blood]

san'itary *a.* promoting health by protection against dirt, *etc.* -sanitar'ium *n.* sanatorium. -sanita'tion *n.* improving of sanitary conditions. [L. *Sanitas*]

Sans'krit *n.* ancient classical language of India. [Sans. *Sam*, together, *kr*. make]

San'ta Claus' in nursery folk lore, gift-bringer of Christmas Eve, riding over the roofs in a sled drawn by reindeer. [Du. *Sint Klaas*, St. Nicholas]

sap *n.* juice of plants. -sap'ling *n.* young tree. [OE. *scep*]

sap *n.* covered trench approaching a besieged place or enemy trench. *-v.t.* construct such trenches. *-v.* i. undermine; destroy insidiously. -sapp'er *n.* one who saps; Royal Engineer. [It. *zappa*, spade]

Sapph'ic *a.* of Sappho, Grecian poetess; verse of 3 lines of 5 feet each, followed by line of 2 feet. *-n.* sapphic verse. [*Sappho*]

sapph'ire (saf-) *n.* blue precious stone. [G. *sappheiros*]

sarcasm *n.* bitter or wounding ironic remarks; such remarks; power of using them. -sarcast'ic *a.* -sarcast'ically *adv.* [G. *sarkasmos*]

sarcophagus *n.* stone coffin; stone used for it. [G. *sarkophagos*]

sard, sar'dius *n.* precious stone, variety of chalcedony. [*Sardis* in Lydia]

sardine' *n.* small fish of herring family, usually packed in oil. [F.]

sardon'ic *a.* of a smile or laughter, bitter, scornful. [L. *sardonius*]

sa'ri *n.* Hindu woman's outer garment, a long straight piece of cotton, silk. [Hind.]

sarong' n. skirtlike garment worn in Asian and Pacific countries. [Malay, *sarung*]

sash *n.* frame forming a window, usually sliding up or down. [F. *chdssis*]

sash *n.* scarf wound around the body. [Arab. *shash*]

Sa'tan *n.* the devil. [Low L.]

sat'chel *n.* small bag, or bag for school books. (L. *saccellus*, a small sack]

sate *v.t.* gratify to the full; glut. [earlier *sade*, make sad]

sat'ellite *n.* in astronomy, planet revolving round another; man-made projectile orbiting a planet; person or country dependent on another. [L. *satellites, pl.*]

satiate *v.t.* satisfy to the full; surfeit. -sa'tiable *a.* -satia'tion *n.* -sati'ety *n.* feeling of having had too much. [L. *satiare-satis*, enough]

sat'in *n.* silk fabric with a glossy surface. -

sateen' *n.* glossy cotton or woolen fabric. -sat'inwood *n.* ornamental wood of a tropical tree. -sat'iny *a.* [F., from It. *seta*, silk]

sat'ire (-Ir) *n.* composition in which vice or folly, or a foolish person, is held up to ridicule; use of ridicule or sarcasm to expose vice and folly. -satir'ic, satirica *a.* -sat'irist *n.* -sat'irize *v.t.* [L. *satura*, poetic medley]

sat'isfy *v.t.* content, meet the wishes of, pay, fulfill, supply adequately; convince; be sufficient. -satisfac'tion *n.* -satisfac'tory *a.* [L. *satisfacere*]

saturate *v.t.* soak thoroughly; cause to dissolve a maximum amount. -satura'tion *n.* -sat'uration point *n.* point at which no more (people, things, ideas, *etc.*) can be absorbed, accommodated, used. etc; in chemistry, the point at. which no more solute can be dissolved in a solution or gaseous material absorbed in a vapor. [L. *saturate*]

Sat'urday *n.* seventh day of the week. Jewish Sabbath. [*Saturn*]

Sat'urn *n.* Roman god; one of the major planets. -sat'urnine *a*, gloomy; sluggish in temperament. -saturn'alia *n.* ancient festival of Saturn; noisy orgy or revel. [L. *Saturnus*, god of agricultura]

sat'yr (-r) *n,* woodland god, part man and part goat. -satyr'ic *a.* [G. *satyros*]

sauce *n.* liquid added to food to give relish. *-v.t.* add sauce to. -sauce'pan *n.* cooking-pot. -sau'cy *a.* impudent, cheeky. -sau'cily *adv.* [F.]

sau'cer *n.* curved plate put under a cup, *etc.*, to catch spilt liquid. [OF. *saussiere*]

saunter *v.i.* walk in leisurely manner, stroll. *-n.* leisurely walk or stroll. [AF. *sauntrer*, adventure]

sausage *n.* minced meat enclosed in a tube of thin membrane. -saus'age-meat *n.* [F. *saucisse*]

sau'té *a.* fried lightly and quickly. [F.]

savage *a.* uncivilized, primitive; wild. *-n.* member of a savage tribe, barbarian. *-v.t.* attack with trampling, biting. sav'agery *n.* -sav'agely *adv.* [F. *sauvage*, fr. L. *silva*, wood]

sav'ant *n.* learned man. [F.]

save *v.t.* rescue, preserve; keep for the future, lay by; prevent the need of. *-v.i.* lay by money. *-prep.* except. *conj.* but. -sa'ving *a*, frugal. *-n.pl.* what is saved, laid by. -sa'vior *n.* deliverer or redeemer; Christ. [F. *sauver*, fr. L. *saluare*]

savoir-faire' (-war-fer') *n.* tact; knowing what to do. -savoir-vivre' *n.* knowledge of polite usages; social adequacy; good breeding. [F.]

sa'vor *n.* characteristic taste. *-v.i.* smack of -sa'vory *a.* having an appetizing taste or smell. *-n.* savory dish at beginning or end of dinner; aromatic mint. [L. *sapor*]

savoy' *n.* variety of cabbage. [*Savoy*]

saw *n.* old saying, maxim. [OE. *sagu*]

saw *n.* tool for cutting wood, *etc.* toothed. *-v.t.* cut with a saw. *-v.i.* make the movements of sawing. -saw'dust *n.* fine wood dust made in sawing. -saw'fish *n.* fish armed with a toothed snout. -saw'mill *n.* one for mechanical sawing of timber. -**saw'pit** *n.* pit in which one of wielders of two-handed saw stands. -**saw'yer** *n.* workman who saws timber. [OE. *saga*]

sax'horn *n.* instrument of the trumpet class. -**sax'ophone** *n.* large instrument like a clarinet. [invented by C. J. *Sax*, a Belgian (d. 1865)]

say *v.t.* utter or deliver with the speaking voice; state; express; take as an example or as near enough; deliver an opinion. -*n.* what one has to say; chance of saying it; share in a decision. -**say'ing** *n.* maxim, proverb. [OE. *secgan*]

scab' *n.* crust formed over a wound; skin disease; disease of plants; somebody who works while his colleagues are on strike. **scabb'y** *a.* -**scab'land s** *pl.n.* type of terrain consisting of bare rock surfaces deeply channelled by glacial floodwaters. [ON. *skabbi*]

scabb'ard *n.* sheath for sword or dagger. [OF. *escalberc*]

scald (skold) *v.t.* injure with boiling liquid or steam; clean with boiling water. -*n.* injury by scalding. [ONF. *escaider*, fr. L. *calidus*, hot]

scald (skold) *n.* ancient Scandinavian poet. [ON. *skaid*]

scale *n.* pan of a balance; weighing instrument. -*v.t.* weigh in scales; have the weight of. [ON. *skal*, bowl]

scale *n.* one of the plates forming the outer covering of fishes and reptiles; thin flakes. -*v.t.* remove the scales from. -*v.i.* come off in scales. -**sca'ly** *a.* -**sca'liness** *n.* [OF. *escale*, husk]

scale *n.* series of musical notes, degrees, or graduations; steps of graduating measuring instrument; relative size, ratio of enlarging or reduction (*e.g.* in a map, *etc.*). -*v.t.* climb; attack with ladders. [L. *scala*, ladder]

sca'lene *a.* of a triangle, having its three sides unequal. [G. *skalenos*]

scallion *n.* variety of shallot; green onion. [L. *cepa Ascalonia*, onion of Ascalon]

scall'op *n.* edible shellfish; edging in small curves imitating the edge of a scallop shell. -*v.t.* shape in this way; cook in a scallop shell or a dish resembling one. [OF. *escalope*, shell]

scalp *n.* skin and hair of the top of the head. -*v.t.* cut off the scalp of; reprimand severely. [contr. of *scallop*]

scalper *n.* small surgical knife. -**scal'per** *n.* engraver's gouge. [L. *scalpere*, cut]

scamp'er *v.i.* run about; run hastily from place to place. -*n.* scampering. [fr. *scamp*, rascal]

scan *v.t.* look at carefully; measure or read (verse) by its metrical feet; examine, search by systematically varying the direction or a radar or sonar beam; glance over quickly. -*n.* -**scann'er** *n.* one that scans. -**scan'sion** *n.* analysis or metrical structure of verse. [L. *scandere*, climb]

scand'al *n.* malicious gossip; feeling that something is an outrage or cause of discussion; thing causing such feeling. **scan'dalize** *v.t.* shock. -**scan'dalous** *a.* outrageous; disgraceful. -**scan'dal-monger** *n.* one who spreads malicious rumors. [G. *skandalon*, cause of stumbling]

scanner *n.* (*compute.*) input device that reads symbols, codes, text, or graphics, by passing a light or laser beam over them.

scant *a.* barely sufficient; not sufficient. -*v.t.* put on short allowance; supply grudgingly. -**scant'y** *a.* -**scant'ily** *adv.* -**scantiness** *n.* [ON. *skamt*, short]

scape *n.* and *v.t.* (*arch.*) escape. -**scape'-goat** *n.* person unwillingly bearing blame due to others. -**scape'grace** *n.* incorrigible fellow. [*escape*]

scap'ula *n.* shoulder-blade. -**scap'ular** *a.* of the shoulder. -**scap'ulary** *n.* small shoulder-garment worn as badge of a religious order. [L.]

scar *n.* mark left by a healed wound, burn or sore. -*v.t.* mark with a scar. -*v.i.* heal with a scar. [ON. *scarth*, cleft]

scar *n.* rocky face of hillside. [ON. *sker*, skerry]

scarce *a.* hard to find; existing or available in insufficient quantity. -**scarce'ly** *adv.* only just; not quite. **scarce'ness** *n.* -**scar'city** *n.* [OF. *escars*]

scare *v.t.* frighten. -*n.* fright or panic. -**sca'ry** *a.* timid. [ON. *skirra*]

scarf *n.* scarfs, scarves, *pl.* long narrow strip of material to put round neck, shoulders, *etc.* [OE. *scearfe*, piece]

scarf *v.t.* join two timbers. [Sw. *scarfa*]

scarify *v.t.* scratch or cut slightly all over; criticize mercilessly. -**scarifica'tion** *n.* [L. *scarificare*]

scar'let *n.* brilliant red color; cloth or clothing of this color, *esp.* military uniform. -*a.* of this color. -**scar'let fe'ver** *n.* infectious fever with a scarlet rash. [Pers. *saqirtat*, broadcloth]

scathe (-TH) *n.* injury. -*v.t.* injure, especially by withering up. -**scathe'less** *a.* unharmed. [ON. *skatha*]

scatter *v.t.* throw or put here and there; sprinkle. -*v.i.* disperse. -**scatt'er-brained** *a.* giddy, thoughtless. [orig. uncertain]

scavenger *n.* one employed in cleaning streets, removing refuse, *etc.* -**scav'enge** *v.i.* clean (streets). -*v.i.* work as a scavenger; originally a kind of Customs Inspector. [OF. *escauuer*, inspect]

scene (sen) *n.* place of the action of a novel, play, *etc.*; place of any action; subdivision of a play; view; episode; stormy conversation, *esp.* with display of temper. -**sce'nery** *n.* stage scenes; natural features of a district. -**sce'nic** *a.* picturesque; of, or on, the stage. -**scenar'io** *n.* written version of a play to be produced by cinematograph. [L. *scena*]

scent (a-) *v.t.* track by smell; detect; give a perfume to. -*n.* smell; liquid perfume. [F. *sentir*, smell]

scep'ter (s-) *n.* ornamental staff as a symbol of royal power; royal or imperial dignity. [G. *skeptron*, staff]

sched'ule (sk-) *n.* plan or procedure of a project; list; timetable. -*v.t.* enter in a schedule; plan to occur at a certain time. [Late L. *scedula*, small scroll]

sche'ma *n.* image to aid the process of thought; synopsis; diagrammatic outline. -

scheme 198 scratch

schemat'ic a. [*scheme*]

scheme (sk-) n. plan or design; project; list or table; outline or syllabus. -v.i. make plans, especially as a secret intrigue. -v.t. plan, bring about. -**schema** n. (*compute.*) logical structure, plan, or method by which data are organized in a database system. -**sche'mer** n. -**sche'ming** a. plotting, intriguing. [G. *schema*, form]

schis'm (sizm) n. division in a church or party. -**schismat'ic** n. and a. -**schis'mat'ical** a. [G. *schisma*, cleft]

schist (shist) n. crystalline rock which splits into layers. -**schist'ose** a. [G. *schiotos*, split stone]

schizophrenia n. split personality; dementia præcox, a mental disorder. -**schizophren'ic** a. [G. *schizein*, cleave, *phren*, mind]

school n. institution for teaching or for giving instruction in any subject; buildings of such institution; time of lessons; group of thinkers, writers, artists, *etc.*, with principles or methods in common. -v.t. educate; bring under control, train. -**school'man** n. medieval philosopher. -**schol'ar** n. one taught in a school; one quick to learn; learned person; person holding a scholarship. -**schol'arly** a. -**schol'arship** n. learning; prize or grant to a student for payment of school or college fees. -**scholast'ic** a. relating to schools or schoolmen; pedantic. [G. *schole*, leisure; place for discussion]

school (sk-) n. shoal (of fish, whales, *etc.*). [Du. *school*, crowd]

schooner (sk-) n. ship having fore and aft sails or two or more masts. [orig. uncertain]

sciatica (si-) n. pain in the sciatic nerve. -**sciat'ic** a. of the hip. [Low L.]

science n. systematic knowledge; investigation of this; any branch of study concerned with a body of observed material facts. -**scientif'ic** a. -**scientif'ically** adv. -**sci'entist** n. [L. *scientia*, knowledge]

scimitar (a-) n. short, single-edged curved sword. [F. *cimeterre*]

scintilla (a-) n. spark. -**scin'tillate** v.i. sparkle. -**scintilla'tion** n. [L.]

scissors (siz'-) n. pl. cutting instrument of two blades pivoted together so that the edges slip over each other. [OF. *cisoires*]

sclerosis n. hardening of bodily organs, tissues *etc.* [G. *skleros*, hard] [*See* **arteriosclerosis**]

scoff (sk-) n. taunt; mocking words. -v.i. jeer, mock. -**scoff'er** n. -**scoff'ing'ly** adv. [of Teut. orig.]

scold (sk-) n. nagging woman. -v.i. find fault noisily. -v.t. rebuke. [ON. *skald*, poet, later lampooner]

sconce n. bracket candlestick on a wall. [orig. screened lantern. OF. *esconce*]

scone (skon) n. round griddle cake. [SC. fr. Du. *schoonbrot*, fine bread]

scoop n. article for ladling; kind of shovel; tool for hollowing out. -v.t. ladle out; hollow out or rake in with a scoop; exclusive newsstory. [of Teut. orig.]

scoot v.i. (*sl.*) move off quickly. -**scoot'er** n. toy consisting of small platform with two wheels and a guiding handle, to carry one person. [Sw. *skjuta*, shoot (v.i.)]

scope n. range of activity or applications room, play. [It. *scopo*, target]

scorch v.i. burn the surface of. -v.i. be burnt on the surface. -**scorched' earth' policy** (of a retreating army) of laying waste as it goes. [orig. uncertain]

score n. group or set of twenty; cut, notch, stroke, or mark; written or printed piece of orchestral music; tally; reason; sake; number of points made in a game, measure of weight, 20 lbs. -v.i. notch or mark; cross out; record; make (points) in a game. -v.i. achieve a success. -**scor'er** n. [ON. *skor*, notch]

scorn n. contempt, derision. [OF. *escarnir*]

scorpion n. small lobster-shaped animal with a sting at the end of its jointed tail. -**Scorpio** n. 8th sign of the zodiac, which sun enters about 22nd October. [L. *scorpio*]

scot n. payment or a person's share of it. -**scotfree'** a. free from payment, punishment, *etc.* [ON. *skot*]

Scot n. native of Scotland. -**Scott'ish** a. (also Scotch, Scots). -**Scots'man** n. -**scott'icism** n. Scottish turn of speech. **Scotch** n. or Scotland; Scotch whiskey. **Scotch' terrier**, short-legged, long-bodied rough terrier. [OE. *Scottas* (pl.), Irishmen]

scoun'drel n. villain. -**scound'relly** a. [orig. uncertain]

scour v.t. clear or polish by rubbing; clear out. [OF. *escurer*]

scourge (skurj) n. whip or lash; an evil pest or plague. -v.t. flog. [OF. *escorgiee*]

scout n. man sent out to reconnoiter; ship used for reconnoitering; small fast airplane; Boy Scout or Girl Scout. -v.i. go out or act as a scout. [OF. *escoute*]

scow n. large flat-bottomed boat. [Du. *schouw*]

scowl v.t. frown gloomily or sullenly. -n. gloomy frown. [of Scand. orig.]

scram v.i. to clear off, to depart hurriedly (when unwanted) [U.S. *slang*]

scram'ble v.i. move along or up by crawling, climbing, *etc.*, struggle with others for; cook (eggs) by stirring them, when broken, in the pan. -n. scrambling; disorderly proceeding. [orig. uncertain]

scrap n. small detached piece of fragment; fight, quarrel. -**scrapp'y** a. -**scrap'-book** n. book in which scraps, cuttings are pasted. [ON. *skrap*]

scrape v.i. rub with something sharp; clean or smooth in this way; rub with harsh noise. -v.i. make an awkward bow. -n. act or sound of scraping; awkward situation, *esp.* one resulting from an escapade. -**scra'per** n. [OE. *scrapian*]

scratch v.t. score or mark a narrow surface wound with claws, nails, or anything pointed; make marks on with pointed instruments; remove from a list. v.i. use claws or nails. -n. wound or mark or sound made by scratching; line or starting point. -a. got together at short notice; impromptu. **-scratch'ily** a. [mixture of earlier *scrat* and *crotch*, both of Teut. orig.]

scrawl v.t. write or draw untidily. -n. something scrawled; careless writing. [orig. uncertain]

scream v.i. utter a piercing cry; whistle or hoot shrilly. -n. shrill piercing cry; (sl.) something ludicrous. **-scream'er** n. [imit. orig.]

screech v.i. and n. scream. **-screechowl** n. barn-owl. [earlier *scratch*, of imit. orig.]

screen n. piece of furniture to shelter from heat, light, draught or observation; anything used for such purpose; sheet or board to display cinema pictures, etc., wooden or stone partition in a church. -v.t. shelter or hide; protect from detection; sift, assort, as coal; examine a person's political antecedents. [OF. *escren*]

screw n. cylinder with a spiral ridge running round it, outside or inside; ship's propeller; turn of a screw; twist; miser; worn-out horse. -v.t. fasten with a screw; press or stretch with a screw; obtain by pressure, extort; work by turning, twist round. [OF. *escroue*]

scrib'ble v.t. wrote or draw carelessly. v.i. write or draw carelessly; make meaningless marks with a pen or pencil. -n. something scribbled. [*scribe*]

scribe n. writer; copyist; author. [L. *scribere*, write]

scrimmage n. scuffle. [*skirmish*]

scrimp v.t. and i. make short or scanty; limit; straiten. **-scrimp'y** a. scanty. [OE. *scrimpan*]

scrip n. small wallet. [OF. escrepe]

scrip n. certificate of holding stocks or shares. [for *subscription* (receipt)]

script n. handwriting; written characters. **-script'ure** n. sacred writings; the Bible. **-script'ural** adv. [L. *scribere, script-*, write]

scrivener n. copyist or clerk. [L. *scrihere, script-*, write]

scroll n. roll or parchment of paper; list; ornament shaped like a scroll of paper. [OF. *escrou*]

scrounge' (-ow-) v.t. and i. (sl.) pinch; cadge. **-scroung'er** n. [orig. unknown]

scrub v.t. clean with a hard brush and water. -n. a scrubbing. **-scrubb'ing- brush** n. [obs. Du. *schrubben*]

scruff n. nape (of neck). [of Teut. orig.]

scrum'mage, scrum n. in Rugby football, close skirmish between opposing forwards. [var. of *scrimmage*]

scru'ple n. small weight; feeling of doubt about a proposed action; conscientious objection. -v.i. hesitate. **-scru'pulous** a. extremely conscientious, thorough; attentive to small points of conscience. **-scrupulos'ity** n. [L. *scrupulus*, small sharp stone]

scru'tiny n. investigation, official examination of votes; searching look. **-scrutineer'** n. examiner o f votes. scrutinize v.t . examine closely. **scru'table** a. [L. *scrutari*, examine closely]

scuf'fle v.i. struggle at close quarters. -n. confused struggle. [Sw. *skuffa*, push]

scull n. oar used for the stern of a boat; short oar used in pairs. -v.t. and i. propel or move

by means of a scull or sculls. [orig. unknown]

sculpture n. art of forming figures in relief or solid; product of this art. -v.t. represent, by sculpture. [L. *sculpere, sculpt-*, carve]

scum n. froth or other floating matter on a liquid; waste part of anything. [OF. *escume*]

scurrilous a. coarse or indecent language. **-scurril'ity** n. [L. *scurrilis*]

scurr'y v.i. run hastily. -n. bustling haste. [orig. uncertain]

scur'vy n. disease due to lack of fresh vegetable food. -a. afflicted with the disease; mean, low, contemptible. [*scurg*]

scut'tle v.i. rush away. [freq. of *scud*]

scut'tle n. lidded opening in the side or deck of a ship. -v.i. make a hole in a ship, esp. to sink it, or to salve the cargo. [OF. *escoutile*, hatchway]

scythe (sith) n. mowing implement consisting of a long curved blade swung by a bent handle held in both hands. -v.t. cut with a scythe. [OE. *sithe*]

sea n. mass of solid water covering most of the earth; broad tract of this; waves; swell. **-sea'board** n. coast. **-sea-cow** n. dugong. **-sea'-dog** n. old sailor. seafaring a. occupied in sea voyages. sea-gull n. gull. **-sea-horse** n. fabulous sea-monster; walrus; warm-water fish remarkable for its horse-like head. **-sea'man** n. sailor. **-sea'weed** n. plant growing in the sea. **-sea'worthy** a. in a fit condition to put to sea. **-sea'plane** n. amphibious aircraft. **-sea'power**, nation's naval strength. **-sea ur'chin** n. marine annual with globular body enclosed in rigid, spine-covered shell. [OE. *sce*]

seal n. amphibious marine animal with flippers as limbs, of which some varieties have valuable fur. -v.i . hunt seals. seal'skin n. skin or fur of seals. **-seal'er** n. man or ship engaged in sealing. [OF. *seolh*]

seal n. piece of metal or stone engraved with a device for impression on wax, etc., impression made by this (on letters, documents, etc.) -v.t. affix a seal to; ratify; mark with a stamp as evidence of some quality; keep close, or secret; settle, as doom. **-seal'ing wax** n. [OF. *seet*, fr. L. *sigillum*, seal]

seam n. line of junction of two edges, e.g., of two pieces of cloth, or two planks; thin layer of stratum. -v.t. mark with furrows or wrinkles. [OE.]

sé'ance n. session of a public body; meeting of Spiritualists. [F.]

sear v.t. scorch or brand with a hot iron; deaden. [OE. *seartan*]

search v.t. look over or through in order to find something; probe into. -v.i. explore. look for something. -n. act of searching; quest. **-search'ing** a. keen thorough. **-search'light** n. electric arelight which sends a concentrated beam in any desired direction. **-search-warrant** n. authorization enabling police to search house etc., [F. *chercher*]

seas'on n. one of the four divisions of the year associated with a type of weather and a stage of agriculture; proper time; period during which something happens, grows, is active, *etc. -v.t.* bring into sound condition; flavor with salt or condiments, *etc.* -seas'onable *a.* suitable for the season. -seas'onal *a.* depending on, or varying with seasons. -seas'oning *n.* flavoring materials. [F. *saison,* fr. L. *satio,* sowing]

seat *n.* thing made or used for sitting on: manner of sitting (of riding, *etc.*); right to sit (*e.g.,* in a council, etc.,); sitting part of the body; locality of a disease, trouble, *etc.,* country house. -v.t. make to sit; provide sitting accommodation for. [ON. *salti*]

sec'ant *a.* cutting. -n. line that cuts another; *(trig.)* line from center of a circle through one end of an arc, cutting the tangent from the other end. [L. *secare,* cut]

secede *v.i.* withdraw from a federation, *etc.* -seces'sion *n.* -seces'sionist *n.* [L. *secedere, secess-,* go apart]

seclude *v.t.* guard from, remove from sight or resort, -seclu'sion *n.* [L. *secludere, seclus-,* shut away]

sec'ond *a.* next after the first. -n. person or thing coming second; one giving aid, *esp.* assisting a principal in a duel; sixtieth part of a minute. -v.t. support further; support (a motion in a meeting) so that discussion may be in order. -sec'ondly *adv.* -sec'ondary *a.* subsidiary, or of less importance; of education, coming between primary and university stages. -sec'ondarily *adv.* -sec'onder *n.* -sec'cond-hand *a.* buy after use by a previous owner, not original. -sec'ond-rate *a.* inferior, mediocre. -sec'ond sight*', faculty of prophetic vision. [L. *secundus*]

se'cret *a.* kept or meant to be kept from general knowledge; hidden, -n. something kept secret. -se'cretly *adv.* se'crecy *n.* a keeping or being kept secret; ability to keep secrets. -se'cretive *a.* uncommunicative. -se'cretiveness *n.* [L. *secretus,* separated]

sec'retary *n.* one employed by another to deal with papers and correspondence, keep records, prepare business, *etc.*; official in charge of certain departments of government. -secreta'rial *a.* -secretar'iat *n.* body of officials led by a secretary; body of secretaries. -sec'retaryship *n.* [Med. L. *secretarius*]

secrete' *v.t.* hide; of a gland, *etc.,* collect and supply a particular substance in the body. [L. *secernere, secret-,* to put apart]

sect *n.* party within a church; religious denomination. -sect'ary *n.* -secta'rian *a.* [L. *sequi, sect-,* follow]

sec'tion *n.* cutting; part cut off, drawing of anything as if cut through. -sec'tional *a.* -sec'tor *n.* a part of a circle enclosed by two radii and the arc which they cut off, a subdivision of the front occupied by an army. [L. *secare, sect-,* cut]

sec'ular *a.* wordly; lay; not monastic; lasting for, or occurring once in, an age-sec'ularist *n.* one who would exclude religion from schools. -sec'ularism *n.* sec'ularize *v.t.* transfer from religious to lay possession or use. -seculariza'tion *n.* [L. *secularis,* fr. *seculum,* age, century]

secure' *a.* safe; free from care; firmly fixed. -v.t. make safe; free (a creditor) from risk of loss; make firm; gain possession of. -secure'ly *adv.* -secu'rity *n.* [L. *secur-us*]

sedate' *a.* calm, collected, serious. **sedate'ly** *adv.* -sed'ative *a.* soothing. -n. soothing drug. -sed'entary *a.* sitting much; done in a chair. [L. *sedere,* sit]

sed'iment *n.* matter which settles to the bottom of liquid. [L. *sedimentum-sedere,* sit]

sedi'tion *n.* talk or speech urging to rebellion. -sedi'tious *a.* [L. *seditio,* a going apart]

seduce' *v.t.* lead astray, persuade to commit some sin or folly; induce (a woman) to surrender her chastity. -seduc'tion *n.* -seduct'ive *a.* alluring, winning. [L. *seducere, seduct-,* lead away]

see *v.t.* perceive with the eyes or mentally; find out, reflect; come to know; interview. -v.i. perceive; understand. -seer *n.* prophet. -see'ing *conj.* since. [OE. *seon*]

see *n.* diocese and work of a bishop. [OF. *sie,* fr. L. *sedere,* sit]

seed *n.* reproductive germs of flowering plants; one grain of this; such grains saved or used for sowing; offspring. -v.t. produce seed. -v.i. sow with seed. -seed'ling *n.* young plant raised from seed. [OE. *soed*]

seek *v.t.* make search or enquiry for. -v.i. search. [OE. *secant*]

seem *v.i.* appear (to be or to do). -seem'ingly *adv.* -seem'ly *a.* becoming and proper. -seem'liness *n.* [ON. *soma*]

seep *v.i.* oak through; ooze. [OE. *sipean*]

seer. *See* see.

see'saw *n.* game in which children sit at opposite ends of a plank supported in the middle and swing up and down, plank used for this. -v.i. move up and down. [redupl. on *saw*]

seethe *v.t.* boil, cook or soak in hot liquid. -v.i. be agitated or in confused movement. [OE. *seothan,* boil]

seg'ment *n.* piece cut off, section; part of a circle cut off by a straight line. [L. *segmentum*]

segregate *v.t.* set apart from the rest. -segrega'tion *n.* [L. *segregate,* remove from the flock, *grex, greg-*]

segue (-gwi) *v.i.* proceed from one section or piece of music to another without a break; (imperative) play on without pause; a musical direction. *n.* practice or an instance of playing music in this way. [It. *seguire,* follow]

seine (son) *n.* large upright fishing net. [F.]

seis'm (sizm) *n.* earthquake. -seis'mic *a.* of earthquakes. -seis'micity *n.* seismic activity; the phenomenon of earthquake activity or the occurrence of artificially produced earth tremors. -seis'mograph *n.* instrument to record earthquakes. -seismol'ogy *n.* science of earthquakes. [G. *seismos,* earthquake]

seize *v.t.* grasp; lay hold of; perceive. -seiz'able *a.* -seiz'ure *n.* a seizing; sudden illness. [F. *saisir*]

sel'dom *adv.* rarely. [OE. *seldan*]

select' *v.t.* pick out, choose. -a. choice, picked; exclusive. -selec'tion *n.* -select'or *n.* [L. *seligere, select-*]

self *pron.* selves *pl.* is used to express emphasis or a reflexive usage. -a. of a color, uniform, the same throughout. -n. one's own

person or individuality. -self- deceit, -decep-
tion n. deceiving oneself, self-denial n. un-
selfishness, denying oneself pleasure. -self-
evident a. explaining itself without proof-
self'ish a. concerned unduly over personal
profit or pleasure, lacking consideration for
others. -self'ishly adv. -self'less a. -
self contained' a. complete in itself, (of a person) reserved. -self-possessed' a. calm, composed. -self-righteous a. smug, believing
oneself better than others. -self'-same a. very
same. -self-seeking a. striving for one's own
advancement only. -self-sufficient a. independent of others, presumptuous. self-will n.
obstinacy. [OE.]

sell v.t. hand over for a price; betray or cheat;
of an idea etc. promote it with 'sales talk'. -v.i.
find purchasers. -n. (sl.) disappointment. -
sell'er n. [OE. sellan]

seman'tic a. concerned with the meanings
of words. - n.pl. science of the meanings of
words. [G. seinantikos, significant]

semaphore n. post with movable arm or
arms used for signaling; system of signaling
by human or mechanical arms. [G. sema, sign,
phoros, bearing]

sem'blance n. appearance; image; likeness.
[F. sembler, seem]

seme'ster n. university or college half-year
course; one of the two, or three, divisions of
the school year. [L. semestris- six months
(course)]

semi- prefix. half as in sem'ibreve n. musical
note half the length of a breve. -sem'icircle n.
half a circle. -semicir'cular a. -semico'lon n.
punctuation mark (;) -sem'iquaver n. musical note half the length of a quaver. -sem'itone
n. musical half note. -sem'i-detach'ed a. of a
house, joined to another on one side only.
-sem'i-fi'nal a. and n. last but one (match) of
series. [L. semi, half]

semiconductor n. (compute.) solid state
electronic switching device that performs
functions similar to an electronic tube. -semi-
conductor memory n. memory system containing thousands of microscopic transistors
and instructions manufactured on a chip of
silicon.

seminal a. pert. to semen or seed; reproductive; capable of developing; influential. [L.
semen, seed]

seminary n. school or college, esp. for
priests. [L. seminarium, seed plot]

Semi'tic a. of Semites. (Jews, Arabs etc.) of
their languages; the languages. [G. Sem,
Shem]

semolin'a n. hard grains left after the sifting
of flour, used for puddings etc. [L. simila,
wheatmeal]

sen'ate n. upper council of a state, university,
etc. -sen'ator n. -senator'ial a. [L. senatus,
council of old men]

send v.t. cause to go or be conveyed; despatch;
discharge. [OE. setidan]

sen'eschal n. steward or major domo of
medieval castle. [OF.]

se'nile a. showing the weakness of old age.
-senil'ity n. [L. senex, old]

se'nior a. older; superior in rank or standing.
-n. an elder person; a superior. -senior'ity n.
[L. compar. of senex, old]

sense n. any of the bodily functions of perception or feeling; sensitiveness of any or all
of these faculties; ability to perceive, mental
alertness; consciousness; meaning;
coherence, intelligible meaning. -sensa'tion
n. operation of a sense, feeling; excited feeling
or state of excitement; exciting event. -
sensa'tional a. -sensa'tionalism n. -
sense'less a. -sense'lessly adv. -sen'sible a.
that can be perceived by the senses; aware,
mindful; considerable; appreciable;
reasonable, wise. -sensibly adv. -sensibil'ity
n. delicacy of perception, feeling. -sen'sitive
a. open to or acutely affected by external impressions; easily affected or altered; respon-
sive to slight changes. -sen'sitively adv. -
sen'sitiveness n. sensitize v.t. make sensitive,
esp. to make (photographic film, etc.) sensitive to light. -senso'rial, sen'sory a. pert. to
senses, sensation. -sen'sual a. depending on
the senses only and not on the mind; given to
the pursuit of pleasure of sense, self-indul-
gent; licentious. -sen'suous a. stimulating or
apprehended by the senses. [L. sensus, fr. sentire, feel]

sen'tence n. judgment passed on criminal by
court or judge; combination of words which
is complete as expressing thought. -v.t. condemn. -senten'tial a. of sentence. [L. sentire,
feel]

sentiment n. a mental feeling; emotion; tendency to be moved by feeling rather than
reason; verbal expression of feeling. -
sentiment'al a. -sentiment'alist n. -
sentimental'ity n. [Fr., fr. L. sentire, feel]

sentinel n. sentry. [F. sentinelle]

sent'ry n. soldier on watch. [fr. sanctuary,
place of safety, shelter for a watchman]

sep'arate v.t. put apart; occupy a place between. -v.i. withdraw, become parted from. a.
disconnected, apart. -sep'arator n. that which
separates, esp. an apparatus for separating
cream from milk. [L. separare]

se'pia n. brown pigment made from a fluid
secreted by the cuttle fish. -a. of this color. [G.
= cuttlefish]

sept'-, [L. septem, seven] -Septem'ber n.
ninth month (seventh in the Roman reckoning). -septenn'ial a. occurring every seven
years. -septent'rional a. northern. -septet(te)
n. music for seven instruments or voices. -
septuagena'rian n. person in his seventies.
-sept'uagint n. the Greek version of the Old
Testament. [L. septem, seven]

sep'tic a. causing or caused by blood poisoning or putrefaction. -sep'sis n. septic state. [G.
septikos]

sepulcher (-ker) n. tomb. -sepul'chral a. -
sep'ulture n. burial. [L. sepulcrum-sepelire,
sepult-, bury]

se'quel n. consequence or continuation. -
se'quent a. following. -se'quence n. connected series, succession. [L. sequelasequi,
follow]

sequest'er v.t. seclude. -sequest'rate v.t.

confiscate; divert to satisfy claims against its owner. [L. *sequestrate*, put in safe keeping]

se'quin *n.* ornamental metal disk on dresses, *etc.*; formerly, a Venetian gold coin. [It. *zecchino*, fr. *zecca*, mint]

sequoi'a *n.* kind of giant conifers of California. [Cherokee chief *Sequoiah*]

sere *a.* dried up, withered. [OE. *sear*]

serenade' *n.* music sung or played at night below a person's window, *esp.* by a lover. -*v.t.* entertain with a serenade. [It. *serenata*, fr. *sereno*, open air]

serene' *a.* calm, tranquil. -serene'ly *a.* -seren'ity *n.* [L. *serenus*]

serf *n.* one of a class of laborers bound to, and transferred with, land. -serf'dom *n.* [L. *servus*, slave]

serg'eant (sarj-ant) *n.* non-commissioned officer; police officer; officer at a law court. -serg'eant-at-arms *n.* ceremonial official responsible for discipline. -sergeant-ma'jor *n.* highest non-commissioned officer. [F. *sergent*, fr. L. *serviens, servient-*, serving]

serial output *n.* (*compute.*) form of output in which the characters are printed letter by letter. *opp.* parallel output.

ser'ies *a.* sequence, succession, set. -se'rial *a.* of and forming a series; published in instalments. -se'rialize *v.t. n.* serial story or publication. -seria'tim *adv.* one after another. [L.]

ser'if *n.* fine cross-line finishing off stroke of letter, as for example at the top and base of H. [orig. uncertain]

serious *a.* earnest, sedate, thoughtful; not jesting; of importance. -se'riously *adv.* [L. *serius*, heavy]

ser'mon *n.* discourse of religious instruction or exhortation spoken or read from a pulpit; any similar discourse. -ser'monize *v.i.* talk like a preacher; compose sermons. [L. *sermo, sermon-*, discourse]

serp'ent *n.* snake; kind of firework; obsolete wind instrument. -serp'entine *a.* like or shaped like a serpent or snake; tortuous. [L. *serpere*, creep]

serra'ted *a.* notched like a saw. -serra'tion *n.* [L. *serra*, saw]

ser'ried *a.* in close order, press shoulder to shoulder. [F. *serrer*, lock]

ser'um (se-r-) *n.* watery animal fluid, *esp.* a thin part of blood as used for inoculation. -ser'ous *a.* [L. = whey]

serve *v.i.* work under another; carry out duties; be a member of a military unit; be useful or suitable or enough; in tennis, start play by striking the ball. -*v.t.* work for, attend on, help to food; supply something; be useful to; contribute to; deliver formally; treat in a specified way. ser'vant *n.* personal or domestic attendant. -ser'vice *n.* state of being a servant; work done for and benefit conferred on another; military, naval, air-force duty; set of dishes, *etc.* -ser'viceable *a.* useful or profitable. -ser'vitude *n.* bondage or slavery. [L. *servire*]

ser'vice *n.* a tree like a mountain ash with a pear-shaped fruit. [L. *sorbus*]

se'same *n.* eastern plant whose seeds yield gingili-oil. o'pen se'same, magic formula to gain entrance. [G.]

ses'sion *n.* meeting of a court, *etc.*; continuous series of such meetings. -ses'sional *a.* [L. *sessio*, fr. *sedere, sess-*, sit]

set *v.t.* cause to sit, put in place; fix, point, put up; make ready; put to music; put in position. *etc.* -*v.i.* of the sun, to go down, become firm or fixed; have a directions. deliberate; formal, arranged beforehand; unvarying. -*n.* a setting; tendency; habit. [OE. *settan*]

set *n.* number of things or persons associated as being similar or complementary or used together, *etc.* ; (tennis) series of games. [OF. *sette, sect*]

settee' *n.* couch. [var. of *settle*]

sett'er *n.* breed of dog which sets (crouches) on scenting game. (*e.g.*, Gordon, Irish, English)[*set*]

set'tle *n.* bench with a back and arms. [OE. *setl*]

set'tle *v.t.* put in order; establish, make firm or secure or quiet; decide upon; bring (a dispute, *etc.*), to an end; pay. -*v.i.* come to rest; subside; become clear; take up an abode; come to an agreement. [OE. *setlan*, fix]

sev'en *a.* and *n.* cardinal number, next after six. -sev'enth *a.* ordinal number. -sev'enth heav'en, state of supreme bliss. [OE. *soefon*]

sev'er *v.t.* separate, divide; cut off. -*v.i.* divide. -sev'erance *n.* -sev'eral *a.* separate; individual; some, a few. -*pron.* a few. -sev'erally *adv.* [F. *seurer*, wean, fr. L. *separate*]

severe' (-ear) *a.* strict; rigorous; simple and austere; hard to do or undo. severe'ly *adv.* sever'ity *n.* [L. *severus*]

sew *v.t.* join with thread. -*v.i.* be occupied in sewing. [OE *seowian*]

sew'er (sia-) *n.* underground drain to remove waste water and refuse. -sew'age *n.* the refuse. [OE. *esseveur*]

sex *n.* state of being male or female; males or females collectively; sexual intercourse. -sex'ism *n.* discrimination on the basis of sex. -sex'ist *a.* and *n.* -sex'ual *a.* sexually *adv.* [L. *sexus*]

sext'ant *n.* instrument with a graduated arc of a sixth of a circle to measure angles, altitudes of a heavenly body, *etc.* [L. *sextans*, sixth part]

sextet' *n.* (*mus.*) composition for six voices, instruments; the singers, players. [L. *sex*, six]

shabb'y *a.* poorly dressed; faded, worn; dishonorable. [OE. *sceabb*, scab]

shack *n.* hut, cabin. [*shake*]

shac'kle *n.* fetter; manacles; link to join two pieces of chain, *etc.*; anything that hampers. -*v.t.* fetter or hamper. [OE. *scacul*, bond]

shade *n.* partial darkness; darker part of anything; depth of color; tinge; shelter or a place sheltered from light, heat, *etc.*; ghost. -*v.t.* screen from light, darken; represent shades in a drawing. -shad'ow *n.* patch of shade; dark figure projected by anything that intercepts rays of light. -*v.t.* cast a shadow over; follow and watch closely. -shad'owy *a.* -sha'dy *a.* [OE. *sceadu*, shadow]

shaft (-a-) *n.* straight rod, stem, or handle; one

of the bars between which a horse is harnessed; entrance boring of a mine; revolving rod for transmitting power. [OE. *sceaft*, shaft of spear]

shag *n.* matted wool or hair; cloth with a long nap; fine cut tobacco. **-shagg'y** *a.* [OE. *sceacga*, head of hair]

shake *v.i.* tremble, totter, vibrate. *-v.t.* cause to shake. *-n.* act of shaking; vibration; jolt. **-sha'ky** *a.* **-sha'kily** *adv.* **-shake'-down** *n.* make-shift bed, as of hay or straw. [OE. *sceancan*]

shall *v. aux.* makes compound tenses to express obligation, command, condition or intention. [OE. *sceal*]

shallot' *n.* small onion. [F. *échalotte*]

shall'ow *a.* not deep. *-n.* shallow place, shoal, sandbank. [ep. *shoal*]

sham *n.* imitation, counterfeit. *-a.* imitation. *-v.t.* and *i.* pretend; feign (sickness). [orig. uncertain]

sha'man *n.* priest of shamanism; medicine man of similar religion. [Russ. fr. *Tungus*]

shamb'les *n.pl.* messy, disorderly thing or place; slaughter-house [OE. *sceamel*, bench]

shame *n.* emotion caused by consciousness of something wrong or dishonoring in one's conduct or state; cause of disgrace. *v.t.* cause to feel shame; disgrace. **shame'faced** *a.* (earlier shame-fast) shy. **-shame'less** *a.* bold, immodest. [OE. *sceamu*]

shampoo' *v.t.* wash (*esp.* hair) with something forming a lather in rubbing. *n.* any of various preparations of liquid soap for washing hair, carpets *etc.* [Hind. *sharnpo*, kind of massager]

sham'rock *n.* trefoil plant taken as the emblem of Ireland. [Ir. *searnrog*]

shanghai' *v.t.* drug (sailor) and convey on board ship for service; force or trick someone into doing something. [*Shanghai*, China]

shank *n.* the lower leg; the shinbone; a stem of a thing. [OE. *sceanca*, leg]

shant'y *n.* hut; ramshackle or temporary house. [F. *chantier*, workshop]

shant'y *n.* sailor's song with chorus sung by crew at work. [*See* **chanty**]

shape *n.* external form or appearance; mold or pattern. *-v.t.* give shape to; mold, fashion, make. **-shape'less** *a.* **-shape'ly** *a.* well-proportioned. [OE. *gesceap* *n.*; *scieppan* *v.*]

shard *n.* broken fragment, *esp.* of earthenware. [OE. *sceard*]

share *n.* blade of a plough [OE. *scear*]

share (sher) *n.* portion; dividend. *-v.t.* give or allot a share. *-v.i.* take a share. **-share'holder** *n.* holder of shares in a company *etc.* [OE. *scearu*, cutting or division]

shark *n.* large, *usu.* predatory, sea fish; grasping person; sharper. [orig. unknown]

sharp *a.* having a keen edge or fine point; apt, keen; brisk; harsh; dealing cleverly but unfairly; shrill; strongly marked, *esp.* in outline. *-n.* in music, a note half a tone above the natural pitch. **-sharp'ly** *adv.* **sharp'en** *v.t.* **-sharp'er** *n.* swindler. **-sharp'ness** *n.* **-sharp'-shooter** *n.* marksman. **-sharp'-set** *a.* hungry, ravenous. [OE. *scearp*]

shatt'er *v.t.* break in pieces. *-v.i.* fly in pieces. [var. of *scatter*]

shave *v.t.* pare away; cut close, *esp.* the hair of the face or head; graze. *-v.i.* shave oneself. *-n.* shaving; narrow escape. **-sha'ver** *n.* (*sl.*) youngster. [OE. *sceafan*, scrape]

shawl *n.* square of fabric mainly used to cover the shoulders. [Pers. *shal*]

she *pron.* third person singular feminine pronoun. [OE. *seo*]

she'a-butt'er *n.* butter derived from W. African shea-tree. [native, *shea*]

sheaf *n.* bundle, *esp.* corn. [OE. *sceaf*]

shear *v.t.* cut through; clip or cut; clip the hair or wool from. *-n.* in *pl.* cutting implement like a large pair of scissors; scissor-shaped erection of beams used as a cranc. **-shear'er** *n.* **-shear'water** *n.* sea bird of the petrel family. [OE. *scieran*]

sheath *n.* close-fitting cover, *esp.* for a knife or sword; scabbard. **-sheathe** *v.t.* put into a sheath. [OE. *scceth*]

shed *n.* roofed shelter used as a store or workshop. [var. of *shade*]

shed *v.t.* cast off, scatter, throw off, divide. *-n.* dividing ridge; hair-parting. [OE. *sceadan*, divider]

sheen *n.* gloss, brightness, luster. **sheen'y** *a.* [OE. *sciene*, beautiful]

sheep *n.* ruminant animal with a heavy coat of wool. **-sheep'ish** *a.* shy, awkwardly bashful. [OE. *sceap*]

sheer *a.* pure; perpendicular. [OE. *scir*, pure, bright]

sheer *v.i.* deviate from a course. **-sheer off'**, avoid, leave. [var. of *shear*, divide]

sheet *n.* large piece of linen, *etc.*, to cover a bed; broad piece of any thin material; large expanse. *-v.t.* cover with a sheet. [OE. *sciete*]

sheet *n.* rope fastened to the corner of a sail. **-sheet'-anchor** *n.* large anchor used only in an emergency. [OE. *sceata*]

shelf *n.* board fixed horizontally (on a wall, *etc.*), on which to put things; underwater ledge. **-shelve** *v.t.* put on a shelf: put off, slope. [LG. *schelf*]

shell *n.* hard outer case of an animal, fruit, *etc.*; explosive projectile; inner coffin; outer part of a structure left when the interior is removed. *-v.t.* take a shell from, or from a shell: fire at with shells. **shell-fish** *n.* sea-animal covered with shell. **-shell'-shock** *n.* nervous or mental disorder caused by shock from bursting shells, bombs, *etc.* [OE. *sciell*]

shelt'er *n.* place or structure giving protection; protection. *-v.t.* give protection to, screen. *-v.i.* take shelter. [orig. uncertain]

shep'herd (shep'-erd) *n.* man who tends sheep. **-shep'herdess** *fem.* [OE. *sceaphirde*, sheep herd]

sher'bet *n.* oriental drink of sugar, water and fruit juices. [Pers.]

sher'iff *n.* county or city officer; chief law-enforcement officer. **-sher'iffdom**, **sher'iffship** *n.* office, area of jurisdiction of sheriff. [OE. *scirgerefa*, shire reeve]

sherr'y *n.* Spanish wine. [wine of *Seres* (now Jerez)]

shield *n.* plate of armor carried on the left arm; protective covering. *-v.t.* cover, screen. [OE. *scield*]

shift *v.t.* move, remove. *-v.i.* remove; change position. *-n.* evasion; expendient; relay of workmen; time of their working; removal; formerly, a woman's undergarment. *-shift'less a.* lacking in resource or character. *-shift'y a.* shuffling, full of evasions. *-shift'iness n.* [OE. *sciftan*, arrange]

shill'ing *n.* formerly, British silver coin = twelve pence. [OE. *scilling*]

shimm'er *v.i.* shine with faint quivering light. *-n.* such light; glimmer. [OE. *seymrian*, shine]

shin *n.* front of the lower leg. *-v.i.* climb with arms and legs. [OE. *scinu*]

shine *v.i.* give out or reflect light. *-n.* brightness. *-shi'ny a.* [OE. *scinan*]

shin'gle *n.* flat piece of wood used as a tile. *-v.t.* cover with shingles; name board; cut (a woman's hair) close. [L. *scindula*, for *scandula*]

shin'gle (-ng-gl) *n.* pebbles on the shore, of river, sea. [fr. *chink*]

shin'gles (-ng-glz) *n.* disease with eruptions often forming a belt round the body; herpes. [L. *cingula*, belt]

shin'ty *n.* game like hockey played by the Scots and Irish. [orig. uncertain]

ship *n.* large sea-going vessel. *-v.t.* put on or send in a ship. *-v.i.* embark; take service in a ship. *-v.i.* *-ship'ment n.* act of shipping; goods shipped. *-shipp'ing n.* ships collectively. *-ship'shape a.* orderly, trim. [OE. *scip*]

shire *n.* county. [OE. *scir*, district]

shirk *v.t.* evade, try to avoid (duty, etc). *-shirk'er n.* [orig. uncertain]

shirt *n.* undergarment for the upper part of the body; blouse. [OE. *seyrte*]

shiv'er *n.* splinter. *-v.t.* shatter. *-v.i.* split into pieces. [ME. *scifre*]

shiv'er *v.i.* tremble, usually with cold or fear. *-n.* act or state of shivering. [orig. uncertain]

shoal *n.* sandbank or bar, shallow; school of fish. *-v.i.* become shallow; collect in a shoal. [OE. *sceald*]

shock *v.t.* horrify, scandalize. *-n.* violent or damaging blow; collision. *-shock'er n.* sensational novel. *-shock'ing a.* [F. *choquer*]

shock *n.* mass of hair. *-a.* shaggy. (obs. *shockdog*, fr. OE. *scucca*, demon]

shod'dy *n.* cloth made of mixed old and new wool. *-a.* worthless, second-rate, of poor material. [orig. unknown]

shoe *n.* covering for the foot, like a boot, but not enclosing the ankle; metal rim or curved bar put on a horse's hoof, various protective plates or undercoverings. *-v.t.* provide with shoes. *-shoe'black n.* one who polishes shoes. *-shoe'horn v.t.* implement to ease heel into shoe. [OE. *scoh*]

shoot *v.i.* move swiftly and suddenly; let off a gun, bow, *etc.*; go after game with a gun; sprout. *-v.t.* pass quickly under or along; dump; discharge; kill or wound with a missile. *-n.* act of shooting; expedition to shoot; young branch or stem. *-shoot'ing n.* area where game

is preserved. [OE. *sceotan*]

shop *n.* place where goods are made, or bought and sold. *-v.i.* visit shops. **shop'lifter** *n.* one who steals from a shop. *-shop'-steward* *n.* trade union representative of factory workers, *etc.* in negotiating with employers. *-shop'walker n.* overseer who directs customers to various departments. [F. *schoppe*, booth]

shore *n.* edge of the sea, or large lake. [Du. *schor*]

shore *n.prop, esp.* for a ship on the slips. *-v.t.* prop. [orig. uncertain]

short *a.* having little length: brief, hasty; friable. *-n.* in *pl.* short trousers coming to. and open at, the knee; underpants of a similar style. *-adv.* abruptly. *-short'age a.* deficiency. *-short'en v.t.* and *i.* **short'bread** *n.* rich cookie made with butter. *-short'coming n.* failing, fault, defect. *-short'hand n.* method of rapid writing by signs or contractions. *-short'ly adv.* soon; briefly. *-short waves n.* (wireless) waves between 10 and 50 meters. [OE. *sceort*]

shot *n.* act of shooting, shooter; missile; lead in small pellets; bill at a tavern; film scene. *-a.* woven so that the color is different according to the angle of the light. [OE. *sceot*]

shoul'der *n.* part of a body to which an arm or foreleg is attached; support or bracket. *-v.t.* put on one's shoulder. *-v.i.* make a way by pushing. *-shoulder'blade n.* shoulder bone; clavicle. [OE. *sculdor*]

shout *n.* loud cry. *-v.i.* utter one. *-v.t.* utter with a very loud voice. [orig. uncertain]

shove *v.t.* and *n.* push. [OE. *scufan*]

shov'el (-uv-) *n.* broad spade with a long or short handle. *-v.t.* lift or move with a shovel. [OE. *scofl*]

show *v.t.* expose to view, point out; guide; accord (favor, *etc.*,). *-v.i.* appear. be visible. *-n.* something shown; display, spectacle. *-show'down n.* disclosure of true state of things. *-show'man n.* *-show'off.* display. [OE. *sceau, ian*, look at]

show'er *n.* short fall of rain; anything coming down like rain. *-v.t.* and *i.* rain. *-show'ery a.* [OE. *scur*]

shred *n.* fragment, torn strip. *-v.t.* break or tear to shreds. [OE. *scread*]

shrew *n.* animal like a mouse; malicious person: scold. *-shrewd a.* intelligent, crafty; coming near the truth. [OE. *screawa*, shrew-mouse]

shriek *v.t.* and *i.* and *n.* (to utter) a loud. piercing cry of alarm, pain, *etc.* [imit. orig.]

shrill *a.* piercing, sharp in tone. *-shrill'y adv.* [imit. orig.]

shrimp *n.* small crustacean of lobster shape. *-v.i.* go catching shrimps. **shrimp'er n.** [orig. uncertain]

shrine *n.* case for relics; altar; chapel; temple. [L. *scrinium*, coffer]

shrink *v.i.* become smaller; retire, flinch. *-v.t.* make shrink. *-shrink'age n.* [OE. *scrincan*]

shriv'el *v.i.* shrink and wrinkle. *-v.t.* wither up; scorch. [orig. uncertain]

shroud *n.* sheet for a corpse; covering. *-pl.* set of ropes to a masthead. *-v.t.* put a shroud on; screen, wrap up (fig.) conceal. [OE. *scrud*, garment]

shrub *n.* woody or bushy plant. -shrubb'y *a.* -shrubb'ery *n.* plantation of shrubs, part of a garden filled with them. [OE. *scrybb*]

shrub *n.* drink of fruit juice, rum, *etc.* [Arab. *sharab*]

shrug *v.i.* raise and narrow the shoulders. as a sign of disdain, *etc.* -*v.t.* move (the shoulders) thus. -*n.* shrugging. [orig. unknown]

shudd'er *v.i.* tremble violently, *esp.* with horror. -*n.* shuddering. -shudd'ering *a.* [of Tent. orig.]

shuf'fle *v.i.* move the feet without lifting them; act evasively. -*v.t.* mix (cards); (with off) evade, pass to another. Also *n.* [orig. uncertain]

shun *v.t.* avoid. [OE. *scrunian*]

shunt *v.t.* move (a train) from one line to another; push aside; switch over. [orig. uncertain]

shut *v.t.* and *i.* close. -shutt'er *n.* movable screen for a window usually hinged to the frame. [OE. *scyttan*]

shut'tle *n.* instrument which threads the wool between the threads of the warp in weaving; similar appliance in a sewing machine; airplane, bus *etc.* traveling to and fro over a short distance. -shuttlecock *n.* cork with cup-shaped fan of feathers stuck in it for use with battledore or badminton racquet. [OE. *scytel*, missile]

shy *a.* timid, bashful, awkward in company; reluctant. -*v.i.* start back in sudden fear; show sudden reluctance. -*n.* sudden start of fear by a horse. -shy'ly *adv.* -shy'ness *n.* [OF. *eschif*]

sib'ilant *a.* having a hissing sound. -*n.* speech sound with a hissing effect. [L. *sibilare*, whistler]

sicc'ate *v.t.* dry. -sicc'ative *a.* drying. [L. *siccare*, *siccat-*, dry]

sick *a.* affected by disease or ill health; tired of; disgusted. -sick'en *v.t.* and *i.* sick'ly *a.* -sick'ness *n.* -sick'bay *n.* on a ship, *etc.*, place for treating the sick. [OE. *seoc*]

side *n.* one of the surfaces of an object, *esp.* upright inner or outer surface; either surface of a thing having only two; part of the body that is to the right or left; region nearer or farther than, or right or left of, a dividing line, *etc.* ; one of two parties or sets of opponents. -*v.i.* take up the cause of. -side'arms *n. pl.* weapons worn at the side. -side'board *n.* piece of furniture for holding dishes, *etc.*, in a dining room. -side'kick *n.* person closely associated with another, *usu.* as subordinate. -side'long *adv.* obliquely. -side'walk *n.* paved walkway for pedestrians at the side of a street. -side'ways *adv.* -si'ding *n.* track added at the side of a railway. -si'dle *v.i.* edge along. -side'show *n.* (auxiliary) fairground show. -side'track *v.t.* shunt; divert. -side'slip *n.* skid. [OE.]

sider'eal *a.* relating to the stars. [L. *sidus, sider-*, constellation]

siege *n.* a besieging of a town or fortifield place. [F. *siege*, seat, siege]

sierr'a *n.* mountain drawn with saw-like ridges. (Sp.]

siest'a *n.* rest or sleep in the afternoon. [Sp. = sixth (hour)]

sieve (siv) *n.* utensil with network or a perforated bottom for sifting. -sift *v.t.* separate coarser portion from finer; solid from liquid. [OE, *site*]

sigh *v.i.* utter a long audible breath. -*n.* such a breath. [OE. *sican*]

sight (sit) *n.* faculty of seeing; a seeing; something seen; device (on a rifle, *etc.*) for guiding the eye; (*sl.*) large number. -*v.t.* catch sight of; adjust sights of. -sight'less *a.* -sight'ly *a.* good to look at. [OE. *sihth*, from *seon*, see]

sign (sin) *n.* movement, mark, or indication to convey some meaning; spoor, trail. -*v.t.* put one's signature to. -*v.i.* make a sign or gesture; affix a signature. -sign'-post *n.* post supporting a signboard, *esp.* to show the way at cross roads. -sign'board (sin-) *n.* board with some device or inscription. [L. *signum*]

sig'nal *n.* sign to convey an order, *etc.*, semaphore, *esp.* on a railway. -*v.t.* make signals to. -*v.i.* give orders, *etc.*, by signals. -*a.* remarkable, striking. -sig'nally *adv.* -sig'nalize *v.t.* make notable. [L. *signalis*]

signature *n.* person's name written by himself; act of writing it. -sig'natory *n.* one of those who sign a document. sig'nature tune', tune announcing a particular performer, radio feature, *etc.* [L. *signore, signat-*]

sig'nify *v.t.* mean; to intimate. -*v.i.* to be of importance. -signif'icant *a.* expressing the importance. -signif'icantly *adv.* -significance *n.* -significa'tion *n.* the meaning. [L. *signum*, sign]

si'lence *n.* stillness, absence of noise; refraining from speech. -*v.t.* make silent. -si'lent *a.* -si'lencer *n.* expansion chamber in internal combustion engine., minimizing sound of exhaust; device to deaden report of firearm. [L. *silentium*]

silhouette' *n.* portrait or picture cut from black paper or done in solid black on white; outline of an object seen against the light. [F. *de Silhouette*, French politician (d. 1767)]

sil'icon *n.* non-metallic base of silica. sil'ica *n.* mineral found in rock-crystal, quartz, *etc.* -sil'icon chip *n.* tiny wafer of silicon forming an integrated circuit in a computer. -silico'sis *n.* stonemason's disease caused by inhaling silicia-dust. [L. *silex, sitic-*, flint]

silk *n.* fiber made by the larvae of certain moths; thread or fabric made from this. -silk'en *a.* -silk'y *a.* -silk'iness *adv.* -silk'ily *a.* [OE. *seole*]

sill *n.* slab of wood or stone at bottom of a door or window. [OE. *syll*]

sill'y *a.* foolish; weak in intellect. -sill'iness *n.* [OE. *gescelig*, happy]

si'lo *n.* pit or tower for storing fodder or grain; underground missile launching site. -si'lage *n.* the fodder, *etc* . [Sp.]

silt *n.* mud deposited by water. -*v.t.* and *i.* fill with silt. [orig. uncertain]

Silu'rian *a./n.* (of) division of Palaeozoic rocks before Devonian. [L. *Silurs*, ancient Welsh tribe]

sil'van *a*. wooded; rural. [L. *silua*, wood]

sil'ver *n*. white precious metal; things made of it; silver coins. -*v.t*. coat with silver. -**sil'very** *a*. -**sil'ver-fish** *n*. small wingless insect, the spring-tail. [OE. *siolfor*]

sim'ian *a*. of apes; ape-like. -*n*. ape; any kind of monkey. [L. *simia*, ape]

sim'ilar *a*. resembling, like. -**sim'ilarly** *adv*. -**similar'ity** *n*. likeness. -**simile** (sim-i-li) *n*. (*rhet*.) comparison, *esp*. in poetry. -**simil'itude** *n*. outward appearance; guise. [L. *similis*]

simm'er *v.t*. and *i*. keep or be just bubbling or just below boiling point; be in a state of suppressed anger or laughter. [imit. orig.]

sim'per *v.i*. smile in a silly or affected way. [orig. uncertain]

sim'ple *a*. plain; straightforward; ordinary, mere. -**sim'ply** *adv*. -**sim'pleton** *n*. foolish person. [L. *simplus*]

sim'ulate *v.t*. pretend to be. -**simulac'rum** *n*. -**simulac'ra** *pl*. shadowy likeness; unreal thing. -**simula'tion** *n*. [L. *simulare*, make like]

simultaneous *a*. occurring at the same time. [L. *simmul*, at the same time]

sin *n*. transgression against divine or moral law, *esp*. one committed consciously; conduct or state of mind of a habitual or unrepentant sinner. -*v.i*. commit sin. -**sin'ful** *a*. of the nature of sin; guilty of sin. -**sin'fully** *a*. -**sinn'er** *n*. [OE. *synn*]

since *adv*. from then till now; subsequently; ago. -*prep*. at some time subsequent to. -*conj*. from the time that; seeing that. [earlier *sithens*, OE. *siththan*, after that]

sincere' *a*. not assumed or merely professed; actually moved by or feeling the apparent motives; straightforward. -**sincere'ly** *adv*. -**sincer'ity** *n*. honesty of purpose; frankness. [L. *sincerus*, pure]

sine (sin) *abbrev*. **sin** (sin) *n*. (trigonometry) in a right-angled triangle the sine of an acute angle is the ratio of its opposite side to the hypotenuse. [L. *sinus*, a bay]

si'necure *n*. office with pay, but no duties. [orig. a church benefice without cure of souls; L. *sine cure*]

sin'ew *n*. tendon. -*pl*. muscles, strength; mainstay or motive power. -**sin'ewy** *a*. [OE. *sinu*]

sing *v.i*. utter musical sounds. -*v.t*. utter (words) with musical modulation; celebrate in song or poetry. -**sing'er** *n*. one who, or that which, sings. [OE. *singan*]

singe (-nj) *v.t*. burn the surface of. -*n*. act or effect of singeing. [OE. *sengan*, make to hiss]

sin'gle (-ng-gl) *a*. one only; alone, separate; unmarried; formed of only one part, fold, *etc*. -*v.t*. pick (out). -**singlet** (-ng-gl-) *n*. undergarment. -**sin'gleton** *n*. single thing; only card of a suit in a hand. -**sin'gly** *adv*. -**sin'gular** *a*. unique; remarkable; odd; denoting one person or thing. -*n*. word in singular. [L. *singuli*, one at a time]

Sinhalese, Singhalese *a*. of people living mainly in Sri Lanka. [Sans. *Sinhalam*, Ceylon]

sin'ister *a*. evil-looking; wicked; ill omened;

in heraldry, on the left-hand side. [L. = on the left hand]

sink *v.i*. become submerged in water; drop, give way, decline. -*v.t*. cause to sink; make by digging out; invest. -*n*. receptacle for washing up with a pipe for carrying away waste water; ditch or tunnel for carrying off sewage; place where evil, corruption collects. -**sink'er** *n*. weight used to sink line. [OE. *sincan*]

sin'uous *a*. curving, winding -**sin'uously** *adv*. -**sinuos'ity** *n*. [L. *sinuosus*]

si'nus *n*. an opening; a hollow; a recess in the shore; a bay; (*surg*.) a cavity in a bone or other part; an abscess with a small orifice (**si'nuses**, **si'nusi** *pl*.) [L. *sinus*, a curve]

sip *v.t*. and *i*. drink in very small draughts. -*n*. portion of liquid sipped. -**sipp'er** *n*. [var. of *sup*]

si'phon *n*. bent tube for drawing off liquids; bottle with a tape at the top through which liquid is forced by pressure of gas inside. (G. = tube]

sir *n*. title of a knight or baronet (with Christian name and surname); public or respectful form of address. [*sire*]

si'ren *n*. legendary female monster supposed to lure sailors to destruction; fog signal; air-raid or fire signal. [L.]

sir'loin *n*. upper part of a loin of beef. [OF. *surloigne*, over loin]

sis'ter *n*. daughter of the same parents or having a common parent. *a*. closely related, exactly similar. -**sis'terly** *a*. -**sis'terhood** *n*. relation of sister; order or band of women. -**sis'ter-in-law** *n*. sister of a husband or wife; wife of a brother. [ON. *systir*]

sit *v.i*. rest on the lower part of the body as on a chair, seat oneself; hold a session; incubate. -*v.t*. sit upon (horse). -**sitt'ing** *n*. act of sitting down or being seated; session, meeting; posing for artist; church seat. [OE. *sittan*]

site *n*. place, situation, plot of ground for, or with, a building. -**sit'uate**, **sit'uated** *a*. placed. -**situa'tion** *n*. place or position; employment or post; state of affairs. [L. *situs*, place]

six *a*. and *n*. cardinal number one more than five. -**sixth** *a*. ordinal number. -*n*. sixth part. -**six'pence** *n*. sum of six pence; silver coin of this value. -**six'penny** *a*. costing sixpence. [OE. *siex*]

size *n*. bigness, dimensions. -*v.t*. sort or estimate by size. [for *assize*]

size *n*. substance resembling glue. -*v.t*. coat or treat with size. [F. *assise*]

sizz'le *v.i*. hiss as when frying. -*n*. hissing sound; great heat. -**sizz'ling** *a*. [imit. orig.]

skate *n*. flat fish. [ON. *skata*]

skate *n*. steel blade with a framework to attach it to a boot, for gliding over ice. -*v.i*. glide on skates. [Du. *schaats*]

skel'eton *n*. bones of an animal. -**skel'eton key**, key used for picking locks —**skel'eton in the cupboard**, hidden domestic secret. [G. = dried up]

sketch *n*. rough drawing; brief account; essay, *etc*.. -*v.t*. make a sketch of. -*v.i*. practice sketching. -**sketch'y** *a*. rough, unfinished. [Du. *schets*]

skew *v.i.* move obliquely. -*a.* slanting, oblique. [OF. *escuer*]

skew'er *n.* pin to fasten meat together. *v.i.* pierce or fasten with a skewer. [orig. uncertain]

ski *n.* long runner fastened to the foot for sliding over snow. -*v.i.* slide on skis. [Norw.]

skid *n.* drag for a wheel; side-slip. -*v.t.* apply a skid to. -*v.i.* of a wheel, slip without revolving, slip sideways. [orig. uncertain]

skiff *n.* small boat. [F. *esquif*]

skill *n.* practical ability, cleverness. [ON, *skil*, distinction]

skill'et *n.* pan with long handle; small cauldron. [ON. *skjola*, pail]

skim *v.t.* rid of floating matter; remove from the surface of a liquid; move over lightly and rapidly; read in this way. -*v.i.* move thus. [OF. *escumer*]

skin *n.* outer covering, *esp.* of an animal or fruit. -*v.t.* remove the skin of. -**skinn'y** *a.* thin. -**skin'flint** *n.* miser, niggard. [ON. *skinn*]

skip *v.i.* leap lightly; jump a rope as it is swung under one. -*v.t.* pass over. -*n.* act of skipping. [orig. uncertain]

skipp'er *n.* captain of a ship. [Du. *scipper*, fr. *scip*, ship]

skirm'ish *n.* fight between small parties, small battle. -*v.i.* fight slightly or irregularly. [F. *escarmouche*]

skirt *n.* lower part of a woman's dress, coat, *etc.*, outlying part. -*v.t.* border; go round. [ON. *skyrta*]

skit *n.* satire or caricature. -**skitt'ish** *a.* frisky, frivolous. [orig. uncertain]

skulk *v.i.* sneak out of the way; lurk; malinger. -**skulk'er** *n.* [Nor. *skulka*, to lurk]

skull *n.* bony case enclosing the brain. [orig. uncertain]

skunk *n.* small N. American animal like a weasel, which defends itself by emitting an evil-smelling fluid; mean fellow. [N. Amer. Ind. *segankw*]

sky *n.* apparent canopy of the heavens; heavenly regions. -**sky-lark** *n.* lark; prank. -**sky-light** *n.* window in roof; **sky-scraper** *n.* very tall building. -**sky'-writing** *n.* smoke writing executed in the sky by an airplane. [ON. = cloud]

slab *n.* thick broad piece. [orig. uncertain]

slack *a.* loose, sluggish, not busy. -*n.* loose part. -*v.t.* mix (lime) with water. -*v.i.* be idle or lazy. -**slack'ly** *adv.* **slack'en** *v.t.* and *i.* [OE. *sloec*]

slack *n.* small coal. **slack'-water** *n.* ebb-tide. [Ger. *schlacke*, dross]

slacks *n.pl.* loose trousers for men or women. [fr. *slack a. q.v.*]

slag *n.* dross of melted metal; spongy volcanic lava. -*v.i.* to form into slag. [Ger. *schlacke*, dross]

slake *v.i.* moderate. -*v.t.* quench; slack (time). [OE. *slacian*]

slam *v.t.* shut noisily; dash down. -*v.i.* shut with a bang. -*n.* noisy shutting or other bang. [imit. orig.]

slander *n.* false or malicious statement about a person. -*v.t.* utter such statement. -**slan'derer** *n.* -**slan'derous** *a.* [F. *esclandre*, fr. L. *scandal*, scandal]

slang *n.* colloquial language. -*v.t.* scold violently. [orig. uncertain]

slant (-a-) *v.t.* and *i.* and *n.* slope; idea; viewpoint. *v.* in a slanting manner. - *a.* sloping, oblique. [orig. uncertain]

slap *n.* blow with the open hand or a flat instrument. -*v.t.* strike thus. -**slap'-dash** *a.* careless, rash, slipshod. *adv.* -**slap'stick** (comedy) *n.* rough knockabout comedy, farce. [imit. orig.]

slash *v.t.* gash; lash. -*n.* gash; cutting stroke. [orig. uncertain]

slat *n.* narrow strip of wood or metal; thin, flat stone. [OF. *esclat*]

slate *n.* kind of stone which splits easily in flat sheets; piece of this for covering a roof or for writing on. -*v.t.* cover with slates. [var. of *slat*]

slaughter *n.* killing *v.t.* kill. -**slaught'erous** *a.* -**slaught'er-** *n.* place for killing animals for food. [ON. *site*, butcher's meat]

slave *n.* captive, person without freedom or personal rights. -*v.i.* work like a slave. -**sla'very** *n.* -**sla'vish** *a.* -**sla'ver** *n.* person or ship engaged in slave traffic. [*slav*]

slay *v.t.* kill. -**slay'er** *n.* [OE. *stean*]

sledge, **sledge-ham'mer** *n.* heavy blacksmith's hammer. [OE. *sleog*]

sledge, **sled** *n.* carriage on runners for sliding on snow; toboggan. -*v.t.* and *i.* [Du. *slede*]

sleep *n.* unconscious state regularly occurring in men and animals. -*v.i.* take rest in sleep, slumber. -**sleep'er** *n.* one who sleeps; sleeping-car. -**sleep'less** *a.* **sleep'iness** *n.* -**sleep'y** *a.* -**sleep'ily** *adv.* -**sleep'ing-sick'ness** *n.* tropical African disease spread by tsetse fly. -**sleepwalker** *n.* one who walks in sleep, somnambulist. [OE. *slcepan*]

sleet *n.* partly-thawed snow-flakes. -*v.i.* rain sleet. [orig. uncertain]

sleeve *n.* part of a garment covering the arm. -**sleeve'less** *a.* [OE. *slicfe*]

sleigh (sla) *n.* sledge. [Du. *sleet*]

sleight (slit) *n.* dexterity. -**sleight'-of-hand'** *n.* conjuring. [OE. *sleegth*]

slender *a.* slim, slight, small. [orig. uncertain]

sleuth *n.* track; bloodhound; relentless tracker; detective. [ON. *sloth*, track]

slice *n.* thin flat piece cut off. -*v.t.* cut into slices. [OF. *esclice*]

slick *a.* smooth; smooth-tongued; smart. -*adv.* deftly. -*v.t.* make glossy. -**slick'er** *n.* waterproof [OE. *slycian*, sleek]

slide *v.i.* slip smoothly along. -*v.t.* cause to slide. -*n.* a sliding track on ice made for or by sliding; sliding part of mechanism. -**slide'-rule** *n.* ruler with sliding graduated scale to simplify calculations. -**sli'ding scale'**, scale of *e.g.* wages, which varies in ratio to the variations of another factor. -**sli'der** *n.* sliding part of a machine *etc.* [OE. *slidan*]

slight (-it) *a.* slim, slender; not substantial; trifling. -*v.t.* disregard; neglect. -*n.* indifference; act of discourtesy. -**slight'ly** *adv.* [ON. *slettr*]

slim *a.* thin, slight; crafty. -*v.i.* reduce, grow thinner. [Du. = *crafty*]

slime *n.* sticky mud. -**sli'my** *a.* -**sli'miness** *n.* [OE. *slim*]

sling *n.* pocket with a string attached at each end for hurling a stone; hanging bandage for a wounded limb; any rope, belt, *etc.*, for hoisting or carrying weights. -*v.t.* throw; hoist or swing by means of a rope. [ON. *slyngua*]

slink *v.i.* move stealthily (*p.t.* and *pp.*, slunk, *pres. p.* slinking). [OE. *slincan*, creep]

slip *n.* twig cut for grafting or planting; long narrow strip; landing place; slope on which ships are built; leash; mistake; act of slipping. -*v.i.* lose one's foothold. -*v.t.* cause to slip; put on or off easily or gently; release (a dog). -**slipp'er** *n.* light shoe for indoor use. -**stipp'ery** *a.* so smooth as to cause slipping or to be difficult to hold or catch. -**slip'shod** *a.* slovenly, careless. - **slip'-way** *n.* sloping launching-way with one end under water. [OE. *slipor*, slippery]

slit *v.t.* cut open, sever. -*a.* cut, torn. -*n.* straight narrow cut. [OE. *slitan*]

slith'er *n.* slip or splinter of wood; long strip. -*v.t.* divide into long, thin or very small pieces. -*v.i.* split; become split off. [OE. *slifan*, split]

slo'gan *n.* Scottish Highland war-cry; catchword, motto. [Gael. *sluagh-ghairm*, army cry]

sloop *n.* one-masted cutter-rigged vessel; small warship. [Du. *sloep*]

slop *n.* dirty liquid; semi-liquid food. -*v.t.* spill or splash. -*v.i.* spill. -**slopp'y** *a.* (*sl.*) weakly sentimental. [OE. *sloppe*]

slope *n.* slant, upward or downward inclination. -*v.i.* move obliquely. -*v.t.* place slanting; (*sl.*) abscond; stroll off. [OE. *aslupan*, slip away]

slot *n.* narrow hole, depression; slit for coins in, *e.g.*, stamp machine. -*v.i.* make a slot or slots in. -**slotted** *a.* (OE. *esclot*]

sloth *n.* sluggishness; sluggish S. Amer. animal. -**sloth'fully** *a.* idle; unwilling to exert oneself. [fr. *slow*]

slouch *n.* stooping, or shambling walk. -*v.i.* walk in this way. -*v.t.* pull down (a hat). [orig. uncertain]

slough (-ow) *n.* bog. [OE. *sloh*]

slough (-uf) *n.* skin shed by a snake; dead tissue from a sore. -*v.i.* of such tissue to be shed. -*v.t.* shed (skin). [of Scand. orig.]

slow *a.* moving at a low rate of speed; behindhand; dull. -*v.i.* slacken speed. -**slow'ly** *adv.* -**slow'ness** *n.* [OE. *slaw*, sluggish]

sludge *n.* slush, sewage. [*slush*]

slug *n.* land snail with no shell; lazy fellow. -**slugg'ard** *n.* -**slugg'ish** *a.* slow moving; lazy. -**slugg'ishness** *n.* [of Scand. orig.]

sluice *n.* sliding gate or door to control a flow of water. -*v.t.* pour water over; drench. [OF. *escluse*]

slum *n.* squalid street or neighborhood. -*v.i.* visit slums. [orig. unknown]

slum'ber *v.i.* sleep. -*n.* sleep. -**slumbrous** *a.* sleepy, inducing slumber. [OE. *sluma*]

slump *v.i.* of prices, *etc.*, to fall suddenly or

heavily. -*n.* such fall. [imit.]

slur *v.t.* pass over lightly; depreciate. -*n.* slight. [orig. uncertain]

slut *n.* a dirty untidy woman. -**slutt'ish** *a.* [orig. uncertain]

sly *a.* cunning, wily; done with artful dexterity. -**sly'ly** *adv.* -**sly'ness** *n.* -on the sly', surreptitiously. [ON. *slcegr*]

smack *n.* taste, flavor. -*v.i.* taste (of). [OE. *smcec*]

small (-awl) *a.* little. -**small'ness** *n.* -**small'pox** *n.* contagious disease. -**small'talk** *n.* polite conversation. [OE. *smcel*]

smart *a.* brisk; clever; trim, well dressed; fashionable. -*v.i.* be very painful; suffer acutely. -*n.* sharppain. [OE. *smeortan*, to be painful]

smash *v.t.* shatter; dash. -*v.i* break. -*n.* heavy blow; wrecked state; accident wrecking vehicles. [fr. *mash*]

smattering *n.* superficial knowledge. -**smatt'er** *v.i.* have a smattering. -**smatt'er** *n.* [orig. unknown]

smear *v.t.* rub with grease, *etc.* -*n.* mark made thus. [OE. *smeoru*, fat]

smell *v.t.* perceive by the nose. -*v.i.* use the nose; give out an odor. -*n.* odor; faculty of perceiving odors by the nose. [orig. unknown]

smelt *v.t.* extract metal from ore. -**smelt'ing-fur'nace** *n.* [obs. Du. *smelten*]

smile *v.i.* assume a pleased or amused expression. -*n.* act of smiling. [orig. uncertain]

smirch *v.t.* make dirty; soil; dishonor. -*n.* mark, blot; stain. [orig. uncertain]

smirk *v.i.* smile affectedly. -*n.* such smile. [OE. *smearcian*]

smite *v.t.* strike; attack; affect, *esp.* with love. [OE. *smitan*, smear]

smith *n.* worker in iron, *etc.* -**smith'y** (-TH-) *n.* his workshop. [OE.]

smock *n.* loose garment with the upper part gathered. -*v.t.* gather by diagonal lines of sewing. -**smock'-frock** *n.* laborer's smock. [OE. *smoc*]

smog *n.* mixture of smoke and fog. [*smoke*, *fog*]

smoke *n.* cloudy mass of suspended particles that rises from fire or anything burning; spell of tobacco smoking. -*v.i.* give off smoke; inhale and expel the smoke of burning tobacco. -*v.t.* expose to smoke (*esp.* in curing fish, *etc.*); consume (tobacco) by smoking. -**smo'ker** *n.* -**smo'ky** *a.* -*n.* smoked haddock. -**smo'kily** *adv.* -**smokestack** *n.* funnel, chimney, from a steam boiler *etc.* -**smoke-screen** *n.* in warfare, cloud of smoke to conceal activities of ships or troops. [OE. *smoca*]

smol'der *v.i.* burn slowly without flame. [orig. uncertain]

smooth (-TH) *a.* not rough, even of surface; plausible. -*v.t.* make smooth. quieten. -**smooth'ly** *adv.* [OE. *smoth*]

smoth'er (-uTH-) *n.* dense smoke, spray, foam, *etc.* -*v.t.* suffocate, suppress. -*v.i.* be suffocated. [OE. *smorian*]

smudge *n.* smear, dirty mark. -*v.t.* make a dirty mark on. [orig. uncertain]

smug *a.* self-satisfied, complacent. -**smug'ly** *adv.* [Low Ger. *smuk*, neat]

smug'gle v.t. bring into a country without payment of legal customs duties. -smugg'ler n. [LG. smuggeln]

smut n. piece of soot, black particle of dirt; disease of grain; lewd or obscene talk. -v.t. blacken, smudge. -smutt'y a. [Low Ger.]

snack n. light meal. -snack'-bar n. bar, counter, for this. [dial. snack, bite]

snag n. stump, esp. a tree-trunk in a river; any obstacle or impediment. [ON. snagi, point]

snail n. slow-moving mollusk with a shell, common in gardens. [OE. sncegel]

snake n. long scaly limbless reptile. -sna'ky a. [OE. snaca]

snap v.i. make a quick bite or snatch. -v.t. snatch or bite; break abruptly; photograph. -n. quick sharp sound; bite; break; photograph. -snap'shot n. instantaneous photography; print of this; shot without deliberate aim. [Du. snappen]

snare n. noose used as a trap. -v.t. catch with one. [ON. snara]

snarl n. growling sound made by an angry dog. -v.i. make this sound; grumble. [imit. orig.]

snarl n. tangle. [fr. snare]

snatch v.i. make a quick grab or bite (at). -v.t. seize, catch. -n. grab; short spell. [cp. snack]

sneak v.i. slink. -n. mean or treacherous person. [OE. snican, creep]

sneer v.i. smile, speak or write scornfully. -n. a sneering. [orig. uncertain]

sneeze v.i. emit breath with a sudden convulsive spasm and noise. -n. sneezing. [OE. fneosan]

snick'er v.t. snigger, giggle. [imit.]

sniff v.i. draw in breath through the nose with a sharp hiss; express disapproval, etc., by sniffing. -v.t. take up through the nose, smell. -n. a sniffing. [imit. orig.]

snip v.t. cut, cut bits off. -n. bit cut off, small cut. -snipp'et n. shred, fragment. [Du. snippen]

snipe n. long-billed marsh-bird. -v.i. shoot at enemy individuals from cover. v.t. hit by so shooting. -sni'per n. [ON. snipe]

sniv'el v.i. sniff to show real or sham emotion, esp. sorrow. [OE. snyflan]

snob n. one who judges by social rank or wealth rather than merit. -snobb'ery n. -snobb'ish a. -snobb'ishly adv. [orig. uncertain]

snoop v.i. pry, sneak around. -snoop'er n. [Du. snoepen]

snooze v.i. take a short sleep, be half asleep. -n. nap. [orig. unknown]

snore v.i. make noises with the breath when asleep. -n. act of snoring. [imit. orig.]

snort v.i. make a noise by driving breath through the nostrils; show defiance; contempt. -n. such noise. [imit. orig.]

snout n. nose of an animal. [OE. snut]

snow n. frozen vapor which falls in flakes. -(sl.) cocaine. -v.i. it snows, snow is falling. -v.t. let fall or throw down like snow; cover with snow. -snow-line n. elevation above which snow does not melt. -snow'y a. [OE. snow]

snub v.t. mortify or repress intentionally; rebuke. -n. snubbing. -snub'nose n. turned-up stumpy nose. [ON. snubba, rebuke]

snuff n. charred candle-wick; powdered tobacco for inhaling through the nose; act of snuffing. -v.t. free (a candle) from snuff; put out; draw up or through the nostrils. v.i. draw air or snuff into the nose. [cp. snuff]

snug a. cosy; trim. -snug'ly adv. -snugg'ery n. cosy room. -snuggle v.i. nestle. [orig. uncertain]

so adv. in such manner; very; the case being such. -conj. therefore; in case that. [OE. swa]

soak v.i. lie in a liquid. -v.t. steep, make throughly wet. -n. a soaking. [OE. socian]

soap n. compound of alkali and oil used in washing. -v.t. apply soap to. -soap'stone n. soft kind of rock, steatite. -soap'y a. [OE. sape]

soar v.i. to fly high.[F. essorer]

sob v.i. catch the breath, esp. in weeping. -n. sobbing. -sob'-stuff n. cheap pathos. [imit.]

so'ber a. temperate; subdued; not drunk. -v.t. and i. make or become sober. -so'berly adv. -sobri'ety n. [L. sobrius]

socc'er n. association football, game between two teams of eleven players using a round ball which is kicked from one to another in order to score goals between goalposts. [fr. association football]

so'cial a. living in communities; relating to society; sociable. -so'cially adv. -so'ciable a. inclined to be friendly, of ready companionship. -sociabil'ity n. -so'ciably adv. -soci'ety n. companionship; living associated with others; those so living; fashionable people collectively; association or club. -sociol'ogy n. social science. -so'cialism n. policy aiming at ownership of means of production and transport, etc., by the community. -so'cialist n. -socialist'tic a. [L. socius, companion]

sock n. short stocking; inner sole, formerly, light shoe worn by actors in comedy; hence, comedy. [L. soccus]

sock v.t. (sl.) hit, punch. [orig. unknown]

sock'et n. hole for something to fit into. [AF. soket, spear-head]

sod n. flat piece of earth with grass; a turf. [orig. uncertain]

so'da n. alkali. -so'da-water n. water charged with gas. [It. -L. solids, firm]

sodd'en a. soaked; like dough; of ground, boggy. [orig. pp. of seethe]

so'dium n. a metallic element found in soda, salt and other compounds. [Latinized from soda]

sod'omy n. unnatural sexual intercourse, esp. between males; anal intercourse. [Sodom (Gen. xviii)]

so'fa n. long padded seat with a back and one or two ends. [F.]

soft a. yielding easily to pressure; not hard; not loud; mild; easy; subdued; over-sentimental. -soft'ly adv. -soft'en (sofn) v.t. and i. [OE. softe]

sogg'y a. soaked, soden, marshly; damp and heavy. [orig. uncertain]

soil *n.* earth, ground. [L. *solum*]

soil *v.t.* and *i.* make or become dirty. -*n.* dirt; sewage. [F. *souiller*]

so'lace *n.* and *v.t.* comfort; consolation in distress. [L. *solari*, comfort]

so'lan *n.* large sea-bird like a goose; gannet. [orig. uncertain]

so'lar *a.* of the sun. -**sola'rium** *n.* sunroom. -**so'lar hea'ting** *n.* heat radiation from the sun collected by heat-absorbing panels through which water is circulated. -**so'lar pan'el** *n.* a panel exposed to radiation of heat from the sun, used for heating water or, when mounted with solar cells, to produce electricity direct, *esp,* for powering instruments in satellites. -**so'lar pow'er** *n.* heat radiation from the sun converted to electrical energy by specially designed steam boilers and turbogenerators. -**so'lar sys'tem,** system of planets, *etc.* revolving round the sun. -**so'lar plex'us,** nerve network at pit of stomach. [L. *sol,* sun]

solder (soi-, sol-, sod-) *n.* an easilymelted alloy used for joining metal. -*v.t.* to join with it. -**sol'dering-iron** *n.* [L. *solidare,* to make solid]

sol'dier *n.* one serving in an army. -*v.i.* serve in the army. -**sol'dierly** *a.* -**sol'diery** *n.* troops. [F. *solde,* pay]

sole *n.* flat of the foot; under part of a boot or shoe, *etc.* -*v.t.* supply with a sole. [F. fr. L. *solea*]

sole *a.* only, unique; single. -**sole'ly** *adv.* only; singly. [L. *solus*]

sol'emn (-M) *a.* serious, grave; formal; impressive. -**sol'emnly** *adv.* -**solem'nity** *n.* - **sol'emnize** *v.t.* celebrate, perform; make solemn. -**solemniza'tion** *n.* [L. *sollemnis,* appointed]

soli'cit (-lis'-) *v.t.* urge; request; entice. - **solicita'tion** *n.* -**soli'citor** *n.* one who solicits; lawyer. -**soli'citous** *a.* anxious. -**solicitude** *n.* [L. *sollicitare*]

sol'id *a.* not hollow; compact; substantial; unanimous. -*n.* body of three dimensions. - **sol'idly** *adv.* -**solid'ity** *n.* -**solid'ify** *v.t.* and *i.* -**solidifica'tion** *n.* -**solidar'ity** *n.* united state. [L. *solidus*]

solid-state circuit *See* semiconductor.

solil'oquy *n.* talking with oneself. - **solil'oquize** *v.i.* [Late L. *soliloquium*]

solitaire' *n.* single precious stone set by itself; game for one. [L. *solus,* alone]

sol'itary *a.* alone, single. -*n.* hermit. - **sol'itude** *n.* [L. *solitarius*]

so'lo *n.* music for one performer; a solo part; motor-bicycle without sidecar. -**so'loist** *n.* - **so'lo flight'**, flight by one person alone. [F.]

sol'stice *n.* period of the year when the sun is overhead at one of the tropics. -**solsti'tial** *a.* [L. *solstitium*]

solve *v.t.* work out, clear up, find the answer of. -**sol'uble** *a.* capable of solution. - **solubil'ity** *n.* -**solu'tion** *n.* answer to a problem; a dissolving; liquid with something dissolved in it. -**sol'vable** *a.* -**sol'vent** *a.* able to pay debts, having more assets than liabilities. -*n.* liquid with a power of dissolving. -

sol'vency *n.* state of being able to pay one's debts. [L. *solvere, solut-,* loosen]

som'ber *a.* dark or gloomy. -**som'berly** *adv.* -**somberness** *n.* (F.)

sombre'ro *n.* wide-brimmed felt hat worn in Mexico. [Sp.]

some (sum) *pron.* portion, quantity. -*a.* one or other; amount of; certain; approximately; **some'body** *n.* -**some'how** *adv.* -**some'thing** *n.* -**some'time** *a.* former. -*adv.* formerly; at some (past or future) time. -**some'times** *adv.* on occasion. -**some'what** *n.* something. -*adv.* to some extent, rather. -**some'where** *adv.* [OE. *sum*]

somersault (sum-) *n.* tumbling head over heels. [F. *soubresant*]

somnolent *a.* sleepy. -**som'nolence** *n.* [L. *somnus,* sleep]

son *n.* male child. -**son'-in-law** *n.* daughter's husband. [OE. *sunu*]

sona'ta (-d-) *n.* piece of music in several movements, mainly for a solo instrumental. -**sonati'na** *n.* short and simple sonata. [It.]

song *n.* singing; poem for singing; notes of certain birds. -**song'ster** *n.* -**song'-stress** *fem.* [OE.]

so'nic *a.* of sound waves. [L. *sonus,* sound]

sonnet *n.* fourteen-line poem with a rhyme system. -**sonneteer'** *n.* [F.]

sonor'ous *a.* giving out deep sound, resonant. -**son'orously** *adv.* -**sonor'ity** *n.* [L. *sonorus-sonare,* sound]

soon *adv.* before long; early; without delay. [OE. *sona,* at once]

soot *n.* black substance formed from smoke. -**soot'y** *a.* [OE. *sot*]

soothe *v.t.* calm, soften; please with soft words. -**sooth'ing** *a.* -**sooth'ingly** *adv.* [OE. *sothian,* show to be true]

sop *n.* piece of bread, *etc.,* soaked in liquid; bribe; something to quieten. -*v.t.* steep in water *etc.* [OE. *sopp*]

sophist *n.* captious reasoner. -**soph'ism** *n.* specious argument. -**sophist'ical** *a.* - **soph'istry** *n.* -**sophisticate** *v.t.* make artificial, spoil, falsify. -**sophistica'tion** *n.* [G. *sophisma*] -**sophistication** *n.* [G. *sophisms*]

soprano *n.* highest voice in women and boys; singer with this voice; musical part for it. [It.]

sor'cerer *n.* wizard. -**sor'ceress** *fem.* - **sor'cery** *n.* witchcraft. [F. *soreier*]

sor'did *a.* mean, squalid. -**sor'didly** *adv.* - **sor'didness** *n.* [L. *sordidus*]

sore *a.* painful; distressed. *adv.* grievously. -*n.* sore place, ulcer or boil, *etc.* -**sore'ness** *n.* -**sore'ly** *adv.* [OE. *sar*]

sorority *n.* club of women, *esp.* a women's student organization formed chiefly for social purposes, *etc.* [L. *soror,* sister]

sorr'ow (-o) *n.* pain of mind, grief. -*v.i.* grieve. -**sorr'owful** *a.* -**sorr'owfully** *adv.* [OE. *sorh*]

sorr'y *a.* distressed; mean, poor. -**sorr'ily** *adv.* [OE. *sarig*]

sort *n.* kind or class. -*v.t.* classify. -**sort'er** *n.* [L. *sors, sort-,* share, lot]

sort'ie *n.* sally by besieged forces. [F.]

SOS *n.* letters of Morse Code sent as an appeal for help by ship at sea; a broadcast appeal for a relative of one dangerously ill; an urgent appeal.

sot *n.* drunkard. -sott´ish *a.* [F. = fool]

sou´fflé *n.* dish made with whisked white-of-egg. [F.]

soul *n.* spiritual part of a human being; person. -soul´ful *a.* expressing elevated feeling. -soul´less *a.* mean, prosaic. -soul food *n.* food, as yams *etc.*, traditionally eaten by southern black Americans. -soul mate *n.* person for whom one has deep affinity. -soul music *n.* type of Black music resulting from addition of jazz and gospel to urban blues style. [OE. *sawol*]

sound *n.* that which is heard; meaningless noise. -*v.i.* make a sound. -*v.t.* cause to sound. -sound´ing *n.* act of sounding; an ascertained depth. [L. *sonus*]

sound *a.* in good condition; solid; of good judgment. -sound´ly *adv.* . thoroughly. [OE. *gesund*, healthy]

sound *n.* channel or strait. (ON. *sund*]

sound *v.t.* find the depth of -*v.i.* find the depth of water. [F. *sonder*]

soup *n.* liquid food made by boiling meat or vegetables. [F. *souse*]

sour *a.* acid; peevish. -*v.t.* and *i.* make or become sour. -sour´ly *adv.* -sour´ness *n.* -sour´dough *n.* leaven; old timer. [OE. *sur*]

source *n.* spring; origin. [F.]

south *n.* cardinal point opposite the north; region, or part of a country, *etc.*, lying to that side. *a.* that is towards the south. *adv.* towards the south. south´erly (suTH-) *a.* -south´ern (suTH-) *a.* -south´wards *a.* and *adv.* -south´wester, sou´-wester *n.* waterproof hat. [OE. *suth*]

souvenir *n.* memory; keepsake. [F.]

sovereign (sov´rin) *n.* king or queen; ruler; formerly, gold coin *a.* supreme; efficacious. -sov´ereignty *n.* [OF. *soverain*]

soviet´ *n.* council, *esp.* of soldiers and workmen, in Russia, forming basis of Russian national government. [Russ.]

sow *n.* female of the swine. [OE. *sugu*]

sow *v.i.* scatter seed. -*v.t.* scatter or deposit (seed); spread abroad. -sow´er *n.* [OE. *sawan*]

soy´a-bean *n.* Eastern edible bean. -soy´a-flour *n.* flour made from it. -soy sauce *n.* salty, dark brown sauce made from fermented soya beans, used *esp.* in Chinese cookery. [Jap. *shoyu*]

spa *n.* medicinal spring; place with one. [*Spa*, in Belgium]

space *n.* extent; period; area; expanse; expanse of the universe; empty place. *v.t.* place at intervals. -spa´cious *n.* roomy. [F. *espace*, fr. L. *spatium*]

spade *n.* tool for digging. [OE. *spadu*]

spades *n.pl.* suit at cards. -*sing.* card of this suit. [Sp. *espada*, sword]

spaghetti (-get´-) *n.* dried wheat-paste in long narrow tubes, thinner than macaroni. [It.]

span *n.* space from thumb to little finger as a measure; extent or space; the stretch of an arch, *etc.*; (airplane) distance between wingtips; team of oxen. -*v.t.* stretch over; measure with the hand; harness or yoke. -spann´er *n.* tool for gripping the nut of a screw. [OE. *spann*]

spaniel *n.* dog with long ears and hair. [OF. *espagneul*, 'Spanish']

spank *v.i.* move with vigor or spirit. -spank´ing *a.* brisk; fine, big. -spank´er *n.* fast-going horse, ship, *etc.* [Dan. *spanke*, strut]

spank *v.t.* slap with the flat of the hand, *esp.* in chastising children. [imit.]

spar *n.* pole, *esp.* as part of a ship's rigging. [On. *sparri*]

spar *v.i.* box; make boxing motions; dispute, *esp.* in fun. [orig. uncertain]

spare *a.* additional, in reserve, not in use. -*v.t.* leave unhurt; abstain from using; do without; give away. spar´ing using little; economical. -spar´ingly *adv.* [OE. *sparian*]

spark *n.* small glowing or burning particle; trace; electric spark igniting explosive mixture in car cylinder. -*v.i.* emit sparks. -spar´kie *v.i.* glitter. [OE. *spearca*]

sparr´ow *n.* small brownish bird, common in towns. [OE. *spearswa*]

sparse *a.* thinly scattered. -sparse´ly *adv.* [L. *spargere*, spars-, scatter]

spar´tan *a.* hardy; frugal. [*Sparta*]

spas´m (-zm) *n.* convulsive muscular contraction. -spasmod´ic *a.* of the nature of a spasm; jerky; intermittent; disjointed. -spa´stic *a.* of, like spasms, spasmodic. [G. *spasmos*]

spat *n. usu. pl.* short gaiter. [short for *spatter-dash*, shield against splashes]

spatt´er *v.t.* splash, cast drops over. -*v.i.* fall in drops. -*n.* slight splash. -spatt´er- dash *n.* protection against splashes. [Du. *spatten*, burst]

spat´ula *n.* broad blade, used for mixing paint, *etc.* [L.]

spawn *n.* eggs of fish. -*v.i.* of fish, to cast eggs. [OF. *espandre*, shed]

speak *v.i.* utter words; converse; deliver a discourse. -*v.t.* utter; communicate with (a passing ship). [OE. *sprecan*]

spear *n.* long pointed weapon, pike. -*v.t.* pierce with a spear. -spear´-side *n.* male side of family *pl* . distaff-side. [OE. *spere*]

spe´cial (spesh-) *a.* beyond the usual; particular, individual; distinct; limited. spe´cially *adv.* -spe´cialist *n.* one who devotes himself to a special subject or branch of a subject. -spe´cialism *n.* -spe´cialize *v.i.* be a specialist. -*v.t.* make special. -special´ty *n.* special product, characteristic, *etc.* [L. *species*, kind, appearance]

spe´cies *n.* class; sub-division; sort or kind. [L.]

specific *a.* characteristic of a thing or kind; definite; specially efficacious for something. -specif´ically *adv.* -spe´cify (-fi) *v.t.* state definitely or in detail. -specifica´tion *n.* detailed description. [L. *species*, kind, appearance]

spe´cimen *n.* individual example; part used to typify a whole. [L. *specimen*]

speck *n.* small spot, particle. *-v.t.* spot. -**speck'le** *n.* and *v.* speck. -**speck'led** *a.* -**speck'less** *a.* spotless [OE. *specca*]

spectacle *n.* show; thing exhibited. *-pl.* arrangement of lenses to help defective sight. -**spectac'ular** *a.* -**specta'tor** *n.* one who looks on. [L. *specere, spect-,* look]

spec'ter *n.* ghost; threatening image. [L. *spec'trum,* vision]

spectrum *n.* -**spec'tra** *pl.* colored band into which a beam of light can be decomposed. -**spec'toscope** *n.* instrument for decomposing light and examining spectra. [L.]

speculate *v.i.* make theories or guesses; engage in risky commercial transactions. -**spec'ulator** *n.* -**spec'ulative** *a.* -**specula'tion** *n.* [L. *speculatus*]

spec'ulum *n.* a mirror; a reflector of polished metal, *esp.* such as that used in reflecting-telescopes. [L. *speculum,* a mirror-*specere,* to look at]

speech *n.* act or faculty of speaking words; language; conversation; discourse. -**speechify** *v.i.* make a speech. -**speech'less** *a.* [OE. *sprxc*]

speed *n.* swiftness; rate of progress. *-v.i.* move quickly; succeed. *-v.t.* further; expedite; bid farewell to. -**speedom'eter** *n.* instrument to show the speed of a moving vehicle. -**speed'y** *a.* -**speed'ily** *adv.* -**speed'way** *n.* track for racing. [OE. *spxd*]

spell *n.* magic formula; enchantment. -**spell'-bound** *a.* entranced. [OE.]

spell *n.* turn of work, *etc.*; bout. [OE. *spelian,* act for]

spell *v.t.* read letter by letter; give the letters of in order. [OF. *espeler*]

speller *n.* zinc. [orig. unknown]

spend *v.t.* lay out; disburse; employ. -**spend'thrift** *n.* wasteful person, prodigal. -**spend'er** *n.* [L. *expendere,* pay]

sperm *n.* animal seed; spawn of fishes, frogs. [G. *sperma*]

sphere *n.* globe; range, province. -**spher'ical** *a.* -**sphe'roid** *n.* body nearly a sphere in shape. [G. *sphaira,* ball]

sphinx *n.* statue, half woman, half lion; enigmatic person. [G. *Sphingx*]

spice *n.* aromatic or pungent vegetable substance; spices collectively; trace. *-v.t.* season with spices. -**spi'cy** *a.* piquant. -**spi'cily** *adv.* [OF. *espice*]

spick and span *a.* new and neat. [*spick, spike,* and ME. *span-new,* ON. *span-nyr,* chip-new]

spi'der *n.* animal which spins a web to catch its prey. -**spi'dery** *a.* [ME. *spithre,* fr. OE. *spinnam,* spin]

spig'ot *n.* peg for a hole in a cask. [orig. uncertain]

spike *n.* ear (of corn, *etc.*); sharp-pointed piece of metal, wood, nail. *-v.t.* drive a spike into, supply with spikes, fasten with spikes. [L. *spica*]

spill *n.* splinter or twist of paper for use as a taper. [OE. *speld,* torch]

spin *v.t.* twist into thread; revolve rapidly. *-v.i.* make thread; revolve rapidly. *-n.* rapid run or ride; spinning. -**spin'dle** *n.* rod or axis for spinning. -**spinn'er** *n.* -**spin'ster** *n.* one who spins. [OE. *spinnan*]

spin'ach (-ij) *n.* edible green vegetable. [OF. *espinage*]

spine *n.* thorn; various things like this; backbone. -**spi'nal** *a.* [L. *spina*]

spin'et *n.* instrument like a small harpsichord. [OF. *espiente*]

spinnaker *n.* large yacht sail spread by a boom. [orig. uncertain]

spin'ster *n.* unmarried woman. [*spin*]

spire *n.* pointed steeple on church or other building; peak, plant, *etc.,* of this form. *-v.t.* and *i.* shoot up; furnish into a spire. [OE. *spir,* sprout, shoot]

spire *n.* coil. -**spi'ral** *n.* continuous curve round a cylinder, like the thread of a screw. *-a.* of this form. -**spi'rally** *adv.* [G. *speira,* coil]

spir'it *n.* soul; ghost; essential character or meaning; courage, liveliness; frame of mind; liquid got by distillation, *esp.* an alcoholic one. *-v.t.* carry away mysteriously. -**spir'itual** *a.* hymn, *esp.* of Black Americans. -**spir'itually** *adv.* -**spir'itless** *a.* -**spir'ituality** *n.* -**spir'itualism, spir'itism** *n.* belief that the spirits of the dead can communicate with living people. -**spiritualist, spir'itist** *n.* -**spir'ituous** *a.* alcoholic. [L. *spiritus,* fr. *spirare,* breathe]

spirt *v.t.* and *i.* send or come out in jet. *-n.* jet. [orig. uncertain]

spit *n.* sharp metal rod to put through meat for roasting; sandy point projecting into the sea. *-v.t.* thrust through; impale. [OE. *spitu*]

spit *v.i.* eject saliva. *-v.t.* eject from the mouth. *-n.* a spitting; saliva. -**spit'tle** *n.* saliva. -**spittoon'** *n.* vessel to spit into. [OE. *spittan*]

spit *n.* spadeful; depth of a spade blade as measure of depth for digging. [OE. *spittan*]

spite *n.* malice. *-v.t.* thwart. -**spite'ful** *a.* -**spite'fully** *adv.* [*despite*]

splash *v.t.* spatter liquid over. *-v.i.* dash, scatter (of liquids). *-n.* sound or result of splashing. -**splash'board** *n.* mudguard. [imit. orig.]

splay *v.t.* spread out; make slanting. *-n.* slanting surface; spread. *a.* slanting. -**splay-foot** *n.* flat foot turned outward. [for *display*]

spleen *n.* organ in the abdomen; irritable or morose temper. -**splenet'ic** *a.* melancholy, irritable. [G. *splen*]

splen'did *a.* magnificent, gorgeous; illustrious; excellent. -**splen'didly** *adv.* -**splen'dor** *n.* [L. *splendidus*]

splice *v.t.* join by interweaving strands; join (wood) by overlapping. *-n.* spliced joint. [Du. *splitsen*]

splint *n.* rigid strip of material for holding a broken limb in position. -**splin'ter** *n.* split-off fragment, chip. *-v.i.* break into fragments. [Du.]

split *v.t.* and *i.* break asunder; (*sl.*) give away (a secret, *etc.*). *-n.* crack or fissure. [Du. *split-ten*]

splurge *n.* ostentatious display. *-v.i.* [orig. unknown]

spoil *v.t.* damage. or injure; pillage; damage the manners or behavior of by indulgence. *-v.i.*

go bad. -n. booty. [L. *spoliate*]

spoke n. radial bar of a wheel; rung of ladder. -**spoke**'shave n. tool for shaping wood. [OE. *spaca*]

spokesman n. one deputed to speak for others. [*speak*]

sponge (-unj) n. marine growth used to absorb liquids. -v.t. wipe with a sponge. -v.i. live craftily at the expense of others. -**spon**'gy a. [L. *spongia*]

spon'sor n. guarantor; patron; one who provides financial backing for an enterprise, *usu.* in return for publicity; one who answers for an infant at baptism; surety. [L.]

spontaneous a. of one's own accord; involuntary; impulsive; self-produced; self motivated. -**spontane**'ity n. -**sponta**'neously. *adv.* [L. *spontaneous*]

spoof n. card game; hoax, trick. -v.f. [mod. *coinage*]

spook n. ghost; specter. [Du.]

spool n. reel. [Du. *spoel*]

spoon n. implement with a shallow bowl at the end of a handle for carrying food to the mouth, *etc.* -v.t. transfer with a spoon. [OE. *spon*, chip]

spoor n. trail of a wild beast. [Du.]

sporad'ic a. occurring at intervals or in small numbers. [G. *sporadikos-sporas, sporad-*, scattered]

spore n. tiny organ of reproduction in plants and protozoa. [G. *spora*, seed]

sport n. pastime; merriment; (*sl.*) one prepared to take a risk, a sporting chance-v.i. amuse onself, take part in a game. *etc.* - **sport**'ive a. playful. -**sports**'man n. one who hunts, shoots, *etc.* -**sports**'manship n. [for *disport*]

spot n. small mark or stain; place. -v.t. mark with spots; detect. -**spot**'less a. -**spot**'lessly *adv.* -**spot**'light n. light thrown on one part of the stage. -**spott**'ed dog n. (*sl.*) plum-pudding. [ON. *spotti*]

spouse n. husband or wife. [OF. *espouse*, fr. L. *sponsus*, promised]

spout v.t. and i. pour out. -n. projecting tube for pouring a liquid; copious discharge. [orig. uncertain]

sprain n. and v.t. wrench or twist (of muscle, *etc.*). [OF. *espreindre*, press out]

sprawl v.i. lie or toss about awkwardly.- n. sprawling position. [OE. *spreawlian*]

spray n. water, *etc.*, flying in small, fine drops. -v.t. sprinkle with spray. [LG. *sprei*]

spread (-ed) v.t. stretch out; scatter. -v.i. become spread.-n. extent. -**spreader** n. - **spread**'-eagle v.t. tie up with outstretched arms and legs. [OE. *spraedan*]

spreadsheet n. (*compute.*) form of computer program that manipulates information and displays it in the form of an electronic ledger; accounting tables.

sprig n. small twig; small headless nail. [orig. uncertain]

spright'ly a. lively, brisk. [fr. *sprite*]

spring v.i. leap; appear; crack. - v.t. produce unexpectedly.- n. flow of water from the earth; first season of the year; leap; recoil; piece of coiled or bent metal with much resilience. - **spring**'bok n. S. African antelope. - **spring**'-tide n. high tide at new or full moon.[OE. *springan*]

sprin'kle (-ng-kl) v.t. scatter small drops on. - **sprink**'ler n. [OE *sprengan*]

sprint v.i. run a short distance at great speed. - n. such run or race. - **sprint**'er n. [of Scand. orig.]

sprite n. fairy. [L. *spiritus*]

sprout v.i. put forth shoots, spring up. - n. shoot. [OE. *sprutan*]

spruce n. variety of fir. - a. neat in dress. [earlier *pruce*, fr. *Pruce*, Prussia]

spry a. active; lively, gay. [orig. unknown]

spud n. small spade-like implement for cutting roots of weeds, *etc.*; (*sl.*) potato. [orig. uncertain]

spur n. pricking instrument attached to a horseman's heel; projection on the leg of a cock; projecting mountain range; stimulus. - v.t. apply spurs to; urge. - v.i. ride hard. [OE. *sporu*]

spurious a. sham. [L. *spurius*]

spurn v.t. reject with scorn. - **spurn**'ing n. [OE. *spornan*, kick]

spurt n. a short sudden effort, *esp.* in a race. - v.i. gush. [var. of *spirt*]

sput'ter v.t. and i. and n. splutter. [imit. orig.]

spu'tum n. spittle. [L.]

spy n. one who enters hostile territory to observe and report. - v.i. act as a spy. - v.t. catch sight of. [OF. *espie*]

squab (-ob) n. unfledged bird; sofa cushion. - a. clumsy; squat. [imit. orig.]

squab'ble n. petty noisy quarrel. - v.i. engage in one. [imit. orig.]

squad (-od) n. small party, esp. of soldiers. - **squad**'ron n. division of a cavalry regiment or of a fleet, or of an air force. [F. *escouade*]

squal'id a. mean and dirty, as slums. - **squal**'or n. [L. *squalidus*]

squall (-awl) n. scream; sudden gust of wind. - v.i. scream. [imit. orig.]

squan'der (-on-) v.t. spend wastefully. [orig. uncertain]

square n. equilateral rectangle; area of this shape; product of a number multiplied by itself; instrument for drawing right angles. - a. square in form honest. - **square meal** n. a substantial meal consisting of enough food to satisfy. - v.t. make square; find the square of; pay; bribe. - v.i. fit, suit. - **square**'ly *adv.* - **square**'-rigg'ed a. having chief sails square on horizontal yards at right angles to keel.[OF. *esquarre*, fr. L. *ex-quadra*]

squash (-osh) v.t. crush flat or to pulp. - n. crowd; game (squash rackets) played with rackets and a rubber ball inside a specially constructed enclosed space. [OF. *esquasser*]

squash n. gourd-like vegetable [Amer. Ind. *asquash*]

squat (-ot) v.i. sit on the heels. - a. short and thick. - **squatt**'er n. one who settles on land without title. [OF. *esquati*, fr.*quatir*, press flat]

squaw n. N. American Indian wife or woman. [N. Amer. Ind. *squa*]

squeak *v.i.* make a short shrill sound. -*n.* such sound. - **squeak′er** *n.* one who betrays an accomplice. [imit. orig.]

squeal *n.* long squeak. - *v.i.* make one; turn informer. [imit. orig.]

squeam′ish *a.* easily made sick; overscrupulous. [AF. *escoymos*]

squeeze *v.t.* press; subject to extortion. - *n.* a squeezing. [OE. *cwiesan*]

squid *n.* cuttle-fish. [var. of *squirt*]

squint *v.i.* have the eyes turned in different directions. - *v.t.* this affection of the eyes; glance. [earlier *asquint*, of uncertain orig.]

squire *n.* country gentleman; lady's escort. -*v.t.* escort (a lady). [*esquire*]

squirm *v.i.* and *n.* wriggle. [imit. orig.]

squirr′el *n.* small graceful animal living in trees and having a large bushy tail. [OF. *escureul*]

squirt *v.t.* and *i.* eject, be ejected, in a jet. -*n.* instrument for squirting; small rapid stream. [orig. uncertain]

stab *v.i.* pierce with a pointed weapon. -*v.i.* strike with such weapon. -*n.* wound so inflicted. [Gael. *stob*, stake]

sta′ble *n.* building for horses. -*v.t.* put into one. [L. *stabulum*, stall]

sta′ble *a.* firmly fixed; resolute. -**sta′bly** *adv.* -**stabil′ity** *n.* -**sta′bilize** *v.t.* and *i.* [L. *stabilis*]

stack *n.* pile or heap, *esp.* of hay or straw; tall chimney. -*v.t.* pile in a stack. [ON. *stakkr*, haystack]

sta′dium *n.* (sta′dia *pl.*) sportsground; arena. [G. *stodion*]

staff *n.* (staffs, staves *pl.*), pole; body of officers or workers; five lines on which music is written. [OE. *stæf*]

stag *n.* male deer. [OE. *stagga*]

stage *n.* raised floor or platform; platform of a theater; dramatic art or literature; scene of action; point of development; stopping-place on a road, distance between two of them. -*v.t.* put (a play) on the stage. -**sta′gy** *a.* theatrical. -**stage -coach** *n.* public passenger coach running between stages. -**stage′-fright** *n.* nervousness before an audience. [OE. *estage*]

stagg′er *v.i.* walk or stand unsteadily. -*v.t.* shock; spread (*e.g.* holidays) over a period to prevent overlapping. -*n.* act of staggering. [ON. *stakra*]

stag′nate *v.i.* to cease to flow, be motionless. -**stag′nant** *a.* -**stagna′tion** *n.* [L. *stagnum*, pool]

staid *a.* of sober and quiet character. [for *stayed*]

stain *v.t.* and *i.* discolor, soil. -*n.* spot or mark; blemish. [for *distain*, OF. *desteindre*]

stair *n.* set of steps, *esp.* as part of a house. -**stair′case** *n.* [OE. *stæger*]

stake *n.* sharpened stick or post; money wagered or contended for; martyrdom. -*v.t.* secure or mark out with stakes; wager-. [OE. *stoca*]

stalactite *n.* deposit of lime like an icicle on roof of a cave. -**stal′agmite** *n.* similar deposit on floor. [G. *stalaktos*, dropping; *stalagmos*, a dropping]

stale *a.* old, lacking freshness. -*n.* urine of horses. -*v.i.* of horses, make water. -**stale′mate** *n.* in chess, a draw through one player being unable to move. [OF. *estate*, spread out]

stalk (-awk) *n.* plant's stem. [OE. *stalu*]

stalk (-awk) *v.i.* steal up to game; walk in a stiff and stately manner. -*v.t.* steal up to. -*n.* a stalking. [OF. *stealcian*]

stall (-awl) *n.* compartment in a stable; erection for the display and sale of goods; seat in the chancel of a church; front seat in a theater, *etc.* -*v.t.* put in a stall. -*v.i.* stick fast; of an airplane, lose flying speed. [OE. *steall*, standing place, *esp.* for cattle]

stallion (stal′-yun) *n.* uncastrated male horse. [OF. *estalon*]

stal′wart *a.* strong, sturdy, brave. -*n.* stalwart person. -**stal′wartness** *n.* [OE. *stoelwierthe*, serviceable]

sta′men *n.* male organ of a flowering plant. [L. = fibre]

stamina *n. pl.* powers of endurance; vigor, vitality. [L. *stamen*, warp, thread]

stamm′er *v.s.* speak with repetitions of syllables, stutter. -*v.t.* utter thus. -*n.* habit of so speaking. [OE. *stamerian*]

stamp *v.i.* put down a foot with force. -*v.t.* impress a mark on; affix a postage stamp. -*n.* stamping with the foot; imprinted mark; appliance for marking; piece of gummed paper printed with a device as evidence of postage, *etc.*; character. [ME. cp. OE. *stempan*]

stampede′ *n.* sudden frightened rush, *esp.* of a herd of cattle, crowd, *etc.* -*v.t.* and *i.* put into, take part in, a stampede. [Sp. *estampido*]

stance *n.* (golf, *etc.*) position, stand; site. [Scot.]

stand *v.i.* have an upright position; be situated; become or remain firm or stationary; be a symbol of, *etc.* -*v.t.* set upright; endure. -*n.* stoppage, a holding firm; something on which a thing may be placed; structure for spectators to stand on for better view. -**stand′ing** *n.* position (in society, *etc.*) -**stand′-point** *n.* position from which things are viewed, judged. [OE. *standan*]

stand′ard *n.* flag; weight or measure to which others must conform; degree, quality; post, *e.g.* lamp-post. -**stand′ardize** *v.t.* [OF. *estendard*, royal banner]

stan′za *n.* group of lines of verse. [It.]

sta′ple *n.* U-shaped piece of metal with pointed ends to drive into wood for use as a ring; main commodity; the fiber of wool. [OE. *stapol*, post]

star *n.* shining celestial body seen as a twinkling point of light; asterisk (*); celebrated player; medal or jewel, *etc.*, of the apparent shape of a star. -*v.i.* adorn with stars; to mark with an asterisk (*). -**stargazer** *n.* astrologer; astronomer. [OE. *steorra*]

starboard *n.* right-hand side of a ship looking forward. -*a.* of, or on, this side. -*v.t.* put (the helm) to starboard. [OE. *steorbord*, steer side (the steering oar being worked on this side)]

starch *n.* substance forming the main food element in bread, potatoes, *etc.*, and used, mixed with water, for stiffening linen, *etc.* -*v.t.*

stiffen with it. [OE. *stearc*, rigid]

stare *v.i.* looked fixedly at; be prominent or obvious. -*v.t.* abash by staring at. -*n.* a staring. [OE. *starian*]

stark *a.* stiff, downright. *adv* . quite (*e.g.* in stark-mad). [OE. *stearc*, hard, strong]

starling *n.* speckled bird. [OE. *starling*, dim. of *steer*]

start *v.i.* make a sudden movement; begin, *esp.* a journey. -*v.t.* begin; set going. -*n.* abrupt movement; advantage of less distance to run in a race. [OE. *styrtan*]

star'tle *v.t.* give a fright to. -**start'ling** *a.* -**start'lingly** *adv.* [OE. *steartlian*]

starve *v.i.* suffer from cold, hunger; die of hunger. -*v.t.* kill or distress with lack of food, warmth, or other necessary thing. -**starve'ling** *n.* starving person. -**starvation** *n.* [OE. *steorfan*, di]

state *n.* condition; politically organized community; rank; pomp. -*v.t.* express in words; fix. -**state'ly** *a.* dignified. -**statement** *n.* expression in words; account. -**states'man** *n.* one able in managing the affairs of a state. -**states'manship** *n.* his art. -**state'room** *n.* separate cabin on a ship. [L. *status*, state, fr. *stare*, stand]

stat'ic *a.* motionless, at rest; dealing with forces in equilibrium. -*n.* in *pl.* the branch of physics studying such forces. [G. *statikos*, causing to stand]

sta'tion *n.* place where a thing stops or is placed; position in life; stopping place for trains. -*v.t.* put in a position. -**sta'tionary** *a.* not moving or not intended to be moved. [L. *statio-stare*, *stat-*, stand]

stationer *n.* one who deals in writing materials, *etc.* -**sta'tionery** *n.* his wares. [orig. tradesman with a *station*]

statistics *n.pl.* numerical facts collected systematically and arranged; study of them. -**statisti'cian**, *n.* one who deals with statistics. -**statist'ic** *a.* -**statist'ically** *adv.* [fr. obs. *statist*, politician]

statue *n.* solid carved or cast image of a person, *etc.* -**stat'uary** *n.* statues collectively. -**statuesque'** *a.* like a statue. -**statuette'** *n.* small statue. [L. *status*]

stature *n.* height (of a person). [F.]

sta'tus *n.* position, rank, 'standing'; position of affairs. [L.]

stat'ute *n.* a written law. -**stat'utory** *a.* [L. *statuere*, *statut-*, set up]

staunch, stanch *v.t.* stop a flow [of blood] from. -*a.* trustworthy, loyal. [OF. *estancher*, stop a flow; *estanche*, watertight]

stay *v.t.* stop. -*v.i.* remain; sojourn; pause. -*n.* a remaining or sojourning. -**stay'-in-strike**, strike in which strikers stay in their place of work. [OF. *ester*, fr. L., *stare*, stand]

stay *n.* support, prop; rope supporting a mast, *etc.* -*pl.* corsets. -*v.i.* prop or support. [OE. *stay*]

stead (-ed) *n.* in stead, in place; in good stead, of service. -**stead'y** *a.* firm; regular; temperate. -**stead'ily** *adv.* -**stead'fast** *a.* firm, unyielding. -**stead'fastly** *adv.* -**steadiness** *n.* [OE. *stede*, position, place]

steak (stak) *n.* slice of meat, fish for grilling, *etc.* [ON. *steik*, roast on a spit]

steal *v.i.* rob; move silently. -*v.t.* take without right or leave. -**stealth** (**stelth**) *n.* secrecy; slinking way. -**stealth'y** *a.* -**stealth'ily** *adv.* [OE. *stelan*]

steam *n.* vapor of boiling water. -*v.t.* cook or treat with steam. -*v.i.* give off steam; rise in vapor; move by steam power. -**steam'er** *n.* vessel for cooking or treating with steam; steam-propelled ship. -**steam'-engine**, engine worked by steam power. [OE.]

steed *n.* (*poet.*) horse. [OE. *steda*, stallion]

steel *n.* hard and malleable metal made by mixing carbon in iron; tool or weapon of steel. -*v.t.* harden. -**steel'y** *a.* [OE. *stele*]

steep *a.* having an abrupt or decided slope. -*n.* steep place. -**steep'ly** *adv.* [OE. *steep*, lofty]

steep *v.t.* soak. [orig. uncertain]

stee'ple *n.* church tower with a spire. **steeplechase** *n.* cross-country horse-race over obstacles. [OE. *stepel*]

steer *v.t.* guide, direct the course of. -*v.i.* direct one's course. -**steer'age** *n.* effect of a helm; part of a ship allotted to the passengers paying lowest fare. -**steers'man** *n.* one who steers a ship. -**steer'ing-wheel** *n.* [OE. *stieran*]

steer *n.* young male ox, bullock. [OE. *steor*, bullock]

stem *n.* stalk; trunk; part of a word to which inflectional endings are added; foremost part of a ship. [OE. *stemm*]

stem *v.t.* check. [ON. *stemma*]

stench *n.* evil smell. [OE. *stenc*]

sten'cil *v.t.* paint with figures, *etc.*, by passing a brush over a pierced plate. -*n.* the plate; pattern made. [orig. uncertain]

stenography *n.* shorthand writing. [G. *stenos*, narrow]

stentorian *a.* very loud. [*Stentor*, a G. warrior who had a very loud voice]

step *v.i.* move and set down a foot. -*v.t.* measure in paces; set up (a mast). -*n.* act of stepping; mark made by the foot; measure, act, stage in a proceeding; board, rung, *etc.*, to put the foot on; degree in a scale; mast socket. -**step'-dance** *n.* solo dance with intricate steps. [OE. *stæppan*]

stepchild *n.* child of a husband or wife by a former marriage. -**stepfather** *n.* -**step'mother** *n.* -**step'brother** *n.* -**step'sister** *n.* [OE. *steop-*, orphaned]

ster'eophonic *a.* (of sound reproduction) using two or more separate microphones to feed two or more loudspeakers through separate channels in order to give spatial effect to sound. -**ster'eo** *a.* /*n.* (of, for) stereophonic sound system. [G. *stereos*, solid, *phone*, sound]

ster'eoscope *n.* instrument in which two pictures taken at different viewpoints are combined into one image with an effect of solidity. -**stereoscop'ic** *a.* [G. *stereos*, solid]

ster'eotype *n.* plate for printing cast from set-up type; something monotonously familiar, conventional, predictable. -*v.t.* make a stereotype from; make into an empty formula. [G. *stereos*, solid] ster'ile a. barren; free from disease germs. -ster'ilize v.t. -ster'ilizer n. apparatus to destroy germs. [L. sterilis]

ster'ling a. of standard value or purity; of solid worth; in British coin. [AF. esterling]

stern a. severe, strict. -stern'ly adv. -stern'ness n. [OE. stierne]

stern n. after part of a ship; rump, tail, of an animal. [ON. stjorn, steering]

stet v.t. "let it stand", proof-reader's direction to cancel previous alteration. [L.]

stethoscope n. instrument for listening to the action of the heart or lungs. [G. stethos, chest]

stevedore n. one who loads or unloads ships. [Sp. estivador, wool-packer]

stew v.t. and i. cook slowly in a closed vessel. -n. food so cooked. -stew'pan n. [OF. estuve, hot bath]

steward n. one who manages another's property; attendant on a ship's passengers; official managing a race-meeting assembly, etc. -stew'ardess fem. [OE. stigweard, major-domo]

stick v.t. jab, stab, fix, fasten. -v.i. adhere, project, come to a stop, etc. -n. rod. -stick'y a. adhesive, viscous. [OE. stician, pierce]

stickler n. one who insists on trifles of procedure, authority, etc. [OE. stihtan, control]

stiff a. rigid; awkward, difficult. [OE. stif]

sti'fle v.t. smother. [earlier stuffle; OF. estouffer]

stig'ma n. brand, mark. -stig'matize v.t. mark out, brand with disgrace. [G.]

stile n. arrangement of steps for climbing a fence. [OE. stigel]

stilett'o n. small dagger. [It.]

still a. motionless, noiseless. -v.t. quiet. -adv. to this time; yet; even. -still'ness n. -still'y a. quiet. -still'born a. born dead. -still life n. painting of inanimate objects. [OE. stille]

still n. apparatus for distilling, esp. spirits. -still'-room n. housekeeper's storeroom. [for distil]

stilt n. one of a pair of poles with footrests for walking raised from the ground. stilt'ed a. stiff in manner, pompous [Du. stelt]

Stil'ton n. kind of cheese. [made famous by an inn at Stilton, England]

stim'ulus n. something that rouses to activity. -stim'ulate v.t. rouse up, spur. -stim'ulant a. producing a temporary increase of energy. -n. drug, etc., doing this. [L. = goad]

sting v.t. thrust a sting into; cause sharp pain to. -v.i. be affected with sharp pain. -n. pointed weapon, often poisoned, of certain insects and animals; thrust, wound, or pain of one. -stin'gy (-ji) a. miserly. [OE. stingan, pierce]

stink v.i. give out a strongly offensive smell. -n. such smell. [OE. stincan]

stint v.t. keep on short allowance. -n. limitation of supply or effect. [OE. styntan, blunt]

stipend n. salary. -stipend'iary a. receiving a stipend. -n. stipendiary magistrate. [L. stipendium]

stip'ple v.t. engrave in dots. -n. this process. [Du. stippelen]

stipulate -v.i. insist on, mention in making a bargain. -stipula'tion n. -stip'ulator n. [L. stipulari, stipulate]

stir v.t. set or keep in motion. -v.i. begin to move, be out of bed. -n. commotion. -stir'-cra'zy a. (sl.) mentally disturbed as a result of being in prison or otherwise confined. [OE. styrian]

stirr'up n. metal loop hung from a strap, support to the foot of a horseman. -stirr'up-cup n. drink given to a departing rider. [OE. stigrap, mount rope]

stitch n. movement of the needle in sewing; its result in the work; sharp pain in the side v.t. and i. sew. -stitch'ery n. [OE. stice, puncture]

stoat n. ermine. [orig. unknown]

stock n. stump or post; stem; handle or piece to hold by; lineage; animals, materials, etc., requisite for farming trade; supply; broth used as a foundation of soup; various sweet-smelling flowers; money invested in a concern. pl. frame of timber supporting a ship while building; frame with holes to confine the feet of offenders. -v.t. supply with, or keep, a stock. -stock'ist n. one who stocks (a particular brand of goods, etc.). -stockbroker n. agent for buying and selling shares in companies. -stock'exchange' n. where stocks are bought and sold; association of stockbrokers. -stock'-jobber n. dealer in stocks and shares. -stock'piling n. -stock'still a. motionless. [OE. stoc, trunk]

stockade n. enclosure of stakes. -v.t. surround with a stockade. [F. estocade]

stock'ing n. close-fitting covering for leg and foot; anything resembling this. [for nether stock, lower hose]

stod'gy a. heavy, dull, indigestible. -stodge n. heavy food. [orig. uncertain]

sto'ic n. philosopher holding virtue to be the highest good and teaching indifference to pleasure and pain; person of great selfcontrol. -sto'ic, sto'ical a. -sto'ically adv. -sto'icism n. [G. stoa, the Porch where Zeno taught this philosophy]

sto'ker n. one who tends a fire. -stoke v.t. and i. tend (a fire). [Du.]

stole n. priestly vestment; a long robe reaching to the feet; women's long scarf of fur or fabric. [G.]

stol'id a. hard to excite; phlegmatic; dull. -stol'idly adv. -stolid'ity n. [L. stolidus]

stom'ach (-mak) n. bag forming the chief digestive organ; appetite; inclination. -v.t. put up with. [G. stomachos, gullet]

stone n. piece of rock; rock; gem; hard seed of a fruit; weight = 14 lbs. -v.t. throw stones at; free (fruit) from stones. -stone'-blind' a. quite blind. -stone'-crop n. plant, the wall-pepper. -stone'deaf' a. -stone pine n. Mediterranean pine tree with branches forming an umbrella shape; umbrella pine. -stone'ware n. heavy common pottery. sto'ny a. -sto'nily adv. [OE. stan]

stonewall v.i. obstruct (government) business; play slow defensive game. [stone and wall]

stool n. chair with no back; place for evacuating the bowels; what is evacuated. [OE. stol, throne]

stoop *v.i.* lean forward or down. -*n.* stooping carriage of the body. [OE. *stupian*, bow]

stop *v.t.* fill up; check, bring to a halt. -*v.i.* cease, stay. -*n.* a stopping or being stopped; punctuation mark; set of organ pipes; lever for putting it in action. **-stopcock** *n.* tap turned by key. **-stop'gap** *n.* temporary expedient, substitute. **-slopp'age** *n.* **-stopp'er** *n.* a plug for closing a bottle. **-stop'over** *n.* stop at an intermediate point during a journey. **-stop'press** *n.* news inserted at last possible minute before printing. **-stop'watch** *n.* watch with hands which can be stopped for exact timing of races. [OE. *stoppian*, to plug]

store *n.* abundance; stock; place for keeping goods. -*pl.* stocks of goods, provisions, *etc.* -*v.t.* stock, furnish, keep. **-stor'age** *n.* [OF. *estorer*, fr. L. *instaurare*, provide]

stork *n.* wading bird. [OE. *store*]

storm *n.* violent wind or disturbance of the atmosphere; assault on a fortress. -*v.t.* take by storm. -*v.i.* rage. **-storm'y** *n.* [OE.]

stor'y *n.* tale; account; horizontal division of a building; plot of book or play; (*sl.*) lie. **-stor'ied** *a.* celebrated in tales. [L. *historia*]

stout *a.* sturdy; fat. -*n.* kind of beer. **stout'ly** *adv.* **-stout'ness** *n.* obesity. [OF. *estout*, proud, fierce]

stove *n.* apparatus for cooking, warming a room, *etc.* [Du.]

stow *v.t.* pack away. **-stow'age** *n.* **-stow'away** *n.* one who hides himself on a ship to obtain passage. [OE. = place]

strad'dle *v.i.* spread the legs wide. -*v.t.* bestride something in this way. [fr. OE. *straed-stridan*, stride]

strag'gle *v.i.* stray, get dispersed. **-strag'gler** *n.* [orig. uncertain]

straight [strat] *a.* without bend; honest; level; in order. -*n.* straight state or part. *adv.* direct. **-straight'en** *v.t.* and *i.* **-straightfor'ward** *a.* open, frank; simple. **-straightfor'wardly** *adv.* **-straightway** *adv.* at once. [ME. *streght*, *p.p.* of *stretch*]

strain *v.t.* stretch tightly; stretch to the full or to excess; filter. -*v.i.* make great effort. -*n.* stretching force; violent effort; injury from being strained; burst of music or poetry; tone of speaking or writing. **-strain'er** *n.* filter. [OF. *estreindre*, fr. L. *stringers*]

strain *n.* breed or race. [OE. *strean*]

strait *a.* narrow, strict. -*n.* channel of water connecting two larger areas. *pl.* position of difficulty or distress. **straitlaced** *a.* puritanical. **-straitjacket** *n.* jacket to confine the arms of maniacs, *etc.* [OF. *estreit*, fr. L. *strictus*]

strait'en *v.t.* make straight, narrow; distress *esp.* by poverty. [OE. *estreit*]

strand *n.* one of the strings or wires making up a rope. [OF. *estran*, rope]

strand *n.* shore of sea or lake. [OE.]

strange (-anj) *a.* unaccustomed, singular. **strangely** *adv.* **-strange'ness** *n.* **-stra'nger** *n.* unknown person; a foreigner; one unaccustomed (to). [OF. *estrange*, fr. L. *extraneus*, -extra, beyond]

stran'gle (-ng-gl) *v.t.* kill by squeezing the windpipe. **-strangula'tion** *n.* [L. *strangulate*, strangulat-]

strap *n.* strip of leather or metal. -*v.t.* fasten with a strap; beat with one. **strapp'ing** *a.* tall and well-made. **strap'hanger** *n.* one who travels in crowded buses, trains, clinging to strap. [var. of *strop*]

stratagem *n.* artifice in war; a trick, device. **-strat'egy** *n.* art of handling troops, ships, *etc.*, to the best advantage. **strat'egist** *n.* **-strate'gic** *n.* [G. *stratagema*, piece of generalship]

stra'tum *n.* (**strata** *pl.*) layer. **-stra'tify** *v.t.* arrange things. **-stratifica'tion** *n.* **-stra'tosphere** *n.* high layer of atmosphere, with constant temperature. [L.]

straw *n.* dry cut stalks of corn. **-straw'berry** *n.* creeping plant producing a red fruit; the fruit. [OE. *streow*]

stray *v.i.* wander, get lost. -*a.* strayed; occasional. -*n.* stray animal, person (as in waits and strays). [*astray*]

streak *n.* long line, band. -*v.t.* mark with streaks. **-streak'y** *a.* [OE. *strica*]

stream *n.* flowing body of water, or other liquid. -*v.i.* flow; run with liquid; float or wave in the air. **-stream'er** *n.* ribbon to stream in the air. **-stream'let** *n.* small stream. **stream'lined** *a.* shaped to offer, when in motion, the minimum resistance to air or water. [OE.]

street *n.* road in a town or village with houses at the side. **-street'car** *n.* vehicle on rails for transporting passengers, *usu.* in a city. **street'wise** *a.* attuned to and adept at surviving in an urban, poor and often criminal environment. also **street-smart** *a.* [Late L. *strata*]

strength *n.* power. **-strength'en** *v.t.* and *i.* [OE. *strengthu*]

stren'uous *a.* energetic, earnest. **stren'uously** *adv.* [L. *strenuus*]

stress *n.* strain; impelling force; effort; emphasis. -*v.t.* emphasize; put mechanical stress on. [OF. *estrecier* and for *distress*]

stretch *v.t.* tighten, pull out; reach out; exert to the utmost. -*v.i.* reach; have elasticity. -*n.* stretching or being stretched; expanse; spell. **-stretch'er** *n.* person or thing that stretches; bar in a boat for a rower's feet; appliance on which an injured person can be carried. **stretch'marks** *n.pl.* marks that remain visible on the abdomen after its distension in pregnancy. [OE. *streccan*]

strew *v.t.* scatter over a surface. [OE. *strewian*]

strict *a.* defined; without exception; stern, not lax or indulgent. **-strict'ly** *adv.* **strict'ness** *n.* **-stric'ture** *n.* critical remark; morbid contraction. [L. *stringers*, *strict*-, tighten]

stride *v.i.* walk with long steps. -*v.t.* pass over with one step. -*n.* step, or its length. [OE. *stridan*]

strident *a.* harsh in tone. **-strid'ulous** *a.* emitting a grating sound. **-stridor** *n.* harsh sound in breathing. [L. *stridere*, creak]

strife *n.* conflict; discord. [OF. *estrif*]

strike *v.t.* hit. -*v.i.* hit; cease work in order to enforce a demand. -*n.* such stoppage of work. **-stri'ker** *n.* **-stri'king** *a.* noteworthy. [OE.

strican]

string *n.* fine cord; row or series; gut, *etc.* cord of a musical instrument. -*v.t.* tie with or thread on string. -*pl.* stringed instruments. -**string'y** *a.* fibrous. [OE. *streng*]

stringent *a.* strict. -**strin'gency** *n.* **string'gently** *adv.* [L. *stringers*, tighten]

strip *v.t.* lay bare, take the covering off. -*v.i.* take off one's clothes. -*n.* long narrow piece. -**strip'ling** *n.* youth com'ic strip, in a newspaper, strip of small pictures telling a story. [OE. *stripan*, plunder]

stripe *n.* narrow mark or band; blow with a scourge. [of. LG. orig.]

strive *v.i.* try hard, struggle. [*strife*]

stroke *n.* blow, attack of paralysis, apoplexy; mark of a pen; completed movement in a series; rower sitting nearest the stern; act of stroking. -*v.t.* set the time in rowing; pass the hand lightly over. [OE. *stracian*]

stroll *v.i.* walk in a leisurely or idle or rambling manner. -*n.* leisurely walk. [orig. uncertain]

strong *a.* powerful, earnest; forceful; pronounced, *e.g.*, a strong flavor. **stron'gest** *a.* (superl.). -**strong'hold** *n.* fortress. -**strong'ly** *adv.* [OE. *strong*]

structure *n.* construction, building, something made of various pieces. -**struc'tural** *a.* -**struc'turally** *adv.* [L. *struere, struct-*, build]

strug'gle *v.i.* contend, fight; proceed or work with difficulty and effort. -*n.* contest, effort. [orig. uncertain]

strum *v.t.* and *i.* play piano, guitar, *etc.*, idly or inefficiently. [imit.]

strut *v.i.* walk affectedly or pompously. -*n.* such gait. -**strut'ting** *n.* and *a.* [OE. *strutian*, stick out stiffly]

strut *n.* rigid support, usually set obliquely. -*v.t.* stay with struts. [orig. uncertain]

strychnine (-k'nen) *n.* poison got from nux vomica seeds, and used in medicine. [G. *strychnos*, nightshade]

stub *n.* tree-stump; end of a cigar, *etc.* -*v.t.* strike (one's toe) on an obstruction. -**stub'bed** *a.* [OE. *stubb*]

stub'ble *n.* stumps of cut grain. [L. *stipula*, dim. of *stipes*, stalk]

stubb'orn *a.* unyielding, obstinate. [*stub*]

stucc'o *n.* and *v.i.* plaster. (It.)

stud *n.* movable double button; nail with large head sticking out; boss. -*v.t.* set with studs. [OE. *studu*, post]

stud *n.* set of horses kept for breeding. -**stud'farm** *n.* [OE. *stod*]

stud'y *n.* effort to acquire knowledge; subject of this; room to study in; sketch. -*v.t.* make a study of; try constantly to do. -*v.i.* be engaged in learning. -**stu'dent** *n.* one who studies. -**stu'dio** *n.* workroom of an artist, photographer, *etc.*, building where film, television or radio shows are made, broadcast, *etc.* -**stu'dious** *a.* **stu'diously** *adv.* [L. *studere*, be zealous]

stuff *n.* material, fabric. -*v.t.* stop or fill up. -*v.i.* eat greedily. -**stuffy** *a.* lacking fresh air. [OE. *estoffe*, fr. L. *stuppa*, tow]

stum'ble *v.i.* trip and nearly fall; slip. *n.* -

stumbling *a.* -**stum'bling block** *n.* obstacle. [ME. *stomelen*]

stump *n.* remnant of a tree, *etc.* when the main part has been cut away; one of the uprights of the wicket at cricket. -*v.i.* walk noisily. -*v.t.* walk heavily; confuse, puzzle; tour making speeches. -**stump'y** *a.* -**stump'orator** *n.* traveling speaker (as using tree-stumps for platforms). [of Teut. orig.]

stun *v.t.* knock senseless. [OF. *estoner*, astonish]

stunt *n.* spectacular effort or feat. [orig. uncertain]

stunt *v.t.* check the growth of. -**stunt'ed** *a.* dwarfed. [OE. *stunt*, dull]

stu'pefy *v.t.* make stupid, deprive of full consciousness. -**stupefac'tion** *n.* [L. *stupere*, be amazed]

stupendous *a.* amazing. [L. *stupendus*]

stu'pid *a.* slow-witted, dull. -**stupid'ity** *n.* -**stu'pidly** *adv.* [L. *stupidus*]

stu'por *n.* dazed state; torpor. [L. *stupor*]

stur'dy *a.* robust, strongly built. -**stur'dily** *adv.* -**stur'diness** *n.* [OF. *estordi*, reckless]

stur'geon *n.* large edible fish yielding caviar and isinglass. [F. *esturgeon*]

stutt'er *v.i.* and *t.* speak with difficulty, *esp.* with repetition of initial consonants; stammer. -*n.* act or habit of stuttering. [frequentative of obs. *stut*]

sty *n.* place to keep pigs in. [OE. *stig*]

sty, stye *n.* inflammation on the eyelid. [OE. *stigend*]

style *n.* manner of writing, doing, etc, ; designation; sort; superior manner or quality; pointed instrument for writing on waxed tablets. -*v.t.* designate. -**sty'lish** *a.* fashionable. -**sty'lishly** *adv.* -**sty'list** *n.* one cultivating style in literary or other execution. -**sty'listics** *n.* a branch of linguistics concerned with the study of characteristic choices in use of language, *esp.* literary language, as regards sound, form, or vocabulary. [L. *stilus*]

suave *a.* smoothly polite. [L. *suavis*, sweet]

sub- *prefix*, meaning under, in lower position, *etc.* Often used separated as abbreviation for the whole compound, *e.g.*, 'sub' = a subscription. [L.]

subcommittee *n.* section of a committee functioning separately. committee

subdivide' *v.t.* divide again. -*v.i.* separate. -**subdivis'ion** *n.* [*divide*]

subdue' *v.t.* overcome; tame; tone down. [OF. *souduire*, fr. L. *subducere*]

sub'ject *a.* liable to, owing allegiance. subject to, conditional upon. -*n.* one owing allegiance; that about which something is predicated; conscious self; topic, theme. -**subject'** *v.t.* make liable, or cause to undergo. -subject'ive *a.* relating to the self; displaying an artist's individuality. -**subjectiv'ity** *n.* [L. *subicere*, subject]

subjoin' *v.t.* add at the end; annex; append. [L. *jungere*, joint]

sub'jugate *v.t.* conquer. [L. *jugum*, yoke]

subjunc'tive *n.* mood used mainly in conditional clauses. -*a.* in or of that mood. [L. *jungere, junct-*, join]

sublet' v.t. of a tenant, let to another the whole or part of what he himself has rented. [let]

sublime' a. inspiring awe. -sub'limate v.t. purify; heat into vapor and allow to solidify again. -n. sublimated substance. -sublimation n. purification of e.g. an emotion. -sublime'ly adv. -sublim'ity n. [L. sublimis, lofty]

sub'marine a. below the surface of the sea. -n. warship that can operate under water. [marine]

submerge' v.t. place under water. -v.i. go under. -also submerse'-submersion n. -submers'ible a. -n. submarine. [L. mergere, mers-, dip]

submit' v.t. put forward for consideration; surrender. -v.i. surrender; urge. submiss'ive a. -submis'sion n. [L. mittere, miss-, put]

subord'inate a. of lower rank or importance. -n. one under the orders of another. -v.t. make or treat as subordinate. [L. ordinare, set in order]

suborn' v.t. bribe to do evil. -subornation n. [L. subornare. equip secretly]

subpoe'na n. writ requiring attendance at a court of law. -v.t. summon by one. [L. sub pœna, under penalty (first words of the writ)]

subscribe' v.t. write one's name at the end of a document; assent; pay or promise to pay (a contribution). -subscri'ber n. -subscription n. [L. scribere, script-, write]

subsequent a. later; coming after. -sub'sequence n. -sub'sequently adv. [L. sequi, follow]

subside' v.i. sink, settle; come to an end. -sub'sidence n. [L. subsidere, settle]

sub'sidy n. money granted, e.g., by the state to an industry, or by one state to another. -sub'sidize v.t. pay a grant to. -subsid'iary a. supplementing. [subsidium, aid]

subsist' v.i. exist. -subsist'ence n. being; livelihood. -subsist'ence allow'ance, allowance for living expenses in special circumstances. [L. sistere, stand]

substance n. matter; particular kind of matter; chief part, essence; wealth. -substan'tial a. solid, big, important. -substan'tially adv. -substantial'ity n. -substantiate v.t. bring evidence for. -substantia'tion n. -sub'stantive a. having independent existence. -n. noun. [L. substare, stand under, be present]

substitute n. thing or person put in place of another. -v.t. put in exchange for. [L. statuere, appoint]

subterfuge n. evasion, lying excuse. [L. fugere, flee]

subterranean a. underground. -subterra'neously adv. [L. terra, earth]

sub'tile (sub'til, sut'-il) a. delicate, rare, tenuous; acute. -sub'tilty n. fineness; dialectic nicety; acuteness. [L. subtilistela, web]

subtle (sut'l) a. ingenious, clever; acute; crafty; tenuous. -subt'ly adv. -subt'lety n. [L. subtilis, fine woven]

subtract' v.t. take away a part. -subtrac'tion n. [L. trahere, tract-, draw]

sub'urb n. outlying part of a city. -suburb'an a. [L. urbs, city]

subvert' v.t. overthrow; corrupt. -subversive a. -subver'sion n. [L. vertere, vers, turn]

sub'way n. underground passage, railway, roadway. [OE. weg]

succeed' (-ks-) v.t. follow, take the place of. -v.i. follow; accomplish a purpose. success' n. accomplishment, attainment; issue, outcome. -success'ful a. -success'fully adv. -success'ion n. a following; series; a succeeding. -success'ive a. -success'ively adv. -success'or n. [L. succedere, success-]

succinct' a. terse, concise. -succinct'ly adv. -succinct'ness n. [L. succingere, succinct-, gird up]

succ'or v.t. and n. help. [L. succurrere]

succulent a. juicy. -succ'ulence n. [L. succulentus-succus, juice]

succumb' (-kum) v.i. yield; die. [L. succumbere, lie down under]

such a. of the kind, quality or degree mentioned; of the same kind. [OE. swilc]

suck v.t. draw into the mouth; roll in the mouth. -n. a sucking. -suck'er n. person or thing that sucks; organ or appliance which adheres by suction; (sl.) mug, dupe. -suc'kle v.t. feed from the breast. -suck'ling n. unweaned child. -suc'tion n. drawing in or sucking, esp. of air. [OE. sucan]

sudd'en a. done or occurring unexpectedly, abrupt. -sudd'enly adv. -sudd'enness n. [F. soudain]

suds n.pl. froth of soap and water. [orig. Du. sudde, ooze]

sue v.t. seek justice from. -v.i. make application or entreaty. [F. suivre, follow]

suède n. soft kid leather with an unglazed surface. [F. = Swedish]

suet n. hard animal fat. [OF. sicu, fr. L. sebum, tallow]

suff'er v.t. undergo; permit. -v.i. undergo pain, hurt, etc. -suff'erable a. -suff'erance n. toleration. -sufferer n. -suff'ering n. trouble, distress. [F. souffrir]

suffice' v.i. be enough. -v.t. meet the needs of. -suffi'cent a. enough. -suffi'ciency n. [L. sufficere]

suffix n. letter or syllable added to the root word. [L. suffigere, suffix, fix under]

suff'ocate v.t. kill by stopping breathing. -v.i. feel suffocated. -suffoca'tion n. [L. suffocate, suffocate]

suff'rage n. vote or right of voting. -suff'ragist n. one claiming a right of voting. -suffragette' n. militant woman suffragist. [L. suffragium]

suffuse' v.t. well up and spread over. -suffu'sion n. [L. suffundere, suffus-]

su'gar (shoog-) n. sweet crystalline vegetable substance. -v.t. sweeten with it. -su'gary a. [Arab. sukkar]

suggest' (sui-) v.t. propose; call up the idea of. -suggest'ible, suggestive a. -suggest'ively adv. -sugges'tion n. [L. suggerere, suggest-]

suicide n. one who kills himself intentionally; self-murder. -suici'dal a. suici'dally adv. [Mod. L. suicidium, fr. ccedere, kill]

suit n. action at law; petition; courtship; set,

esp. of outer clothes; one of the four sets in a pack of cards. -*v.t.* go with, be adapted to; meet the desires of, make fitting, *etc.* -*v.i.* be convenient. -**suit'able** *a.* fitting, convenient. -**suit'ably** *adv.* -**suitabil'ity** *n.* -**suite** *n.* set of things going or used together, *esp.* furniture; retinue. -**suit'or** *n.* one who sues; wooer. -**suit'case** *n.* portable traveling-case for clothes, *etc.* [F. *suite*]

sul'fate *n.* salt of sulfuric acid. [L.]

sul'fur *n.* pale-yellow non-metallic element. -**sul'furous** *a.* -**sulfu'ric** *a.* sulfu'reous *a.* [L.]

sull'en *a.* resentful, ill-humored; dismal. -**sull'enly** *adv.* [var. of *solemn*]

sull'y *v.t.* stain, tarnish. [F. *souiller*]

sul'tan *n.* Mohammedan sovereign. sulta'na *n.* mother, wife, daughter of a sultan; small kind of raisin. [Arab.]

sul'try *a.* hot and close. -**sul'triness** *n.* [obs. *v. sulter*, var. of *swelter*]

sum *n.* amount, total; arithmetical problem. -*v.t.* add up. -**summ'ary** *a.* done quickly. -*n.* abridgement or statement of the chief points of a longer document, speech, *etc.* -**summ'arily** *adv.* -**summ'arize** *v.t.* -**summa'tion** *n.* an adding up. -**sum up**, recapitulate. [F. *somme*, L. *summa*]

summ'er *n.* second season. -*v.i.* pass the summer. -**summ'ery** *a.* [OE. *sumor*]

summ'it *n.* top; peak. [F. *sommet*]

summ'on *v.t.* demand the attendance of, call on; gather up (energies, *etc.*). summ'ons *n.* call, authoritative demand. [L. *summonere*]

sump'tuary *a.* regulating expenditure, -**sumptuous** *a.* lavish, magnificent. -**sumptuously** *adv.* -**sump'tuousness** *n.* [L. *sumptus*, expense]

sun *n.* luminous body round which the earth revolves; its rays. -*v.t.* expose to the sun's rays. -**Sun'belt** *n.* the Southern states of the U. S. *a.* -**Sun'day** *n.* first day of the week. -**sun'down**, **sun'set** *n.* action of the sun dropping below the horizon at the end of the day; the time at which it does this- **sun'flower** *n.* plant with large golden flowers like pictures of the sun. -**sunn'y** *a.* -**sun'less** *a.* -**sun'bathing** *n.* exposure of the body to sun's rays. -**sun'rise**, **sun'up** *n.* action of the sun rising above the horizon at the beginning of the day, the time at which it does this. -**sun'stroke** *n.* collapse from excessive exposure to the sun. [OE. *sunne*]

sun'dae *n.* ice-cream with fruit, nuts, *etc.* [orig. uncertain]

sup *v.t.* take by sips. -*v.i.* take supper. -*n.* sip of liquid. [OE. *supan*]

su'per- *prefix*, makes compounds with meaning of above, in excess, *e.g.* superabundant *a.* excessively abundant, superhuman *a.* more than human. *etc* . These are not given where the meaning and derivation may easily be found from the simple word. [L. *super*, above]

superann'uate *v.t.* pension off, or discharge as too old. -**superannua'tion** *n.* [L. *annus*, year]

superb' *a.* splendid, grand, impressive. superb'ly *adv.* [L. *superbus*, haughty]

supercil'ious *a.* indifferent and haughty. -superciliously *adv.* -**supercil'iousness** *n.* [L. *supercilium*, eyebrow]

supereroga'tion *n.* a doing more than duty requires. -**supererog'atory** *a.* [L. *erogare*, pay out]

superfi'cial *a.* of or on a surface; without depth. -**superficial'ity** *n.* [L., fr. *facies*, face]

super'fluous *a.* extra, unnecessary. [L. *superfluere*, overflow]

superintend' *v.t.* have charge of overlook. [L. *intenders*, attend to]

supe'rior *a.* upper, higher in position or rank or quality; showing a consciousness of being so. -**superior'ity** *n.* [L.]

super'lative *a.* of or in the highest degree. -*n.* superlative degree of an adjective or adverb. [L. *superlativus*]

su'perman *n.* ideal man, of an ideal and higher type; person of extraordinary powers. [trans. of Ger. *Ubermensch*]

supernat'ural *a.* above nature; occult; miraculous; spiritual. -**supernat'urally** *adv.* [*natural*]

supernu'merary *a.* in excess of the normal number. -*n.* supernumerary person or thing. [L. *numerus*, number]

supersede' *v.t.* set aside; supplant; take the place of -**superses'sion** *n.* [L. *supersedere*, *supersess* -, be superior to]

supersonic *a.* of waves of greater frequency than sound; faster than sound. [L. *sonus*, sound]

superstition *n.* religion or opinion or practice based on a belief in luck or magic. -**supersti'tious** *a.* -**supersti'tiously** *adv.* [L. *superstitio*]

supervise *v.t.* superintend. -**supervi'sion** *n.* -supervi'sor *n.* [L. *videre*, *vis-*, see]

su'pine *a.* indolent; negligent; inactive. [L. *supinus*, lying on one's back]

supp'er *n.* last meal of the day when dinner is not the last. -**supp'erless** *a.* [F. *souper*, fr. LG. *supen*, sup]

supplant' *v.t.* take the place of, *esp.* unfairly. -supplant'er *n.* [L. *supplantare*, trip up]

sup'ple *a.* pliable; lithe; compliant. -*v.t.* sup'ply *adv.* -sup'pleness *n.* [L. *supplex*]

supplement *n.* something added to fill up, supply a deficiency. -*v.t.* add to. supplement'al *a.* -supplement'ary *a.* [L. *supplere*, fill up]

supplicate *v.t.* and *i.* beg humbly. -supplica'tion *n.* -supp'licatory *a.* supp'liant *a.* petitioning. -*n.* petitioner. [L. *supplicate*, fr. *plicare*, bend]

supply' *v.t.* furnish; *s* ubstitute for. -*n.* a supplying, substitute; stock, store. [L. *supplere*, fill up]

support' *v.t* . hold up; assist; sustain. -*n.* a supporting or being supported, or means of support. -support'able *a.* tolerable. -support'er *n.* adherent. [L. *supportare*, fr. *portare*, carry]

suppose' *v.t.* assume as a theory; take for granted; accept as likely. -**suppo'sable** *a* . -suppositi'on *n.* -**suppositi'tious** *a.* sham. [F. *supposer*]

suppress' *v.t.* put down, restrain, keep or withdraw from publication. -suppres'sion *n.* [L. *supprimere*, suppress-]

supreme' *a.* highest. -supreme'ly *adv.* -suprem'acy *n.* [L. *supremus*]

surcharge *n.* excessive charge or load; additional charge. -*v.t.* exact such charge. [*charge*]

sure *a.* certain; trustworthy; strong, secure. -*adv.* certainly. -sure'ly *adv.* -sure'ty *n.* certainty; one who makes himself responsible for the obligations of another. [F. *sur*, fr. L. *securus*]

surf *n.* foam of breaking waves on a beach. -surf'y *a.* -surfing *n.* sport of riding the incoming waves on a surfboard. [orig. uncertain]

sur'face (-fis) *n.* outside face of a body; plane; top, visible side; lifting or controlling surface of an plane. [F.]

sur'feit (-fit) *n.* excess. -*v.t.* and *i.* feed to excess. [F. *surfaire*, overdo]

surge *v.i.* move in large waves. -*n.* a great wave. [L. *surgere*, rise]

sur'geon (-in) *n.* medical expert who performs operations. -sur'gery *n.* treatment by operation; doctor's consulting room. -surg'ical *a.* -sur'gically *adv.* [F. *chirurgien*, fr. G. *cheirourgos*, lit. hand worker]

sur'ly *a.* morose, ill-tempered. [fr. *sir-ly*, orig. like an arrogant master]

surmise *v.t.* and *i.* and *n.* guess. [OF. fr. *surmettre*, accuse]

surmount' *v.t.* get over, overcome. surmount'able *a.* [F. *surmonter*]

sur'name *n.* family name. [*name*]

surpass' *v.t.* outdo. [F. *surpasser*]

sur'plice (-plis) *n.* loose white vestment worn by clergy and choristers. sur'pliced *a.* [OF. *surpeli s*]

sur'plus *n.* what remains over or in excess. *a.* excess. [F.]

surprise' *n.* what takes unawares; emotion roused by being taken unawares; a taking unawares. -*v.t.* cause surprise to. -surprising *a.* [OF., fr. *surprendre*, lit. overtaken]

surrealism *n.* movement in the creative arts, which endeavors to express the subjective and subconscious. -surreal *a.* of the world of the subconscious; dreamlike. -surrealist *n.* [*real*]

surrender *v.t.* hand over. -*v.i.* yield. -*n.* act of surrendering. [OF. *surrendre*, hand over]

surreptitious *a.* done secretly or stealthily. -surrepti'tiously *adv.* [L. *subripere*, snatch]

surrogate *n.* deputy, *esp.* of a bishop. -*a.* -surr'ogate motherhood or surrogacy *n.* role of a woman who bears a child on behalf of a couple unable to have a child, either by articial insemination from the man or implantation of an embryo from the woman. -surr'ogate moth'er *n.* [L. *surrogatus*]

surround' *v.t.* be or come all round. -*n.* border. [OF. *suronder*, overflow]

sur'tax *n.* additional tax. -*v.t.* impose one on. [F. *surfaxe*]

surveill'ance *n.* close watching. [F. *veiller*, fr. L. *vigilare*, watch]

survey' *v.t.* view; measure or map (land). -sur'vey *n.* a surveying. -survey'or *n.* [OF. *veir*, fr. L. *videre*, see]

survive' *v.t.* outlive; come alive through. -*v.i.* continue to live or exist. **survi'val** *n.* -surviv'alist *n.* person who believes in ensuring personal survival of a catastrophic event by arming himself and often by living in the wild. sur'viv'atism *n.* -survi'vor *n.* [L. *super-vivere*, overlive]

suscep'tible *a.* sensitive; impressionable. -susceptibil'ity *n.* [L. *suscipere*, *suscept-*, receive]

suspect' *v.t.* have an impression of the existence or presence of, be inclined to believe; doubt the innocence of. *a.* of suspected character. -*n.* (sus'-) suspected person. -suspi'cion *n.* a suspecting or being suspected. -suspi'cious *a.* suspiciously *adv.* [L. *suspicere*, suspect-, lit. look up at]

suspend' *v.t.* hang up; sustain in fluid; cause to cease for a time, keep inoperative. -*v.i.* suspend'er *n.* -suspend'-ers *n.pl.* straps for supporting trousers, skirt *etc.* -suspense' *n.* state of uncertainty. -suspen'sion *n.* state of being hung up, or debarred. -suspensory *a.* [L. *suspendare*, suspense]

sustain' *v.t.* keep or hold up; endure; confirm. -sustain'able *a.* -sus'tenance *n.* food. -sustenta'tion *n.* maintenance. [OF. *sostenir*, fr. L. *sustinere*, hold up]

su'ture *n.* act of joining together, as the exterior parts of a wound; the seam or joint that unites two bones, *esp.* of the skull. -*v.t.* to stitch up. [L. *sutura*, -*suere*, to sew]

svelte *a.* lithe, slender. [F.]

swab (-ob) *n.* mop; pad of surgical wool. -*v.t.* clean with a swab. -swabb'er *n.* [orig. uncertain]

swad'dle (-od-) *v.t.* swathe. -swadd'ling bands (-clothes) *n.pl.* clothes in which an infant is swathed. [fr. *swathe*]

swagg'er *v.i.* strut; talk boastfully. -*n.* strutting gait; boastful or overconfident manner. [orig. uncertain]

swall'ow *n.* migratory bird with a skimming flight. [OE. *swealwe*]

swall'ow (-ol-o) *v.t.* cause or allow to pass down the gullet. -*n.* an act of swallowing. [OE. *swelgan*]

swamp (-omp) *n.* bog. -*v.t.* entangle in a swamp; overwhelm, flood. -swamp'y *a.* [of LG. orig. cp. *sump*]

swan (-on) *n.* large water bird with graceful curved neck. -swan'-song *n.* fabled song of swan before its death; last work of poet, musician. [OE.]

swank *n.* (*sl.*) brag; display. -*v.i.* show off. -swank'y *a.* [Sc.]

swap, swop *v.t.* and *i.* and *n.* (*sl.*) exchange. (ME. *swappen*]

swarm *n.* large cluster of insects; vast crowd. -*v.i.* of bees, to emigrate in a swarm; gather in larger numbers. [OE. *swearm*]

swarm *v.i.* climb grasping with hands and knees. [orig. uncertain]

swash'buckler *n.* swaggerer; blustering braggart. [obs. *swack*, strike] swasti'ka *n*. form of cross with arms bent at right-angles. [Sanskrit *swastika*, fortunate]

swathe *v.t.* cover with wraps or bandages. [OE. *swathian*]

swathe, swath *n*. band of mown grass or corn or track cut by scythe. [OE. *sweceth*]

sway *v.i.* swing unsteadily. -*v.t.* make to do this; govern; wield. -*n.* swaying motion; government. [LG. *swajen*, swing in the wind]

swear *v.t.* promise on oath; cause to take an oath. -*v.i* . use profane oaths. [OE. *swerian*]

sweat (swet) *n*. moisture oozing from the skin. -*v.i.* exude sweat; toil. -*v.t.* cause to sweat; employ at wrongfully low wages. -sweat'er *n*. woolen jersey. [OE. *swcetan*]

swede *n*. variety of turnip. [for Swedish *turnip*]

sweep *v.i.* pass quickly or magnificently; extend in a continuous curve. -*v.t.* clean with a broom; carry impetuously. -*n.* sweeping motion; wide curve; range; act of cleaning with a broom; long oar; one who cleans chimneys. [OE. *swapan*]

sweep'stake *n*. gamble in which the winner takes the stakes contributed by all. [*sweep* and *stake*]

sweet *a.* tasting like sugar; agreeable; tuneful; in good condition. -*n.* sweet part; sweetmeat. -*pl.* sweet dishes at table; delights. -sweet'bread *n*. animal's pancreas as food. -sweet'-brier *n*. wild rose. -sweetmeat *n*. piece of confectionery. -sweetheart *n*. lover. -sweetpea' *n*. plant of the pea family with bright flowers. [OE. *swete*]

swell *v.i.* expand. -*v.t.* cause to expand. -*n.* act of swelling or being swollen; heave of the sea after a storm; mechanism in an organ to vary the volume of sound. [OE. *swellan*]

swelt'er *v.i.* be oppressive, or oppressed, with heat. [OE. *sweltan*, die]

swerve *v.i.* swing round, change direction during motion; deviate. -*n.* a swerving. [OE. *sweorfan*]

swift *a.* rapid, quick, ready. -*n.* bird like a swallow. -swift'ly *adv.* [OE.]

swill *v.t.* pour water over or through; drink greedily. -*v.i.* drink greedily. -*n.* a rinsing; liquid food for pigs. [OE. *swillan*, wash]

swim *v.i.* support and move oneself in water; float; be flooded; have a feeling of dizziness. -*v.t.* cross by swimming. -*n.* spell of swimming. -swimm'er *n*. [OE. *swimman*]

swind'ler *n*. cheat. -swin'dle *v.t.* and *i* and *n*. cheat. [Ger. *schwindler*]

swine *n*. pig. -swine'herd *n*. [OE. *swin*]

swing *v.i.* move to and fro, *esp.* as a suspended body; revolve; (*sl.*) be hanged. -*v.t.* cause to swing; suspend. -*n.* an act of swinging; a seat hung to swing on. [OE. *swingan*]

swipe *n*. sweeping blow. -*v.t.* give a sweeping blow to; (*sl.*) steal. [var. of *sweep*]

swirl *v.i.* move with an eddying motion. -*v.t.* cause to do this. -*n.* such motion. [of Scand. orig.]

swish *v.i.* swing a rod, *etc.*, with an audible hissing sound; move with a similar sound. -*v.t.* swing cane thus. -*n.* the sound; stroke with a cane, *etc.* [imit.]

switch *n*. flexible stick or twig; mechanism to complete or interrupt an electric circuit, *etc.*; on railway, two movable rails for transferring locomotive or train from one set of tracks to another. -*v.t.* strike with a switch; affect (current, *etc.*) with a switch; swing round abruptly. -switch'back *n*. short railway in steep undulations as a fairground amusement. -switch'blade *n*. pocket-knife with a spring-operated blade which opens at the release of a button. -switch'board *n*. board with switches to connect telephones, *etc.* [orig. uncertain]

swiv'el *n*. mechanism of two parts which can resolve the one on the other. -*v.t.* and *i.* turn on a swivel. [OE. *swifan*, revolve]

swoon *v.i.* and *n*. faint. [ME. *swowenynge*]

swoop *v.i.* come down like a hawk. -*n.* an act of swooping. [OE. *swapan*, sweep]

swop *v.i.* barter, exchange. -*n.* (orig. strike hands in bargaining.) [imit.]

sword (sord) *n*. weapon, long blade for cutting or thrusting. -sword'-fish *n*. fish with a long sharp upper jaw. -sword'play *n*. fencing. [OE. *sweord*]

sycamore *n*. tree allied to maple and plane. [G. *sykomoros*]

sycophant *n*. flatterer. -sycophant'ic. *a.* -syc'ophancy *n*. obsequiousness. [G. *sykophantes*, informer]

syllable *n*. division of a word as a unit for pronunciation. -syllab'ica. [G. *syliambanein*, take together]

syll'abus *n*. programme; outline. [by a misunderstanding for G. *sittube*, label of a parchment]

syllogism (-j-) *n*. form of logical reasoning consisting of two premises and a conclusion. -syllogist'ic *a.* [G. *syllogismos*, reckoning together]

sylph *n*. sprite. [coined by Paracelsus]

sym'bol *n*. sign; thing representing or typifying something. [G. *symbolon*, token]

symmetry *n*. proportion between parts, balance of arrangement between two sides; regularity. [G. *symmetria*, fr. *metron*, measure]

sympathy *n*. feeling for another in pain, *etc.*; sharing of emotion, interest, desire, *etc.* [G. *sympatheia*, fr. *pathos*, feeling]

symphony *n*. (*mus.*) important composition, in several movements, for full orchestra. [G. *phone*, sound]

sympo'sium *n*. drinking party; friendly discussion; set of magazine articles by various writers on the same subject. [G. *symposion*, fr. *posis*, drinking]

symp'tom *n*. sign, token; change in the body indicating its health or disease. symptomat'ic *a.* [G. *sympotoma*]

synagogue *n*. Jewish congregation; its meeting-place. [G. *synagoge*, assembly]

synch'ronize *v.t.* make agree in time. -*v.i.* happen at the same time. [G. *synchronl-ein*]

synch'rotron *n*. device for acceleration of stream of electrons. [G. *sun*, together, *chronos*, time]

syn'cope (*pl.*) *n*. fainting; syncopated spelling, *etc.* -syn'copate *v.t.* shorten by the omission of an interior element (in words, music, *etc.*) -syncopa'tion *n.* [G. *synkope,* dashing together]

synd'rome *n.* symptoms occurring together in a disease. [G. *syn,* together, *dramein,* run]

syn'onym *n.* word with the same meaning as another. -synon'ymous *a.* -synonym'ity *n.* [G. *synonymso*]

synop'sis *n.* a summary. -synop'tic *a.* having the same viewpoint. [G. *synopsis,* seeing together]

syn'tax *n.* part of grammar treating of the arrangement of words. -syntact'ic *a.* -syntact'ically *adv.* [G. *syntaxis,* arrangement together]

synth'esis *n.* a putting together, combination *esp.* of ideas, theories, *etc.* -syn'thesize *v.t.* [G. *synthesis*]

synthet'ic *a.* (*colloq.*) artificial. -synthetically *adv.* [G. *sunthelikos*]

syph'ilis *n.* infectious venereal disease. -syphilit'ic *a.* [coined (1530) by a doctor of Verona]

syringe' *n.* instrument for drawing in liquid by a piston and forcing it out in a fine stream or spray; squirt; (*med.*) injecting instrument. -*v.t.* spray with a syringe. [G. *syrinx,* shepherd's pipe, reed]

syr'up *n.* thick solution of sugar; treacle, *etc.* -syr'upy *a.* [Arab. *sharab,* fr. *shariba,* drink]

sys'tem *n.* complex whole; organization; method; classification. -systemat'ic *a.* methodical. -systemat'ically *adv.* -sys'tematize *v.t.* reduce to system. [G. *systems,* what stands together]

sys'tole *n.* shortening of long syllable; contraction of heart and arteries for expelling blood and carrying on circulation. -systol'ic *a.* contracting; of systole. [G. *syn,* together, *stellein,* place]

T

tab *n.* tag, label, short strap; bill, check; surveillance. [orig. uncertain]

tabb'y *n.* brindled cat; she-cat. [F. *tabis,* striped taffeta]

tabernacle *n.* tent or booth; religious meeting-house. [L. *taberna,* hut]

ta'ble *n.* piece of furniture consisting mainly of a flat board supported by legs, brackets, *etc.*, about three feet from the ground; tablet; food; set of facts or figures arranged in lines or columns. -*v.t.* lay on a table. -ta'ble-cloth *n.* cloth of linen, *etc.*, to cover table at mealtimes. -tab'ular *a.* shaped or arranged like a table. -tab'ulate *v.t.* arrange (figures, facts, *etc.*) in tables. -tabula'tion *n.* [L. *tabula*]

tab'leau *n.* -tab'leaux *pl.* dramatic situation. [*table*]

tab'loid *n.* illustrated popular newspaper with brief sensational headlines. -concentrated, very short. [Trademark]

taboo' *n.* setting apart of a thing as sacred or accursed; ban or prohibition. *a.* put under a taboo. -*v.t.* to put under a taboo. [Polynesian]

tac'it (tas'-) *a.* implied but not spoken. tac'itly *adv.* -tac'iturn *a.* talking little, habitually silent. -taciturn'ity *n.* [L. *tacere,* be silent]

tack *n.* small nail; long loose stitch; rope at the corner of a sail; course of a ship obliquely to windward. -*v.t.* nail with tacks; stitch lightly; beat to windward with tacks; change from one tack to another. [ONF. *toque,* fastening]

tack *n.* food. -hard tack, ship's biscuit. [for *tackle*]

tac'kle *n.* equipment, apparatus, *esp.* lifting appliances with ropes. -*v.t.* take in hand; grip. [LG. *takel*]

tack'y *a.* shabby, seedy, common; characterized by a lack of style. [orig. uncertain]

tact *n.* skill in dealing with people or situations. -tact'ful *a.* -tact'less *a.* tact'fully *adv.* -tact'lessly *adv.* tact'ile *a.* of or relating to the sense of touch. [L. *tactus-tangere, tact-,* touch]

tactics *n. pl.* art of handing troops or ships in battle; science of strategy. tact'ical *a.* -tacti'cian *n.* [G. *la taktika,* matters of arrangement]

tad'pole *n.* young frog in the tailed stage. [ME. *taddepol,* 'toad-head']

tag *n.* ragged end; pointed end of lace, *etc.* [of Scand. orig.]

tail *n.* projecting continuation of the backbone at the hinder end of an animal; any tail-like appendage. -tailed *a.* -tail'less *a.* tail'spin *n.* spiral dive of airplane. [OE. *taegel*]

tail'or *n.* maker of outer clothing. [F. *tailleur,* tailor, cutter]

taint *n.* stain; infection; moral infection. *v.t.* stain slightly; corrupt. -*v. i.* become corrupted. [for *attaint*]

take *v.t.* grasp, get hold of, get; receive, assume, adopt; accept; understand; consider; carry or conduct; captivate. -*v. i.* be effective. -take'-off *n.* of a plane, *etc.*, rise from the ground. [ON. *taka*]

talc *n.* white or green mineral of soapy feel; powder made from it. [Arab. *talq*]

tale *n.* story; number, count. [OE. *talu,* speech, number]

tal'ent *n.* natural ability or power; ancient weight or money. [L. *lalenturn,* money of account]

tal'isman *n.* object supposed to have magic powers. -talisman'ic *a.* [G. *telesma,* payment, religious rite]

talk (tawk) *v.i.* speak or converse. -*v.t.* express in speech; use (a language); discuss. -*n.* speech; conversation; rumor. -talkative *a.* [fr. *tale*]

tall *a.* high; of great stature; (*sl.*) of a story, to be taken with a pinch of salt. [OE. *getoel,* swift, prompt]

tall'ow *n.* melted and clarified animal fat. [LG. *talg*]

tall'y *n.* notched rod for keeping accounts; account so kept; reckoning. -*v.t.* record by a tally. -*v. i.* agree, correspond. [F. *tailler,* cut]

Tal'mud *n.* collection of volumes containing Jewish civil and canonical law. -Talmud'ic *a.* [Heb. *talmud,* instruction]

tal′on *n.* claw. [F. = *heel*]

tame *a.* not wild; domesticated: unexciting, uninteresting. *-v.t.* make tame. [OE. *tam*]

tamp′er *v.i.* interfere (with) improperly; meddle. [var. of *temper*]

tan *n.* crushed oak-bark; color of this. *v.t.* make into leather; make brown. **tann′in** *n.* astringent substance got from oak-bark, *etc.* [of Celt. orig.]

tan′dem *adv.* one behind the other. *-n.* vehicle with two horses one behind the other; bicycle for two riders one behind the other. [L. = *at length*]

tang *n.* pungent taste, odor; kind of seaweed. [ON. *tangi*, point]

tan′gent (-j-) *a.* touching, meeting without cutting. *-n.* line tangent to a curve. **-tangen′tial** *a.* **-tangen′tially** *adv.* [L. *tangere, tangent-*, touch]

tangent (tan′-jent) abbrev. **tan** *n.* (*trigonometry*) in a right-angled triangle, the tangent of an acute angle is the ratio of the perpendicular to the base. [fr. L. *tangere*, to touch]

tangerine′ *n.* kind of small orange. [F. Tanger, Tangiers]

tan′gible *a.* that can be touched; definite. **-tangibil′ity** *n.* [L. *tangibilis*]

tan′gle *v.t.* twist together in a muddle. *-n.* tangled mass, kind of edible seaweed. [orig. uncertain]

tang′o (-ng-go) *n.* S. American dance. [orig. uncertain]

tank *n.* storage vessel for liquids, *esp.* a large one; (*mil.*) heavily armed and armored tracked vehicle used in modern warfare. **-tank′er** *n.* vessel designed to carry petroleum in bulk. [Port, *tanque*]

tan′ner *n.* one who tans; (*sl.*) sixpence. **tannery** *n.* place where hides are tanned. [OE. *tannere*]

tantalize *v.t.* torment by presenting and then taking away something desired. [fr. punishment of Tantalus, king of Phrygia]

tantamount *a.* equivalent in value or signification; equal. [L. *tantus*, so great, and E. *amount*]

tan′trum *n.* outburst of temper. [orig. unknown]

tap *n.* hollow plug for drawing off liquid; valve with a handle to regulate or stop the flow of a fluid in a pipe, *etc.* *-v. t.* put a tap in; draw off. [OE. *tæppa*]

tap *v. t.* strike lightly but with some noise. *-n.* slight blow or rap. [imit.]

tape *n.* narrow long strip of fabric, paper, *etc.* **-tape′worm** *n.* flat worm parasitic on animals. [OE. *teppa*]

ta′per *n.* long wick covered with wax; thin candle. *-v.i.* become gradually thinner towards one end. *-v.t.* make thus. [OE. *tapur*]

tap′estry *n.* fabric decorated with woven designs in colors. [F. *tapisserie*]

tar *n.* thick black liquid distilled from coal, resinous wood, *etc.* *-v.t.* coat with tar. **-tarr′y** *a.* [OE. *teru*]

tarantula *n.* large, poisonous spider of Southern Europe. [Taranto, in Italy]

tard′y *a.* slow, behindhand. **-tard′ily** *adv.* **-tard′iness** *n.* [L. *tardus*, late]

tar′get *n.* mark to aim at in shooting; small shield. [ON. *targa*, shield]

tar′iff *n.* list of charges. [It. *tariffa*]

tar′nish *v.t.* discolor (*esp.* metal). *-v.i.* become stained, lose shine. *-n.* discoloration. [F. *ternir*, become dull, dingy]

tarpaulin *n.* canvas treated with tar or oil. [ME. *palyoun*, canopy]

tart *n.* open pie of fruit, *etc.*; small covered fruit pie. [F. *tarte*]

tart *a.* sour. [OE. *teart*, severe]

tart′an *n.* woollen cloth woven in a pattern of stripes crossing at right angles. [OF. *tartarin*, rich fabric imported through Tartary]

tar′tar *n.* crust deposited on the teeth; deposit on wine-casks, *etc.* **-tartar′ic** *a.* [F. *tartre*]

task *n.* piece of work set or undertaken. *-v.t.* put a task on, take to task, to reprove. **-task′master** *n.* [ONF. *tasque*, fr. L. *taxare*, appraise]

tass′el *n.* bunch of threads on a knob as an ornament. [OF. = 'little heap']

taste *v.t.* perceive or try the flavor of, eat or drink; experience. *-v.i.* have a flavor. *n.* small quantity; flavor; judgment in matters of beauty, style, *etc.* **-taste′ful** *a.* **-taste′fully** *adv.* **-taste′less** *a.* [OF. *taster*, touch, handle]

tatt′er *n.* rag. **-tatterdema′lion** *n.* ragged fellow. [of Teut. orig.]

tat′tle *v.i.* gossip; talk idly; give away secrets. *-n.* [Flem. *tateln.* stammer]

tattoo′ *n.* beat of drum and bugle-call; military spectacle, earlier *taptoo*: lights out, or closing time for taverns. [Du. *tap toe*, 'shut the tap to']

tattoo′ *v.t.* mark the skin in patterns, *etc.*, by pricking and filling the punctures with coloring matter. *-n.* mark so made. [Polynesian]

taunt *n.* reproach, insulting words. *-v.t.* insult, reproach bitterly. [OF. *tanter*]

Taur′us *n.* the Bull, 2nd sign of the zodiac, which sun enters on 21st April. [L.]

taut *a.* drawn tight. [orig. uncertain]

tav′ern *n.* inn or ale-house. [F. *taverner* fr. L. *taberna*, hut]

taw′dry *a.* showy but cheap and without taste. **-taw′drily** *adv.* [St. Audrey's fair (Oct. 17th) where trinkets were sold]

tawn′y *a.* yellowish-brown. *-n.* this color. [F. *tanné*, tanned]

tax *v.t.* exact a contribution to the cost of government; examine accounts; put a burden or strain on. *n.* charge imposed; a burden. **-taxa′tion** *n.* **-tax′able** *a.* **tax′-payer** *n.* [L. *taxare*, reckon]

tax′i- (cab) *n.* motor-cab for hire with driver. **-tax′i** *v.i.* go in a taxi; (of an airplane) run along the ground under its own power. *-pres. part.* **-tax′ying.** **- taxim′eter** *n.* instrument for measuring the time and distance to reckon the charge for a cab fitted with it. [abbrev. of taximeter. *See* tax]

tax′idermy *n.* art of stuffing animals. **taxi′dermist** *n.* [fr. G. *taxis*, arrangement, and *derma*, skin]

tea *n.* dried leaves of a plant cultivated in China, India, *etc.*; infusion of it as a beverage; various herbal infusions; afternoon meal at which tea is served. [Du. *thee* (fr. Chin.)]

teach *v.t.* instruct; impart knowledge of, direct; discipline. *-v.i.* act as teacher. **teach'er** *n.* [OE. *toecan*]

teak *n.* East Indian tree; the very hard wood obtained from it. (Malayalam *tekka*)

teal *n.* small water-fowl allied to the duck. [orig. uncertain]

team *n.* set of animals, players of a game, *etc.*, associated in an activity. **-team'ster** *n.* one who drives a team of draught animals; driver of a motortruck, *esp.* as an occupation. [OE.]

tear *n.* drop of fluid in, or failing from, the eye. **-tear'ful** *a.* **-tear'less** *a.* **-tear'drop** *n.* **-tear'-stained** *a.* **-tear'-gas** *n.* irritant gas causing watering of the eyes. [OE.]

tear (tar) *v.t.* pull apart, rend. *-v.i.* become torn; rush. *-n.* rent. [OE. *teran*]

tease *v.t.* pull apart the fibers of, torment; irritate. *-n.* one who torments. **-teas'ing** *a.* [OE. *toesan*]

teat *n.* nipple of a female breast; artificial substitute for this. [F. *tette*]

technical (tek-) *a.* of or used in an art, *esp.* an industrial art; belonging to a particular art. **-technical'ity** *n.* state of being technical; that which is technical. **-tech'nically** *adv.* **-technique'** *n.* method of performance. **techni'cian** *n.* **-technol'ogy** *n.* systematic knowledge of industrial arts. **technol'ogist** *n.* [G. *techne*, art, craft]

te'dium *n.* boredom or quality of boring. **-te'dious** *a.* wearisome. **-te'diously** *adv.* [L. *toedium*, fr. *toedere*, weary]

tee *n.* (*golf*) small peg or sand-heap from which the ball is played off at each hole. [orig. unknown]

teem *v.i.* abound with, swarm, be prolific. [OE. *tieman*]

teens *n. pl.* years of youth, between 12 and 20. **-teen'ager** *n.*

teethe (-TH) *v.i.* cut teeth. [fr. *teeth*]

teeto'tal *a.* abstaining or pledged to abstain from intoxicating drink; relating to such abstinence or pledge. **-teeto'taler** *n.* [elaboration of *total*]

tel- *prefix*, at a distance. [G. = far off] **-telecommunications** *n* transmission of data signals in digital, audio, or video form. **-tel'egraph** *n.* apparatus for sending messages mechanically to a distance, as by semaphore, electricity, *etc.* *-v.t.* and *i.* communicate by telegraph. **-tel'egram** *n.* message sent by telegraph. **-telekine'sis** *n.* motion caused by spirit or psychic force. **-telep'athy** *n.* action of one mind on another at a distance. **-telepath'ic** *a.* **-telepath'ically** *adv.* **-tel'ephone** *n.* apparatus for communicating sound to a distance. *-v.t.* and *i.* communicate or speak by telephone. **tel'escope** *n.* instrument of lenses to see things more clearly at a distance. **telescop'ic** *a.* **-televi'sion** *n.* seeing at a distance by the use of wireless transmission.

tell *v.t.* narrate, make known; count. *-v. i.* give an account; be of weight or importance. **-tell'er** *n.* **-tell'ing** *a.* effective. **-tell'tale** *a.* indicating, betraying (secrets, *etc.*). *-n.* teller of secrets. **-tell'off** *v.t.* berate. [OE. *tellan*]

temerity *n.* rashness. **-temera'rious** *a.* foolhardy. [F. *témérité*, fr. L. *temeritas*]

temp'er *v.t.* harden; bring to proper condition; restrain, moderate. *-n.* degree of hardness of steel, *etc.*; mental constitution, frame of mind; anger, *esp.* in noisy outburst. **-temp'erament** *n.* mental constitution. **-temperament'al** *a.* **-temperament'ally** *adv.* **-temp'erate** *a.* showing or practicing moderation. **-temp'erance** *n.* moderation, self-restraint. **-temp'erately** *adv.* **-temp'erature** *n.* degree of heat or coldness. [L. *temperate*, proportion duly]

temp'est *n.* violent storm. **-tempest'uous** *a.* **-tempest'uously** *adv.* [L. *tempestas*, weather, storm]

template *n.* pattern or guide. (*compute.*) plastic cutout used for drawing computer flowcharting symbols.

tem'ple *n.* building for worship, or to house a deity. [L. *templum*]

tem'ple *n.* flat part on either side of the head above the cheekbone. [L. *temporal* pl.]

tem'po *n.* (*music*) time, rate; rhythm. [It.]

temp'oral *a.* relating to time, or to this life or world; secular. **-temporal'ity** *n.* **temp'orary** *a.* lasting or used only for a time [L. *tempus*, *tempor-*, time]

tempt *v.t.* try; try to persuade, *esp.* to evil. **-tempt'er** *n.* **-temptress** *n. fem.* **tempta'tion** *n.* [OF. *tempter*, fr. L. *temptare*, test]

ten *n.* and *a.* cardinal number next after nine. **-tenth** *a.* ordinal number. **tenth'ly** *adv.* [OE. *tien*]

ten'able *a.* that may be held or defended. [F.]

tenacious *a.* holding fast. **-tenac'ity** *n.* [L. *tenax-tenere*, hold]

ten'ant *n.* one who holds lands or house, *etc.*, on a rent, or lease. [F. fr. L. *tenere*, hold]

tend *v.t.* take care of. **-tend'er** *n.* vessel attending a larger one; carriage for fuel and water attached to a locomotive. [for *attend*]

tend *v.i.* incline; make in direction of **tend'ency** *n.* **-tend'er** *v. t.* offer. *-n.* offer; what may legally be offered in payment. [L. *tendere*, stretch]

tend'er *a.* delicate, soft; fragile; gentle, loving, affectionate. **-tend'erly** *adv.* **tend'erness** *n.* **-tend'erfoot** *n.* new comer on plains; novice. **-tend'er loin** *n.* undercut of sirloin; (*sl.*) district of a city known for vice, corruption *etc.* [F. *tendre*, fr. L. *tener*]

tend'on *n.* sinew attaching a muscle to a bone, *etc.* [G. *tenon*, sinew]

tend'ril *n.* slender curling stem by which a climbing plant attaches itself to anything. [F. *tendre*, stretch]

ten'ement *n.* piece of land or a house; part of a house forming a separate dwelling; block of flats. [L. *tenere*, hold]

ten'et *n.* doctrine. [L. = 'he holds']

ten'nis *n.* game in which a ball is struck between players on opposite sides of a net in a covered court; variation of this played on a grass or other court (also called lawn tennis). [F. *tenez*, take; (called by the server)]

ten'on *n.* tongue on the end of a piece of wood, *etc.*, to fit into a mortise. [F.]

ten'or *n.* meaning; trend; male voice between alto and bass, music for this; singer with this voice. [L.]

tense *n.* modification of a verb to show time of action, *etc.* **-ten'sity** *n.* [OF. *tens*, fr. L. *tempus*, time]

tense *a.* stretched tight. **-ten'sile** *a.* capable of being stretched. **-ten'sion** *n.* stretching or strain when stretched; mental strain. [L. *tendere*, *tens-*, *tent-*, stretch]

tent *n.* portable shelter of canvas. **-tent'pole** *n.* **-tent'-peg** *n.* [F. *tente*, fr. L. *tendere*, stretch]

tentacle *n.* feeler. **-tent'ative** *a.* done as a trial. **-n.** attempt. **-tent'atively** *adv.* [L. *tentare*, try]

tenuous *a.* thin. [L. *tenuitas-tenuis*, slender]

tepee' *n.* American Indian skin-tent. [Sioux = *dwelling*]

tep'id *a.* moderately warm; lukewarm. [L. *tepidus*]

tequila *n.* strong Mexican liquor. [Tequila, district of Mexico]

term *n.* limit or end; fixed day for regular payment, *e.g.* rent; period during which courts sit, schools are open, *etc.* **-pl.** conditions, mutual relationship; word or expression. **-v.t.** name. **-term'inal** *a.* at or forming an end. **-n.** terminal part or structure. **-term'inate** *v.t.* bring to an end. **-v.i.** come to an end. **-termina'tion** *n.* study of terms; set of technical terms or vocabulary. **-terminolo'gical** (-j-) *a.* **term'inus** *n.* finishing point; station at the end of a railway. [L. *terminus*, limit]

ter'mite *n.* the so-called white ant. [L. *termes*, woodworm]

tern *n.* sea-bird allied to the gull. [Ice. *therna*]

tertiary *a.* in threes; proceeding in threes. [L. *terni*, three each]

Terpsich'ore *n.* Muse of dancing. [G.]

terrace *n.* raised level place, level cut out of a hill; row or street of uniform houses. **-v.t.** form into a terrace. [F. *terasse*, fr. *terre*, earth]

terra-cotta *n.* hard unglazed pottery, *a.* brownish-red color. [It. = *cooked earth*]

terr'ain *n.* a region or tract of land; ground considered in relation to, *e.g.*, military operations. [F.]

terrest'rial *a.* of the earth; of land. [L. *terrestris*, fr. *terra*, earth]

terr'ible *a.* causing fear; (call.) excessive. **-terr'ibly** *adv.* **-terrif'ic** *a.* terrible, awesome. **-terrif'ically** *adv.* **terr'ify** *v.t.* frighten. **-terr'or** *n.* state of great fear. **-terr'orize** *v.t.* force or oppress by fear. **terrorism** *n.* **-terr'orist** *n.* [L. *terrère*, frighten]

terr'ier *n.* small dog of various breeds, orig. for following a quarry into a burrow. [F., fr. *terre*, earth]

territory *n.* region; land subject to a ruler. **-territo'rial** *a.* relating to a territory. [L. *territorium*]

ter'tiary *a.* third. [L. *tertius*, third]

test *n.* means of trial. **-v. t.** try, put to the proof. **-test pi'lot** *n.* pilot who flies aircraft of new

design to test performance in air. **-test tube** *n.* narrow cylindrical glass vessel used in scientific experiments. [OF. *test*, pot]

testament *n.* will; one of the two divisions of the Bible. **-testament'ary** *a.* **-test'ate** *a.* that has left a will. [L. *testamentum*]

test'icle *n.* male genital organ. [L. *testiculus*]

test'ify *v.i.* bear witness. **-v.t.** bear witness to. **-test'imony** *n.* evidence. **testimo'nial** *n.* certificate of character, ability, *etc.*; gift by a number of persons to express their regard for the recipient. [L. *testis*, witness]

test'y *a.* irritable, short-tempered. [OF. *testif*, heady, obstinate]

tet'anus *n.* lockjaw; rigidity of some or all muscles. [G. *tetanos*, muscular spasm]

teth'er *v. t.* tie up (a horse, *etc.*), with a rope. **-n.** rope or chain for fastening a grazing animal; limit of endurance (end of one's tether). [ON. *tjothr*]

tet'ragon *a.* figure with four angles and four sides. **-tetrag'onal** *a.* **-tetrahe'dron** *n.* solid contained by four plane faces. [G. *tetra*, four]

tet'rarch *n.* in Roman Empire, ruler of 4th part of a province. [G. *tetra*, four, *arches*, ruler]

Teuton'ic *a.* of, pert. to, Germanic race, *e.g.* Germans, Scandinavians, English. [L. *Teutonicus*, from the Teutones]

text *n.* actual words of a book, passage, *etc.*; main body of a literary work; letterpress; passage from the Scriptures, *etc.*, *esp.* as the subject of a discourse. **-text'book** *n.* manual of instruction. **-text editing** *v.t.* procss of changing, adding, or deleting material on a computer. **-text'ual** *a.* of or in a text. [L. *textus-texere*, text-, weave]

text'ile *a.* woven; capable of being woven; relating to weaving. **-n.** a woven fabric. [L. *textilis*]

text'ure *n.* the character or structure of a textile fabric. [L. *texere*, *text-*, weave]

than (TH-) *conj.* and *prep.* introduces second part of a comparison. [OE. *thanne*]

thank *v.t.* give thanks to, express gratitude to. **-thanks** *n. pl.* words of gratitude. **-thank'ful** *a.* feeling grateful. **-thankless** *a.* having or bringing no thanks. [OE *thanc*]

that (TH-) *a.* demonstrates or particularizes. *fem. pron.* particular thing meant. **-adv.** as. **-rel. pron.** which, who. **-conj.** introduces noun or adverbial clauses. [OE. *thcet*]

thatch *v.t.* roof (a house) with straw or similar material. **-n.** straw used in thatching. [OE. *thæc*, roof]

thaw *v. t.* and *i.* melt. **-n.** a melting (of frost, *etc.*). [OE. *thawian*]

the (TH-) is the definite article. [that]

the'ater (-ter) *n.* place where plays are performed; drama or dramatic works generally; surgical operating room. **theat'rical** *a.* of or for the theater; showy, spectacular. **-theat'rically** *adv.* **-theat'ricals** *n. pl.* amateur dramatic performances. [G. *theatron*]

theft *n.* stealing. [OF. *thiefth*]

their (THir) *a.* **-pron.** belonging to them. [ON. *theirra*]

the'ism *n.* belief in divine creation of the universe without denial of revelation. **the'ist**

n. [G. *theos*, god]

them *pron.* objective case of they; those persons or things. [ON. *theim*]

theme *n.* subject of a composition; essay. [G. *theme*, proposition]

then (TH-) *adv.* at that time; next; that being so. [OE. *thanne*]

theol'ogy *n.* science treating of God. - **theoc'racy** *n.* government by God. - **theocrat'ic** *a.* [G. *theos*, god]

the'orem *n.* proposition which can be demonstrated by argument. -**the'ory** *n.* supposition to account for something; system of rules and principles; rules and reasoning, *etc.*, as distinguished from practice. [G. *theorems*, proposition to be proved]

theosophy *n.* any of various ancient and modern systems of esoteric philosophy by which the soul may attain to knowledge of, and ultimate union with, the universal spirit. [G. *theosophos*, wise in the things of God]

therapeutic *a.* relating to healing. -*n.* in *pl.* art of healing. -**ther'apy** *n.* curative treatment. [G. *therapeutikos*]

there (TH-) *adv.* in that place, to that point. -**there'fore** *adv.* in consequence, that being so. [OE. *thcer*]

ther'mal *a.* of or pertaining to heat. -**therm** *n.* unit of heat; unit of 1,000 calories. -**ther'mic** *a.* thermal. -**thermom'eter** *n.* instrument to measure temperature. -**thermomet'ric** *a.* [G. *therme*, heat]

thermodynamics *n. pl.* science dealing with conversion of heat into mechanical energy. [G. *thermos*, hot]

thermostat *n.* automatic regulator of temperature. -**thermostat'ic** *a.* [G. *thermos*, hot]

thesaurus *n.* treasury; storehouse; *esp.* a collection of words and phrases; a lexicon or encyclopedia. [L. -G. *thesauros*, *tithenae*, place]

the'sis *n.* proposition; dissertation. [G.]

thes'pian *a.* of the drama. [*Thespis*, founder of Greek drama]

they *pron.* third person plural pronoun. [ON. *their*]

thick *a.* having great thickness, not thin; dense, crowded; viscous; foggy. -**thick'ly** *adv.* -**thick'en** *v. t.* and *i.* -**thick'ness** *n.* dimension of anything measured through it, at right angles to the length and breadth. -**thick'et** *n.* thick growth of small trees. -**thick'set** *a.* set closely together; sturdy and solid in limbs and frame. [OE. *thicce*]

thief *n.* thieves *pl.* one who steals. **thieve** *v.t.* and *i.* steal. [OE. *theof*]

thigh *n.* upper part of the leg above the knee. [OE. *theoh*]

thim'ble *n.* metal cover for the fingertip in sewing. [OE. *thymel*, fr. thumb]

thin *a.* not thick; of little density; loose, not closely packed. -*v.t.* and *i.* make or become thin. -**thin'ness** *n.* [OE. *thynne*]

thing *n.* material object; any possible object of thought. [OE. = assembly for deliberation; affairs; matters]

think *v.i.* have one's mind at work; reflect;

hold an opinion. -*v.t.* conceive or consider in the mind. -**think'er** *n.* [OE. *thencan*]

third *a.* ordinal number corresponding to three. -*n.* third part. -**third degree'**, drastic police methods to make a prisoner 'talk'. [ver. of *thrid*, fr. three]

thirst *n.* feeling caused by lack of drink. *v. i.* feel the lack of drink. -**thirst'y** *a.* thirst'ily *adv.* [OE, *thurst*]

thirteen' *a.* and *n.* number, three and ten. -**thirt'y** *n.* and *a.* number, three times ten. [OE. *threotyne; thritig*]

this, these *pl.* -*dem. a.* and *pron.* denotes a thing or person near, or just mentioned, *etc.* [OE.]

this'tle (-*sl*) *n.* prickly plant with a purple flower. [OE. *thistel*]

thong *n.* narrow strip of leather. -*v.t.* sew with thongs. [OE. *thwang*, strap]

thor'ax *n.* part of the body between neck and belly. [G. = breastplate]

thorn *n.* prickle on a plant; bush noted for its thorns. -**thorn'y** *a.* [OE.]

thor'ough *a.* complete, painstaking. - **thor'oughly** *adv.* -**thor'oughbred** *a.* of pure breed. -*n.* purebred animal, *esp.* horse. - **thor'oughfare** *n.* road or passage open at both ends; right of way. [var. of *through*]

those *a.* and pron. *pl.* of that. [OE. *thas*]

thou *pron.* (*arch.*) second person singular pronoun. [OE. *thu*]

though *conj.* in spite of the fact that. -*adv.* for all that. [OE. *theah*]

thought (thawt) *n.* process of thinking; what one thinks; a product of thinking; meditation. -**thought'ful** *a.* engaged in meditation; considerate. -**thought'less** *a.* careless, heedless, inconsiderate. [OE. *thoht*]

thou'sand (-z-) *a.* and *n.* cardinal number, ten hundreds. [OE. *thusend*]

thrash, **thresh** *v.t.* of corn, *etc.*, beat out the grains of. -**thrash** *v.t.* beat, whip. [OE. *threscan*]

thread (-ed) *n.* fine cord; yarn; ridge cut spirally on a screw. -*v.t.* put a thread into; put on a thread; pick (one's way, *etc.*). **thread'bare** *a.* worn, with the nap rubbed off. [OE. *thrced*]

threat (-et) *n.* announcement of what the speaker intends to do if his orders or wishes are not complied with. -**threat'en** *v.t.* and *i.* utter threats against. **threat'ening** *a.* menacing. [OE. *pressure*]

three *n.* and *a.* cardinal number, one more than two. [OE. *threo*]

threshold (-old) *n.* the bar of stone or wood forming the bottom of the framework of a door. [OE. *therscold*, fr. *therscask*, tread]

thrift *n.* saving, economy. [fr. thrive]

thrill *v.t.* send -a nervous tremor of emotion through. -*v. i.* feel one. -*n.* such emotional tremor. -**thrill'er** *n.* (*sl.*) sensational story. -**thrill'ing** *a.* exciting. [OE. *thyrlian*, pierce]

thrive *v. i.* grow well; flourish, prosper. [ON. *thrifa*, grasp]

throat *n.* front of the neck; either or both of the passages through it. -**throat'y** *a.* of voice, hoarse. [OE. *throte*]

throb *v. i.* beat or quiver strongly. -*n.* a throbbing. [orig. uncertain]

thrombosis *n.* formation of a bloodclot in artery or vein. (G. *thrombos*, clot]

throne *n.* seat of state, *esp.* of a king. *v. t.* place on a throne. [G. *thronos*]

throng *n. v.t.* , and *i.* crowd. [OE. *gethrana*, fr. *thringan*, press]

throt'tle *v.t.* and *i.* strangle. [fr. *throat*]

through *prep.* from end to end of, *adv.* from end to end; to the end. **throughout'** *adv.* in every part. -*prep.* in every part of [OE. *thurh*]

throw *v.t.* fling; bring down. -*n.* an act or distance of throwing. -**throw'back** *n.* reversion to an ancestral type. [OE. *thrawan*, to twist]

thrush *n.* song-bird. [OE. *thrysce*]

thrush *n.* throat and mouth disease of children; foot disease of horses. [orig. uncertain]

thrust *v. t.* push, stab, drive. -*v. i.* lunge, stab; push one's way. -*n.* lunge or stab with sword, *etc.* [ON. *thrysta*]

thud *n.* dull heavy sound, as of a brick falling on earth. -*v. i.* make a thud. [imit. orig.]

thug *n.* one of a body of Indian assassins in early 19th c.; cutthroat; ruffian. [Hind.]

thumb *n.* short thick finger, the one which can be opposed to the others. -*v.t.* handle or dirty with the thumb. **thumb'tack** *n.* tack with a large flat head for pressing into a surface with the thumb. [OE. *thuma*]

thump *v. t.* strike heavily. -*n.* dull heavy blow; sound of one. [imit.]

thunder *n.* loud noise accompanying lightning. -*v. i.* of thunder, to sound. -*v. t.* utter loudly. -**thun'derbolt** *n.* lightning flash as agent of destruction. -**thun'dery** *a.* -**thun'derous** *a.* [OE. *thunor*]

Thurs'day *n.* fifth day of the week. [OE. *thunresdaeg*, day of Thor or thunder]

thus *adv.* in this way; therefore. [OE.]

thwack *v.t.* and *n.* whack. [imit.]

thwart *v.t.* foil, frustrate. *adv.* across. [ON. *thuert*, across]

thwart *n.* seat for a rower across a boat. [OE. *thofte*, rower's bench]

thy *pron.* or *a.* (*poss.* of *thou*) belonging to thee. [var. of *thine*]

thy'roid (gland) *n.* ductless gland at front of neck; chief cartilage of larynx. [G. *thyreos*, shield, *eidos*, form]

tiar'a *n.* jeweled head-ornmanent. [G.]

tib'ia *n.* shin-bone; flute. [L.]

tic *n.* spasmodic twitch in the muscles of the face; tic douloureux. [F.]

tick *n.* mite in hair or fur. [Teut. orig.]

tick *n.* mattress case. [G. *theke*, case]

tick *n.* slight sound as of a watch movement; -*v.i.* make the sound; small mark -*v.t.* mark with a tick. [imit.]

tick *n.* (*sl.*) credit. -**give tick**, sell on credit. [ticket]

tick'et *n.* card or paper entitling to admission, travel, *etc.*; label. -*v.t.* attach a label to. [F. *étiquette*, label]

tickle *v.i.* itch. -*v.t.* make itch with light touches, *etc.* -**tick'lish** *a.* sensitive to tickling;

requiring care or tact in handling. [orig. uncertain]

tide *n.* season or time; rise and fall of the sea happening twice each lunar day; stream. -*v.i.* tide over, get over or surmount. -*v.t.* enable someone to do this. -**ti'dal** *a.* of or resembling a tide. [OE. *tid*, time]

ti'dings *n.* news; happenings; a report. [fr. *betide*]

ti'dy *a.* orderly, neat. -*v.t.* put in order. [orig.]

timely. *See* tide

tie *v. t.* fasten, bind; restrict. -*n.* that with which anything is bound; cravat; bond; drawn game with equal points; match. [OE. *teag n.*; *tigan v.*]

tier *n.* row, rank, *esp.* rising in a series. [F. *tirer*, draw]

ti'ger *n.* large carnivorous animal with striped coat. -**ti'gress** *fem.* [G. *tigris*]

tight *a.* firm; tense, taut; fitting close; not allowing the passage of water, *etc.*; (*colloq.*) drunk. -**tights** *n. pl.* tight-fitting elastic garments. -**tight'en** *v.t.* and *i.* **tight'ly** *adv.* [ON. *thettr*, watertight]

tile *n.* slab of baked clay, porcelain, *etc. v.t.* cover with tiles. [L. *tegula*]

till *n.* drawer for money in a shop. [orig. uncertain]

tilt *v.t.* cultivate. -**till'er** *n.* lever to move a rudder of a boat. [OF. *telier*, weaver's beam]

tilt *n.* canvas cover or hood for a wagon; stern-sheets of boat, *etc.* [orig. uncertain]

tilt *v.t.* and *i.* slope, slant. -*n.* inclination from the vertical. [OE. *tealt*, unsteady]

tilt *v.i.* take part in a medieval combat with lances, joust. -*n.* combat for mounted men with lances. [orig. uncertain]

tim'ber *n.* wood for building, *etc.* **tim'bered** *a.* made or partly made of wood. [OE. = house or material suitable to make one]

time *n.* existence as a succession of states; hour; duration; period; point in duration. -*v. t.* choose or note the time of. -**time'ly** *a.* seasonable. -**time'ous** *a.* opportune, seasonable. -**time'piece** *n.* watch or clock. -**time'-honored** *a.* respected because old. -**timetable** *n.* schedule of times, *e.g.*, of working hours, trains, *etc.* [OE. *tima*]

tim'id *a.* diffident; lacking courage. [L. *timidus*, fr. *timere*, fear]

tin *n.* malleable white metal; vessel of tin or tinned iron. -*v. t.* coat with tin; put in a tin, *esp.* for preserving (food). -**tinn'y** *a.* of sound, light and unmusical, like clash of tin. [OE.]

tin'der *n.* dry easily-burning material used to catch a spark from flint and steel. [OE. *tynder-tendan*, kindle]

tine *n.* tooth, spike of fork, antler, harrow, *etc.* [OE. *tind*]

tinge *v.t.* color or flavor slightly. -*n.* slight trace. [L. *tingere*, dye]

tingle *v.i.* vibrate; thrill; feel 'pins and needles' [var. of *tinkle*]

tink'er *n.* mender of pots and pans. -*v. i.* work in clumsy or amateur fashion. [fr. noise of his work]

tin'kle *v.i.* give out a series of light sounds like a small bell. -*v. t.* cause to do this. -*n.* sound or action of this. [imit.]

tin'sel *n.* thin metal plates, cord, *etc.* , for decoration; anything sham and showy. [F. *étincelle*, spark]

tint *n.* color; tinge. *-v. t.* dye, give a tint to. [L. *tingere*, dye]

ti'ny *a.* very small. [orig. uncertain]

tip *n.* slender or pointed end of anything; piece of metal, leather, *etc.* , protecting or softening a tip. *-v.t.* put a tip on. **tip'staff** *n.* sheriffs officer, who carried a tipped staff. **-tip'toe** *v.i.* walk on one's toes. **-tiptop'** *a.* of the best quality or highest degree. [of Teut. orig.]

tip *n.* small present of money; piece of useful private information. *-v.t.* give a tip to. **-tip'ster** *n.* one who sells tips about races. [orig. a *cant* word]

tip *v.t.* upset. *-v.i.* topple over. *-n.* place for tipping carts, emptying out rubbish, *etc.* **-tip'-cat** *n.* game in which a spindle of wood is struck into the air by hitting one of the pointed ends with a stick; the piece of wood struck. [orig. type. of unknown orig.]

tip *v.t.* touch lightly. *-n.* children's game in which a pursuer touches one of the others pursued, who then becomes the pursuer. -[var. of *tap*]

tip'sy *a.* drunk or partly drunk. [fr. *tip*, upset]

tirade' *n.* long speech, generally vigorous and hostile; harangue. [It. *tirata*, volley]

tire *n.* and *v.* attire; rim of metal, rubber, *etc.* , round a wheel. *-v.t.* put one on. [attire]

tire *v.i.* become weary or fatigued. *-v.t.* fatigue. **-tire'some** *a.* wearisome, irritating. [OE. *tiorian*, exhaust]

ti'ro *n.* (also **tyro**) beginner, novice. [L. *raw* recruit]

tiss'ue *n.* fine woven fabric *esp.* of gold or silver; substance of an animal body, of a plant *etc.* **-tiss'ue-paper** *n.* very thin paper. [F. *lissu*, woven]

titan'ic (ti-) *a.* huge, gigantic. [G. *Titanes*, family of giants]

tithe (-TH) *n.* tenth part, *esp.* of agricultural produce paid as a tax. *-v.t.* exact tithes from. [OE. *teotha*, tenth]

tit'illate *v.t.* tickle, stimulate agreeably. **-titilla'tion** *n.* [L. *titillare*]

ti'tle *n.* heading, name of a book; name, appellation; legal right or document proving it. **-tit'le-deed** *n.* document confirming ownership. **-ti'tle-page** *n.* page at beginning of book bearing title, author's name and publishers' imprint. [L. *titulus*]

tit'ular *a.* so in name or title only; held by virtue of a title. [*See* **title**]

to *prep.* towards, in the direction of, as far as; used to introduce a comparison, ratio, indirect object, infinitive mood, *etc.* *-adv.* to the required or normal state or position. **-to-do'** *n.* fuss, commotion. [OE.]

toad *n.* animal like a frog. **-toad'stool** *n.* fungus like a mushroom, but usually poisonous. **-toad'y** *n.* one who fawns or curries favor unworthily. *-v.i.* do this. **toad'-eater** *n.* sycophant. [OE. *tadige*]

toast *v.t.* brown at the fire; warm; drink the health of. *-n.* slice of bread browned at the fire;

a health; person toasted. **-toast'master** *n.* one whose duty is to announce toasts at a banquet. [OF. *toster*, fr. L. *torrere*, *tort-*, parch]

tobacco *n.* plant of which the leaves are used for smoking; prepared leaves. [Sp. *taboco*]

tobog'gan *n.* sledge for sliding down a slope of snow or ice. *-v.i.* slide on one. [Canadian Ind. *tobakun*]

today' *n.* this day; present time. *-adv.* on this day. [*to* and *day*]

toddle *v.i.* walk with unsteady short steps. *-n.* a toddling. **-todd'ler** *n.* little child. [orig. uncertain]

toe *n.* digit of the foot. *-v. t.* reach or touch with the toe. [OE. *ta*]

to'ga *n.* mantle of a Roman citizen. [L.]

togeth'er *adv.* in company, simultaneously. [OE. *togoedere*]

togs *n. pl.* (*sl.*) clothes. [L. *toga*]

toil *v.i.* labor. *-n.* heavy work or task. **toil'some** *a.* **-toil'-worn** *a.* [OF. *touillier*, fr. L. *tudiculare*, stir]

toil'et *n.* process of dressing; articles used in this; manner of doing it, style of dress; dressing-table; cover for it; lavatory. [F. *toilette*]

toils *n. pl.* nets for catching game. [F. *toile*, fr. L. *tela*, cloth, web]

to'ken *n.* sign or object used as evidence; symbol. **-to'ken-pay'ment**, nominal payment as symbol only. **-to'ken-strike'**, workmen's strike intended merely as a gesture. [OE. *tæn*]

tol'erate *v.i.* put up with. **-tol'erant** *a.* disinclined to interfere with others ways or opinions. **-tol'erance** *n.* **tol'erantly** *adv.* [L. *tolerare*]

toll *n.* tax, *esp.* for the use of a bridge or road. **-toll-gate**. [OE.]

toll *v.t.* make (a bell) ring slowly at regular intervals; announce a death thus. *-v.i.* ring thus. *-n.* action or sound of tolling. [obs. *toll*, draw, pull]

toma'to *n.* plant with bright red yellow, fruit; the fruit, [Mex. *tomatl*]

tomb *n.* grave or monument over one. [G. *tymbos*, funeral mound]

tom'boy *n.* romping boyish girl. [*Tom* and *boy*]

tom'-cat *n.* male cat. [Tom]

tome *n.* volume, large ponderous book, [G. *tomos*]

tomorr'ow *n.* day after to-day. *adv.* on the next day after this one. [*morrow*]

ton (tun) *n.* measure of weight, 20 cwt.; unit of a ship's carrying capacity. **tonn'age** *n.* carrying capacity; charge per ton; ships. [var. of *tun*]

tondo *n.* round painting, carved relief, or other work of art.

tongs (-z) *n. pl.* large pincers, *esp.* for handling coal, *etc.* [OE. *tang*]

tongue (tung) *n.* muscular organ inside the mouth, used for speech, taste, *etc.*; various things shaped like this; speech; language. [OE. *tunge*]

tonight' *n.* this night; the coming night. *-adv.* on this night. [night]

ton'sil *n.* gland at the side of the throat.
ton'sillitis *n.* inflammation of the tonsils. [L.
tonsillce pl.]

too *adv.* in addition; in excess, more than
enough; also. [stressed form of to]

tool *n.* implement or appliance for mechanical operations. -*v.t.* work on with a tool. [OE.
tol]

tooth *n.* teeth *pl.* ivory process of the jaw;
anything resembling this. -**tooth'some** *a.*
pleasant to eat. [OE. *toth*]

top *n.* highest part; platform on a ship's mast.
-*v.t.* cut off, put on, pass, or reach, a top. -
top'hole *a.* (*sl.*) first-rate **top'most** *a.* [OE.]

top *n.* toy which spins on a point. [orig. un-
certain]

to'paz *n.* precious stone of various colors;
humming bird. [G. *topazos*]

top'ic *n.* subject of a discourse or conversation. -**top'ical** *a.* of a topic; up-to-date, having
news value. [G. *topos*, place]

topography *n.* description of a place; its features. -**topograph'ic** *a.* -**topograph'ically**
adv. -**topog'rapher** *n.* [G. *topos*, place]

top'ple *v. i.* fall over. [top]

topspin *n.* forward rolling (rotating) motion
imparted to a ball hit in tennis, billiards or to
a thrown ball.

torch *n.* twist of hemp, *etc.*, soaked in tar or
oil to burn as a portable light. **torch'light** *n.*
-**torch'bearer** *n.* [F. torche]

toreador' *n.* bull-fighter, *esp.* one who fights
on horseback. [Sp.]

tor'ment *n.* suffering or agony of body or
mind. -**torment'** *v. t.* afflict; tease. **torment'or**
n. [L. *tormentum*]

torna'do *n.* whirlwind; violent storm. [Sp.
tronada, fr. *tronar*, to thunder]

torpe'do *n.* cigar-shaped missile filled with
explosives and propelling itself underwater
by compressed air engines after discharge
from a ship. -*v.t.* strike or sink with a torpedo.
-**torpe'do-boat** *n.* [usually destroyer] [L. =
numbness; cramp-fish]

tor'pid *a.* sluggish, dormant. -**torpid'ity** *n.*
-**tor'por** *n.* torpid state. [L. *torpere*, be torpid]

torque (tork) *n.* collar or like ornament of
twisted gold or metal; in mechanics, rotating
or twisting forces. [L. *torquire*, twist]

torr'ent *n.* rushing stream. -**torren'tial** *a.* [L.
torrens, torrent-, boil]

torr'id *a.* hot, scorching; dried up with heat.
[L. *torrere*, burn or boil]

tor'sion *n.* twist. [L, *torquere*, twist]

tort *n.* breach of legal duty. [F.]

tortellini *n.* small, rounded pieces of pasta
dough filled with cheese or chopped meat,
served with tomato, cheese, or cream sauce.

tort'uous *a.* winding, twisting, not
straightforward. [L. *torquere*, twist]

tor'toise *n.* four-footed reptile covered with
a shell of horny plates. [Late L. *tortuca*]

tort'ure *n.* infliction of severe pain. -*v. t.* subject to torture. -**tort'urer** *n.* **tort'ure-cham-
ber** *n.* [L. *torquere*, twist]

toss *v. t.* throw up or about. -*v. i.* be thrown, or
fling oneself, about. -*n.* act of tossing. -

toss'pot *n.* toper. [orig. uncertain]

tot *n.* very small thing; small quantity, *esp.* of
a drink; tiny child. [orig. uncertain]

tot *v.t.* add up. -*v. i.* (with up) amount to. -*n.*
addition sum. [orig. uncertain]

to'tal *n.* whole amount. -*a.* complete, entire.
-*v. t.* add up; amount to. -**total'ity** *n.* -
totaliza'tor *n.* machine which registers total
totalita'rian *a.* of a government, in complete
control of the nation's resources. (L. *totus*, all]

to'tem *n.* tribal badge or emblem, usually an
animal. -**totem'ica.** [N. Amer. Ind., hereditary
emblem]

totter *v. i.* walk unsteadily, begin to fall [orig.
uncertain]

touch (tuch) *v.t.* put the hand on, come into
contact with; reach; move the feelings of (*sl.*)
borrow from. -*v.i.* call; (with on) refer to. -*n.*
a touching; slight blow, stroke, contact,
amount, *etc.* [F. *toucher*]

touch'y (tuch'-) *a.* over-sensitive, easily offended. [earlier *tetchy*, fr. OF. *entechio*]

tough (tuf) *a.* strong and pliable, not brittle;
sturdy; difficult; needing effort to bite. -
tough'ness *n.* -**tough'en** *v. t.* and *i.* [OE. *toh*]

toupee' *n.* false hair, wig. [F.]

tour *n.* a traveling round. -*v.t.* travel through.
-*v.i.* travel. -**tour'ist** *n.* one who travels for
pleasure. [F. fr. *tourner*, turn]

tournament *n.* a meeting for knightly contests; a meeting for games or athletic contests.
-**tour'ney** *n.* a tournament. [F. *tournoyer*, fr.
tourner, turn]

tourniquet *n.* bandage which can be
tightened by twisting a crosspiece put through
it to stop bleeding. [P.]

tout *v.i.* solicit custom (usually in an undesirable fashion). -*n.* one who does this. [OE.
totian, look out for]

tow *n.* hemp or flax fiber. [OE.]

tow *v.t.* drag at the end of a reopen. a towing,
being towed; vessel in tow. -**tow'age** *n.* [OE.
togian, draw]

tow'ard *a.* docile (also **tow'ardly**). -
towards (tordz) *prep.* in the direction of. (also
toward'). [OE. *toweard*]

tow'el *n.* cloth for wiping off moisture after
washing. -**tow'eling** *n.* material used for
towels. [OF. *touaille*]

tow'er *n.* tall building or part of a building;
fortress. -*v.i.* rise aloft, stand very high. [F.
tour, fr. L. *turris*]

town *n.* collection of dwellings, *etc.* larger
than a village. -**town'ship** *n.* division of a
county. [OE. *tun*, homestead]

tox'ic *a.* poisonous, due to poison. - **toxi'city**,
toxication *n.* -**toxicol'ogy** *n.* science of
poisons. -**tox'in** *n.* poison, *usu.* of bacterial
origin. [G. *taxikon*, arrow poison]

toy *n.* plaything. -*v. i.* act idly, trifle. [Du. *tuig*,
tools]

trace *n.* chain or strap by which a horse pulls
a vehicle; track left by anything; indication;
minute quantity. -*v. t.* follow the course or track
of, find out; make a plan of, draw. [L. *trahere*,
tract-, draw]

trache'a *n.* windpipe. -**trache'al, trache'an**
a. [L. *trachia*]

track *n.* mark or line of marks, left by the passage of anything; path; course. *v.t.* follow up the track of, *esp.* in hunting. [F. *trac*]

tract *n.* space of land, *etc.* , area. [L. *tractus*, a stretching out]

tract *n.* pamphlet, *esp.* a religious one. **tract'ate** *n.* treatise. [L. *tractare*, handle]

tract'able *a.* easy to manage, docile. [L. *tractare*, handle]

trac'tion *n.* action of drawing. **trac'tion-engine** *n.* steam or motor engine for drawing; steam-roller. **tract'or** *n.* self-propelling agricultural implement, *e.g.*, plow. **-tract'or feed** *n.* in computer technology, the automatic movement of a continuous roll of edge-perforated paper through the platen of the printer. [L. *trahere, tract-*, draw]

trade *n.* commerce, traffic; practice of buying and selling; any profitable pursuit; those engaged in a trade. -*v. i.* engage in trade. *-v. t.* buy and self-, barter. **trade mark** *n.* distinctive mark on a maker's goods. **-tra'der** *n.* **-trades'man** *n.* shopkeeper; mechanic. **trade-u'nion** *n.* society of workmen for protection of their interests. **-trade'wind** *n.* wind blowing constantly towards the equator in certain parts of the globe. [LG. *cognate* with tread]

tradition *n.* body of beliefs, facts, *etc.*, handed down from generation to generation without being reduced to writing; process of handing down, **-tradi'tional** *a.* **-tradi'tionally** *adv.* [L. *traditio* a handing over]

traffic *n.* passing to and fro of pedestrians, vehicles, *etc.* , in a road or street, *etc.*; trade. -*v.i.* trade. **-trafficker** *n.* trader. [F. *trafic*]

trag'edy (-j-) *n.* drama showing the ruin or downfall of the principal character, dealing with the sorrowful or terrible side of life; this type of drama. **-trag'ic** *a.* of, or in the manner of, tragedy; (journalism) disastrous; appalling. **-trag'ically** *adv.* **-trage'dian** *n.* player in tragedy; **tragicom'edy** *n.* play with both tragic and comic elements. [G. *tragoidia*- lit. 'goat- song']

trail *v.t.* drag behind one; follow the track of. -*v.i.* be drawn behind; hang loosely. *n.* thing that trails; back end of a guncarriage; track or trace. **-trail'er** *n.* road vehicle drawn by an automobile, *esp.* one that is designed to serve as a dwelling, office *etc.* when parked; film scenes shown as preliminary advertisement for a cinema film. [OF. *trainer*, tow]

train *v.t.* cause to grow in a particular way; educate, instruct, exercise; aim (a gun). -*v.i.* follow a course of training, *esp.* to achieve physical fitness for athletics. *n.* trailing part of a dress; body of attendants; fuse or trail of powder to a mine; line of railway vehicles joined to a locomotive; collection of vehicles, *etc.* , *esp.* in military use. **-trainee'** *n.* person being trained. [F. *trainer*, drag]

trait *n.* distinguishing characteristic. [F. = line, stroke, feature]

trait'or *n.* one who betrays or is guilty of treason. [L. *traditor*, fr. *tradere*, hand over]

trajectory *n.* line of flight of a projectile. [L.

trajicere, traject-, cast across]

train *n.* mining wagon-road; line of rails; truck running on rails; car for passengers running on rails laid through streets. **tram'car** *n.* **-tram'way** *n.* rails for trams in a street. [of LG. origin]

tramp *v.i.* walk heavily, travel on foot, *esp.* as a vagabond or for pleasure. -*v.t.* cross on foot. *-n.* an act of tramping; walk; vagabond; cargo-boat. **-tram'ple** *v.t.* tread under foot. [of Teut. orig.]

trampoline *n.* tough canvas sheet stretched horizontally with elastic cords *etc.* over frame for gymnastic, acrobatic use. [It. *trampoline*, springboard]

trance (-a-) *n.* state of suspended consciousness, *esp.* from rapture or ecstasy; catalepsy. [F. *transe*; (orig. passage from life to death)]

tran'quil (-ng-kw-) *a.* calm, quiet. **tran'quilly** *adv.* **-tranquil'ity, tranquil'ity** *n.* **-tranquil'ize, tranquillize** *v.t.* **tranquil'izer, tranquillizer** *n.* one that tranquilizes; drug used to reduce anxiety. [L. *tranquillus*]

trans- *prefix*, across, through, beyond. [L.] **-transact'** *v.t.* carry on or through; conduct (an affair, *etc.*). **-transac'tion** *n.* **-transcend'** *v.t.* exceed, surpass. **transcend'ent** *a.* **-transcend'ence** *n.* **transcendent'al** *a.* surpassing experience; super-natural; abstruse. **-trancendent'alism** *n.* **-transcribe'** *v.t.* copy out. **-trans'cript** *n.* copy. **-transfer'** *v.t.* make over; move from one place to another. **trans'fer** *n.* a transferring or being transferred. **-transform'** *v.t.* change the shape or character of. **-transforma'tion** *n.* **-transform'er** *n.* (*elec.*) apparatus for transforming voltage of alternating current. **-transgress'** *v.t.* break (a law); sin. **-tran'sient** *a.* passing away. **-tran'sience** *n.* **-tran'sit** *n.* passage, crossing. **-transi'tion** *n.* change from one state to another. **-transi'tional** *a.* **-tran'sitory** *a.* transient. **-translate'** *v.t.* move (a bishop) from one see to another; turn from one language into another. **-transla'tion** *n.* **-transla'tor** *n.* **-translu'cent** *a.* letting light pass, semi-transparent-**translu'cent** *n.* **transmigrate** *v.i.* of the soul, to pass into another body. **-transmigra'tion** *n.* **transmit'** *v. t.* send or cause to pass to another place, person, *etc.* **-transmute'** *v.t.* change in form, properties, or nature. **-transmuta'tion** *n.* **-transpar'ent** *a.* letting light pass without distortion, that can be seen through distinctly; obvious. **-transpire'** *v.t.* exhale. -*v.i.* exhale; come to be known. **transpira'tion** *n.* **-transplant'** *v.t.* move and plant again in another place. **-transplanta'tion** *n.* **-transport'** *v.t.* convey from one place to another; carry into banishment; enrapture. **-trans'port** *n.* means of conveyance; ships, vehicles, *etc-*, used in transporting stores; ship so used. **-transpose'** *v.t.* change the order of, interchange; put music into a different key. **-transubstantia'tion** *n.* change in essence or substance. **-trans'verse** *a.* lying across, at right angles. **transom** *n.* cross-piece; lintel. [corrupt. of F. *traversin*, crosspiece]

trap *n.* snare, contrivance for catching game,

etc.; movable covering for an opening, *esp.* through a ceiling, *etc.*; two-wheeled carriage; arrangement of pipes to prevent escape of gas, *etc. -v.t.* catch, entrap. -**trap'door** *n.* door in a floor or roof. -**trapp'er** *n.* [OE. *troeppe*]

trap *v.t.* ornamental coverings *usu.* for a horse. -**trapp'ings** *n. pl.* caparison; equipment, ornaments. [F. *drop*, cloth]

trapeze' horizontal bar suspended from two ropes. [L. *trapezium*]

trash *n.* worthless refuse; rubbish. **trash'y** *a.* -**trash'iness** *n.* [orig. uncertain]

trau'ma *n.* wound, injury; shock. -**traumat'ic** *a.* [G. = *wound*]

trav'ail *v.i.* labor or be in labor. -*n.* toil; pains of childbirth. [F. = *work*]

trav'el *v.i.* journey. -*v. t.* journey through. -*n.* journeying. -*pl* .account of traveling. -**trav'eler** *n.* -**trav'elogue** *n.* travel talk or film. [var. of *travail*]

trav'erse *v.t.* cross, go through or over; oppose. [F. *traverser*]

trav'esty *n.* comic imitation. -*v. t.* ridicule by a travesty. [F. *travestir*, disguise]

trawl *n.* net dragged along the bottom of the sea. -*v. i.* fish with one. -**trawl'er** *n.* trawling vessel. [OF. *trailler*, drag]

tray *n.* shallow flat receptacle used for holding or carrying small articles; any similar utensil of metal, plastic, wickerwork, *etc.* [OE. *trig*]

treachery *n.* deceit, betrayal. **treach'erous** *a.* -**treach'erously** *adv.* [F. *tricherie*, OF. *trecherie*, trickery]

tread *v. t.* set foot on. -*v. i.* walk. *n.* a treading; fashion of walking; upper surface of a step, tyre, *etc.* -**trea'dle** *n.* lever worked by the foot to turn a wheel. [OE. *tredan*]

trea'son *n.* treachery; breaking allegiance. -**trea'sonable** *a.* constituting treason. -**trea'sonous** *a.* [F. *trahison*, fr. L. *tradition* handing over]

treas'ure (trezh-) *n.* riches, stored wealth or valuables. -*v.t.* prize; store up. **treas'urer** *n.* official in charge of funds. **treas'ury** *n.* place for funds or treasure, *esp.* of a state; govt. dept. in charge of the public revenue. [G. *thesauros*]

treat *v.t.* deal with, act towards; apply remedies to. -*v. i.* negotiate. -*n.* entertainment, pleasure given. -**treat'ise** *n.* book on a given subject. -**treat'ment** *n.* [F. *traiter*, fr. L. *tractare*, handle]

treat'y *n.* contract between states. [OF. *traiter* fr. L. *tractare*]

tre'ble (treb'l) *a.* threefold. -*n.* soprano voice; part of music for it; singer with such voice. -*v.t.* and *i.* increase three-fold. **treb'ly** *adv.* [L. *triplus*]

tree *n.* large perennial plant with a woody trunk; beam. [OE. *treow*]

tree stucture *n.* (*compute.*) database format using master records, linked to several subordinate records, each of which is linked to only one master record.

trek *v.i.* journey by bullock-wagon; journey overland. [Du. *trekken*, drag]

trellis *n.* lattice or grating of light bars fitted crosswise. -*v. t.* screen or supply with trellis.

[F. *treillis*]

trem'ble *v.i.* quiver, shake. -*n.* a trembling. [L. *tremere*, quake]

tremen'dous *a.* causing fear or awe; vast, immense. [L. *tremere*, quake]

trem'olo *n.* (*mus.*) tremulous effect on a sustained note, a shake. [L. *tremere*, quake]

trem'or *n.* a trembling. -**trem'ulous** *a.* quivering easily; timorous. [L. *tremere*, quake]

trench *v.t.* cut grooves or ditches in. -*v. i.* infringe. -*n.* long narrow ditch, *esp.* as a shelter in war. -**trench'ant** *a.* cutting, incisive. -**trench'er** *n.* wooden plate. **trench'erman** *n.* hearty eater. [F. *trancher*, to cut]

trend *v.i.* have a general direction. -*n.* direction or tendency. -**trend'setter** *n.* person or thing that creates, or may create, a new fashion. -**trend'setting** *a.* -**trendy** *a.* very fashionable; faddish. [OE. *trendan*]

trepidation *n.* state of alarm; trembling from fear. [L. *trepidatio*]

tres'pass *n.* wrongdoing; wrongful entering on another's land. -*v. i.* commit trespass. [OF. *trespasser*, pass across]

tress *n.* lock of hair. (F. *tresse*)

tres'tle (-sl) *n.* bar fixed on pairs of spreading legs and used as a support. [OF. *trestel*, fr. L. *transtrum*, crosspiece]

triangle *n.* plane figure with three angles and three sides; percussion instrument. -**triang'ular** *a.* [L. *triangulum*]

tribe *n.* race or subdivision of a race of people. -**tri'bal** *a.* [L. *tribus*]

tribulation *n.* misery, trouble, affliction. [L. *tribulare*, oppress]

trib'une *n.* popular leader; speaker's platform; bishop's throne. -**tribu'nal** *n.* lawcourt; bench of judges, *etc.* [L. *tribunus*, protector of the commons]

trib'ute *n.* tax paid by one state to another; speech or act of homage. **trib'utary** *a.* paying tribute; auxiliary. *n.* stream flowing into another. [L. *tributum*]

trick *n.* stratagem; feat of skill or cunning; cards played in one round. -*v.t.* cheat. -**trick'ery** *n.* -**trick'ster** *n.* **trick'sy** *a.* sportive; deceptive; crafty. **trick'y** *a.* crafty; ticklish. [ONF. *trique*]

trick *v.t.* deck, attire. (Celt. orig.]

trickle *v.i.* flow slowly or in drops. [for *strickle*, fr. *strike*, in sense of flow]

tri- prefix. three. [L. fr. *tres*, or G. *treis*, three] -**tri'color** *a.* three colored. -*n.* tricolor flag, *esp.* the French one. **tri'cycle** *n.* vehicle like a bicycle, but with three wheels. -**tri'dent** *n.* three-pronged fork. -**trienn'ial** *a.* happening every, or lasting, three years.

tri'fle *n.* insignificant thing or matter; pudding of sponge-cake, whipped cream, *etc.* -*v.i.* act or speak idly. -**tri'fling** *a.* unimportant. -**tri'fler** *n.* [OF. *trufle*, mockery]

trigg'er *n.* catch which releases a spring, *esp.* to fire a gun, *etc.* [earlier tricker, Du. , *trekker*, fr. *trekken*, pull]

trigonom'etry *n.* branch of mathematics dealing with the relations of the sides and angles of triangles. **trigonomet'rical** *a.* -

trigonom'eter n. [fr. G. trigonon, triangle]

trill v.i. sing with a quavering voice. sing lightly. -n. such singing. [It; trillare, of imit. orig.]

tril'ogy n. series of three related dramas or novels. [G. trilogia, series of three tragedies]

trim v.t. prune; adjust, put in good order. -v.i. shuffle, act as a timeserver. n. order, state of being trimmed. a. neat, smart; in good order. [OE. trymman, arrange, make firm]

trinitrotol'uene (abbrev. **TNT**) n. a high explosive. [nitric acid, toluene]

trin'ity n. state of being threefold; three persons of the Godhead. -**trinitar'ian** n. and a. [L. trinitas]

trink'et n. small ornament for the person. [orig. uncertain]

trio. See triple.

trip v. i. run lightly, skip; stumble. -v. t. cause to stumble. -n. light step; stumble; journey, excursion. [OF. triper, dance]

tripe n. stomach of a ruminant animal prepared for food; (sl.) rubbish. [F. entrails]

trip'le a. threefold. -v. t. and i. treble. **trip'ly** adv. -**trip'let** n. three of a kind. **tri'o** n. group of three; music for three performers, etc. -**tri'partite** a. having three parts. -**trip'licate** a. three-fold. v.t. make threefold. -n. state of being triplicate; one of a set of three copies. **triplica'tion** n. -**tri'pod** n. stool or stand, etc., with three feet. -**trip'tych** n. carving or picture in three compartments. [L. fr. tres, three]

tri'sect v.t. to divide into three (usually equal) parts. -**trisection** n. [L. fr. tres, three, secare, sectu, to cut]

trite a. hackneyed; worn out. [L. tritus, to rub]

tri'umph n. great success, victory; exultation. -v.i. achieve great success or victory; exult. -**triumph'ant** a. -**triumph'al** a. [L. triumphus]

tri'umvir n. one of three men joined equally in an office. -**trium'virate** n. [L. back formation fr. L. trium virorum, of three men]

triv'et n. an iron bracket or stand for putting a pot or kettle on. [OE. trefet fr. L. tripes, triped-, tripod]

triv'ial a. commonplace, trifling. **triviality** n. [L. trivialis]

troll v. t. pass (cup) round; sing heartily. [orig. uncertain]

troll n. diminutive supernatural being in Scandinavian mythology. [ON.]

troll'ey n. form of small truck; pole and wheel by which a tramcar collects power from overhead wire. -**trolley bus** n. an omnibus which is similarly powered. [orig. uncertain]

trom'bone n. large brass wind-instrument of which one part slides in and out of the other. [It.]

troop n. crowd of persons or animals; unit of cavalry. -pl. soldiers. -v.i. move in a troop. -**troop'er** n. a cavalry-soldier; state policeman. [F. troupe]

tro'phy n. memorial of a victory, in war, sport, the chase, etc. [F. trophée]

trop'ic n. either of two circles in the heavens or round the earth where the sun seems to turn at a solstice. -pl. hot regions between the tropics. -**trop'ical** a. [trope]

troposphere n. lowest layer of Earth's atmosphere bounded by stratosphere. [G. trope, turning, sphaira, sphere]

trot v.i. of a horse, move at medium pace, lifting the feet in diagonal pairs; of a person, etc., run easily with short strides. -n. action of trotting; a brisk, steady pace. -**trott'er** n. horse which trots; (sl.) foot; pig, sheep's foot for eating. [F. trotter]

troth n. faith. [var. of truth]

trou'ble (trub'l) v.t. disturb, afflict. -v.i. be agitated or disturbed. -n. disturbance, agitation; inconvenience; distress; confusion. -**troub'lous** a. -**troub'lesome** a. [F. trouper]

trough (trof) n. long open vessel; hollow between two waves. [OE. trog]

trounce v. t. beat severely, thrash. **trouncing** n. [orig. uncertain]

troupe n. company of actors, acrobats, etc. -**troup'er** n. [F.]

trou'sers n. pl. two-legged outer garment with legs reaching to the ankles. [earlier trouse, Gael. triuohas]

trousseau n. outfit of clothing, esp. for a bride. [F.]

trout n. freshwater fish esteemed as food. [OE. truht]

trow v.i. trust; believe. [OE. treowian, trust]

trow'el n. small tool like a spade for spreading mortar, lifting plants, etc. [Late L. truella, small ladle]

tru'ant n. one absent from duty without leave, esp. a child so absent from school. [F. truand, vagabond]

truce n. temporary cessation of fighting. [pl. of OE. treow, agreement]

truck v.t. and i. barter; exchange. -n. barter; payment of workmen in goods; (colloq.) rubbish. -**truck farm** n. small farm specializing in growing vegetables for market. [F. troquer]

truck n. open vehicle for heavy goods; kind of barrow; disk at a masthead. -v. t. transport by truck. [G. trochileia, pulley]

truc'ulent a. ferocious, inclined to fight, belligerent. [L. truculentus]

trudge v.i. walk laboriously. -n. laborious walk. [earlier truss, pack (off)]

true a. in accordance with facts; faithful; exact, correct. -**truth** (-oo-) n. state of being true; something that is true. -**tru'ism** n. self-evident truth. **tru'ly** adv. -**truth'ful** a. -**truth'fully** adv. [OE. treow, faith]

truf'fle n. edible fungus growing underground. [OF. truffe]

trump n. card of a suit temporarily ranking above the others. -v.t. take (a trick) with a trump. -v.i. trump up, get up, fabricate. [earlier triumph]

trum'pery a. showy, but worthless. -n. worthless finery. [F. tromperie, deceit]

trum'pet n. metal wind instrument like a horn. -v.i. blow a trumpet or make a sound like one. -v. t. proclaim. . [F. trompette]

truncate v.t. cut short. [L. truncare, truncate, fr. truncus, trunk]

trunk n. main stem of a tree; person's body

without or excluding the head and limbs; box for clothes, *etc.*; elephant's or other proboscis. [OF. *tronc*, L. *truncus*, trunk]

truss *v.t.* fasten up, tie up. *-n.* support; bundle (of hay, *etc.*). [F. *trousser*, pack]

trust *n.* confidence, firm belief, property held for another; state of being relied on; combination of producers to do away with competition and keep up prices. *-v. t.* rely on, believe in. **-trustee'** *n.* one legally holding property on another's behalf. **trustee'ship** *n.* **-trust'ful** *a.* **-trust'worthy** *a.* **-trust'y** *a.* [ON. *traust*]

truth. *See* true.

try *v.t.* test; conduct a judicial enquiry; attempt; cause to suffer. *-v. i.* attempt something, endeavor. *-n.* attempt. **-tri'al** *n.* **-try-sail** *n.* small fore-and-aft sail set with gaff, storm sail. [F. *trier*, to sift]

tryst *n.* appointment to meet. [OF. *tristre*, hunting station]

Tsar. *See* Czar.

tset'se *n.* small African fly carrying germ of sleeping-sickness. [Bechuana]

tub *n.* open wooden vessel like the bottom half of a barrel; bath. *-v.t.* and *i.* bathe. [Du. *tobbe*]

tube *n.* pipe, long narrow hollow cylinder. **-tu'bular** *a.* [L. *tubus*]

tu'ber *n.* swelling on the roots of certain plants, *e.g.* potato. **-tu'berous** *a.* [L. *lump*]

tu'bercle *n.* granular small tumor in consumptive lungs, *etc.*, **-tuber'cular** *a.* **tuberculo'sis** *n.* disease, *esp.* of the lung, marked by the presence of tubercles and a characteristic bacillus, *esp.* consumption of the lungs. [L. *tuberculum*, dim. of *tuber*, lump]

tu'berose *n.* plant with tuberous root and sweet-scented, creamy flowers. [L. *tuberose*, tuberous]

tuck *v. t.* gather or stitch in folds; draw or roll together. *-n.* stitched fold; food, *esp.* dainties eaten by schoolboys. [orig. *tug*, OE. *tucian*, illtreat]

Tues'day *n.* third day of the week. [OE. *Tiwesdoeg*, day of *Tiw*, Teutonic god of war]

tuft *n.* bunch of feathers, threads, *etc.* knot; cluster. [F. *touffe*]

tug *v. t.* pull hard or violently. *-n.* violent pull; steamship used to tow other vessels. [orig. obscure]

tui'tion *n.* teaching. [L. *twitio*]

tu'lip *n.* plant of the lily family with bright bell-shaped flowers. [OF. *tulipe*, fr. Pers. *dulband*, turban]

tum'ble *v. i.* fall; turn somersaults. *-v. t.* throw down; rumple. *-n.* fall; somersault. **-tum'bler** *n.* acrobat; round-bottomed drinking-glass; variety of pigeon. [OE. *tumbian*, dance]

tu'mid *a.* swollen, distended. [L. *tumere*, to swell]

tu'mor *n.* abnormal growth on the body. [L. *tumere*, to swell]

tu'mulus *n.* burial mound. **-tu'mular** *a.* [L.]

tu'mult *n.* uproar, commotion; confusion of mind. **-tumult'uous** *a.* [L. *tumultus*, fr. *tumere*, swell]

tun *n.* large cask. [OE. *tunne*]

tun'dra *n.* flat, treeless, marshy plains of *n.* Russia and Siberia. [Lapp]

tune *n.* melody; concord; adjustment of a musical instrument. *-v, t.* put in tons. **tune'ful** *a.* **-tune'fully** *adv.* **-tu'ner** *n.* [var. of *tone*]

tung'sten *n.* rare metal with high melting-point. **-tung'stic** *a.* [Sw. *tung*, heavy, *sten*, stone]

tu'nic *n.* short military coat; garment of similar shape. [L. *tunics*]

tunn'el *n.* artificial underground passage. *-v.t.* and *i.* make a tunnel (through). **-tunn'eler** *n.* [OF. *tonel*, dim. of ME. *tonne*, tun]

tur'ban *n.* man's headdress made by coiling a length of material round a cap or the head. **-tur'banned** *a.* [Pers. *dulband*]

tur'bid *a.* muddy, thick. **-turbid'ity** *n.* [E. *turbare*, disturb]

tur'bine *n.* kind of water-wheel; rotary steam or gas engine. [F.]

tur'bulent *a.* riotous, in commotion. [F. -L. *turbulentus*]

tureen' *n.* dish for soup. [earlier *terreen*, F. *terrine*, earthenware pot]

turf *n.* short grass with the earth bound to it by the matted roots; sod. *-v. t.* lay with turf. [OE. = *sod*, peat]

tur'key *n.* large bird reared for food. [Turkey-cock, orig. the guinea-fowl, the present bird being American]

tur'moil *n.* confusion and bustle; disturbance; agitation. [orig. uncertain]

turn *v.t.* make move round or rotate; shape on a lathe; change, reverse, alter position of, *etc.* *-v.i.* move round; change; become, *etc.* *-n.* act of turning; walk; rotation; part of a rotation; performance; inclination; *etc.* **turn'key** *n.* jailer. **-turn'over** *n.* act of turning over; in business, amount of money changing hands; kind of pie with top flapped over. **-turn'pike** *n.* gate across a road where tolls are paid, toll gate; toll road, or one formerly maintained as one; main road. **-turn'stile** *n.* revolving gate for controlling admission of people. **-turn'table** *n.* revolving platform. [L. *tornare*, fr. *tornus*, lathe]

turn'ip *n.* plant with a round root used as a vegetable or fodder. [*turn* and OE. *næp*, L. *napus*]

turp'entine *n.* resin got from certain trees; oil or spirit made from this. [L. *terebinthina*, resin of the terebinth]

turp'itude *n.* baseness. [L. *turpitudo*]

tur'quoise *n.* opaque blue precious stone. [F. = Turkish]

turr'et *n.* small tower; revolving tower for a gun on a ship, tank or fort. [OF. *tourete*, dim. of *tour*, tower]

tur'tle *n.* common wild dove. [OE.]

tur'tle *n.* sea-tortoise; its shell. **-turn'tur'tle**, capsize. **-tur'tleneck** *n.* closefitting turnover collar; sweater with such a collar. [corrupt. of F. *tortue*, tortoise]

tusk *n.* long pointed tooth sticking out from a mouth. **-tusk'er** *n.* animal with tusks fully developed. [OE. *tux*]

tus'sle *n.* struggle. *-v.i.* [dial *touse*]

tu'telage *n.* guardianship. **-tu'telary** *a.*

protecting. [L. *tutela*]

tu'tor *n.* person giving lessons privately, or to individuals in a college; guardian. **tutor'ial** *a.* [L. , fr. *tueri, tut-,* see to]

tuxe'do *n.* semi-formal dinner jacket. [Tuxedo Park, N. Y.]

twain *a.* two. *-n.* a pair, couple; two persons or things. [OE. *twegen*]

twang *n.* ringing sound as of plucked string. *-v. i.* and *t.* make, cause to make, such sound. [imit.]

tweak *v.t.* pinch and twist or pull. *-n.* act of tweaking. [OE. *twiccian*]

tweed *n.* rough-surfaced woolen cloth, usually of mixed colors. [for *tweel,* var. of *twill*]

tweez'ers *n. pl.* small forceps or pincers. [earlier *tweeses, pl.* of obs. *twee,* F. *étui,* case for instruments]

twelve *n.* and *a.* cardinal number, two more than ten. **-twelfth** *a.* ordinal number. **-twelve'month** *n.* year. [OE. *twelf*]

twent'y *n.* and *a.* cardinal number, twice ten. **-twent'ieth** *a.* ordinal number. [OE. *twentig*]

twice *adv.* two times. [OE. *twiges*]

twig *n.* small branch. [OE.]

twilight *n.* half light after sunset or before dawn. [*twi-,* two]

twill *n.* fabric woven so as to have a surface of parallel diagonal ridges. *v.t.* weave thus. [OE. *twili*]

twin *n.* one of a pair, *esp.* of children born together. *-a.* being a twin. [OE. *twinn,* twofold]

twine *v.t.* and *i.* twist or coil round. *-n.* string. [OE. *twin*]

twinge *n.* momentary sharp pain; (fig.) qualm, as of conscience. [OE. *twengan v.*]

twin'kle *v.i.* shine with dancing or quivering light. *-n.* twinkling; flash; gleam of amusement in eyes or face. **-twink'ling** *n.* instant. [OE. *twinclian*]

twirl *v.t.* and *i.* turn or twist round quickly, spin round. [orig. uncertain]

twist *v.t.* and *i.* make or become spiral, by turning with one end fast. *-n.* at twisting; something twisted. [OE.]

twitch *v.i.* give a momentary sharp pull; jerk. *-v.t.* pull at thus. *-n.* such pull or jerk; spasmodic jerk. [OE. *twiccian,* pluck]

twitt'er *v.i.* of birds, utter a succession of tremulous sounds. *-n.* such succession of notes. [imit.]

two *n.* and *a.* cardinal number, one more than one. **-two-faced** *a.* having two faces; insincere. **-two'fold** *adv.* and *a.* [OE. *two*]

tycoon' *n.* important business man. [Jap. *taikun,* great prince]

tympanums *n.* ear-drum. **-tympan'ic** *a.* of or like a drum. [L. fr. G.]

type *n.* class; characteristic build; specimen, block bearing a letter used for printing; such pieces collectively; state of being set up for printing. *-v.t.* print with a typewriter. **-type'writer** *n.* keyed writing machine. **-ty'pist** *n.* **-typ'ical** *a.* typically *adv.* **-typ'ify** *v.t.* serve as a type or model of **-typog'raphy**

n. art of printing; style of printing.

typhoon' *n.* violent cyclonic hurricane. [Chin. *tai fung,* big wind]

ty'phus *n.* contagious fever. [G. *typhos,* vapour]

ty'rant *n.* oppressive or cruel ruler. **tyrann'ical** *a.* [G. *tyrannos,* absolute ruler]

U

ubiq'uity *n.* a being everywhere at the same moment. **ubiquitous** *a.* [L. *ubique,* everywhere]

U'-boat *n.* German submarine. [Ger. *unterseeboot,* under-sea boat]

udd'er *n.* mammary gland or milk-bag of a cow, *etc.* [OE. uder]

ug'ly *a.* unpleasing or repulsive to the sight; ill-omened; threatening. **-ug'liness** *n.* [ON. *uggligr,* fr. *uggr,* fear]

uh'lan *n.* German light cavalryman. [Ger. fr. Tatar]

ukulele *n.* four-stringed guitar. [Hawaiian]

ul'cer *n.* open sore. **-ul'cerate** *v. i.* form an ulcer. *-v.t.* make ulcerous. **-ul'cerous** *a.* **-ulcera'tion** *n.* [L. *ulcus, ulcer-*]

ul'ster *n.* man's, woman's, long caped overcoat. [*Ulster*]

ulterior *a.* situated beyond; beyond what appears. [L., compar. of *ultra,* beyond, on the other side]

ultimate *a.* last, farthest. **-ult'imately** *adv.* **-ultima'tum** *n.* final proposal the rejection of which causes war. **-ult'imo** *adv.* in last month. [L. *ultimus,* superl. of *ultra,* beyond]

ultramarine' *a.* beyond the sea. *n.* blue pigment. **-ultramont'ane** *a.* south of or beyond the Alps; favorable to the absolute authority of the Pope. **ultrason'ics** *n.* science of waves beyond the frequency of sound. **-ultravi'olet** *a.* beyond the violet (of rays of the spectrum). [L. *ultra,* beyond]

umbel *n.* flower cluster in which a number of stalks, each bearing a flower, radiate from a common center. [L. *umbella,* dim. of *umbra,* a shade]

um'ber *n.* dark brown pigment. [It. (*terra d'*) ombra, shadow (earth)]

umbilical *a.* of the navel. **-umbil'icus** *n.* [L. *umbilicus*]

um'brage *n.* sense of injury, offense. **umbrage'ous** *a.* shady. [L. *umbra,* shadow]

umbrella *n.* a light folding circular cover of silk, *etc.,* on a steel framework, carried in the hand to protect against rain. [L. *umbra,* shadow]

um'pire *n.* person chosen to decide a question; person chosen to decide disputes and enforce the rules in a game. *-v.i.* act as umpire in. *-v.i.* act as umpire. [ME. *nomper,* fr. F. *non pair,* not equal (*i. e.,* odd man called in when arbitrators disagreed)]

ump'teen *n.* (*sl.*) indefinite number, quite a lot. [*umpty,* morse for dash]

un- *prefix.* makes compounds negativing the idea of the simple words, *e.g.* **-unarmed** *a.* not armed. **-unfast'en** *v.t.* loosen or remove the fastening. **untruth'** *n.* lie. These are only given where the meaning or derivation cannot easily be found from the simple word. [OE.]

unan'imous *a.* of one mind, agreeing. [L. *unanimus -unus*, one, *animus*, mind]

unassum'ing *a.* modest, not bold or forward. [*an-* and L. *assumere*]

uncann'y *a.* weird, mysterious. -uncann'iness *n.* [OE. *can*, know]

un'cate *a.* hooked. [L. *uncus*, hook]

unc'le (unk'l) *n.* brother of a father or mother; husband of an aunt. [F. *oncle*, fr. L. *avunculus*, uncle on mother's side]

uncon'scious *a.* not knowing, unaware; insensible. -*n.* hidden or repressed part of thought. [*un-* and L. *conscius*]

uncout *a.* clumsy, without ease or polish. -uncouth'ly *adv.* -uncouth'ness *n.* [OE. *un-cuth*, unknown]

unction *n.* anointing; soothing words or thought; fervor of words or tone; imitation of this; affected enthusiasm. -unc'tuous *a.* full of unction; greasy. [L. *unctio*, fr. *ungere*, *unct-*, anoint]

un'der *prep.* below, beneath; bound by, included in; in the time of. -*adv.* in a lower place or condition -*a.* lower. underbred'*a.* ill-bred. -und'er-carriage *n.* landing structure of aircraft. undercharge'*v.t.* charge less than the proper amount. -*n.* too low a charge. underhand'*a.* unfair, sly. -underhung'*a.* with the lower part projecting beyond the upper. -un'derling *n.* subordinate. underneath' *adv.* below. -*prep.* under. underpass'*n.* road or passage for traffic or pedestrians which passes underneath a highway or railroad.-undershirt'*n.* collarless garment for wearing underneath a shirt. -un'dershot *a.* moved by water passing under. -un'der strapper *n.* underling, subordinate. -un'dertow *n.* current beneath surface moving in a different direction from surface current; back-wash; and numerous other compounds of *under* which need no explanation. [OE. *under*]

undergrad'uate *n.* university student who has not yet taken a degree. [*graduate*]

und'erground *a.* subterranean; secret -go und'erground, of a political organization, continue its activities in secret. -*n.* underground railway. [*ground*]

understand *v.t.* see the meaning of, infer; take for granted. -*v. i.* be informed. -p. p. understood. -understand'ing *n.* intelligence. [OE. *understanan*]

understudy *v.t.* study an actor's part so as to be able to take his place in emergency. -*n.* one who does this. [*study*]

undertake' *v.t.* make oneself responsible for; enter upon a task, *etc.* [ME. *undertaken*]

un'dertaker *n.* one who undertakes; one who manages funerals. [*under* and *take*]

un'derwrite *v.t.* agree to pay, take up shares in, *e.g.*, in marine insurance, *etc.* [trans. of *subscriber*]

un'dulate *v.i.* move in waves or like waves. -undula'tion *n.* -un'dulatory *a.* [L. *unda*, wave]

undu'ly *adv.* too much, excessively, wrong-

ly, improperly. [*due*]

unfrock' *v.t.* strip a monk, priest, of his gown, *i.e.*, his office. [*frock*]

ungain'ly *a.* awkward, uncouth, clumsy [ON. *gegn*, convenient]

uxi'guent *n.* an ointment. -ung'uentary *a.* [L. *unguentum*]

ung'ulate *a.* having hoofs. [L. *unguis*, nail]

unhinge' *v.t.* take from hinges; unbalance, *esp.* -uniformly [*hinge*]

u'nicorn *n.* a fabulous animal like a horse, with a single long horn. [L. *unicorns*, fr. *cornu*, horn]

uni- prefix one. [L. *unus*, one]

u'niform *a.* not changing, unvarying; conforming to the same standard or rule. -*n.* uniform dress worn by members of the same body, *e.g.*, soldiers, nurses, *etc.* -u'niformly *adv.* -uniform'ity *n.* [L. *uniformis*]

unify *v.t.* bring to unity or uniformity. unifica'tion *n.* [Med. L. *unificare*]

u'nion *n.* joining into one; state of being joined; result of being joined; federation. combination of societies, *etc.*; trade union. -u'nionist *n.* supporter of union. u'nionism *n.* [F.]

unique' *a.* being the only one of its kind. [F. fr. L. *unicus*]

u'nison *n.* agreement, harmony; sounding at the same pitch. [L. *uni and sonus*]

u'nit *n.* single thing or person; standard quantity. -unitar'ian *n.* member of a Christian body that denies the doctrine of the Trinity. -unitar'ianism *n.* [L. *unus*]

unite' *v.t.* join into one, connect. -*v.i.* become one, combine. -u'nity *n.* state of being one; harmony. -United Nations Organization organization founded in 1945 for maintaining peace and settling international difficulties by arbitration. [L. *unire*, *-itus*, to unite]

uni'verse *n.* whole of creation, all existing things. -univer'sal *a.* relating to all things or all men; applying to all members of a community. -univer'sally *adv.* -universal'ity *n.* [L. *universus*, lit. 'turned to one', *unus*]

university *n.* educational institution for study, examination and conferment of degrees in all or most of the important branches of learning. [L. *universitas*]

unkempt' *a.* of rough or uncared-for appearance. [OE. *cemban*, comb]

unless' *conj.* if not, except when; save. [for *on less*]

unru'ly *a.* badly behaved, ungovernable; turbulent. [*rule*]

until' *prep.* up to the time of. *conj.* to the time that; with a negative, before. [*See* till]

un'to *prep.* to. [*See* to]

untouchable *n.* Hindu below the caste level. -*a.* [*touch*]

untoward' *a.* inconvenient; inopportune. [arch. toward, propitious]

unwield'y *a.* large and cumbersome; difficult to handle. [wield]

up *adv.* in or to a higher position, a source, an activity, *etc.*; quite. -*prep.* to or towards the source, *etc.* -up'ward *a.* and *adv.* -up'wards *adv.* [OE.]

up- *prefix* makes compounds mostly of obvious meaning, *e.g.*, **upbringing** *n.* bringing up. **-uphold** *v.t.* hold up, support, *etc.* **upbraid'** *v.t.* scold, reproach; reprove severely. **-upbraid'ing** *n.* abuse, reproach. - **upbraid'ingly** *adv.* [orig. uncertain]

upholsterer *n.* one who provides carpets, hangings, or covers chairs, *etc.* **upholst'er** *v.t.* to put coverings on, supply carpets, *etc.* - **upholst'ery** *n.* [earlier *upholder*, in ME. a broker]

upon' *prep.* on. [OE. *uppon*]

upp'er *a.* higher, situated above. *-n.* upper part of a boot or shoe. [up]

upp'ish *a.* self-assertive. [up]

up'right *a.* erect; honest, just. *-n.* thing standing upright, *e. g.*, post in a framework. [right]

up'roar *n.* tumult, disturbance. **uproar'-ious** *a.* **-uproar'iously** *adv.* [Du. *oproer*, stirring up]

upset' *v. t.* overturned. overturned. *-n.* an upsetting; trouble. **-up'set price** *n.* price below which goods at auction may not be sold. [set]

up'shot *n.* outcome, conclusion, final result. [orig. *deciding shot*]

up'start *n.* one suddenly raised to wealth, power, *etc.* [start]

ura'nium *n.* hard white radioactive metal. [*Uranus*, planet]

urbane' *a.* polished, courteous. **urban'ity** *n.* **-ur'ban** *a.* relating to a town or city. [L. *urbanus*, of a city, urbs]

urch'in *n.* sea urchin; hedgehog; mischievous boy; boy or youngster. [F. *hérisson*, fr. L. *ericius*, hedgehog]

Ur'du *n.* Hindustani. [for *zaban-i-urdu*, language of the camp]

urge *v.t.* drive on; entreat or exhort earnestly. *-n.* strong impulse. **-ur'gent** *a.* pressing; needing attention at once; importunate. **-ur'gently** *adv.* **-ur'gency** *n.* [L. *urgere*]

urine *n.* fluid secreted by the kidneys. **u'ric** *a.* **-u'ric acid** *n.* **-u'rinate** *v. t.* discharge urine. **-u'rinal** *n.* . place for urinating. [L. *urina*]

urn *n.* vase with a foot and usually a rounded body. [L. *urna*]

ur'sine *a.* of, like, a bear. [L. *ursus*, bear]

urtica'ria *n.* nettle-rash. (L. *urtica*, nettle]

us *pron.* obj. case of *we.* [OE.]

use *n.* employment, applications to a purpose; profit, serviceableness; need to employ; habit. **-use** *v. t.* employ, avail oneself of, accustom. **-u'sable** (-z-) *a.* **u'sage** (-s-) *n.* act of using; custom; customary way of using. **-use'ful** (-s-) *a.* **-use'fully** *adv.* **-usefulness** *n.* **use'less** *a.* **-use'lessly** *adv.* **-use'lessness** *n.* **-u'sual** (-z-) *a.* habitual, ordinary. **-u'sually** *adv.* [L. *usus*, use]

ush'er *n.* doorkeeper, one showing people to seats, *etc.*; formerly an underteacher. *v.t.* introduce, announce. [F. *huissier*, fr. L. *ostiarius-stium*, door]

us'quebaugh (-kwi-baw) *n.* whiskey. [Ir. and Gael. *iusge*, water, *beatha*, life]

usurp' *v.t.* seize wrongfully. **-usurp'er** *n.* - **usurpa'tion** *n.* [L. *usurpare*]

u'sury (-z-) *n.* lending of money at excessive interest; such interest. **u'surer** *n.* **-usu'rious** *a.* [L. *usura*]

utensil *n.* vessel or implement, *esp.* in domestic use. [L. *utensilis*, fr. *uti*, use]

u'terus *n.* womb. **-u'terine** *a.* [L.]

utility *n.* usefulness; useful thing. *a.* serviceable. **-utilita'rianism** *n.* doctrine that the morality of actions is to be tested by their utility, *esp.* that the greatest good of the greatest number should be the sole end of public action. **utilita'ria** *a.* **-u'tilize** *v. t.* make use of. **-utiliza'tion** *n.* [L. *utilitas*, fr. *uti*, use]

ut'most *a.* extreme, farthest. *-n.* one's best endeavor. [OE. *ut*, out]

Uto'pia *n.* imaginary state with perfect political, social, conditions or constitution. - **Uto'pian** *a.* visionary. [Sir T. More's imaginary country (in book published 1516), fr. G. *ou*, not, *topos*, place]

utt'er *a.* complete, total. **-utt'erly** *adv.* [OE. *uttera*, compar. of *ut*, out]

utt'er *v.t.* express, emit audibly; put in circulation. **-utt'erance** *n.* uttering; expression in words; spoken words. [ME. *uttren*, fr. *adv. utter*]

u'vula *n.* pendent fleshy part of the soft palate. **-u'vular** *a.* [Med. L. dim. of *uva*, bunch of grapes]

uxorious *a.* excessively fond of one's wife. [L. *uxorius*, fr. *uxor*, wife]

V

vacate' *v.t.* quit, leave empty. **-va'cant** *a.* unoccupied; without thought, empty. **va'cantly** *adv.* **-va'cancy** *n.* emptiness; situation unoccupied. **-vaca'tion** *n.* act of vacating; scheduled period when school is suspended; period away from work or home for recreation. [L. *vacare*, be empty]

vac'cinate (-ks-) *v.t.* inoculate with vaccine *esp*, as a protection against smallpox. - **vaccina'tion** *n.* **-vac'cinator** *n.* **-vac'cine** *n.* virus of cowpox. [L. *vacca*, cow]

va'cillate (vas'-) *v.i.* waver. **-vacilla'tion** *n.* [L. *vacillate*, vacillate]

vac'uum *n.* place devoid of matter; place from which air has been practically exhausted. **-vac'uous** *a.* vacant. **vacu'ity** *n.* - **vac'uum clean'er**, suction cleaner for sweeping, dusting, *etc.* [L. *vacuus*, empty]

vademe'cum *n.* manual, pocket companion. [L. = go with me]

vag'abond *a.* having no fixed dwelling. *-n.* wanderer; idle scamp. **vag'abondage** *n.* [L. *vagari*, wander]

vagar'y *n.* freak; unaccountable proceeding. *-(pl.)* **vagar'ies.** (prob. fr. L. *vagare*, to wander]

va'grant *n.* tramp. *-a.* on tramp; wandering idly. **-va'grancy** *n.* [OF. *walcrer*, wander]

vague *a.* indefinite; not distinct; mentally unprecise. **-vague'ly** *adv.* **vague'ness** *n.* [L. *vagus*, wandering]

vain *a.* worthless, useless; conceited; foolish. **-va'nity** *n.* [L. *vanus*, empty]

vainglo'ry *n.* self-glorification from vanity.

-vainglo'rious a. [*vain* and *glory*]

val'ance n. short curtain round a bedstead, above window-curtains, *etc*. val'anced a. [orig. uncertain]

vale n. valley. [L. *vallis*]

valedic'tion n. farewell. -valedic'tory a. [L. *valedicere, valedict-*, say farewell]

va'lences, va'lency n. combining power of element or atom. [L. *valere*, be strong]

val'entine n. picture, set of verses, *etc*., sent to a sweetheart on the 14th February; sweetheart chosen on that day. [Saint Valentine]

valer'ian n. flowering herb used in medicine. [F. *valériane*]

val'et (-a, or -et) n. manservant looking after his master's clothes, *etc*. [F.]

valetudinary a. sickly. -valetudina'rian n. person obliged or disposed to live the life of an invalid. [L. *valetudinarius*, fr. *valetudo*, state of health]

Valhall'a n. in Scandinavian mythology, place of immortality for heroes slain in battle. [ON. *valr*, slain, *höll*, hall]

valiant a. brave. [F. *vaillant*]

val'id a. sound; binding in law. valid'ity n. -val'idate v. t. [L. *validus*, strong]

valise' n. traveling bag. [F.]

vall'ey n. (vall'eys pl.) low area between hills. [F. *vallee*]

val'or (-er) n. personal bravery or courage. -val'orous a. [OF. *valour*]

val'ue n. worth, price; equivalent. -v. t. to estimate a value of; to care for. - val'uable a. capable of being valued; of great value. -n. a valuable thing. valua'tion n. -val'ueless a. -val'uer n. [L. *valere*, be worth]

valve n. device to control the passage of a fluid, gas, *etc*., through a pipe; thermionic valve (q.v.). -val'vular a. [L. *valva*, leaf of folding door]

vamp n. upper leather of a shoe. -v.t. and i. (*music*) improvise an accompaniment. [OF. *avanpie* (i. e. *avant pied*) part of the shoe covering the front of foot]

vamp'ire n. blood-sucking animal, person, ghost *etc*.; (*sl*.) person who preys on others. -vamp n. (*sl*.) a flirt. (Slav. *vampir*]

van n. leading division of an army or fleet. -van'guard n. [F. *avant-garde*, fr. *avant*, in front]

van n. covered road or rail vehicle, *esp*. for goods. [short for *caravan*]

vandalism n. barbarous destruction of works of art *etc*.; malicious destruction or defacement of property. -vandal n. vandalize v.t. [L. *Vandalus*, Vandal]

vane n. weather cock. [OE. *fana*, flag]

vanill'a n. plant of the orchid kind; extract of this for flavoring. [Sp. *vainilla*, small pod]

van'ish v.i. disappear. [L. *evanescere*, fr. *vanus*, empty]

van'ity n. worthless pleasure or display; conceit of one's appearance, ability, *etc*. [L. *vanitas, -atis*]

van'quish v.t. conquer. [OF. *vainquir*, fr. L. *vincere*]

van'tage (va-) n. advantage, *esp*. in lawn tennis; condition favoring success. [AF. *vantage*]

vap'id a. flat, dull, insipid; savorless. vapid'ity n. [L. *vapidus*]

va'por (-er) n. gaseous form of a substance more familiar as liquid or solid; steam or mist; invisible moisture in the air. -va'porize a. turn into vapor, fine mist. -va'porous a. [L. *vapor*]

var'icose a. of a vein, morbidly dilated. [L. *varicosus-varix*, dilated vein]

var'let n. page, attendant; pert rascal. [OF. dim. of *vassal*]

var'nish n. resinous solution put on a surface to make it hard and shiny. -v.t. apply varnish to. [F. *vernis*]

var'y (var'-i) v.t. change. -v.i. be changed; become different. -var'iable a. -variabil'ity n. -var'iance n. state of discord. -var'iant a. different. -n. different form. -varia'tion n. - var'iegate v.t. diversify by patches of different colors. variegation n. -vari'ety n. state of being varied or various; varied assortment; sort or kind. -var'ious a. manifold, diverse, of several kinds. [L. *varius*, various]

vase n. vessel, jar. -vas'cular a. of, or having, vessels for conveying sap, blood, *etc*. [L. *vas*, with dim. *vasculum*]

Vas'eline n. brand of petroleum which is a transparent yellowish semi-solid substance used in ointments, pomades, as a lubricant, *etc*. [Trademark]

vass'al n. holder of land by feudal tenure; dependant. -vass'alage n. [F.]

vast (-a-) a. very large. -vast'ly adv. vast'ness n. [L. *vastus*]

vat n. large tub. [OE. *foet*, cask]

Vat'ican n. collection of buildings, including the palace of the Pope, at Rome; the papal authority. [L. *Mons Vaticanus*, a hill in Rome]

vaudeville n. popular song, light theatrical production interspersed with comic songs; variety concert. [from F. *Vau* (*Val*) *de Vire*, in Normandy]

vault n. arched roof; arched apartment; cellar. -v.t. build with an arched roof. [L. *voluta*, turned]

vault v.i. spring or jump with the hands resting on something. -v. t. jump over in this way. -n. such jump. [F. *volter*]

vaunt v.i. boast. -v.t. boast of. -n. boast. [F. *vanter*]

veal n. calf flesh used as food. [OF. *veel*, fr. L. *vitulus*, calf]

vedette' n. mounted sentinel. [F.]

veer v.i. change direction (*e.g.* wind); change one's opinion. [F. *virer*]

veer v.t. (*naut*.) slacken or let out (rope). [Du *vieren*]

veg'etable (-j-) a. of, from, or concerned with, plants. -n. plant, *esp*. one used for food. -vegeta'rian n. one who does not eat meat. -vegeta'rianism n. -veg'etate v. i. live the life of a plant. vegeta'tion n. plants collectively; the plants growing in a place; process of plant growth. [L. *vegetus*, lively, flourishing]

ve'hement a. forcefully eager, impetuous. - ve'hemently adv. -ve'hemence n. (L. *vehemens*]

ve'hicle *n.* carriage, cart, or other conveyance on land; means of expression; liquid which serves as medium for medicinal substances, *etc.* -vehic'ular *a.* [L. *vehiculum,* fr. *vehere,* carry]

veil *n.* piece of material to cover the face and head; pretext. -*v.t.* cover with, or as with, a veil. [L. *velum*]

vein *n.* tube in the body taking blood to the heart; rib of a leaf or insect's wing; fissure in rock filled with ore; streak. -*v. t.* mark with streaks. -ve'nous *a.* [L. *vena*]

veld (felt) *n.* (*S. Africa*) open country, thinly wooded grassland. [Du. *veld,* field]

vell'um *n.* parchment of calf skin prepared for writing on or bookbinding. [L. *vitulus*]

veloc'ipede (-os'-) *n.* early bicycle without pedals, moved by striking the feet on the ground. [F.]

velo'city *n.* speed, rate of speed. [L. *velax, veloc-,* swift]

velours' *n.* kind of hatter's plush; fabric resembling velvet. [F.]

vel'vet *n.* silk fabric with a thick, short pile. -vel'vety *a.* smoothly soft like velvet. -velveteen' *n.* cotton fabric resembling velvet. (L. *villus,* nap]

ve'nal *a.* guilty of taking, prepared to take, bribes. -venal'ity *n.* [L. *veaalis,* fr. *venum,* that which is for sale]

vend *v.t.* sell; peddle. -vend'or *n.* vend'ible *a.* [L. *vendere*]

vendetta *n.* blood-feud. [It.]

veneer' *v.t.* to cover with a thin layer of finer wood. -*n.* such covering. [earlier *fineer,* Ger. *furnieren*]

ven'erable *a.* worthy of reverence; aged; hallowed by age. -ven'erate *v. t.* - veneration *n.* [L. *venerari,* worship]

vene'real *a.* from, or connected with, sexual intercourse. [L. *venereus,* fr. *venus, vener-,* love]

vene'tian-blind *n.* window blind of thin slats of wood, slanted to admit light and air. [Venice]

ven'geance *n.* revenge, retribution for wrong done. -venge'ful *a.* -venge'fully *adv.* [F. *veneer,* fr. L. *vindicate*]

ve'nial *a.* pardonable. -venial'ity *n.* [L. *venia,* pardon]

ven'ison *n.* flesh of deer as food. [F. *venaison,* L. *venatio,* hunting]

ven'om *n.* poison, *esp.* of a snake; spite. ven'omous *a.* [L. *venenum*]

vent *n.* small hole or outlet. -*v. t.* give outlet to (*e.g.* air, one's feelings, *etc.*) [F.]

ventilate *v.t.* supply with fresh air; bring into discussion. -vent'ilator *n.* ventila'tion *n.* [L. *ventilare,* fan]

ventricle *n.* cavity or hollow in the body, *esp.* in the heart or brain. -ventric'ular *a.* [L. *venter,* belly]

ventril'oquist *n.* one who can so speak that the sounds seem to come from some other person or place. -ventril'oquism *n.* - ventrilo'quial *a.* [*ventricle*]

ven'ture *n.* undertaking of a risk, speculation. -*v.t.* risk. -*v.i.* dare; have courage to do something or go somewhere. -ven'turesome *a.* -vent'urous *a.* [ME. *aventure,* adventure]

ven'ue *n.* district in which a case is tried; meeting place; scene (of some event). [Med. L. *vicinetum,* area from which a jury was summoned]

vera'cious *a.* truthful. -vera'city (-as'-) *n.* [L. *verax, verac-*]

veran'da, veran'dah *n.* open gallery or portico at the side of a house. [Port. *veranda*]

verb *n.* part of speech which asserts or declares. -verb'al *a.* of, by, or relating to, words. -verb'ally *adv.* -verba'tim *adv.* word for word. -verb'iage *n.* excess of words. -verbose' *a.* wordy. -verbos'ity *n.* [L. *verbum,* word]

verbe'na *n.* kinds of fragrant plant including wild vervain. [L.]

ver'dant *a.* green. -verd'ure *n.* greenery. [OF. *verd,* green, fr. L. *viridis*]

ver'dict *n.* decision of a jury; opinion reached after examination of facts, *etc.* [OF. *veir dit,* true word]

verdigris' *n.* green rust on copper. [OF. *vert de Grece,* Greek green]

verd'ure. *See* verdant.

verge *n.* edge, brink. -ver'ger *n.* bearer of a wand of office; usher in a church. [L. *virga,* wand]

verge *v.i.* be on the border of, come close to. [L. *vergere,* turn]

ver'ify *v.t.* prove or confirm the truth of. - verifi'able *a.* -verifica'tion *n.* ver'itable *a.* true, genuine. -ver'itably *adv.* -ver'ity *n.* truth. -ver'ily *adv.* truly. -verisimil'tude *n.* appearance of truth. [L. *verus,* true]

ver'juice *n.* sour fruit juice: [F. *verjus*]

vermicell'i *n.* Italian pasta of flour, *etc.,* made in long thin tubes. [It.]

verm'icide *n.* substance to destroy worms. -verm'iform *a.* shaped like a worm. -verm'ifuge *n.* substance to drive out worms. [L. *vermis,* worm]

vermil'ion *n.* bright red color or pigment. -*a.* of this color. [L. *vermiculus,* dim. of *vermis,* worm]

ver'min *n.* injurious animals, parasites, *etc.* -ver'minous *a.* [L. *vermis,* worm]

ver'mouth *n.* liqueur of wormwood. [L. *vermis,* worm]

vernacular *a.* of language, idiom, *etc.,* of one's own country *n.* mother tongue; homely speech. [L. *vernaculus,* domestic]

vern'al *a.* of spring. [L. *ver,* spring]

vernier *n.* small sliding scale for obtaining fractional parts of the subdivisions of a graduated scale. [Vernier, F. mathematician (d. 1637)]

ver'onal *n.* hypnotic drug. [G.]

vers'atile *a.* capable of dealing with many subjects. -versatil'ity *n.* [F.]

verse *n.* line of poetry; short division of a poem or other composition. -ver'sify *v. t.* turn into verse. -*v.i.* to write verses. **versifica'tion** *n.* [OE. *fers*]

versed *a.* skilled; proficient. [F. *versé*]

ver′sion *n.* a translation; an account or description. [L. *vertere,* translate]

ver′so *n.* back of an object; left-hand page. [L. *vertere, vers-,* turn]

ver′sus *prep.* against. [L.]

vert′ebra *n.* single section of a backbone. **-vert′ebrate** *a.* having a backbone. **-vert′ebral** *a.* [L.]

vert′ex *n.* **-vert′ices** *pl.* summit. [L. *vertex, -icis,* summit]

vert′ical *a.* upright; overhead. [fr. L. *vertere,* to turn]

verti′go *n.* giddiness. **-verti′ginous** *a.* dizzy. [L.]

ver′vain *n.* wild verbena, much used in ancient magic. [OF. *verveine*]

verve *n.* inspired enthusiasm; life, vigor, *esp.* in creative work, [F.]

ver′y *a.* true, real. *adv.* extremely, to a great extent. [OF. *verai,* true]

Ve′ry light *n.* colored flare fired from pistol to illuminate, or as signal. [Samuel Very, inventor]

ves′icle *n.* small blister, bubble, or cavity. **-vesic′ular** *a.* (L. *vesica,* bladder]

ves′pers *n. pl.* evening church service. [L. *vesper,* evening star]

vess′el *n.* any utensil or appliance for containing, *esp.* for liquids; ship. [OF. *vaissel,* fr. L. *vas,* vase]

vest *n.* sleeveless garment worn beneath a suit coat, waistcoat. **-v.t.** endow. **-v.i.** be in a person's authority. **-vest′ment** *n.* robe or official garment. **-vest′ry** *n.* room attached to a church for keeping vestments, holding meetings, *etc.* **-vest′ure** *n.* clothing, a covering. [L. *vestis,* garment]

Ves′ta *n.* Roman goddess of the home. **ves′ta** *n.* kind of match. **-ves′tal** *a.* pure, chaste, of Vesta. [L.]

vestibule *n.* entrance hall, passage, or space between outer and inner doors. [L. *vestibulum,* porch]

vest′ige *n.* trace or mark. [L. *vestigium,* footprint]

vetch *n.* plant of the bean family used for fodder, *esp.* the tare. [L. *vicia*]

vet′eran *n.* person who has served a long time, *esp.* a soldier with much service. [L. *veteranus*]

veterinary *a.* of, or for, the diseases of domestic animals. **-vetinar′ian** *n.* one skilled in the medical treatment of animals. *n.* [L. *veterinarius*]

ve′to *n.* power of rejecting a piece of legislation, or preventing it from coming into effect; any prohibition. **-v. t.** enforce a veto against; forbid with authority. [L. = I forbid]

vex *v.t.* annoy or distress. **-vexa′tion** *n.* **vexatious** *a.* **-vexed** *a.* annoyed; much discussed. [L. *vexare,* shake]

vi′able *a.* born alive, capable of living and growing; practicable. [L. *vita,* life]

vi′aduct *n.* bridge over a valley for road or rail. [L. *via,* way]

vi′al, phi′al *n.* small glass bottle for holding liquids. [G. *phiale,* flat vessel]

vi′ands *n. pl.* food. [F. *viande*]

vi′brate *v.i.* move to and fro rapidly and continuously, oscillate, quiver. **-v.t.** cause to do this. **-vibra′tion** *n.* **-vibra′tor** *n.* **vibra′tory** *a.* **-vi′brant** *a.* [L. *vibrare,* shake]

vic′ar *n.* clergyman; deputy. **-vic′arage** *n.* vicar's house. **-vicar′ial** *a.* **-vicar′ious** *a.* done or suffered by one person on behalf of another. **-vicar′iously** *adv.* [L. *vicarius,* substitute]

vice *n.* fault or blemish; evil or immoral habit or practice. **-vi′cious** *a.* **-vi′ciously** *adv.* [L. *vitium*]

vice *- prefix.* **-vicere′gent** *n.* holder of delegated authority. **-vice′roy** *n.* ruler acting for a king in a province or dependency. **-vicere′gal** *a.* **-vice′reine** *n. fem.* viceroy's wife. **-viceroy′alty** *n.* [L. = in place of]

vice ver′sa *adv.* other way round. [L.]

vicinity *n.* neighborhood. [L. *vicinitas vicinus,* neighborhood]

vicissitude *n.* change of fortune. **-pl.** ups and downs. [L. *vicissitude*]

victim *n.* person or animal killed as a sacrifice; one injured by accident or so that an object may be gained by another. **- vic′timize** *v.t.* make a victim of- **victimiza′tion** *n.* [L. *victima*]

vic′tor *n.* conqueror or winner. **-vic′tory** *n.* winning of a battle, *etc.* **-victor′ious** *a.* **-victor′iously** *adv.* [L.]

victo′ria *n.* light horse-carriage with folding hood. [Queen Victoria]

victual (vit′l) *n.* (*usu.* in *pl.*) food. **-v. t.** supply with food. **v.i.** obtain supplies [L. *victualia,* fr. *vivere, vict-,* live]

vid′eo *a.* relating to vision or the transmission or production of television image. **-n.** apparatus for recording television programs and viewing pre-recorded video tapes. **- vid′eophone** *n.* telephonic device in which there is both verbal and visual communication between parties. **vid′eo tape** *n.* magnetic tape on which to record images for use in the video machine. [L. *videre,* to see]

vie *v.i.* contend, enter into competition. [OF. *envier,* challenge]

view *n.* survey by eyes or mind; picture; scene; opinion; purpose, **-v. t.** took at, examine, survey. **-viewless** *a.* invisible- [F. *vue*]

vig′il (-j-) *n.* a keeping awake, a watch; eve of a feast day. **-vig′ilant** *a.* **vig′ilance** *n.* [L. *vigilia,* watchfulness]

vignette′ (vin-yet′) *n.* illustration in a book not enclosed in a definite border; portrait showing only head and shoulders with the background shaded off; slight word-sketch. [F.]

vig′or (-ger) *n.* force, strength, activity. **vig′orous** *a.* **-vig′orously** *adv.* [L. *vigor-vigere,* be strong]

vi′king *n.* Northern sea-rover of the eighth-tenth centuries. [ON. *vikingr,* or perh. fr. OE. *wicing,* fr. *wic,* camp]

vile *a.* base, mean, bad. **-vil′ify** *v.t.* speak ill of. **-vilifica′tion** *n.* [L. *vilis*]

vill′a *n.* country or suburban house. (L. *manor*]

vill'age n. assemblage of dwellings in the country. **-vill'ager** n. dweller in a village. [L. villa, manor]

vill'ain (-in) n. feudal serf (also **vill'ein**); scoundrel. **-vill'ainous** a. **-vill'ainy** n. [Low L. villanus]

vim n. (sl.) vigor, force, energy. [L. vis. strength]

vinaigrette' n. savory sauce, esp. for salads; small bottle of smelling salts. [F.]

vin'dicate v.t. establish the truth or merit of, clear of charges. **-vindica'tion** n. **-vin'dicator** n. **-vin'dicatory** a. **vindic'tive** a. revengeful; inspired by resentment. [L. vindicate, avenge]

vine n. climbing plant which bears grapes: **-vine'yard** n. vine farm, or plantation of vines. **-vi'nery** n. greenhouse for grapes. **-vi'nous** a. of, or due, to wine. **-vin'tage** n. gathering of the grapes; the yield; wine of a particular year. **-vint'ner** n. dealer in wine. [L. vinum, wine]

vine'gar n. an acid liquid got from wine and other alcoholic liquors. [F. vinaigre, fr. aigre, sour]

vi'ol n. medieval instrument like a violin. **violin'** n. fiddle. **-vi'ola** n. tenor fiddle. **violoncell'o** (-chel'-) n. large bass violin. **violin'ist** n. **-violoncell'ist** n. [F. viole; It. viola]

vi'ola n. single-colored variety of pansy. [L. = violet]

vi'olate v.t. outrage, desecrate; infringe. **viola'tion** n. **-vi'olator** n. [L. violare, violate-]

vi'olent a. of great force; marked by, or due to, extreme force of passion or fierceness. **-vi'olence** n. **-vi'olently** adv. [F.]

vi'olet n. plant with a small bluish purple flower; the flower; color of it. -a of this color. [L. viola]

vi'per n. venomous snake. [L. vipera]

vira'go n. abusive woman. [L.]

vir'gin n. girl or woman who has not had sexual intercourse with a man. -a. chaste unsullied; fresh, untilled (of land). **vir'ginal** a. -n. kind of harpsichord. **virgin'ity** n. [L. virgo, virgin-]

Vir'go n. the Virgin, 6th sign of the zodiac, which sun enters about 22nd August. [L.]

viridesc'ent a. greenish, turning green. **viri'dity** n. freshness, greenness. [L. viridis, green]

vir'ile a. manly; strong; procreative. **vir'ility** n. [L. virilis, fr. vir, man]

virtu' n. artistic excellence, objects of art or antiquity collectively. [It. virtu, virtue]

vir'tue n. moral goodness; good quality; inherent power. **-vir'tual** a. so in effect though not in name. **-vir'tually** adv. **vir'tuous** a. morally good; chaste. **vir'tuously** adv. **virtuo'so** n. one with special skill in a fine art. **-virtuos'ity** n. such a skill. [L. virtus]

vi'rus n. poison; disease, infection. **vir'ulent** a. poisonous; bitter, malignant. **virulently** adv. **-vir'ulence** n. [L.]

vi'sa n. endorsement on passport to show that it has been examined, [F.]

vis'age (-z-) n. face; expression. [F.]

vise n. appliance with a screw jaw for holding things while working on them. (F. vis., screw)

vis'cera (vis-e-ra) n. pl. internal organs; entrails. **-vis'ceral** a. [L.]

viscid a. sticky, of a consistency like treacle. **-vis'cose** n. form of cellulose used in making rayon. **-vis'cous** a. viscid. **-viscid'ity** n. **viscos'ity** n. [L. viscum, birdlime]

vis'count (vi-kownt) n. peer of rank next above a baron. **-viscount'ess** fem. (Of. visconte, 'vice-count]

vis'ion n. sight. **-vis'ionary** a. unpractical, dreamy. -n. one full of fancies. **-vis'ible** a. that can be seen. **visibil'ity** n. **-vis'ibly** adv. **-vis'ual** a. of sight. **-vis'ual dis'play u'nit** (abbrev. VDU) n. screen attached to a computer on which the information is displayed. **vis'ualize** v.t. make visible; form a mental image of. **-visualization** n. [L. videre, vis-, see]

vis'it v.t. go, or come, and see. -n. a visiting. **-vis'itor** n. **-vis'itant** n. visitor. **-visita'tion** n. formal visit or inspection; affliction or plague. [vision]

vi'sor, vi'sard, viz'ard n. movable front part of a helmet covering the face. [F. visière, fr. vis, face]

vista n. view, esp. between trees. [It., fr. L. videre, see]

vi'tal a. necessary to, or affecting life. **vi'tally** adv. **-vital'ity** n. life, vigor. **vi'talize** v.t. give life to. [L. vita, life]

vitamin n. factor in certain foodstuffs regarded as essential to life and health. [L. vita, life]

vi'tiate (vish'-), v.t. spoil, deprive of efficacy. **-vitia'tion** n. [L. vitiare]

vit'reous a. of glass; glassy. **-vit'rify** v.t. and i. [L. vitrum, glass]

vit'riol n. sulfuric acid; caustic speech. **vitriol'ic** a. [Low L. vitreous]

vituperate v.t. abuse in words, revile. -v.i. use abusive language. **vitupera'tion** n. **vitu'perative** a. [L. vituperate, vituperate, fr. vitium, fault]

vivacious a. lively, animated, gay. **-viva'city** n. [L. vivax, vivac-, fr. vivere, live]

viva'rium n. place to keep living creatures. [L.]

vivid a. bright, intense; clear, lively, graphic. **-viv'idly** adv. **-viv'ify** v.t. animate, inspire. [L. vividus]

viviparous a. bringing forth young alive. [L. vivus, alive, parere, bring forth]

vivisection n. dissection or experiment on living bodies of animals, etc. **viv'isector** n. [L. virus, alive, secare, cut]

vix'en n. female fox; spiteful woman. **vix'enish** a. [OE. fem. of fox]

vizard. See visor.

viz'ier n. minister of state in a Muslim country. (Turk. vezir)

vocable n. word. **-vocab'ulary** n. list of words; stock of words used. [L. vocabulum, fr. vocare, call]

vo'cal a. of, with, or giving out, voice. **vo'calist** n. singer. **-vo'cally** adv. **vo'calize** v.t. utter with the voice. **voca'tion** n. calling. **voca'tive** n. in some languages, the case of nouns used in addressing a person. [L. vox, voice]

vocif'erate *v.t.* and *i.* shout. **-vocif'erous** *a.* shouting, noisy. **-vocifera'tion** *n.* [L. *vox*, voice]

vod'ka *n.* Russian spirit distilled from rye. [Russ. dim. of *voda*, water]

vogue *n.* fashion. [F.]

voice *n.* sound given out by a person in speaking or singing, *etc.*; quality of the sound; expressed opinion; share in a discussion; verbal forms proper to relation of subject and action. *-v. t.* give utterance to. **-voice'less** *a.* (F. *voix*, fr. L. *vox*, voc-]

void *a.* empty. *-n.* empty space. *-v.t.* empty out. [OF. *voit*]

voile *n.* thin cotton fabric. [F.]

vol'atile *a.* evaporating quickly; lively. **volatil'ity** *n.* **-volat'ilize** *v.t.* and *i.* [L. *volatilis*, flying]

volca'no *n.* mountain with a hole through which lava, ashes, smoke, *etc.*, are discharged. **-volcan'ic** *a.* [L. *Vulcanus*, Vulcan (whose forge was supposed to be below Etna)]

vole *n.* kinds of small rodent, as water-vole, field-vole, *etc.* [for *vole-mousse*, fr. Norw. *voll*, field]

voli'tion (-ish'-) *n.* act or power of willing. **-voli'tional** *a.* [Med. L. *volitio*]

voll'ey *n.* simultaneous discharge of weapons or missiles; rush of oaths, questions, *etc.* in sport, kick, stroke at moving ball before it hits the ground. *-v.t.* discharge in a volley. *-v. i.* fly in a volley. **-voll'eyball** *n.* team game where a large ball is hit by hand over a high net. [F. *volée*, flight, orig. at tennis]

volt'age *n.* electromotive force measured in volts. **-volt** *n.* unit of electromotive power. [A. Volta, 1745-1827]

voluble *a.* with incessant or abundant speech. **-volubil'ity** *n.* **-vol'ubly** *adv.* [L. *volvere*, *volut-*, roll]

vol'ume *n.* book, or part of a book, bound; mass; bulk, space occupied. **-volu'minous** *a.* bulky, over ample. [L. *volumen*]

voluntary *a.* having, or done by, free will. *-n.* organ solo in a church service. **vol'untarily** *adv.* **-volunteer'** *n.* one who offers service, joins a force, *etc.*, of his own free will. *-v.i.* offer oneself. [L. *voluntas*, wish, will]

voluptuous *a.* of or contributing to the pleasures of the senses. **-volup'tuary** *n.* one given to luxury and sensual pleasures. [L. *voluptas*, pleasure]

vol'ute *n.* spiral scroll-like ornament found *esp.* in Ionic capitals; genus of shellfish like whelks. **-volu'ted**, **volu'tion** *n.* whorl, spiral; convolution. [L. *volvere*, roll]

vom'it *v.t.* eject from the stomach through the mouth. *-v.t.* be sick. *-n.* matter vomited. [L. *vomere*, vomit-]

voo'doo *n.* African black magic practiced in Haiti, *etc.*; one skilled in this. [W. Afr. *vodu*]

voracious *a.* greedy, ravenous. **-vora'city** *n.* voraciously *adv.* [L. *vorax*, *vorac-*]

vor'tex *a.* vortices *pl.* whirlpool; whirling motion. [L.]

vo'tary *n.* one vowed to a service or pursuit. **-vo'taress** *fem.* **-vo'tive** *a.* given or consecrated by vow. [L. *votum*, vow]

vote *n.* formal expression of a choice; individual pronouncement, or right to give it, in a question or election; result of voting; that which is given or allowed by vote. *v.i.* give a vote. *-v. t.* grant or enact by vote. **-vo'ter** *n.* [L. *votum*, vow]

vouch *v.i.* vouch for, make oneself responsible for. *-v. t.* guarantee. **-vouch'er** *n.* document proving the correctness of an item in accounts. **-vouchsafe'** *v.i.* condescend to grant or do something. [OF. *vochier*]

vow *n.* solemn promise, *esp.* a religious one. *-v.t.* promise or threaten by vow. [F. *vœu*, fr. L. *vovere*, vot-]

vow'el *n.* vocal sound pronounced without stoppage or friction of the breath; letter standing for such sound. [F. *voyelle*, fr. L. *vocalis* (*littera*), vocal (letter)]

voy'age *n.* journey, *esp.* a long one, by water. *-v.i.* make a voyage. [F]

vulcanize *v.t.* treat (rubber) with sulfur at a high temperature. **-vul'canite** *n.* rubber so hardened. **-vulcanization** *n.* [Vulcan; See **vol'cano**]

vul'gar *a.* of the common people; common; coarse, not refined; offending against good taste. **-vulga'rian** *n.* vulgar fellow, *esp.* a rich one. **-vul'garly** *adv.* **vul'garism** *n.* word or construction used only by the uneducated. **-vulgar'ity** *n.* **vul'garize** *v. t.* make vulgar or too common. **-vulgariza'tion** *n.* **-vul'gar fractions** common fraction, as distinct from decimals. **-vul'gar tongue'**, vernacular. [L. *vulgaris*, fr. *vulgus*, common people]

Vul'gate *n.* 4th cent. Latin version of the Bible made by St. Jerome [L. *vulgatus*]

vulnerable *a.* not proof against wounds; offering an opening to criticism, *etc.* [L. *vulnerare*, wound]

vul'pine *a.* of foxes; foxy; crafty, cunning. [L. *vulpinus*, of the fox, *vulpes*]

vul'ture *n.* large bird which feeds on carrion. [L. *vultur*]

W

wab'ble. See **wobble.**

wad (wod) *n.* small pad of fibrous material, used *esp.* to pack charge in a gun; money, notes. *-v. t.* line, pad, stuff, *etc.*, with a wad. **-wadd'ing** *n.* stuffing. [orig. unknown]

wad'dle *v. i.* walk like a duck. [wade]

wade *v.i.* walk through something that hampers movement, *esp.* water. **-wa'der** *n.* person or bird that wades; high waterproof boot. [OE. *wadan*]

wad'i *n.* dry bed of a stream. [Arab.]

wafer *n.* thin cake or biscuit; the Host; disk of paste for fastening papers. *-v. t.* fasten with a wafer. **-waf'fle** *n.* kind of pancake. **-waffle-iron** *n.* [Du. *wafel*]

waft *v.t.* convey smoothly through air or water. *-n.* breath of wind, odor, etc, [orig. uncertain]

wag *v.t.* cause to move to and fro. *-v.i.* shake, swing. *-n.* merry fellow (orig. waghalter, rascal). **-wagg'ery** *n.* **-wagg'ish** *a.* **-wag'tail** *n.* small bird with a wagging tail. [OE. *wagian*]

wage *n.* payment for work done (usu. in *pl.*). -*v. t.* carry on. -**wa'ger** *n.* and *v.t.* and *i.* bet. [ONF. *wage*, for *gage*, pledge]

wag'gle *v.t.* wag. [fr. *wag*]

wag'on *n.* four-wheeled vehicle for heavy loads. -**wag'oner** *n.* -**wagonette'** *n.* four-wheeled horse carriage with lengthwise seats. [Du. *wagen*, carriage]

waif *n.* homeless person, *esp.* a child. **waifs and strays**, the homeless destitute; odds and ends. [ONF.]

wail *n.*, *v.t.* and *i.* lament. [ON. *vœla*]

wain *n.* farm wagon. [OE. *wœgn*]

wains'cot *n.* wooden lining of the walls of a room, *esp.* oak. -*v.t.* line thus. [LG. *wagenschot*]

waist *n.* part of the body between hips and ribs; various central parts. **waistcoat** *n.* sleeveless garment worn under a coat. [ME. *waste*, growth, fr. *wax*, grow]

wait *v.i.* await. -*v.i.* be expecting, attend; serve at table. -*n.* act of waiting; carol singer. -**wait'er** *n.* attendant on guests in restaurant, hotel, *etc.* -**wait'ress** *fem.* [ONF. *waitier*, lurk, lie in ambush]

waive *v.t.* forgo; renounce (a right, claim). (ONF. *waiver*, renounce]

wake *v.i.* rouse from sleep. -*v.t.* rouse from sleep; stir up. -*n.* watch by a dead person; holiday. -**wa'ken** *v.t.* wake. **wake'ful** *a.* [OE. *waccian*]

wake *n.* track left by a ship, airplane, *etc.*, track. (Du. *wak*]

wake'-rob'in *n.* mild arum, cuckoopint. [*wake*]

wale, weal *n.* streak left by the blow of a stick or whip. [OE. *walu*]

walk (wawk) *v. i.* move on the feet at an ordinary pace; cross by walking. -*v. t.* cause to walk. -*n.* slowest gait of animals; occupation or career; path, *etc.* for walking; spell of walking for pleasure, *etc.* -**walk'er** *n.* -**walk'way** *n.* pedestrian passage, *usu.* suspended *e.g.* between buildings. [OE. *wealean*, roll]

Walkman *n.* small portable cassette recorder with light headphones. [Trademark]

wall (wawl) *n.* structure of brick, stone, *etc.*, serving as a fence, side of a building, *etc.*; surface of one. -*v.t.* supply with a wall; block up with a wall. -**wall'flower** *n.* sweet smelling garden flower, often growing on walls. [L. *vallum*]

wall'a(h) *n.* man, agent. -**competition wallah**, Indian civil servant appointed by competitive examination. [Hind. *wale*, doer]

wallaby *n.* small kangaroo. [Austral.]

wall'et (wol-) *n.* small bag; pocketbook for paper-money, *etc.* [var. of *wattle*]

walleyed (wawl-id) *a.* having eyes with pale irises. [ON. *vald-eygthr*]

wall'op *v. t.* beat, flog. -*n.* beating, blow; (*sl.*) draught beer. [ONF. *waloper*]

wall'ow *v. i.* roll in mire, water, *etc.* -*n.* act of wallowing. [OE. *wealwian*]

wal'nut (wawl-) *n.* large nut with a crinkled shell splitting easily into two halves; the tree. [OE. *wealh*, foreign]

wal'rus (wol-) *n.* large seal-like sea animal with long tusks. [Dan. *hvalros*]

waltz (wawlts) *n.* dance. -*v. i.* dance it. [Ger. *walzer-watzen*, roll]

wam'pum *n.* strings of shells, beads, used by N. American Indians as money. [N. Amer. Ind.]

wan (won) *a.* pale, sickly-complexioned, faint-looking. [OE. *wann*, lurid]

wand (wond) *n.* stick, usually straight and slender. [ON. *vondr*]

wand'er (won-) *v.i.* roam; ramble; deviate from one's path; be delirious. [OE. *wandrian*].

wanderlust *n.* travel urge. [Ger.]

wane *v.i.* and *n.* decline. [OE. *wanian*]

wang'le *v.t.* manipulate, manage in a skillful way. [orig. uncertain]

want (wont) *n.*, *v.t.* and *i.* lack. [ON. *vant*]

want'on (won-) *a.* unrestrained; playful; dissolute; without motive. -*v.i.* frolic. -*n.* wanton person. [ME. *wanto-wen*]

wap'iti (wop-) *n.* large N. American deer. [N. Amer. Ind. *wapitik*]

war *n.* fighting between nations; state of hostility. -*v.i.* make war. -**war'fare** *n.* hostilities. -**war'like** *a.* -**war'monger** *n.* spreader of war propaganda. **war'paint** *n.* paint, adornments assumed by N. American Indians before battle. **war'ship** *n.* naval vessel of any type used in warfare. -**warr'ior** *n.* fighter. [ONF. *werre*, F. *guerre*]

war'ble (wor-) *v.i.* sing with trills. **warb'ler** *n.* [ONF. *werbler*]

ward (wawrd) *n.* guardianship; minor under care of a guardian; division of a city, or hospital, *etc.* -*pl.* indentations of the bead of a key or lock. -*v.t.* guard. **ward'er** *n.* prison keeper. -**ward'ress** *fem.* -**ward'ship** *n.* -**ward'robe** *n.* piece of furniture for hanging clothes in. **ward'room** *n.* officers' mess on a warship. -**ward'en** *n.* president or governor. -**ward'enship** *n.* [OE. *weard*, ONF. *warder*, F. *garder*]

ware *n.* goods; articles collectively. **ware'house** *n.* store-house; large commercial establishment. [OE. *waru*]

ware *a.* on guard. -*v. t.* beware; keep clear of. -**wa'riness** *n.* suspicious care, caution. [OE. *woer*]

war'lock *n.* wizard, sorcerer. [OE. *waer*, truth, compact, *leogan*, to lie]

warm *a.* moderately hot; ardent. -*v.t.* and *i.* heat. -**warm'ly** *adv.* **warm'th** *n.* [OE. *wearm*]

warn *v.t.* caution, put on guard. -**warn'ing** *n.* [OE. *warnian*]

warp *n.* lengthwise threads in a loom; rope. -*v.t.* twist; move by a rope fastened to a buoy. -*v.i.* become twisted. [OE. *weorpan*, throw]

warr'ant *n.* authority; document giving authority. -*v.t.* authorize; guarantee. **warr'anly** *n.* justification, guarantee. [ONF. *warant*, F. *garant*]

warr'en *n.* ground occupied by rabbits. [ONF. *warenne*, F. *garenne*]

wart (wort) *n.* hard growth on the skin. -**wart'y** *a.* [OE. *wearte*]

war'y *a.* cautious; watchful; on the defensive. -**war'ily** *adv.* [fr. *ware*]

wash (wosh) v.t. clean with liquid; carry along with a rush of water; color lightly. v.i. wash oneself-, stand washing. -n. an act of washing; clothes washed at one time; sweep of water, esp. set up by moving ship; thin coat of color. -wash′er n. one who or that which washes; ring put under a nut. -wash′y a. diluted. wash out n. (sl.) failure, ineffectual effort. -wash-leather n. akin to chamois leather. -wash-stand n. stand holding basin and water-jug. [OE. wascan]

wasp n. striped stinging insect resembling a bee. -wasp′ish a. irritable; spiteful. [OE. wœsp, wœps]

wass′ail n. drinking bout; liquor for it. -v. i. carouse. [OE. wes heil, be hale('your health')]

waste v. t. expend uselessly, use extravagantly; lay desolate. -v. i. dwindle; pine away. -a. wasted; desert. -n. what is wasted; act of wasting; desert. -wast′age n. -waste′ful a. -waste′fully adv. wast′er n. -waste′ful a. -waste′fully adv. -wast′er n. -wast′rel n. useless person, profligate. [ONF. waster, F. gâter, fr. L. vastare, destroy]

watch (woch) n. state of being on the lookout; spell of duty; pocket clock. -v. t. observe closely; guard. -v. i. be on watch, be wakeful. -watch′ful a. -watch′fully adv. -watch′man n. -watch′keeper n. officer of the watch. -watch′maker n. watch′word n. rallying-cry. [OE. wœcce]

wat′er n. transparent tasteless liquid, the substance of rain, rivers, etc., transparency of a gem. -v. t. put water on or into; cause to drink. -v.i. take in or obtain water. -wat′ery a. -wat′er-bailiff n. customs official who inspects vessels entering and leaving port; official in charge of fishing rights and prevention of poaching. -wat′er-boat′man n. kind of water-beetle. -wat′ercress n. moisture loving salad plant. -wat′erfall n. fall of water (river, stream) over a perpendicular drop. -wat′erglass n. solution (sodium silicate) for preserving eggs. -wat′erlil′y n. water-plant with floating leaves and large flowers. -wat′er-logged a. soaked, filled with water so as to be unseaworthy. -wat′ermark n. mark made in paper during manufacture and visible on holding the paper to the light. wat′erproof a. not letting water through. -n. waterproof garment. -watertight a. [OE. wœter]

watt (wot) n. unit of electric power. [J. Watt, engineer (d. 1819)]

wat′tle (wot-) n. hurdle of wicker. -v. t. make into basket-work. [OE. watel]

watt′le n. pendent skin of bird's throat; species of Australian, S. African, etc., acacia. [orig. unknown]

waul, wawl, v. i. cry as cat; squall. [imit-]

wave v.i. move to and fro; beckon; have an undulating shape. -v. t. move to and fro; give the shape of waves; express by waves. -n. act or gesture of waving; ridge and trough of water, etc.; vibration. wa′vy a. -wa′vily adv. [OE. wafian, brandish]

wa′ver v.i. hesitate, be irresolute. wa′verer n. [fr. wave]

wax v.i. grow, increase. [OE. weaxan]

wax n. yellow plastic material made by bees; this or similar substance used for sealing, making candles, etc. -v.t. put wax on. -wax′works n. pl. display of figures modelled in wax. [OE. weax, beeswax]

way n. track; direction; method. way′farer n. traveler, esp. on foot. waylay′ v.t. lie in wait for. -way′ward a. capricious, perverse. -way′wardly adv. -way′wardness n. [OE. weg]

we pron. first person plural, pronoun. I and others. [OE.]

weak a. lacking strength. -weak′ly a. weak; sickly. -weak′ly adv. -weak′en v.t. and i. -weak′ling n. feeble creature. -weak′ness n. [ON. vickr]

weal n. well-being. [OE. wela]

weal. See wale.

weald n. open or wooded country; the Weald, formerly wooded, between the N. and S. Downs, England. [OE. weald]

wealth (welth) n. riches; abundance. -wealth′y a. [OE. weld]

wean v.t. accustom to food other than mother's milk. -wean′ling n. newly weaned child. [OE. wenian, accustom]

weap′on (wep′n) n. implement to fight with. [OE. woepen]

wear v.t. carry on the body; show consume. -v.i. last; become impaired by use. -n. act of wearing; impairment; things to wear. -wear′er n. -wear′ing a. exhausting. [OE. woerian]

wear′y a. tired. -v.t. and i. tire. wear′ily adv. -wear′iness n. -wear′isome a. [OE. werig]

weas′el (-z-) n. small animal related to the ferret, etc. [OE. wesle]

weath′er (weTH-) n. atmospheric conditions. -a. towards the wind. -v.t. affect by weather; sail to windward of, come safely through. -weath′ercock n. revolving vane to show which way the wind blows. -weath′ered a. (archit.) slightly inclined, to throw off water. [OE. weder]

weave v.t. form in texture or fabric by interlacing. -v.i. make by crossing. threads, etc., thread one's way (among). n. texture. -weav′er n. [OE. wefan]

web n. woven fabric; net spun by a spider; membrane between the toes of waterfowl. [OE. webb]

wed v.t. marry; to unite closely. -wedd′ing n. marriage. -wed′lock n. marriage. [OE. weddian]

wedge n. piece of material sloping to an edge. -v.t. fasten or split with a wedge; stick by compression or crowding. [OE. wecg]

Wed′nesday n. fourth day of the week. [OE. wodnesdoeg, day of Woden, or Odin]

wee a. small, little, tiny. [ME. we, bit]

weed n. plant growing where it is not desired. -v.t. and i. pull out weeds. -weed′y a. [OE. weod, herb]

weeds n. pl. widow's mourning garments. [OE. woed, garment]

week n. period of seven days. -week′ly a. happening, done, etc., once a week. -week′ly adv. once a week. [OE. wicu]

ween *v.i.* think, imagine. [OE. *wenan*]

weep *v.i.* shed tears. -*v.t.* lament. -weep'ing-will'ow, willow with drooping boughs. (OE. *wepan*]

wee'vil *n.* beetle harmful to grain, *etc.* [OE. *wifel*, beetle]

weft *n.* cross threads in weaving; woof [OE. *wefta*, fr. *wefan*, weave]

weigh *v.t.* find the weight of, raise, as in weigh anchor. -*v.i.* have weight. **weight** *n.* force exerted by the earth on a body; heavy mass; object of known mass for weighing; importance. -*v.t.* add a weight to. -**weight'y** *a.* -**weight'ily** *adv.* [OE. *wegan*, carry]

weir *n.* dam across a river. [OE. *wer*]

weird *a.* unearthly. [OE. *wyrd*, fate]

wel'come *a.* received gladly. -*n.* kindly greeting. -*v.t.* receive gladly or hospitably. [*well* and *come*]

weld *v.t.* unite (hot metal) by hammering or compressing; unite closely. -*n.* welded joint. [var. of *well*]

wel'fare *n.* well-being; prosperity. [*well* and *fare*]

wel'kin *n.* sky. [OE. *wolcen*, cloud]

well *adv.* in good manner or degree. -*a.* in good health; suitable. -well-being *n.* health and contentment; prosperity. well-bred *a.* polite, mannerly; (of horse) coming from good stock. -well-favored *a.* good-looking, handsome. -well-nigh *adv.* almost. -well-off *a.* fortunate-well-to-do *a.* prosperous. [OE. *wel*]

well *n.* deep hole for water; spring. -*v. i.* flow out or up. [OE. *wiella*]

well'ingtons *n. pl.* knee-length rubber boots worn in wet weather. [Duke of Wellington]

Welsh *a.* of Wales. -*n.* language, or people, of Wales. [OE. *wcelisc*, foreign]

welsh, welch *v.t.* and *i.* (of bookmaker) abscond without paying debts. -welsh'er *n.* [uncertain]

welt *n.* seam; leather rim put on a boot-upper for the sole to be attached to; wale. -*v.t.* provide a shoe with a welt; thrash. [orig. uncertain]

welt'er *v.i.* roll or tumble. -*n.* turmoil. (M. Du. *welteren*]

wen *n.* tumor forming a permanent swelling beneath the skin. [OE.]

wench *n.* damsel. [OE. *wencel*, child]

wend *v.i.* go. [OE. *wendan*, turn]

went *v.i. p.t.* of go. [*wend*]

wer'wolf, were'wolf *n.* human being able to turn into a wolf. [OE. *werwulf*, man-wolf]

Wes'leyan *a.* of Wesley or the Church founded by him. -*n.* member of that church. [J. Wesley (d. 1791)]

west *n.* part of the sky where the sun sets; part of a country, *etc.*, lying to this side. *a.* that is toward this region. *adv.* to the west. -west'erly *a.* -west'ward *a.* and *adv.* -west'wards *adv.* -west'ern *a.* [OE.]

wet *a.* having water or other liquid on a surface or being soaked in it; rainy. -*v.t.* make wet. -*n.* moisture, rain. -wet' blankets damping influence. -wet nurse, nurse who suckles a child not her own. [OE. *woot*]

weth'er (-TH-) *n.* castrated ram. [OE.]

whack *v.t.* hit, *esp.* with a stick. -*n.* such a blow. [imit.]

whale *n.* large fish-shaped sea animal. whale-back *n.* vessel with turtle-deck; vessel with upper deck of this type, used for carrying grain. -whale'bone *n.* springy substance from the upper jaw of certain whales. -wha'ler *n.* man or ship employed in hunting whales. [OF. *hwæl*]

wharf (hworf) *n.* quay for loading and unloading ships. -wharf'age *n.* accommodation or dues at a wharf. -wharf'inger *n.* -wharf owner. [OE. *hwerf*, shore]

what (hwot) *pron.* which thing? that which. -*a.* which. -whatev'er *pron.* anything which; of what kind it may be. whatsoev'er *a.* [OE. *hwcet*]

wheat *n.* cereal plant with thick four-sided seed-spikes, of which bread is chiefly made. -wheat'en *a.* [OE. *hwæte*]

wheat'ear *n.* small bird, one of the chats. [corrupt. of white-arse]

whee'dle *v.t.* and *i.* coax. [orig. uncertain]

wheel *n.* circular frame or disk with spokes revolving on an axle. -*v.t.* convey by wheeled apparatus or vehicles; cause to turn or change direction. -*v.i.* revolve; change direction. -wheel'-barrow *n.* barrow with one wheel. -wheel'wright *n.* maker or repairer of wheels. [OE. *kweol*]

wheeze *v. i.* to breathe with difficulty and noise. -*n.* (*sl.*) joke; trick. -wheez'y *a.* [ON. *hvæsa*, hiss]

whelk *n.* shell-fish. [OE. *weoloc*]

whelm *v. t.* submerge, overbear, destroy. [orig. uncertain]

whelp *n.* pup or cub. -*v. i.* and *t.* produce whelps. [OE. *hwelp*]

when *adv.* at what time. -*conj.* at the time. -whenev'er *adv.* and *conj.* at whatever time. [OE. *hwænne*]

whence *adv.* from what place. [fr. *when*]

where *adv.* and *conj.* at what place. whereas' *conj.* considering that, while, on the contrary. -where'fore *adv.* why. *conj.* consequently. -wherev'er *adv.* at whatever place. -where'withal *n.* means; resources. [OE. *hwar*]

wherr'y *n.* light shallow boat or barge. [orig. unknown]

whet *v.t.* sharpen. -whet'stone *n.* stone for sharpening tools. [OE. *hwettan*]

wheth'er (-TH-) *a.* and *pron.* which of the two. -*conj.* introduces first of two alternatives, of which second may be expressed or implied. [OE. *hwæther*]

whey *n.* watery part of milk. -whey'ey, whey'ish *a.* [OE. *hwæg*]

which *a.* asks for a selection from alternatives. -*pron.* which person or thing; thing 'who.' [OE. *kwilc*]

whiff *v.t.* and *i.* and *n.* puff. [imit.]

while *n.* space of time. -*conj.* in the time that. -*v.t.* pass (*time*, usually idly). **whilst** *adv.* [OE. *hwil*]

whim *n.* caprice, fancy. -whim'sical *a.* delicately fanciful. -whimsical'ity *n.* [orig. uncertain]

whim′brel *n.* small curlew. [imit.]

whim′per *v.i.* cry or whine softly. **whim′pering** *v.i.* cry or whine softly. **whim′pering** *a.* such cry. [imit.]

whin′ *n.* gorse, furze. **-whin′-chat** *n.* small bird found among gorse, the stone-chat. [of Scand. orig.]

whine *n.* long-drawn wail. *v.i.* make one. [OE. *hwinan*]

whinn′y *v.i.* neigh joyfully. **-n.** such neigh. [imit.]

whip *v.t.* apply a whip to; thrash; lash. *v.i.* dart. **-n.** lash attached to a stick for urging or punishing. **-whip′cord** *n.* thin hard cord. **-whip′hand** *n.* superiority, advantage. **-whipp′er-snapper** *n.* small child; insignificant person. [orig. uncertain]

whipp′et *n.* coursing dog like a small greyhound. [orig. uncertain]

whirl *v.t.* and *i.* swing rapidly round. **-n.** whirling movement. **-whirl′igig** *n.* spinning toy. **-whirl′pool** *n.* circular current. **-whirl′wind** *n.* wind whirling round a forward-moving axis. [ON. *hvirfill*, ring]

whir, whirr *n.* sound as of rapid beating or whirling. [imit.]

whisk *v.t.* and *i.* brandish, sweep, or beat lightly. **-n.** light brush; flapper; egg-beating implement. **-whisk′er** *n.* hair of a man's face. [of Teut. orig.]

whiskeys, whisk′y *n.* spirit distilled from various grains. [for *usquebaugh,* Ir. *uisge beatha,* water of life]

whisp′er *v.t.* and *i.* speak with rustling breath instead of voice. **-n.** such speech. [OE. *hwisprian*]

whist *n.* card game. [var. of *whisk*]

whis′tle (-sl) *n.* sound made by forcing the breath through rounded and nearly closed lips; any similar sound; instrument to make it. **-v.i.** make such sound. **-v.t.** utter or summon, *etc.,* by whistle. **whis′tler** *n.* [OE. hwistle]

whit *n.* jot. [OE, *wiht,* thing]

white *a.* of the color of snow; pale; light in color. **-n.** color of snow; white pigment; white part. **-white-ant** *n.* termite. **white′bait** *n.* small edible fish. **-white drugs** *n. pl.* harmful narcotics; dope. **white elephant** *n.* useless or incongruous gift. **-White House** *n.* executive department of the U.S. government; official residence of the president of the U.S. in Washington D.C. **-white-line** *n.* safety line on road. **-white-livered** *a.* cowardly. **-whi′ten** *v.t.* and *i.* **-white′ness** *n.* **white-paper** *n.* government report on any recent investigation. **-white slave** *n.* woman or child abducted or sold for purposes of prostitution. **-white′smith** *n.* tinsmith. **-white′wash** *n.* liquid mixture for whitening. **-v.t.** apply this, clear of imputations. **-whi′ting** *n.* dried chalk; small sea-fish. **-whi′tish** *a.* [OE. *hwit*]

whith′er (-TH-) *adv.* to what place. **whithersoev′er** *adv.* [OE. *hwider*]

whit′low *n.* inflamed swelling on a finger. [orig. uncertain]

whit′tle *v.t.* cut or carve with a knife; pare away. [OE. *thwitan,* cut]

whiz *n.* violent hissing sound. **-v.i.** move with such sound; make it. [imit.]

who *pron.* (*obj.* whom) relative and interrogative pronoun, always referring to persons. **-whoev′er** *pron.* any one or everyone that. [OE. *hwa*]

whole (h-) *a.* complete; healthy; all. **-n.** complete thing or system. **-who′lly** *adv.* **-whole′meal** *a.* of flour which contains the whole of the grain. **whole′sale** *n.* sale of goods by large quantities. **-a.** dealing by wholesale; extensive. **-whole′saler** *n.* **-whole′some** *a.* producing a good effect, physically or morally. [OE. *hal,* hale, uninjured]

whoop *v.t.* and *i.* and *n.* about. **-whoop′ing-cough** *n.* disease marked by a whooping breath. [F. *houper*]

whore (h-) *n.* prostitute. [ON. *hora*]

whorl *n.* turn of a spiral; ring of leaves, *etc.* **-whorl′ed** *a.* [OE. *hweorfan,* turn]

whor′tleberry *n.* bilberry. [earlier *hurtleberry,* fr. OE. *hortan,* bilberries]

whose *pron.* possess. of who, which. [OE. *hwces-hwa,* who]

why *adv.* and *conj.* for what cause; wherefore. **-interj.** of surprise, *etc.* **-n.** the reason or purpose of anything. [OE. *hwi*]

wick *n.* strip or thread feeding the flame of a lamp or candle. [OE. *weoce*]

wick′ed *a.* evil, sinful. **-wick′edly** *adv.* **-wick′edness** *n.* [ME. *wikke,* feeble]

wick′er *n.* plaited osiers, *etc.,* for baskets. **-a.** **-wick′erwork** *n.* basketwork. [ME. *wikir,* osier]

wick′et *n.* small gate; in cricket, a set of three stumps and bails. [AF. *wiket,* F. *guiche*]

wide *a.* broad; far from the mark. **wi′den** *v. t.* and *i.* **-wide′ly** *adv.* **-width** *n.* **-wide′-awake** *a.* alert. **-n.** kind of soft felt hat. [OE. *wid*]

wid′geon *n.* kind of wild duck. [orig. uncertain]

wid′ow *n.* woman whose husband is dead and who has not married again. *v. t.* make a widow of. **-wid′ower** *n.* man whose wife has died and who has not married again. **-wid′owhood** *n.* [OE. *wydewa*]

wield *v.t.* hold and use. **-wield′y** *a.* manageable. [OE. *gewieldan,* govern]

wife *n.* wives *pl.* woman married to a man. **-wife′ly** *a.* [OE. *wif,* woman]

wig *n.* artificial hair for the head. [for *periwig* -O Du. *peruyk*]

wight *n.* American Indian's hut or tent. [N. Amer. Ind.]

wild (wild) *a.* not tamed or domesticated; not cultivated (as wildflowers); savage; excited, rash. **-wild′ly** *adv.* **-wild′ness** *n.* **-wil′derness** *a.* desert. **-wild fire** *n.* burning liquid used formerly in sea-fights, Greek fire. **-like wild′fire** *adv.* very quickly. [OE. *wilde*]

wile *n.* trick. **-wi′ly** *a.* artful. [OE. *wil*]

will *v. aux.* forms moods and tenses indicating intention or conditional result. *v.i.* have a wish. **-v.t.** wish intend, purpose; leave as a legacy. **-n.** faculty of deciding what one will do; purpose, wish; directions written for disposal of property after death. **-will′ing** *a.* ready; given cheerfully. **-will′ingly** *adv.* **-will′ingness** *n.*

-will'y-nill'y *adv.* willing or unwilling. [OE. *willan*]

will-o'-the-wisp *n.* light flitting over marshes; elusive person or hope. [E. = William of the torch]

will'ow *n.* tree such as the weeping willow with long thin flexible branches; its wood. **-will'owy** *a.* lithe and slender. **will'ow pattern** famous pattern on china *etc.*, illustrating a Chinese legend. [OE. *welig*]

wilt *v.i.* droop; fade; go limp. *-v.t.* make to wilt. [orig. uncertain]

wim'ple *n.* covering for head and extending round cheeks and neck, worn by nuns. [OE. *wimple*]

win *v.t.* get by labor or effort; reach; allure; be successful in. *-v.i.* be successful. **-winn'er** *n.* [OE. *gewinnan*]

wince *v.i.* flinch. *-n.* a flinching from pain, *etc.* IOF. *guenchir*, shrink]

win'cey *n.* cotton cloth with wool filling. **-winceyette'** *n.* cotton cloth. [orig. uncertain]

winch *n.* crank; windlass. [OE. *wince*, pulley]

wind *n.* air in motion; breath. -(wind) *v.t.* sound by blowing. **-wind'fall** (-awl) *n.* fallen fruit; piece of good luck. **-wind'jamm'er** *n.* sailing ship. **-wind'mill** *n.* mill worked by sails. **-wind'pipe** *n.* passage from throat to lungs. **-wind'shield** *n.* in car, motorcycle, *etc.*, sheet of strong glass for protection in front of driver. **-wind'surfing** *n.* sport of sailing standing up on a sailboard that is equipped with a mast, sail, and wishbone boom; boardsailing. **-wind'y** *a.* exposed to winds; (*sl.*) timid, fearful. **-wind'ward** (-ord) *n.* side towards the wind. **-wind'flower** *n.* wood anemone. [OE.]

wind (wind) *v.i.* twine; vary from a direct course. *-v.t.* twist round, wrap; make ready for working by tightening a spring. **-wind'lass** *n.* machine which hauls or hoists by wrapping rope round an axle. [OE. *windan*]

win'dow *n.* hole in a wall (with or without glass), to admit light. [ON. *vindauge*, 'wind-eye]

wine *n.* fermented juice of the grape, or other fruit. **-wine box** *n.* wine sold in a cubic carton, having a plastic lining and a tap for dispensing. **-wine grow'er** *n.* a person engaged in cultivating vines in order to make wine. **-wine grow'ing** *n.* **wine press** *n.* apparatus for squeezing grapes in order to extract juice for wine making. **-wine tas'ting** *n.* an occasion for sampling a number of wines. **-wine tas'ter** *n.* [OE. *win*, fr. L. *vinum*]

wing *n.* limb a bird uses in flying; flight; lateral extension; plane. *v.t.* cross by flight; supply with wings; disable. *-v.i.* fly. [ON. *voengr*, wing]

wink *v.i.* close and open an eye; connive with (*at*). *-n.* an act of winking. [OE. *wincian*]

win'kle *n.* periwinkle. [OE. *wincle*]

winn'ow *v.t.* blow free of chaff. [OE. *winduian*, winnow]

win'some *a.* charming, attractive. [OE. *wynsum*, fr. *wynn*, joy]

win'ter *n.* fourth season. *-v. i.* pass the winter. *-v. t.* tend during winter. **-win'try** *a.* **-win'ter-**

green *n.* evergreen plant; flavoring obtained from oil extracted from the plant. **-win'ter quarters** *n. pl.* quarters for troops during winter. [OE.]

wipe *v.t.* rub so as to clean. *-n.* a wiping. [OE. *wipian*]

wire *n.* metal drawn into the form of cord; (*coll.*) telegram. *-v. t.* provide, catch, fasten with, wire; send by telegraph. **wi'ry** *a.* like wire, tough. **-wire'less** *n.*, *a.* and *v. t.* telegraphy or telephony without connecting wires. **-wire'drawn** *a.* strained, over-subtle. **-wire'-pulling** *n.* use of influence behind the scenes. **-wire'tap** *v.t.* and *i.* make a connection to a telegraph or telephone wire in order to obtain information secretly. **-wire'-tapper** *n.* [OE. *wir*]

wise *a.* sagacious; having intelligence and knowledge. **-wis'dom** *n.* **-wise'ly** *adv.* **wis'dom-tooth**, large back-tooth cut in one's later 'teens. [OE. *wis*]

wise *n.* manner. [OE. *wise*]

wise'acre *n.* foolish pretender to wisdom. [Du. *wijssegger*, soothsayer]

wish *v.i.* have a desire. *-v. t.* desire. *-n.* desire or thing desired. **-wish'ful** *a.* **wish'ful think'ing**, beliefs colored by one's wishes. [OE. *wyscan*]

wisp *n.* twisted handful, usually of straw, *etc.* [orig. uncertain]

wisteria *n.* climbing plant with pale purple flowers. [C. Wistar (d. 1818)]

wist'ful *a.* longing. **-wist'fully** *adv.* **wist'fulness** *n.* [orig. uncertain]

wit *n.* sense; intellect; ingenuity in connecting amusingly incongruous ideas; person gifted with this power. **-witt'y** *a.* **-witt'ily** *adv.* **-witt'icism** *n.* witty remark. **-witt'ingly** *adv.* on purpose. [OE. *witt*, fr. *witan*, know]

witch *n.* woman said to be endowed with black-magical powers. **-witch'craft** *n.* **witch'ery** *n.* **-witch'ing** *a.* weird. **witch'doc'tor** *n.* medicine-man, magician. [OE. *wicca*]

witch'-elm, **wych'-elm** *n.* variety of elm. **-witch'-hazel** *n.* **-witch'-alder** *n.* [OE. *wice*, bending, drooping]

with *prep.* in company or possession of-, against; in relation to; through. **-withal'** *adv.* also, likewise. **-withdraw'** *v. t.* and *i.* draw back, retire. **-withdraw'al** *n.* **-withhold'** *v. t.* keep, hold back, restrain. **-within'** *prep.* and *adv.* in, inside. **-without'** *adv.* outside. *-prep.* lacking. **-withstand** *v. t.* oppose. [OE.]

withe, **with'y** *n.* tough, flexible twig, willow. [OE, *withthe*]

with'er *v.i.* fade. *-v.t.* cause to fade; blight. [var. of *weather*]

with'ers *n. pl.* ridge between a horse's shoulder-blades. [OE. *withre*, resistance]

wit'ness *n.* testimony; one who sees something; one who gives testimony. *-v.i.* give testimony. *-v.t.* see; attest; see and sign as having seen. [OE *witnes*, evidence]

wiz'ard *n.* sorcerer, magician. [*wise*]

wiz'ened *a.* shriveled, dried up, withered. [OE. *wisnian*, shrink]

woad *n.* blue dye. [OE. *wad*]

wobb'le v.i. shake, be unsteady. -n. swaying movement. [L. Ger. wabbeln]

woe n. grief -**woe'begone** a. sorrowful. -**woe'ful** a. -**woe'fully** adv. [OE. wa]

wold. See weald.

wolf (woolf) n. wolves pl. wild beast allied to the dog. -**wolf's-bane** n. aconite. [OE. wulf]

wolf'ram n. ore containing iron, manganese and tungsten. -**wolf'ramite** n. important ore of tungsten. [Ger.]

wol'verine n. rapacious N. American animal, the glutton, carcajou; its fur. (wolf)

wom'an (woo-) n. wom'en pl. adult human female; female sex. -**wom'an-hood** n. -**wom'anly** a. -**wom'anish** a. wom'ankind n. [OE. wifmann, wife-man, female]

womb n. female organ of conception and gestation, the uterus. [OE. wamb, belly]

wom'bat n. Australian marsupial animal resembling the opossum. [native]

won'der (wun-) n. marvel; emotion excited by an amazing or unusual thing. v.i. feel this emotion. -**won'derful** a. won'derfully adv. -**won'drous** a. won'drously adv. -won'derment n. [OE. wundor]

wont n. custom. -**wont'ed** a. habitual. [OE. gewun, usual]

woo v.t. court, seek to marry. -**woo'er** n. -**woo'ing** n. and a. [OE. wogian]

wood n. tract of land with growing trees; substance of trees, timber. -**wood'en** a. wood'y a. -**wood'bine** n. honeysuckle. wood'cock n. bird like a snipe. -**wood'-cut** n. engraving on wood. -**wood'land** n. woods, forest. -**wood'pecker** n. bird which searches tree-trunks for insects. wood'man n. forester. -**wood'craft** n. knowledge of woodland conditions. wood'ruff n. woodland plant with small white fragrant flowers. -**wood'winds** n. pl. clarinet, oboe, etc., in an orchestra. [OE. wudu, forest]

woof n. threads that cross the warp in weaving, the weft. [OE. owef]

wool n. soft hair of the sheep and certain other animals. -**wool'en** a. -**wooll'y** a. [OE. wull]

word (wurd) n. single symbol used in speaking or writing, a unit of speech; information; promise. -v.t. express in words. -**word'y** a. -**word'ily** adv. [OE.]

work (wurk) n. labor; task; something made or accomplished. -pl. factory. -v. t. cause to operate; make, shape. -v.i. apply effort; labor; operate; ferment; be engaged in a trade, profession, etc. -**work'able** a. -**work'er** n. -**work'house** n. institution for paupers. -**work'man** n. manual worker. -**work'manship** n. skill of a workman; way a thing is finished, style. -**work'shop** n. place where things are made. -**work'top** n. a surface in a kitchen, often of heat resistant laminated plastic, that is used for food preparation. [OE. woerc]

world (wurld) n. universe; sphere of existence; mankind; society. -**world'ling** n. one given up to affairs of this world. **world'ly** a. engrossed in temporal pursuits. [OE. weorold]

worm (wurm) n. small limbless creeping creature, shaped like a snake; thread of a screw. -v. i. crawl. -v. t. work (oneself) in insidiously; extract (a secret) craftily. **worm'eaten** a. eaten by worms; old, out-of-date. [OE. wyrm, serpent]

worm'wood (wurm-) n. bitter herb; (fig.) bitterness. [OE. wermod]

worr'y (wur'i) v.t. seize or shake with teeth; trouble, harass. -v.i. be unduly concerned. -n. useless care or anxiety. **worr'ying** a. [OE. wyrgan, strangle]

worse (wurs) a. and adv. comparative of bad or badly. -**worst** a. and adv. superlative of bad or badly. -**wors'en** v. t. and i. [OE. wiersa]

wor'ship (wur-) n. reverence, adoration. -v.t. adore; love and admire. **wor'shipful** a. -**wor'shiper** n. [OE. weorthscipe, 'worthship']

wor'sted (wur-) n. woolen yarn. [fr. Worstead, in Norfolk, England]

wort n. plant, herb; infusion of malt before fermentation. [OE. wyrt]

worth (wurth) a. having value specified; meriting. -n. merit, value. -**wor'thy** (-TH-) a. -**wor'thily** adv. -**wor'thiness** n. -**worth'less** a. [OE. weorth]

wound n. injury, hurt by cut, stab, etc. -v. t. inflict a wound on; pain. -**wound'ing** a. [OE. wund]

wrack n. sea-weed, esp. the kind burned as kelp; wreckage. [var. of wreck]

wraith n. apparition of a person seen shortly before or after death. [ON. vörthr, guardian]

wran'gle (-ng-gi) v.i. quarrel or dispute noisily. -n. act of doing this. [ME. wrangela]

wrap v.t. cover, esp. by putting something round; put round. -n. loose garment; covering. -**wrapp'er** n; [earlier wiap, of uncertain orig.]

wrath n. anger. -**wrath'ful** a. -**wrath'fully** adv. -**wrathfulness** n. [OE. = angry]

wreak v.t. inflict (vengeance, etc.). [OE. wrecan, avenge]

wreath n. something twisted into ring form; garland. -**wreathe** v.t. surround; form into wreath; wind round. [OE. wrath, fillet]

wreck n. destruction of a ship by accident; wrecked ship; ruin; something ruined. -v.t. cause the wreck of. -**wreck'age** n. [OE. wræc, fr. wrecan, drive]

wren n. very small brown bird, allied to the goldcrest. [OE. wrenna]

wrench n. violent twist; tool for twisting or screwing. -v.t. twist; distort; seize forcibly. [OE. wrenc, trick]

wrest v.t. take by force; twist violently. n. tool for tuning a harp, etc. -**wres'tle** (-sl) v.i. contend by grappling and trying to throw down. -**wres'tler** n. [OE. wræslan]

wretch n. miserable creature. -**wretch'ed** a. miserable; worthless. -**wretch'edness** n. -**wretch'edly** adv. [OE. wræcca, outcast]

wrig'gle v. t. and i. move sinuously like a worm. -n. quick twisting movement. [fr. obs. wrig]

wright n. workman, maker, e.g. wheelwright. [OE. wyrhta, worker]

wring v.t. twist, squeeze, compress; extort; pain. [OE. wringan]

wrin'kle (-ng-kl) *n.* slight ridge on a surface. *-v.t.* makes wrinkles in. *-v.i.* become wrinkled. [OE. *wrincle*]

wrist *n.* joint between the hand and the arm. *-wrist'let n.* band worn on the wrist. *-wrist-watch' n.* watch worn on wrist. [OE]

write *v.i.* mark paper, *etc.*, with the symbols which are used to represent words or sounds; compose; send a letter. *v.t.* set down in words; compose; communicate in writing. *-writ n.* a formal or legal document. *-wri'ter n.* penman; author. [OE. *writan*]

writhe *v.i.* twist or roll body about, as in pain; to squirm (with shame, *etc.*) [OE. *writhan*]

wrong *a.* not right or good or suitable. *n.* that which is wrong; harm; evil. *-v.t.* do wrong to. *-wrong'ly adv.* *-wrong'ful a.* *-wrong'fully adv.* [OE. *wrang*, injustice]

wroth *a.* angry. [fr. *wrath*]

wrought' *p.t.* of *work.*

wrung' *p.p.* and *p.t.* of wring.

wry *a.* turned to one side, distorted. **wry'neck** *n.* small bird which twists its neck thus. [OE. *wrigian*, twist]

wyandotte *n.* breed of domestic fowls. [name of Amer. Ind. tribe]

X

X-rays' *n. pl.* invisible short-wave rays used in surgery to take photographs of the bones, etc., inside the human frame. [X = the unknown]

xanth'ic (zan-) *a.* yellowish. *-xanth'ism n.* a condition of skin, fur, or feathers in which yellow coloration predominates. [G. *xanthos*, yellow]

xantipp'e (zan-tip'-i) *n.* shrewish woman, scold. [wife of Socrates]

xen'on *n.* gaseous element of the atmosphere. [G. *zenos*, stranger]

xenopho'bia *n.* morbid fear of strangers. [G. *zenos*, stranger]

xo'anon *n.* primitive image of a god, carved, *esp.* originally, in wood, and supposed to have fallen from heaven. [G. *xuo*, scrape, smooth]

xy'lograph *n.* wood-engraving, impression from wood-block. *-xylog'raphy n.* wood-engraving. *-xylog'rapher n.* wood-engraver. *-xylograph'ic a. pert.* to xylography. [G. *xylon*, wood, *graphein*, write]

xy'loid *a.* woody, like wood. [G. *xylon*, wood, *eidos*, form]

xy'lonite (zi) *n.* celluloid.

xylophone *n.* musical instrument of wooden bars which vibrate when struck. [G. *xylon*, wood]

xy'lorimba (zi) *n.* large xylophone with an extended range of five octaves. [fr. *xylophone* and *marimba*]

Y

yacht (yot) *n.* light vessel for racing or pleasure. *-v.i.* cruise or race in a yacht. **yachts'man** *n.* [Du. *jacht*]

yahoo' *n.* brute in human form. [coined by Swift in *Gulliver's Travels*]

yak *n.* long-haired Tibetan ox. [Tibetan]

yam *n.* tropical plant with large edible tuber, the sweet potato. [Senegalese *nyami*, eat]

yam'mer *v.i.* talk in a sad voice, complain; talk continuously, *usu.* loudly. [OE. *geomar*, sad]

Yank'ee *n.* inhabitant of U.S.A. *esp.* of New England, or of the Northern States. *-a.* belonging to U.S.A. [orig. uncertain]

yap *n.* and *v.i.* bark (of small dog). [imit.]

yapp *n.* bookbinding with limp leather cover projecting over the edges. [Yapp, London bookseller]

yard *n.* unit of measure, 36 inches; that length of anything; spar slung across a ship's mast to extend sails. *-yard'arm n.* either half of a long slender beam or pole used to support a square sail. [OE. *gierd*, rod]

yard *n.* piece of enclosed ground around a building [OE. *geard*]

yarn *n.* spun thread of fiber prepared for weaving, knitting, *etc.*; tale. *-v. i.* tell a tale. [OE. *gearn*]

yash'mak *n.* veil worn by Muslim women. [Ar. *yashmaq*]

yaw *v.i.* fall off from a course in steering a ship. [orig. uncertain]

yawl *n.* small yacht, boat. [Du. *jol*]

yawn *v.i.* gape; open the mouth wide, *esp.* in sleepiness. *-n.* the act of yawning. [OE. *ganian*]

ye *pron.* you. [OE. *gea*]

year *n.* time taken by one revolution of the earth round the sun, about 365¼ days; twelve months. *-year'ling n.* animal one year old. *-year'ly adv.* every year, once a year. *-a.* happening, *etc.*, once a year. [OE. *gear*]

yearn (yern) *v. i.* feel a longing or desire. [OE. *giernan*]

yeast *n.* substance used as a fermenting agent, *esp.* in raising bread. *-yeast'y a.* frothy, fermenting. [OE. *gist*]

yell *v.i.* cry out in a loud shrill tone. *-n.* loud, shrill cry. [OE. *gellan*]

yell'ow *a.* of the color of lemons, gold, *etc.* *-n.* this color. *-a.* (*fig.*) envious, jealous. *-* (*coll.*) cowardly. *-yell'ow fever n.* acute infectious disease of tropical Amer. and W. Africa. *-yell'owhammer n.* yellow bunting. *-yell'ow press'* sensational journalism. *-* **yell'ow rain** *n.* a type of yellow precipitation described in parts of S.E. Asia and alleged by some to be evidence of chemical warfare. [OE. *geoly*]

yelp *v.s.* give a quick, shrill cry. *-n.* such cry. [OE. *gielpan*, boast]

yeo'man *n.* man owning and farming a small estate. *-yeo'manry n.* yeomen collectively; territorial cavalry force. [contra. of young man]

yes *interj.* affirms or consents, gives an affirmative answer. *-yes'man n.* servile person who never dares to disagree. [OE. *gese*]

yesterday *n.* day before today. [OE. *giestrandæg*]

yet *adv.* now, still; hitherto. *conj.* but, at the same time, nevertheless, however. [OE. *giet*]

yew *n.* evergreen tree with dark leaves; its wood. [OE. *iw*]

Yidd'ish *n.* Jewish dialect of corrupt Hebrew, German and other elements. [Ger. *jüdisch,* Jewish]

yield *v.t.* give or return as food; give up, surrender. *-v.i.* produce; surrender, give way. *-n.* amount produced; profit, or result. [OE. *gieldan,* pay]

yo'del *v.i.* warble in a falsetto tone. *-n.* falsetto warbling as practiced by Swiss mountaineers. [Ger. *jodeln*]

yo'ga *n.* Hindu discipline of deep meditation aiming at union of soul with God; exercises associated with this. *-yogi* *n.* devotee of yoga. [Sans. = *union*]

yog'urt, yogh'urt *n.* thick, custard-like preparation of curdled milk. [Turk. *yoghurt*]

yoke *n.* wooden bar put across the necks of two animals to hold them together and to which a plow, *etc.*, may be attached; various objects like a yoke in shape or use; bond or tie. *-v.t.* put a yoke on; couple, unite. [OE. *geoc*]

yo'kel *n.* rustic. [orig. unknown]

yolk *n.* yellow part of an egg. [OE. *geoloca,* fr. *geolu,* yellow]

yon *a.* that or those over there. **-yon'der** *a.* yon. *adv.* over there, in that direction. [OE. *geon*]

yore *n.* past. [OE. *geara-gear,* year]

you *pron.* plural of the second person pronoun, but used also as a singular. (OE. *eow*]

young (yung) *a.* not far advanced in growth, life or existence, not yet old; vigorous. *-n.* offspring. **-young'ster** *n.* child, *esp.* an active or lively boy. [OE. *geong*]

your *pron.* belonging to you. **-yours** *pron.* **-yourself** *pron.* [OE. *eower*]

youth *n.* state or time of being young; state before adult age; young person; young people. **-youth'ful** *a.* [OE. *geogoth*]

yule *n.* Christmas festival. **-yule-log** *n.* **-yuletide** *n.* [OE. *geol*]

yuppie *n.* wealthy young person. **-a.** [fr. *y*oung *up*wardly-*m*obile *p*rofessional]

Z

za'ny *n.* clown. [It. Giovanni, John]

zeal *n.* fervor, keenness. **-zeal'ous** *a.* **-zeal'ously** *adv.* **-zeal'ot** *n.* fanatic. [G. *zeros*]

ze'bra *n.* striped animal like a horse, native of Africa. [Port.]

ze'bu *n.* domestic animal of Asia and eastern Africa, resembling ox, but with large hump. [F.]

Zen *n.* Japanese school of Buddhism teaching contemplation and meditation. *a.* [Jap.]

zena'na *n.* women's quarters in high-caste Indian houses. [Pers. *zanana,* fr. zan, woman]

zen'ith *n.* point of the heavens directly above an observer. [Arab. *samt,* a road]

zeph'yr (zefer) *n.* west wind; gentle breeze. [G. *zéphyros,* west wind]

Zepp'elin *n.* German airship, used in World War I. [Count Zeppelin]

ze'ro *n.* nothing; figure 0; point on a graduated instrument from which positive and negative quantities are reckoned. **ze'ro hour** in military operations, time from which each item on the program is at an interval stated. [It., fr. Arab. *sifr,* cipher]

zest *n.* relish. **-zest'ful** *a.* **-zest'fully** *adv.* [F. = slice of lemon peel for flavoring]

zig'zag *n.* line bent by a series of angles. **-a.** forming a zigzag. **-adv.** with a zigzag course. *-v. i.* move along in a zigzag course. [F.]

zinc *n.* white metal. *-v.t.* coat with it [Ger. *zink*]

zinc'ograph, **zinc'o** *n.* design in relief on zinc plate; print made from this. *-v.t.* and *i.* etch on zinc, reproduce thus. **zincog'rapher** *n.* **-zincog'raphy** *n.* **zincograph'ic** *a.* [G. *zink*]

zing'aro *n.* gypsy. **-zing'ari** *pl.* [It.]

zinn'ia *n.* plant allied to the aster, with brightly colored flowers. [J. G. Zinn (d. 1759)]

Zi'on *n.* (hill in) ancient Jerusalem; Israel; the people of Israel; Christianity; paradise. **-Zi'onism** *n.* movement to found and support a Jewish homeland in Palestine. **-Zi'onist** *n.* advocate of this. [Heb. *tsiyon,* hill]

zip code *n.* five-figure number used in postal addresses designed to facilitate delivery of mail. [fr. *z*one *i*mprovement *p*lan]

zip'per *n.* quick-fastening device for clothes. [imit.]

zir'con *n.* mineral, Ceylon stone, varieties of which include jocinth and jargoon. **-zircon'ic** *a.* [Arab. *zarquin*]

zither(n) *n.* flat, stringed instrument with 29-42 strings. [Ger.]

zo'diac *n.* imaginary belt of the heavens outside which the sun, moon, and chief planets do not pass and divided crosswise into twelve equal areas (signs of the zodiac), each named after a constellation. **-zo'diacal** *a.* [G. *zodiakos,* fr. *zoon,* animal (the constellations being named mainly after animals)]

zom'bie(e) *n.* African snake deity; in American voodooism, corpse given appearance of life by sorcery. [W. African *zambi,* fetish]

zone *n.* girdle; encircling band; any of the five belts into which the tropics and the arctic and antarctic circles divide the earth. **-zo'ning** *n.* town-planning according to zonal areas, residential, *etc.* [G.]

zool'ogy *n.* natural history of animals. **-zoolo'gical** *a.* **-zool'ogist** *n.*

zoo *n.* short for zoological gardens, place where wild animals are kept for show. **-zo'olite** *n.* fossil animal. **zo'ophyte** *n.* plant-like animal, *e.g.* a sponge. [G. *zoos,* living]

Zoroas'trian, Zorathus'trian *a.* pert. to Persian religion of Zoroaster (Zorathustra). *-n.* adherent of this.

zy'gote *n.* fertilized egg cell. [G. *zygon,* yoke]

zymot'ic *a.* of, or caused by, fermentation; of a disease, due to multiplication of germs introduced into the body from outside. [G. *zimotikos,* fr. *zume,* leaven]